The Sociology of Health, Healing, and Illness

With thorough coverage of inequality in health care access and practice, this leading textbook has been widely acclaimed by teachers as the most accessible of any available. It introduces and integrates recent research in medical sociology and emphasizes the importance of race, class, gender, and sexuality throughout.

This new edition leads students through the complexities of the evolving Affordable Care Act. It significantly expands coverage of medical technology, end-of-life issues, and alternative and complementary health care—topics that students typically debate in the classroom. While the COVID-19 pandemic emerged after this edition of the text was originally submitted, material has been added in Chapters 3, 10, and 13 about it. Many new text boxes and enhancements in pedagogy grace this new edition, which is essential in the fast-changing area of health care.

New to this edition:

- More text boxes relating the social aspects of medicine to students' lives.
- Expanded coverage leading students through the complex impacts of the ACA and health care reform.
- Greater emphasis on sexual minority health and LGBTQ+ persons' experiences in the health care system.
- Expanded coverage of medical technology, end-of-life issues, and alternative and complementary health care.
- "Health and the Internet" sections are updated and renovated to create more interactive student assignments.
- New end-of-chapter lists of terms, with key terms as flash cards on the companion website.
- An updated instructor's guide with test bank.

Gregory L. Weiss earned his PhD from Purdue University and is now Professor Emeritus of Sociology at Roanoke College. During his career, he has been an honored teacher (winning numerous college, statewide, regional (SSS), and national (ASA's Section on Teaching and Learning)) awards, a dedicated researcher and writer (author of *Grass Roots Medicine* and co-author of *Experiencing Social Research* and the ASA publication on *Creating an Effective Sociology Assessment Program* as well as dozens of scholarly articles), and active in the community in a variety of health- and animal-related organizations.

Denise A. Copelton, PhD, is Associate Professor of Sociology at The State University of New York (SUNY), College at Brockport. One of the first social scientists to study celiac disease and gluten-free eating, her work has been published in *Social Science & Medicine, Sociology of Health & Illness, Advances in Gender Research*, and *Deviant Behavior*, among others outlets. She is co-author (with Amy Guptill and Betsy Lucal) of *Food & Society: Principles and Paradoxes*, now in its second edition. She regularly teaches courses on introductory sociology, sociology of health and illness, sociology of families, and deviance. Her college-wide leadership was recognized in 2019 with the prestigious SUNY Chancellor's Award for Faculty Service.

TENTH EDITION

THE SOCIOLOGY OF HEALTH, HEALING, AND ILLNESS

Gregory L. Weiss and Denise A. Copelton

Routledge
Taylor & Francis Group

NEW YORK AND LONDON

10th edition published 2021
by Routledge
52 Vanderbilt Avenue, New York, NY 10017

and by Routledge
2 Park Square, Milton Park, Abingdon, Oxon, OX14 4RN

Routledge is an imprint of the Taylor & Francis Group, an informa business

© 2021 Taylor & Francis

The right of Gregory L. Weiss and Denise A. Copelton to be identified as authors of this work has been asserted by them in accordance with sections 77 and 78 of the Copyright, Designs and Patents Act 1988.

First edition published by Prentice Hall 1994
Ninth edition published by Routledge 2017

Library of Congress Cataloging-in-Publication Data
Names: Weiss, Gregory L., author. | Copelton, Denise A., author.
Title: The sociology of health, healing, and illness / Gregory L. Weiss and Denise A. Copelton.
Description: 10th edition. | New York, NY : Routledge, 2020. | Includes bibliographical references and index.
Identifiers: LCCN 2019058418 (print) | LCCN 2019058419 (ebook) | ISBN 9780367233556 (hardback) | ISBN 9780367253882 (paperback) | ISBN 9780429279447 (ebook)
Subjects: LCSH: Social medicine—United States. | Medical ethics—United States. | Medical care—United States.
Classification: LCC RA418.3.U6 W45 2020 (print) | LCC RA418.3.U6 (ebook) | DDC 362.10973—dc23
LC record available at https://lccn.loc.gov/2019058418
LC ebook record available at https://lccn.loc.gov/2019058419

ISBN: 978-0-367-23355-6 (hbk)
ISBN: 978-0-367-25388-2 (pbk)
ISBN: 978-0-429-27944-7 (ebk)

Typeset in Bembo
by Apex CoVantage, LLC

Visit the eResources: www.routledge.com/9780367253882

To Janet

To Brian, Mathilda and Margaret

To all of the health care professionals who have given so much of themselves to provide care to patients during the COVID-19 pandemic.

With much appreciation to former co-author, Lynne Lonnquist.

Contents

CHAPTER THREE
SOCIAL EPIDEMIOLOGY   40

CHAPTER FOUR
SOCIETY, DISEASE, AND ILLNESS   75

CHAPTER FIVE
SOCIAL STRESS   111

CHAPTER TWELVE
THE PHYSICIAN–PATIENT RELATIONSHIP: BACKGROUND AND MODELS   307

CHAPTER THIRTEEN
PROFESSIONAL AND ETHICAL OBLIGATIONS OF PHYSICIANS IN THE PHYSICIAN–PATIENT RELATIONSHIP   333

CHAPTER FOURTEEN
THE HEALTH CARE SYSTEM OF THE UNITED STATES   354

Tables and Figures

TABLES

FIGURES

Preface

The tenth edition of this textbook has been updated to reflect the very important changes that have occurred in the US health care system in the last 3 years and in matters related to the sociology of health, healing, and illness. It reflects medical sociology's commitment to analyzing patterns of disease and illness, health- and illness-related behaviors, health care workers, and the health care system.

In preparing this tenth edition, we have sought to retain and strengthen the emphases and features of the earlier editions, to thoroughly update patterns, trends, and statistics, and to present new material that reflects important changes in health care in society and important advancements in medical sociology. As an illustration, although the COVID-19 pandemic emerged after this edition of the text was already submitted, we later added material in Chapters 3, 10, and 13 about the pandemic.

KEY EMPHASES WITHIN THE TEXT

This edition of the text maintains the same five emphases as the earlier editions. *First, we provide broad coverage of the traditional subject matter of medical sociology and include both new perspectives and research findings on this material.* The core areas of medical sociology (the influence of the social environment on health and illness, health and illness behavior, health care practitioners and their relationships to patients, and the health care system) all receive significant attention within the text. Naturally, statistics throughout the text have been updated to provide timely analysis of patterns and trends. Recent research findings and theoretical insights have been incorporated in every chapter. Attention devoted to relatively new areas in the field has not reduced coverage of

traditional areas such as social stress, illness behavior, and the physician–patient relationship.

Second, we have continued to emphasize emerging areas of analysis in medical sociology and recent work within the field. Recent health care reform efforts in both the public and private domains continue to have dramatic effects on almost every aspect of health care. We describe these effects throughout the text.

We also continue to incorporate key medical ethics issues throughout the text. These issues represent some of the most important health-related debates occurring in the United States today, and many medical sociologists have acknowledged the importance of understanding these policy debates and setting them within a sociological context. We have attempted to provide balanced and comprehensive coverage of several of these issues (especially in Chapters 13 and 16 and in the discussion questions and cases at the ends of chapters).

We work hard to keep this book as up to date as possible and to reflect the most recent developments related to health, healing, and illness. For example, this tenth edition provides extended analysis of a wide range of topics, including the following:

- Introduction of key new concepts, including
  - Pregnancy-related mortality ratio
  - Health social movements
  - Competency-based standards in medical education
  - The glass escalator
  - High-deductible health plans
  - Value-based care.
- Addition of new "In the Field" boxes, including
  - The COVID-19 pandemic
  - Coping methods of college students
  - Perceived discrimination as a stressor

- Oath-taking in medical schools
- The business side of egg freezing.
- Introduction to new topics, including
  - *Healthy People 2030*
  - The recent measles outbreak and anti-vaccination efforts
  - Changes in the physician's workplace
  - The American Hospital Association's "Value Initiative"
  - Medical care in the Central African Republic, sometimes identified as the world's unhealthiest country.
- Increased coverage of many topics, including
  - E-cigarettes
  - Medical marijuana and CBD oil
  - Self-help initiatives
  - Sexual harassment in medicine
  - Physician impairment
  - Medical school curricular reform
  - Patient-centered care
  - Changes in medical practice
  - The HPV vaccination controversy
  - The opioid crisis, including its negative impact on life expectancy and mortality
  - International physicians
  - Nurse demographics
  - The nursing shortage and efforts to recruit men into nursing
  - Nursing burnout
  - Disease and illness in developing countries
  - Developments related to palliative care
  - Recent developments in the health care systems of Canada, China, and the United Kingdom, and increased attention to European models for health insurance
- Thorough coverage of The Patient Protection and Affordable Care Act, including its successes and failures and continuing efforts both to dismantle it and to extend it.

Third, the extensive coverage of gender, race, and class issues as they relate to health, healing, and illness has been enlarged in several chapters and significant coverage is now given to sexual minorities, including transgender issues. We want students to constantly be exposed to the important influence of these factors and others on matters related to health and illness. The chapters on social epidemiology, social stress, health and illness behaviors, nursing, the profession of medicine and medical education, and the physician–patient relationship all give special emphasis to these matters.

Fourth, we continue to emphasize key social policy questions. Timely questions and issues addressed include

- Performing regular, routine HIV checks
- Providing clean needles to people using injectable drugs
- Taxing sugary food and beverages
- Mandating HPV and measles vaccinations
- Public financing of free medical education
- Recruiting physicians, nurses, and other health care workers from developing countries
- Striking by medical providers
- Permitting religious exemption laws
- Legalizing medical marijuana
- Allowing further consolidation and merger of American hospitals
- Maximizing use of expensive advanced health care technologies
- Considering new organ donation policies in Singapore and Israel.

Fifth, we have attempted to prepare a text that is informative. We want readers to become aware of the many contributions of medical sociology to understandings of health, healing, and illness, and to become intrigued by the provocative issues and debates that exist in medical sociology and in the health care field. We also want readers to find this book readable and interesting.

Both of us have enjoyed structuring our classrooms to enable as much reflection, critical thinking, and student participation as possible. We have found that there is simply not time for some of the classroom activities that we most enjoy (e.g., reading and then discussing a provocative paperback, watching a good documentary and critically analyzing it together, or using student panels to introduce issues) if we feel obligated to lecture on all the material in each chapter. On the other hand, we do want students to become familiar with the important contributions of the field. When we use this book, we spend some time lecturing on parts of it, adding to certain discussions and presenting some of the material in an alternative manner. However, our students are able to grasp much of the book on their own, enabling us to supplement and create additional types of learning experiences. The available instructor's guide provides further information on how we have combined successfully the chapter material with lectures, videos, and discussions.

What are the key pedagogical features of this text?

- Clear organization within chapters and a clear writing style
- "In the Field" boxed inserts that provide illustrations of key points made in the chapters
- "In Comparative Focus" boxed inserts that examine a selected health topic or issue in another country or countries
- Meaningful tables and charts with the most recent data available at the time of writing this edition of the book
- Illustrative photographs, many of which were taken specifically for use in this book
- Chapter summaries
- End-of-chapter "Health on the Internet" references and questions
- End-of-chapter "Discussion Cases"
- End-of-chapter "Glossary" sections
- References conveniently provided at the end of each chapter
- A glossary is available as an e-Resource at www.routledge.com/9780367253882.

Three additional facets of the book are important to us and help to describe its place within the field. *First, we consider one of the strengths of the book to be the large number of research studies cited to illustrate key points.* We do this to demonstrate to students the empirical basis of sociology, the origin of sociological knowledge, and the fascinating types of research conducted in medical sociology. We hope it inspires students to consider interesting research projects.

We have worked hard to identify theoretically meaningful and methodologically sound studies that contribute important knowledge to our understanding of health, healing, and illness. While making heavy use of research conducted by medical sociologists, we also include appropriate material from other social sciences, from the government, and from the medical professional literature. We believe that this is helpful in forming the most comprehensive understanding of the topics covered in the book.

A second facet of our book that is important to us is that we provide balanced coverage on key issues. This does not mean that our book lacks critical perspective or analysis. In fact, readers will find no shortage of critical questions being asked. However, our objective is to expose students to arguments on both sides of the issues, and to challenge them to consider the soundness of reasoning and quality of evidence that are offered.

Finally, we hope that this text reflects a genuine understanding of some very important and complex issues. Both of us have had many opportunities to experience various dimensions of the health care system. Between the two of us, we have been able to apply and extend our medical sociological training through work in a free health clinic, in a family planning clinic, in self-help groups, in hospital bioethics groups, on the human rights committee of a state psychiatric hospital, on the Navajo reservation, and in voluntary health agencies. Although we have not substituted our personal experiences for more general understandings developed through sound theory and research, we believe that our experiences have helped us to develop a better understanding of certain issues and assisted us in being able to illustrate important concepts and patterns.

Ultimately, our hopes for student-readers remain the same as with the earlier editions—that they gain an appreciation of how the sociological perspective and social theory contribute to an understanding of health, healing, and illness, and of the manner in which social research is used to study these processes. In addition, we hope that readers perceive some of the many wonderfully exciting issues that are studied by medical sociologists.

Acknowledgments

We are deeply grateful to the many people who have made helpful suggestions and comments to us about the first nine editions of this book. Our appreciation is extended to the following individuals: James R. Marshall, SUNY–Buffalo, School of Medicine; Lu Ann Aday, University of Texas, School of Public Health; Paul B. Brezina, County College of Morris; Janet Hankin, Wayne State University; Naoko Oyabu-Mathis, Mount Union College; Judith Levy, University of Illinois at Chicago; Mike Farrall, Creighton University; John Collette, University of Utah; Raymond P. Dorney, Merimack College; C. Allen Haney, University of Houston; Arthur Griel, Alfred College; Larry D. Hall, Spring Hill College; Patricia Rieker, Simmons College; Deborah Potter, Brandeis University; John Schumacher, University of Maryland, Baltimore County; Lisa Jean Moore, College of Staten Island; Ilona Hansen, Winona State University; William H. Haas III, University of North Carolina at Asheville; Robert D. Ruth, Davidson College; Eldon L. Wegner, University of Hawaii at Manoa; Diane S. Shinberg, University of Memphis; Juyeon Son, University of Wisconsin–Oshkosh; Matthew Carlson, Portland State University; Linda Grant, University of Georgia; Ande Kidanemariam, Northeastern State University; Mark Bird, College of Southern Nevada; Daphne Pedersen, University of North Dakota; Abby Johnston, Baptist College of Health Sciences; Angelique Harris, Marquette University; and to Professors Mary Kreutzer, Neveen Shafeek Amin, and Shawn Bauldry for their helpful comments and suggestions as reviewers.

Gregory L. Weiss
Denise A. Copelton

CHAPTER 1

A Brief Introduction to the Sociology of Health, Healing, and Illness

Learning Objectives

- Identify and explain the major historical factors that led to the development of medical sociology as a subfield of sociology.

- Identify and give specific examples of the four major categories of focus within medical sociology.

- Explain how the sociological perspective, sociological theory, and social research methods can be applied to the study of health, healing, and illness.

- Discuss the orientation of medical sociologists to their research in this early part of the twenty-first century.

Until the second half of the twentieth century, matters pertaining to health, healing, and illness were viewed as the primary domain of physicians, other health care practitioners, and scholars in biology and chemistry. Neither medicine nor sociology paid much attention to each other. This changed dramatically in the ensuing decades as the paths of sociology and medicine increasingly converged. This chapter presents a brief introduction to the sociology of health, healing, and illness—a subfield of sociology commonly referred to as medical sociology.

DEFINITION OF MEDICAL SOCIOLOGY

Ruderman (1981:927) defines **medical sociology** as "the study of health care as it is institutionalized in a society, and of health, or illness, and its relationship to social factors." The Committee on Certification in Medical Sociology (1986:1) of the American Sociological Association (ASA) provided the following elaboration:

Medical sociology is the subfield which applies the perspectives, conceptualizations, theories, and methodologies of sociology to phenomena having to do with human health and disease. As a specialization, medical sociology encompasses a body of knowledge which places health and disease in a social, cultural, and behavioral context. Included within its subject matter are descriptions and explanations or theories relating to the distribution of diseases among various population groups; the behaviors or actions taken by individuals to maintain, enhance, or restore health or cope with illness, disease, or disability; people's attitudes and beliefs about health, disease, disability and medical care providers and organizations; medical occupations or professions and the organization, financing, and delivery of medical care services; medicine as a social institution and its relationship to other social institutions; cultural values and societal responses

1

with respect to health, illness, and disability; and the role of social factors in the etiology of disease, especially functional and emotion-related.

Clearly, the focus of medical sociology is broader than just "medicine." In fact, the title of this book was intentionally selected to connote that medical sociology includes a focus on health (in the positive sense of social, psychological, and emotional wellness), healing (the personal and institutional responses to perceived disease and illness), and illness (as an interference with health).

Sociologists study health, healing, and illness because they are a central part of the human experience, because they help us understand how society works, because they reflect patterns of social relationships, and because these understandings can contribute to helping address problems in the health care field. Sociologists emphasize that explanations for health and illness and for healing practices must go beyond biological and individualistic factors by examining the important influence of social context.

HISTORICAL DEVELOPMENT OF MEDICAL SOCIOLOGY

Setting the Foundation: The Importance of Social Factors in Health and Illness

It is difficult to identify any single event as the "starting point" of the field of medical sociology. Some of the basic insights of the field were even present among society's earliest philosophers and physicians. Many physicians in ancient times perceived an essential interrelationship among social and economic conditions, lifestyle, and health and illness. This understanding has been an integral part of medical thinking in some (though not all) civilizations ever since.

Often cited as a key historical figure who paved the way for medical sociology is Rudolf Virchow, the great mid-nineteenth-century German physician (and the founder of modern pathology). Virchow identified social and economic conditions as primary causes of an epidemic of typhus fever in 1847, and he lobbied for improved living conditions for the poor as a primary preventive technique. He argued against biomedical reductionism—attempting to reduce every disease and illness to a biological cause—and contended that medicine is largely a social science that needs to consider the influence of social context on health and illness.

The Turn of the Century: Development of Social Medicine

The late nineteenth century and the early twentieth century were a period of heightened awareness of the need for social programs to respond to health crises. These were years of social upheaval caused in part by the effects of the Industrial Revolution and rapid urban growth (and, in the United States, a tremendous influx of largely poor and unskilled immigrants). In 1915, Alfred Grotjahn published a classic work, *Soziale Pathologie*, documenting the role of social factors in disease and illness and urging development of a social science framework for reducing health problems. The term **social medicine** was coined to refer to efforts to improve public health.

However, an important crosscurrent was occurring simultaneously. The development of the germ theory of disease enabled physicians to treat more successfully the acute infectious diseases that plagued society. This reinforced a belief that medicine could rely solely on biological science. The discipline of sociology was still in its infancy and unable to provide sufficient documentation of the need for a complementary focus on social conditions.

The Early to Mid-twentieth Century: More Studies on Health and Medicine

Several important precursors to medical sociology occurred in the first half of the twentieth century. Social surveys became an important research technique, and many focused on health and living conditions. Sociologists often worked with charity organizations and settlement houses, which also became subjects for study. By the 1930s and 1940s, many sociological studies of the medical field appeared, including Talcott Parsons's 1939 work on the medical professions. Political scientist Oliver Garceau (1941) contributed to the political sociology of medicine by analyzing the political life of the American Medical Association. George Rosen (1944) studied increasing specialization in medicine. Oswald Hall (1946) studied the informal organization of medical practice in an American city (Rosen, 1976).

The 1950s and 1960s: The Formal Subdiscipline Emerges

The formal emergence of medical sociology as a field of study occurred in the 1950s and 1960s. The most important stimuli were changes in health, healing, and illness, external recognition of the field, and its institutionalization within sociology.

Changes in Health, Healing, and Illness. Based on analysis by Rodney Coe (1970) and others, the development of medical sociology was facilitated by four changes that occurred or were occurring in medicine in the 1950s and 1960s:

1. *Changing patterns of disease and illness.* During this time, the primary causes of disease and illness shifted from acute infectious diseases (e.g., influenza and tuberculosis) to chronic, degenerative diseases (e.g., heart disease and cancer). Because the factors that lead to degenerative diseases are more obviously tied to social patterns and lifestyle, the necessity for sociological contributions became more apparent.
2. *The impact of preventive medicine and public health.* The focus in public health was shifting from germs and immunology to the social

conditions such as poverty and poor housing that underlie many diseases and illnesses.
3. *The impact of modern psychiatry.* The development of the field of psychiatry led to increased interest in the psychosociological basis for many diseases and illnesses and in the importance of effective interaction between patients and practitioners.
4. *The impact of administrative medicine.* Medical organizations such as hospitals and health insurance companies were becoming increasingly complex, creating greater need for researchers with organizational expertise.

External Recognition and Legitimation. Two key events during the 1950s and 1960s contributed to the increased interest in and legitimation of medical sociology. First, medical schools began to hire more sociologists. Although medical sociology was not always well integrated into the curriculum, the move symbolized an increasing recognition of sociology's potential contribution to understanding disease and illness. Second, government agencies and private foundations initiated significant financial funding for medical sociology. The National Institutes of Health and the National Institute of Mental Health sponsored sociological research in medicine and subsidized training programs for graduate students in sociology. The Russell Sage Foundation provided significant funding of programs to increase the use of social science research within medicine.

Institutionalization of Medical Sociology. Two additional events contributed to the institutionalization of medical sociology. In 1959, medical sociology was accepted as a formal section of the ASA—an important step in bringing recognition to the field and enabling recruitment of new members. Second, in 1965, the ASA assumed control of an existing journal in medical sociology and renamed it the *Journal of Health and Social Behavior.* Now the official ASA journal for medical sociology, it is a key mechanism for medical sociologists to share their research.

Since then, the field has flourished. The ASA section on medical sociology currently has approximately 1,000 members (there are more than 13,000 ASA members), and is the third largest (of 52) interest sections within the association. Medical sociologists publish in a wide variety of journals in sociology, public health, and medicine and are increasingly employed in health planning, community health education, education of health professionals, government at all levels, and health care administration in addition to colleges and universities. See the "In the Field" box on Major Topics in Medical Sociology for one way of organizing the field's major topics.

IN THE FIELD

MAJOR TOPICS IN MEDICAL SOCIOLOGY

The four major categories of interest in medical sociology with specific topics of analysis and sample research questions (that will be answered in the appropriate chapters) are as follows:

Category #1: The Relationship Between the Social Environment and Health and Illness

Social Epidemiology—the study of patterns and trends in the causes and distribution of disease and illness within a population. Research question: Why is the infant mortality rate in the United States higher for African Americans than for whites?

Social Stress—the study of the imbalance or unease created when demands on a person exceed resources to deal with them. Research question: Why do women report higher levels of stress?

Category #2: Health and Illness Behavior

Health Behavior—the study of behaviors intended to promote positive health. Research question: Why does society focus on changing individual behaviors rather than the social circumstances that influence individual behaviors?

Experiencing Illness and Disability—the study of the ways that people perceive, interpret, and act in response to illness and disability. Research question: What factors cause people to interpret medical symptoms in very different ways?

Category #3: Health Care Practitioners and Their Relationship With Patients

Physicians and the Profession of Medicine—the study of medicine as a profession and the role of medicine within society. Research question: How does the high number of medical malpractice suits influence physicians and the practice of medicine?

Medical Education and the Socialization of Health Providers—the study of the education and socialization of physicians in medical school. Research question: What are the key value orientations that students learn in medical school?

Nurses, Advanced Practice Practitioners, and Allied Health Workers—the study of issues pertaining to non-physician health care providers. Research question: Why are physicians more supportive of physician assistants than they are of nurse practitioners?

Complementary and Alternative Healing Practices—the study of healers and healing practices outside conventional medicine. Research question: Why do many people simultaneously use both medical doctors and alternative healers?

The Physician–Patient Relationship—the study of patterns in how physicians and patients relate to each other and the factors that influence these patterns. Research question: To what extent do men and women physicians interact differently with patients?

Category #4: The Health Care System

The Health Care System—the study of the organization, regulation, financing, and important problems in the health care system and efforts to enact change. Research question: What effect is health care reform having on the health care system?

Health Care Delivery—the study of the many kinds of organizations that provide health care services. Research question: What are the causes and consequences of the increasing use of retail store clinics for primary care?

The Social Effects of Health Care Technology—the study of the social consequences and public policy choices of new health care technologies. Research question: What effects does legalizing physician-assisted death have on the dying experience?

Comparative Health Care Systems—the study of health care systems in other countries. Research question: What facets of health care are emphasized in countries around the world?

Foundational and Emerging Areas of Interest

All fields of inquiry are built on certain foundational topics yet remain open to new and emerging areas of interest. Within medical sociology, four particular topics are of rapidly expanding interest.

Issues Related to Health Care Reform. Concerns about the high cost of health care and the lack of or inadequate access that millions of Americans have to quality health care has led to recent reform efforts in the United States. A massive shift in the structure of insurance plans occurred in the 1990s and early 2000s, and major health care reform legislation (the Patient Protection and Affordable Care Act—commonly known as Obamacare) was passed in 2010. Hankin and Wright (2010:S10), in an editorial entitled "Reflections on Fifty Years of Medical Sociology" in the *Journal of Health and Social Behavior*, state:

> The work for medical sociologists is just beginning as we enter a new era of health care reform. Not only can we offer insights about how to implement reform, but we can also examine the intended and unintended consequences of transforming the health care system and the extent to which these structural changes actually improve population health.

These changes have had tremendous effects on the health care system and are examined throughout this book.

Issues Related to Technological Advancements in Medicine. Rapid advancements in medical technologies have dramatically changed the practice of medicine and how we conceptualize the human body. Medical sociologists are examining these technologies and their effects on the delivery of health care, the financing and regulation of health care, the provision of information to patients, the sharing of information among patients, and the reform of the health care system.

> Across the half-century lifespan of the (ASA) Medical Sociology Section, during which sweeping changes have impacted American society as a whole, technologies have changed dramatically, too, from large "machines at the bedside" to tiny pills and devices that enter into and transform human bodies, and information technologies that have altered if not restructured health care provision.
>
> (Casper and Morrison, 2010:S121)

We examine many of these technologies in this text, from life-saving technologies to the significant development of use of social media by health care providers and patients.

Issues Related to Medical Ethics.   Many technological advancements in medicine have raised important and provocative ethical questions. Sociological analysis and insights are extremely important in genuinely understanding these matters (DeVries et al., 2007). In recent years, medical sociologists have become more active in studying (1) values, attitudes, and behaviors of people relative to ethical issues in medicine (e.g., attitudes about genetic research and human cloning) and how they are influenced by various social factors, (2) social policy questions (e.g., on new reproductive technologies or the termination of treatment for the terminally ill), and (3) social movements (e.g., the pro-life and pro-choice movements) that have developed around these ethical issues. DeVries and Subedi (1998:xiii) describe sociology's role as "lifting bioethics out of its clinical setting, examining the way it defines and solves ethical problems, the modes of reasoning it employs, and its influence on medical practice."

Issues Related to Globalization.   Increasing globalization with respect to health and medicine is apparent in several ways. For example, climate change is affecting conditions that relate to health and disease all over the world. Recent disease epidemics—such as COVID-19, Ebola, and SARS—demonstrate the worldwide spread of disease. As the provision of health care becomes more and more expensive, countries around the world find it increasingly difficult to sustain an adequate health care system and seek to learn from each other. Medical schools increasingly have formal relationships with health institutions in other countries. Several chapters in this book describe the increasing attention given by medical sociology to global health care issues.

SOCIOLOGY'S CONTRIBUTION TO UNDERSTANDING HEALTH, HEALING, AND ILLNESS

Sociology is "the scientific study of social life, social change, and the social causes and consequences of human behavior" (American Sociological Association, 2013:1). It is the discipline with primary responsibility for studying social interaction among people, groups and organizations, and social institutions, and examining how these interactions influence and are influenced by the larger culture and social structure of society.

Three particular aspects of sociology contribute in important ways to understanding health, healing, and illness: (1) the sociological perspective, (2) the construction of social theories to explain why things happen as they do, and (3) the scientific foundation of the discipline.

The Sociological Perspective

Sociology is one of many perspectives used to acquire knowledge about the world. History, biology, chemistry, anthropology, psychology, economics, political science, philosophy and religion, clinical medicine, and other disciplines all contribute to our understanding of the medical field. Sociology's primary focus is to understand social interaction, groups and organizations, and how social context and the social environment influence attitudes, behaviors, and social organization.

The **sociological perspective** requires an ability to think about things in a manner other than that to which many individuals are accustomed. Often we think very individualistically about human behavior. If a particular teenager begins smoking cigarettes, or a particular man is very reluctant to see a physician when ill, or a particular medical resident feels abused by superiors, we may attempt to understand the behavior by focusing on the particular individual or the particular situation. However, sociology attempts to understand these behaviors by placing them

C. Wright Mills (1916–1962) coined the term "sociological imagination" to refer to the ability to see how individuals' *personal* troubles are influenced by large-scale, social (public) issues.

Source: © Archive Photos/Getty Images.

in social context—that is, by looking for social patterns and examining the influence of social forces or circumstances that have an impact on individual behavior.

C. Wright Mills, an enormously influential sociologist, referred to this ability to see how larger social patterns (public issues) influence individual behavior (personal troubles) as the **sociological imagination** (Mills, 1959). Consider the following:

1. Almost all adult smokers began smoking as teenagers; few adults begin smoking.
2. Men are more reluctant than women to see a physician.

3. Pharmaceutical drugs are more expensive in the United States than in any other country.

Sociologists attempt to understand these very important social patterns by placing them in social context. It is not just one adult smoker who started as a teen—that is the common pattern. So we try to find the social forces and the social arrangements that make it common for teens but not for adults to initiate smoking.

It is not just one man who is more reluctant than one woman to see a physician. If it was, there might be an individual explanation. Instead, men in general show more reluctance than women in general, so we are talking about some social force that influences men and women differently. What is it that creates this greater physician-aversion for men?

Finally, it is not just one drug that is more expensive in the United States than in other countries. If it was, there might be something in particular about that drug. In fact, almost all drugs in the United States are more expensive—many are much, much more expensive—so there must be some larger explanation. This is what Mills meant when he said that sociologists try to identify and explain the "public issues" (the larger social forces) that lead to "personal troubles."

The Construction of Social Theories

Sociologists attempt to describe social patterns and then find cause-and-effect relationships that explain them. In *Invitation to Sociology* (1963), Peter Berger describes sociology as searching for the general in the particular—attempting to determine how particular facts or individual behaviors may generate and reflect social patterns.

All science, natural and social, assumes that there is some underlying order in the universe. Events, whether they involve molecules or human beings, are not haphazard. They follow a pattern that is sufficiently regular for us to be able to make generalizations—statements that apply not just to a specific case but to most cases of the same type. . . . Generalizations are crucial to science because they place isolated, seemingly meaningless events in patterns we can understand. It then becomes possible to analyze relationships of cause and effect and thus to explain why something happens and to predict that it will happen again under the same conditions in the future.

(Robertson, 1987:6)

Grand Theoretical Orientations in Sociology.   Three grand (meaning all-encompassing) theoretical orientations have dominated the field of sociology. These orientations are fundamental images of society that guide sociological thinking. They are all-encompassing in that they offer a perspective to unify all observed uniformities in social behavior or social organization.

Functionalism (or structural functionalism) views society as a system (a structure) with interdependent parts (e.g., the family, the economy, and medicine) that work together to produce relative stability. Each of these parts is assumed to have positive consequences (or functions) and may have negative consequences (or dysfunctions) for the society as a whole. When each part operates properly, a stable and relatively harmonious society exists.

Given this image of society, functionalists are adept at identifying the effective integration of societal parts. For example, functionalists might identify the manner in which the value that America places on science and discovery has led to significant advancements in medical knowledge and to the development of new forms of medical technology.

Conflict theory views society as a system largely dominated by social inequality and social conflict. Societies are viewed as being in a constant state of change, characterized by disagreements over goals and values, competition among groups with unequal amounts of power, and hostility. Conflict theorists perceive whatever societal order exists to be dictated by the most powerful groups rather than being based on the value consensus envisioned by functionalists.

Given this image of society, conflict theorists are skillful at utilizing a critical perspective and identifying social inequities. In this regard, medical sociologists have an opportunity to comment critically on perceived problems and inequities in the health care system and to offer a critical perspective on the functioning of the system. For example, conflict theorists point out that a primary reason why many low-income women deliver premature, low-birth-weight babies is their inability to access adequate prenatal care.

While functionalism and conflict theory view society from a macro perspective (examining society as a whole), **interactionism** (or symbolic interactionism) focuses on small-scale, day-to-day interactions among people. Interactionists view society as the ultimate outcome of an infinite number of interpersonal interactions in which individuals interpret social messages and base their responses on these interpretations.

In medicine, interactionists have shown how physicians sometimes utilize particular communication strategies (e.g., using brief, closed-ended questions and interrupting patient comments) to reinforce dominance and bolster role distance.

Mid-Range Theoretical Orientations in Sociology.   While the previously mentioned grand theories are all-encompassing, most sociological research is guided more directly by theories that attempt to explain a specific behavior or social condition. These are called **"mid-range" theories**—a term coined by the distinguished sociologist Robert Merton. For example, in Chapter 6 we compare the Health Belief Model and the Theory of Reasoned Action—each a mid-range theory formulated to understand why some people but not others participate in health-promoting behaviors.

The Scientific Foundation of the Discipline

Charon and Vigilant (2008) maintain that sociology rests on both an objective and critical foundation. Sociology is a social science and sociological researchers have typically followed the same basic model of science and scientific research as their colleagues in the natural and physical sciences. These techniques rely on empirical procedures to obtain quantifiable data designed to test specific hypotheses and on the objectivity of scientists—that is, attempting to prevent biases from influencing the conduct of the work or the conclusions drawn.

The Scientific Process. A model of the **scientific process** is provided in Figure 1.1. According to this model, once a particular sociological question is identified, the researcher scours the literature (typically academic books and journals) to learn what research has already been done and determine what is already known about the subject. This work guides the researcher in formulating a mid-range *theory*, or general explanation, about why things happen as they do regarding the particular issue being studied.

Based on this theory, the researcher deduces one or more specific *hypotheses* (statements predicting what will be found in the research). These hypotheses must be capable of being found to be accurate or inaccurate. She then designs a research study to test the accuracy of the hypotheses, and selects a sample of people from the population about whom she collects data.

Once the data have been collected and analyzed, the researcher seeks to draw empirical generalizations from the research. She draws conclusions about the accuracy of the hypotheses and the appropriateness of the theory that guided the research. Conclusions may lend additional credence to the theory, or suggest that the theory needs to be modified, or be so inconsistent with the theory that a major revision is needed. If the results of the research are published or presented, the study will join others on the subject and be available for the next researcher doing a literature review on the subject.

Data–Collection Techniques. In this section we describe some of the most important data-collection techniques used by medical sociologists. Other techniques, such as specific epidemiological techniques, are described where appropriate in the text.

1. *Survey research.* **Survey research** is the most commonly used data-gathering technique in sociology. It involves the systematic collection of information about attitudes and behaviors through personal or telephone interviews or self-administered questionnaires (increasingly done online). Survey research is particularly helpful in studying attitudes or values—subjects that cannot easily be studied in other ways—and obtaining self-reported data on health and response to illness. Survey researchers must follow proper sampling techniques to ensure that the sample is representative of the population of interest.

2. *Experimental research.* **Experimental research** seeks to identify cause-and–effect relationships between specified variables in carefully controlled conditions. It is typically conducted in a laboratory but also can be done in natural

Figure 1.1 The Scientific Process

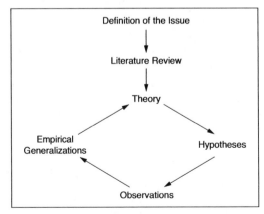

Source: Adapted from Walter L. Wallace (ed.). *Sociological Theory: An Introduction*, Copyright (2017) by Routledge. Reprinted by permission of Routledge.

settings. In the ideal case, two groups—the experimental group and the control group—are formed. The groups should be as similar as possible, except that only the experimental group receives the experimental condition or independent variable (the potential "cause"). Whatever change occurs in the dependent variable (the potential "effect") from the beginning to the end of the experiment can then be attributed to the independent variable. Experimental research is used in health settings for purposes such as testing the effectiveness of health education materials, innovations in teaching medical students, and new payment mechanisms.

3. *Observational research.* **Observational research** involves systematic observation of people in their natural environment. While it may be more difficult to be systematic when using this technique (although an extensive array of techniques to support systematic study is available), it does enable observation of actual behaviors rather than reports of behavior or behaviors performed in artificial settings. Important observational studies have been conducted in such diverse settings as hospitals, mortality review conferences, and patient self-help groups.

4. *Use of existing statistics.* Many demographers (those who study population size, composition, and distribution) and other medical sociologists study health problems and society's reaction to them by drawing on recorded vital and social statistics. Researchers may examine birth and death records, medical charts and insurance forms, and any compiled statistics on mortality, morbidity, medical resources, or any other aspect of health care systems.

Getting at Socially Constructed Reality. Although the scientific method continues to dominate in sociology, most sociologists acknowledge that reality is often more subjective than objective. These perspectives direct sociology to help us to understand the "socially constructed" nature of belief systems about health, illness, and healing practices. Cultures vary in their perception of what constitutes good health, in factors that shape health (e.g., Chinese belief in the presence of a vital spirit in the body), and in views of appropriate healing procedures (e.g., the importance of social support in Navajo healing). We further examine these perspectives in this text in chapters on social stress, illness behavior, and alternative healing practices.

THE ROLE OF THE MEDICAL SOCIOLOGIST IN THE TWENTY-FIRST CENTURY

What will be the future role of the medical sociologist? Perhaps three aspects will be most important.

First, the most important objective of the medical sociologist will continue to be to demonstrate and emphasize the important influence of cultural, social-structural, and institutional forces on health, healing, and illness. Medical sociologists must be ever more vigilant in using their "theoretical and methodological skills to address interesting and important questions" in order to ensure that the sociological perspective continues to influence public discussion (Pescosolido and Kronenfeld, 1995:19).

Second, medical sociologists need to maintain their spirit of free and critical inquiry (Bloom, 1990). Responding to an article that suggested that some physicians were concerned about sociologists' more liberal ideology, Mechanic (1990:89) wrote:

> It seems clear that these commentators . . . prefer a sociology that is adjunct to medical activity and accepting of its basic premises. Such a sociology would simply be a servant to medicine, not fulfilling its larger responsibility to understand medicine as a social, political, and legal endeavor; to challenge its curative and technological imperatives;

to examine equity of care in relation to class, race, gender, age, character of illness, and geographic area; and to study the appropriate goals and objectives for health care in the context of an aging society with an illness trajectory dominated by chronic disease.

Finally, medical sociologists should continue to seek interdisciplinary collaboration. In the early years of the field, medical sociologists debated whether their primary focus should be on the **sociology of medicine** (i.e., advancing sociological theory and method through research in the medical field) or on the **sociology in medicine** (i.e., making practical contributions to the practice of medicine) (Straus, 1957). While many medical sociologists have clearly identified more with one or the other of these approaches, the distinction has blurred over time, and today most researchers understand that good sociological research can simultaneously contribute to the development of medical sociology *and* to improved health care (Bird, Conrad, and Fremont, 2000). Many refer to this as **sociology with medicine**. Straus (1999) suggested that it is even possible to take a critical perspective while working in a medical setting, as long as it is perceived as constructive, objective, and not blatantly antagonistic.

Mechanic (1995:1492) noted that "the major health problems facing national systems are complex and multifaceted and not easily amenable to analysis from the perspective of any single discipline." Coe (1997:6) encouraged working with other social scientists (as well as others involved in health research) as a way of creating "opportunities to strengthen a sociological perspective" and deepening "our understanding of the complexities of human behavior in the context of health and illness." Zussman (2000) wrote persuasively about how genuine understanding of ethical issues in medicine can be derived from utilizing both normative reflection (the primary approach of medical ethics) and empirical description (the primary contribution of sociology). Brown (2013) called for interdisciplinary work among medical sociologists and environmental sociologists and linking their work with environmental health science. Several medical sociologists (Fremont and Bird, 1999; Pescosolido, 2006, 2011; Seabrook and Avison, 2010) have recently urged greater effort to integrate social and biological explanations of matters related to health, healing, and illness.

SUMMARY

Medical sociology emerged as a scholarly field of inquiry in the 1950s and 1960s. Four factors were primarily responsible for this emergence: (1) a shift from acute infectious diseases to chronic degenerative diseases as major sources of morbidity and mortality, (2) increased focus on behavioral factors related to health and illness, (3) increased recognition of the importance of the patient–physician relationship, and (4) the increasingly complex structure of the health care system. Simultaneously, outside agencies (e.g., medical schools and government agencies) were taking an increasing interest in the field, and medical sociology was becoming institutionalized as a special interest section in the ASA.

Sociology's contributions to the study of health, healing, and illness emanate from the sociological perspective (the understanding that human behavior is largely shaped by the groups to which people belong and by the social interaction that takes place within those groups), sociology-based grand (functionalism, conflict theory, and interactionism) and mid-range (more specifically focused) theoretical approaches, and the scientific foundation and critical perspective of the discipline.

The most important tasks of medical sociology are to demonstrate and emphasize the important influence of cultural, social-structural, and institutional forces on health, healing, and illness, and to maintain a spirit of free and critical inquiry while recognizing the value and necessity of interdisciplinary research and work on health and illness.

HEALTH ON THE INTERNET

This chapter discusses recent calls for health researchers in various disciplines to work more closely together. Learn more about three of the social science disciplines that investigate health, healing, and illness by checking out their websites.

Medical sociology: https://www.asanet.org/ asa-communities/sections/medical-sociology
Medical anthropology: www.medanthro.net
Health psychology: www.health-psych.org.

What is the main focus of each of these fields? What similarities and differences do you note?

DISCUSSION QUESTIONS

1. To understand better the approach and work of medical sociologists, select a recent article from the *Journal of Health and Social Behavior* or *Social Science and Medicine* (written by a sociologist) or any journal assigned by your professor. Identify its main subject, theoretical approach, data-collection technique, and main findings. How does the approach of a medical sociologist differ from that of a medical journalist or that of a layperson attempting to understand some subject related to health, healing, and illness? Identify a specific question related to medical sociology or an issue that you might be interested in studying.

2. The health and medical sector is an extraordinarily broad and important component of society. One way of identifying the importance of health, healing, and illness in society is to note the extent to which the social institution of medicine is closely interwoven with all or almost all other social institutions. Describe how the social institution of medicine interrelates to each of the following nine social institutions.

science	government	economy
education	family	law
religion	the arts	recreation

GLOSSARY

conflict theory	mid-range theory
experimental research	observational research
functionalism	scientific process
interactionism	social medicine
medical sociology	sociological imagination

sociological perspective
sociology in medicine
sociology of medicine

sociology with medicine
survey research

REFERENCES

American Sociological Association. 2013. "What is Sociology?" Retrieved May 10, 2013 (www.asanet.org/employment/careers21st_whatissociology.cfm).

American Sociological Association, Committee on Certification in Sociology. 1986. *Guidelines for the Certification Process in Medical Sociology.* Washington, DC: American Sociological Association.

Berger, Peter L. 1963. *Invitation to Sociology: A Humanistic Perspective.* New York: Doubleday.

Bird, Chloe E., Peter Conrad, and Allen M. Fremont. 2000. "Medical Sociology at the Millennium." Pp. 1–10 in *Handbook of Medical Sociology* (5th ed.), edited by Chloe E. Bird, Peter Conrad, and Allen M. Fremont. Upper Saddle River, NJ: Prentice Hall.

Bloom, Samuel W. 1990. "Episodes in the Institutionalization of Medical Sociology: A Personal View." *Journal of Health and Social Behavior* 31(1):1–10.

Brown, Phil. 2013. "Integrating Medical and Environmental Sociology with Environmental Health." *Journal of Health and Social Behavior* 54(2):145–164.

Casper, Monica J., and Daniel R. Morrison. 2010. "Medical Sociology and Technology: Critical Engagements." *Journal of Health and Social Behavior* 51(S1):120–132.

Charon, Joel, and Lee G. Vigilant. 2008. *The Meaning of Sociology* (8th ed.). Upper Saddle River, NJ: Prentice Hall.

Coe, Rodney M. 1970. *Sociology of Medicine.* New York: McGraw-Hill.

———. 1997. "The Magic of Science and the Science of Magic: An Essay on the Process of Healing." *Journal of Health and Social Behavior* 38(1):1–8.

DeVries, Raymond, and Janardan Subedi. 1998. *Bioethics and Society: Constructing the Ethical Enterprise.* Upper Saddle River, NJ: Prentice Hall.

DeVries, Raymond, Leigh Turner, Kristina Orfali, and Charles L. Bosk. 2007. *The View from Here: Bioethics and the Social Sciences.* London: Blackwell.

Fremont, Allen M., and Chloe E. Bird. 1999. "Integrating Sociological and Biological Models: An Editorial." *Journal of Health and Social Behavior* 40(2):126–129.

Garceau, Oliver. 1941. *The Political Life of the American Medical Association.* Cambridge, MA: Harvard University Press.

Grotjahn, Alfred. 1915. *Soziale Pathologie.* Berlin: August Hirschwald Verlag.

Hall, Oswald. 1946. "The Informal Organization of the Medical Profession." *Canadian Journal of Economic and Political Science* 12(1):30–44.

Hankin, Janet R., and Erik R. Wright. 2010. "Reflections on Fifty Years of Medical Sociology." *Journal of Health and Social Behavior* 51(S):10–14.

Mechanic, David. 1990. "The Role of Sociology in Health Affairs." *Health Affairs* 9(1):85–97.

———. 1995. "Emerging Trends in the Application of the Social Sciences to Health and Medicine." *Social Science and Medicine* 40(11):1491–1496.

Mills, Wright C. 1959. *The Sociological Imagination.* New York: Oxford University Press.

Parsons, Talcott. 1939. "The Professions and Social Structure." *Social Forces* 17(4):457–467.

Pescosolido, Bernice A. 2006. "Of Pride and Prejudice: The Role of Sociology and Social Networks in Integrating the Health Sciences." *Journal of Health and Social Behavior* 47(3):189–208.

———. 2011. "Taking the 'Promise' Seriously: Medical Sociology's Role in Health, Illness, and Healing in a Time of Social Change." Pp. 3–20 in *Handbook of the Sociology of Health, Illness, and Healing: A Blueprint for the 21st Century,* edited by Bernice A. Pescosolido, Jack K. Martin, Jane D. McLeod, and Anne Rogers. New York: Springer.

Pescosolido, Bernice A., and Jennie J. Kronenfeld. 1995. "Health, Illness, and Healing in an Uncertain Era: Challenges from and for Medical Sociology." *Journal of Health and Social Behavior* 51(Extra Issue):5–33.

Robertson, Ian. 1987. *Sociology* (3rd ed.). New York: Worth Publishers.

Rosen, George. 1944. *The Specialization of Medicine.* New York: Froben Press.

———. 1976. "Social Science and Health in the United States in the Twentieth Century." *Clio Medica* 11(4):245–268.

Ruderman, Florence A. 1981. "What Is Medical Sociology?" *Journal of the American Medical Association* 245(9):927–929.

Seabrook, James A., and William R. Avison. 2010. "Genotype–Environment Interaction and Sociology: Contributions and Complexities." *Social Science and Medicine* 70(9):1277–1284.

Straus, Robert. 1957. "The Nature and Status of Medical Sociology." *American Sociological Review* 22(2):200–204.

———. 1999. "Medical Sociology: A Personal Fifty-Year Perspective." *Journal of Health and Social Behavior* 40(2):103–110.

Wallace, Walter L. (ed.). 2017. *Sociological Theory: An Introduction.* New York: Routledge.

Zussman, Robert. 2000. "The Contributions of Sociology to Medical Ethics." *Hastings Center Report* 30(1):7–11.

CHAPTER 2

The Development of Scientific Medicine

Learning Objectives

- Explain how medical belief systems fluctuated from the earliest civilizations to the Hippocratic Era to the Medieval Era to the Renaissance and to the development of scientific medicine.

- Identify and discuss three significant contributions of Hippocrates to the understanding of health, healing, and illness.

- Describe the practice of medicine in early America.

- Identify and discuss the effects of the Civil War on medical knowledge and on the practice of medicine.

- Compare and contrast the views of Paul Starr and Vicente Navarro on the "cultural authority of medicine."

Today's healing practices and health care systems developed through centuries of efforts to understand disease and illness and to find effective means to protect and restore health. Understanding this historical development is important both as an end in itself and as a means to better understand current patterns.

Compiled histories of medicine are not in short supply, but few of these histories attempt to place the development of medicine within a social context. A *sociological* approach to the history of medicine includes at least the following: (1) a *sociology of medical knowledge*—that is, the ways in which societies socially construct medical knowledge; (2) the development and evolution of the primary activities in which physicians engage, including patient education, prevention, examination and diagnosis, prognosis, curative techniques, and palliative care (relief from suffering); (3) the evolution of the organization of medical practice, including medical specialization and the relationship to hospitals and corporations; (4) the development of hospitals and their changing role within society; and (5) the development and evolution of public health measures, including nutrition, sanitation, and public education (McKeown, 1970; White, 2009).

This chapter gives some attention to all these themes but focuses primarily on the first by describing the historical development of scientific medicine and tracing the ascendancy of scientific medical authority in America. It demonstrates that the discovery and acceptance of medical knowledge can be understood only in social context and are, at the very least, partially dependent on both cultural values (including orientation toward medicine) and the configuration of powerful interests within society. In particular, notice the following:

1. The constantly shifting character (Cassady, 1991) of medicine as understanding of disease causation shifts between a supernatural and scientific basis, as the role and popularity of alternative healing philosophies ebb and flow.

2. The constant struggle of medical researchers to discover causes and cures of disease, and the typically long time lag before major discoveries are accepted and impact patient care.
3. The important impact on medicine of other major institutions in society, including government, religion, family, and science.
4. The constantly evolving view of the nature and inevitability of disease and of the patient's responsibility for self-care.

A BRIEF HISTORY OF MEDICINE

One of the most significant events in the development of scientific medicine was the discovery that many diseases can be traced to specific causes such as bacteria, viruses, and parasites. Chief credit for this discovery is typically assigned to Louis Pasteur's formulation of the germ theory of disease in the 1860s and 1870s. Prior to this time, both laypersons and professionals used a multitude of approaches and explanations to understand the causes of disease and illness. The first part of this chapter traces this development of scientific medical knowledge.

EARLY HUMANS

Although the first forms of writing did not appear until between 4000 and 3000 BC, paleontologists have used human remnants such as teeth, bones, and mummies, as well as works of art, to study early disease and its treatment. They have learned that disease and injury are as old as humankind (and the presence of bacteria and viruses far older). There is evidence of tumors, fractures, parasitic diseases, arthritis, osteomyelitis, and dental caries that pre-date written communication. How did early humans interpret these medical calamities?

Primitive man, noting the rising and setting of the sun and moon, the progress of the seasons, the birth, growth, and inevitable death of plants, animals, and humans, did not take long to arrive at the supposition that these phenomena did not occur by chance . . . it seemed logical to suppose that they were ordered by some all-powerful god, or gods, and equally logical was the belief that fortune and misfortune were signs of the gods' pleasure or displeasure.

(Camp, 1977:11)

Supernatural Belief Systems

These "magico-religious" or **supernatural explanations of disease** evolved into complex belief systems. Diseases were caused either by direct intervention of a god or spirit or through a sorcerer (a mortal in control of supernatural forces), or through the intrusion of some foreign object into the body—a spirit or demon, or something more tangible, such as a stone or pebble (Magner and Kim, 2017).

Early humans used several divination procedures (e.g., crystal gazing or trances) to read the intentions of the supernatural. Once the diagnosis was made, appropriate cures were employed. Religious rituals such as prayer, magic spells, and exorcism were used when the origin of the disease was traced to supernatural forces, and more physical means including a "sucking-out" procedure, artificially induced vomiting, and "bloodletting" (draining blood from the body to extract the foreign presence or redistribute the blood, a practice that survived for centuries) were used in cases of object intrusion (Magner and Kim, 2017).

The most amazing procedure used was skull **trephination**—utilizing sharpened stones to drill or carve a hole in the skull. The exact purpose of trephination is unknown, but many believe it was done to release evil spirits. The holes drilled were of various sizes and configurations depending upon the diagnosis. Fossil studies demonstrate that many patients survived the surgery, and some received additional trephinations years after the original.

Trephination is considered by many to be the first surgical technique. It involved carving a circular section from the skull to reduce pressure or release evil spirits causing sickness. It likely started as long as 7,000 years ago and continued for perhaps 2,500 years.

Source: © Paul Bevitt/Alamy Stock Photo.

THE FIRST PHYSICIANS

Specialists (often religious figures) emerged to serve as intermediaries with the gods. **Shamans** (or "witch doctors" or "medicine men"), were highly revered, much-feared individuals who often provided effective medical care. Many were adept at observing animals and noting the plants and herbs they used for relief, and many practiced trial-and-error medicine—experimenting with a variety of substances or procedures to identify the most effective ones. The kinds of diseases that were most common in early societies—rheumatic diseases, digestive disorders, skin diseases, and gynecological disorders—were problems more amenable to cures available at that time than would be epidemic diseases, such as typhoid

and smallpox, which many believe were not yet present.

Of course, these techniques were only part of the medical arsenal of the shaman. Prayer and incantation, ritualistic dancing, and sacrifices were also used to capture the attention of the gods. These techniques also increased the patient's confidence in the cures being attempted—an important psychotherapeutic benefit (Magner and Kim, 2017).

FOUR ANCIENT CIVILIZATIONS

Ancient Chinese Civilization

For much of human history, knowledge was passed from generation to generation orally in the form of songs and stories, as formal systems of writing did not exist. While Chinese medicine dates back to about 5000 BC, the earliest written records of it date to only about 3000 BC. The *Huang-Di Nei-Jing* (*Yellow Emperor's Cannon of Internal Medicine*), written between 300 and 200 BC, is supposedly a record of the emperor's conversations with his esteemed physician that occurred around 2650 BC.

The *Huang-Di Nei-Jing* consists of both a theoretical section (discussing interactions between the internal organs, the sense organs, and brain waves) and a practical section (describing acupuncture practices). The book deals extensively with the concept of yin and yang, which understands bodily organs as interdependent and existing in a harmonious state when the individual is healthy. Disease occurs when the natural harmony within and between organs is lost. Therefore, the goal of treatment is to restore the body's natural harmony (Cohen, 2013).

Our understanding of early Chinese medicine also comes from the work of archaeologists. For example, two graves from about 2,000 years ago included ancient silk scrolls with references to 247 herbal substances used for medicinal purposes, and the grave of a physician from about the same time included 92 wooden bamboo slips with pharmaceutical data listing 30 prescriptions and referring to a hundred herbal medicines (Cohen, 2013).

Ancient Egyptian Civilization

Egyptian medical practices have received considerable attention due to Egypt's reputation as an especially healthy civilization and to an abundance of surviving written material. Ancient Egyptian medicine was very advanced for its time. Mummification ceremonies involved removing organs—including the intestine, pancreas, liver, spleen, heart, lungs, and brain (Nunn, 2002). This enabled physicians to develop anatomical knowledge and to understand the functions of most organs, contributing to somewhat effective treatments and even to effective dentistry.

Most Egyptian physicians focused on a particular disease or a particular part of the body. Given the hot and dusty desert conditions, most specialized in eye care. Physicians were also religious leaders, and each was devoted to a different god. As a result, they tended to focus on whatever diseases were associated with their deity. They also wrote codes of medical ethics centuries before Hippocrates.

The theories and techniques of Ancient Egyptian medicine were highly regarded by other cultures and studied by early Greek physicians, forming the basis of many of their medical advancements. Imhotep—an African engineer, architect, scribe, priest, builder of tombs, and possibly a physician—lived in the 2600s BC and is referred to as the "Historical Father of Medicine." He produced journals (now lost) on surgery, anatomy, pathology, diagnosis, and experimental scientific observation and possibly built the first hospital (Makah and Jalil, 2009).

Ancient Mesopotamian Civilization

Ancient Mesopotamia is a region in Western Asia that roughly corresponds today to parts of Iraq, Kuwait, Saudi Arabia, Syria, and Turkey. It is the site of some of the most important developments in human history including the invention of the wheel, the planting of the first cereal crops, and the development of mathematics and astronomy.

Along with ancient Egyptian medicine, the Babylonians (part of Mesopotamia) introduced the concepts of diagnosis, prognosis, physical examination, and prescriptions. The **Code of Hammurabi** (a Babylonian king who lived from 1728 to 1686 BC), is possibly the first codified set of guidelines regarding responsibilities of physicians, and other writings (including the Ebers Papyrus (see Image 2.2) addressed disease causation, symptoms, and medical therapy (Teall, 2014).

Georg Ebers papyrus from the U. S. National Medical Library at the National Institutes of Health. This papyrus recounts the case of a "tumor against the god Xenus and recommends do thou nothing there against." It is also noted that the heart is the center of the blood supply with vessels attached for every member of the body. (Public Domain)

Ancient Indian Civilization

The development of medicine in India can be traced to the Indus Valley civilization (ca. 3300–1300 BC). Archaeological remains portray involvement of the Indus people in concocting drugs from plants, animal products, and minerals. More substantial evidence is provided in the Vedic civilization that flourished from about 1000 BC forward. There, evidence reflects concern with demons, curses, and poisoning, details about using plants for healing, and the possible origin of Ayurveda and Ayurvedic medicine—one of India's main medical systems (Ranganayakulu, 2015).

Ayurveda means complete knowledge for long life. It synthesizes traditional herbal practices and new therapies based on the thoughts of Buddha and other thinkers. Ayurveda posits that life and health are not predetermined, and life can be prolonged by human effort. Therapies include use of herbal drugs, massage, sauna, exercise, diet, bloodletting (including leeching), and surgery. Lengthy volumes—on topics such as anatomy, embryology, diagnosis, surgery, epidemics, and pharmacology—also include reflective passages on topics such as the origin of humans (Ranganayakulu, 2015).

GREEK AND ROMAN SOCIETIES

During the last 2,000 years BC, Greece was an especially remarkable civilization, making substantial contributions to areas such as medicine, philosophy, art, theater, and government. In the beginning of this era, religion and medicine were still inextricably linked. Apollo, the sun god, was also god of health and medicine and believed to be the inventor of the healing art. According to Greek legend, Aesculapius was the son of Apollo and such a brilliant healer that by the eighth century he was considered the Greek god of health.

Priest-physicians practiced the healing ceremony of *temple sleep*. Patients would come to temples called *asklepieia* to purify themselves (bathe), fast, read about the cures of former patients, and make offerings to Aesculapius. They were given drugs to induce sleep, and during the night, harmless "sacred" snakes would crawl around the patients and lick their wounds. Attendants would later apply salves, and according to lore, patients were cured (Magner and Kim, 2017).

Hippocrates—The "Father of Medicine"

Simultaneously, a more empirically based medicine was developing, and many physicians enjoyed favorable reputations. Ancient Greece is often regarded as the first culture to apply scientific thinking to the art of healing and produce doctors whose methods were in many respects comparable to those of modern physicians The most renowned of these physicians is **Hippocrates** of Cos (460–377 BC)—the "Father of Medicine." Hippocrates was well educated, became a successful and much beloved physician, and was an esteemed teacher. He is best known for three major contributions:

1. *The principle of natural, rather than supernatural, explanations for disease.* The most important contribution of Hippocrates to medicine is the understanding that disease is a natural process and that symptoms are the body's reactions to disease. Hippocrates emphasized that the body has its own means of recovery and that a healthy person is one in a balanced mental and physical state (Green, 1968:31).

   Hippocrates subscribed to the **humoral theory of disease**—the dominant approach for centuries. The humoral theory postulates that there are four natural elements in the world (air, earth, fire, and water) and four natural properties (hot, cold, dry, and wet). In the body, the elements are blood (hot), phlegm (cold), yellow bile (dry), and black bile (wet). A person is healthy when these four humors are in balance and when the individual is in balance with the environment. Sickness results from imbalance, which is detected by physical symptoms. A warm forehead (fever) indicates excessive heat; a runny nose is a sign of excessive phlegm. Appropriate cures seek to restore balance. Cold food was a remedy for heat-related diseases, and a very dry environment was recommended for excessive phlegm. He further emphasized that the chief function of the physician is to aid the natural forces of the body.

Following Hippocrates' beliefs, Greek physicians studied the case history of patients, asking questions and attempting to learn as much as possible from the patient before arriving at a diagnosis. This two-way interaction between patient and doctor became a foundation in the history of medicine.

The Greeks were also surgeons, and some of the equipment they used is recognizable today. Greek physicians used medical tools such as forceps, scalpels, tooth-extraction forceps and catheters, and even syringes for drawing pus from wounds. The Greeks also knew how to splint and treat bone fractures, as well as add compresses to prevent infection.

2. *His writings.* One of the most important sets of medical writings ever collated is the *Corpus Hippocraticum*—more than 70 books, monographs, and essays covering a variety of medical topics. Hippocrates wrote of the importance of observing disease progression and described his own copious note-taking of medical histories, symptoms, and reactions to therapy when treating his patients. He encouraged physicians to treat the whole patient, not just a particular organ or symptom (Porter, 2006).

3. *His teaching of human compassion and ethical standards.* The first section of the **Hippocratic Oath** (see the accompanying box "The Hippocratic Oath") expresses reciprocal commitments made by physicians and their apprentices, and establishes teaching as a primary obligation of the

physician. The second part is a brief summary of ethical guidelines. Some of the pledges—for example, against performing abortion, cutting for stone, and facilitating a suicide—raise questions, since they were common practices at the time even by Hippocratic physicians (Nuland, 1995). Nevertheless, the oath commanded significant attention then as it does now.

Despite the popularity of Hippocrates, Greece could be described as an "open medical marketplace" comprising several types of religious, magical, and empirical medical practitioners. Because there was no medical licensing, anyone could be a healer, and physicians reflected a multitude of medical philosophies.

Hippocrates of Cos, the "Father of Medicine," advocated natural rather than supernatural explanations for disease.

Source: © INTERFOTO/Alamy.

Roman Medicine

Medicine did not develop in Rome to the same extent it did in Greece. Mostly, Roman households ministered to the sick in their own families, often using treatments similar to those used in early societies. Beginning in the third century BC (Rome was founded in 753 BC), Greek physicians began filtering into Rome. At first, these physicians were persecuted, partly out of a jealousy that Rome was not producing its own physicians. Cato the Censor (234–149 BC), the man given credit for being the first important writer in Latin, prohibited all in his family from using these physicians (he relied instead on raw cabbage taken internally and rubbed on the body as a medicinal cure). Pliny the Elder is said to have remarked that "the honour of a Roman does not permit him to make medicine his profession, and the Romans who begin to study it are mercenary deserters to the Greeks" (Camp, 1977).

However, Roman medicine made significant contributions to health care by emphasizing the importance of nutrition and exercise and implementing elaborate sanitation procedures. Romans created the now famous aqueduct system as a means of delivering a continual supply of fresh drinking water and established public fountains and public baths. They passed ordinances requiring street cleanliness, signaling knowledge of the importance of hygiene, waste disposal sanitation, and a fresh water supply for general health.

Roman medicine also further developed surgery and physicians frequently performed successful surgical procedures. They treated war wounds, removed growths, did reconstruction surgery, and boiled equipment prior to surgery to ensure its sterility.

IN THE FIELD

THE HIPPOCRATIC OATH

I swear by Apollo the physician, and Aesculapius, Hygeia, and Panacea and all the gods and goddesses, that, according to my ability and judgment, I will keep this oath and this covenant:

To reckon him who taught me this Art equally dear to me as my parents, to share my substance with him, and relieve his necessities if required; to look upon his offspring on the same footing as my own brothers, and to teach them this Art, if they shall wish to learn it, without fee or stipulation; and that by precept, lecture, and every other mode of instruction, I will impart a knowledge of the Art to my own sons, and those of my teachers, and to disciples who have signed the covenant and have taken an oath according to the law of medicine, but no one else.

I will follow that system of regimen which, according to my ability and judgment, I consider for the benefit of my patients, and abstain from whatever is deleterious and mischievous.

I will give no deadly medicine to anyone if asked, nor suggest any such counsel; and in like manner I will not give to a woman an abortive remedy. With purity and with holiness I will pass my life and practice my Art.

I will not cut persons labouring under the stone, but will leave this to be done by such men as are practitioners of this work.

Into whatever houses I enter, I will go into them for the benefit of the sick, and will abstain from every voluntary act of mischief and corruption; and, further, from the seduction of females or males, of freemen and slaves.

Whatever, in connection with my professional practice, or not in connection with it, I see or hear, in the life of men, which ought not to be spoken of abroad, I will not divulge, as reckoning that all such should be kept secret.

While I continue to keep this Oath unviolated, may it be granted to me to enjoy life and practice the Art, respected by all men, in all times. But should I trespass and violate this Oath, may the reverse be my lot.

Galen

The most renowned medical figure of this era is Galen, a physician whose ideas dominated much of medicine for the next 12 centuries. Born in Asia Minor in AD 131, he studied Hippocratic medicine (and its rival theories) and eventually migrated to Rome at the age of 34. There he became famous as a physician, author, and medical researcher.

Galen made extensive contributions to the understanding of anatomy. Because he was prevented by Roman law from using human cadavers for study, Galen relied on the dissection of monkeys and pigs and the study of the skeletons of criminals. Based on these studies, he refuted several common medical notions (e.g., that blood vessels originate in the brain) and added to existing knowledge about bones, muscle groups, the brain, and various nerves. He also believed strongly in *pneuma*—that certain vital spirits (but not blood) circulated throughout the body (Magner and Kim, 2017).

Galen vehemently discouraged others from further investigating his work. Although we now know many of his theories to be false, they were extremely influential during his time and for subsequent centuries. On the other hand, his title as the "Father of Experimental Physiology" seems well deserved, as he was probably the foremost medical experimentalist until the 1600s.

THE MEDIEVAL ERA

The collapse of the Western Roman Empire, generally pegged at AD 476, was due to many reasons—both internal (political corruption, an overreliance on slavery, and military overspending) and external (the rise of the Eastern Empire and the migration of so-called *barbarians*, including Huns, Goths, and Vandals. In the East, the Byzantine Empire (which became Constantinople, and now Istanbul) survived and became a center of civilization. The time period between (roughly) AD 500 and 1500 is referred to as the Medieval Era.

Monastic Medicine

Medical practice in the first half of this era is known as **monastic medicine** because it was based in the monastery and officially controlled by the Christian Church. The Church was hostile to physicians because it believed that disease and illness are beneficial tests of faith and commitment to the church. The prevailing belief was that illnesses were a punishment by God, possession by the devil, or a result of witchcraft.

Given that diseases were thought to be religious in origin, religious cures were most appropriate. Medieval cures largely consisted of prayers, penitence, pilgrimage, intercession of saints, or other signs of religious devotion. Each disease and body part had a patron saint who could inflict pain and enact cures. For example, if one had a toothache, prayer was made to Saint Apollonia.

A common treatment in medieval medicine was "bloodletting" or bleeding, thought to allow disease or illness to leave the blood. The individual who generally performed such procedures was known as a "barber" and traveled to towns performing minor surgeries, such as teeth pulling. The red and white striped pole which is a familiar sight in front of barber shops today originated with this practice of barbers as medieval medicine practitioners.

(Abrams, 2009:1)

According to the Church, efforts to cure disease apart from religious intervention represented a form of blasphemy. In reality, many people from all stations in life considered secular healing an appropriate complement to religious healing and often used the services of herbalists, midwives, wise women, and lay specialists. These practitioners are largely responsible for preserving the medical knowledge passed on to them and ensuring its transmission to later generations.

IN THE FIELD

A MEDIEVAL JOKE

If you want to be cured of
I don't know what—
Take this herb of
I don't know what name

Apply it
I don't know where
And you will be cured
I don't know when.

Islamic Medicine

The commonwealth of Islam was founded in 622 by Mohammed. During the next 100 years, his followers conquered almost half of the world known at that time. By 1000, the Arab Empire extended from Spain to India.

The development of Islamic medicine arose out of an ambitious movement in the ninth century to translate Greek texts into Arabic. However, it went beyond this in collating and synthesizing medical principles from many of the ancient traditions, making it the most sophisticated approach to medicine during the Medieval Era.

Islamic medicine recognized that the various parts and organs (skeletal, nervous, circulatory, and reproductive) of the body existed in an interrelated physical system. Understanding of the specific functions of these systems, however, was limited by the lack of empirical data. For example, the movement of blood from the heart was recognized but not the return of blood back to the heart.

The various organs and systems within the body were referred to as the *naturals*. However, Islamic medicine believed that outside factors (*non-naturals*) also influence health. These factors included air quality, exercise, diet, sleep, digestion, and psychic states (including stressfulness, moods, and attitudes). The doctrine of the non–naturals highlights the themes of moderation and balance that also dominated medieval Islamic thinking on the healthy body (Conrad, 1995).

An interesting aspect of Islamic medicine is that the physical presence of the patient was not deemed absolutely necessary for an accurate diagnosis. A family member with no medical background could describe a relative's illness to a physician or bring in a written account or a urine sample, and the physician would identify the problem and prescribe a therapy without direct recourse to the patient (Conrad, 1995).

Scholastic Medicine

The second half of the Medieval Era is referred to as the time of **scholastic medicine**. In 1130, a proclamation from the Council of Clermont responded to growing public disillusionment with medical care by forbidding monks from practicing medicine. The cited reasons were that it was too disruptive to the peace and order of monastic sequestration. So medicine became the province of secular clergy, and universities began to play a prominent role in the education of physicians. Although it is impossible to fix the precise date at which universities in the modern sense first developed, twelfth- and thirteenth-century schools became centers where a variety of disciplines were taught (probably the most important legacy of the Middle Ages) (Magner and Kim, 2017).

During this time period, many small towns and cities developed. Given their only rudimentary sanitation practices and the lack of any effective medical care, disease spread quickly, and devastating epidemics occurred. Leprosy reached a peak in the thirteenth century, scurvy epidemics were common, and the bubonic plague—**Black Death** raged in Europe in the 1340s, killing an estimated 43 million people in 20 years—one-third of Europe's population (Porter, 2006).

MEDICINE IN THE RENAISSANCE

The fifteenth and sixteenth centuries—the Renaissance—represent a rebirth in the arts and philosophy, scientific endeavor, technological advancement, and medicine. The scholarly blinders of the Middle Ages were discarded in favor of *humanism*, which stressed the dignity of the individual, the importance of this life (not solely the afterlife), and spiritual freedom. Greek, Roman, and Islamic medicine received significant attention. As church control of medicine declined, medical research increased. The printing of books led to a much greater sharing of ideas.

Andreas Vesalius

A key early event of the Renaissance was the refutation of many of Galen's ideas. Andreas Vesalius (1514–1564), a product of a Brussels medical family, contradicted Galen's description of anatomy. Using corpses purchased from grave robbers, he discovered that Galen's descriptions accurately portrayed monkeys but in many respects, not humans. He thought if Galen was wrong about anatomy, he might be wrong about his other conclusions (e.g., pneuma). Yet allegiance to Galen's ideas was so strong that Vesalius was dismissed from his university position for this heresy, and his career as an anatomist was finished (although he later became a court physician).

Medical Specialization

During the Renaissance, the medical specialization that had begun in the ninth and tenth centuries became more pronounced. *Physicians* were those who had graduated from a school of medicine. They provided diagnosis and consultation and were expected to bear themselves as gentlemen to match the demeanor of their wealthy patients. *Surgeons* were lower in status because they practiced skills learned in apprenticeship. Their primary responsibilities were to treat external complaints (e.g., wounds and abscesses), repair broken bones, and perform minor surgeries. In some areas, *barber surgeons* performed major surgery (often on the war-wounded) and many also practiced bloodletting. Approximately equal in prestige to surgeons, *apothecaries* dispensed herbs and spices prescribed by physicians and, especially in the countryside, often took on a physician's duties. Nevertheless, self-medication and lay healing were still very common in the Renaissance.

MEDICINE FROM 1600 TO 1900

The Seventeenth Century

At the start of the seventeenth century, there were still many significant misunderstandings about human anatomy and the causes of disease and illness (belief in the four body humors still prevailed). But there began a push to draw upon insights from both ancient civilizations and the Renaissance. Francis Bacon (1561–1626) argued, as Hippocrates and others had done, for natural explanations of diseases that could be understood through systematic observation and experimentation. The development of modern science was about to occur.

William Harvey. The most important physiological advancement in the century was the confirmation by Englishman William Harvey (1578–1657) of the circulation of blood. Though the idea had been suggested by others earlier in history, Harvey was the first to offer experimental and quantitative proof.

While Harvey maintained a clinical practice throughout his life, he devoted himself to medical investigation in anatomy and physiology. Through analysis of dissected and vivisected animals, observation of the weakening heartbeat of animals as they were about to die, and various forms of experimentation on human heartbeat, Harvey proved that the contraction of the heart drove blood into the major arteries toward the body's peripheries. When the heart rested between beats, it filled with blood carried to it by the veins.

Although Harvey's finding removed a key obstacle to medical progress, the discovery was met with skepticism by some and open hostility by others. It had little influence on the treatment of patients during Harvey's time (even in his own practice). Routinely, the process of incorporating new knowledge or techniques into medical practice occurred very slowly (Nuland, 1995).

The Eighteenth Century

The eighteenth century—the "Age of Enlightenment"—is marked by efforts to collate the advancements of the preceding century and further refine knowledge in all fields, including medicine. Sound scientific thinking was making steady progress, and advances in biology, physics, and chemistry were converging to form a rational scientific basis for every branch of clinical medicine. People perceived that they were living at a special time of rapid growth, more open intellectual inquiry, advancement in the arts, literature, philosophy, and science, and freer political expression.

Development of a Modern Concept of Pathology. Although medical progress had been achieved in many areas, understanding of disease causation in the early eighteenth century was little different than it had been 2,500 years earlier. Many still advocated the humoral theory or some variation of it; others traced disease to climatic conditions or focused on structural explanations such as the condition of the pores.

The understanding that diseases are attached to particular organs is traceable to Giovanni Battista Morgagni (1682–1771), an Italian physician and professor of anatomy at the University of Padua. Based on his systematic and thorough note-taking of patients' symptoms, Morgagni developed the *anatomical concept of disease*—that diseases could be traced to particular pathology in individual organs. He directed medicine to seek the originating localized disturbance in a particular organ. It may seem strange to us today that for so long physicians did not connect patients' symptoms with the corresponding pathological condition. And even those who challenged the prevailing notions of the day, like Andreas Vesalius and William Harvey, relied primarily on the old ways in the actual treatment of patients.

The Emergence of Public Health and Preventive Medicine. The eighteenth century also witnessed a return to interest in public health. Attention focused on the unsanitary conditions that prevailed in industry, the armed forces, prisons, and hospitals. The lack of public sanitation in cities and contaminated water supplies were seen as significant threats to health, and individuals were encouraged to attend to personal hygiene.

The foremost accomplishment of this movement was the discovery of an effective preventive measure against smallpox, a leading cause of death among children. Edward Jenner (1749–1823), a British country doctor, heard that milkmaids infected by cowpox developed an immunity to smallpox. Through experimentation (on humans), Jenner demonstrated that persons vaccinated against cowpox did not develop the disease. Although initially regarded with suspicion, it was a signal event in the history of preventive medicine. Once it became common to immunize and inoculate people and animals against diseases, the medical world exploded in new directions (Magner and Kim, 2017).

Alternative Paths of Medicine. While discussing the advancement of ideas later confirmed by science, competing theories and treatments of the day are often overlooked. The discoveries of Morgagni and Jenner, for example, do not mean that medicine was not simultaneously taking alternative routes. For example, William Cullen of Edinburgh (1712–1790) founded a medical system based on *nervous forces*—that all diseases were a result of overstimulation or an inability to respond to stimulation. Appropriate cures included stimulants and depressants. Edinburgh-trained James Graham established a "Temple of Health and Hymen" in London. The temple was filled with beautiful young virgins attired in skimpy costumes who would sing to the sick, an approach that seemed logical to Graham, who believed illness could only be cured in the presence of beautiful sights and sounds (Camp, 1977).

The Nineteenth Century

The Industrial Revolution began in England and spread to Europe and the United States. The development of large industries with many jobs pulled large numbers of workers into concentrated areas. The world was not prepared to deal with the consequences of this urbanization process. Cities that emerged around industries were severely overcrowded, typically unsanitary, and often lacked safe procedures for food and water storage, producing unhealthy living environments.

Hospital Medicine. The first half of the nineteenth century is known mostly for the importance that physicians and medical researchers attached to clinical observation. Whereas medicine in the Middle Ages was centered in monasteries and libraries and in the Renaissance (as in antiquity) was centered on the individual sickbed, in the nineteenth century, for the first time, it was centered on the hospital.

Hospitals had existed for centuries but increased rapidly in number in the 1800s in response to the massive migration of people to newly developing cities. Communicable diseases became commonplace, and many urban migrants contracted typhoid fever and tuberculosis. Admission to a hospital was the only resort. These patients provided an unprecedented opportunity for clinicians and researchers to observe the sick and search for common patterns in their symptomology, disease progression, and response to medication. By the 1830s, especially in Paris, physician-researchers were increasingly taking advantage of the opportunity to separate patients by condition and specialize in particular conditions to expand medical knowledge (Weisz, 2003). Simultaneous advances in science and technology (e.g., the invention of the stethoscope by Laennec) were extremely important events of this era, but the immediate course of medicine was more strongly influenced by clinical observation in hospitals.

Laboratory Medicine. The laboratory became the focus in the second half of the century. The work of Morgagni and others fixed attention on pathology in particular organs, but no one knew what caused something in the organ to go awry. Many theories existed, and each sought *the* answer to unlock this key mystery. The absence of a correct answer was repeatedly made obvious by the absence of effective cures.

> They bled their patients, and they puked them and purged them and blistered them as their professional forefathers had always done; they confused the metabolisms of the sick with dazzling combinations of botanicals whose real actions were only partially known, and often not known at all. They stimulated in cases whose cause was thought to be too little excitation, and they tried to induce a touch of torpor when the opposite was the case. In short, except when the need for amputation or lancing was obvious, the healers didn't really know what they were doing.
>
> (Nuland, 1995:306)

Discovery of the Cell. Needed knowledge was produced by the German pathologist Rudolf Virchow (1821–1902). Virchow pinpointed the cell as the basic physiological matter and understood that disease begins with some alteration in the normally functioning, healthy cell. Effective treatment depends on restoring the cell to normality or at least terminating abnormal development.

Ironically, while Virchow's discovery of the human cell appropriately led to study of the physiological changes involved in disease progression, Virchow was a leading proponent of the importance of environmental influences on health and illness. He understood that social class, occupation, and involvement in social networks did as much to create sickness as cellular changes. He considered medicine to be a social science and sought to address harmful social conditions. The final 30 years of his life were largely devoted to explorations in the fields of anthropology and archaeology, the development of public health measures in his hometown of Berlin, and advocating for democratic reform and political and cultural freedom in Germany. He was a much beloved figure in Germany at the time of his death.

The Germ Theory of Disease. One more question remained. What causes a cell to begin to change? What condition initiates the disease process? At various points in history, medical researchers had speculated on the existence of microorganisms, but the speculation never inspired any substantial following. From the 1830s through the 1860s, various researchers observed bacteria under the microscope (minute organisms were first observed under a microscope by its inventor, Leeuwenhoek, in 1675), but their significance was not understood.

The key figure in the development of the **germ theory of disease** is Louis Pasteur (1822–1895), a French chemist now called the "Father of Modern Medicine." In 1857, Pasteur

Louis Pasteur, called the "Father of Modern Medicine," is credited with discovering the role of microorganisms as a cause of many human diseases.

Source: © Georgios Kollidas/Fotolia.

countered prevailing understandings by demonstrating that fermentation (he lived in the wine region) was not solely a chemical event but also the result of various microorganisms. By 1862, he disproved the notion that bacteria were spontaneously generated.

However, it was not until 1877, after 20 years of research on microorganisms, that Pasteur turned to human diseases. He identified the specific bacteria involved in anthrax and chicken cholera and, with several of his pupils, identified other disease-causing bacteria and developed effective vaccinations against them. By 1881, the germ theory of disease was generally accepted. With the impetus provided by Pasteur, one bacteriological discovery after another occurred. Between 1878 and 1887, the causative agents for gonorrhea, typhoid fever, leprosy, malaria, tuberculosis, cholera, diphtheria, tetanus, pneumonia, and epidemic meningitis were discovered (Magner and Kim, 2017).

The success of these efforts inspired an exciting period in medical history. Researchers would focus on a particular disease, identify the organism that caused it, determine how it invaded the body, and create a vaccine to prevent it. The mass media—newspapers, magazines, health education pamphlets, radio, motion pictures, and even comic books—all promoted medical advancements (Hansen, 2009).

At first, however, it was understood only that vaccines worked. It required another 10 years to understand why—that the body produces antibodies in response to the presence of a disease, and that these antibodies remain in the body to fight the disease on future exposures (Magner and Kim, 2017).

Progress in Surgery. Considerable progress in surgery also occurred during this time due to three essential advancements: (1) an understanding of the "localized" nature of disease (when surgeons believed that diseases were caused by generalized forces, like humors, it made little sense to remove a particular area or organ); (2) an ability to control the patient's pain in the surgical process (which occurred in incremental stages based on trial and error throughout the nineteenth century); and (3) an ability to prevent wound infection. Throughout history, surgeons recognized that almost all surgeries (even "successful" ones) resulted in a frequently fatal infection in the wound site. ("The operation was a success, but the patient died.") Surgery performed in hospitals was especially likely to result in infection.

The importance of "asepsis" (surgical cleanliness) was discovered by Sir Joseph Lister (1827–1912), an English surgeon. Lister's concern was prompted by the large percentage (almost half) of his amputation patients who died as a result of infection. Initially convinced that infection was caused by the air that came into contact with the wound, Lister altered his thinking when he read descriptions of Pasteur's work. By the mid-1860s, he realized that sepsis (an inflammatory response throughout the body to infection) was caused by bacteria in the air rather than by the air itself. Lister learned that applying carbolic acid to the wound, his hands, the surgical instruments, and the dressings used to close the wound prevented sepsis (Magner and Kim, 2017).

THE ASCENDANCY OF MEDICAL AUTHORITY IN AMERICA

Early America

The Early Colonists. The earliest colonists endured an excruciatingly difficult voyage across the ocean (typically requiring 3 or more months) only to be met with tremendous hardship upon arrival. Although warned about the danger of disease by their sponsor, the London Company, the Jamestown settlers in 1607 were more concerned about being attacked by Indians. They selected a site for their new home that had a military advantage (being able to see up and down the river) but was limited by an inadequate food supply and brackish water. Six months after their arrival, 60 of the 100 who landed had died from dietary disorders or other diseases.

The Plymouth Colony in Massachusetts had a similar experience. Due to an outbreak of scurvy and other diseases, only 50 of the 102 arrivals survived the first 3 months. Epidemics and other infectious diseases (e.g., malaria, dysentery, typhoid fever, influenza, smallpox, scarlet fever, yellow fever, and tuberculosis) were the primary killers (Green, 1968).

The colonists also brought from Europe several contagious diseases (e.g., measles, smallpox, and mumps) that had been unknown in the Americas. Lacking immunity to these diseases, Native American populations were very susceptible and were decimated in continuing outbreaks.

Some historians estimate that up to 90 percent of Native Americans died in this process (Cassady, 1991).

Although health problems were rampant in the colonies, conditions for slaves were especially bad. Subjected to massive overwork, poor food, housing, and sanitation, and inadequate medical care, the health of slaves was very poor in both an absolute and relative sense.

Early Medical Practitioners. Medical care was provided by colonists (often clergy) who had some formal education (not necessarily in medicine). The only known medical work published in America in the 1600s was by the Reverend Thomas Thatcher of the Old South Church in Boston. The Reverend Cotton Mather (1663–1728) (precocious, vain, and fanatical about witches) is often called the first significant figure in American medicine. Though a full-time clergyman, Mather read widely about medicine, wrote numerous treatises and books on anatomy and therapeutic medicine, and is known for an understanding of inoculation far beyond that of his contemporaries.

There were a few trained physicians and surgeons who had migrated to the colonies from Europe, and it was common for young men to attach themselves to these physicians as apprentices (typically for 4 to 7 years). However, in colonial America, people from all walks of life took up medicine and referred to themselves as physicians. Many added the physician's duties to another job, such as food merchant, wig maker, or cloth manufacturer (Starr, 1982). Much medical care was delivered by the apothecary. Although apothecaries primarily made their living by providing drugs and medical preparations, they also gave medical advice, dressed wounds, and even performed amputations (Magner and Kim, 2017). Many colonists would never have seen a trained physician in their life.

There was little in the way of professionalized medicine. The first comprehensive hospital in the United States (the Pennsylvania Hospital in Philadelphia) was not built until 1751 (and the second not until 20 years later in New York); the first formalized medical school (at the College of Philadelphia) was established in 1765; and the first state medical society (in New Jersey) organized in 1766.

Domestic Medicine. Given these conditions, it is not surprising that families assumed primary responsibility for protecting the health of family members and providing therapeutic agents when they were sick. Women stored medicinal herbs just as they did preserves, made up syrups, salves, and lotions, bandaged injuries, and were expected to tend to sick family members. They called on other family and friends in the community for advice, and sometimes sought the assistance of an older woman in the community known for her healing knowledge (Cassady, 1991; Starr, 1982).

Domestic medicine was supported by an ideology that individuals and families were capable of providing for the ill. Texts on domestic medicine (typically written by physicians) were available, as was advice through newspapers, almanacs, and word of mouth. Medical jargon was criticized as unnecessary and discouraging people from family treatment.

The Revolution to the Mid-1800s

Although there were only about 3,500 physicians in the country at the start of the Revolutionary War (and only 400 of these had a university medical degree), medicine was making progress. Many of the physicians were as competent as the times allowed, and they took their responsibility to apprentices seriously. Many of America's founders, such as Benjamin Franklin, John Adams, and Thomas Jefferson, were captivated by the spirit of science, although that developed in medicine in America only much later (Abrams, 2013).

Americans who could afford formal medical education often traveled to the University of Edinburgh, then considered the world's finest medical school, or other European centers. By the turn of the century, the country had established four medical schools (Pennsylvania, Columbia, Harvard, and Dartmouth), each of which sought to offer excellence in medical training (but with a minimum of faculty members; Dartmouth had a one-man medical faculty for over a decade).

The most famous American physician of this era was Benjamin Rush (1745–1813), who, after serving an apprenticeship in the colonies, earned a medical degree from the University of Edinburgh. Rush, a signer of the Declaration of Independence and strong advocate for temperance and the abolition of slavery, wrote extensively on his medical observations and made substantial contributions to the understanding of yellow fever and psychological problems. He argued against the common stigmatization of the mentally ill, and urged that those with mental health problems be treated with kindness and humaneness (Magner and Kim, 2017).

Nevertheless, he preached and practiced many of the medical errors of the day. He believed that all symptoms and sickness were traceable to just one disease—a *morbid excitement* induced by *capillary tension*, and he recommended and used bloodletting and purging as common cures (Magner and Kim, 2017). He also had the perception that mental illness could be shaken from a person. He devised chairs suspended from the ceiling, and attendants swung and spun mentally ill patients for hours.

America's experience in the Revolutionary War highlighted the lack of accurate knowledge about disease. The annual death rate in the Continental army was approximately 20 percent; 90 percent of war deaths were the direct result of disease (Green, 1968). See the accompanying box "The Death of a President" on the use of bloodletting as a factor in George Washington's death.

IN THE FIELD

THE DEATH OF A PRESIDENT

In December 1799, the president went out riding and got caught in a cold freezing rain, hail, and snow. When he returned to the house, he went to dinner without changing his wet clothes. He quickly came down with a cold, hoarseness, and a severe sore throat.

He was feeling worse the next morning, and three physicians were called in. A mixture of molasses, vinegar, and butter was provided, but it brought on near fatal choking. A short time later, a bloodletter was added to the team. At various points during the day, blood was removed from the patient: 12 to 14 ounces at 7:30 A.M., an additional 18 ounces at 9:30 A.M., and another 18 ounces at 11:00 A.M. Despite continued pleadings by his wife for caution, another 32 ounces of blood were let at 3:00 P.M. At 4:00 P.M., calomel (mercurous chloride) and tartar emetic (antimony potassium tartrate) were administered.

After a brief spell of improvement, his condition began to weaken. Various poultices and compresses were applied. Around 10:00 P.M., he whispered burial instructions to a friend. A few minutes later, the recently retired first president of the United States, George Washington, died.

Did the attempted cure kill the former president? The bloodletting did not help and probably hastened Washington's death. It is now generally agreed that Washington had acute bacterial epiglottitis. The youngest of the three physicians had argued unsuccessfully to do a very new technique at the time, a tracheotomy, to assist Washington's breathing. That might have worked and prolonged his life (Morens, 1999; Wallenborn, 1997).

The Status of Medicine. Despite these advancements, medicine remained a downgraded occupation. Physicians had little genuine understanding of disease causation and few effective treatments. Sometimes their cures were helpful (e.g., using willow bark, a source of aspirin, or rose hips, the ripened fruit of the rose bush and a good source of vitamin C, for fevers). Other remedies may not have been helpful, but neither were they harmful (e.g., using fried daisies for a compress, or putting feverish patients in a tent with burning tobacco). However, some cures were very harmful (e.g., bleeding, purging, amputation for any broken limb, and trephination). Diseases that are now treatable meant certain death then. Epidemics were terrifying. Most accidents proved fatal.

Alternative Philosophies. For a variety of reasons, physicians were poorly paid (and often not paid at all). These reasons include: (1) the fact that family medicine was preferred by many, (2) the difficulty in seeing a substantial number of patients in a day (people lived far apart and efficient transportation was lacking), (3) the inability of many patients to pay for care (much care was provided on credit but never reimbursed), and (4) the fact that many people offered themselves as physicians (without licensure requirements, there was virtually unlimited entry into the field). Given these conditions, many could not justify the cost of formal education. Through the first half of the 1800s, physicians enjoyed little prestige (Starr, 1982).

Many alternative healing philosophies (medical sects) competed throughout this time period. "Thomsonianism" was created by Samuel Thompson (1769–1843), a New Hampshirite, who had unhappy experiences with "regular" physicians. His motto was "Every man his own physician." He believed that disease resulted from insufficient heat, and could be countered by measures that would restore natural heat (e.g., steam baths that would promote intense sweating, and

hot botanicals such as red pepper). Over three decades, Thompson's influence grew, and he attracted many followers (Steele, 2005).

A second important medical sect, homeopathy, was founded by a German physician, Samuel Hahnemann (1755–1843), who viewed diseases as being primarily of the spirit. Homeopaths believed diseases could be cured by drugs that produced the same symptoms when given to a healthy person (the homeopathic law of "similars"—that like cures like). The rationale was that after a patient had taken a homeopathic medicine, their natural disease would be displaced by a weaker, but similar, artificial disease that the body could more easily overcome (Starr, 1982). For example, homeopaths view coughing as the body's effort to deal with foreign substances in the lung. Whereas medical doctors would typically try to suppress the cough, homeopaths would regard this as stifling the body's natural curative processes.

Conventional physicians (referred to as allopaths and as practicing allopathic medicine) were vocally critical of homeopaths and others who practiced forms of medicine contrary to the allopaths. They sought to discredit them, often refused to interact with them, and attempted to drive them from the field of medicine. You can read more about the relationship between conventional and alternative medicine in Chapter 11.

1850 Onward

At least three events of major significance during the second half of the nineteenth century and the first half of the twentieth century combined to "professionalize" medicine.

The Civil War. War dramatizes both the technological strengths and weaknesses of a society. Despite the ferocity of battle between the Union and Confederate forces, disease and illness represented the most lethal forces of the Civil War. An estimated 618,000 persons were killed during the Civil War—one-third from battle fatalities and two-thirds from disease and illness. Diarrhea and dysentery were the major killers, while numerous deaths were caused by smallpox, typhoid, yellow fever, pneumonia, scarlet fever, and infection from surgical procedures.

The wounded often lay on the battlefield for days until a conflict subsided and they could be moved. Wounds commonly became infected. Surgery was very primitive. Although anesthesia was often used, it typically took the form of alcohol or opium. In some instances, the patient was hit in the jaw to knock him out, or the patient would simply bite down on a piece of wood or even a bullet (hence the expression "bite the bullet") as a distraction.

To remove a bullet, the surgeon would put his unwashed hand in the open wound, squish around until the bullet was found, and pull it out. Scalpels used for amputation (there were approximately 60,000 amputations during the Civil War—75 percent of all operations) were not washed, the blade was often dull, and whatever sharpening occurred was done on the surgeon's boot sole. Surgeons bragged about the speed with which they could amputate a limb (the best were called 1½-minute men). Almost everyone got infections, and many died from them. For comparison purposes, in Vietnam, 1 in every 75 wounded soldiers died; in World War II, 1 in 33 wounded died; and in the Civil War, 1 in 7 wounded died.

The lack of effective medical care was obviously frustrating but it inspired several ways of improving care both on the battlefield and in society in general. Military physicians were encouraged to observe patients systematically and undertake whatever kind of experimentation might produce helpful knowledge (Devine, 2014). Professional nursing was begun during the Civil War as a means of assisting in the treatment of wounded soldiers. The ambulance corps was initiated to move the wounded from the battlefield to field hospitals. These experiences helped

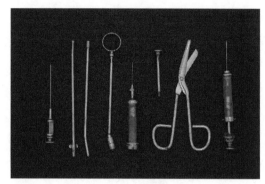

As late as the Civil War, undergoing any kind of surgery was a very risky ordeal.

medical personnel learn about sanitation and other public health measures.

Medical Advancements. As discussed earlier, the discovery by Pasteur that microorganisms cause disease is considered by many to be the most important medical discovery ever made. Coupled with Lister's recognition of the importance of sepsis and Wilhelm Roentgen's (1845–1923) discovery of X-rays and their diagnostic utility in the 1890s, much improved diagnosis was possible. These advancements meant that medical knowledge required specialized training.

The germ theory of disease stimulated a massive and effective assault on infectious disease through immunization and treatment. The decades from the 1920s through the 1940s represent years of peak pharmacological success—a time when one "magical bullet" after another was discovered. Insulin was discovered in 1921, and vitamin C was isolated in 1928 (enabling better understanding of vitamin deficiency diseases), the same year that a vaccine for yellow fever was produced. The potential for sulfa drugs (in preventing the growth or multiplication of bacteria) was realized in the 1930s, and the ability of penicillin to kill bacteria was fully understood by the 1940s. For a time, great optimism was engendered that all diseases and illnesses could be eradicated.

An unfortunate consequence of this focus on germ-caused disease was the turning away of attention from the "whole person." Some of the most valuable lessons to be learned from the Hippocratic tradition, such as the influence of lifestyle, the importance of inner harmony and moderation in life, the mind–body connection, and the importance of person-oriented medicine, were lost in the rush to identify microorganismic culprits and methods of conquering them. It would be decades before the importance of these themes would be remembered.

The Organization of Professional Medicine.

During the first half of the nineteenth century, several localities and states formed professional medical societies. While there was considerable variation in their objectives and activities, each focused primarily on promoting the professionalization of medicine. On May 5, 1847, 250 physicians representing many of these medical societies and some medical schools met in Philadelphia to establish a national medical society, the **American Medical Association (AMA)**.

The motivation to establish the AMA was partly ideological and partly economic. Competition from homeopaths and other alternative healers was limiting financial success for physicians and reducing pride in the field. Physicians openly sought more esteem and condemned those who used alternative approaches (Magner and Kim, 2017; Steele, 2005). In part, the motivation for creating the AMA was similar to Hippocrates' motivation for writing his famous oath—to establish visible standards for the practice of medicine so as to gain greater confidence from the general public.

The AMA identified its chief goals as (1) the promotion of the science and art of medicine, (2) the betterment of public health, (3) the standardization of requirements for medical degrees, (4) the development of an internal system of licensing and regulation, and (5) the development of a code of medical ethics.

However, it would be years before the AMA would develop intó an important force in medicine. Several states and some medical schools opposed uniform standards in education and licensing requirements. There was general public sentiment against legitimizing a particular medical orientation, as it was not clear that the brand of medicine offered by the AMA was superior to the many alternative healing philosophies in existence.

Forces Stimulating Professionalization

Three pivotal events strengthened the position of the AMA. First, the development of the germ theory of disease offered medical schools a sound approach to disease causation and treatment, and provided the public with a clear rationale for preferring formally trained physicians.

Second, the AMA was eventually successful in achieving one of its key goals—**medical licensure** requirements. The AMA and the country's top medical schools argued that licensure would restrict the practice of medicine to those who had been formally trained and were able to demonstrate competency. Opposition stemmed both from those who wanted to maximize the choices people had available for medical practitioners and from the administrations of many of the lower-quality medical schools who feared that their graduates would not be able to pass a licensure exam. By the early 1900s, the battle had largely been won, as most states required a license to practice medicine.

These two events were necessary but not sufficient in the AMA's drive for professional authority. By 1900, there were approximately 110,000 physicians in the United States, but only 8,000 of them belonged to the AMA. Reorganization of the AMA in 1901 (tightening the relationship among local, state, and national associations and increasing the power of the governing board) provided a boost, but one more thing was needed—control of medical education.

In the late 1800s and early 1900s, there was considerable variation in the quality of America's medical schools. More than 400 medical schools had been created in the United States in the 1800s (more than twice as many as exist today.) Some, like Harvard and Johns Hopkins, offered sound training in the basic sciences and substantial clinical experience under close supervision, and had excellent resources. The majority, however, were not linked to a university and did not have access to the faculty, library resources, and facilities provided in the better schools. In many cases, admission standards were nonexistent, and there was no training provided in the basic sciences and little or no clinical supervision. As late as the 1870s, one physician was quoted as saying that

> it is very well understood among college boys that after a man has failed in scholarship, failed in writing, failed in speaking, failed in every purpose for which he entered college; after he has dropped down from class to class; after he has been kicked out of college; there is one unfailing city of refuge—the profession of medicine.
>
> (Numbers, 1985:186)

The Flexner Report. The AMA contracted with the Carnegie Foundation to study the quality of medical education. They hired Abraham Flexner, an American educator, to conduct a comprehensive study of all medical schools in the United States and Canada. Upon hearing of this study, many schools closed immediately rather than risk being condemned. Flexner's team visited the 155 remaining schools. His final report, the **Flexner Report**, issued in 1910, praised the efforts of many schools (Harvard, Western Reserve, McGill, Toronto, and especially Johns Hopkins) but lambasted those that offered inferior programs. He recommended that the number of schools be reduced to 31 and that medical education be subjected to formal regulation.

The Great Trade of 1910

The only national standards available for accrediting medical schools were those that had been prepared by the Council on Medical Education (CME) of the AMA. In 1910, the states and the federal government made a deal with the AMA. In return for providing the best possible health care system, the CME would be given complete power over the education and licensing of physicians, including the power to establish standards for medical schools. In this **Great Trade of 1910**, the AMA was given a near exclusive right to regulate the medical profession. With the knowledge supplied by the germ theory of disease and the organizational legitimacy provided by the states and federal government, the powerful position of the AMA was secured. In turn, the AMA institutionalized scientific medicine as the foundation of America's health care system.

PERSPECTIVES ON THE ASCENDANCY OF MEDICAL AUTHORITY

Attempts to interpret and explain the ascendancy of scientific and professional medicine (i.e., medical authority) in the United States have followed various lines. Two contrasting approaches—those of Paul Starr and Vicente Navarro—are summarized here.

Paul Starr

Paul Starr's Pulitzer Prize–winning *The Social Transformation of American Medicine* (1982) is a fascinating and well-documented description and analysis of the evolution of the medical profession in America. Recall that in the late 1800s and early 1900s, there were many competing orientations to medicine in addition to the scientific medicine being embraced by the AMA. Many people objected to any one of the orientations being promoted by the government as being best and believed that everyone should be free to choose their type of physician just as they were able to choose their preferred religion.

The first part of Starr's book describes the rise of medical authority based on scientific medicine in America. It explains how medical practice was transformed from a relatively weak and poorly regarded occupation into a powerful and prestigious "sovereign" profession. Starr acknowledges the important contribution of the advancement of science to the professionalization of medicine, but he contends that something more is needed to explain medicine's acquisition of economic power, political influence and ability to shape the health care system.

For Starr, the key "something more" is development of a **cultural authority of medicine**. Cultural authority of medicine refers to the public's trust in professional medicine, its willingness to comply with its recommendations, and its willingness to see professional medicine as "legitimate" medicine. It is reflected in the fact that the general public and legislators even allow professional medicine to set its own conditions of practice. Starr emphasizes that professions must "persuade" publics that they are deserving of cultural authority—that it cannot be forcibly obtained.

Paul Wolpe summarizes this point:

A profession's power rests on its consensually granted authority over a specific, cultural tradition. Knowledge and maintenance of that tradition is the profession's social capital, and it must guard that capital from challenges while projecting an aura of confidence, competence, trust, and self-criticism. Professions institutionalize control over social capital by establishing licensing procedures, internally-run educational institutions, and self-regulation. But institutional legitimacy, while somewhat self-sustaining, also depends on ongoing public acceptance of a profession's claim of exclusive expertise over a realm of specialized knowledge. Lacking broad coercive powers, professions have developed strategies to protect their socially granted right to interpret their particular cultural tradition.

(Wolpe, 1985:409)

Once in possession of this important cultural authority, Starr suggests that professions develop a social authority (Max Weber's notion of using laws or rules or bureaucratic protocol) to further entrench their position. Starr delineates five changes that provided social authority to medicine: (1) The growth of hospitals created a desire for hospital privileges and referrals, which caused physicians to become more colleague dependent and less patient dependent. (2) Gaining control of medical education and the licensure process enabled the profession to restrict entry into the field and shape the evolution of the profession. (3) Having medicine viewed as a special type of field legitimated the expenditure of enormous sums of public money for hospital construction, medical education, medical research, and public health. (4) Physicians gained nearly complete control over conditions of medical practice (e.g., the setting of fees), and established significant political influence. (5) Medicine established very clear professional boundaries that were to be respected by others.

By the 1920s, the ascendancy of medical authority was clear. According to Starr, this occurred largely because the public believed in professionalized medicine (cultural authority) which allowed it to further secure its position of dominance through mechanisms of social authority.

The triumph of the regular profession depended on belief rather than force, on its growing cultural authority rather than sheer power, on the success of its claims to competence and understanding rather than the strong arm of the police. To see the rise of the profession as coercive is to underestimate how deeply its authority penetrated the beliefs of ordinary people and how firmly it had seized the imagination even of its rivals.

(Starr, 1982:229)

Vicente Navarro

An alternative view of the ascendancy of medical authority in America is presented by sociologists and medical historians who follow a social conflict approach. Vicente Navarro, a Marxist scholar who has written extensively about medicine, disagrees with three assumptions he finds in Starr's approach.

> Starr's interpretation of America sees the past and present structure of power in the United States as reflecting the wishes of the majority of Americans. To see the structure of power in America as the outcome of what Americans want, however, is to beg the question of which Americans. If by Americans it is meant the majority of Americans, then two assumptions are being made. One is that the majority of Americans share a set of beliefs, values, and wants that provide an ideological cohesiveness to the totality of the unit called America. The other assumption is that the majority of Americans have had and continue to have the power to determine what happens both in the private sector of America (through market forces) and in the public sector (through representative public institutions). To these two assumptions Starr adds a third: the dominant ideologies and positions become dominant through their powers of persuasion rather than through coercion and repression of alternative ideologies and positions.
>
> (Navarro, 1984:515)

Navarro emphasizes that Americans have been and continue to be "divided into classes, races, genders, and other power groupings, each with its own interests, set of beliefs, and wants that are in continuous conflict and struggle" (Navarro, 1984:515). These groups have different levels of power, and interact within a dominant–dominated framework. In society in general and within medicine, powerful groups are decisive due to the resources they have acquired. They get their way not because they successfully persuade, but because they have sufficient power to coerce and repress the less powerful.

According to Navarro, the ascendancy of medical authority occurred (and the corporatization of medicine is now occurring) not because people willed it and not because they were persuaded that it was in their interests, but because it served the interests of powerful societal groups (the government, those sufficiently wealthy to afford medical education and private health care, and corporations). These groups are often motivated by self-interest and greed, and they ignore public values and preferences (e.g., for universal coverage for health care) that they judge not to be in their interest.

SUMMARY

The study of the history of medicine is important both to understand earlier peoples and events and to decipher ways in which modern ideas and practices have evolved. Understanding of disease shifted from supernatural explanations in early humans to a slightly more empirical basis in Egyptian, Mesopotamian, and Indian society to natural causes in the Greco-Roman era. Hippocrates, the "Father of Medicine," encouraged careful observation of sickness in patients, a close relationship between physician and patient, and ethical guidelines for physician behavior.

The centrality of religion's role in medicine re-emerged during the Medieval Era but ultimately became overshadowed by the scientific perspective,

which emerged during the Renaissance. Particularly important was Pasteur's development of the germ theory of disease. Diseases were common in colonial America, trained physicians were few, accurate medical knowledge was limited, and most families cared for their own sick members. Physicians had little training, low prestige, and earned little money. The development of the germ theory of disease led to other medical discoveries, much improved medical care, and widespread public health and disease prevention programs.

The AMA was established in 1847, although it did not become a powerful voice for medicine for several decades. The two key events in the institutionalization of the AMA were (1) the establishment of licensure requirements in states, thus controlling entry into the field, and (2) the federal government's granting of authority to the AMA to control standards in medical education.

Paul Starr emphasizes that medical authority ascended in the United States largely because the medical profession persuaded people that such power was in their best interest (cultural authority). Vicente Navarro contends that the profession of medicine and the health care system have evolved in ways determined by and in the interest of powerful groups.

HEALTH ON THE INTERNET

There are several informative sites about Hippocrates, his writings, and recent updates of his work. Read the Introductory Note, the Oath of Hippocrates, and the Law of Hippocrates at

www.bartleby.com/38/1/

Consider the following questions:

1. The final paragraph of the Introductory Note contains an aphorism about the art of the physician. What is the meaning of this statement? What does it say about the physician–patient relationship? Have you observed any occasions when a physician seemed to be practicing this art?
2. Point 2 in the Law of Hippocrates identifies several personal traits that Hippocrates believes should be found in persons seeking to become a physician. What do these traits say about Hippocrates' view of physicians? Are any of the traits surprising to you?
3. In what ways is the Law of Hippocrates consistent with the Oath of Hippocrates, and in what ways does it differ?
4. There are now many contemporaneously written oaths to which physicians and other health care providers pledge, and no graduating student recites the exact Hippocratic Oath. In 2015, more than half of medical graduates recited an oath written at their own school (only 9 percent did so in 1982). Search online, identify one alternative oath, and compare and contrast it with the Hippocratic Oath.

DISCUSSION QUESTION

In his seminal work *The Structure of Scientific Revolutions* (published in 1962), Thomas Kuhn describes the history of science as a series of eras, each guided by a dominant paradigm (i.e., a theoretical perspective or general understanding of things). This is "normal science," and it is sustained through education and research apprenticeships whereby young scientists are socialized into the prevailing paradigm.

Occasionally, new theoretical insights or empirical findings appear that question the dominant paradigm. If these "anomalies" are infrequent or isolated occurrences, consensus around the dominant paradigm will be undisturbed. However, if these contradictory perspectives persist and are accepted, a "scientific revolution" may occur wherein the old paradigm is replaced by a new one. Kuhn sees scientific progress as occurring more through these revolutions than evolution.

Based on your reading of this chapter and other familiarity you have with the history of medicine, would you say Kuhn's view is or is not applicable to the advancement of medical knowledge? Have the progression of medical knowledge and the understanding of the causes of disease occurred incrementally in an evolutionary process? Or have there been one or more revolutions in understanding disease and illness wherein new paradigms have become accepted? Cite specific examples both of incremental, evolutionary change *and* complete paradigm shift, and revolutionary change.

GLOSSARY

American Medical Association (AMA)
Ayurveda
Black Death
Code of Hammurabi
cultural authority of medicine
domestic medicine
Flexner Report
germ theory of disease
Great Trade of 1910
Hippocrates

Hippocratic Oath
humoral theory of disease
Islamic medicine's "naturals" and "non-naturals"
medical licensure
monastic medicine
scholastic medicine
shaman
supernatural explanations of disease
trephination

REFERENCES

Abrams, Jeanne E. 2009. "Medieval Medicine." *Med-Help.Net.* Retrieved November 5, 2018 (www.medhelp.net/med-ancient-medieval-medicine.html).

———. 2013. *Revolutionary Medicine: The Founding Fathers and Mothers in Sickness and in Health.* New York: New York University Press.

Camp, John. 1974, 1977. *The Healer's Art: The Doctor through History.* New York: Taplinger Publishing Company.

Cassady, James H. 1991. *Medicine in America: A Short History.* Baltimore, MD: The Johns Hopkins University Press.

Cohen, Leslie. 2013. "Early Texts of Traditional Chinese Medicine—An Ancient and Sophisticated Medical System." Retrieved November 7, 2018 (http://decodedpast.com/traditional-chinese-medicine-earliest-written-records/1159).

Conrad, Lawrence I. 1995. "The Arab-Islamic Medical Tradition." Pp. 93–138 in *The Western Medical Tradition: 800 BC to 1800 AD*, edited by Lawrence I. Conrad, Michael Neve, Vivian Nutton, Roy Porter, and Andrew Wear. Cambridge: Cambridge University Press.

Devine, Shauna. 2014. *Learning from the Wounded: Civil War and the Rise of American Medical Science.* Chapel Hill, NC: The University of North Carolina Press.

Green, John R. 1968. *Medical History for Students.* Springfield, IL: Charles C. Thomas.

Hansen, Bert. 2009. *Picturing Medical Progress from Pasteur to Polio: A History of Mass Media Images and Popular Attitudes in America.* New Brunswick, NJ: Rutgers University Press.

Kuhn, Thomas S. 1962. *The Structure of Scientific Revolutions.* Chicago, IL: University of Chicago Press.

Magner, Lois N., and Oliver J. Kim. 2017. *A History of Medicine* (3rd ed.). Boca Raton, FL: CRC Press.

Makah, Jonathan, and Marques Jalil. 2009. *The Healing of the Gods: Imhotep, Health and Healing in Ancient Kemet (Egypt).* Seattle, WA: CreateSpace Independent Publishing Platform.

McKeown, Thomas. 1970. "A Sociological Approach to the History of Medicine." *Medical History* 14(4):342–351.

Morens, David M. 1999. "Death of a President." *New England Journal of Medicine* 341(24):1845–1849.

Navarro, Vicente. 1984. "Medical History as Justification Rather than Explanation: A Critique of Starr's *The Social Transformation of American Medicine.*" *International Journal of Health Services* 14(4):511–527.

Nuland, Sherwin B. 1995. *Doctors: The Biography of Medicine.* New York: Knopf.

Numbers, Ronald L. 1985. "The Rise and Fall of the American Medical Profession." Pp. 185–196 in *Sickness and Health in America: Readings in the History of Medicine and Public Health* (2nd ed.), edited by Judith W. Leavitt and Ronald L. Numbers. Madison, WI: University of Wisconsin Press.

Nunn, John F. 2002. *Ancient Egyptian Medicine*. Norman, OK: University of Oklahoma Press.

Porter, Roy. 2006. *The Cambridge History of Medicine*. Cambridge, MA: Cambridge University Press.

Ranganayakulu, Potturu. 2015. *Ayurveda: A Historical Perspective*. New Delhi, India: Pangea Publishers.

Starr, Paul. 1982. *The Social Transformation of American Medicine*. New York: Basic Books.

Steele, Volney. 2005. *Bleed, Blister, and Purge*. Missoula, MT: Mountain Press Publishing Company.

Teall, Emily K. 2014. "Medicine and Doctoring in Ancient Mesopotamia." *Grand Valley Journal of History* 3(1):1–8.

Wallenborn, White M. 1997. "George Washington's Terminal Illness: A Modern Medical Analysis of the Last Illness and Death of George Washington." *The Papers of George Washington*. Retrieved March 15, 2019 (http://gwpapers.virginia.edu/resources/articles/illness/).

Weisz, George. 2003. "Medical Specialization in the Nineteenth Century." *Bulletin of the History of Medicine* 77(3):536–575.

White, Kevin. 2009. *An Introduction to the Sociology of Health and Illness*. London: Sage Publications.

Wolpe, Paul R. 1985. "The Maintenance of Professional Authority: Acupuncture and the American Physician." *Social Problems* 32(5):409–424.

CHAPTER 3

Social Epidemiology

Learning Objectives

- Define the term "social epidemiology" and identify the major research techniques used by epidemiologists.

- Identify and describe the five major stages of the epidemiological transition. Discuss the changing presence of acute infectious diseases and chronic degenerative diseases during these stages.

- Explain the poor performance of the United States relative to other countries regarding life expectancy, infant mortality, and maternal mortality.

- Explain how social class, race, and gender influence life expectancy, mortality, and morbidity in the United States.

- Describe how the meaning of "disability" has changed in the United States in the last 20 years. Identify social factors that influence the likelihood of disability.

The field of **social epidemiology** focuses on understanding the causes and distribution of diseases and impairments within a population. Early in its history, epidemiologists concentrated primarily on identifying the microorganisms responsible for epidemics of acute infectious diseases. Utilizing the germ theory of disease (see Chapter 2), epidemiologists achieved much success in identifying the responsible agents. As populations became less susceptible to infectious diseases and less likely to die from them, chronic degenerative diseases such as coronary heart disease and cancer became more prominent. This shift emphasized the importance of social characteristics (including gender, race, and social class), lifestyle, and the social and physical environment (including such things as employment status, stress, exposure to toxic substances, and participation in social networks) as underlying factors of disease and illness.

THE WORK OF THE EPIDEMIOLOGIST

The work of the epidemiologist has been compared to that of a detective or investigator. Epidemiologists scrutinize data on death and disease within societies, often searching for patterns or linkages within population subgroups (e.g., among men or women, or among people living in cities or rural areas) or other meaningful changes over time. If a pattern or trend is detected, the task of the epidemiologist is to explain it—that is, to identify a cause-and-effect relationship. This may require an understanding of how the disease is contracted, how it has been or could be spread, and why it is more common among some groups than others.

Increasingly, epidemiologists subscribe to a "web of causation" approach based on their belief that most disease patterns must be explained by multiple factors involving the disease agent, the human host, and the social and physical environment. McKinlay (1996) suggests the addition of a fourth target: social systems. He argues that individual health behaviors cannot sensibly be separated from system influences such as government reimbursement policies, priorities of health facilities, and the behavior of health providers. In conducting their research, epidemiologists use a variety of data-gathering techniques, including (1) examination of medical records and databases from physicians, hospitals, schools, employers, insurance companies, public health departments, and birth and death records, (2) systematic health examinations, (3) health-focused surveys, and (4) experimentation under tightly controlled conditions.

The leading health surveillance organization in the world is the **World Health Organization (WHO)**, created in 1948 under the auspices of the United Nations. Headquartered in Geneva, Switzerland, with offices around the globe, the WHO monitors the world health situation and world health trends, provides technical support to countries, enters into programmatic partnerships, establishes norms and protocols, and helps set the world health research agenda.

In 1950, the United States created a nationwide system of disease surveillance, now called the **Centers for Disease Control and Prevention (CDC)**, that provides ongoing evaluations of and systematic responses to disease conditions. CDC workers analyze data to understand disease outbreaks, determine their likely effects on the

The World Health Organization is the leading epidemiological agency in the world.

Source: © yui/Shutterstock.

population, and identify and enact efforts to control or stop them. The CDC reports these data weekly to health departments, government agencies, academic facilities, and the public through the *Morbidity and Mortality Weekly Report (MMWR)*.

Although epidemiologists are constantly studying disease and illness patterns, the public often only hears of their work during an emergency situation as in recent outbreaks of the H1N1, Zika, and Ebola viruses. Most recently, terms such as social distancing, contact tracing, and community spread have entered the common lexicon due to the emergence of coronavirus disease 2019 or COVID-19. The accompanying box, "The COVID-19 Pandemic," discusses this newest global health emergency.

IN THE FIELD

THE COVID-19 PANDEMIC

In late December 2019, health officials in Wuhan, China confirmed dozens of cases of a pneumonia-like respiratory illness of unknown origin. The illness spread rapidly throughout Wuhan city, Hubei Province, and mainland China. On January 8, 2020, officials announced the pathogen causing

it, a novel coronavirus later named Severe Acute Respiratory Syndrome Coronavirus 2 (SARS-CoV-2). The disease it causes was termed coronavirus disease 2019 or COVID-19 (Taylor, 2020).

Coronaviruses are a large family of viruses that can infect animals and humans. Some

(Continued)

(*Continued*)

cause mild respiratory illnesses in humans (i.e., the common cold), while others cause more severe illness such as Severe Acute Respiratory Syndrome (SARS) and Middle East Respiratory Syndrome (MERS). Like SARS and MERS, COVID-19 is an emerging infectious disease— a new disease not previously seen in humans. Consequently, the population has no immunity and there is yet no vaccine or drug treatment. Unlike SARS and MERS, which are not easily spread, COVID-19 is readily transmitted through respiratory droplets. When these virus-containing droplets enter the respiratory tract (by breathing or touching one's nose, mouth, or eyes after touching a contaminated surface), transmission occurs. With an estimated incubation period up to 14 days, even asymptomatic persons can transmit the virus (Sauer, 2020).

Symptoms range from mild to severe and include fever, cough, shortness of breath, sore throat, chills, muscle pain, headache, and loss of taste or smell (Centers for Disease Control and Prevention, 2020b). Older adults, those in nursing or long-term care facilities, and persons with underlying medical conditions including asthma, chronic lung disease, serious heart conditions, liver disease, severe obesity, and the immunocompromised are at heightened risk (Centers for Disease Control and Prevention, 2020a). Treatment consists of supportive care (treating symptoms), with severe cases requiring hospitalization, oxygen, and mechanical ventilation.

By the end of January, COVID-19 had spread to Japan, South Korea, Thailand, and the United States. On January 30 the WHO declared a global health emergency, and on March 11 declared COVID-19 a global pandemic (Taylor, 2020).

By the end of March, the US led the world in total cases with over 81,000 infections and 1,000 deaths (Taylor, 2020). When hospitals in virus hotspots like New York City were in danger of being overwhelmed with patients, field hospitals were set up and refrigerated trucks brought in to house the dead. Ventilators and bronchodilators such as albuterol inhalers were in short supply, and the cache of personal protective equipment (e.g., N95 masks and face shields) that medical personnel and first responders relied on to keep them safe from infection were quickly depleted (Cook, 2020; Kates, 2020).

Throughout February and March, as the global death toll climbed and the virus spread to new regions, local, regional, and national governments widely adopted emergency public health measures. They encouraged people to practice social distancing by staying 6 feet away from others. They exhorted (sometimes required) persons who travelled to affected areas to self-quarantine. They encouraged frequent hand washing and disinfection of commonly used surfaces, enacted stay-at-home and work-from-home orders, restricted international travel, closed schools and nonessential businesses, and cancelled cultural and sporting events to curb the spread of the virus and prevent hospitals from being overwhelmed with patients (Taylor, 2020).

Social distancing made a difference, as early hotspots such as Wuhan, South Korea, and Italy saw the number of new cases drop. By late April, some countries began loosening restrictions and opening parts of their economies (Taylor, 2020). The pandemic took a heavy toll on the global economy, shuttering factories, disrupting supply chains, and, in the US (with its weaker social safety net relative to other industrialized countries), creating a massive spike in unemployment not seen since the Great Depression and leaving millions without health insurance. Jobless claims exceeded 20 million in just four weeks (Schwartz, 2020).

The pandemic's economic cost was high, but so was its human cost. According to the WHO, by April 26, 2020, the total number of confirmed infections globally was nearly 3 million, and the total number of confirmed deaths was 194,000 (World Health Organization, 2020). In the US, the elderly and African-Americans were especially hard hit (CBS News, 2020).

Although the full economic and human cost is not yet known, it is clear that the COVID-19 pandemic will leave a major global mark.

THE EPIDEMIOLOGICAL TRANSITION

Prior to large-scale migrations of people and urbanization, the threat of infectious (communicable) disease and epidemics was minimal. However, once people began to move from one region of the world to another, and once crowded and unsanitary cities emerged within nations, **acute infectious diseases** (e.g., pneumonia and tuberculosis) began to spread more quickly and lingered longer. As societies further develop and modernize, morbidity and mortality change systematically to **chronic degenerative diseases** (e.g., heart disease and cancer). To capture this **epidemiological transition**, Omran (1971) divided the mortality experience of humankind into three stages—the Age of Pestilence and Famine, the Age of Receding Pandemics, and the Age of Degenerative and Human-Made Diseases.

The Age of Pestilence and Famine existed throughout the world for thousands of years and still exists in many of the world's developing countries. Lack of proper nutrition, poor sanitation, and unclean drinking water lead to continuing epidemics of infectious and parasitic diseases, such as influenza, pneumonia, diarrhea, and smallpox.

Infants, children, and women of reproductive age are at particularly high risk during this era, and are even now often the victims of nutrition-related diseases. Infant mortality rates (IMRs) remain very high today in many developing countries, where more than 1 in every 10 babies dies during the first year of life. Moreover, adult health in developing countries is a serious and continuing problem. Historically, life expectancy during the Age of Pestilence and Famine was between 20 and 40 years, although life expectancy in most of the world's developing countries today exceeds that. In several African countries, however, life expectancy remains less than 60 years.

In the late 1800s and early 1900s, industrialization and urbanization led to increased societal wealth. Significant improvements occurred in sanitation (e.g., cleaner water supplies and more effective sewage systems) and standard of living (especially the availability of nutritious food). Advances in medical knowledge and public health swept across countries. These changes led to the Age of Receding Pandemics—a transition stage—in which the risk of death from infectious and parasitic diseases declines, and the risk of death from degenerative diseases increases. People began to survive into older age, and as they did so, became more likely to experience and die from heart disease, cancer, and other chronic degenerative diseases. Historically, during this stage, life expectancy was about 50 years.

The Age of Degenerative and Human-Made Diseases arrived in the mid-1900s with the stabilization of death from acute infectious diseases at a relatively low level, and with mortality from degenerative diseases significantly increasing and becoming the most common cause of death. During this third stage, mortality rates dropped considerably from earlier times, and life expectancy reached approximately 70 years or more.

At one time, it was generally believed that the decline in mortality experienced during the third period put life expectancy at about its biological limit. However, in the mid-1960s, an unexpected and rapid decline in deaths from major degenerative diseases began to occur. This decline first affected middle-aged people, but eventually the lives of older people were also extended.

Thus, modern societies have entered a fourth period of epidemiological transition—the Age of Delayed Degenerative Diseases. During this era, the risk of dying from chronic degenerative diseases continues but is pushed back to older ages. Both reduction in behavioral risk factors (e.g., a decline in cigarette smoking) and advances in medical technology have been responsible for this shift (Olshansky and Ault, 1986).

Recently, Gaziano (2010) has proposed that a fifth epidemiological stage—the Age of Obesity and Inactivity—is now underway and has been for the last few decades. He suggests that the progress made in postponing disease and mortality to later stages of life is being undermined by an epidemic of obesity. Data from the National Health and Nutrition Examination Surveys (NHANES), conducted biannually since 1999, indicate that rates of obesity among US adults and children have increased significantly since the survey began. The 2015–2016 survey revealed that 39.8 percent of US adults and 18.5 percent of US children were obese (Hales et al., 2017). If not addressed, this excess weight will lead to an increased risk of coronary heart disease, stroke, hypertension, diabetes, cancer, joint disease, sleep apnea, asthma, and other chronic conditions. These final two "Ages" raise new questions about the health of the population. Will the prolonging of life continue? If so, will that result in additional years of health or additional years of disability? Will healthier lifestyles and the postponement of chronic disease retard the aging process? Will death from other diseases increase?

One thing is certain: unless the Age of Obesity and Inactivity dramatically reverses recent improvements in life expectancy, all segments of the elderly population are expected to increase in absolute numbers. The US Census Bureau (2018c) projects that the US population aged 65 years and over will increase to over 73.0 million by 2030 (when all baby boomers—those born between 1946 and 1964—will have turned 65), constituting a full 20 percent of the population. By 2035, adults aged 65 and over will outnumber children for the first time in US history.

Recent Alarming Trends in Infectious Diseases

In the last several years, societies around the world have faced two alarming epidemiological trends: the emergence of new diseases and the declining ability to successfully treat some diseases already present.

New diseases like COVID-19, Zika, and Middle East respiratory syndrome (MERS), have captured worldwide attention in the last few years. Since 1980, the world has confronted about three new pathogens a year. What is causing this surge in new diseases? At least five important explanations exist.

1. *Population growth.* Population growth leads to a greater concentration of people in increasingly crowded urban environments, allowing infections to emerge and spread quickly.
2. *Increased travel.* Worldwide travel increases the chances of a pathogen being contracted in one area and unwittingly transported to another.
3. *Climate change.* Vector-borne diseases are those spread by insects such as mosquitos, ticks, and spiders. Warming temperatures allow vectors to thrive, increasing the risk of disease to human populations.
4. *Deforestation and natural habitat loss.* Cleared land collects rainwater more than rainforests, providing more suitable breeding grounds for mosquitos. Loss of habitat through deforestation and human encroachment bring animals into greater contact with humans, increasing the potential for disease. For example, Lyme disease increased in the United States because of our encroachment upon and fragmentation of woodland habitat, increasing the mouse population and bringing tick-carrying mice and deer into closer contact with humans (Akhtar, 2016).
5. *The global trade in wildlife and production of animals for food.* About two-thirds of emerging pathogens come from other animals. The United States is one of the largest importers and exporters of animals. As demand for food, skins, and entertainment increases, so does the risk of infectious disease (Akhtar, 2016).

Second, epidemiologists have discovered a pattern that could be tremendously disruptive to the epidemiological transition. Several infectious diseases, including tuberculosis (TB), syphilis, gonorrhea, and bacterial pneumonia, are increasingly resistant to the antibiotics that have been successful in defeating them. Malaria (spread by a parasite) was all but eradicated in the world in 1965. But today more than 200 million people worldwide are infected annually and more than 400,000 died in 2017 (World Health Organization, 2018d). Once almost conquered in the United States, tuberculosis (a bacterial disease affecting the lungs) has re-emerged with more than 9,000 reported US cases in 2017 (Centers for Disease Control and Prevention, 2018b). Globally, approximately 10 million people became ill with TB in 2017, and 1.6 million died from it. Sixty-two percent of new TB cases in 2017 occurred in the Southeast Asia and Western Pacific regions, with another 25 percent of cases in Africa (World Health Organization, 2018c).

Several patterns related to infectious disease are evident in these two problems. First, they represent a global problem. About one-third of all deaths in the world today are attributable to infectious disease—the single biggest killer. Second, these diseases are becoming an increasing threat in the United States. Even prior to the emergence of COVID-19, infectious diseases represented the third leading cause of death in the United States, and the mortality rate from infectious disease has jumped in the last 20 years. Third, many of the previously successful antibiotic treatments for these diseases are no longer effective. Some infectious diseases have become resistant to traditional drugs, and more will become so. Drug resistance occurs as a result of inappropriate or inadequate use of antibiotics (e.g., medical providers prescribe antibiotics when they are not medically necessary, or patients prematurely stop taking them). According to the WHO (2018c), an estimated 558,000 TB cases worldwide in 2017 were resistant to rifampicin, the first-line drug treatment, and 82 percent of these were resistant to multiple drug treatments. Methicillin-resistant *Staphylococcus*

aureus (commonly known as MRSA) has long been a problem in hospitals. The number of patients contracting it spiked in the 1990s (when more than 125,000 people in the United States were hospitalized each year), although recent studies show the incidence has now significantly decreased. Finally, the response to infectious disease must be at the worldwide level. Yet both the CDC and WHO maintain that the current state of preparedness for outbreaks of disease epidemics is inadequate, as the rampant global spread of COVID-19 illustrates.

The next section offers an introduction to several key concepts and measurement techniques in epidemiology—life expectancy, mortality, infant mortality, maternal mortality, morbidity, and disability—and examines current rates and trends within the United States and around the world.

LIFE EXPECTANCY AND MORTALITY

Life Expectancy

Using both current mortality data and projections, **life expectancy** rates reflect the average number of years that a person born in a given year can expect to live. The average life expectancy at birth throughout the world is about 69.8 years, but this statistic camouflages significant variation. Life expectancy is about 79 years in "more developed" countries, but only about 69 years in "less developed" countries (United States Census Bureau, 2018b). Life expectancy has increased significantly in most countries in the last 20 years, especially in several large developing countries, such as China and India.

Despite the fact that it spends significantly more money on health care than any other country, the United States compares poorly to other countries in life expectancy. Among countries with a population of at least 5 million, the United States ranks only 24th in life expectancy, and among 228 comparison countries of any size, the United States ranks only 45th (United States Census Bureau, 2018b).

About two-thirds of the gap between the United States and other countries is explained by Americans' higher likelihood of dying before the age of 50 years, especially from causes other than disease. These causes include drug poisoning (largely from alcohol, prescription opioid abuse, and heroin), gun-related violence (both suicide and homicide—the rate of firearm homicides is 20 times higher in the United States than in other countries), and motor vehicle crashes (Ho, 2013; Storrs, 2016). Table 3.1 identifies estimated life expectancy in the year 2018 for countries with a population over 5 million.

Trends.   Since 1900, life expectancy in the United States has increased by more than 30 years to 80.1 years in 2018. This does not mean a significant increase has occurred in the life span (the maximum biological age). Rather, it occurs primarily because fewer babies die in the first year of life—something that significantly reduces average life expectancy. Males and females who survived these stages could expect to live on average almost as long as males and females do today.

Longer life expectancy together with a lower fertility rate (i.e., the rate of reproduction of women in their most fertile years—aged 15 to 44 years) has resulted in a larger proportion of the US population being over 65 years of age. Just 4 percent of the population was 65 years or older in 1900. Today it is 15 percent, and people aged 65 years or older are the fastest growing segment of the population (US Census Bureau, 2019).

This "aging" of the American population has many implications. A greater number of elderly persons will require significant increases in the supply of primary and specialty health care, short-term hospitalization, and extended care. Their numbers will also provide a formidable voting bloc and lobbying force to ensure that their needs will not be overlooked. Because extended care can be very expensive, increasing numbers of the elderly may need to reside with their adult children, thus

TABLE 3.1   Life Expectancy at Birth, 2018 in Countries with a Population of More Than 5 Million

Country	Life Expectancy in 2018
Highest 25	
Japan	85.5
Singapore	85.5
Hong Kong	83.1
Israel	82.7
Switzerland	82.7
South Korea	82.5
Australia	82.4
Italy	82.4
Sweden	82.2
Canada	82.0
France	82.0
Norway	82.0
Spain	81.8
Austria	81.7
Netherlands	81.5
Belgium	81.2
Finland	81.0
Denmark	81.0
Ireland	81.0
Germany	80.9
Portugal	80.9
United Kingdom	80.9
Greece	80.8
Taiwan	80.4
United States	80.1
Lowest 10	
South Sudan	42.6
Afghanistan	52.1
Zambia	53.0
Somalia	53.2
Central African Republic	53.3
Mozambique	54.1
Niger	56.3
Uganda	56.3
Chad	57.5
Congo	58.1

Source: US Census Bureau, International Data Base. 2018b. "Mortality Indicators by Sex for Region Summary. Life Expectancy, Both Sexes." Retrieved June 2, 2019 (www.census.gov/data-tools/demo/idb/informationGateway.php).

requiring a family member to take on a full-time caregiving role, or necessitating the use of home health care services. Many elderly persons and their families will be faced with having to determine the relative value of quality versus quantity of life and the extent to which high-technology medicine will be employed (Sade, 2012).

Although US life expectancy has increased overall since 1900, it has not increased continuously. In fact, the rate of increase has declined in recent years (i.e., the pace of change has slowed) and since 2015, US life expectancy has decreased slightly (Ho and Hendi, 2018; Murphy et al., 2018). Comparing data from 18 high-income countries, Ho and Hendi (2018) found that other high-income countries have also experienced this decline, but their life expectancy rebounded. They concluded, "Declines in life expectancy in the USA differ from those in other countries in that they are more concentrated at younger ages (0–65 years) and largely driven by increases in drug overdose mortality related to its ongoing opioid epidemic" (Ho and Hendi, 2018: 1).

Mortality

Mortality refers to the number of deaths in a population. Whereas death itself is easy to document, determining the actual cause can be problematic because death may result from a combination of many factors. In the United States, an attempt is made to classify each death according to the *International Statistical Classification of Diseases, Injuries, and Causes of Death,* which consists of a detailed list of categories of diseases and injuries. Although this system is valuable, it is not totally reliable due to the problems in diagnosing the actual underlying cause of death—something especially difficult for some chronic diseases.

Measurement. Mortality rates are reported in ratios such as the **crude death rate (CDR)**. The crude death rate refers to the number of deaths per year per 1,000 people in a population. In 2018, the crude death rate worldwide was 7.7, and the rate in the United States was 8.2. South Sudan had the highest death rate in the world (19.3), and Qatar had the lowest (1.6) (CIA, 2019).

Trends. The crude death rate in the United States has declined by almost 50 percent since 1900. Females, both black and white, enjoyed the largest decrease, while black males saw the smallest decrease. However, between 1999 and 2013, mortality rates for middle-aged (45–64 years) non-Hispanic whites increased, due largely to increasing death rates from drug and alcohol poisonings (i.e., overdoses), suicide, and chronic liver diseases and cirrhosis, reversing a century-long downward trend and paralleling recent drops in life expectancy among this group (Case and Deaton, 2015).

Additionally, the major causes of death have changed substantially (see Table 3.2). In 1900, the major killers were infectious diseases such as influenza and pneumonia, gastrointestinal diseases, and TB. Today, death is most likely to result from a chronic degenerative disease. Of the top ten causes of death in the United States in 2016, seven were chronic degenerative diseases. The top ten causes of

TABLE 3.2 The Ten Leading Causes of Death in the United States, 1900 and 2016

1900	2016
1. Influenza and pneumonia	Heart disease (635,260)
2. Tuberculosis	Cancer (598,038)
3. Gastroenteritis	Accidents (161,374)
4. Heart disease	Lung disease (154,596)
5. Cerebral hemorrhage	Stroke (142,142)
6. Kidney disease	Alzheimer's disease (116,103)
7. Accidents	Diabetes (80,058)
8. Cancer	Influenza and pneumonia (51,537)
9. Certain diseases of infancy	Kidney disease (50,046)
10. Diphtheria	Suicide (44,965)

Source: Heron, Melonie. 2018. "Deaths: Leading Causes for 2016." *National Vital Statistics Reports* 67(6):77.

death collectively accounted for 74.1 percent of all deaths in 2016, but the top two causes of death—heart disease and cancer—accounted for nearly 49 percent of all deaths (Heron, 2018). Deaths from almost all chronic, degenerative diseases are occurring at later ages. To an increasing extent, people are now dying of multiple system diseases—being afflicted with more than one fatal disease.

Sociodemographic Variations in Life Expectancy and Mortality

Socioeconomic Status (SES). People with high socioeconomic status have a distinct advantage over the less affluent with regard to life expectancy. The effect of income and education on life expectancy is clear, and holds for both men and women and across a variety of racial and ethnic groups. People with low incomes live approximately 7 years less than the more affluent, and, in all groups, those with less than a high school degree have the shortest life expectancy, whereas those with a college degree or higher have the highest life expectancy (Montez et al., 2011). Among white males, college and graduate degree holders average about 12 additional years of life expectancy compared with those with less than a high school degree (Olshansky et al., 2012). Moreover, this disparity in life expectancy by education has actually increased in recent years (Spittel, Riley, and Kaplan, 2015).

What explains the relationship between SES and life expectancy, and why is this relationship becoming stronger? There are many reasons why more highly educated people live longer. **Fundamental cause theory (FCT)** has often been used to focus on the importance of personal resources such as knowledge, money, power, prestige, and social connections to explain the life expectancy advantage of the more educated (Masters, Link, and Phelan, 2015). For example, higher levels of education are associated with greater opportunities for employment, economic security, a sense of personal control, social ties, less overall stress, healthier and safer living and working environments, and a more nutritious diet. Because the highly educated have more financial resources and greater access to health services, they use more preventive and curative services.

But why is SES becoming more important? Hayward, Hummer, and Sassoon (2015) propose that technological development has elevated the importance of educational attainment—particularly advanced education—for enabling access to health care knowledge and other health care resources, and that this may be reflected in longer life expectancy.

Race and Ethnicity. In the United States, non-Hispanic whites have a much longer life expectancy than most racial and ethnic minority groups (except Asians). Life expectancy for non-Hispanic blacks lagged behind that for the total population throughout the twentieth century, but since 1990 the gap has decreased. However, in 2016, non-Hispanic whites still lived an average of 3.7 years longer than non-Hispanic blacks (see Table 3.3). The leading causes of death for non-Hispanic blacks are the same as for non-Hispanic whites (heart disease, cancer, lung diseases, and stroke), although blacks die from these diseases at an earlier age.

See the box, "What Explains Continuing Racial Differences in Mortality?" for a further examination of this issue.

TABLE 3.3   Life Expectancy at Birth by Race, Ethnicity, and Gender, 2016

Total	Male	Female
Non-Hispanic White		
78.5	76.1	81.0
Non-Hispanic Black		
74.8	71.5	77.9
Hispanic		
81.8	79.1	84.2
Overall, all races/ethnicities		
78.6	76.1	80.3

Source: National Center for Health Statistics. 2018. *Health, United States, 2017: With Special Feature on Mortality.* Hyattsville, MD.

WHAT EXPLAINS CONTINUING RACIAL DIFFERENCES IN MORTALITY?

Continuing racial differences in life expectancy and mortality represent an obvious and critical social disparity in the United States. In 2016, whites in the United States averaged nearly 4 years longer life expectancy than blacks. This represents some reduction in the disparity in the last 15 years, but is still a large difference.

What causes these racial differences? If there were meaningful biological differences between racial groups, this might partially explain them. However, racial categories are not genetic or biological categories and racial groupings do not capture meaningful biological or genetic differences. Instead, racial categories are historical and social constructs that capture important differences in both the social circumstances faced by, and the social resources available to, various groups. To explain racial disparities in life expectancy and mortality, we must examine the dual roles of social structure and social stratification (Williams and Sternthal, 2010).

Williams and Sternthal define social structure as "enduring patterns of social life that shape an individual's attitudes and beliefs, behaviors and actions, and material and psychological resources" (2010:S18–19). Social class is an important social structure that impacts racial disparities because of how socioeconomic status and race are intertwined (e.g., blacks are three times more likely than whites to be below the poverty level). Socioeconomic differences in income, wealth, and education explain some, but not all, of the racial disparities in life expectancy and mortality. One study determined that approximately 38 percent of the black–white mortality differential is due to income differences (Otten et al., 1990). In another study, Wong et al. (2002) tested the relative impact of education and race on mortality differentials for various causes of death. They found that racial disparities in death rates and life expectancy persist for nearly every cause of death, even after equalizing education.

Residential segregation is another important structural condition impacting racial differences in life expectancy and mortality (Williams and Sternthal, 2010). As Williams and Jackson (2005) explain, due to residential segregation, blacks often live in poorer neighborhoods than do whites of similar income. Neighborhood affects educational and employment opportunities, which in turn influence income and access to health insurance. High unemployment rates and low wages are associated with higher rates of out-of-wedlock births and single-parent households, which are in turn related to lower levels of supervision and elevated rates of violent behavior. Poorer neighborhoods are more often exposed to environmental toxins. Perception of neighborhood safety relates to the ability to get adequate physical exercise. Both the tobacco and alcohol industries often target their products at poorer neighborhoods. Thus the neighborhood in which one lives is associated with a wide variety of factors that ultimately influence mortality rates. The persistence of racially segregated housing means blacks and whites are exposed to vastly different structural opportunities that impact health.

Finally, social inequality in the form of persistent racism and racial discrimination also plays a role in racial differences in life expectancy and mortality. In 2003, the Institute of Medicine published *Unequal Treatment: Confronting Racial and Ethnic Disparities in Health Care* (Smedley, Stith, and Nelson, 2003)—a book based on thorough investigation of research on black–white health differentials. While acknowledging the important influences described earlier, the book focused attention on what health care providers and health care systems could do to reduce or eliminate the disparity. Part of their analysis examines racial

(Continued)

(Continued)

differences in health care services even after socioeconomic differences are controlled. They highlight several studies showing that differences between blacks and whites in treatment for heart disease are not explained by severity of disease or by other clinical factors, and that these treatment differences lead to higher mortality for black patients. Other studies have documented racial differences in the use of diagnostic tests, in the provision of cancer treatment, and in drug therapy for AIDS patients.

A key feature of *Unequal Treatment* relates to recommendations on what can be done at both the macro and micro levels to address these disparities. One recommendation is to make all health care providers aware of how unconscious racial bias impacts their work. To enhance ability and skill in working with patients from diverse backgrounds, all providers should undergo cross-cultural education focusing on (1) *attitudes* (cultural sensitivity and awareness), (2) *knowledge* (of cultural groups), and (3) *skills* (in working with patients from different cultural backgrounds).

Preliminary data on COVID-19 bears this out, with higher mortality reported among African Americans in New York City, Chicago, Louisiana, Michigan, and New Jersey (CBS News, 2020; Levenson, 2020). Persistent structural racism is to blame. Because African–Americans are more likely to work in service occupations deemed essential (e.g., retail grocery, transportation and delivery services, etc.) and are less likely to hold jobs in which they can telecommute; they are at higher risk of contracting the virus that causes COVID-19. Lack of access to health care services and higher rates of underlying conditions (also a result of institutional racism) lead to disproportionately high COVID-19 fatalities among African-Americans.

Hispanics are now the largest racial/ethnic minority group in the United States, comprising about 17.6 percent of the population (US Census Bureau, 2019). Although Hispanics (a broad term covering several groups with important differences) are more likely than non-Hispanic whites to be below the poverty level and less likely to have health insurance—conditions almost universally related to poorer health and higher death rates—they have a lower death rate. As reported in Table 3.3, in 2016, Hispanics had a life expectancy of 81.8 years—3.1 years more than the national average. This is sometimes referred to as the "Hispanic Paradox."

What explains the Hispanic advantage in life expectancy and mortality? Some suggest it is a matter of selective migration—that healthier Hispanics are more likely to migrate to the United States. However, this explanation has been largely disproved. On the other hand, Hispanics are significantly less likely than whites to smoke cigarettes, leading to lower death rates from heart disease and cancer, and to an overall lower death rate (Fenelon, 2013). Dietary factors and the strong family life and support networks found in many Hispanic families also may be protective. Despite these protective factors, preliminary data on COVID-19 deaths reveal higher mortality rates among Hispanic-Americans compared to whites, likely due to a higher risk of exposure to the virus that causes COVID-19 among Hispanics in the workplace (Levenson, 2020).

Asian and Pacific Islanders, another strikingly diverse population, represent about 6.7 percent of the population (US Census Bureau, 2019). Included among this group are well-established Asian American populations (Japanese, Chinese, and Filipinos) and recent immigrants and refugees from Southeast Asia. The Asian American population is one of the healthiest in the country, with the longest life expectancy overall (about 87 years). Leading causes of death mirror those of other population groups, but rates are lower. As with Hispanics, lower rates of cigarette smoking contribute significantly to this advantage.

Gender. Women have a longer life expectancy than men. At birth, female infants can expect to live about 81 years, compared with just 76 years for males. Within racial groups, white female infants are expected to live almost 5 years longer than their white male counterparts, and black females nearly 6.5 years longer than black male infants. Mortality rates for all four leading causes of death in the United States—heart disease, cancer, accidents, and lung disease—are higher for men than for women.

Females have a biological advantage over males from the beginning of life, as demonstrated by lower mortality rates at both the prenatal and neonatal (i.e., first 28 days) stages of life. However, the sizeable gap in life expectancy between men and women can be traced to an interrelationship among several biological and sociocultural influences. These are discussed in the accompanying box, "Why Do Women Live Longer Than Men?"

IN THE FIELD

WHY DO WOMEN LIVE LONGER THAN MEN?

In the United States, women live approximately 5 years longer than men. Is this an inescapable gender-based feature? No. In the early part of the twentieth century, there was little difference in life expectancy between men and women, and by 1920, women lived only about 2 years longer than men. Although women live longer than men in all developed countries, in some agriculturally based societies men live longer than women. These patterns reflect the importance of social and cultural influences, not genetic determination. Systematic analyses of gender differentials in mortality point to two primary reasons: (1) differences in health-related behaviors and circumstances and (2) differences in the manner in which health services are used.

In the United States, women are more likely to experience acute illnesses such as upper respiratory tract infections and gastroenteritis and have higher rates of certain chronic debilitating (but not usually life-threatening) conditions such as anemia, thyroid conditions, colitis, and arthritis. Men are more likely to have life-threatening chronic conditions such as cancer, stroke, and liver disease (Bird and Rieker, 2008).

This pattern can be traced to behavioral differences. Over most of the age span, men are more likely than women to die of cancer. This can be traced to a greater likelihood of cigarette smoking, men's greater propensity to drink

alcohol excessively, and men being more likely to be exposed to cancer-causing agents in the workplace. Differences in reproductive anatomy and the effects of sex hormones also play a role and help to explain the greater likelihood of women dying from certain types of cancer, such as breast cancer.

Men are more likely to die in automobile accidents (studies show that men drive more miles but also drive faster, less cautiously, and violate more traffic regulations), to die in on-the-job accidents, to commit suicide, or to be victims of homicide. Whether or not male sex hormones create a predisposition to more aggressive behavior, socialization experiences relative to alcohol consumption, the use of guns, physical risk-taking, and assumption of risky jobs set the pattern (Stillion and McDowell, 2001–2002).

In addition, women are more likely than men to seek medical care. Women perceive more symptoms, take them more seriously, and are more willing to see a physician about them. They are more likely to have a regular source of medical care, use more preventive care, see physicians more often, be prescribed medications, and be hospitalized (Bird and Rieker, 2008). Often, men would benefit from earlier and increased medical attention as a means of earlier diagnosis of and intervention in diseases that become life-threatening.

INFANT MORTALITY

Measurement

In 2017, approximately 4.1 million infants died within 1 year of their birth. Of these, 1 million died on the same day they were born, and 2.5 million died within the first month after birth (World Health Organization, 2018b). The **infant mortality rate** (IMR) records the number of deaths of persons less than 1 year of age for every 1,000 babies born alive in a given year.

Epidemiologists divide infant mortality rate into two components—the **neonatal mortality rate** (deaths among infants in the first 28 days of life) and the **post-neonatal mortality rate** (deaths between 29 days and 1 year of life). Although infant mortality rates are sometimes used as an indicator of the quality of health care within a country, the post-neonatal mortality rate is actually a better indicator for two reasons. First, deaths in the first 28 days of life are often a direct consequence of genetic problems or difficulties in the birthing process. Second, using the neonatal rate to assess quality or delivery of care creates an illogical situation. The better health care technology gets at sustaining an early life, but one that it cannot sustain over the long term, the higher the neonatal mortality rate and the lower the evaluation of the health care system (i.e., babies who die during birth are not counted in infant mortality rates, but babies who are sustained and given a chance at life but die in the first 28 days are counted). The post-neonatal mortality rate is a better reflection of babies who die due to socioenvironmental conditions.

Both the infant mortality rate and postneonatal mortality rates are considered strong measures of a country's health care because they reflect social and economic conditions including public health practices, the overall health of women, the quality of health care services, and access to health care services.

Trends

The infant mortality rate (IMR) in the United States has steadily declined since the early 1900s, although there has been little reduction in the last several years (Mathews, MacDorman, and Thoma, 2015). Between 1950 and 2018, the mortality rate for infants dropped from 29.2 per 1,000 live births to a rate of 5.7. The long-term improvement is a result of factors such as improved socioeconomic status, better housing and nutrition, clean water, and pasteurized milk. Medical discoveries such as antibiotics and immunizations, better prenatal care and delivery, and technological breakthroughs in infant care (such as neonatal intensive care and new surgical techniques) have also been important.

Despite this decrease in the IMR, the United States ranks far below most nations that have comparable (or even fewer) resources (see Table 3.4). Japan, Singapore, Norway, and Finland are world leaders—all with an infant mortality rate at or below 2.5. In recent years, most of these countries have experienced a more rapid reduction in the rate of infant deaths than the United States.

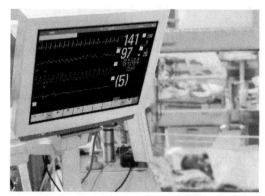

Hospital neonatal intensive care units provide specialized intensive care for sick and premature newborns. Despite their prevalence in the United States, the US infant mortality rate lags behind that of most modern countries.

Source: © beerkoff/Fotolia.

TABLE 3.4   Infant Mortality Rates, 2018 in Countries with a Population of More Than 5 Million

Country	Number of Deaths Under 1 Year/1,000 Live Births
Lowest 24, plus the United States	
Japan	2.0
Singapore	2.3
Norway	2.5
Finland	2.5
Czechia	2.6
Portugal	2.6
Sweden	2.6
Hong Kong	2.7
South Korea	3.0
Denmark	3.2
France	3.2
Italy	3.2
Spain	3.3
Austria	3.4
Belgium	3.4
Germany	3.4
Israel	3.4
Netherlands	3.5
Belarus	3.6
Ireland	3.6
Switzerland	3.6
Australia	4.2
United Kingdom	4.2
Taiwan	4.3
United States	5.7 (ranked 32nd)
Highest 10	
Afghanistan	108.5
Somalia	93.0
South Sudan	90.4
Central African Republic	84.3
Niger	79.4
Chad	71.7
Mali	67.6
Congo	66.7
Sierra Leone	66.7
Angola	65.8

Source: US Census Bureau. 2018a. "Mortality Indicators by Sex for Region Summary. Infant Mortality Rate, Both Sexes." International Data Base. Retrieved June 2, 2019 (www.census.gov/data-tools/demo/idb/informationGateway.php).

Countries with the highest infant mortality rates are mostly located in sub-Saharan Africa. In the country with the highest rate—Afghanistan—the rate is more than 100, which means that more than 1 in 10 babies die in the first year of life. The United States' rate ranks only 32nd best among countries with a population of more than 5 million, and only 57th best among all countries in the world.

Some researchers have asked if there are differences among countries in the method by which infant mortality is calculated, and, if so, whether this differential reporting contributes to the relatively higher IMR in the United States. The answer to the first part of this question is yes—some countries use a variation of the IMR formula, and this variation contributes to a modest reduction in the rate of infant deaths. Most countries—including the United States—consider all babies born alive when calculating IMR. Some other countries—for example, Ireland and Poland—consider only babies with a birth weight of at least 500 g. Thus the smallest and most vulnerable babies—those most likely to die—are excluded. This has the consequence of lowering their IMR. France and the Netherlands include only babies with a birth weight of at least 500 g, or of at least 22 weeks' gestation (MacDorman and Mathews, 2009).

However, in response to the second part of the question, researchers have calculated the magnitude of the difference in the IMR caused by the formula variations, and have discovered that they have a very small overall effect (MacDorman and Mathews, 2009). Given that most countries use the same formula as the United States, and given the small number of babies excluded from being counted in the other countries relative to the number of births counted, there is validity in comparing countries internationally. Although there might be some modest movement upward or downward in the ranking for any given country, there should be considerable consistency. In all calculations, the United States has a high relative IMR (Heisler, 2012).

Causes

By far, the single most hazardous condition for infants is low birth weight. In 2016, 8.1 percent of live births were of low birth weight (less than 2,500 g—about 5.5 pounds), and an additional 1.4 percent were very low birth weight (less than 1,500 g) (National Center for Health Statistics, 2018). Low birth weight is the primary determinant of approximately 75 percent of all deaths in the first month and 60 percent of all infant deaths. Low-birth-weight babies are also at risk of congenital anomalies such as malformations of the brain and spine, heart defects, and long-term disabilities such as cerebral palsy, autism, mental retardation, and vision and hearing impairments.

What factors increase the likelihood of a baby being low birth weight? At a micro level, low birth weight has been linked to the age of the mother (younger women have a more difficult time sustaining a healthy pregnancy), maternal smoking and use of alcohol or other drugs, and inadequate prenatal care. About two-thirds of low-birth-weight babies are born prematurely (defined as before the 37th week of a typical 40-week pregnancy).

Estimates are that half of the infant deaths due to low birth weight would be preventable with early and adequate prenatal care (most women at risk for delivering a low-birth-weight baby can be identified at an initial visit and monitored for factors such as inadequate nutrition, substance use, hypertension, urinary tract infections, and other potential risks to the fetus). Important issues such as weight gain, exercise, breastfeeding, and immunizations can be discussed.

In the United States, 6.2 percent of mothers who gave birth in 2016 received late or no prenatal care (Osterman and Martin, 2018). Mothers who do not receive prenatal care are three times more likely to give birth to a low-weight baby, and their babies are five times more likely to die in the first year of life. Many European countries attribute their lower infant mortality rate to the provision of early and adequate prenatal care to all women.

At a macro level, several social structural (social, economic, and political) factors directly impinge on the infant mortality rate. One study of state infant mortality levels compared the influence of social structural factors (such as percentage of persons in poverty, percentage of blacks and Hispanics in the population, amount of residential segregation, and political voting patterns) and health services variables (such as number of physicians relative to the population, and proportion of state expenditures on health care). The researchers found that the social structural factors were more strongly related to the rate of infant mortality (Bird and Bauman, 1995). Despite the appeal of focusing only on individual-level explanatory factors, social structural factors are very important influences of infant mortality.

Variations by Race and Socioeconomic Status

The overall infant mortality rate masks a significant discrepancy among mothers of different racial-ethnic and socioeconomic backgrounds (see Table 3.5). The infant mortality rate for non-Hispanic black mothers is significantly higher than for non-Hispanic white mothers (11.4 versus 4.9, respectively). Rates are also higher among low-income mothers. Low-income and black women are more likely to give birth in their teenage years and experience more health problems during pregnancy, but they are less likely to receive early and adequate prenatal care. In the United States in 2016, 4.3 percent of non-Hispanic white women received late or no prenatal care, but the corresponding percentages were 10.0 percent for non-Hispanic black, 12.5 percent for American Indian/Alaskan Native, and 19.2 percent for Native Hawaiian/Pacific Islander women (Osterman and Martin, 2018). These factors lead to a higher likelihood of giving birth prematurely and of having a low-birth-weight baby, and a higher infant mortality rate. In 2016, 11.5 percent of black women and 9.9 percent of American Indian/Alaskan Native women delivered a preterm infant (less than 37 weeks) compared to only 7.1 percent of non–Hispanic whites (National Center for Health Statistics, 2018).

As with racial differences in life expectancy and mortality, explanations for persistent racial disparities in infant mortality stress social structural factors. One classic study documented the effects of poverty (the fact that blacks are more likely to be below the poverty level), racial segregation (segregated black, urban communities being more likely to be toxic environments lacking in city services and medical services and having an inflated cost of living), and political empowerment (the black infant mortality rate is lower in cities with greater black political power, perhaps due to reduced feelings of hopelessness and greater availability of and inclination to use appropriate health services) (LaVeist, 1993).

MATERNAL MORTALITY

Every day in the world, more than 800 women die from pregnancy- or childbirth-related complications, totaling more than 300,000 maternal deaths yearly. More than 95 percent of these deaths occur in the developing world. Although this number is large, it actually represents a reduction of more than 40 percent since 1990. Several sub-Saharan African nations have decreased their rate by more than half during this time (World Health Organization, 2018a).

Maternal death is defined as the number of women who die while pregnant or within 42 days of termination of pregnancy, from any cause related to or aggravated by the pregnancy or its management. The **maternal mortality rate (MMR)** is the number of maternal deaths per 100,000 live births. The rate is about 12 per 100,000 live births in developed countries, but about 239 per 100,000 live births in developing

TABLE 3.5   Infant Deaths per 1,000 Live Births by Race/Ethnicity of Mother, United States, 2016

Race/Ethnic Origin	Rate
Overall, All Races/Ethnicities	5.8
Hispanic	5.0
Non-Hispanic	
White	4.9
Black	11.4
American Indian/Alaskan Native	9.4
Asian	3.6
Native Hawaiian/Other Pacific Islander	7.4

Source: Adapted from Centers for Disease Control and Prevention. 2019b. "User's Guide to the 2016 Period Linked Birth/Infant Death Public Use File, Table 3.1." National Center for Health Statistics. Retrieved June 7, 2019 (www.cdc.gov/nchs/data_access/vitalstatsonline.htm).

countries. The risk of a woman in a developing country dying from a pregnancy- or birth-related cause during her lifetime is more than 27 times higher than for a woman in a developed country (World Health Organization, 2018a). Nonetheless, MMR rates have been declining in most of the world and importantly, in many developing countries (Kassebaum et al., 2014). The accompanying box, "Mortality Patterns in Developing Countries," discusses explanations for the higher mortality rates there.

Why do women die as a result of pregnancy and childbirth? The most common reason is that they die from complications during and immediately following birth. Most of these complications develop during pregnancy, but others exist before pregnancy and are worsened by it. Around 75 percent of complications result from one or more of five conditions—severe bleeding (mostly occurring after birth), infections (mostly post birth), eclampsia or elevated blood pressure during pregnancy, complications of delivery, and unsafe abortions. Other complications result from having certain diseases (e.g., malaria or

IN COMPARATIVE FOCUS

MORTALITY PATTERNS IN DEVELOPING COUNTRIES

Worldwide, life expectancy increased more in the twentieth century and the first part of the twenty-first century than in all previous human history, with the biggest increases in the most recent years. Average life expectancy in the world increased from 48 years in 1955 to 66 years at the turn of the century, to 70 years in 2013, and is expected to increase to about 73 years by 2025.

However, these data camouflage continuing disparities between the world's wealthiest and poorest nations. Overall mortality, maternal mortality, and infant mortality rates remain high in the developing world. In many developing countries, the focus is more on "child mortality" (i.e., death in the first 5 years of life) than solely on infant mortality. This is because children aged 2 to 5 years are at continued high risk in these countries—a situation unlike that in industrialized countries. Worldwide, an estimated 7 million children die each year (more than 19,000 per day) before their fifth birthday. Although an extremely high number, it represents a large decrease since 1990, when about 12 million children under the age of 5 years died each year. The major causes of these deaths are lack of access to clean water, inadequate nutrition, expensive vaccines, and lack of skilled birthing attendants.

The experience of Pakistan illustrates the influence of economic and social development on infant mortality rates. Despite having a high infant mortality rate, little progress has been made in reducing the number of infant deaths. Pakistan has the highest rate of first-day deaths in the world, and more than 200,000 babies die annually in the first year of life.

Concerned about this pattern, Agha (2000) identified two primary factors that account for the lack of progress. First, socioeconomic inequality in Pakistan concentrates political power in a powerful rural elite. Throughout the 1980s and early 1990s, economic planning was built around the "trickle-down theory"—that efforts should be made to promote economic flourishing of the upper classes with the expectation that their success would filter down to the lower classes. The failure of this policy resulted in substantial disparities in income, education, nutrition, and access to quality housing, sanitary conditions, and clean water—all factors implicated in infant mortality rates.

Second, gender inequity contributes to the high infant mortality rate. Relative to Pakistani men, women tend to be poorer, less educated, and have lower social and legal status, making the health of Pakistani women and children a lower national priority. Additionally, more highly educated women have fewer children, stop procreation at an earlier age, and have longer spacing between births—all factors that positively impact the health and sustainability of newborns (Agha, 2000).

AIDS) during pregnancy (World Health Organization, 2018a).

Most of these complications develop during pregnancy, and most are preventable or treatable. The provision of adequate family planning services, prenatal care, and postpartum care, and clean, safe surgical procedures attended by a skilled health worker—such as a physician, nurse, or midwife—would dramatically reduce MMR even further (World Health Organization, 2018a). It is also essential that pregnant women in whom complications develop have access to emergency obstetrical care. This entails upgrading rural health centers and referral hospitals and ensuring they have the necessary drugs, supplies, and equipment, such as magnesium sulfate for eclampsia, antibiotics for infection, and basic surgical equipment for cesarean sections (Rosenfield, Min, and Freedman, 2007).

In contrast to the decreasing maternal mortality rate in most countries, the US rate has actually increased since the 1980s. The US National Vital Statistics System has not published an *official* maternal mortality rate since 2007, due to discrepancies in how states record maternal deaths. Nevertheless, researchers have estimated the US MMR using sophisticated statistical models to correct for reporting inconsistencies. Excluding Texas and California, MacDorman et al. (2016) estimated the MMR in 2014 was 23.8 per 100,000 live births, representing a 26.6 percent increase from 2000 when the rate was only 18.8 per 100,000 live births.

Clearly at a time when the World Health Organization reports that 157 of 183 countries studied had decreases in maternal mortality between 2000 and 2013, the United States maternal mortality rate is moving in the wrong direction. Among 31 Organization for Economic Cooperation and Development countries reporting maternal mortality data, the United States would rank 30th, ahead of only Mexico.

(MacDorman et al., 2016:7)

California is unique among states in showing a marked decline in maternal mortality during this time. California's MMR decreased by 57 percent between 2006 and 2013 (from 16.9 to 7.3 per 100,000 live births) due largely to concerted statewide efforts addressing the two largest contributors to maternal death—hemorrhage and preeclampsia (MacDorman et al., 2016; Main, 2018).

In 1986, the CDC created a new system, the Pregnancy Mortality Surveillance System, to collect more rigorous national data on maternal and pregnancy-related death. This led to the development of a new statistic, the **pregnancy-related mortality ratio (PRMR)**. Like the MMR, the PRMR reports the number of pregnancy-related deaths per 100,000 live births. The PRMR defines a pregnancy-related death as the death of a woman during pregnancy or within 1 year of the

end of a pregnancy from any cause related to or aggravated by the pregnancy or its management. It therefore differs from the MMR by counting deaths up to 1 year (not just 42 days) postpartum (Centers for Disease Control and Prevention, 2019a). The PRMR increased from 7.2 deaths per 100,000 live births in 1987 to 17.2 in 2015. Thus, whether using estimates of the MMR or the newer PRMR, all indications are that US maternal deaths have increased over the past several decades.

Yet significant variations exist among population subgroups. Black and American Indian/Alaskan Native women's PRMR is over three times and two and a half times, respectively, that of white women. Table 3.6 reports the pregnancy-related mortality ratio for various sociodemographic groups in the United States. Clearly,

TABLE 3.6 Pregnancy-Related Mortality Ratios (PRMR), by Sociodemographic Characteristics of Mothers, 2011–2015

Race/Ethnicity[1]

White	13.0
Black	42.8
American Indian/Alaskan Native	32.5
Asian/Pacific Islander	14.2
Hispanic	11.4

Highest Level of Education

Less than high school	19.8
High school graduate	24.2
Some college	14.8
College graduate or higher	9.4

Marital status

Married	13.1
Not married	22.8

[1] Women identified as white, black, American Indian/Alaskan Native and Asian/Pacific Islander were non-Hispanic. Hispanic women could be of any race.

Source: Adapted from Petersen, et al. 2019. "Vital Signs: Pregnancy-Related Deaths, United States, 2011–2015, and Strategies for Prevention, 13 States, 2013–2017." *Morbidity and Mortality Weekly Report* 68(18): 423–429.

mothers with less education, the unmarried, and those with lower levels of education are at highest risk.

Why is maternal mortality increasing in the United States? Some is due to more accurate record-keeping, but researchers agree the most important factors include more women beginning pregnancy with pre-existing chronic conditions (e.g., hypertension, diabetes), more women giving birth at later ages, a dramatic increase in cesarean section births, and continued absence of appropriate prenatal care (especially among low-income and minority women) (World Health Organization, 2018a). Because 1 out of 4 pregnant women in the United States experiences a major complication, such as high blood pressure or hemorrhage, prenatal care benefits both pregnant women and babies.

MORBIDITY

Morbidity refers to the amount of disease, impairment, and accident in a population. For several reasons, morbidity is more difficult to measure than mortality. The definition of illness varies considerably from one individual to another and from one group to another. Some people have a disease and do not realize it; others think they have a disease although there is no clinical confirmation. In the case of COVID-19, asymptomatic persons may never seek testing yet still be infected, while symptomatic persons may never receive confirmation due to lack of access to testing. For many illnesses, individuals may use home care instead of professional care, so the illness is never officially reported. In cases where a physician is consulted, the results of the examination may or may not be reported, since the law does not require the reporting of all diseases. While certain communicable diseases, such as TB and chicken pox, are reportable, others, such as cancer and heart disease, are not. If written records (e.g., hospital records) are used,

only professionally treated cases will be counted, resulting in an underestimation.

Much of the morbidity data we rely on is gathered through surveys such as the National Health Interview Survey. Although sampling techniques ensure a representative population, accurate data still depend on respondents' memories, and reporting still reflects individual perceptions of illness.

Measurement

Two epidemiological techniques—incidence and prevalence—are used to determine the social and ecological distribution of disease and illness.

Incidence and Prevalence. The **incidence** of disease, impairment, or accident refers to the number of new cases added to the population within a given period. For example, one could report the incidence of AIDS in the United States during the last year—this would include the number of people newly diagnosed in the last 12 months. **Prevalence** refers to the total number of cases of a condition present at a given time. The prevalence of AIDS in the United States today would be the total number of living people who have been diagnosed with AIDS. Together, incidence and prevalence help identify disease patterns. In the case of COVID-19, reported incidence and prevalence figures in the United States will likely undercount the true spread and extent of the disease due to limited test availability, especially in the early months of the pandemic.

Patterns and Sociodemographic Variations in Morbidity

In this section, we examine the relationship between morbidity and age, socioeconomic status, race, gender, and sexuality. This information is supplemented by the box, "The Link Between Health and Positive Social Relationships."

IN THE FIELD

THE LINK BETWEEN HEALTH AND POSITIVE SOCIAL RELATIONSHIPS

In the last 30 years, medical sociologists have attempted to understand better the impact of social relationships on health and illness. A key finding is that engagement in positive social relationships has a significant impact on health. Adults who are more socially connected have healthier lives and longer life expectancy than their more socially isolated peers. They are less likely to suffer from a host of diseases and illnesses (including heart disease, high blood pressure, and cancer) and do better when these diseases occur (Umberson and Montez, 2010).

How does participation in positive social relationships benefit health? Umberson and Montez (2010) identify three pathways. First, social relationships increase the likelihood of engaging in healthy behaviors and disengaging from unhealthy ones. Interaction with others may create a sense of responsibility toward them (e.g., a parent may become more health conscious as a role model for children or to be better able to care for them). This is a behavioral explanation.

Linked to this benefit is **social capital theory**, which posits that we may gain valuable resources from our social networks. These networks might provide helpful health information, assist in enabling health-promoting behaviors, increase access to beneficial resources, and

add to an individual's self-esteem and positive self-concept (Song and Lin, 2009).

Second, a psychosocial explanation asserts that social relationships can provide a variety of psychosocial benefits. They may be an important source of emotional support, enhance mental health, assist in handling stress, and provide for greater happiness and purpose in life. A recent study of Latino sexual minorities found that those who were actively involved in local lesbian, gay, bisexual, and transgender organizations were better able to deal with social stigmatization, felt higher levels of social support, and were less likely to engage in potentially health-harming sexual risk behaviors (Ramirez-Valles et al., 2010).

Third, supportive relationships have beneficial effects on the immune system, the endocrine system, and the cardiovascular system, and they reduce the negative bodily effects of social stress. This is a physiological explanation.

Of course, not all social relationships are positive, and participation in a negative relationship can exact health detriments in addition to failing to provide health benefits. In both cases, participation in social relationships influences health throughout the life course and has a cumulative impact on health.

Age. The health of children in the United States has changed dramatically in the past four decades. One by one, the major infectious diseases that used to imperil children have been eliminated or significantly reduced by widespread immunization. Smallpox has been eliminated, and polio will be soon. Diphtheria, scarlet fever, cholera, tetanus, pneumonia, mumps, and whooping cough are increasingly uncommon; however, many of these diseases continue to plague children

in developing countries. Although more than 75 percent of children in the United States receive all their immunizations by their third birthday, some children, especially in inner-city and rural areas, do not. Some claim that basic immunizations cause adverse reactions (claims that have been thoroughly disproven), leaving some parents ambivalent about immunizations.

As the prevalence of infectious diseases decreased, epidemiologists have focused increased attention on four other conditions that contribute to morbidity among children and adolescents:

1. *Poor diet and lack of exercise.* Poor nutrition, lack of exercise, and the resulting obesity among adolescents have become major problems. Since the 1980s, rates of overweight and obesity among children and adolescents have increased significantly. Data from the 2015–2016 NHANES showed that 18.4 percent of children aged 6 to 11 years were obese, and 20.6 percent of adolescents aged 12 to 19 years were obese (Hales et al., 2017).

   This pattern has been created by twin conditions—an increasing percentage of adolescents eating less nutritious, high-fat, high-sugar diets (as per most fast food) and a decreasing percentage getting the recommended amount of exercise. While these same patterns characterize adults, patterns set in adolescence are especially difficult to break. Poor diet and lack of exercise are related to elevated risks for many diseases, including heart disease, cancer, diabetes, depression, and stroke.

2. *Use of tobacco, alcohol, and other drugs.* Cigarette smoking among young people has decreased in the last few years with the popularity of e-cigarettes (discussed more in Chapter 6) surpassing that of cigarettes. In 2018, 8 percent of high school students and 2 percent of middle school students smoked cigarettes, while 4.9 percent of middle school students and nearly 21 percent of high school students used e-cigarettes (Centers for Disease Control and Prevention, 2019c). Cigarette smoking is related to an increased likelihood of developing many chronic diseases, including cancer, heart disease, depression, and lung disease.

   Alcohol use among high school students has also decreased significantly since the early 1990s. In 2017, 60.4 percent had ever drunk alcohol, 30 percent were current drinkers, and 13.5 percent binge drank (Kann et al., 2018). Underage drinking is associated with a variety of health problems, including impaired brain development, memory problems, alcohol poisoning, alcohol dependence, and car crashes.

   In the last decade, the proportion of high school students who ever used illicit drugs other than marijuana (specifically cocaine, inhalants, heroin, methamphetamines, hallucinogens, and ecstasy) declined significantly from 22.6 percent in 2007 to 14.0 percent in 2017. Nearly 36 percent of high school students have tried marijuana, 14 percent reported ever misusing prescription opioids, and less than 2 percent ever used injected drugs. Declines occurred across all subgroups of high school students (Centers for Disease Control and Prevention, 2018a).

   The health problems associated with illicit drug use depend on the specific drug, but they are many and can be serious. More than 40,000 people die from drug overdoses each year—more than half of these deaths are from prescription pills, and about 10,000 are due to heroin. Illicit drug use also puts adolescents at risk for violence, sexually transmitted infections (STIs), and unwanted pregnancy.

3. *Sexual activity and pregnancy.* Over the past decade, teenage sexual activity has declined significantly and contraceptive use has increased. In 2017, 39.5 percent of high school students reported ever having sex and only 28.7 percent were currently sexually active. Just over half of those who were currently sexually active reported using a condom during their last sexual encounter, down from 61.5 percent in 2007. However, declines in condom use were accompanied by an increased use of hormonal birth control (30 percent). Sexually active individuals who do not use condoms are at increased risk of HIV and other STIs, while those who do not use condoms or other forms of birth control are at risk of both STIs and unintended pregnancy (Centers for Disease Control and Prevention, 2018a).

   Teen birthrates declined steadily and are now at their lowest recorded levels (about

210,000 teenage girls give birth each year). However, the teenage birth rate in the United States is substantially higher than in other developed countries. Teenage mothers are less likely to finish school or be employed, and are more likely to have low-birth-weight babies (Centers for Disease Control and Prevention, 2018a).

4. *Violence.* Physical abuse is an increasingly recognized problem, as are emotional and sexual abuse. Reported physical and sexual abuse cases have increased since 1980, although this is partially due to improved reporting. In 2016, an estimated 676,000 children in the United States (a rate of 9.1 victims per 1,000 children, up from 8.8 in 2012) were confirmed by Child Protective Services to have been the victims of maltreatment, including neglect, physical abuse, emotional abuse, custodial interference, and sexual abuse (US Department of Health and Human Services, 2018).

Children who experience maltreatment are more likely to suffer a variety of negative health outcomes, both long- and short-term, including impaired brain development, impaired cognitive learning, and depression, and are at higher risk for heart, lung, and liver disease, high blood pressure, and cancer (Child Welfare Information Gateway, 2019).

The proportion of high schoolers threatened or injured with a weapon at school decreased between 2007 and 2017, and those experiencing physical or sexual dating violence also decreased between 2015 and 2017. The proportion of high schoolers bullied at school has remained relatively constant since 2009, hovering around 19 percent, and those electronically bullied also has not changed significantly (about 15 percent in 2017) (Centers for Disease Control and Prevention, 2018a).

At the other end of the age spectrum, health among the elderly has improved in recent years as a result of better diet, more exercise, and more accessible health care. Despite the fact that health problems increase in the later years, elderly people today are more likely to rate their health as good compared to earlier generations, and fewer report disabling physical conditions. This assessment is consistent with physician evaluations, and occurs even though people in their later years are more likely to experience multiple health ailments, such as heart disease, cancer, high blood pressure, diabetes, declining cognitive ability, hearing impairment, and arthritis. It is common for those over 65 to see multiple physicians (e.g., primary care physician, cardiologist, pulmonologist, oncologist, and others) and take ten or more prescriptions on a regular basis.

However, among the middle-aged (specifically, persons 45–54 years) the picture is more complex. Morbidity among middle-aged non-Hispanic whites increased after 1998, evidenced by declines in self-reported health and mental health, increased reports of pain, and greater difficulties with activities of daily living (eating, bathing, etc.). This increase mirrors decreases in life expectancy and increases in mortality among middle-aged whites noted earlier, and highlights the importance of deteriorating economic situations on health status (Case and Deaton, 2015).

Socioeconomic Status. Nearly 1 in every 7 Americans lives in a family with an income below the federal poverty level, and more than 20 percent of children under 18 years of age are in such families. House, Kessler, and Herzog (1990) studied the relationship between socioeconomic status and level of health (measured by number of chronic conditions, functional status, and limitation of daily activities) at various ages. They discovered a vast amount of preventable morbidity and functional limitations in the lower socioeconomic stratum of American society, and that the discrepancy between the poor and non-poor was especially great for those between the ages of 35 and 75 years.

Figure 3.1 is a representation of one model of how poverty influences morbidity and mortality. Persons in the lower social class are more likely to live and work in areas with hazardous chemico-physical conditions and are less likely to be involved in supportive social networks. These conditions lead to higher levels of psychological stress. The poor are more likely to engage in certain health-damaging behaviors (e.g., cigarette smoking and getting too little exercise, although heavy drinking occurs more in higher SES groups) in part due to the high level of stress (Shaw et al., 2014). The harmful lifestyle behaviors, the high levels of stress, and the lack of support networks all contribute to increased morbidity and a greater likelihood of mortality. Since the poor often cannot afford preventive or therapeutic care, health problems frequently do not receive immediate attention and serious conditions worsen.

Despite stay-at-home orders during the COVID-19 pandemic, low SES groups were more likely to work in essential services exempt from such orders (e.g., retail grocery sales, delivery, and transportation services), putting them at higher risk of infection. Unlike middle-class office workers who can telecommute, blue-collar workers seldom have this option. Because these same patterns tend to fall along racial lines, racial-ethnic minorities also tended to have higher COVID-19 infection rates than whites (CBS News, 2020; Levenson, 2020).

Race and Ethnicity.   One of the most discouraging health-related trends in the United States in the last decade has been the worsening

Figure 3.1   The Cycle of Poverty and Pathology

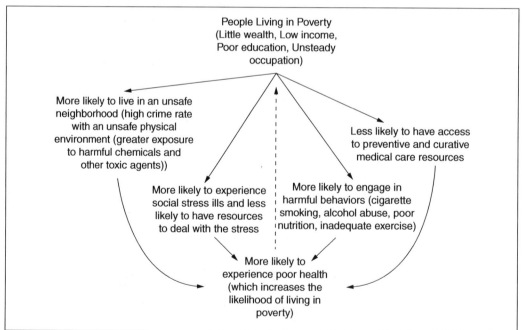

Source: Adapted from Diana B. Dutton, "Social Class, Health, and Illness," pp. 31–62 in *Applications of Social Science to Clinical Medicine and Health Policy*, edited by Linda H. Aiken and David Mechanic. Copyright 1986 by Rutgers, the State University. Reprinted by permission of Rutgers University Press.

state of health of African Americans. Rates of morbidity are higher for blacks than for whites for most diseases, including heart disease, cancer, diabetes, pneumonia and influenza, liver disease and cirrhosis, accidental injuries, and AIDS. Blacks experience more health problems than whites early in life, and their health deteriorates more rapidly. Some, but not all, of this health disadvantage is due to the lower economic standing of blacks. For example, Sudano and Baker (2006) identified education, income, and net worth as being more influential than lifestyle and health insurance in explaining racial–ethnic differences in declines in self-reported overall health. However, at all ages and at all levels of socioeconomic standing, blacks have more health problems than whites (Ferraro and Farmer, 1996). Moreover, education confers fewer health advantages to blacks than it does to whites, creating a situation of "diminishing returns." For example, Farmer and Ferraro (2005) found that self-rated health for whites, but not blacks, improves with higher levels of education.

Research has found that race creates an added burden on the health of blacks. Williams (2012) contends that this added burden derives from three primary factors:

1. Indicators of SES are not equivalent across race. Compared to whites, blacks and Hispanics have lower levels of earning, less wealth, and less purchasing power at every educational level.
2. Health is affected by adversity over the entire life course—not just at the current time. The cumulative impact of social and economic adversity takes a toll on the body, producing a higher burden of disease (and death) for racial minorities. This is sometimes referred to as a "weathering" effect (Forde et al., 2019).
3. Discrimination—both institutional (e.g., residential segregation that leads to more health-harmful neighborhoods in which minorities live) and individual (which has been found to

be a significant source of health-harming psychological distress).

The health of Asians and Pacific Islanders is as varied as the people are diverse. The level of health of those born within the United States and established in the culture is very similar to that of the population as a whole, but on most major indicators, Asians and Pacific Islanders are the healthiest of all racial/ethnic groups in the country. This is true especially for Chinese, Japanese, and Korean Americans.

However, Asian Americans are at especially high risk for certain diseases. Asian Americans are the only segment of the US population for whom cancer is the leading cause of death. Rates of lung cancer (due mostly to higher rates of cigarette smoking), liver cancer, and stomach cancer are a particular problem. Rates of hepatitis B and tuberculosis are also higher than in the general population. Additionally, inaccurate stereotyping of COVID-19 as a Chinese or Asian disease has led to violence and discrimination against Asian-Americans.

Most Hispanic groups—especially Mexican and Cuban Americans—compare favorably with whites on rates of morbidity, and fare better than blacks. On the other hand, Puerto Ricans fare less well than whites on morbidity indicators. Rates of diabetes, tuberculosis, and HIV/AIDS are all of special concern. As with other groups, Hispanics below the poverty level are at special risk.

The Mexican Americans who are most at risk of morbidity are the approximately 1 million farmworkers who do exhausting work, have high rates of accidents, and have limited access to health care providers. Groups on both sides of the US–Mexico border contend with serious air and water pollution, poor sanitation, considerable overcrowding, and illegally dumped hazardous wastes.

Gender. Although men have a higher prevalence of fatal conditions and thus higher mortality rates, women have higher morbidity rates for most acute illnesses (including infectious and respiratory diseases) and most chronic conditions. Scholars offer five explanations for gender differences in morbidity:

1. *Biological risks.* Males are at some health disadvantage due to the female's intrinsic protection from certain genes and hormones. Reproductive conditions (pregnancy, childbirth, and disorders of puerperium) account for a substantial amount—but not all—of the morbidity differential, even at ages 17 to 44 years.

2. *Acquired risks due to differences in work and leisure activities, lifestyle and health habits, and psychological distress.* Acquired risks are different for men and women. Some health-harming behaviors, such as smoking cigarettes, excessive alcohol consumption, and occupational hazards, are more common among men. Others, such as less active leisure activities, being overweight, stress and unhappiness, and role pressures are associated more with women. Most analysts perceive this to be the most important explanation for gender differences in mortality, and an important part of the explanation for gender differences in morbidity.

3. *Psychosocial aspects of symptoms and care.* People perceive symptoms, assess their severity, and decide what to do to relieve or cure health problems differently. Gender differences in response to illness may stem from childhood or adult socialization that it is more acceptable for women to reflect upon and discuss symptoms and concerns. Physiological conditions such as menstruation, pregnancy, breastfeeding, and menopause may encourage women to pay more attention to their bodies and be more observant of physiological changes. Research confirms that women place higher value on health and have more of a preventive orientation. This may be the other most important explanatory factor in morbidity differentials.

4. *Health-reporting behavior.* Women are more willing to acknowledge symptoms and illness and to seek care. In one study, women were significantly more likely than men to report headache-related disability and seek health care services for headaches, even after controlling for severity of the headache (Celetano, Linet, and Stewart, 1990). Depending on the source of the data, part of these differences may relate to continuing differences in the socioeconomic position of men and women. Women are less likely than men to be employed, so they can more easily arrange a medical visit. If a family member is ill, it is more likely that the woman will call in sick, since women on average earn less than men, and in many families it is the wife's "duty" to care for sick children or be home on school holidays.

5. *Prior experience with health care and caretakers.* Men use fewer health care services. As a result of their greater participation in self-care and greater attentiveness to health status, women may derive more benefit from seeing a health care provider and receive more positive reinforcement for their attentiveness (Verbrugge, 1990).

Sexual Minorities. Traditionally defined as persons who identify as lesbian, gay, and bisexual, the term "sexual minority" also now encompasses those who identify as transgender, queer or questioning, intersex, and non-binary, and may include persons who identify as heterosexual, but engage in sexual activities with persons of the same sex. For brevity, we use the term sexual minorities or LGBTQ+.

Historically, health disparities research in sexual minority communities was dominated by a focus on HIV/AIDS, reflecting both the seriousness of the health threat HIV/AIDS posed and the ways homophobia and heterosexism blinded researchers to other important health disparities affecting the LGBTQ+ community. The addition of questions about sexual and gender identity on national health surveys now permits a wider examination of how sexual minorities fare (relative to non-sexual minorities) across a variety of health measures. Recent research shows that sexual minorities experience higher rates of poor mental health and activities limitations, and have higher rates of alcohol and drug use. Sexual minority women also have higher rates of obesity than non-sexual minority women.

Stigma and discrimination are believed to play significant roles in health disparities within the LGBTQ+ community. However, different age cohorts face different lifetime exposures to stigma and discrimination, as perceptions and social acceptance of LGBTQ+ persons change. As Fredriksen-Goldsen et al. (2013:1806) explain, "older adults came of age during a time when same-sex relationships were criminalized and severely stigmatized and same-sex identities were socially invisible." Although still not enjoying full legal protections, LGBTQ+ youth today are coming of age at a time when same-sex marriage is legal across the United States and social acceptance of sexual minorities is much greater. Consequently, it is important to examine health disparities within the LGBTQ+ community across different age groups.

The Youth Risk Behavior Survey (YRBS) found significant health disparities between sexual minority and non-sexual minority high school students. In fact, for every variable examined, including measures of sexual behavior, substance use, violence victimization, and mental health and suicide, sexual minority youth were at significantly higher risk than non-sexual minority youth (Centers for Disease Control and Prevention, 2018a).

Using data from the 2001–2010 waves of the National Health and Nutrition Examination Survey (NHANES) for respondents aged 20 to 49 years, Operario and colleagues (2015) found higher rates of multiple health problems among sexual minority men and women. After adjusting for sociodemographic factors, compared to their heterosexual counterparts, sexual minority men had an increased risk of testing positive for HIV and genital herpes, and both sexual minority men and women had increased odds of reporting 15 or more poor mental health days during the past 30 days. Finally, sexual minority women were more likely than heterosexual women to report heavy alcohol use, smoking more than 100 cigarettes, and ever using marijuana and other illicit drugs (i.e., cocaine, heroin, methamphetamine, or injection drugs).

A study of older LGBTQ+ persons (aged 50 years and over) in Washington State found that some disparities seen in mid-life sexual minorities persist into later life, including higher rates of disability, poor mental health, and smoking, and, for lesbians and bisexual women, excessive drinking and obesity. As well, conditions typical of older adults are more prevalent among older sexual minority adults, including for women heightened risks of cardiovascular disease and for men poor physical health and excessive drinking (Fredriksen-Goldsen et al., 2013). The greater health burden for older LGBTQ+ adults means health services for sexual minorities must be a high priority.

DISABILITY

What it means to be "disabled" or to have a **disability** has undergone significant revision in the last 30 years. Historically, Western societies viewed disability as a personal tragedy and individual failing, with a focus on deficits, abnormalities, and functional limitations. Often, definitions of disability centered on having at least one designated disabling physical condition. For example, a person with one arm or leg would be considered to have a disability. Societal attitudes ranged from sympathy to indifference to exclusion (Barnes and Mercer, 2010).

Many sociologists criticize this approach as focusing too much on individuals outside of any social context. They prefer a **social model of disability**, which posits that restrictions in activities or functions are the result of a society that has not made appropriate accommodations. According to David Mechanic (1995:1210):

> In the older conception, while disability deserved public sympathy and assistance, it was viewed in essence as a personal problem that required considerable withdrawal from usual activities. The contemporary view has had a transformative influence in its implication that persons with almost any impairment can meet most of the demands of everyday living if they adopt appropriate attitudes and if physical, social, and attitudinal barriers are removed.

From this perspective, disability occurs only when there is an absence of "fit" between the capabilities of persons and the physical environment in which they live. This gap can partially be addressed at the individual level (e.g., by modifying the impairment, increasing patient motivation, and teaching coping strategies), but must also be addressed through social policy and environmental remediation (e.g., by providing assistive devices, removing unnecessary physical barriers, and ensuring fair treatment). In the last few years, an abundance of research has demonstrated the importance of the "built environment" in reducing barriers to full participation in society (Barnes and Mercer, 2010; Clarke et al., 2011).

The World Health Organization (2019:1) defines disabilities as

> an umbrella term, covering impairments, activity limitations, and participation restrictions. An *impairment* is a problem in body function or structure; an *activity limitation* is a difficulty encountered by an individual in executing a task or action; while a *participation restriction* is a problem experienced by an individual in involvement in life situations. Disability is a complex phenomenon, reflecting an

interaction between features of a person's body and features of the society in which he or she lives.

An example of this evolution in thinking would be to consider the situation of a disabled person failing to find employment. Traditionally, such a failure would be considered an individual shortcoming. However, given that the employment rate is much lower for disabled persons than the rest of the population, it is viewed more appropriately as a structural problem—work environments are configured in such a way as to be inappropriate for people with disabilities—or as reflecting discriminatory attitudes toward disabled people (Barnes and Mercer, 2010). See the accompanying box, "The Importance of the Americans with Disabilities Act."

Measurement of disability varies from one study to another—that is, the identification of who is and is not disabled or what is and is not a disability is not always the same. Nevertheless, in 2011, the World Health Organization and the World Bank estimated that 1 billion people around the world live with a disability, and 80 percent of these individuals live in developing countries. Those with disabilities are more than twice as likely to find health care providers unprepared to meet their needs, nearly three times more likely to be denied care, and four times more likely to be treated badly (World Health Organization and World Bank, 2011).

According to the **Behavioral Risk Factor Surveillance System (BRFSS)**, one-quarter of the US population reported one or more disabilities in 2016. Table 3.7 identifies the percentage of selected population subgroups with a disability, and Table 3.8 reports the proportion with specific

IN THE FIELD

THE IMPORTANCE OF THE AMERICANS WITH DISABILITIES ACT

Throughout much of its history, the United States made few efforts to create a society in which people with disabilities could participate

as freely and fully as possible. The virtually impenetrable barriers that occurred throughout workplaces and public settings prevented full participation of individuals with functional limitations.

The signature change in this approach occurred in 1990 with the passage of the Americans with Disabilities Act (ADA), a civil rights law that aimed to provide "equality and inclusion into all facets of life, while offering an inspiring model that much of the world would come to embrace" (Gostin, 2015:2231).

In 2015, 25 years after the passage of the ADA, many individuals and groups reflected on the consequences of the legislation and on Supreme Court rulings relative to it. Many pointed out positive changes in access to public services, such as crosswalks with curb cuts for wheelchair access, more buildings that enable changing floors without climbing steps, pedestrian signals that assist people with vision difficulties, and more accessible vehicles.

Despite these changes, substantial disparities remain in employment, housing, transportation, and other areas that lead to less access and ultimately poorer health for those with disabilities. Access problems remain for using some types of diagnostic imaging equipment and even equipment as basic as a weight scale, for participating in certain types of wellness programs, for communicating for deaf people, and in having medical providers feel comfortable and competent in working with people with disabilities. The Supreme Court heard several cases involving interpretation of the ADA, and early on they defined disability so narrowly that it prevented many of the advancements Congress had intended. Congress passed with broad support the ADA Amendments Act of 2008, which overturned many of these decisions and added protections for a more broadly defined group of disabled persons. The Patient Protection and Affordable Care Act—referred to as the ACA or Obamacare (see Chapter 14)—was passed in 2010 and contains provisions specifically to address health inequities for people with disabilities, including more systematic data gathering, new standards for medical equipment to increase accessibility, and helping health care professionals become more competent in "disability culture" (Peacock, Iezzoni, and Harkin, 2015).

TABLE 3.7   Percentage of the US Population With One or More Disabilities, 2016

Characteristic	Percentage		
	Age 18–44 years	Age 45–64 years	Age 65+ years
With any physical difficulty	16.6	28.6	41.7
Men	15.2	27.1	40.9
Women	17.9	30.1	42.3
Poor[1]	27.8	57.9	59.6
Near Poor	20.1	44.5	53.1
Not Poor	9.3	16.6	31.9
White	16.3	26.2	40.2
Black	18.1	35.5	46.7
Hispanic	17.6	35.5	50.5
American Indian/Alaskan Native	27.7	49.2	54.9

[1] Those with incomes <100% of the federal poverty line (FPL) are poor; those with incomes ≥100% to <200% FPL are near poor; those ≥200% FPL are not poor.

Source: Okoro, Catherine A., NaTasha D. Hollis, Alissa C. Cyrus, and Shannon Griffin-Blake. 2018. "Prevalence of Disabilities and Health Care Access by Disability Status and Type Among Adults—United States, 2016." *Morbidity and Mortality Weekly Report* 67 (August 17):882–871.

TABLE 3.8   Prevalence of Any Disability and Disability Type Among Individuals Aged 18 or Older, United States, 2016

Disability Status in US Population	Percentage
With any disability (some people with more than one disability)	25.7
Hearing difficulty	5.9
Vision difficulty	4.6
Cognition difficulty	10.8
Mobility difficulty	13.7
Self-care difficulty	3.7
Independent living difficulty	6.8

Source: Okoro, Catherine A., NaTasha D. Hollis, Alissa C. Cyrus, and Shannon Griffin-Blake. 2018. "Prevalence of Disabilities and Health Care Access by Disability Status and Type Among Adults—United States, 2016." *Morbidity and Mortality Weekly Report* 67 (August 17):882–871.

disabling conditions. American Indian/Alaskan Natives have the highest rates of disabilities across all three age groups examined, while whites have the lowest. Women report slightly more disabilities than men, regardless of age. The likelihood of having a disability is highest among those with the least education, and it decreases as level of education increases. People in the lowest-income groups are two to three times more likely to have a disability as people in higher-income groups. Their lack of financial means often results in lack of access to needed services. This in turn hinders the successful management of a chronic medical condition, and makes it more difficult to live successfully in the community (Okoro et al., 2018).

Disability is related to age—persons aged 65 years or older are two and a half times more likely than younger people to have a disability. Disability among seniors has declined over the last few decades due to better nutrition, higher levels of education, improved economic status, and medical advances. However, between 2000 and 2015, rates of disability among the middle-aged (those 45 to 64 years) grew for all but the most highly educated (i.e., those with at least a college degree), with the least educated (i.e., less than high school) experiencing the biggest increase. Researchers point to the worsening economic well-being of middle- and working-class families during this period as one possible explanation (Zajacova and Montez, 2017). Unless the trend is reversed, it will lead to higher rates of disability among the elderly.

Health status and disability status often are related, as many health problems arise from or are related to the main cause of disability. These secondary conditions often are linked to living conditions. For example, pressure sores and musculoskeletal disorders are common among those confined to a wheelchair or bed. Not only can these complicating medical conditions arise from immobility or inactivity, but they may also be a result of the progression of the original disabling condition, such as visual impairment among diabetics. Of course, it is also possible for a person to be disabled and be in good health (e.g., someone who is blind).

SUMMARY

Prior to large-scale migration and urbanization, acute infectious diseases and epidemics presented relatively little threat to humans. The development of easier modes of travel and the emergence of cities brought with them outbreaks of infectious disease. With the development of the germ theory of disease and other advances in medicine, as well as greater understanding of the importance of social factors in the transmission of diseases, the threat of infectious diseases was reduced and replaced by a higher incidence and greater likelihood of death from chronic degenerative diseases.

This chapter examines key patterns and trends related to measures of life expectancy, mortality, infant mortality, maternal mortality, morbidity, and disability. Across indicators, there has been improvement over time in both developed and developing countries, but rates are typically still of great concern in less developed countries. Rates in the United States have improved over time, but the United States still compares unfavorably to many countries.

Within the United States, there continue to be wide inequities on most indicators by gender, race and ethnicity, socioeconomic status, age, and for sexual minorities. These disparities require continued analysis and efforts at remediation.

HEALTH ON THE INTERNET

1. One way to stay abreast of mortality and morbidity data is to check the CDC's *Morbidity and Mortality Weekly Report* on the Internet (www.cdc.gov/mmwr/). After you enter the website, click on "Y" in the top A–Z Index, and then click on "Youth Violence."

   What is *youth violence*? What are the four types of *risk factors* and the three types of *protective factors* (and specific examples of each) associated with youth violence? What are some *consequences* of youth violence? What are some *prevention strategies* for youth violence? What is the significance of violence being included in the website of a center for "disease control"?

2. Listen to or read one of the reports from the National Public Radio special series on US maternal mortality titled "Lost Mothers: Maternal Mortality in the United States," located at:

   www.npr.org/series/543928389/lost-mothers

   Prepare a short report on the segment you selected. In your report, identify at least two similarities between information in the segment and material in the chapter, as well as two important items from the segment not discussed in the chapter.

DISCUSSION CASES

1. As this chapter demonstrates, epidemiologists provide valuable information for understanding and controlling diseases. However, data gathering can conflict with the rights of individuals. For example, identification of individuals with STIs, collection of names of their sexual partners, and contacting these partners can infringe on the autonomy and privacy of individuals even as they assist in promoting public health. It is therefore extremely important that epidemiologists carry out their responsibilities while adhering to ethical principles of respect, justice, and equity.

   Discuss these issues as they relate to the following case. Thomas Hoskins is a 21-year-old full-time college student who is also employed 30 hours per week. The pressures of school, work, and a marriage on the rocks have been adding up. Three weeks ago, he went out with friends, drank too much, and ended up sleeping with a woman he met at the bar. Tests confirm that he now has gonorrhea. While giving him an injection, his physician tells him that all sexually transmitted diseases must be reported to the state health department.

   Thomas is panic-stricken. He fears that his wife will find out (she has friends who work for the health department), and that if she does, their marriage will be over. He pleads with the physician to make an exception to his duty to report. This is his first extramarital sexual contact, and he assures the physician it will be his last.

   Should the physician make an exception in this case and not comply with the state mandatory reporting law? Or should physicians always report regardless of the circumstances?

2. Life expectancy in the United States has increased to about 80 years and is continuing to increase. Many demographers anticipate that life expectancy will top out at around 88 years for females and 82 years for males. However, Donald Loria, a professor at the New Jersey Medical School, believes that the average could reach 100 years in the next few decades just with continued gradual increases, and 110 or 120 years with

revolutionary advances in health and medicine (Curtis, 2004). Some others do not see this as being likely or possible.

But what if this happened? What if average life expectancy reached 100 or 110 years by mid-century? Identify the changes that would occur in social institutions if 30 or 40 percent of the population was aged 65 years or older (up from today's 13.5 percent). If we knew that this change was going to occur within the next five decades, what social planning could be done to accommodate it?

GLOSSARY

acute infectious diseases
Behavioral Risk Factor Surveillance System (BRFSS)
Centers for Disease Control and Prevention (CDC)
chronic degenerative diseases
crude death rate (CDR)
disability
epidemiological transition
epidemiology
fundamental cause theory (FCT)
incidence
infant mortality rate (IMR)

life expectancy
maternal mortality rate (MMR)
morbidity
mortality
neonatal mortality rate
post-neonatal mortality rate
pregnancy-related mortality ratio (PRMR)
prevalence
sexual minority
social capital theory
social epidemiology
social model of disability
World Health Organization (WHO)

REFERENCES

Agha, Sohail. 2000. "The Determinants of Infant Mortality in Pakistan." *Social Science and Medicine* 51(2):199–208.

Akhtar, Aysha. 2016. "Why Are We Seeing an Explosion of New Viruses Like Zika?" *HuffPost World Economic Forum*. Retrieved December 15, 2018 (www.huffingtonpost.com/aysha-akhtar/).

Barnes, Colin, and Geof Mercer. 2010. *Exploring Disability: A Sociological Introduction* (2nd ed.). Malden, MA: Polity Press.

Bird, Chloe E., and Patricia P. Rieker. 2008. *Gender and Health: The Effects of Constrained Choices and Social Policies*. New York: Cambridge University Press.

Bird, Sheryl T., and Karl E. Bauman. 1995. "The Relationship Between Structural and Health Services Variables and State-Level Infant Mortality in the United States." *American Journal of Public Health* 85(1):26–29.

Case, Anne and Angus Deaton. 2015. "Rising Morbidity and Mortality in Midlife among White Non-Hispanic Americans in the 21st Century." *Proceedings of the National Academy of Sciences of the United States of America* 112(49):15078–15083.

CBS News. 2020. "African Americans Comprise More than 70% of COVID-19 Deaths in Chicago, Officials Say." Retrieved April 26, 2020 (www.cbsnews.

com/news/african-americans-comprise-more-than-70-percent-of-covid-19-deaths-in-chicago-mayor-says-2020-04-06/).

Celetano, David D., Martha S. Linet, and Walter F. Stewart. 1990. "Gender Differences in the Experience of Headache." *Social Science and Medicine* 30(12):1289–1295.

Centers for Disease Control and Prevention. 2018a. "Youth Risk Behavior Survey—Data Summary & Trends Report: 2007–2017." *Division of Adolescent and School Health, National Center for HIV/AIDS, Viral Hepatitis, STD, and TB Prevention.* Retrieved June 8, 2019 (www.cdc.gov/healthyyouth/data/yrbs/).

———. 2018b. "Tuberculosis, Data and Statistics." Retrieved June 3, 2019 (www.cdc.gov/tb/statistics/default.htm).

———. 2019a. "Pregnancy Mortality Surveillance System." Retrieved June 7, 2019 (www.cdc.gov/reproductivehealth/maternalinfanthealth/pregnancy-mortality-surveillance-system.htm).

———. 2019b. "User's Guide to the 2016 Period Linked Birth/Infant Death Public Use File, Table 1." *National Center for Health Statistics.* Retrieved June 7, 2019 (www.cdc.gov/nchs/data_access/vitalstatsonline.htm).

———. 2019c. "Youth and Tobacco Use." Retrieved June 8, 2019 (www.cdc.gov/tobacco/data_statistics/fact_sheets/youth_data/tobacco_use/index.htm.

———. 2020a. "Groups at Higher Risk for Severe Illness." Retrieved April 26, 2020 (www.cdc.gov/coronavirus/2019-ncov/need-extra-precautions/groups-at-higher-risk.html).

———. 2020b. "Symptoms of Coronavirus." Retrieved April 26, 2020 (https://www.cdc.gov/coronavirus/2019-ncov/symptoms-testing/symptoms.html).

Central Intelligence Agency. 2019. "World Factbook." Retrieved June 4, 2019 (www.cia.gov/library/publications/resources/the-world-factbook/).

Child Welfare Information Gateway. 2019. *Long-term Consequences of Child Abuse and Neglect.* Washington, DC: United States Department of Health and Human Services, Children's Bureau.

Clarke, Phillipa J., Jennifer A. Ailshire, Els R. Nieuwenhuijsen, and Marike W. de Kleijn-de Frankrijker. 2011. "Participation Among Adults with Disability: The Role of the Urban Environment." *Social Science and Medicine* 72(10):1674–1684.

Cook, Jeffrey. 2020. "Critical Inhaler Medication Shortage Looms as Coronavirus Cases Soar." *ABC News.* Retrieved April 26, 2020 (https://abcnews.go.com/Health/critical-inhaler-medication-shortage-looms-coronavirus-cases-soar/story?id=69759965).

Curtis, Wayne. 2004. "The Methuselah Report." *AARP Bulletin* 43:5–7.

Dutton, Diana B. 1986. "Social Class, Health, and Illness." Pp. 31–62 in *Applications of Social Science to Clinical Medicine and Health Policy,* edited by Linda H. Aiken and David Mechanic. New Brunswick, NJ: Rutgers University Press.

Farmer, Melissa M., and Kenneth F. Ferraro. 2005. "Are Racial Disparities in Health Conditional on Socioeconomic Status?" *Social Science and Medicine* 60(1):191–204.

Fenelon, Andrew. 2013. "Revisiting the Hispanic Mortality Advantage in the United States: The Role of Smoking." *Social Science and Medicine* 82(April):1–9.

Ferraro, Kenneth F., and Melissa Farmer. 1996. "Double Jeopardy to Health Hypothesis for African-Americans: Analysis and Critique." *Journal of Health and Social Behavior* 37(1):27–43.

Forde, Allana T., Danielle M. Crookes, Shakira F. Suglia, and Ryan T. Demmer. 2019. "The Weathering Hypothesis as an Explanation for Racial Disparities in Health: A Systematic Review." *Annals of Epidemiology* 33(May):1–18.

Fredriksen-Goldsen, Karen I., Hyun-Jun Kim, Susan E. Barkan, Anna Muraco, and Charles P. Hoy-Ellis. 2013. "Health Disparities Among Lesbian, Gay, and Bisexual Older Adults: Results from a Population-Based Study." *American Journal of Public Health* 103(10):1802–1809.

Gaziano, J. Michael. 2010. "Fifth Phase of the Epidemiologic Transition: The Age of Obesity and Inactivity." *Journal of the American Medical Association* 303(3):275–276.

Gostin, Leonard, O. 2015. "The Americans with Disabilities Act at 25: The Highest Expression of American Values." *Journal of the American Medical Association* 313(22):2231–2235.

Hales, Craig M., Margaret D. Carroll, Cheryl D. Fryar, and Cynthia L. Ogden. 2017. "Prevalence of Obesity among Adults and Youth: United States, 2015–2016." *NCHS Data Brief,* 288. Hyattsville, MD: National Center for Health Statistics.

Hayward, Mark D., Robert A. Hummer, and Isaac Sassoon. 2015. "Trends and Group Differences in the Association Between Educational Attainment and United States Adult Mortality: Implications for Understanding Education's Causal Influence." *Social Science and Medicine* 127(February):8–18.

Heisler, Elayne J. 2012. *The United States Infant Mortality Rate: International Comparisons, Underlying Factors, and Federal Programs.* Washington, DC: Congressional Research Service (www.fas.org/sgp/crs/misc/R41378.pdf).

Heron, Melonie. 2018. "Deaths: Leading Causes for 2016." *National Vital Statistics Reports* 67(6):77.

Ho, Jessica Y. 2013. "Mortality Under Age 50 Accounts for Much of the Fact That US Life Expectancy Lags That of Other High-Income Countries." *Health Affairs* 32(3):459–467.

Ho, Jessica Y., and Arun S. Hendi. 2018. "Recent Trends in Life Expectancy across High Income Countries: Retrospective Observational Study." *BMJ* 362:k2562 (https://doi.org/10.1136/bmj.k2562).

House, James S., Ronald Kessler, and A. Regula Herzog. 1990. "Age, Socioeconomic Status, and Health." *The Milbank Quarterly* 68(3):383–411.

Kann, Laura, Tim McManus, William A. Harris, Shari L. Shanklin, Katherine H. Flint, Barbara Queen, Richard Lowry, David Chyen, Lisa Whittle, Jemekia Thornton, Connie Lim, Denise Bradford, Yoshimi Yamakawa, Michelle Leon, Nancy Brener, and Kathleen A. Ethier. 2018. "Youth Risk Behavior Surveillance—United States, 2017." *Morbidity and Mortality Weekly Report* 67(8):479.

Kassebaum, Nicholas J., Amelia Bertozzi-Villa, Megan S. Coggeshall, Katya A. Shackelford, et al. 2014. "Global, Regional, and National Levels and Causes of Maternal Mortality during 1990–2013: A Systematic Analysis for the Global Burden of Disease Study 2013." *The Lancet* 384(9947):980–1004.

Kates, Graham. 2020. "N95 Mask Shortage Comes Down to This Key Material: 'The Supply Chain Has Gotten Nuts.'" Retrieved April 26, 2020 (www.cbsnews.com/news/n95-mask-shortage-melt-blown-filters/).

LaVeist, Thomas A. 1993. "Segregation, Poverty, and Empowerment: Health Consequences for African Americans." *The Milbank Quarterly* 71(1):41–64.

Levenson, Eric. 2020. "Why Black Americans Are at Higher Risk for Coronavirus." *CNN*. Retrieved April 26, 2020 (www.cnn.com/2020/04/07/us/coronavirus-black-americans-race/index.html).

MacDorman, Marian, and T.J. Mathews. 2009. "Behind International Rankings of Infant Mortality: How the United States Compares with Europe." *NCHS Data Brief* 23. National Center for Health Statistics.

MacDorman, Marian F., Eugene Declercq, Howard Cabral, and Christine Morton. 2016. "Recent Increases in the U.S. Maternal Mortality Rate: Disentangling Trends from Measurement Issues." *Obstetrics and Gynecology* 128(3):447–455.

Main, Elliott K. 2018. "Reducing Maternal Mortality and Severe Maternal Morbidity through State-Based Quality Improvement Initiatives." *Clinical Obstetrics and Gynecology* 61(2):319–331.

Masters, Ryan K., Bruce G. Link, and Jo C. Phelan. 2015. "Trends in Educational Gradients of 'Preventable Mortality': A Test of Fundamental Cause Theory." *Social Science and Medicine* 127(February):19–28.

Mathews, T.J., Marian MacDorman, and Marie E. Thoma. 2015. "Infant Mortality Statistics from the 2013 Period Linked Birth/Infant Death Data Set." *National Vital Statistics Reports* 64(9).

McKinlay, John B. 1996. "Some Contributions from the Social System to Gender Inequalities in Heart Disease." *Journal of Health and Social Behavior* 37(1):1–26.

Mechanic, David. 1995. "Sociological Dimensions of Illness Behavior." *Social Science and Medicine* 41(9):1207–1216.

Montez, Jennifer K., Robert A. Hummer, Mark D. Hayward, Hweyoung Woo, and Richard G. Rogers. 2011. "Trends in the Educational Gradient of United States Adult Mortality from 1986 through 2006 by Race, Gender, and Age Group." *Research on Aging* 33(2):145–171.

Murphy, Sherry L., Xu Jiaquan, Kenneth D. Kochanek, and Elizabeth Arias. 2018. *Mortality in the United States, 2017.* NCHS Data Brief 328. Hyattsville, MD: National Center for Health Statistics.

National Center for Health Statistics. 2018. *Health, United States, 2017: With Special Feature on Mortality.* Hyattsville, MD: National Center for Health Statistics.

Okoro, Catherine A., NaTasha D. Hollis, Alissa C. Cyrus, and Shannon Griffin-Blake. 2018. "Prevalence of Disabilities and Health Care Access by Disability Status and Type Among Adults—United States, 2016." *Morbidity and Mortality Weekly Report* 67 (August 17):882–871.

Olshansky, Jay S., Toni Antonucci, Lisa Berkman, Robert H. Binstock, Axel Boersch-Supan, John T. Cacioppo, Bruce A. Carnes, Laura L. Carstensen, Linda P. Fried, Dana P. Goldman, James Jackson, Martin Kohli, John Rother, Yuhui Zheng, and John Rowe. 2012. "Differences in Life Expectancy Due to Race and Educational Differences Are Widening, and Many May Not Catch Up." *Health Affairs* 31(8):1803–1813.

Olshansky, Jay S., and A. Brian Ault. 1986. "The Fourth State of the Epidemiologic Transition: The Age of Delayed Degenerative Diseases." *The Milbank Quarterly* 64(3):355–391.

Omran, Abdel R. 1971. "The Epidemiologic Transition: A Theory of the Epidemiology of Population Change." *Milbank Memorial Fund Quarterly* 49(4):309–338.

Operario, Don, Kristi E. Gamarel, Benjamin M. Grin, Ji Hyun Lee, Christopher W. Kahler, Brandon D.L. Marshall, Jacob J. van den Berg, and Nickolas D.

Zaller. 2015. "Sexual Minority Health Disparities in Adult Men and Women in the United States: National Health and Nutrition Examination Survey, 2001–2010." *American Journal of Public Health* 105(10):e27–34.

Osterman, Michelle J.K., and Joyce A. Martin. 2018. "Timing and Adequacy of Prenatal Care in the United States, 2016." *National Vital Statistics Reports* 67(3):1–14.

Otten, Mac W., Steven M. Teutsch, David F. Williamson, and James F. Marks. 1990. "The Effect of Known Risk Factors on the Excess Mortality of Black Adults in the United States." *Journal of the American Medical Association* 263(6):845–850.

Peacock, Georgina, Lisa I. Iezzoni, and Thomas R. Harkin. 2015. "Health Care for Americans with Disabilities—25 Years after the ADA." *New England Journal of Medicine* 373(10):892–893.

Petersen, Emily E., Nicole L. Davis, David Goodman, Shanna Cox, Nikki Mayes, Emily Johnston, Carla Syverson, Kristi Seed, Carrie K. Shapiro-Mendoza, William M. Callaghan, and Wanda Barfield. 2019. "Vital Signs: Pregnancy-Related Deaths, United States, 2011–2015, and Strategies for Prevention, 13 States, 2013–2017." *Morbidity and Mortality Weekly Report* 68(18):423–429.

Ramirez-Valles, Jesus, Lisa M. Kuhns, Richard T. Campbell, and Rafael M. Diaz. 2010. "Social Integration and Health: Community Involvement, Stigmatized Identities, and Sexual Risk in Latino Sexual Minorities." *Journal of Health and Social Behavior* 51(1):30–47.

Rosenfield, Allan, Caroline J. Min, and Lynn P. Freedman. 2007. "Making Motherhood Safe in Developing Countries." *New England Journal of Medicine* 356(14):1395–1397.

Sade, Robert M. 2012. "The Graying of America: Challenges and Controversies." *Journal of Law, Medicine and Ethics* 40(1):6–9.

Sauer, Lauren M. 2020. "What Is Coronavirus?" *Johns Hopkins Medicine*. Retrieved April 26, 2020 (www.hopkinsmedicine.org/health/conditions-and-diseases/coronavirus).

Schwartz, Nelson D. 2020. "'Nowhere to Hide' as Unemployment Permeates the Economy." *The New York Times*, April 16. Retrieved April 26, 2020 (www.nytimes.com/2020/04/16/business/economy/unemployment-numbers-coronavirus.html).

Shaw, Benjamin A., Kelly McGeever, Elizabeth Vasquez, Neda Agahi, and Stefan Fors. 2014. "Socioeconomic Inequalities in Health After Age 50: Are Health Risk Behaviors to Blame?" *Social Science and Medicine* 101(January):52–60.

Smedley, Brian D., Adrienne Y. Stith, and Alan R. Nelson (eds.). 2003. *Unequal Treatment: Confronting Racial and Ethnic Disparities in Health Care.* Washington, DC: Institute of Medicine.

Song, Lijun, and Nan Lin. 2009. "Social Capital and Health Inequality: Evidence from Taiwan." *Journal of Health and Social Behavior* 50(2):149–163.

Spittel, Michael L., William T. Riley, and Robert M. Kaplan. 2015. "Educational Attainment and Life Expectancy: A Perspective from the NIH Office of Behavioral and Social Sciences Research." *Social Sciences and Medicine* 127(February):203–205.

Stillion, Judith M., and Eugene E. McDowell. 2001–2002. "The Early Demise of the 'Stronger' Sex: Gender-Related Causes of Sex Differences in Longevity." *Omega* 44(4):301–318.

Storrs, Carina. 2016. "Why Americans Don't Live as Long as Europeans." Retrieved December 15, 2018 (www.cnn.com/2016/health/ american-life-expectancy-shorter-than-europeans/ index.html).

Sudano, Joseph J., and David W. Baker. 2006. "Explaining US Racial/Ethnic Disparities in Health Declines and Mortality in Late Middle Ages: The Roles of Socioeconomic Status, Health Behaviors, and Health Insurance." *Social Science and Medicine* 62(4):909–922.

Taylor, Derrick Bryson. 2020. "A Timeline of the Coronavirus Pandemic." *The New York Times*. Retrieved April 26, 2020 (www.nytimes.com/article/coronavirus-timeline.html)

Umberson, Debra, and Jennifer K. Montez. 2010. "Social Relationships and Health: A Flashpoint for Health Policy." *Journal of Health and Social Behavior* 51(S1)54–66.

US Census Bureau. 2018a. "Mortality Indicators by Sex for Region Summary. Infant Mortality Rate, Both Sexes." *International Data Base.* Retrieved June 2, 2019 (www.census.gov/data-tools/demo/idb/informationGateway.php).

———. 2018b. "Mortality Indicators by Sex for Region Summary. Life Expectancy, Both Sexes." *International Data Base.* Retrieved June 2, 2019 (www.census.gov/data-tools/demo/idb/informationGateway.php).

———. 2018c. "Older People Projected to Outnumber Children for First Time in United States History." Retrieved June 3, 2019 (www.census.gov/newsroom/press-releases/2018/cb18-41-population-projections.html).

———. 2019. "2013–2017 American Community Survey 5-Year Estimates." *American FactFinder.* Retrieved

May 29, 2019 (https://factfinder.census.gov/bkmk/table/1.0/en/ACS/17_5YR/DP05/0100000US).

US Department of Health and Human Services. 2018. "Child Maltreatment 2016." *Administration for Children and Families, Administration on Children, Youth and Families, Children's Bureau.* Retrieved June 17, 2019 (www.acf.hhs.gov/cb/research-data-technology/statistics-research/child-maltreatment).

Verbrugge, Lois M. 1990. "Pathways of Health and Death." Pp. 41–79 in *Women, Health and Medicine— A Historical Handbook,* edited by Rima D. Apple. New York: Garland Publishing, Inc.

Williams, David R. 2012. "Miles to Go Before We Sleep: Racial Inequities in Health." *Journal of Health and Social Behavior* 53(3):279–295.

Williams, David R., and Pamela B. Jackson. 2005. "Social Sources of Racial Disparities in Health." *Health Affairs* 24(2):325–334.

Williams, David R., and Michelle Sternthal. 2010. "Understanding Racial-ethnic Disparities in Health: Sociological Contributions." *Journal of Health and Social Behavior* 51(S):S15–S27.

World Health Organization. 2018a. "Maternal Mortality, Key Facts." Retrieved June 4, 2019 (www.who.int/news-room/fact-sheets/detail/maternal-mortality).

———. 2018b. "Newborns: Reducing Mortality." Retrieved June 5, 2019 (www.who.int/news-room/fact-sheets/detail/newborns-reducing-mortality).

———. 2018c. "Tuberculosis, Key Facts." Retrieved June 3, 2019 (www.who.int/en/news-room/fact-sheets/detail/tuberculosis).

———. 2018d. "World Malaria Report, 2018." Retrieved June 3, 2019 (www.who.int/malaria/publications/world-malaria-report-2018/report/en/).

———. 2019. "Disabilities." Retrieved June 27, 2019 (www.who.int/topics/disabilities/en/).

Wong, Mitchell D., Martin F. Shapiro, W. John Boscardin, and Susan L. Ettner. 2002. "Contribution of Major Diseases to Disparities in Mortality." *New England Journal of Medicine* 347(20):1585–1592.

World Health Organization and World Bank. 2011. *World Report on Disability.* Geneva, Switzerland: World Health Organization.

Zajacova, Anna, and Jennifer Karas Montez. 2017. "Physical Functioning Trends among US Women and Men Age 45–64 by Education Level." *Biodemography and Social Biology* 63(1):21–30.

CHAPTER 4

Society, Disease, and Illness

Learning Objectives

- Distinguish between "fundamental causes," proximate risk factors," and "genetic factors" as causes of disease.

- Identify and discuss three important patterns of disease in the world's developing countries.

- Explain the traditional under-representation of women and racial and ethnic minorities

in medical research. Discuss the harm created by this under-representation.

- Identify and discuss the most important fundamental causes of disease discussed in this chapter.

- Identify and explain the most important proximate risk factors related to heart disease and to cancer—the two leading causes of death in the United States.

The most common types of diseases within a society and their distribution among the population are determined by a wide range of factors, including the presence of disease agents, characteristics of the social, economic, physical, and biological environment, and demographic characteristics and lifestyles of the people. In every society, these factors lead to some groups being more vulnerable to disease than others and being more likely to contract specific diseases.

THE SOCIAL ETIOLOGY OF DISEASE

Explaining both the occurrence of particular **acute infectious diseases** and **chronic degenerative diseases** within a society and their distribution within the population begins with identification of the cause or causes of each disease (i.e., their **etiology**). After the **germ theory of disease** was developed in the late 1800s, the identification of the bacterium or virus responsible for most acute infectious diseases was relatively straightforward. However, tracing the

origin of most chronic degenerative diseases has been more complicated, for at least four reasons:

1. Most chronic degenerative diseases, such as cancer and heart disease, have multiple causes that may be related to diet, exercise, personality type, smoking and drinking behavior, stress, social support, and more. It is very difficult to measure the amount, duration, and effect of each factor on an individual.

2. With chronic degenerative diseases, there is a long latency period between the influence and the consequence, making it difficult to determine cause-and-effect relationships. Plus, not everyone engaged in a harmful lifestyle or exposed to a carcinogenic substance will develop degenerative disease. Cancer often appears 20 or more years after exposure to the carcinogenic substance, and some lifetime smokers never get lung cancer.

3. It is difficult to determine how much of a behavior or substance is necessary to trigger a disease. Almost any substance taken in sufficiently large quantities can be health

damaging. Many regulations on substances are based on the idea that there is a threshold of exposure below which there is no danger to health. Others believe there are only lower levels of danger.

4. The validity of generalizations from animal testing to humans is an unresolved question. The amount of a substance required to cause cancer in an animal and in a human may be different. There are many toxicologists on both sides of this issue. Some years ago, when limits on human consumption of saccharin were contemplated based on laboratory tests on rats, one critic suggested that diet soft drinks should be labeled "Warning: Extensive use of this product has been shown by scientists to be dangerous to your rat's health."

To fully understand disease causation and distribution, it is important to understand both **social determinants of health** (fundamental causes and proximate risk factors) and genetic factors.

Social Determinants of Health

In *Why Are Some People Healthy and Others Not? The Determinants of Health of Populations*, Evans, Barer, and Marmor (1994) sought to explain why diseases are not randomly distributed within societies. They synthesized research from several disciplines and included studies conducted in the United States and other countries. While not discounting the influence of heredity on disease causation, they concluded that the primary determinants of health and the distribution of diseases within society are embedded in the social structure of society.

Hertzman, Frank, and Evans (1994) identified six causal pathways through which one's position in the social structure can determine health status or likelihood of disease:

1. *Physical environment.* Some individuals are more likely than others to be exposed to the potentially harmful effects of physical, chemical, and biological agents. The presence of harmful substances in the workplace (e.g., hydrocarbons in coal), in the home (e.g., lead paint), or in the neighborhood (e.g., proximity to a landfill) serve as a pathway to ill health. See the accompanying box, "Climate Change and Health."

2. *Social environment (and psychological response).* Some persons live in a more stressful social environment than others (e.g., at the workplace or school, within the family, or with social responsibilities), and some have less access to supportive social relationships.

3. *Differential susceptibility.* Some persons receive more discrimination based on personal characteristics. For example, opportunities for occupational success are influenced partially by physical traits such as appearance and height. A tall person with an attractive appearance may gain some occupational advantages (and greater income) over a shorter person with a more disheveled appearance.

4. *Individual lifestyle.* Some people live a healthier lifestyle than others, but often lifestyle decisions are shaped by social forces. For example, individuals who grow up in a family of cigarette smokers are themselves more likely to smoke, and people who reside in safer neighborhoods are more likely to get adequate physical exercise outdoors.

5. *Differential access to/response to health care services.* Some persons (e.g. those with more financial resources) have greater access to health care services, differential propensity to use services, and differential benefit of services received.

6. *Reverse causality.* Sometimes health status may influence a person's position in the social structure rather than the other way. For example, the relationship between income and sickness might exist because the sick become poor rather than because the poor become sick. However, with the exception of chronic mental illness, the authors find little empirical support for this pathway.

IN THE FIELD

CLIMATE CHANGE AND HEALTH

The climate change issue has become entangled in political discourse in the United States, and the scientific understanding of climate change and its medical consequences are sometimes lost in political posturing. The international scientific community overwhelmingly accepts the idea that climate change is occurring as a consequence of human behavior. Global surface temperatures today are about 0.6 degrees Celsius higher than the average for the last century. As of 2018, the five hottest years on record were 2016, 2015, 2017, 2018, and 2014. Atmospheric carbon dioxide was at its highest level in at least 800,000 years. Ocean temperatures have warmed, amounts of snow and ice have diminished, and the sea level has risen. Extreme temperature events (sometimes hot and sometimes cold, sometimes wet and sometimes dry) are causing considerable disruption to ecosystems, agriculture, the availability of clean air and water, and a host of human health conditions.

Ninety-seven percent of climate scientists have concluded that climate change is very likely due to human activities, especially the release of greenhouse gases into the atmosphere. The primary source of greenhouse gas emissions is fossil fuels (e.g., coal, oil, and gas) used to provide electricity, heat, transportation, and industrial energy. As greenhouse gases build up in the earth's atmosphere, they cause heat from the earth to become trapped. This leads to a rise in temperature and increased likelihood of situations like floods and droughts.

This has an impact on human health in important but indirect ways. There are no diseases that directly result from climate change. However, climate change is a "risk amplifier"—it makes other diseases more likely. Heart attacks and heart failure increase substantially in very warm weather. Many infectious diseases flourish in very warm weather. Warm weather attracts mosquitos that can carry diseases such as malaria and West Nile virus. Lung cancer, asthma, and other respiratory diseases increase due to the presence of more toxins in the air. Expected declines in crop productivity and availability of clean water could lead to more nutritional diseases and increased diarrheal problems. Environmental conditions could lead to increases in neurological diseases such as Parkinson's disease and Alzheimer's disease (Krueger, Biedrzycki, and Hoverter, 2015).

Due to the health-related considerations, health care leaders from around the world are involved in efforts to reduce greenhouse gases. International conferences have been held for physicians, nurses, public health specialists, and other health care professionals. The World Health Organization, the Centers for Disease Control and Prevention, the World Medical Association, and several national medical associations are taking leadership on the health issues, are serving as role models in changing their sources of energy, are educating the public that climate change is a serious health-related issue and not just fodder for political bickering, and are demonstrating the importance of global connectedness in addressing vital issues.

These social determinants of health can be divided into two types—**fundamental causes and proximate risk factors**. *Proximate risk factors* of disease and illness refer to health–related individual behaviors, and include diet, exercise, use of tobacco and alcohol, control of stress, and other aspects of lifestyle. Epidemiologists have amassed volumes of research linking these factors to the onset of specific diseases and illnesses, which we examine in depth later in this chapter and in

Chapters 5 and 6. *Fundamental causes* of disease and illness refer to underlying social conditions such as socioeconomic status, social inequality, community and neighborhood characteristics, exposure to stressful life events, and access to a supportive social network. These fundamental causes help to shape health and disease by influencing participation in proximate risk factors (e.g., influencing the likelihood of smoking cigarettes) and by providing access to important resources (e.g., money and social connectedness) that can bolster health and enable receipt of preventive or curative medical care (Link and Phelan, 1995, 2000).

> Key resources such as knowledge, money, power, prestige, and beneficial social connections can be used no matter what the risk and protective factors are in a given circumstance. . . . If the problem is cholera, for example, a person with greater resources is better able to avoid areas where the disease is rampant, and highly resourced communities are better able to prohibit entry of infected persons. If the problem is heart disease, a person with greater resources is better able to maintain a heart-healthy lifestyle and get the best medical treatment available. (Phelan, Link, and Tehranifar, 2010:S29)

Education is an example of an underlying social condition and component of SES that has significant impact on the occurrence of disease and illness. In Chapter 3, we discussed the advantage the highly educated have in terms of life expectancy. Not surprisingly, this advantage also exists with respect to disease and illness. The fact that more highly educated people are healthier is well documented and occurs through four pathways. First, well-educated persons are more likely to be employed, work full-time at a fulfilling job, and have high income with little economic hardship—all of which have a positive impact on health. Second, the well-educated have a greater sense of control over their lives and health, and have higher levels of social support—both of which are associated with good health. Third, well-educated persons are less likely to smoke and more likely to get adequate exercise and drink in moderation—all of which have a positive impact on health (Margolis, 2013; Ross and Wu, 1995). Finally, more highly educated people are more likely to have health insurance and are better able to obtain medical care.

For two specific examples of the importance of fundamental causes in the United States, see the boxes "Toxic Air and America's Schools" and "The Water Crisis in Flint, Michigan."

IN THE FIELD

TOXIC AIR AND AMERICA'S SCHOOLS

Air samples taken outside Meredith Hitchens Elementary School in Addyston, Ohio, showed high levels of chemicals coming from the plastics company across the street. The Ohio Environmental Protection Agency (EPA) concluded that the risk of getting cancer there was 50 times higher than what the state considers acceptable. School district officials closed the school. The air outside 435 other schools across the country appears to be even worse.

The newspaper *USA Today*, working with researchers from Johns Hopkins University and the University of Massachusetts, Amherst, spent 8 months using the most up-to-date computer modeling process for tracking industrial pollutants outside schools across the nation. Their research led to a ranking of 127,800 schools based on the level of nearby toxic chemicals and health hazards. These findings are important because children are especially susceptible to airborne pollutants, as they breathe in more air relative to their weight than adults do (Heath, Morrison, and Reed, 2008; Morrison and Heath, 2008).

How could such a condition exist? Many states have no laws regulating where schools can be built. In building new schools, school districts often look for inexpensive land (10 percent of the 435 worst schools had been built in the last decade). Inexpensive land can often be found near heavy (and often polluting) industry. Throughout most of the first decade of the 2000s, the EPA was less aggressive in pursuing polluting industries and had never done research of this type. Residents of low-income communities typically have less influence on local decision making than do residents of more affluent communities. One result is that low-income schools are more likely to be located near polluting industries, and the children in those schools are more likely to have to breathe unclean air.

IN THE FIELD

THE WATER CRISIS IN FLINT, MICHIGAN

Flint, Michigan, is a community of 100,000 people and is disproportionately poor and black. It was once a thriving automobile city, home to the first General Motors factory. However, in the late 1960s, General Motors began disinvesting in the community, factory jobs were lost, and urban decay settled in. In its heyday, General Motors employed 80,000 people in Flint. By 2006, only 8,000 employees remained. Many prosperous residents moved to the suburbs or out of Flint altogether, and the city began struggling financially.

By 2011, a financial emergency was declared (the city was bankrupt), and a city administrator was appointed by the governor. In 2014, in order to save money, the decision was made to switch the city water supply from Detroit's system using treated Lake Huron water to the untreated and highly polluted Flint River.

Shortly after the water supply transition, the General Motors plant complained that the water was creating rust on newly machined parts, and the plant was given permission to change to a different water supplier. For months, city residents also complained that their water was contaminated. It was discolored, smelly, and foul tasting, and skin rashes appeared after people bathed in it, but city officials maintained that the water was safe to drink.

When they did not get an adequate response at the local or state level, or from the

Activists in Lansing, Michigan, picket Governor Rick Snyder's annual State of the State speech, calling for him to resign because of the state's handling of the water crisis in Flint.

Source: © Jim West/Alamy Stock Photo.

(Continued)

(Continued)

Environmental Protection Agency, local residents hired scientists from Virginia Tech to investigate their water. Researchers found nearly 17 percent of water samples taken throughout the city had elevated lead levels above 15 parts per billion, the federal threshold at which corrective action must be taken. Flint officials had failed to treat the water with an anticorrosive agent, and the highly polluted river water had caused lead to leach from the supply pipes. By the time researchers confirmed the high lead levels, Flint residents had been consuming the water for a year. A local pediatrician reported that elevated blood-lead levels in children had nearly doubled since 2014. High levels of lead can lead to a variety of physical health and other problems, including anemia, decreased IQ, and slower growth. Some of the damage might not manifest for years, and the developmental problems are not reversible.

Between June 2014 and October 2015, Flint suffered an outbreak of Legionnaire's disease (the third largest outbreak in US history) that many believe was due to the water switch. Fecal coliform bacteria were detected in city water in 2014, likely due to the city's failure to chlorinate the water sufficiently to disinfect it. "Ironically, the city's corrective measure—adding more chlorine without addressing other underlying issues—created a new problem: elevated levels of total trihalomethanes (TTHM), cancer-causing chemicals that are by-products of the chlorination of water" (Denchak, 2018:8). In October 2015, amid mounting national criticism, Flint switched back to Detroit water.

In 2016, a coalition of residents and community organizations sued the city, demanding proper water testing and treatment, the replacement of lead pipes in the water system, and installation of filters or free bottled water distribution to all residents unable to access bottled water distribution sites that had been set up throughout the city. A March 2017 settlement agreement required "replacing the city's thousands of lead pipes with funding from the state, and guaranteeing further funding for comprehensive tap water testing, a faucet filter installation and education program, free bottled water through the following summer, and continued health programs to help residents deal with the residual effects of Flint's tainted water" (Denchak, 2018:11).

Since remedial action began, the city's water quality has improved and now meets or exceeds federal standards. However, the damage to Flint residents' health cannot be undone and mistrust of city and state officials runs high (Smith, Bosman, and Davey, 2019).

Genetic Factors in Health

Knowledge about the role of genetic transmission of disease has increased substantially in the last several years with the successful mapping of the approximately 25,000 genes within each human. The **Human Genome Project**, which was completed in 2003, has provided knowledge now being used to better understand the role of genes with respect to a variety of diseases (National Human Genome Research Institute, 2019).

Given the importance of fundamental causes and proximate risk factors in affecting disease and illness, what role does genetic transmission play?

Essentially, genes affect disease and illness in two primary ways:

1. *As the specific cause of approximately 4,000 "genetic diseases," including Down syndrome, cystic fibrosis, Tay–Sachs disease, Huntington's disease, and sickle-cell anemia.* Some diseases are monogenic—they can be traced to a single gene. For example, chromosome 21 is the site of genes for Down syndrome, Lou Gehrig's disease, and epilepsy. More diseases are polygenic—they result from several genes acting together. These have more complicated

causal relationships about which much more needs to be known. While genetic diseases represent a small component of all diseases, they are especially apparent early in life.

2. *As a factor that increases the likelihood of occurrence of many other diseases, including heart disease, some types of cancer, Alzheimer's disease, and diabetes.* In these cases, an individual's genetic makeup renders it either more or less likely that environmental factors will trigger a particular disease. An even greater number of diseases follow this multifactorial path in which interplay between genes and the environment causes a disease to occur (National Human Genome Research Institute, 2019).

Excited by knowledge about genes and their implications for disease and illness, some people envision a future in which all disease can be understood through genetic roots. However, this perspective ignores all our existing knowledge about social pathways to disease and illness. Both genetic and sociological research need to continue, along with efforts to integrate the two perspectives, or at least utilize both in seeking to understand why disease and illness occur as they do (Fletcher and Conley, 2013). As an illustration, Beaman (2008)

cites the fact that the genetic tendency to obesity is only observed in societies that produce a surplus of food. This example points to the need for the work of both biologists and sociologists to unravel the contributions of genes and social factors to particular diseases and conditions.

This is exactly what Pescosolido et al. (2008) did in a study attempting to understand alcohol dependence. Using data from the Collaborative Study on the Genetics of Alcoholism, they tested propositions about alcohol dependence based on three sociological theories and on the influence of the GABRA-2 gene (which has been linked to alcoholism). They found strong evidence that the GABRA-2 gene increases the likelihood of alcohol dependence in men only, that childhood deprivation enhances the gene's expression in alcohol dependence, and that having a strong socially supportive network almost completely eliminates the effects of the gene. In this case, consideration of both genetic and social influences provides the most complete understanding. As more is learned about the genetic origin of or influence on particular diseases and on the interplay between genes and social factors, advances in preventive medicine and patient outcomes are likely (Tuckson, Newcomer, and De Sa, 2013).

Medical research is a foundation for advances in understanding disease causation and the evaluation of new therapeutic agents. The National Institutes of Health (NIH) is the leading medical research organization in the United States.

Source: © Tyler Olson/Fotolia.

THE INTERRELATIONSHIP OF PROXIMATE RISK FACTORS AND FUNDAMENTAL CAUSES: THE CASE OF DEVELOPING COUNTRIES

In Chapter 3, we used the *epidemiological transition* to explain the general shift from acute infectious diseases to chronic degenerative diseases within societies as they modernize. Because the pace of this transition has accelerated in recent years, developing countries in the world today are confronted with a **double disease burden**. While they are still at a point in development where they have to deal with acute infectious diseases (such as malaria and tuberculosis), they are already facing increased rates of the chronic degenerative diseases (such as heart disease

and cancer) that predominate in industrialized countries. As developing countries industrialize and urbanize, people are adopting more affluent Western lifestyles, including high-fat diets, greater use of tobacco and alcohol, and less physical activity. These changes will lead to an increased incidence of chronic, degenerative diseases. However, this double disease burden is uneven across socioeconomic groups within developing countries, with poorer communities suffering disproportionately from both infectious and chronic conditions, while wealthier communities escape much of the morbidity and mortality from infectious disease (Agyei-Mensah and de-Graft Aikins, 2010; Frenk et al., 1989). See the accompanying box, "Disease and Illness Patterns in Worldwide Perspective."

IN COMPARATIVE FOCUS

DISEASE AND ILLNESS PATTERNS IN WORLDWIDE PERSPECTIVE

The main causes of death and sickness around the world have changed significantly in the last 10 to 20 years, with chronic degenerative diseases (also called non-communicable diseases because they are not transmitted from person to person) becoming more and more important. The **Global Burden of Disease Study** (GBD) is a collaborative effort by more than 3,600 researchers in over 145 countries that aims to understand death, sickness, and disability in countries around the world. Since 1990, the GBD has compiled morbidity and mortality data from more than 350 diseases and injuries (Institute for Health Metrics and Evaluation, 2019).

Various reports since the GBD began have found that people are living longer nearly everywhere around the world and fewer children are dying, but that people are more often dealing with chronic, non-communicable diseases that typically occur later in life. Seventy-three percent of deaths worldwide in 2017 were from non-communicable causes. Key

findings are that heart disease and stroke are the leading causes of death around the world, that diabetes, lung cancer, and motor vehicle accidents are increasingly common causes of death, and that certain conditions such as malnutrition and childhood infectious diseases are decreasing as causes of death. However, the health of people aged 10 to 24 years has not kept pace with that of older persons, and injuries (especially from traffic accidents), suicide, homicide, AIDS, and complications of childbirth account for most deaths in this age category (Roth et al., 2018).

The World Health Organization (2017a) highlighted the following ten facts on the state of global health in 2015:

1. Life expectancy at birth increased globally by 5 years between 2000 and 2015.
2. Babies born in 2015 had a Healthy Life Expectancy (HLE)—the expected years of life in good health—of 63.1 years. However, HLE for girls/women remains higher than for boys/men.

3. Over 16,000 children under the age of 5 years died every day in 2015, and most could have been saved with simple interventions.
4. Preterm birth was the leading killer of newborn babies in 2015.
5. An estimated 2.6 million babies were stillborn in 2015. Inconsistent registrations of stillbirths make exact counts difficult.
6. There were 1.3 million deaths in 2015 that were hepatitis-related. Hepatitis is an inflammation of the liver. The most common forms of hepatitis have viral causes.
7. Non-communicable diseases accounted for 37 percent of deaths in low-income countries (an increase of 14 percentage points since 2000) and over 70 percent of deaths globally in 2015.
8. Cardiovascular diseases accounted for 31 percent of all deaths in 2015, making it the leading cause of death in the world (most could be prevented or delayed by healthy diet, regular physical exercise, and by not using tobacco).
9. Diabetes is one of the top ten causes of death and disability. The global death rate from diabetes per 100,000 population increased 38 percent from 2000 to 2015.
10. Injuries caused 5 million fatalities in 2015, with 27 percent of these from traffic-related causes.

To assist in handling this critical situation in developing countries, a broad program for research and empowerment called the **health transition (HT)** has been developed (Caldwell, 1993). The program is grounded in three themes (Gallagher, Stewart, and Stratton, 2000):

1. *The importance of equitable distribution of income and wealth.* Health progress occurs more rapidly in countries without huge disparities in wealth. Some relatively poor countries that do not have sharp divisions in wealth (e.g., China and Cuba) have made more headway in reducing death rates than some relatively wealthier countries with greater inequality (e.g., Iran).
2. *The importance of public and community health.* The decline in the death rate in industrialized countries resulted more from public health measures than from advances in clinical medicine. Therefore, developing countries are being urged to invest in social policies that emphasize improvements in food and water supply, sanitation, access to primary health care, community development, and greater opportunities for women in education, employment, and public life. Countries are being discouraged from investing available funds in high-technology medicine that has much more limited impact.
3. *The importance of lifestyle and behavioral factors.* While proximate risk factors such as diet, tobacco smoking, and sexual behavior are important in industrialized countries because of their link to chronic diseases, they are especially important in developing countries because of their link to infectious diseases. Emphasis is encouraged on such behaviors as drinking only safe water (which might necessitate considerable travel and inconvenience), limiting family size to a number that can be economically supported, and using a condom for non-monogamous sex.

An example of such a framework is the United Nations' 2030 Agenda for Sustainable Development, which sets an ambitious timeline for achieving seventeen broad goals. While several goals address global health indirectly through such issues as gender equity, poverty, and economic development, goal 3 addresses health directly by setting specific targets for, among other things, ending epidemics of AIDS, malaria, and other infectious diseases, reducing traffic-related morbidity and mortality, and strengthening tobacco control initiatives (United Nations, 2019).

In the remainder of this chapter, five significant but very different diseases and conditions in American society are examined. Coronary heart disease and cancer are the two leading causes of death in the United States. HIV/AIDS is a relatively recently identified disease that quickly became a pandemic. It appears to be in transition from a fatal disease to a controllable chronic condition. Alzheimer's disease was first identified in the early 1900s as a disease of mental deterioration in mid- and late adult life. It is currently the only one of the ten leading causes of death in the United States for which there is no cure. Mental illness and severe mental disorders have long been studied, and a considerable body of research has developed around their etiology. Nevertheless, they are still sometimes considered less "legitimate" than physical diseases and illnesses, and they often receive less government funding.

CORONARY HEART DISEASE (CHD)

The Cardiovascular System

The body's cardiovascular system transports necessary nutrients, oxygen, and water to all the body's tissues, carries substances such as disease-fighting antibodies wherever they are needed, and removes carbon dioxide and other waste products. The pumping of the heart stimulates the flow of blood, which is the transportation system. For the heart to function properly (it beats about 100,000 times a day, pumping about 1,800 gallons of blood), it must receive an adequate supply of blood from the three main coronary arteries and their smaller branches. Heart disease occurs when this system is disrupted.

Coronary heart disease (CHD, sometimes called ischemic heart disease) occurs when the inner surface (or inner layers) of any artery become thickened, resulting in narrowing and hardening of the artery, decreasing the amount of blood that can flow through it. This is usually caused by a build-up of cholesterol plaques and other fatty substances or a blood clot. If the blood flow is severely restricted, the person may feel a tightening sensation or squeezing feeling in the chest that may radiate into the left arm and elsewhere. CHD is the most common form of cardiovascular disease (American Heart Association, 2018).

If a coronary artery becomes completely blocked, the heart may not receive enough blood to fulfill its normal workload. This may lead to a heart attack—that is, sudden and irreversible damage to the heart muscle. Other forms of heart disease can occur involving the heart valves, the veins, or the heart muscle itself. Heart disease is the most common cause of death in the United States.

IN THE FIELD

THE HISTORICAL UNDER-REPRESENTATION OF WOMEN AND RACIAL AND ETHNIC MINORITIES IN BIOMEDICAL RESEARCH

The physiology and social position of women and men and blacks and whites differ in ways that relate to disease and illness. Gender and racial/ethnic groups show different propensities to different diseases. Therapeutic and pharmacological agents affect people differently. For these reasons, biomedical research must be conducted on samples that reflect population differences (within or among studies) if they are to benefit all people. Amazingly, this is often not the case. Dresser (1992:24) summarized the issue:

> The failure to include women in research populations is ubiquitous. An NIH-sponsored study

showing that heart attacks were reduced when subjects took one aspirin every other day was conducted on men, and the relationship between low-cholesterol diets and cardiovascular disease has been almost exclusively studied in men. Yet coronary heart disease is the leading cause of death in women. Similarly, the first 20 years of a major federal study on health and aging included only men. Yet two-thirds of the elderly population are women. The recent announcement that aspirin can help to prevent migraine headaches is based on data from males only, even though women suffer from migraines up to three times as often as men.

The list goes on: studies on AIDS treatment frequently omit women, the fastest growing infected population. An investigation of the possible relationship between caffeine and heart disease involved 45,589 male research subjects. . . . Moreover, the customary research subject not only is male but is a white male. African Americans, Latinos, and other racial and ethnic groups have typically been excluded.

Criticism of this research discrimination led to a major research initiative—the Women's Health Initiative—which was started in 1991 to study heart disease and stroke, cancer, and osteoporosis in women of all races and all socioeconomic strata. The successful effort to bring this issue to public attention and to enlist Congress in creating this program was directed by a number of important groups, including many sociologists (Auerbach and Figert, 1995). Spending on women's health research reached an all-time high.

Two years later, the National Institutes of Health Revitalization Act of 1993, which required that all federally funded studies include women as well as men, and racial and ethnic minorities as well as whites, was passed. Additional policies were implemented in 2001.

However, change has come slowly. In 2015, for example, the Food and Drug Administration approved a prescription drug for women with low libido. A limitation was that alcohol consumed while taking the drug could lead to serious side effects. This conclusion came from a study that included 25 individuals—23 men and 2 women. Despite the fact that men and women metabolize alcohol differently, the study essentially ignored female subjects (Shumaker, 2015).

How do researchers justify these discriminatory practices? Some cite research tradition (Duster, 2006). Some cite the benefits of studies with homogeneous samples—the more alike the samples, the more that variation can be attributed to the intervention under study. Some argue that women's hormonal changes during the menstrual cycle would complicate studies, that women who become pregnant during the research could jeopardize the study, and that women volunteers are more difficult to obtain.

However, none of these justifications is adequate. Critics point out that comparable studies could be conducted on groups other than white males, or statistical controls could be used within heterogeneous samples. Hormonal changes during the menstrual cycle are part of reality; rather than being viewed as somehow distorting the results, efforts need to be made to understand the influence of personality type on heart disease and the influence of aspirin on migraine headaches, and so on, in women, given their particular physiology. It makes just as much sense to say that the absence of a menstrual cycle ought to disqualify males for fear of skewed results (Dresser, 1992; Merton, 1993).

The need for more medical research and more sociologically informed medical research on traditionally under-represented groups is complicated by the fact that funding for the National Institutes of Health (NIH)—the primary medical research organization in the United States—varies from one presidential administration to another. Without a stronger commitment by the federal government, progress in understanding and treating diseases and in understanding differences among racial, ethnic, and gender groups will stagnate.

Prevalence, Incidence, and Mortality

In 2017, about 28.2 million living adults in the United States had been diagnosed with heart disease (more than 11 percent of the adult population). More than 600,000 people die each year from heart disease, which makes this the leading cause of death in the United States (American Heart Association, 2018). It is the most common cause of death for both men and women. Every year about 790,000 Americans have a heart attack, and 15 percent die from it (Centers for Disease Control and Prevention, 2019b).

Men and women are about equally likely to have heart disease, but because there are more women than men in the population, more women than men have heart disease, and more women than men die from it each year. Heart disease is the leading cause of death for both men and women (about 1 in 4 deaths for both), but women are more likely to die from a heart attack than men are. Under the age of 50 years, heart attacks in women are twice as likely to be fatal as those in men. See the accompanying box, "Differing Treatment for Women's Heart Attacks."

Heart disease is the leading cause of death among whites, blacks, Hispanics, and American Indians/Alaskan Natives, although death rates are considerably higher for blacks. Heart disease is second only to cancer for Asian Americans and Pacific Islanders. Disproportionately high rates of CHD deaths are found in black men (a heart disease death rate twice that in white women) and among people living in the southeastern part of the country.

IN THE FIELD

DIFFERING TREATMENT FOR WOMEN'S HEART ATTACKS

Why do women heart attack victims fare worse than men? Data show that heart attacks strike more women than men in the United States, that death rates from heart disease are higher for women than for men, and that women who have a heart attack have longer stays in hospital and more complications while they are there.

Recent research has discovered several explanations for these findings. People—including physicians—may still think of heart disease as being more of a "man's disease." Research has shown that women who have certain conditions, such as high cholesterol and high blood pressure, are less likely than men to be told that these are risk factors for heart disease and are less likely to have beneficial medications such as statins prescribed.

Heart attacks are often manifested differently in women and men. While both women and men may feel tightness or pain in the chest, women are more likely to display symptoms such as nausea, vomiting, shortness of breath, and pain in the back or jaw. If not familiar with these different symptoms, neither the woman nor her physician may immediately suspect a heart attack.

Finally, when women under the age of 55 years arrive at a hospital in the midst of a heart attack, research has discovered that they are less likely to receive angioplasty or a stent to immediately open clogged arteries, and are more likely to die in the hospital during that visit than are men in the same situation. If the artery blockages do not look so severe as those commonly observed in males (even though they may actually be doing more harm to the arteries), medical providers may not be as quick to diagnose heart disease.

All of these conditions could be remedied by comprehensive research on women's heart disease. However, only about 20 percent of subjects in clinical trials for heart disease are women, and even when they are included, researchers often do not focus on gender differences in their analysis.

Etiology

The five major proximate risk factors for CHD are (1) cigarette smoking, (2) poor diet (especially if reflected by high levels of cholesterol and high blood sugar), (3) physical inactivity, (4) obesity (mostly resulting from poor diet and lack of exercise), and (5) high blood pressure (this is both a disease and a risk factor for other diseases).

Cigarette Smoking. According to the World Health Organization (2019c), tobacco is the single biggest cause of premature adult death throughout the world, killing more than half of users and more than 8 million people annually. Studies in the United States determined that cigarette smoking is the biggest risk factor for sudden cardiac death, that smokers have a two to four times higher risk than nonsmokers of having a heart attack, and that smokers are approximately 30 percent more likely than non-smokers to experience fatal coronary heart disease (Centers for Disease Control and Prevention, 2019c).

Moreover, there is extensive danger in breathing in **environmental tobacco smoke (ETS)**— that is, other people's tobacco smoke. Nonsmokers exposed to secondhand smoke at home

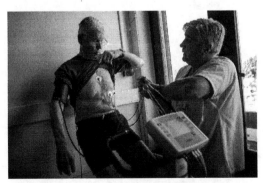

Advances in heart disease treatment have led to the creation of cardiac rehabilitation centers around the country. These facilities offer heart and healthy living education, constantly monitored physical exercise, and emotional support for living healthily and happily with CHD.

or work have a 25 to 30 percent higher risk of developing heart disease than other nonsmokers (Centers for Disease Control and Prevention, 2018c). Nationally, this equates to approximately 45,000 deaths from CHD annually as a result of breathing ETS.

Poor Diet. Eating a diet high in fruits and vegetables, whole grains and high-fiber foods, and fish, and low in saturated and trans fats, cholesterol, and salt protects heart health. Those who eat poor diets often have high levels of blood sugar and cholesterol. *Cholesterol* is a type of fat (lipid) that can build up in the bloodstream. It is transported in the bloodstream via lipoproteins. Most blood cholesterol is carried into the circulatory system by low-density lipoproteins (LDLs), where it may be deposited and accumulate on the arterial walls, causing restriction of blood flow. Cholesterol is also carried on high-density lipoproteins (HDLs), which actually help remove plaque from the arteries. The greater the ratio of LDL to HDL, the more likely it is that cholesterol plaque build-up will occur. As this ratio increases, the risk of heart disease increases. People with high cholesterol levels have about twice the risk of heart disease as people with lower levels.

Physical Inactivity. Not engaging in sufficient physical activity can lead to heart disease both directly and indirectly (by increasing the likelihood of developing other medical conditions, such as high blood pressure, high cholesterol, and high blood sugar, that also increase the risk of heart disease).

Obesity. Based on measures of body mass index (BMI) (defined as weight in kilograms divided by height in meters squared), less than 30 percent of American adults are a healthy weight (BMI between 18.5 and 24.9). Approximately one-third are overweight (BMI between 25 and 29.9), and another one-third are obese (i.e., significantly overweight, BMI of 30 or higher) (National Center for Health Statistics, 2018).

Regular exercise is important for preventing heart disease and other chronic degenerative diseases. However, too few Americans actually get the recommended amount of weekly exercise.

Obesity increases the likelihood that cholesterol, blood sugar, and blood pressure will all be too high. Being overweight increases the likelihood of heart disease, and being obese significantly increases the likelihood of heart disease—especially if the extra weight is concentrated around the waist. Obesity is a major factor in more than 100,000 deaths from heart disease in the United States annually.

High Blood Pressure. Approximately one-third of American adults have high blood pressure (defined as a pressure of 140/90 mmHg or higher, or taking antihypertensive drugs), which is the major cause of strokes and deaths from strokes and one of the major causes of heart attacks and deaths from heart attacks (Centers for Disease Control and Prevention, 2016). Several factors are associated with high blood pressure. Generally, the older people get, the more likely they are to develop high blood pressure. People whose parents have high blood pressure are more likely to develop it, and blacks are more likely than whites to suffer from the disease. When a person has high blood pressure together with obesity, smoking, high blood cholesterol levels, or diabetes, the risk of stroke or heart attack increases substantially.

Other Factors. Other factors that contribute to the risk of heart disease include family history (having a family history of heart disease, especially in one's parents or siblings and at an early age, elevates CHD risk), diabetes (which increases CHD risk partly due to its effects on cholesterol and blood sugar levels), and poor dental health, such as chronic gum disease. High levels of social stress can underlie all of these proximate risk factors and contribute directly to CHD.

Trends

The death rate from heart disease declined dramatically over the past few decades (by 50 percent in the last 35 years and by 22 percent between 2005 and 2015). The percentage of deaths due to heart disease has declined, and heart failure typically now occurs much later in life (usually after the age of 70 years). Much of this sharp decline is due to changing lifestyle. Reduction in the number of cigarette smokers is most important, but changes in diet (and more effective drugs) have brought cholesterol levels down, and blood pressure levels are lower than a decade ago. Improved medical therapies, including initial treatment for those with chest pain or having a heart attack, bypass surgery, and long-term rehabilitation, also play a role (American Heart Association, 2018).

Worldwide. Globally, cardiovascular diseases (primarily coronary heart disease and stroke) are responsible for about 31 percent of all deaths and represent the most common cause of death throughout the world. Heart disease alone is responsible for more than 7 million deaths each year—more than 13 percent of all deaths (World Health Organization, 2017b).

CANCER

Cancer is a group of diseases characterized by the uncontrolled growth (often forming masses of tissue called tumors) and spread of abnormal cells. Normally the body's cells reproduce themselves in an orderly manner, with worn-out or injured tissues being replaced or repaired. Should abnormal (cancer) cells develop, the body's immune system will usually defeat and eliminate them. Tumors that are "benign" are non-cancerous and do not spread, whereas "malignant" tumors are cancerous. When the cancer cells remain at their original site, the disease is said to be localized; when they spread and invade other organs or tissue, the disease is said to have metastasized (American Cancer Society, 2019).

Cancer can cause considerable pain, as various tubes within the body (e.g., esophageal, intestinal, and urinary bladder) become obstructed or as the expanding tumor destroys additional healthy tissue. Infections often occur. A cancerous tumor unsuccessfully removed or destroyed eventually causes death.

Prevalence, Incidence, and Mortality

Current estimates are that 15.5 million Americans alive now have been diagnosed with cancer (some are now cancer-free), and an additional 1.7 million people are diagnosed with cancer each year. About 1 in 2 men and slightly more than 1 in 3 women will be diagnosed with cancer at some point in their lifetime. These figures do not include the estimated 3.3 million people diagnosed annually with skin cancer (discussed later in this chapter). About 77 percent of all cancers are diagnosed in persons aged 55 years or older (American Cancer Society, 2019).

Cancer is the second leading cause of death in the United States, claiming about 600,000 lives each year. Among adults aged 40 to 79 years, cancer is the leading cause of death. Almost 1 in 4 deaths is caused by cancer. Due mostly to cigarette smoking, the national death rate from cancer rose for most of the twentieth century and peaked in 1991. The rate has fallen since then, due mainly to decreases in the number of cigarette smokers,

but also partly due to earlier detection and better treatment (American Cancer Society, 2019).

Table 4.1 lists the most common sites of newly diagnosed cancer, by incidence and by mortality. For men, the prostate, lungs, and colon and rectum are the most common new cancer sites, while for women, the breast, lungs, and colon and rectum are the most common. Lung cancer is by far the most lethal cancer, accounting for 24 and 23 percent of all cancer deaths in men and women, respectively.

Cancer usually develops in older people, with 80 percent of all diagnoses in people aged 50 years or older. People of lower socioeconomic status have a much higher likelihood of developing cancer and dying from it than those with higher SES. This is especially true with regard to education. Non-Hispanic white and black men with less than a high school education are almost three times more likely to die from cancer than their counterparts with a college education or higher. The disparity is highest for lung cancer, reflecting the higher rate of smoking among those with less education, but it also reflects less physical activity and poor diet among these groups and slow treatment once cancer has developed (American Cancer Society, 2019).

Cancer incidence and mortality rates at almost all body sites are higher for blacks than whites. The 5-year survival rate is 7 percentage points higher in whites. Studies of racial disparities in cancer point to socioeconomic explanations. African Americans are more likely to be in poverty and to have lower levels of education, and are less likely to have health insurance. Lack of health insurance leads to less preventive care, later detection of cancer, and less likelihood of high-quality treatment (American Cancer Society, 2019).

Hispanics, Asian Americans and Pacific Islanders, and American Indians and Alaskan Natives overall have somewhat lower cancer incidence and mortality rates than whites. However, all

TABLE 4.1   Leading Sites of New Cancer Cases and Deaths, 2019 Estimates

Estimated New Cases		Estimated Deaths	
Female	**Male**	**Female**	**Male**
Breast 268,600 (30%)	Prostate 174,650 (20%)	Lung and bronchus 66,020 (23%)	Lung and bronchus 76,650 (24%)
Lung and bronchus 111,710 (13%)	Lung and bronchus 116,440 (13%)	Breast 41,760 (15%)	Prostate 31,620 (10%)
Colon and rectum 67,100 (7%)	Colon and rectum 78,500 (9%)	Colon and rectum 23,380 (8%)	Colon and rectum 27,640 (9%)
Uterine corpus 61,880 (7%)	Urinary bladder 61,700 (7%)	Pancreas 21,950 (8%)	Pancreas 23,800 (7%)
Skin melanoma 39,260 (5%)	Skin melanoma 57,220 (7%)	Ovary 13,980 (5%)	Liver 21,600 (7%)
Thyroid 37,810 (4%)	Kidney and renal pelvis 44,120 (5%)	Uterine 12,160 (4%)	Leukemia 13,150 (4%)
Non-Hodgkin lymphoma 33,110 (4%)	Non-Hodgkin lymphoma 41,090 (5%)	Liver 10,180 (4%)	Esophagus 13,020 (4%)
Kidney and renal pelvis 29,700 (3%)	Oral & pharynx 38,140 (4%)	Leukemia 9,690 (3%)	Urinary bladder 12,870 (4%)
Pancreas 26,830 (3%)	Leukemia 35,920 (4%)	Non-Hodgkin lymphoma 8,460 (3%)	Non-Hodgkin lymphoma 11,510 (4%)
Leukemia 25,860 (3%)	Pancreas 29,940 (3%)	Brain and nervous system 7,850 (3%)	Brain and nervous system 9,910 (3%)
All sites 891,480 (100%)	All sites 870,970 (100%)	All sites 285,210 (100%)	All sites 321,670 (100%)

*Excludes basal and squamous cell skin cancers and in situ carcinoma, except urinary bladder

Source: American Cancer Society. 2019. *Cancer Facts and Figures 2019*. Atlanta, GA: American Cancer Society.

these groups have a higher rate of cancer due to infection (especially in the stomach, liver, and cervix). Because lifestyle relates so closely to cancer risk, more research is needed to determine the precise reasons for their overall lower susceptibility (American Cancer Society, 2019).

Etiology

Environmental cancer-producing substances, or *carcinogens,* are found in the food and drugs we ingest, the water we drink, the air we breathe, the occupations we pursue, and the substances with which we come into contact. Particular carcinogens are related to the development of cancer in particular locations. For example, the World

Health Organization (2019a) estimates that outdoor air pollution causes up to 200,000 lung cancer deaths each year. Five important proximate risk factors are (1) cigarette smoking, (2) poor diet, (3) excessive alcohol consumption, (4) obesity, and (5) overexposure to sunlight.

Cigarette Smoking.   The strong relationship between cigarette smoking and heart disease is duplicated for cancer. Smoking is associated with high rates of lung cancer as well as cancer of the mouth, pharynx, larynx, esophagus, pancreas, uterine cervix, kidney, and bladder. The American Cancer Society estimates that cigarette smoking is responsible for 30 percent of all cancer deaths and more than 80 percent of all lung cancer deaths. People who smoke are about 25 times more likely to develop lung cancer than are non-smokers (American Cancer Society, 2019). Alone, smoking greatly increases risk, but with other carcinogens (e.g., poor diet), the risk is even greater. Environmental tobacco smoke also causes cancer in non-smokers. An estimated 5,840 non-smoking adults were diagnosed with lung cancer in 2014 as a result of breathing secondhand smoke (American Cancer Society, 2019).

Poor Diet.   Research demonstrates a clear link between diet and the incidence of cancer, although some cancers are more closely aligned with dietary factors than others. For example, consumption of red meat and processed meat account for approximately 5 percent and 8 percent, respectively, of colorectal cancers, while low dietary fiber and low calcium consumption each account for between 9 and 10 percent of such cancers (Islami et al., 2018). In general, the type of diet that protects heart health also protects against cancer.

International variations in cancer mortality are illuminating. For example, higher rates of cancers of the colon, rectum, breast, and prostate are found in Western countries in which diets are relatively high in meat and fat but low in fruits, vegetables, and whole grains. On the other hand, stomach cancer rates are higher in countries in which diets are relatively high in starch, contain small amounts of meats and fats, and frequently use pickled, salted, smoked, or other preserved foods. High-fiber foods lower the risk of colon cancer, and diets rich in vitamins A and C reduce the risk for cancers of the larynx, esophagus, stomach, and lung.

Excessive   Alcohol   Consumption. Drinking in moderation can have some health benefits, but excessive alcohol consumption is a risk factor for cancer as it is for heart disease. Excessive alcohol consumption is the primary cause of cirrhosis of the liver, a grave disease that puts people at high risk of developing liver cancer, a type of cancer with a generally poor prognosis. Cancers of the mouth, larynx, throat, and esophagus are all linked to excessive alcohol consumption, especially in combination with use of tobacco products. For each of these cancers the risk increases substantially with intake of more than two drinks per day (American Cancer Society, 2019).

Obesity.   People who are obese are at increased risk for several types of cancer, including breast, colon and rectum, esophagus, gall bladder, kidney, pancreas, uterus, and thyroid. In the United States, obesity may be a prime contributor in about 5 percent of cancer cases in men and 11 percent in women (American Cancer Society, 2019). However, a nutritious diet and adequate physical activity bolster general health and the body's ability to ward off disease.

Overexposure to Sunlight.   Almost all the 5 million cases of non-melanoma skin cancer diagnosed each year in the United States are sun related. If detected early, these cancers are fairly routine to remove. Much more dangerous is malignant melanoma skin cancer, which is less related to the amount of sun exposure over a lifetime and more related to one or a couple of intense episodes of sunburn (often early in life).

In the United States, risk of overexposure to ultraviolet radiation also occurs during artificial skin tanning. The association of tanning and skin cancer in adulthood is well established and is especially apparent among individuals with early childhood and adolescent exposure (use of a tanning bed before the age of 30 years increases the risk of melanoma by 75 percent). The National Institutes of Health have declared tanning beds to be a carcinogen, and the World Health Organization lists tanning beds among the most dangerous types of cancer-causing substances (Ladizinski et al., 2013).

Nevertheless, there are over 50,000 indoor tanning facilities in the United States, and it is a US$5 billion annual industry. An estimated 30 million Americans use tanning beds each year, with college students being heavy users. Recently, some states and localities have tightened regulations to prevent use of tanning beds by people under 18 years of age, and the Food and Drug Administration recommends making this national law. Some countries have outlawed all use of tanning beds (Ladizinski et al., 2013).

Other Factors. Other factors considered primary carcinogens include exposure to harmful substances (e.g., hydrocarbons and benzene) in the workplace, excessive exposure to radiation, and excessive exposure to environmental pollutants (e.g., petroleum products, synthetic organic chemicals, and insecticides). About 5 percent of all cancers are strongly hereditary. In these cases, an inherited gene alteration confers a high risk of developing a particular type of cancer.

Trends

A key trend is the increasing rate of survival for people with cancer. In the early 1900s, few people diagnosed with cancer had any likelihood of long-term survival. By the 1930s, about 20 percent of cancer patients survived at least 5 years. This percentage increased to about 50 percent in the 1970s to about 60 percent in the 1990s and is now 69 percent. Table 4.2 shows the 5-year survival rates for selected cancer sites for 1987–1989 and 2008–2014. Moreover, up to 80 percent of children now survive cancer, and recent efforts to protect them against long-term complications have been increasingly successful.

Improved survival rates are due both to early detection of cancer and to significantly improved treatment effectiveness. The probability of early detection and survival varies considerably according to the cancer's anatomical location. However, if cancer is still localized when detected, the survival rate for most types of cancer leaps to over 80 percent (American Cancer Society, 2019).

Worldwide. Globally, about 17 million new cases of cancer were diagnosed in 2018. About 1 in 6 deaths is due to cancer—about 9.5 million in 2018. Cancer was the second leading cause of death in 2016 (after cardiovascular disease) worldwide and in high-income countries, and is the third leading cause of death in medium-income

TABLE 4.2   Five-Year Survival Rates (Percent) for Selected Cancer Sites

Site	1987–1989	2008–2014	Percentage Point Difference
Prostate	83	99	16
Kidney	57	75	18
Uterine cervix	70	69	−1
All sites	55	69	14
Colon and rectum	60	66	6
Oral	54	68	14
Leukemia	43	65	22
Ovary	38	48	10
Lung and bronchus	13	20	7
Pancreas	4	9	5

Source: American Cancer Society. 2019. *Cancer Facts and Figures 2019*. Atlanta, GA: American Cancer Society.

countries (after cardiovascular disease and infectious/parasitic diseases). Although better screening and lifestyle changes (especially decreases in cigarette smoking) have reduced the prevalence of cancer in high-income countries, cancer rates are increasing in low- and middle-income countries. This is due both to an aging of the population and to the fact that, as countries modernize, they often adopt Western-style behaviors such as eating more junk food, smoking, and not getting enough exercise (American Cancer Society, 2018).

HIV/AIDS

Acquired immunodeficiency syndrome (AIDS) is an infectious disease caused by the *human immunodeficiency virus (HIV)*. If untreated, HIV disables the immune system, permitting normally controllable infections to overcome the body and ultimately kill the person. Unlike some other viruses, the human body cannot get rid of HIV (Centers for Disease Control and Prevention, 2019d).

Without treatment, persons who have contracted HIV typically remain in a latent (asymptomatic) stage for up to 8 to 10 years (with early treatment, it is much longer). During this time, the person may show no symptoms but is capable of transmitting the virus to others. In fact, studies indicate that the virus may be 100 to 1,000 times more contagious during the first 2 months after infection. Because tests to identify the presence in the body of antibodies to HIV—the means by which exposure to the virus is determined—are not reliable for up to 2 months following exposure, these months represent a critical time for transmission.

The transition to AIDS itself occurs when significant suppression of the body's immune system leads to other medical conditions or diseases. Common among these are chronic, unexplained weight loss, chronic fevers, night sweats, constant diarrhea, swollen glands, and thrush (a thick, white coating on the tongue). As AIDS progresses, the patient typically experiences debilitating bouts of pneumonia, chronic herpes infections, seizures, and dementia, and ultimately death (Centers for Disease Control and Prevention, 2019d).

Prevalence, Incidence, and Mortality

Because HIV has a long latency period, and because most Americans have never been tested for exposure to the HIV virus, it is difficult to calculate precisely the number of individuals who are HIV-positive. Epidemiologists use sophisticated statistical models to estimate the prevalence of HIV, including both diagnosed and undiagnosed cases, based on information about diagnosed infections (all states are required to report HIV positive results to the Centers for Disease Control and Prevention) and other data (Centers for Disease Control and Prevention, 2018b).

The CDC estimates that approximately 1.1 million Americans were living with HIV in 2017 (with nearly 1 in 7 unaware they were HIV positive) (Centers for Disease Control and Prevention, 2019d). New HIV infections peaked at about 150,000 a year in the mid-1980s but have decreased to less than 40,000 annually since 2012 (Centers for Disease Control and Prevention, 2018b).

More than 15,000 people with HIV died in 2016 in the United States and outlying territories (Centers for Disease Control and Prevention, 2019d). Xu and colleagues (2018:11) report that HIV-related mortality increased significantly after 1987, peaked in 1995, and then "decreased an average of 33.0% per year from 1995 through 1998, and 6.2% per year from 1999 through 2016" due to the availability of more effective treatments.

In 2015, about 77 percent of persons with HIV/AIDS (and 82 percent of new cases that year) were men. HIV is most commonly transmitted between the ages of 25 and 34 years (Centers for Disease Control and Prevention, 2018b).

Blacks and Hispanics constitute a disproportionate number of persons with HIV/AIDS and have disproportionately high death rates. In 2017, blacks were 13 percent of the US population but represented 43 percent of newly diagnosed HIV infections; Hispanics were 18 percent of the population but 25 percent of new HIV diagnoses. The death rates for blacks and Hispanics infected with HIV were 6.5 and 1.72 times higher, respectively, than for whites in 2016. There is no evidence that race per se is a biological risk factor for vulnerability to the disease. Instead, high rates of unemployment and despair in inner-city areas, with associated drug use and less accurate knowledge about AIDS, help account for the higher rates among blacks and Hispanics (Centers for Disease Control and Prevention, 2019d).

Etiology

HIV is transmitted through the exchange of bodily fluids—blood, semen, pre-seminal fluid, rectal fluids, vaginal fluids, and breast milk—from a person who has HIV. These fluids must come in contact with a mucous membrane or damaged tissue or be directly injected into the bloodstream (from a needle or syringe) for transmission to occur. Mucous membranes are found inside the rectum, vagina, penis, and mouth. Therefore exchange can occur through coital sex, anal sex (a common means of transmission for men who have sex with men because the tissue of the rectal wall is very thin and easily penetrated by the virus), or oral sex (extremely rare but theoretically possible), through passing HIV-contaminated blood (e.g., via a blood transfusion, sharing of needles by intravenous drug users, or reuse of contaminated needles for medical injections), and from an infected mother to a child (either prenatally or through breastfeeding).

The three most common transmission methods in the United States are male-to-male sexual contact, heterosexual contact, and injection drug use. Research has determined that HIV is more easily transmitted from men to women than vice versa, in part because the vagina is a more receptive contact surface than a man's penis. The risk of transmission of infection from mother to child during pregnancy, birth, or breastfeeding is high in the case of an HIV-positive mother who is not taking medication. However, recommendations to test all pregnant women for HIV and start HIV treatment immediately have led to a reduction in the number of babies who are born with HIV (Centers for Disease Control and Prevention, 2019d).

Trends

The most remarkable development in recent years with regard to HIV/AIDS is the discovery of both effective prevention and therapy. The most groundbreaking treatment method is pre-exposure prophylaxis (PrEP)—a daily pill that can be taken by persons who are HIV-negative. When taken consistently, it lowers the risk of HIV infection from sex by up to 92 percent and from injection drug use by more than 70 percent. The CDC and the US Preventive Services Task Force recommend that all persons aged 15 to 65 years (as well as younger and older people at increased risk) and all pregnant women be tested for HIV on a regular basis, and that those in high-risk groups be tested annually and take PrEP. The cost of PrEP is high at about US$13,000 per year per patient.

In addition, after years of research around the world, an effective antiretroviral therapy (ART) has been discovered for HIV. For HIV-positive individuals who receive ART, life expectancy at diagnosis approximates that of uninfected persons. There are still some complications—some countries struggle to find the resources to pay for all of the needed ART, some ART recipients develop health problems from long-term therapy or from multidrug interactions, and affected individuals must commit to daily treatment that may interfere with life's other responsibilities. About 60 percent of those taking ART in 2015 adhered to the daily treatment, although adherence rates vary. For example, older persons have higher adherence rates than younger ones, and cisgender persons—those whose gender identity matches their assigned sex at birth—have higher adherence rates than transgender persons. The most common reasons for missing a dose include forgetting to take it (36.6 percent), changes in daily routine (25.2 percent), falling asleep (20.4 percent), and problems getting or paying for the medication (14.9 percent) (Centers for Disease Control and Prevention, 2018a). Although programs are available to help finance PrEP and ART for those who cannot afford it, financial and social barriers (e.g., stigma, denial, dealing with life's daily struggles) remain. Additionally, both patients and physicians may not understand the need for ongoing treatment (e.g., studies show that many physicians are unaware of recent PrEP drugs).

To see an online interactive visual of the distribution of AIDS cases in the United States, go to Emory University's website (www.AIDSVu.org) and click on the national map.

Worldwide. In the late 1970s, HIV spread silently around the world, unrecognized and unnoticed. Although the first case was officially recognized in the United States in 1981, the vast scope of the infection was not realized until the mid-1980s. It is now considered a worldwide pandemic. Although an accurate prevalence rate is difficult to determine, an estimated 37 million people worldwide were living with HIV in 2017, with 1.8 million newly infected that year. An estimated 940,000 people died of AIDS in 2017. Altogether, more than 35.4 million people have died from AIDS-related diseases since the epidemic began (UNAIDS, 2019a). Figure 4.1 portrays the global AIDS situation.

ALZHEIMER'S DISEASE

Alzheimer's disease (AD) is a chronic, degenerative, dementing illness of the central nervous system. It is the most common cause of *dementia*—a condition that involves personality change, emotional instability, disorientation, memory loss, loss of verbal abilities, and an inability to care for oneself. Other specific symptoms of AD are intellectual impairment, depression, agitation, and delusions.

In order to diagnose AD, an extensive evaluation is necessary, including a complete medical history, interviews with the patient and family members, mental status examination, physical and neurological examination, and formal neuropsychological testing. Multiple clinical trials are currently underway to slow or stop the progression of AD.

Currently, there are some medications available to help people carry out everyday activities, to slow down the progression of loss of thinking, memory, or speaking skills, and to assist with certain behavioral symptoms. However, they do not stop or reverse the underlying disease process, and typically only help for a few months to a couple of years. Researchers are also exploring several lifestyle factors (e.g., diet, exercise, stress, and sleep problems) that may influence the risk of AD and age-related cognitive decline. Many studies have found links between brain health and heart disease, diabetes, and depression. Taking steps to reduce the risk of those conditions—through physical exercise, not smoking, limiting intake of high-fat and high-sugar foods, cholesterol and blood pressure control, and maintaining social and intellectual engagement—may also reduce one's risk of AD (National Institute on Aging, 2019).

In 2011, Congress enacted the National Plan to Address Alzheimer's Disease. It set a target date of 2025 for developing methods of prevention and effective treatment. Nevertheless, relative to funding for other leading causes of death, Alzheimer's disease research is severely underfunded.

Figure 4.1   Global HIV Trends, 1990–2017

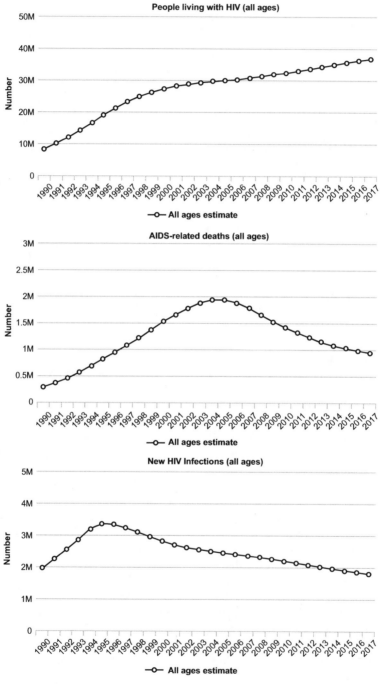

Source: UNAIDS. 2019b. *Graphs*. Geneva, Switzerland: UNAIDS. (https://aidsinfo.unaids.org/).

IN COMPARATIVE FOCUS

AIDS: THE KILLING FIELDS IN AFRICA

The devastating effects of HIV/AIDS take their greatest toll on the world's less developed countries. While HIV rates have stabilized and/or declined in most developed countries and in an increasing number of developing countries (especially in sub-Saharan Africa and the Caribbean), they continue to escalate in some other developing countries (especially in North Africa, the Middle East, Eastern Europe, and Central Asia). Today, 95 percent of people infected with HIV live in a developing country.

Historically, sub-Saharan Africa was the site of the greatest problems. In the early and mid-2000s, for 16 countries in the world—all in sub-Saharan Africa—more than 10 percent of their population aged 15 to 49 years were HIV infected. In South Africa and Zimbabwe, the figure was more than 20 percent.

In addition to its human toll, AIDS wreaks havoc on the entire social fabric of nations. Because most of those infected had acquired HIV by their twenties or thirties, there was a significant shortfall of workers and an increase in the number of people unable to financially support themselves. Life expectancy dropped sharply. Millions of children were orphaned (more than 20 million children worldwide have lost one or both parents to AIDS). In some countries, there were more people in their sixties and seventies than in their thirties and forties, which meant that there was inadequate support for elders. Some countries experienced a significant drop in their national wealth.

Why did HIV/AIDS spread so rapidly in sub-Saharan Africa? Several circumstances had an effect. Many African men in rural villages form a migrant labor pool that migrates to large cities, mining areas, or large commercial farming areas. Their wives typically remain at home to take care of the children. These long absences from home make common the use of prostitutes (most of whom are infected) or multiple sexual partners, thus increasing the opportunities for the virus to be spread. The desire to have a large family led many men to be reluctant to use a condom when back home, which meant that their wives then became vulnerable to infection. In addition, health education programs were frequently unsuccessful, leaving many rural areas where knowledge of HIV/AIDS was inadequate.

Finally, there was not enough money to provide the necessary care. During this time, the United States spent almost US$900 million annually fighting about 55,000 new AIDS cases a year, while all of Africa spent about US$150 million fighting 4 million new cases a year. There was insufficient medicine, and stark inability to pay for AIDS treatment. Despite the increasing effectiveness of drug combinations in reducing suffering and extending life, only about 2 percent of Africans with AIDS were getting treatment as late as 2003 and 2004.

In 2003, new efforts were initiated in the United States and around the world to commit more money to battling HIV/AIDS in the developing world. The United States pledged increased contributions (up to US$3 billion in 2004); the World Health Organization and the United Nations started a new program to bring antiretroviral drugs to those afflicted; the United Nations, the World Bank, the Global Fund to Fight AIDS, Tuberculosis, and Malaria, and former President Clinton created a joint plan to buy and distribute inexpensive, generic AIDS drugs in poor countries; and actor Richard Gere with MTV and VH1 and two of India's largest entertainment networks began creating AIDS Awareness Programs.

Over the last decade, marked progress has been made. Globally, new AIDS cases have decreased tremendously, the number of HIV-positive people receiving treatment increased to 21.7 million in 2017, and AIDS-related mortality has decreased by 51 percent since 2004. Although not all sub-Saharan African countries have lowered the number of new infections or involved more patients in drug programs, many others have made significant progress (Kaiser Family Foundation, 2019).

Prevalence, Incidence, and Mortality

It is difficult to determine the prevalence of AD for a number of reasons. Because onset is often slow and symptoms may go unnoticed or misinterpreted, and because there is no cure for the disease, many people with AD may not seek medical attention. In the United States, more than 5.8 million were living with AD in 2019 (see Figure 4.2). About 3 percent of those aged 65–74 years, 17 percent of those 75 to 84 years, and 32 percent of those aged 85 and over have AD. Because more women live to older ages, they account for nearly two-thirds of Alzheimer's sufferers. More than 121,000 people died from AD in 2017, and the numbers are increasing (Alzheimer's Association, 2019).

In addition to age, race influences the likelihood of contracting Alzheimer's. African Americans are almost twice as likely as whites to have AD and other forms of dementia, and Hispanics are about 1.5 times more likely to have one of these conditions. The late onset form of AD is most common among blacks. In 2013, scientists identified a new gene mutation linked to AD that is more common among blacks. This finding has opened up new areas of research (Alzheimer's Association, 2019).

The progression of AD varies from person to person. On average, someone afflicted with AD survives for up to 10 years or more before dying, although some individuals survive for up to 25 years. Alzheimer's is now the sixth leading cause of death in the United States, and is growing more rapidly than any other cause of death (see Figure 4.3).

Etiology

Although scientists have made significant progress in understanding the etiology of AD, they do not yet know the exact cause. Currently the two most promising lines of explanation relate to two kinds of brain abnormalities. The first is a plaque comprised of beta amyloid that forms on brain cells. When the immune system activates to address the problem, the brain becomes inflamed. Over time, these plaques build up in the brain. The second abnormality is the presence

Figure 4.2 Number of Alzheimer's Cases

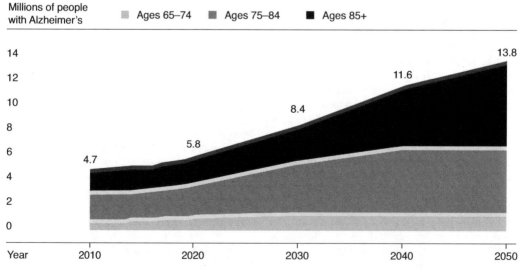

Source: Alzheimer's Association. 2019. *2019 Alzheimer's Facts and Figures*. Chicago, IL: Alzheimer's Association.

Figure 4.3 Percentage Changes in Selected Causes of Death (All Ages) Between 2000 and 2017

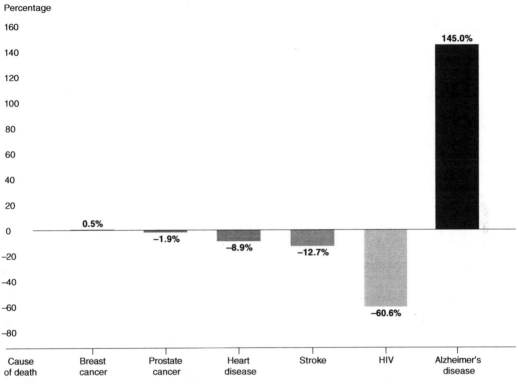

Created from data from the National Center for Health Statistics.

Source: Alzheimer's Association. 2019.*2019 Alzheimer's Facts and Figures*. Chicago, IL: Alzheimer's Association.

of molecular tangles inside brain cells, which can ultimately kill the cells.

Researchers have now identified three genes that, when mutated, cause abnormalities in brain cells. These mutations are inheritable, and virtually everyone who inherits one develops AD by the age of 60 years. However, later onset AD also has a large genetic component. Individuals who have one affected parent are three times more likely to develop AD, and those with two affected parents are five times more likely to do so. It appears that genes are not causative of AD, but simply make one more susceptible to it when exposed to certain environmental triggers. Much current research is focused on understanding these triggers, and researchers are making headway in finding a drug that could melt

away the plaque. Currently, the most definitive diagnosis of AD is made after death, by examining the brain tissue for plaques and tangles (National Institute on Aging, 2019).

Trends

Projections indicate that, without an effective cure or preventive mechanism, the prevalence of AD will increase substantially in the next 50 years as numbers of people in the oldest age groups increase. By 2050, nearly 14 million people in the United States will have AD (Alzheimer's Association, 2019).

This trend will affect health care and the health care system in important ways, increasing the need for caregivers for advanced cases and for support for partners and other family members. In 2018, more than 16 million caregivers for people with dementia provided more than 18.5 billion hours of unpaid care. Awareness of these needs in the medical community has increased dramatically in the last three decades, and is largely a result of research and focus by sociologists and the efforts of a small number of dedicated neuroscientists, the National Institute on Aging (NIA), and the Alzheimer's Disease and Related Disorders Association (ADRDA) advocacy group (Alzheimer's Association, 2019).

There will also be important financial consequences. The annual costs of caring for Alzheimer's patients and those with other forms of dementia are expected to increase from US$290 billion in 2019 to US$1.1 trillion in 2050, when people aged 65 years or older will represent 20 percent of the population. Because Medicare and Medicaid pay for approximately 67 percent of AD-related costs, the financial stability of these programs will be challenged (Alzheimer's Association, 2019).

Worldwide. Approximately 50 million people worldwide have dementia, and as much as 60 to 70 percent of these is Alzheimer's related. Extensions to life expectancy and the aging of the world population signal substantial future growth in the worldwide prevalence of Alzheimer's, which will have a significant economic impact (World Health Organization, 2019b).

MENTAL ILLNESS

It is difficult to define mental illness, in part due to the sociocultural basis for determining what orientations or behaviors are indicative of a mentally ill person. Some conditions (e.g., homosexuality) that were once considered mental illnesses are no longer categorized as such. Some conditions (e.g., having visions) that are considered evidence of mental illness in some cultures are considered perfectly natural in others. Research even indicates that members of different cultures manifest very different symptoms in response to the same clinical psychopathology—for example, schizophrenics in some cultures are loud and aggressive, whereas in other cultures they are quiet and withdrawn.

Moreover, everyone has impairments in functioning or "problems in living" from time to time, and many people consult with mental health professionals such as psychiatrists, clinical psychologists, social workers, and marriage and family counselors about these problems. Most are seeking help with marital or other family relationships, work-related problems, stress, or a lack of self-confidence. Some conditions are more intense, persist longer, and require more significant treatment.

Although mental illness can be categorized in a variety of ways, the most common mental illnesses include the following (WebMD, 2019):

1. *Anxiety disorders*, which are the most common types of mental illness, involve an unusually grave form of fear or dread about certain situations. Although everyone experiences anxiousness sometimes, these disorders refer to a persistently high level of anxiety that may result in a physiological change, such as chest pains. Anxiety disorders include phobias (an abnormally intense level of fear about something that may be harmless), obsessive-compulsive disorders (behaviors that must be performed in order to avoid anxiety or respond to an obsession), and posttraumatic stress disorder (experiencing a traumatic event and then continuing to feel the trauma even after the event has ended).

2. *Mood disorders* (also called affective disorders) affect a person's day-to-day emotional state and may manifest in lasting feelings of excessive sadness or hopelessness (*depression*), periods of extreme happiness, or fluctuations between the two (*bipolar disorder*).

3. *Psychotic disorders* are severe mental disorders that involve abnormal thinking or perception. These include hallucinations (seeing or hearing things that are not real), delusions (believing things that are not true despite evidence to the contrary), incoherent speech, and

schizophrenia (which may involve a combination of these symptoms).

4. *Eating disorders* involve a preoccupation with food and an irrational fear of being fat. Examples of these disorders include anorexia nervosa (self-starvation), bulimia (periods of overeating followed by purging), and cycles of binge-eating.

5. *Impulse control and addiction disorders* are manifested in individuals who cannot resist engaging in behaviors that may be harmful to them and which they wish to avoid. These include kleptomania (stealing), compulsive gambling, and compulsive use of alcohol and/or other drugs.

6. *Personality disorders* refer to extreme and persistent personality traits that are distressing to the individual and typically cause problems in their interactions with other people. These conditions include paranoia (extreme distrustfulness of other people) and antisocial personality disorder (extreme and distressing personality traits that disrupt normal social functioning).

7. *Obsessive–compulsive disorder* (OCD) occurs when people are plagued by constant thoughts or fears that cause them to perform certain rituals or routines. The disturbing thoughts are called obsessions, and the rituals are called compulsions. An example is a person with an unreasonable fear of germs who constantly washes their hands.

8. *Post-traumatic stress disorder* (PTSD) refers to conditions that can develop following a traumatic and/or terrifying event, such as a sexual or physical assault, the unexpected death of a loved one, or a natural disaster. People with PTSD often have lasting and frightening thoughts and memories of the event and tend to be emotionally numb.

See the accompanying box, "College Students and Mental Health Concerns," for a discussion of the kinds of mental disorders most commonly experienced by college students.

IN THE FIELD

COLLEGE STUDENTS AND MENTAL HEALTH CONCERNS

College students now report a higher incidence of mental illness than ever before. About 1 college student in 4 has a diagnosable mental disorder, and about 1 in 5 presenting to the counseling center has a serious mental health concern. Anxiety has long been the most common issue among students, but today it is experienced at a more intense and overwhelming level. Within the last 12 months, nearly 1 student in 6 has been diagnosed with or treated for anxiety. Reports of depression (experienced by more than one-third of students at some point during college, and the most common reason for dropping out of college) and social anxiety have also increased over time. Many students report being overwhelmed by their responsibilities.

Causes include increasing academic pressure, the demands of multiple responsibilities (e.g., school, work, organizations, and family),

overprotective parents, and compulsive engagement with social media. Some college counseling center directors believe that today's generation of students is not as resilient as earlier generations were and are less independent. They have a more difficult time when they have to struggle to succeed, especially if they read on social media about how well everyone else is supposedly doing.

About half of those who seek care at the mental health center have already had some form of counseling before college, and 1 in 3 has previously been treated with psychiatric medications. Higher rates may also be due in part to a greater willingness to seek treatment due to the reduction in stigma associated with mental disorders, and to increased efforts to encourage students in need to visit the counseling center (Center for Collegiate Mental Health, 2016).

The most widely used classification system for mental disorders is the *Diagnostic and Statistical Manual of Mental Disorders, Fifth Edition (DSM-5)* (2013), prepared by a task force of the American Psychiatric Association. It is the system used by mental health professionals, many social workers, courts, and insurance providers. The *DSM-5* assesses each disorder on the basis of the nature and severity of clinical symptoms, relevant history, related physical illnesses, and recent adaptive functioning, especially with regard to the quality of social relationships.

The *DSM* is a very controversial document. Critics charge that its definitions of disorders and the ability of clinicians to apply those definitions lack validity because they are subjectively based. An example is the fact that homosexuality was listed as a mental disorder through the first two editions of the book. When a large number of members of the American Psychiatric Association (APA) challenged this perspective in the 1970s, the APA voted to delete homosexuality from the list of disorders. Critics charged that nothing "objective" about homosexuality had changed—only its subjective interpretation. Horwitz (2007) contends that *DSM* diagnoses sometimes fail to distinguish between genuine individual pathology and entirely understandable distress caused by discouraging life experiences, such as chronic subordination, the inability to achieve valued goals, and the loss of important attachments. Others posit that the *DSM* lacks reliability—that is, it is used inconsistently by different clinicians. Studies have shown that clinicians often disagree about diagnosis and do not uniformly diagnose defined conditions. Studies that show that the race or gender of a patient influences the diagnosis offer further evidence of a lack of reliability. Many mental health organizations have asked for an independent review of the document. The *DSM* is widely used and has some utility but carries with it some serious problems.

Prevalence, Incidence, and Mortality

There are several major data sources that are now used to estimate the prevalence of mental disorders in the population. Population surveys (such as those conducted by CDC's National Health Interview Survey and the Behavioral Risk Factor Surveillance Survey) and surveys of health care use measure the occurrence of mental illness, associated risk behaviors (e.g., alcohol and drug abuse) and chronic conditions, and use of mental health–related care and clinical services.

In the United States, an estimated 20 percent of adults (43.4 million people in 2015) experience some form of mental illness each year. One in 25 would be classified as being serious. Most of these disorders are treatable, but because of potential stigma and financial concerns, many do not seek needed treatment. An estimated 50 percent of people will experience at least one mental illness during their lifetime (Centers for Disease Control and Prevention, 2018d).

Additionally, about 1 in 5 children between the ages of 3 and 17 years will have a diagnosable mental disorder in any given year. The most common mental disorder among children is attention deficit hyperactivity disorder (ADHD), which occurs in just over 9 percent of children. With regard to other disorders, 7.4 percent of children currently have a diagnosed behavioral or conduct problem, 7.1 percent suffer from anxiety, and 3.2 percent have depression. Boys are more prone to ADHD, behavioral or conduct problems, and anxiety, while girls are more likely to have depression (Centers for Disease Control and Prevention, 2019a).

Medical sociologists typically employ a "social consequences" approach when studying mental illness—that is, they examine how social arrangements and social processes affect mental health and the likelihood of obtaining treatment for mental health problems (Aneshensel, 2005). Among the aspects of social structure commonly studied are socioeconomic status, race, gender, and marital status. See the accompanying box, "The Effects of Neighborhood on Mental Health."

IN THE FIELD

THE EFFECTS OF NEIGHBORHOOD ON MENTAL HEALTH

Considerable research has found that neighborhood context has an important effect on psychological distress and mental health. Disordered neighborhoods, common in disadvantaged areas, may produce such psychological states in residents as anxiety, anger, depression, and subjective alienation—that is, a sense of separation between oneself and others. Often this heightens one's sense of powerlessness and of mistrust of others. Ross (2011) has theorized that mistrust is likely to develop in neighborhoods where perceived threat is common and where resources to deal with the threat are scarce. A strong sense of personal control might be helpful in reducing the negative effects of this environment, but that orientation is often eroded by the environment. Feeling a sense of powerlessness and mistrust is in itself psychologically distressing.

These negative effects begin in childhood and carry through to later life. Because neighborhoods are often the limit of adolescents' social world, living in a violent and threatening neighborhood has an early influence on thoughts about self (self-efficacy), which in turn affects emotional health. Studies in disadvantaged neighborhoods have found high levels of anxiety and depression among young people (Dupere, Leventhal, and Vitaro, 2012), and these adolescent experiences can negatively affect cognitive health in later life. This negative influence has been linked especially to personal socioeconomic status—that is, the decline in mental health was most apparent in those who themselves were poor in addition to living in a disadvantaged neighborhood (Aneshensel et al., 2011).

Socioeconomic Status and Race. With the possible exception of anxiety and mood disorders, the highest levels of psychological distress occur among socially disadvantaged groups. Rates of schizophrenia, personality disorders characterized mainly by antisocial behavior and substance abuse, and depression are highest in the lowest socioeconomic groups.

There are three possible explanations for the high prevalence of mental disorders among the poor. The *genetic* explanation asserts that genetic inheritance predisposes members of the lower class to mental disorders. This theory has not received research support. The *social selection/drift* explanation maintains that mentally ill people may drift downward in the social structure, or that mentally healthy individuals tend to be upwardly mobile, thus leaving a "residue" of mentally ill people. Although research indicates that mental health problems do tend to prevent upward social

mobility, it has not been found that they lead to downward mobility. A third explanation—*social causation*—posits that people in lower socioeconomic groups live in a social environment that is more stressful, and that they are more vulnerable to the effects of this stress because they lack the personal and financial resources to obtain the help they need (Aneshensel, 2009). The economic deprivation, dangerous physical environment, less healthy lifestyle, and unstable personal relationships that often accompany poverty all threaten mental health (Eaton, Muntaner, and Sapag, 2010). This approach has received the most empirical support, although none of these three explanations is totally satisfactory.

The relationship between race and mental health disorders depends upon the particular disorder being studied. Although blacks are more likely than whites to be in the lower socioeconomic strata, they do not have higher overall rates of mental illness and disorder (Williams, Costa, and Leavell, 2010). In cases of particular disorders in which rates for blacks are higher than for whites, socioeconomic status accounts for most of the gap (Spence, Adkins, and Dupre, 2011).

Gender. In contrast to the clear differences between men's and women's physical health, the overall incidence of mental illness in men and women is about the same. However, overall rates camouflage differences in the likelihood of developing specific illnesses. For example, rates of mood and anxiety disorders—including depression—are consistently higher in women, and rates of personality disorders, substance abuse, and suicide are consistently higher in men (Bird and Rieker, 2008). These differences are due to both biological and sociocultural factors. Some research has focused on hormonal differences and chromosomal differences between women and men as explanatory factors for differential mental health, but the evidence is insufficient to allow conclusions to be drawn. On the other hand, it is known that differences in behavior are at least partially the result of socialization into prescribed roles for men and women. This pattern is examined in more detail in Chapter 5.

Marital Status. Research consistently finds that married people experience better mental health than unmarried people, and that married men are even healthier mentally than married women. This is partially due to the social and emotional support received from stable, supportive relationships that can protect against the psychological consequences of difficult life situations. It may also reflect the fact that the mentally ill are less likely to be married, and thus the differences between levels of mental health are a result of a selection process rather than of marriage itself (Turner and Gartrell, 1978).

One study (Frech and Williams, 2007) discovered that both men and women who were depressed prior to marriage experienced greater psychological benefits from marriage than those

who were not previously depressed. They postulate that the added emotional support and companionship of marriage and the reduction in social isolation by linking the person to a wider circle of friends and relatives are responsible for this benefit. All men and women experience greater benefits from a marriage when it offers a high level of happiness and a low level of conflict. Thus, it should be understood that the benefits of marriage for mental health vary based on certain conditions and circumstances.

Etiology

There are three primary approaches to understanding the etiology of mental illness—the biogenic or physiological approach (also called the medical model), the environmental or social approach, and a combination of the two, the *gene-environment approach*. The traditional biogenic view of mental illness is that it is an observable and measurable condition, stemming from individual psychological or biological pathology, which is amenable to proper treatment.

Many sociologists have challenged this way of thinking and support a social approach. They argue that definitions of mental illness rely more on subjective social judgments than on objective facts. Thoits (1985) believes that the mental illness label is applied when a behavior is inconsistent with (1) *cognitive norms* (i.e., one's thinking is at odds with norms), (2) *performance norms* (i.e., one's behavior is at odds with norms), or (3) *feeling norms* (i.e., one's feelings are at odds with the range, intensity, and duration of feeling expected in a given situation). She posits that violations of feeling norms are the most common basis for labeling someone as mentally ill.

Finally, a third school of thought advocates for a combination of the two approaches. Those who support the gene-environment approach contend that neither biogenic nor social factors can be dismissed, and that a comprehensive explanation requires both.

Trends

Some sociologists who focus on the "sociology of mental health" have challenged the desirability of thinking in terms of clinical diagnoses at all and suggest that we focus on measurements that reflect the true range of human feelings and emotions. Mirowsky and Ross (2002:152) encourage a "human science" that centers on life "as people feel it, sense it, and understand it," and that includes consideration of human suffering even if it does not fall within pre-formulated diagnostic categories. Kessler (2002) also sees greater value in thinking in terms of dimensional assessments (placing each individual on a continuum of psychological distress without identifying a specific point at which a mental illness begins), rather than the traditional procedure of making categorical assessments (each individual either has a mental illness or does not). These ideas have genuine potential for reshaping our approach to understanding human suffering and mental distress.

A positive development is that public discourse about mental health and mental illness is perhaps more open than ever before, and more people than ever are seeking treatment. Nevertheless, mental disorders continue to receive less public attention than physical ailments despite the very large percentage of people who experience some type of mental disorder each year. In the political arena, coverage of mental health services was a controversial provision in the failed Clinton health care reform package in the early 1990s and the successful Obama reform legislation of 2010. For some, providing for mental health needs lacked the legitimacy of providing coverage for other diseases. Perhaps the biggest battle yet to be won in treating mental disorders is to convince politicians and others of the vast importance of making these services more widely available.

Worldwide. More than 450 million people across the globe suffer from mental illnesses. Schizophrenia, depression, epilepsy, dementia, alcohol dependence, and other mental, neurological, and substance-use disorders make up 13 percent of the global disease burden, surpassing both cardiovascular disease and cancer. According to the World Health Organization (WHO), mental illnesses account for more disability in developed countries than any other group of illnesses, including cancer and heart disease.

SUMMARY

Social epidemiologists help us understand the social etiology (causes) and distribution of disease and illness. In addition to the disease agent, they give attention to proximate risk factors, fundamental causes (underlying social conditions), and genetic factors. The *epidemiological transition* explains the historical shift from dominance of acute infectious diseases to dominance of chronic degenerative diseases.

In the United States, heart disease and cancer are the two most common causes of death. Together, they account for over 45 percent of annual deaths. Although the rate of heart disease has decreased substantially in recent decades, it remains the number one killer of Americans. Overall, cancer rates increased until 1991, but leveled off in the 2000s. Both diseases are influenced by fundamental causes and proximate risk factors. Cigarette smoking, diet, and physical exercise are major risk factors for both. High blood cholesterol, high blood pressure, and social stress are also major risk factors for heart disease, while excessive consumption of alcohol, overexposure to the sun, and overexposure to environmental pollutants are other key risk factors for cancer.

AIDS begins with HIV infection and is transmitted by body fluids through sexual activity, unsterile needles, infected blood supplies, and the placenta. It is a major health problem around the world, and its impact has been particularly severe in Africa. Progress has been made in developing drugs to decrease the likelihood of contracting AIDS, and in long-term survival rates. The disease is currently in transition from a fatal disease to a chronic disease.

Alzheimer's disease is a disease of mental deterioration that begins in mid- to late life and affects millions of people in the United States and especially in other developed countries. There have been advances in our understanding of the disease, but there is still no cure for it.

Approximately 1 in 5 Americans experiences some form of mental disorder each year. Although patterns vary by type of mental illness, people in lower socioeconomic groups experience more mental illness (for many reasons, including neighborhood disorder, higher levels of stress, and less access to medical resources).

HEALTH ON THE INTERNET

Life expectancy varies considerably from state to state. To examine life expectancy in each state go to the following website, run by the Kaiser Family Foundation:

www.kff.org/statedata/

Click on "Health Status" from the list on the left. Under "Categories & Subcategories" select "Life Expectancy" and then click the link to view the state data. Arrange the resulting list from high to low by clicking the upward arrow on the life expectancy column. How does your state compare to others? What factors might plausibly explain your state's ranking? Select three or four factors you think might be most influential. Then, use the Kaiser Family Foundation website to locate data on these factors. (For example, you could check rates of obesity in your state and compare these to rates in states with the highest life expectancy.) Write a short summary of what you find and explain whether or not the data you collected supported your suppositions.

DISCUSSION CASE

Consider the following issue related to social epidemiology:

The World Health Organization, the United Nations Programme on HIV/AIDS, the Centers for Disease Control and Prevention, and the United States Preventive Services Task Force have all recently called for routine HIV testing without specific consent in all doctors' offices, clinics, and hospitals unless patients explicitly refuse to be tested. The WHO and UN have emphasized the importance of testing even healthy-looking individuals. They point out that this would lead to increased life expectancy for those who are HIV-positive (with proper medication, those diagnosed early with the disease can now basically expect to have a normal length of life, whereas those diagnosed with AIDS in the later stages die within months), and reduce the likelihood that those who are HIV-positive but unaware of this (an estimated 200,000 more people in the United States) would pass the disease on to others (drugs have now reduced the likelihood of transmitting the disease by 96 percent). However, a significant backlash has occurred among people who do not wish to see pretest counseling eliminated, and who say that the lingering stigma associated with AIDS makes the risk of disclosure too great, especially when many people still cannot access treatment.

Address the following questions:

1. What are the individual and societal consequences of offering regular routine HIV testing?
2. What values underlie the arguments for and against this proposal?
3. Should our society support/adopt this approach?

GLOSSARY

acute infectious diseases
chronic degenerative diseases
Diagnostic and Statistical Manual of Mental Disorders,
  Fifth Edition (DSM-5)
double disease burden
environmental tobacco smoke (ETS)
etiology

fundamental causes
germ theory of disease
Global Burden of Disease Study (GBD)
health transition (HT)
Human Genome Project
proximate risk factors
social determinants of health

REFERENCES

Agyei-Mensah, Samuel, and Ama de-Graft Aikins. 2010. "Epidemiological Transition and the Double Burden of Disease in Accra, Ghana." *Journal of Urban Health: Bulletin of the New York Academy of Medicine* 87(5):879–897.

Alzheimer's Association. 2019. *2019 Alzheimer's Facts and Figures.* Chicago, IL: Alzheimer's Association. Retrieved June 21, 2019 (www.alz.org/media/Documents/alzheimers-facts-and-figures-2019-r.pdf).

American Cancer Society. 2018. *Global Cancer Facts & Figures* (4th ed.). Atlanta, GA: American Cancer Society.

———. 2019. *Cancer Facts and Figures 2019.* Atlanta, GA: American Cancer Society.

American Heart Association Council on Epidemiology and Prevention Statistics Committee and Stroke Statistics Subcommittee. 2018. "Heart Disease and Stroke Statistics-2018 Update: A Report from the American Heart Association." *Circulation* 137(12):e67–492.

American Psychiatric Association. 2013. *Diagnostic and Statistical Manual of Mental Disorders, Fifth Edition (DSM-5).* Arlington, VA: American Psychiatric Association.

Aneshensel, Carol S. 2005. "Research in Mental Health: Social Etiology Versus Social Consequences." *Journal of Health and Social Behavior* 48(3):221–228.

———. 2009. "Toward Explaining Mental Health Disparities." *Journal of Health and Social Behavior* 50(4):377–394.

Aneshensel, Carol S., Michelle J. Ko, Joshua Chodosh, and Richard G. Wright. 2011. "The Urban Neighborhood and Cognitive Functioning in Late Middle Age." *Journal of Health and Social Behavior* 52(2):163–179.

Auerbach, Judith D., and Anne E. Figert. 1995. "Women's Health Research: Public Policy and Sociology." *Journal of Health and Social Behavior* 36(Extra Issue):115–131.

Beaman, Peter. 2008. "Exploring Genetics and Social Structure." *American Journal of Sociology* 114(S1):v–x.

Bird, Chloe E., and Patricia P. Rieker. 2008. *Gender and Health: The Effects of Constrained Choices and Social Policies.* New York: Cambridge University Press.

Caldwell, John C. 1993. "Health Transition: The Cultural, Social, and Behavioural Determinants of Health in the Third World." *Social Science and Medicine* 36(2):125–135.

Center for Collegiate Mental Health. 2016. *2015 Annual Report.* University Park, PA: Pennsylvania State University.

Centers for Disease Control and Prevention. 2016. "High Blood Pressure Fact Sheet." Retrieved June 20, 2019 (www.cdc.gov/dhdsp/data_statistics/fact_sheets/fs_bloodpressure.htm).

———. 2017a. "Heart Disease Fact Sheet." Retrieved June 23, 2019 (www.cdc.gov/dhdsp/data_statistics/fact_sheets/fs_heart_disease.htm).

———. 2018a. "Behavioral and Clinical Characteristics of Persons with Diagnosed HIV Infection—Medical Monitoring Project, United States, 2015 Cycle." *HIV Surveillance Special Report* 20. Retrieved June 24, 2019 (www.cdc.gov/hiv/library/reports/hiv-surveillance.html).

———. 2018b. "Estimated HIV Incidence and Prevalence in the United States, 2010–2015." *Surveillance Supplemental Report* 23(1):77. Retrieved June 23, 2019 (www.cdc.gov/hiv/library/reports/hiv-surveillance.html).

———. 2018c. "Health Effects of Secondhand Smoke." Retrieved June 22, 2019 (www.cdc.gov/tobacco/data_statistics/fact_sheets/secondhand_smoke/health_effects/index.htm).

———. 2018d. "Learn About Mental Health." Retrieved June 24, 2019 (www.cdc.gov/mentalhealth/learn/index.htm).

———. 2019a. "Data and Statistics on Children's Mental Health." *Centers for Disease Control and*

Prevention. Retrieved June 24, 2019 (www.cdc.gov/childrensmentalhealth/data.html).

———. 2019b. "Heart Disease Facts." Retrieved April 25, 2019 (www.cdc.gov/heartdisease/facts.htm).

———.2019c."Health Effects of Cigarette Smoking."*Centers for Disease Control and Prevention.* Retrieved June 22, 2019 (www.cdc.gov/tobacco/data_statistics/fact_sheets/health_effects/effects_cig_smoking/index.htm).

———. 2019d. "HIV/AIDS." Retrieved June 23, 2019 (www.cdc.gov/hiv/).

Denchak, Melissa. 2018. "Flint Water Crisis: Everything You Need to Know." *Natural Resources Defense Council.* Retrieved June 20, 2019 (www.nrdc.org/stories/flint-water-crisis-everything-you-need-know).

Dresser, Rebecca. 1992. "Wanted: Single, White Male for Medical Research." *Hastings Center Report* 22(1):24–29.

Dupere, Veronique, Tama Leventhal, and Frank Vitaro. 2012. "Neighborhood Processes, Self-Efficacy, and Adolescent Mental Health." *Journal of Health and Social Behavior* 53(2):183–198.

Duster, Troy. 2006. "Lessons from History: Why Race and Ethnicity Have Played a Major Role in Biomedical Research." *The Journal of Law, Medicine, and Ethics* 34(3):487–496.

Eaton, William W., Carles Muntaner, and Jaime C. Sapag. 2010. "Socioeconomic Stratification and Mental Disorders." Pp. 226–255 in *A Handbook for the Study of Mental Health: Social Contexts, Theories, and Systems* (2nd ed.), edited by Theresa L. Scheid and Tony N. Brown. New York: Cambridge University Press.

Evans, Robert G., Morris L. Barer, and Theodore R. Marmor. 1994. *Why Are Some People Healthy and Others Not? The Determinants of Health of Populations.* New York: Aldine de Gruyter.

Fletcher, Jason M., and Dalton Conley. 2013. "The Challenge of Causal Inference in Gene-Environment Interaction Research: Leveraging Research Designs from the Social Sciences." *American Journal of Public Health* 103(S1): S42–S45.

Frech, Adrianne, and Kristi Williams. 2007. "Depression and the Psychological Benefits of Entering Marriage." *Journal of Health and Social Behavior* 48(2):149–163.

Frenk, Julio, Joseé L. Bobadilla, Jaime Sepúlveda, and Malaquias Loópez Cervantes. 1989. "Health Transition in Middle-Income Countries: New Challenges for Health Care." *Health Policy and Planning* 4(1):29–39.

Gallagher, Eugene B., Thomas J. Stewart, and Terry Stratton. 2000. "The Sociology of Health in Developing Countries." Pp. 389–397 in *Handbook of Medical Sociology* (5th ed.), edited by Chloe Bird, Peter Conrad, and Allen M. Fremont. Upper Saddle River, NJ: Prentice Hall.

Heath, Brad, Blake Morrison, and Dan Reed. 2008. "When Schools Are Built, Toxic Air Rarely Considered." *USA Today*, December 30, pp. 1–2.

Hertzman, C., J. Frank, and R.G. Evans. 1994. "Heterogeneities in Health Status and the Determinants of Population Health." Pp. 67–92 in *Why Are Some People Healthy and Others Not? The Determinants of Health of Populations*, edited by Robert G. Evans, Morris L. Barer, and Theodore R. Marmor. New York: Aldine de Gruyter.

Horwitz, Allan V. 2007. "Transforming Normality into Pathology: The DSM and the Outcomes of Stressful Social Arrangements." *Journal of Health and Social Behavior* 48(3):211–222.

Institute for Health Metrics and Evaluation. 2019. "Global Burden of Disease (GBD)." Retrieved June 20, 2019 (www.healthdata.org/gbd).

Islami, Farhad, Ann Goding Sauer, Kimberly D. Miller, Rebecca L. Siegel, Stacey A. Fedewa, Eric J. Jacobs, Marjorie L. McCullough, Alpa V. Patel, Jiemin Ma, Isabelle Soerjomataram, W. Dana Flanders, Otis W. Brawley, Susan M. Gapstur, and Ahmedin Jemal. 2018. "Proportion and Number of Cancer Cases and Deaths Attributable to Potentially Modifiable Risk Factors in the United States: Potentially Preventable Cancers in US." *CA: A Cancer Journal for Clinicians* 68(1):31–54.

Kaiser Family Foundation. 2019. "The Global HIV/AIDS Epidemic." Retrieved June 24, 2019 (www.kff.org/global-health-policy/fact-sheet/the-global-hivaids-epidemic/).

Kessler, Ronald C. 2002. "The Categorical Versus Dimensional Assessment Controversy in the Sociology of Mental Illness." *Journal of Health and Social Behavior* 43(2):171–188.

Krueger, J., Paul Biedrzycki, and Sara P. Hoverter. 2015. "Human Health Impacts of Climate Change: Implications for the Practice and Law of Public Health." *Journal of Law, Medicine, and Ethics* 43(S1):79–82.

Ladizinski, Barry, Kachiu C. Lee, Renata Ladizinski, and Daniel G. Federman. 2013. "Indoor Tanning Amongst Young Adults: Time to Stop Sleeping on the Banning of Sunbeds." *Journal of General Internal Medicine* 28(12):1551–1553.

Link, Bruce G., and Jo C. Phelan. 1995. "Social Conditions as Fundamental Causes of Disease." *Journal of Health and Social Behavior* Extra Issue:80–94.

———. 2000. "Evaluating the Fundamental Cause Explanation for Social Disparities in Health." Pp. 33–46 in *Handbook of Medical Sociology* (5th ed.), edited by Chloe E. Bird, Peter Conrad, and Allen M. Fremont. Upper Saddle River, NJ: Prentice Hall.

Margolis, Rachel. 2013. "Educational Differences in Healthy Behavior Changes and Adherence among Middle-Aged Americans." *Journal of Health and Social Behavior* 54(3):353–368.

Merton, Vanessa. 1993. "The Exclusion of Pregnant, Pregnable, and Once-Pregnable People (a.k.a. Women) from Biomedical Research." *American Journal of Law and Medicine* 19(4):379–445.

Mirowsky, John, and Catherine E. Ross. 2002. "Measurement for a Human Science." *Journal of Health and Social Behavior* 43(2):152–170.

Morrison, Blake, and Brad Heath. 2008. "Health Risks Stack Up for School Kids near Industry." *USA Today*, December 8, pp. 1, 6, 7, 10, 11.

National Center for Health Statistics. 2018. *Health, United States, 2017: With Special Feature on Mortality*. Hyattsville, MD: National Center for Health Statistics.

National Human Genome Research Institute. 2019. "The Human Genome Project." *Genome. Gov*. Retrieved June 20, 2019 (www.genome.gov/human-genome-project).

National Institute on Aging. 2019. "Alzheimer's Disease Fact Sheet." Retrieved June 23, 2019 (www.nia.nih.gov/health/alzheimers-disease-fact-sheet).

Pescosolido, Bernice A., Brea L. Perry, J. Scott Long, Jack K. Martin, John I. Nurnberger, and Victor Hesselbrock. 2008. "Under the Influence of Genetics: How Transdisciplinarity Leads Us to Rethink Social Pathways to Illness." *American Journal of Sociology* 114(S1):S171–S201.

Phelan, Jo C., Bruce G. Link, and Parisa Tehranifar. 2010. "Social Conditions as Fundamental Causes of Health Inequalities: Theory, Evidence, and Policy Implications." *Journal of Health and Social Behavior* 51(S1):S28–S40.

Ross, Catherine E. 2011. "Collective Threat, Trust, and the Sense of Personal Control." *Journal of Health and Social Behavior* 52(3):287–296.

Ross, Catherine E., and Chia-ling Wu. 1995. "The Links between Education and Health." *American Sociological Review* 60(5):719–745.

Roth, Gregory A., Degu Abate, Kalkidan Hassen Abate, Solomon M. Abay, Cristiana Abbafati, Nooshin Abbasi, et al. 2018. "Global, Regional, and National Age-Sex-Specific Mortality for 282 Causes of Death in 195 Countries and Territories, 1980–2017: A Systematic Analysis for the Global Burden of Disease Study 2017." *The Lancet* 392(10159):1736–1788.

Shumaker, Erin. 2015. "Sexism in the Doctor's Office Starts Here." Retrieved January 29, 2016 (www.huffpost.com/entry/women-are-excluded-from-clinical-trials_n_5637ad65e4b0c66bae5d36ba).

Smith, Mitch, Julie Bosman, and Monica Davey. 2019. "Flint's Water Crisis Started 5 Years Ago. It's Not Over." *The New York Times*, April 25.

Spence, Naomi J., Daniel E. Adkins, and Matthew E. Dupre. 2011. "Racial Differences in Depression Trajectories among Older Women: Socioeconomic, Family, and Health Influences." *Journal of Health and Social Behavior* 52(4):444–459.

Thoits, Peggy A. 1985. "Self-Labeling Processes in Mental Illness: The Role of Emotional Deviance." *American Journal of Sociology* 91(2):221–249.

Tuckson, Reed V., Lee Newcomer, and Jeanne M. De Sa. 2013. "Accessing Genomic Medicine: Affordability, Diffusion, and Disparities." *Journal of the American Medical Association* 309(14):1469–1470.

Turner, R. Jay, and John W. Gartrell. 1978. "Social Factors in Psychiatric Outcome: Toward the Resolution of Interpretive Controversies." *American Sociological Review* 43(3):368–382.

UNAIDS. 2019a. "Global HIV & AIDS Statistics—2018 Fact Sheet." Retrieved June 23, 2019 (www.unaids.org/en/resources/fact-sheet).

———. 2019b. "Graphs." Retrieved June 21, 2019 (https://aidsinfo.unaids.org/).

United Nations. 2019. "United Nations Sustainable Development Goals." Retrieved June 20, 2019 (www.un.org/sustainabledevelopment/).

WebMD. 2019. "Types of Mental Illness." Retrieved June 24, 2019 (www.webmd.com/mental-health/mental-health-types-illness).

Williams, David R., Manuela Costa, and Jacinta P. Leavell. 2010. "Race and Mental Health: Patterns and Challenges." Pp. 268–290 in *A Handbook for the Study of Mental Health: Social Contexts, Theories, and Systems* (2nd ed.), edited by Teresa L. Scheid and Tony N. Brown. New York: Cambridge University Press.

World Health Organization. 2017a. "Ten Facts on the State of Global Health." Retrieved June 19, 2019 (www.who.int/features/factfiles/global_burden/en/).

———. 2017b. "Cardiovascular Diseases (CVDs)." Retrieved June 23, 2019 (www.who.int/news-room/fact-sheets/detail/cardiovascular-diseases-(cvds)).

———. 2019a. "Cancer Prevention." Retrieved June 21, 2019 (www.who.int/cancer/prevention/en/).

———. 2019b. "Dementia." Retrieved June 23, 2019 (www.who.int/news-room/fact-sheets/detail/dementia).

———. 2019c. "Tobacco." Retrieved June 22, 2019 (www.who.int/news-room/fact-sheets/detail/tobacco).

Xu, Jiaquan, Sherry L. Murphy, Kenneth D. Kochanek, Brigham Bastian, and Elizabeth Arias. 2018. "Deaths: Final Data for 2016." *National Vital Statistics Reports* 67(5):76.

CHAPTER 5

Social Stress

Learning Objectives

- Explain the process of social stress as presented in the stress model, including reference to social stressors, appraisal, mediators, and stress outcomes.

- Distinguish between life events and chronic strains as they affect social stress. Identify and explain the five key types of chronic strains.

- Apply the concept "social construction of reality" to the appraisal process.

- Identify and discuss the major ways in which individuals cope with stress and use social support to deal with it.

- Explain how social class, race, sexual orientation, and gender can each affect social stress.

Few health-related concepts have captured both the research interest of scientific investigators and the popular imagination as much as "social stress." This reflects both the substantive appeal of the concept for researchers in medicine and the biological and behavioral sciences, as well as attempts by individuals to understand and take responsibility for their own health.

This chapter presents a brief description of the historical development of the concept, an introduction to the various ways stress is conceptualized, and a model of social stress that attempts to capture its causes, mediating effects, and outcomes. Current research into stress as it is related to social class, race, sexual orientation, and gender is also presented.

DEFINITION OF STRESS

The term "stress" is used in countless ways. It can refer to events or circumstances (e.g., an examination) that cause unease, to the general unease we feel during such events, to the specific bodily responses to such events (e.g., rapid

heartbeat), or to the mind's and body's attempts to deal with the unease in order to recapture a sense of wellness.

Most researchers include in the concept of stress some reference to the resulting state in an individual who has experienced various demands. Stoklos (1986:35) defines **stress** as "a state of imbalance within a person, elicited by an actual or perceived disparity between environmental demands and the person's capacity to cope with these demands." Stress occurs in response to "strainful and threatening circumstances in the environment" and has clearer boundaries than states such as anxiety or depression, which are more global, more diffuse, and may exist "even in the absence of specific threats" (Pearlin and Schooler, 1978:4).

HISTORICAL DEVELOPMENT OF THE STRESS CONCEPT

The idea of stress has existed for centuries. As discussed in Chapter 2, such historical luminaries as Hippocrates believed in the humoral theory of illness—that positive health results from a mind and body in harmony—and this is perhaps the earliest characterization of an individual who is not "stressed out." Hippocrates' belief in the self-healing powers of the body is also consistent with an understanding of the body's adaptation to stress.

Historical records indicate that in the fourteenth century the term was equated with hardship and affliction, and in nineteenth-century medicine stress was cited as a cause of ill health, as many diseases were attributed by physicians to conditions of "melancholia," "grief," or "despair." Clearly, by the 1800s, there was widespread recognition of the link between mind and body.

Ironically, Pasteur's demonstration that bacteria cause disease (the germ theory of disease) led many physicians and medical researchers to confine their attention to such germ-caused diseases in the hope of finding specific disease etiology and appropriate "magic bullets." In doing so, many of them abandoned interest in the less concrete areas of attitudes and emotions.

Walter Cannon and Hans Selye

Early in the twentieth century, Walter Cannon, an American physiologist, used the term **homeostasis** to describe a state in which the body's physiological processes are in balance and properly coordinated. He identified many highly specific physiological (adaptive) changes made by the body in response to hunger, thirst, extreme cold, pain, and intense emotions.

Cannon described a "fight or flight" reaction. When circumstances offered the opportunity for success (or there was no choice), humans would fight; in the face of overwhelming odds, they would seek flight. Physiological changes such as sugar entering the bloodstream to provide a rapid source of energy, heavy breathing to provide

more oxygen, and acceleration of the heart to provide more fuel and oxygen occur to enhance the individual's reaction.

However, Cannon noted that whereas this resource mobilization was functional for early humans, today it is often activated when it is not useful—on a first date, for example—and may be harmful as it exhausts the individual.

Hans Selye, an endocrinologist at McGill University, is often cited as the classic figure in stress research. Hoping to discover a new sex hormone, Selye experimentally injected laboratory rats with hormones. Typical reactions were enlarged adrenal glands, shrunken immune systems, and bleeding ulcers. To confirm these effects, he injected non-hormonal substances into a control group of rats and, surprisingly, observed a similar reaction. He realized that the response was a general reaction rather than a substance-specific one. The physiological reaction was termed "stress," and the trio of responses (alarm, adaptation, and exhaustion) was called the "general adaptation syndrome."

Based on this work, Selye eventually pinpointed a truth with which people could immediately identify—in our daily lives, we all experience stressful situations. These situations upset our body's equilibrium—our homeostasis—and make us more susceptible to mild diseases and illnesses. If stressful situations persist over an extended period, the body's resources become depleted and more severe disease or illnesses—or even death—may result.

A MODEL OF SOCIAL STRESS

Several researchers have developed models to describe the processes involved in stress. The model presented in Figure 5.1 is influenced by several of these models, but especially by Morton Lieberman (1982), Pearlin and Aneshensel (1986), and Pearlin and Bierman (2013).

While stress is a broad intellectual concept, this model highlights the importance of using the sociological perspective to understand the following:

1. The nature and dynamics of how social forces and circumstances (stressors) create stressful situations.
2. How the perception or appraisal of stressors affects the manner in which they are handled.
3. How the appraisal of stressors affects the enactment of social roles (and strain created in these roles).
4. How social resources influence the likelihood of stressful circumstances occurring, the appraisal of these circumstances, the extent to which role enactment is problematic, the ability of individuals to cope and the coping mechanisms they use, and the extent to which the stressful circumstances result in negative stress outcomes.

Figure 5.1   A Model of the Stress Process

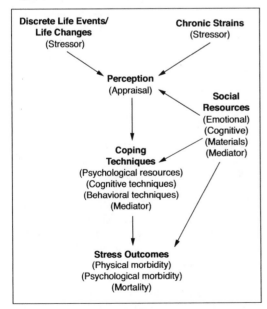

STRESSORS

Many sociologists focus attention on understanding social stressors—that is, social factors that contribute to stress. These factors range from broad social forces (for example, a war or severe economic downturn) to individuals' personal social environments (for example, divorce or loss of someone close).

Stressors and the Sociological Perspective

Attempts to understand human behavior must consider the importance of broader social forces and social organization. A key insight of sociology is that all human behavior, even that which seems very individualistic, is shaped by larger forces in the social environment.

As an example, the French sociologist Émile Durkheim (1858–1917) helped stimulate interest in identifying ways in which individual behaviors are shaped by larger social forces. In his book *Suicide*, first published in 1897 (and translated in 1951), Durkheim focused on what might seem the most individual of human behaviors and described how it is influenced by social forces. Durkheim asked the following questions: If suicide is an entirely personal, individual behavior, why do rates of suicide vary from one social group to another? Why are suicide rates higher among men than women, among the unmarried than the married, and among Protestants than Catholics? And why do patterns in suicide rates persist over time?

Durkheim found his answer in the extent and nature to which individuals were integrated into a group or society. On this basis, he explained suicide as being most likely to occur (1) when an individual is insufficiently integrated within a group and has few social bonds (e.g., an elderly person whose lifetime partner dies and who feels as if there is little reason to go on living), (2) when an individual identifies so strongly with a social group that they are willing to sacrifice their life for the group (e.g., a kamikaze pilot), or (3) when an individual feels a sense of normlessness during times when society's norms and values are undergoing upheaval or rapid change (e.g., during periods of rapid economic upturn or downturn). Durkheim's analysis is an excellent example of the **sociological imagination** (see Chapter 1)—the ability to see how personal troubles (e.g., thoughts of suicide) are influenced by wider social forces (e.g., changes in the state of the economy or the extent of social integration). We take this same perspective to understand social stress. The accompanying box, "Are Cell Phones a Social Stressor? The Impact of Cultural Change," provides an example of individual lifestyle (and stress) affected by a technological change.

IN THE FIELD

ARE CELL PHONES A SOCIAL STRESSOR? THE IMPACT OF CULTURAL CHANGE

Sociologists and psychologists often demonstrate how global events and changes in culture and social structure affect levels of stress (Wheaton and Montazer, 2009). But could a technological change as simple as the cell phone be part of stress-producing cultural change? Consider the following:

1. *Cell phones are one example (but only one example) of the accelerating rate of new technologies within society.* Ask yourself what technologies exist in society today that did not exist when your parents were your age. Consider the fields of medicine, communication, information technology, transportation, and recreation. Changes within these areas and others represent some of the most transformative changes ever within our society.

2. *Cell phones are a major contributor to peoples' constant accessibility and corresponding decline in privacy.* When the parents of today's 18- to 25-year-olds were in college, the most common form of communication with family and friends back home was a personal letter, and a common source of information was the hard-copy (a term that did not exist) encyclopedia. With the speeding up of communication by e-mail, texting, tweeting, twittering, and social networking, we are now almost constantly "on." We can "connect" to almost anyone immediately, and we are constantly available to others. Information about anything is almost immediately available to us, and information about us is easily accessible by others. Menzies (2005) in *No Time: Stress and the Crisis of Modern Life* refers to this as the decline of the "face-to-face world" and the emergence of the "hyperworld." Agus (2011) asserts that these technologies allow even very short periods of time to be productive or entertaining. By constantly keeping our brains busy with digital input, we are missing out on the benefits of downtime—allowing the brain to process, to create, and even to rest.

3. *Cell phones contribute to the compression of time and space.* Work occupies an increasing part of our lives while leisure time diminishes. We feel pressure to multitask in order to accomplish things simultaneously. We need constantly changing images to retain our attention. Reading of books has declined. Life is more fragmented. A comment from your bf may cause u 2 lol. Altheide (1995) states that "An increasing array of life is processed rather than lived, recorded rather than remembered and tracked rather than understood." Trying to keep up makes it

difficult not to exceed your "optimal level of stimulation."

4. *The benefits and problems associated with cell phone use are interrelated with use of social media.* In 2018, there were just over 3 billion social media users worldwide. In the United States, an area of highest penetration along with East Asia, there were about 244 million users. Facebook was the largest platform (2.2 billion worldwide accounts) followed by YouTube and WhatsApp (very popular in Latin America and among US Latinos and owned by Facebook). Eighty-eight percent of 18–29 year-olds use at least one social media form, as do 78 percent of those 30 to 49, 64 percent of those 50 to 64, and 37 percent of those age 65 and older. Use of Snapchat, Instagram, and Twitter is much higher among 18- to 24-year-olds than older groups.

Research has found that early fears of mass addiction have not materialized (although 4 out of 5 teens sleep or used to sleep with their cell phone under their pillow) and that it is not social media itself but rather the pattern and frequency of use that sometimes create serious problems. This "problematic social media use" (PMSU) has been linked for a minority of users to problems such as interference with real-life relationships, participation in dangerous activities such as checking social media while driving, and an increased likelihood of mental health issues such as depression, anxiety, and loneliness (Ariel et al., 2017).

The cell phone industry itself is not very popular; it receives more complaints than any other industry. It is not clear whether adults or teens will be more likely to access a new website created by Consumers Union, called EscapeCellHell.org.

Types of Stressors

Sociologists have distinguished between two major types of stressors: specific **life events** and more enduring life problems called **chronic strains**.

Life Events.   Life events are important specific events or experiences that interrupt an individual's usual activities and require some adjustment. These may be either anticipated (or scheduled) life events (e.g., marriage, divorce, or the beginning or ending of a school year) or unanticipated (unscheduled) life events (e.g., the death of a loved one, a sudden failure, or the sudden loss of a job). Research has begun to explore the importance of anticipatory events—that is, those that might happen in the future (e.g., failing out of school or being a victim of a crime). The very anticipation of such events might be a stressor in itself.

One popular scale—the Social Readjustment Rating Scale (Holmes and Rahe, 1967)—contains a list of 43 events that were evaluated by a panel of judges with regard to the level of readjustment that each required. The most stressful life events were identified as the death of a spouse, divorce, marital separation, and a jail term. At the other end of the scale were minor violations of the law, Christmas, and vacations.

Does experiencing undesirable life events have a negative impact on health? Yes, although even in cases of a traumatizing life event, the effect typically does not persist over a long period of time. Researchers do continue to detect a relationship between adverse life events and certain depressive disorders, but the effects are not large and they generally dissipate within 3 months.

Chronic Strains.   The second major type of stressor—chronic strains—refers to the relatively enduring problems, conflicts, and threats people face in their daily lives. These include family problems with partners, parents, or children; love or sex problems; problems at work or in school; and problems in any site that involves competition. These are likely to be important problems because they involve major social roles and extremely important social relationships. Pearlin (1989) uses the term "role strain" to refer to these problems. The five most common types of role strain are listed here.

1. *Role overload* occurs when the combination of all the role demands placed on an individual exceed that individual's ability to meet them. College students who add several activities (such as employment, club participation, athletics, and a serious relationship) to studying often feel role overload. So also might employees who are assigned more work than they can handle and adults adding caregiving responsibilities of elderly parents to house maintenance, food preparation, and child-rearing.

2. *Interpersonal conflicts within role sets* include problems and difficulties that arise within complementary role sets, such as wife–husband, parent–child, and worker–supervisor. These are the types of strain that often touch people most deeply. Marriage (or other long-term relationship) is typically the center of our most intimate relationships, the context of many of our most far-reaching decisions (e.g., about children, major purchases, degree of egalitarianism), and the role set in which many spend the most time. Therefore, interpersonal conflict in the form of marital dissatisfaction, emotional and physical abuse, and separation and divorce are especially troubling.

   Pearlin (1983) identified specific sources of strain in marriages: (1) a perception that the spouse does not recognize or accept "quintessential" elements of one's self—that he or she fails to authenticate what is judged to be an especially prized aspect of the self-image; (2) a belief that the spouse is failing to fulfill basic marital expectations such as wage earning or housekeeping; (3) a feeling that the spouse is failing to provide even minimal levels of affection or that sexual relations are insufficiently satisfying; and (4) a belief that reciprocity has broken down—that one partner is investing more in the relationship than the other and that one is more thoughtful of the other.

3. *Inter-role conflict* occurs when the demands of two or more roles held by a person are incompatible, and these demands cannot simultaneously be met. On a small scale, genuine conflict occurs whenever any health care worker is "on call" and gets called to the hospital just as he or she is about to participate in a family function (e.g., a child's dance recital or school play). Being a responsible health care worker *and* a loving parent are both very important roles, but on the night in question the child will be disappointed. In a marriage of two people who are equally dedicated to their careers, an elderly parent or young child who requires significant attention during the day will force some resolution of an inter-role conflict.

4. *Role captivity* is the term used by Pearlin to describe situations in which an individual is in an unwanted role—that is, the person feels an obligation to do one thing but prefers to do something else (Pearlin, 1983). A retired person who wishes to continue working and a person who is working but wishes to retire are both held in role captivity. A college student who is forced by parents to attend college and a college-age person who wants to go to college but cannot afford it are both role captives. The captive situation can also occur within families. Feeling trapped in an unhappy marriage can be an extremely stressful situation. Sometimes children in families can be role captives, as is illustrated by the stressfulness of growing up in a family with parental alcoholism.

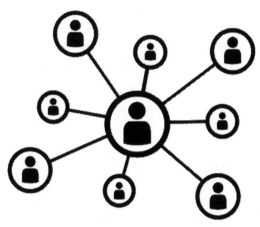

Sociological research increasingly shows that participation in positive social relationships is an important contributor to good physical and mental health and can play a significant role in recovering from illness.

Source: © djvstock/Fotolia.

5. *Role restructuring* occurs in situations in which long-established patterns or expectations undergo considerable restructuring. Pearlin (1989) offers such examples as a rebellious adolescent who desires more independence, an apprentice who grows frustrated with her mentor, and adult children who assume increased responsibilities for aging parents. He notes that the transition can be more difficult when it is forced by circumstances (rather than voluntary effort), and when the transition involves redistribution of status, privilege, or influence over others.

Of course, not all chronic stressors are related to problems carrying out one's roles. Pearlin (1989) also refers to "ambient stressors"—those that do not attach to any particular role. An example would be living in a very noisy place.

Three final points about life events and chronic strains deserve attention:

1. Chronic strains are a more powerful determinant of depressive disorders and other health problems than are discrete life events. Their persistence, emergence in important areas such as marriage and work, and presence throughout the course of each day give them powerful force within our lives.

2. Valid and reliable measurement of chronic strains is especially complicated. For example, it may be difficult to determine the actual "chronicity" of a strain. Interpersonal conflict within a marriage is rarely a linear phenomenon—it often ebbs and flows, sometimes swinging back and forth between happiness and sadness, and does so with uneven intensity. How then does one accurately measure the length of time for which discord has occurred?

3. Life events and chronic strains may accumulate over time and often overlap. Specific life events may alter the existence or meaning of chronic strains. An example is the effect of sudden job loss (a discrete life event) on division of labor within the household (possibly a chronic strain). Moreover, life events may create new strains or magnify existing strains, as when sudden job loss creates ongoing marital discord. This helps explain the fact that the cumulative amount of stress experienced during childhood can have a long-term negative impact on psychological distress and increases the risk of poor mental health later in life (Bjorkenstam et al., 2015).

APPRAISAL OF STRESSORS

Appraisal and the Sociological Perspective

As discussed in Chapter 1, **interactionists** believe that social life comprises a myriad number of episodes of daily social interactions in which people communicate verbally and non-verbally and engage in a constant process of interpreting others' messages and responding to these interpretations. According to interactionism, the world is not so much imposed upon the individual, dictating or strongly influencing behavior, as it is created by the individual through the exchange of these verbal and non-verbal symbols. Berger and Luckmann (1967) assigned the term **social construction of reality** to identify this pattern.

A classic example of the interactionist perspective is found in the work of W. I. Thomas (1863–1947). Thomas recognized that individuals are affected by events only to the extent to which those events are perceived. In other words, neither life events nor chronic strains are in and of themselves stressful. They are simply situations or occurrences in which the likelihood of a stressful response is increased. It is the perception of these events and their interpretation—what an individual believes the implications of the events or strains to be—that is stressful. The **Thomas theorem** is often summarized as "if situations are defined as real, they are real in their consequences." It is the perceived world, whether it is perceived accurately or not, that becomes the basis for response (Thomas and Thomas, 1928).

The Appraisal Process. Whenever any potentially stressful life event or chronic strain occurs, we immediately evaluate or appraise its significance for us. We try to determine the effect of the situation on us. We may consider what occurred in a similar situation in the past or think about what we have heard or read about it. We may assess the availability of resources to help deal with the event. We will calculate the stressfulness of the event not only in absolute terms but also relative to whatever helping resources are available.

The appraisal process does not involve the "real" event but the individual's *perception* of the real event. To the extent that perceptions differ, individuals will respond differently to the same "real" circumstances. Being laid off from a job may be perceived by some as a tragic event, whereas others may view it as an unsolicited step in searching for a better job.

MEDIATORS OF STRESS: COPING AND SOCIAL SUPPORT

The same stressful circumstances do not lead to the same stress outcomes in all people. Other factors exist that can modify the stressor–stress outcome relationship. These additional factors are referred to as **mediators of stress**; they are so identified because research has demonstrated their potential to influence or modify (i.e., mediate) the effects of stressors. This section focuses on coping and social support—the two types of mediators that have received the most attention.

Mediators and the Sociological Perspective

Several sociological concepts and perspectives contribute to an understanding of the mediating role of coping and social support. A classic illustration of the way the social environment influences our self-image (and thus our feelings of confidence in dealing with social stress) is Charles Horton Cooley's (1864–1929) theory of the **looking-glass self**. Cooley illustrated the way that reality is socially constructed by describing the process by which each person develops a self-image. According to this theory, we come to see ourselves as we believe other people see us. Consciously or subconsciously, we attempt to interpret how we are viewed by others (and the judgment being placed on that view), and we gradually develop a self-image consistent with what we perceive (Cooley, 1964). If I believe that people with whom I interact see me as a very humorous person, I will probably see myself that way. However, if others never laugh at my jokes and convey to me that I need a sense-of-humor transplant, I'm not likely to see myself as being very funny.

Coping

Coping refers to the personal responses that people make in order to prevent, avoid, or control emotional distress. It includes efforts to (1) eliminate or modify the stressful situation so that it will not be a continuing problem, (2) control the meaning of the problem by "cognitively neutralizing" the situation, and (3) control the stress created by the situation (e.g., through stress management techniques).

Specific Coping Techniques. There are three types of specific coping techniques—psychological resources, cognitive techniques, and behavioral techniques.

1. Psychological resources are "the personality characteristics that people draw upon to help them withstand threats posed by events and objects in their environment" (Pearlin and Schooler, 1978:5). Three such characteristics have received the most attention:

   a. Individuals with positive feelings about self—*positive self-esteem*—have been shown to cope better with stressful situations. This may be due to greater self-confidence, a feeling that one is held in high regard by others (recall Cooley's looking-glass self), and/or a real or perceived assessment of one's previous ability to handle the stressful situation (Thoits, 2013).

   b. Individuals with a feeling of being in control, controlling their own destiny, and being able to master situations (i.e., *internal control*) have been shown to cope better with stressors than individuals who see themselves as being less competent and who believe that their life is controlled by luck, fate, or outside others (i.e., *external control*). People who have a high sense of mastery of situations are less likely to report negative stress outcomes (Ross and Mirowsky, 2013).

   c. Individuals characterized by a trait referred to by Kobasa (1979) as *hardiness* are better able to handle stress. Hardy individuals exhibit a strong commitment to work, family, friends, and other causes and interests, accept change as a challenge rather than as a foe, and have a feeling of personal control over their life (internal control).

2. Cognitive techniques involve the assignment of specific interpretations to a stressful event in order to control its meaning (i.e., to neutralize its stressfulness). One might deny that the event is happening or tell oneself that the event is not as crucial as it might seem, that it will be over soon, that it might even be a good challenge, or that other people have been in this situation and survived. Many people rely on their spiritual beliefs or participation in religious activities to help them to find meaning in uncontrollable life events.

3. Behavioral techniques can also be used to help cope with a stressful event. Individuals might focus on developing and implementing a plan to reduce or eliminate the stressor. Some individuals use biofeedback or yoga or other meditative techniques to help to reduce stressfulness (research supports the health value of these techniques). Many people try to temporarily get their mind off the object of despair by engaging in an alternative, distracting activity, such as listening to music, engaging in some physical activity (increasingly, exercise is being shown by research to be an especially helpful mediator of stress, in both the short and long term), or using alcohol or some other drug. More than one of our students has resorted to the old adage, "When the going gets tough, the tough go shopping."

Are all coping techniques equally effective in all situations? The answer is no. Therefore, the larger and more varied one's coping repertoire, the more likely it is that one can cope with any stressful situation. In general, however, problem-focused strategies that deal directly with the stressor lead to more positive health outcomes than strategies that include mentally distancing oneself from the stressor, wishful thinking, self-blame, and simply emphasizing the positive. Individuals who have effective coping strategies develop confidence in their ability to deal with stressors and experience fewer uncontrollable events in their lives (Thoits, 2006).

There have been several interesting studies of the specific kinds of coping techniques used in particular circumstances. For example, Schwab (1990) identified five primary coping strategies used by married couples who had experienced the death of a child: (1) seeking a release of tension through talking, crying, exercising, and writing about the death, (2) concentrating on avoiding painful thoughts and feelings by engaging in diversionary activities such as work around the house, (3) cognitively dealing with the situation by reading materials on loss and grief, (4) helping others and/or contributing to a cause, and (5) relying on religiously based beliefs that their child is in a better place and that the family will someday be reunited.

IN THE FIELD

STRESS AND THE COPING STYLES OF COLLEGE STUDENTS

The college experience presents students with a wide range of new challenges that may lead to stress. A recent national survey of college students (American College Health Association, 2018) found that (sometimes) 87 percent felt overwhelmed by all they had to do, 83 percent felt exhausted (not by physical activity), 61 percent felt overwhelming anxiety, 52 percent felt things were hopeless, and 39 percent felt so depressed that it was difficult to function. While everyone feels stress at some times in life, these percentages are alarming and especially because they continue to increase.

A 2015 study of 67,000 college students at 108 institutions found that 1 in 4 students experiencing stress in the previous year had been diagnosed with or treated for a mental health problem. Twenty percent of all students surveyed had thought about suicide, 9 percent had attempted suicide, and nearly 20 percent had injured themselves (Liu et al., 2018). Today, about one-third of all college students seek counseling for stress at some point during their college years.

Research has determined that the most commonly identified sources of stress for college students are:

1. Increased academic demands in terms of workload and pressure to earn high marks. Research typically finds this to be the most common reason for college student stress.
2. Financial pressures including the amount of loans taken on by self or family and the pressure to get a job while attending school.

3. Diminished contact with family members especially homesickness in the first year.
4. Interpersonal relationships with roommates, romantic partners, and new friends.
5. Concerns about future plans.

Individuals feeling stress often exhibit certain signs (American Institute of Stress, 2018), including:

Emotional	Physical
Feelings of agitation or irritability	Tension headaches and other muscle pains
Inability to relate	Chest pain, rapid heartbeat, shortness of breath
Lowered self-esteem, loneliness, depression	Stomach aches, pains, nausea
Feeling overwhelmed or out of control	Shakiness, clammy or sweaty hands, tinnitus
Behavioral	**Cognitive**
Sudden change in appetite	Being forgetful and disorganized
Avoidance of tasks and responsibilities	Inability to focus or concentrate
Increased use of alcohol, smoking, or drugs	Constantly worrying
Nervous behaviors (e.g., fidgeting or nail biting)	Incessant stream of thoughts
	Difficulty with memories

Given the reported high levels of stress and the ensuing negative health outcomes, it is clear that many college students are not successfully mediating the sources of stress. This leads to the question: How do college students cope with stress? To answer this question, it is helpful to divide coping strategies into two categories: those that deal directly with the stressor and those that do not.

Much stress research has identified that coping strategies that deal directly with the stressor are most effective. Specific direct coping actions include acknowledging the existence of the stressor, accurately appraising the stressor and its potential effects, and formulating a specific plan to deal with the stressor (that is, problem-solving). Spending time with one's support network, or in more critical situations seeking out professional help, are also included here. These techniques have routinely been discovered to be most effective in controlling the potential threat and to minimizing negative health outcomes.

Unfortunately, many college students rely on coping strategies that avoid dealing directly with the stressor. These techniques include denying the existence of the stressor, avoiding thinking about the stressor, or simply ruminating about it. Over- or under-eating, using alcohol or other drugs, spending compulsively, and procrastinating with social media or streaming services are included in this category. These techniques do not typically mediate the stress-negative health outcomes relationship and may even become stressors themselves (Coiro, Bettis, and Compas, 2017; Metzger et al., 2017).

Social Support

Social support refers to resources that people receive from their social relationships and their membership in groups. This support may be (1) emotional (e.g., caring, concern, sympathy, and encouragement), (2) cognitive (e.g., information and advice useful in dealing with problems), or (3) material (e.g., child care and transportation). The most important social relationships with respect to health tend to vary over the life course—parents typically are most important for children, peer networks become increasingly important in adolescence, intimate partners are key in adulthood, and adult children often become most important in later life (Umberson, Crosnoe, and Reczek, 2010).

The Effect of Social Support on Stress and Stress Outcomes. People who have meaningful social ties and perceive positive social support tend to have better physical and mental health and are better able to adjust to such events as loss of a partner, unemployment, and criminal victimization. Conversely, people who feel that they are isolated (i.e., who feel lonely and do not have social support) or who feel socially disconnected (i.e., who have a small social network and infrequently participate in social activities) experience higher levels of physical and mental health problems (Cornwell and Waite, 2009). This effect occurs as early as adolescence, through the teenage and adult years, and into later life. In all cases, the more social ties people have, the better their health (Yang et al., 2016).

Two primary models have been developed to explain this relationship.

The **main effects model of social support** asserts that social support contributes directly to well-being and positive health, and that these beneficial effects occur even in the absence of stress. The overall sense of well-being that social support provides, the feeling of being accepted, the knowledge that others care and are available, and the degree of comfort within one's social environment may contribute to inner feelings of contentment and outer expressions of good health.

The **buffering effects model of social support** asserts that the beneficial effects of social support occur only in the presence of stress. By acting as a buffer, social support may decrease the likelihood of negative stress outcomes. The support offered by others, according to this model, provides some sense of security and confidence that stressful circumstances can be handled, and perhaps even that specific assistance in handling the situation will be available. Research has shown that people with larger social networks and stronger ties to those in their networks are better able to avoid illness and recover from it (Smith and Christakis, 2008).

Although research findings are not completely consistent, the wealth of evidence shows that both types of effects occur—that social support does contribute directly to positive health, and that it serves an important buffering effect at times of high stress (Thoits, 2011).

The complexity of the relationship between social support and stress must be emphasized. Often it is impossible to disentangle stressors and their mediators. This is something of a "double whammy"—certain circumstances both add to the stressfulness of life and detract from available social support at the same time. For example, much research has confirmed the stressfulness of unemployment and its relationship to depression. However, research has demonstrated that unemployment carries an extra burden. Following job loss, social support from one's partner and fellow workers often diminishes. At the very time when social support is especially needed, it becomes less readily offered. Thus the psychological distress traditionally linked to job loss may actually be due to both job loss and the reduction in social support that often accompanies it.

STRESS OUTCOMES

In one sense, identification of specific "outcomes" or "ills" of stress is remarkably simple—all of us can relate various ailments that we have suffered to stress. In another sense, however, making specific linkages can be quite difficult because stress leads to a wide variety of outcomes through a wide variety of pathways. In any case, it is clear that when one's level of stress cannot successfully be mediated through coping and social support, negative stress outcomes are likely to occur. In

other words, stress has a very significant impact on ill health.

In attempting to bring some order to the variety of ills produced by stress, Brown (1984) suggested the following categorization:

1. *Bona fide emotional disturbances* such as anxiety, insomnia, tension headaches, depression, neuroses, phobias, hysterias, and hypochondriasis. These are major factors in aging, sexual impotency, alcoholism, drug abuse, sleep disorders, and learning problems.

2. *Abnormal behaviors* such as compulsive behaviors, aggression, withdrawal, criminal activities, battered child/partner/parent syndrome, and sexual deviation. Some research is now beginning to examine "road rage" and other types of rage as a response to accumulated stress.

3. *Psychosomatic illnesses* such as hypertension, coronary heart disease, ulcers, and colitis.

4. *Worsening of genuine organic illnesses* such as epilepsy, migraine, herpes zoster, coronary thrombosis, and rheumatic arthritis.

Grouped somewhat differently, we might say that unchecked stress increases the likelihood of psychological morbidity (e.g., anxiety and depression), physical morbidity (e.g., coronary heart disease and cancer), and mortality (Pearlin and Aneshensel, 1986).

Pathways Between Stress and Disease

Stress responses may be produced voluntarily or involuntarily (see Figure 5.2). A sudden noise or other unanticipated event works through the hypothalamus in the brain (the center of primitive and automatic responses), which stimulates the sympathetic nervous system (and the larger brain system), which arouses the body for action. The cerebral cortex then evaluates the genuine danger presented by the stressor and determines whether the state of arousal is necessary.

Figure 5.2   The Physiological Pathways of the Stress Response

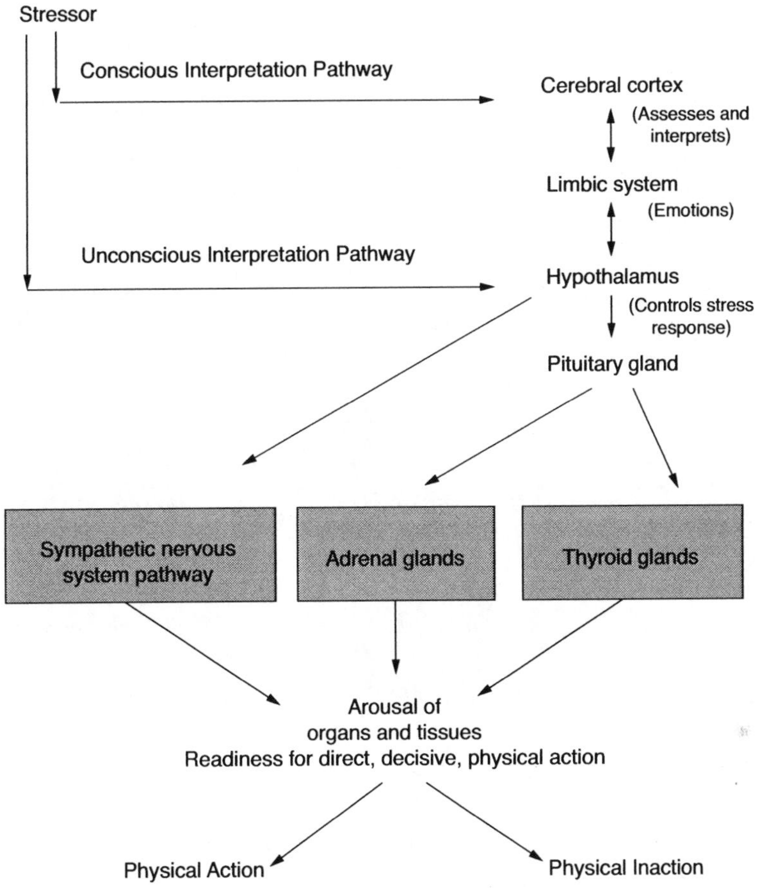

Source: Clint Bruess and Glenn Richardson. *Decisions for Health* (4th ed.). Dubuque, IA: Brown and Benchmark Publishers, 1995.

The pathway for voluntary responses begins in the cerebral cortex, which assesses and interprets the stressor, and then moves through the limbic system (the center of emotions) and the hypothalamus to the pituitary gland, which activates the adrenal glands and thyroid gland to secrete hormones to trigger the body's stress response (if that is judged to be appropriate by the cerebral cortex).

The specific responses made by the body include a sharp increase in blood pressure and increased respiration (to increase the availability of oxygen), an increase in blood sugar levels (to provide energy for muscles), increased muscle tension (to enable quick applications of strength), a release of thyroid hormone (to speed up metabolism for energy), a release of cholesterol in the blood (for endurance fuel), and a release of endorphins (the body's natural painkillers). Ultimately, stress may lead to disease through wearing down bodily organs, weakening the body's immune system, or developing health-impairing behaviors (e.g., increased cigarette smoking or alcohol consumption) in reaction to stress.

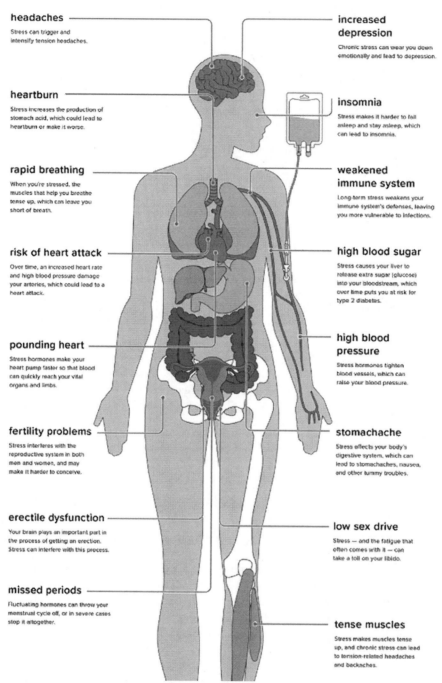

headaches
Stress can trigger and intensify tension headaches.

heartburn
Stress increases the production of stomach acid, which could lead to heartburn or make it worse.

rapid breathing
When you're stressed, the muscles that help you breathe tense up, which can leave you short of breath.

risk of heart attack
Over time, an increased heart rate and high blood pressure damage your arteries, which could lead to a heart attack.

pounding heart
Stress hormones make your heart pump faster so that blood can quickly reach your vital organs and limbs.

fertility problems
Stress interferes with the reproductive system in both men and women, and may make it harder to conceive.

erectile dysfunction
Your brain plays an important part in the process of getting an erection. Stress can interfere with this process.

missed periods
Fluctuating hormones can throw your menstrual cycle off, or in severe cases stop it altogether.

increased depression
Chronic stress can wear you down emotionally and lead to depression.

insomnia
Stress makes it harder to fall asleep and stay asleep, which can lead to insomnia.

weakened immune system
Long-term stress weakens your immune system's defenses, leaving you more vulnerable to infections.

high blood sugar
Stress causes your liver to release extra sugar (glucose) into your bloodstream, which over time puts you at risk for type 2 diabetes.

high blood pressure
Stress hormones tighten blood vessels, which can raise your blood pressure.

stomachache
Stress affects your body's digestive system, which can lead to stomachaches, nausea, and other tummy troubles.

low sex drive
Stress — and the fatigue that often comes with it — can take a toll on your libido.

tense muscles
Stress makes muscles tense up, and chronic stress can lead to tension-related headaches and backaches.

Stress can have a powerful impact on the organs throughout the body.

THE ROLE OF SOCIOECONOMIC STATUS, RACE, SEXUAL ORIENTATION, AND GENDER IN SOCIAL STRESS

Sociologists have clearly shown the importance of social structure in influencing both exposure to stressors and access to social and personal resources to deal with stressors. Studies examining the relationship between social stress and key demographic factors such as socioeconomic status, race, sexual orientation, and gender have been especially helpful. Each of these factors influences stress and the likelihood of negative health outcomes influenced by stress.

Socioeconomic Status (SES)

People with lower socioeconomic status have higher rates of psychological distress and mental health problems than the more affluent. There are two main possible explanations for this. The **exposure hypothesis** asserts that people with lower socioeconomic status are exposed to more stressful life experiences than those in the middle or upper classes, that higher rates of distress are a logical result of this exposure (Lantz et al., 2005), and that these stressful experiences (such as economic strain) are of the type that accumulate over the course of one's life (Pearlin et al., 2005).

An example would be the fact that people with more education often have less psychological distress than those with less education. People with a higher level of education tend to have higher-paying and more fulfilling jobs that offer more mental challenge and work autonomy and tend to have more economic resources (Mirowsky and Ross, 2003). A second example relates to the neighborhood in which one lives. Living in a neighborhood with abundant social stressors such as crime, harassment, and various forms of disorder and decay has been shown to increase distress and ultimately lead to negative health outcomes (Hill, Ross, and Angel, 2005). Individuals living in areas with high levels of industrial activity may stress about the industrial pollution and hazardous wastes to which they are exposed and feel a sense of powerlessness because they do not have the financial resources to relocate (Downey and Van Willigen, 2005).

The **vulnerability hypothesis** asserts that stressful life experiences have a greater impact on those with lower socioeconomic status and a greater capacity to lead to negative stress outcomes. This greater vulnerability has been traced to three factors—inadequate financial resources, greater use of ineffective coping strategies, and less access to social support networks.

First, people with lower socioeconomic status not only experience more of several stressful life events (e.g., job instability and loss, chronic health problems, and poorer quality of housing) but, by definition, they also have fewer financial resources available to deal with these problems. For example, purchasing health insurance might be a partial solution to health care worries, but financial limitations may eliminate this option.

Second, people with lower socioeconomic status are less likely to have psychological traits (e.g., high self-esteem, internal control, and confidence dealing with stressors) that buffer stress and are more likely to use ineffective coping strategies (e.g., avoidance) in responding to stressful situations. These patterns may be linked to socialization experiences. For example, growing up in a family unable to secure the health care it needs may encourage feelings of powerlessness and external control.

Third, aspects of living with low socioeconomic status may reduce the likelihood of establishing or maintaining supportive social resources. While the evidence is mixed on this point, it does appear, for example, that people with lower socioeconomic status are less likely to have a confidant on whom they can rely.

Race

For more than 30 years, research has demonstrated that African Americans have higher rates of psychological distress than whites. A key question has

IN THE FIELD

THE EFFECT OF PERCEIVED DISCRIMINATION ON HEALTH: THE IMPORTANT ROLE OF STRESS

Many social scientists have explored the meaning of discrimination, the ways it is expressed and received, its consequences, and efforts to remediate it. In general, discrimination is making a distinction in favor of or against a person based on membership in a group to which the person belongs rather than on individual merit. Discrimination has been embedded in America since its founding, and countless instances still occur based on age, gender, race, ethnicity, sexual orientation, religion, gender identity, body shape and size and countless other factors.

A vast scholarly literature shows that exposure to discrimination is very stressful. This occurs whether the discrimination is institutional—that is, built into society's institutions in the form of educational or employment discrimination—or interpersonal—that is, discrimination that occurs between people at the personal level (Williams, 2018). Studies have consistently found that experiencing discrimination is associated with both poorer physical health (such as heart disease and certain types of cancer, hypertension, and mortality) and poorer mental health (such as depression and anxiety). Even the anticipation of interacting with a prejudiced person can activate these chemical changes (Sawyer et al., 2012).

Recently, scholars have shown that stress is the (or a) key variable linking discrimination and negative health outcomes. Experiencing discrimination is stressful, and when that stress occurs, potentially health-harming chemical changes occur within the body. These include acute increases in blood pressure and heart rate, release of stress hormones (cortisol) and increase in the body's toxicity (called oxidative stress). Exposure to chronic stress can lead to wear and tear on the body and accelerate disease processes including heart disease, neural apathy, hypertension, stroke, diabetes, and atherosclerosis and increase the likelihood of depression and anxiety.

Two additional points are especially important. These negative health effects occur for all groups that experience discrimination-based stress. For example, research has shown that same-sex couples (Frost et al., 2017) and genderqueer or nonbinary college students (Jones, Mendenhall, and Myers, 2016) experience higher levels of stress and negative health outcomes in response to discrimination.

Second, research from a life course perspective continues to document that experiencing adversity, such as discrimination, early in life is associated with negative health outcomes later in life. In one study, individuals who reported facing discrimination in adolescence had worse self-reported health in a data collection almost 30 years later, whatever their experience was in adulthood (Yang et al., 2018).

been whether this difference can solely or largely be attributed to an economic disparity or whether perception of racial discrimination exerts an independent effect on stress level. Considerable research now shows that both economic standing *and* race exhibit strong effects on stress level. The second explanation is examined more fully in the accompanying box,

"The Effect of Perceived Discrimination on Health: The Important Role of Stress."

A question also emerges about the experience of individuals who hold more than one disadvantaged status. For example, a gay black man might experience prejudice and discrimination because he is black *and* because he is gay. The **double** disadvantage hypothesis asserts that people who hold more than one disadvantaged status may experience worse health than their counterparts with only one disadvantaged status or with none. The evidence with regard to this hypothesis is mixed, but recently Grollman (2014) used national survey data in the United States and found a strong relationship between holding multiple disadvantaged statuses and health. People with multiple disadvantaged statuses were more likely than others to experience major depression, poor physical health, and functional limitations. In part, this was due to a greater likelihood of exposure to interpersonal discrimination.

Sexual Orientation

In the last two decades, an increasing number of studies have focused on the physical and mental health status of lesbian, gay, bisexual, transgender, and queer (LGBTQ+) people and on the role of social stress in their health. Although research samples have often been small, research has found that sexual minorities have more physical and mental health problems than heterosexuals. Several scholars have identified the stress associated with being a sexual minority in a hetero–normative society as underlying these health differences (e.g., Frost, Lehavot, and Meyer, 2015).

Ueno (2010) identified six specific mechanisms that contribute to this greater stress, including an increased likelihood of experiencing:

1. Physical and sexual victimization
2. Discrimination (including name-calling and job discrimination)
3. Negative life events (including job loss and friendship dissolution)
4. Chronic strains (including arguments with parents)
5. A deficiency in psychosocial resources (including family rejection)
6. A deficiency in psychological resources (including lower self-esteem and possible internalization of others' homophobia).

Green (2008) studied the path by which these mechanisms affect sexual minorities. He found that urban gay men faced significant stressors in their everyday lives, including avoidance by others, stigmatization, and rejection. These stressors led directly to lowered self-esteem, a perceived lack of social support, and a decrease in feelings of personal control, which led to greater feelings of anxiety and depression.

In addition, recent studies of the role of stress in the lives of transgender people have found they frequently feel stigmatized in health care encounters; they find that medical providers have not received training in dealing with their particular needs and thus interact with them with ambivalence and uncertainty, and that these experiences push transgender persons away from receiving adequate medical care. This also leads to higher rates of negative health experiences (Hughto, Reisner, and Pachankis, 2015). The extra stress and extra difficulties in obtaining appropriate medical care due to being in a sexual minority group clearly affect morbidity and mortality. These extra stressors may also lead to higher rates of health-damaging behaviors among sexual minorities, such as drug and alcohol use.

There is even a clear-cut influence of the level of anti-gay prejudice in the community in which one lives and negative health outcomes for sexual minority group members. Studies show elevated risks of depression, cardiovascular diseases, suicide, and homicide for gay, lesbian, bisexual, transgendered, and queer people living in communities with high levels of prejudice against them. One study found that these differences translated into a shorter life expectancy (by approximately 12 years) for sexual minority group members living in areas with high levels of prejudice (Hatzenbuehler et al., 2014). This is consistent with research that found that same-sex couples living in states with legally sanctioned marriage reported better health than those living in states with antigay constitutional amendments (Kail, Acosta, and Wright, 2015).

Gender

Women have higher rates (perhaps double) of psychological distress and depression than men. As Rosenfield (1989:77) summarized, these differences are found "across cultures, over time, in different age groups, in rural as well as urban areas, and in treated as well as untreated populations." Consistently, these differences are greater among the married than the unmarried, although distress is greater in women regardless of marital status.

As important as this pattern is, only recently has significant attention been focused on women as subjects in stress research. This lack of attention has been especially obvious in the area of occupational health research, where early research on women was often conducted primarily in order to secure a better understanding of men's stress. The consequence of this inattention is that much remains to be learned about the reasons for the high rates of distress in women.

A wide variety of plausible explanations for the gender disparity in stress have been advanced and tested.

1. Women are exposed to more discrete, stressful life events than are men. This differential exposure hypothesis has not been supported by most research studies. However, Marchand et al. (2016), in a study of 2,000 workers in 63 workplaces, did find evidence that women employees were less likely to utilize their skill set on the job, and were more likely to be overqualified for their job, to be employed part-time, and to juggle work obligations to fulfill home obligations. Women's greater likelihood of taking on a caregiver role necessitating some change in work status also supports this explanation.

2. Women include more people in their social network, care more about these people, and are more emotionally involved in the lives of people around them. Consequently, they are more apt to feel stress when others in their network are feeling stress (Kessler and McLeod, 1984). Women are more likely than men to be both providers and recipients of support, although both men and women rely more on women for support during stressful times. Whereas married women use both their spouse and their friends as confidants, married men tend to rely solely on their wives (Edwards, Nazroo, and Brown, 1998).

3. Women are more vulnerable than men to stress due to their socialization to respond more passively, to introject rather than to express anger, and to use less effective coping skills (Kessler and McLeod, 1984). There is some research to support this notion. However, countering this research is the fact that women appear to cope with many crises as well as or better than men (e.g., women typically deal better with the death of a partner, with financial difficulties, and with marital separation and divorce).

4. Continuing power differences between women and men in society and within many families lead to gender disparity in distress. Women's relative lack of decision-making power within the family and the lesser resources and decreased prestige attached to the conventional feminine role of housewife cause and reflect this power differential. How does this affect psychological state?

   Low power implies less actual control over the environment and thus lower perceptions of personal control. With diminished assessments of their ability to act on and affect their social world, individuals experience greater psychological distress. Thus . . . women have higher rates of anxious and depressive symptoms because their positions of lower power produce lower actual control and thus lower perceived control than those of men (Rosenfield, 1989:77–78).

5. A final perspective asserts that the size of the gender disparity in social stress has been exaggerated and misinterpreted. Aneshensel, Rutter, and Lachenbruch (1991) argue that most stress research has focused on a single disorder or

stress outcome and then has assumed that those who have this disorder are victims of stress and those without the disorder are not. For example, much of the research that found that women report higher rates of depression than men concludes that women experience more stress. However, they argue that most research has focused on outcomes that are more common in women and has neglected to study antisocial personality and alcohol abuse—dependence disorders more common among men. If the full gamut of stress outcomes is considered, women and men may be found to experience comparable levels of stress.

Gender, Work, and Psychological Distress. These explanations suggest that women's level and type of participation in the workplace exert much influence on the gender disparity in distress. This leads to an avenue for study, namely comparing women who are full-time workers outside the home (both married and unmarried) with those who are employed part time and those who are not employed outside the home. If it is simply a matter of "social roles," the benefits and liabilities of working should be the same for men and women. If, on the other hand, the effects of employment for men and women are different, then the influence of gender is more apparent.

Studies addressing these questions have not always produced a coherent picture. Some research has found a reduced disparity in gender distress when the wife is employed, but other research has not. Moreover, some research that identifies smaller differences traces them to increased distress in men rather than a decrease in distress in women. Most research has pointed to positive effects for women who work outside the home, but other research has failed to find differences between employed women and housewives. Even when such a difference is discovered, both groups of women have higher distress scores than employed men. The accompanying box, "Does Marriage Lead to More or Less Stress?" adds to this discussion.

Efforts to sort through these research findings have produced three primary perspectives—role overload, role enhancement, and role context. The "role overload" perspective asserts that there is only so much time and energy available in the day. When women have to combine homemaking, child-rearing, and full-time employment responsibilities, there is role overload—too much work and too many responsibilities, which is obviously a stressful situation. The same combination of activities may not overload men because they engage in fewer homemaking and child-rearing activities—even when their partner is employed. Because many women feel primary responsibility for household obligations, and many men do not, it can be more psychologically distressing for women to occupy the multiple roles of partner, parent, and worker.

This same pattern exists relative to work obligations outside normal work hours. Does the frequency of receiving work-related contact outside of normal working hours (potential inter-role conflict) create guilt for individuals? The answer is yes, but these consequences occur for women only—men feel much less resentment (Glavin, Schieman, and Reid, 2011).

The "role enhancement perspective" asserts that the more roles any person fulfills, the greater are the opportunities for social contacts, satisfaction, and self-esteem, and consequently better health and psychological well-being. According to this theory, feelings of anxiety or depression ought to be inversely related to the number of role involvements. This may occur directly or indirectly as contacts made through employment often become the most important non-kin source of social support for women who work outside the home.

The third perspective—the "role context perspective"—asserts that employment outside the home has neither inherently positive nor inherently negative consequences for stress level, but rather it is dependent on particular factors within the personal, family, and work environments, and on the

IN THE FIELD

DOES MARRIAGE LEAD TO MORE OR LESS STRESS?

Married people report less stress than those who are not married (see Figure 5.3).

Compared with married adults of the same age, those who are single, cohabiting, divorced, or widowed all have higher levels of psychological distress, anxiety, and depression. (Very young married adults are the only exception—they report as much depression as their unmarried counterparts.) This relationship is strong and cannot be explained by a selection factor (i.e., that those with higher well-being are more likely to get married) (Mirowsky and Ross, 2003).

Why does this relationship occur? The most important reason is that married people have higher-quality, more supportive relationships. They receive more emotional support—a greater sense of being cared about, loved, esteemed, and valued as a person. Although there is much

Figure 5.3   Marital Status and Health

Healthfully Married

Married adults tend to be healthier than divorced, widowed or never married adults, a new report from the Centers for Disease Control and Prevention suggests.

Percentage of adults in fair or poor health by age and marital status, 1999–2002

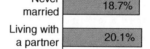

45–64 YEARS

Married	12.8%
Widowed	24.9%
Divorced or separated	20.7%
Never married	18.7%
Living with a partner	20.1%

18–44 YEARS

Married	4.5%
Widowed	14.1%
Divorced or separated	10.5%
Never married	5.2%
Living with a partner	6.8%

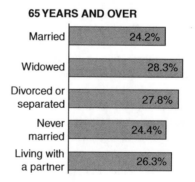

65 YEARS AND OVER

Married	24.2%
Widowed	28.3%
Divorced or separated	27.8%
Never married	24.4%
Living with a partner	26.3%

NOTE: Fair or poor health status is based on the question, "Would you say [person's] health is excellent, very good, good, fair or poor," results based on interviews with 127,545 adults.

Source: Centers for Disease Control and Prevention. "Marital Status and Health: United States, 1999–2002." Advance Data, Number 351 (Atlanta, GA: Centers for Disease Control and Prevention, 2004).

variation, in general they are happier in their personal relationships. Married people are also more likely to experience economic well-being and less likely to experience economic hardship or crisis (Mirowsky and Ross, 2003).

Is it better to be happily single than unhappily married? The answer is yes. Studies show that it is healthier to live alone than with a partner who does not provide supportive qualities. One 12-year study found that happily married women in their forties and fifties were less likely to develop heart disease and stroke than their single counterparts, but that single women were less likely to develop these conditions than the unhappily married (Troxel et al., 2005). Over the last few decades, the health of single individuals has become more

similar to that of married people, while the health of the widowed, divorced, and separated compared with married people has gotten even worse (Liu and Umberson, 2008).

Do men and women benefit equally from marriage in terms of health? The answer is no. Although both benefit, men benefit more. There are three main reasons for this. (1) Women experience greater child-rearing stress because they often have primary child-rearing responsibility. (2) Women more often experience work–family conflict because they have more child-rearing responsibilities whether or not they are employed outside the home. (3) Wives tend to provide more emotional support for husbands than husbands do for wives.

"meaning" attached to work and familial roles (Simon, 1997). What are these additional factors?

1. *The woman's desire to work outside the home.* Waldron and Herold (1986) demonstrated the importance of attitude toward the effects of employment. Based on a national sample of middle-aged women, they found that for women who desired to work outside the home, employment had beneficial effects and non-employment had detrimental effects. No specific effects were noted for women who had unfavorable or neutral attitudes toward outside employment.

2. *The woman's perception of the balance of benefits and liabilities in outside employment.* The greater the "role integration"—that is, the balance of role satisfaction and role stress within and between roles—the greater the sense of well-being. Thoits (1986) posits a curvilinear relationship between the number of role involvements and well-being—that is, there is role enhancement up to a certain threshold, whereupon role overload begins. Well-being is also affected by the compatibility of the work role with other roles (e.g., child care), the extent to which each can be handled, and

the amount of spousal support received for the work career.

For women, the presence of young children reduces the mental health benefits of full- and part-time employment, but the positive benefits increase as children get older. For men, the presence of young children does not affect the level of employment-related mental health benefits. This is consistent with the idea that women's lives more than men's lives are shaped around the needs and experiences of others, including spouses and children. We can understand the effect of employment on mental health for men without knowing about their children, but for women, employment benefits are very much related to whether or not there are young children in the family (Leupp, 2017).

In addition, perception of the trajectory of one's work career (whether one perceives career movement in an upward or downward direction, and whether one perceives responsibilities and compensation to be appropriate for one's position) affects work satisfaction and ultimately health. Both objective and subjective occupational mobility predict health patterns—upward mobility is associated with better health, and downward mobility is associated with worse health. However, perception of mobility is the better predictor (Wilkinson, Shippee, and Ferraro, 2012).

3. *Qualities of the work environment itself.* Because women, on average, occupy lower-level work positions than men, they are subject to greater stress relative to work conditions, mistreatment, sexual harassment, and job instability. Lower-level positions often offer less work autonomy or control, and have less work complexity. Work complexity refers to the amount of variability in the job and is an indicator of its degree of challenge, its level of interest, the extent to which it is psychologically gratifying, and the likelihood that it will contribute to the individual's self-esteem (Pugliesi, 1995). These job factors are related to higher levels of psychological distress.

Even when women move into positions of increased job authority, they do not necessarily experience the same benefits as men. Pudrovska and Karraker (2014) studied the relationship between gender, job authority, and depression. They defined job authority as having the ability to hire and fire and to influence pay. As expected, they found that men without authority in their position were more likely to experience depression than men in authority positions. However, the reverse was found for women—those without job authority were less depressed than women with job authority.

What could cause this contrary pattern? The authors contend that the difference is due to gendered cultural expectations for men and women in the workplace. The exercise of job authority may be seen as consistent with traditional masculine stereotypes that emphasize power, ambition, and dominance. For women, however, exercising job authority may be inconsistent with traditional normative expectations, such as nurturance, empathy, and attachment. This may lead to a workplace that is more accepting of men authorities than of women authorities—a situation that increases stress and has a negative impact on health for women decision makers.

Women's perception of gender discrimination at work adds another important source of stress for women that is linked with negative health outcomes (Pavalko, Mossakowski, and Hamilton, 2003). In a comparison of male and female employees from three national surveys, Harois and Bastos (2018) found that among women, perceptions of gender discrimination, and to a certain extent, sexual harassment, are significantly and negatively associated with self-reported health. Women with such workplace experiences did report both poorer mental health and poorer physical health. Moreover, women with multiple forms of mistreatment reported even worse mental and physical health. The authors concluded that gender-based workplace mistreatment continues to explain some of the gap between men and women in health.

SUMMARY

Stress is defined as "a state of imbalance within a person, elicited by an actual or perceived disparity between environmental demands and the person's capacity to cope with these demands." The configuration of the stress process can be stated in this way: Various stressful situations (or stressors) occur and are appraised by the individual as to their degree of threat. Individuals are forced to cope with those involving some threat; stressors that are unsuccessfully resolved lead to negative stress outcomes. Throughout the process, social support can help to mediate the stress–stress outcome relationship.

Stressors are of two basic types—specific life events and chronic strains (the latter being more enduring problems in everyday life). Pearlin has classified chronic strains according to problems created in discharging our role obligations: (1) role overload, (2) interpersonal problems within role sets, (3) inter-role conflict, (4) role captivity, and (5) role restructuring and to ambient stressors—those that are enduring but not tied to occupancy of a particular role.

Interpretation and appraisal of stressors are key aspects of the stress process. It is the perceived threat, rather than the actual threat, to which a person responds. If a threat is perceived, the individual may activate certain coping responses (psychological, cognitive, and behavioral techniques) from his or her repertoire and also use social support. Negative stress outcomes occur when individuals engage in health-impairing behaviors, such as cigarette smoking, or because of specific psychophysiological changes, including weakening of the immune system.

Certain groups have higher rates of psychological distress—those with lower socioeconomic status (who are exposed to more stressful life events and have fewer resources with which to combat them), African Americans, sexual minorities, and women (possibly due to women being exposed to more stressful life events, caring more about others' problems, being especially vulnerable to stress due to the effects of socialization, and responding to having less access to power within families and within society). Employment affects stress level differently for women than for men; this may be due to the fact that women often maintain primary responsibility for household tasks and child-rearing, even when they are in the labor force.

HEALTH ON THE INTERNET

A significant trend in the United States is the rapidly increasing number of households that are caring for elderly relatives (often taking them into their homes). More than 44 million Americans (more than 1 in 5) provide this caregiving today—a collective 37 billion hours of unpaid caregiving worth US$470 billion. Ten million of these caregivers are "millennials" (aged 18 to 34 years) who are caring for adult family members. The number is expected to increase in the coming years. This trend is a consequence of both the increasing number of people living into their eighties and nineties, often with limitation on their ability to care for themselves, *and* the very high cost of assisted living and nursing home care. Research has found that providing care often has

a negative impact on both the physical and mental health of the caregiver.

To learn more about the relationship between caregiving and social stress, check out the following:

  https://www.womenshealth.gov/a-z-topics/
  caregiver-stress

Answer the following questions: How is "caregiver" defined? Who provides caregiving services? What activities do caregivers often provide?

What is **caregiver stress**? What are the signs and symptoms of caregiver stress? How does caregiver stress affect health? What can caregivers do to prevent or relieve stress?

DISCUSSION CASE

The stress process as it relates to socioeconomic status, race, sexual orientation, and gender was discussed in this chapter. Think about social stress

as it relates to racial and ethnic minorities and women students at your college or university. Are racial/ethnic minority and/or women students more likely (or less likely) to face any particular stressful discrete life events than those faced by all students? Are racial/ethnic minority and/or women students more likely (or less likely) to face any of the five sources of chronic strain (role overload, interpersonal conflicts within role sets, inter-role conflict, role captivity, and role restructuring) or ambient stressors than those faced by all students?

Do racial/ethnic minority students cope with stress or use social support differently than other students? Do women students cope with stress or use social support differently than men students?

GLOSSARY

buffering effects model of social support
caregiver stress
chronic strains
coping
discrimination
double disadvantage hypothesis
exposure hypothesis
homeostasis
interactionism
life events

looking-glass self
main effects model of social support
mediators of stress
social construction of reality
social support
sociological imagination
stress
Thomas theorem
vulnerability hypothesis

REFERENCES

Agus, David B. 2011. *The End of Illness*. New York: Free Press.

Altheide, David. 1995. *An Ecology of Communication: Cultural Formats of Control*. Piscataway, NJ: Aldine Transaction.

American College Health Association. 2018. *National College Health Assessment II: Fall 2017 Reference*. Hanover, MD: American College Health Association.

American Institute of Stress. 2018. "Stress Effects." Retrieved December 4, 2019 (www.stress.org/stress-effects#50).

Aneshensel, Carol S., Carolyn M. Rutter, and Peter A. Lachenbruch. 1991. "Social Structure, Stress, and Mental Health: Competing Conceptual and Analytic Models." *American Sociological Review* 56(2):166–178.

Ariel, Shensa, Cesar G. Escobar-Viera, Jaime E. Sidani, Nicholas D. Bowman, Michael P. Marshal, and Brian A. Primack. 2017. "Problematic Social Media Use and Depressive Symptoms Among United States Young Adults: A Nationally Representative Sample." *Social Science and Medicine* 82(June):150–157.

Berger, Peter L., and Thomas Luckmann. 1967. *The Social Construction of Reality: A Treatise in the Sociology of Knowledge*. Garden City, NY: Anchor Books.

Bjorkenstam, Emma, Bo Burstrom, Lars Brannstrom, Bo Vinnerljung, Charlotte Bjorkenstam, and Anne R. Pebley. 2015. "Cumulative Exposure to Childhood Stressors and Subsequent Psychological Distress." *Social Science and Medicine* 142(October):109–117.

Brown, Barbara B. 1984. *Between Health and Illness*. New York: Bantam Books.

Bruess, Clint, and Glenn Richardson. 1995. *Decisions for Health* (4th ed.). Dubuque, IA: Brown & Benchmark Publishers.

Centers for Disease Control and Prevention. 2004. "Marital Status and Health: United States, 1999–2002." Advance Data, Number 351. Atlanta, GA: Centers for Disease Control and Prevention.

Coiro, Mary Jo, Alexandra H. Bettis, and Bruce E. Compas. 2017. "College Students Coping with Interpersonal Stress: Examining a Control-Based Model of Coping." *Journal of American College Health* 65(3):177–186.

Cooley, Charles H. 1964. *Human Nature and the Social Order*. New York: Schocken.

Cornwell, Erin Y., and Linda J. Waite. 2009. "Social Disconnectedness, Perceived Isolation, and Health Among Older Adults." *Journal of Health and Social Behavior* 50(1):31–48.

Downey, Liam, and Marieke Van Willigen. 2005. "Environmental Stressors: The Mental Health Impacts of Living near Industrial Activity." *Journal of Health and Social Behavior* 46(3):289–305.

Durkheim, Émile. (trans.) 1951. *Suicide: A Study in Sociology*. New York: The Free Press.

Edwards, Angela C., James Y Nazroo, and George W. Brown. 1998. "Gender Differences in Marital Support Following a Shared Life Event." *Social Science and Medicine* 46(8):1077–1085.

Frost, David M., Allen J. LeBlanc, Brian de Vries, Eli Alston-Stepnitz, Rob Stephenson, and Cory Woodyatt. 2017. "Couple-Level Minority Stress: An Examination of Same-Sex Couples' Unique Experiences." *Journal of Health and Social Behavior* 58(4):455–472.

Frost, David M., Keren Lehavot, and Ilan H. Meyer. 2015. "Minority Stress and Physical Health Among Sexual Minority Group Members." *Journal of Behavioral Medicine* 38(1):1–8.

Glavin, Paul, Scott Schieman, and Sarah Reid. 2011. "Boundary-Spanning Work Demands and Their Consequences for Guilt and Psychological Distress." *Journal of Health and Social Behavior* 52(1):43–57.

Green, Adam I. 2008. "Health and Sexual Status in an Urban Gay Enclave: An Application of the Stress Process Model." *Journal of Health and Social Behavior* 49(4):436–451.

Grollman, Eric A. 2014. "Multiple Disadvantaged Statuses and Health: The Role of Multiple Forms of Discrimination." *Journal of Health and Social Behavior* 55(1):3–19.

Harois, Catherine E., and Joao L. Bastos. 2018. "Discrimination, Harassment, and Gendered Health Inequalities: Do Perceptions of Workplace Mistreatment Contribute to the Gender Gap in Self-Reported Health? *Journal of Health and Social Behavior* 59(2):283–299.

Hatzenbuehler, Mark L., Anna Bellatorre, Yeonjin Lee, Brian K. Finch, Peter Muennig, and Kevin Fiscella. 2014. "Structural Stigma and All-Cause Mortality in Sexual Minority Populations." *Social Science and Medicine* 103(February):33–41.

Hill, Terrence D., Catherine E. Ross, and Ronald J. Angel. 2005 "Neighborhood Disorder, Psychophysiological Distress, and Health." *Journal of Health and Social Behavior* 46:170–186.

Holmes, Thomas H., and Richard H. Rahe. 1967. "The Social Readjustment Rating Scale." *Journal of Psychosomatic Research* 11(2):213–218.

Hughto, Jaclyn M.W., Sari L. Reisner, and John E. Pachankis. 2015. "Transgender Stigma and Health: A Critical Review of Stigma Determinants, Mechanisms, and Interventions." *Social Science and Medicine* 147(December):222–231.

Jones, Kayla, Sarah Mendenhall, and Charlsie A. Myers. 2016. "The Effects of Sex and Gender Role Identity on Perceived Stress and Coping Among Traditional and Nontraditional Students." *Journal of American College Health* 64(3):205–213.

Kail, Ben L., Katie L. Acosta, and Eric R. Wright. 2015. "State-Level Marriage Equality and the Health of Same-Sex Couples." *American Journal of Public Health* 105(6):1101–1105.

Kessler, Ronald C., and Jane D. McLeod. 1984. "Sex Differences in Vulnerability to Undesirable Life Events." *American Sociological Review* 49(5):620–631.

Kobasa, Suzanne C. 1979. "Stressful Life Events, Personality, and Health: An Inquiry into Hardiness." *Journal of Personality and Social Psychology* 37(1):1–11.

Lantz, Paula M., James S. House, Richard P. Mero, and David R. Williams. 2005. "Stress, Life Events, and Socioeconomic Disparities in Health: Results from the Americans' Changing Lives Study." *Journal of Health and Social Behavior* 46(3):274–288.

Leupp, Katrina. 2017. "Depression, Work and Family Roles, and the Gendered Life Course." *Journal of Health and Social Behavior* 58(4):422–441.

Lieberman, Morton A. 1982. "The Effects of Social Supports on Responses to Stress." Pp. 764–783 in *Handbook of Stress: Theoretical and Clinical Aspects*, edited by Leo Goldberger and Shlomo Breznitz. New York: The Free Press.

Liu, Cindy H., Courtney Stevens, Sylvia H.M. Wong, Miwa Yasui, and Justin A Chen. 2018. "The Prevalence and Predictors of Mental Health Diagnoses and Suicide Among United States College Students: Implications for Addressing Disparities in Service Use." *Depression and Anxiety*. Retrieved December 1, 2019 (https://doi.org/10.1002/da.22830).

Liu, Hui, and Debra Umberson. 2008. "The Times They Are A Changin': Marital Status and Health Differentials from 1972 to 2002." *Journal of Health and Social Behavior* 49(3):239–253.

Marchand, Alain, Jaunathan Bilodeau, Andree Demers, Nancy Beauregard, Pierre Durand, and Victor Y. Haines. 2016. "Gendered Depression: Vulnerability or Exposure to Work and Family Stressors?" *Social Science and Medicine* 166(October):160–168.

Menzies, Heather. 2005. *No Time: Stress and the Crisis of Modern Life.* Vancouver: Douglas & McIntyre.

Metzger, Isha W., Claire Bevins, Casey D. Calhoun, Tiarney D. Ritchwood, Amanda K. Gilmore, Regan Stewart, and Kaitlin E. Bountress. 2017. "An Examination of the Impact of Maladaptive Coping on the Association Between Stressor Type and Alcohol Use in College." *Journal of American College Health* 65(8):534–541.

Mirowsky, John, and Catherine E. Ross. 2003. *Social Causes of Psychological Distress* (2nd ed.). Hawthorne, NY: Aldine de Gruyter.

Pavalko, Eliza K., Krysia N. Mossakowski, and Vanessa J. Hamilton. 2003. "Does Perceived Discrimination Affect Health? Longitudinal Relationships between Work Discrimination and Women's Physical and Emotional Health." *Journal of Health and Social Behavior* 44(1):18–33.

Pearlin, Leonard I. 1983. "Role Strains and Personal Stress." Pp. 3–32 in *Psychosocial Stress: Trends in Theory and Research*, edited by Howard B. Kaplan. New York: Academic Press.

———. 1989. "The Sociological Study of Stress." *Journal of Health and Social Behavior* 30(3):241–256.

Pearlin, Leonard I., and Carol S. Aneshensel. 1986. "Coping and Social Supports: Their Functions and Applications." Pp. 417–437 in *Application of Social Science to Clinical Medicine and Health Policy*, edited by Linda H. Aiken and David Mechanic. New Brunswick, NJ: Rutgers University Press.

Pearlin, Leonard I., and Alex Bierman. 2013. "Current Issues and Future Directions in Research into the Stress Process." Pp. 325–340 in *Handbook of the Sociology of Mental Health*, edited by Carol S. Aneshensel, Jo C. Phelan, and Alex Bierman. New York: Springer.

Pearlin, Leonard I., Scott Schieman, Elena M. Fazio, and Stephen C. Meersman. 2005. "Stress, Health, and the Life Course: Some Conceptual Perspectives." *Journal of Health and Social Behavior* 46(2):205–219.

Pearlin, Leonard I., and Carmi Schooler. 1978. "The Structure of Coping." *Journal of Health and Social Behavior* 19(1):2–21.

Pudrovska, Tetyana, and Amelia Karraker. 2014. "Gender, Job Authority, and Depression." *Journal of Health and Social Behavior* 55(4):424–441.

Pugliesi, Karen. 1995. "Work and Well-Being: Gender Differences in the Psychological Consequences of Employment." *Journal of Health and Social Behavior* 36(1):57–71.

Rosenfield, Sarah. 1989. "The Effects of Women's Employment: Personal Control and Sex Differences in Mental Health." *Journal of Health and Social Behavior* 30(1):77–91.

Ross, Catherine E., and John Mirowsky. 2013. "The Sense of Personal Control: Social Structural Causes and Emotional Consequences" Pp. 379–402 in *Handbook of the Sociology of Mental Health*, edited by Carol S. Aneshensel, Jo C. Phelan, and Alex Bierman. New York: Springer.

Sawyer, Pamela J., Brenda Major, Bettina J. Casad, Sarah S. M. Townsend, and Wendy B. Mendes. 2012. "Discrimination and the Stress Response: Psychological and Physiological Consequences of Anticipating Prejudice in Interethnic Interactions." *American Journal of Public Health* 102(5):1020–1026.

Schwab, Reiko. 1990. "Paternal and Maternal Coping with the Death of a Child." *Death Studies* 14(5):407–422.

Simon, Robin W. 1997. "The Meanings Individuals Attach to Role Identities and Their Implications for Mental Health." *Journal of Health and Social Behavior* 38(3):256–274.

Smith, Kristen P., and Nicholas A. Christakis. 2008. "Social Networks and Health." *Annual Review of Sociology* 34:405–429.

Stoklos, D. 1986. "A Congruence Analysis of Human Stress." Pp. 35–64 in *Stress and Anxiety: A Sourcebook of Theory and Research*, edited by Charles D. Spielberger and Irwin G. Sarason. Washington, DC: Hemisphere.

Thoits, Peggy A. 1986. "Multiple Identities: Examining Gender and Marital Status Differences in Distress." *American Sociological Review* 51(2):259–272.

———. 2006. "Personal Agency in the Stress Process." *Journal of Health and Social Behavior* 47(4):309–323.

———. 2011. "Mechanisms Linking Social Ties and Support to Physical and Mental Health." *Journal of Health and Social Behavior* 52(2):145–161.

———. 2013. "Self, Identity, Stress, and Mental Health." Pp. 357–377 in *Handbook of the Sociology of Mental Health*, edited by Carol S. Aneshensel, Jo C. Phelan, and Alex Bierman. New York: Springer.

Thomas, William I., and Dorothy S. Thomas. 1928. *The Child in America: Behavior Problems and Programs.* New York: Alfred A. Knopf.

Troxel, Wendy M., Karen A. Matthews, Linda C. Gallo, and Lewis H. Kuller. 2005. "Marital Quality and Occurrence of the Metabolic Syndrome in Women." *Archives of Internal Medicine* 165(9):1022–1027.

Ueno, Koji. 2010. "Mental Health Differences Between Young Adults with and Without Same-Sex Contact: A Simultaneous Examination of Underlying Mechanisms." *Journal of Health and Social Behavior* 51(4):391–407.

Umberson, Debra, Robert Crosnoe, and Corinne Reczek. 2010. "Social Relationships and Health Behavior." *Annual Review of Sociology* 36:139–157.

Waldron, Ingrid, and Joan Herold. 1986. "Employment, Attitudes toward Employment, and Women's Health." *Women and Health* 11(1):79–98.

Wheaton, Blair, and Shirin Montazer. 2009."Stressors, Stress, and Distress." Pp. 171–199 in *A Handbook for the Study of Mental Health: Social Context, Theories, and Systems* (2nd ed.), edited by Teresa L. Scheid and Tony N. Brown. New York: Cambridge University Press.

Wilkinson, Lindsay R., Tetyana P. Shippee, and Kenneth F. Ferraro. 2012. "Does Occupational Mobility Influence Health Among Working Women? Comparing Objective and Subjective Measures of Work Trajectories." *Journal of Health and Social Behavior* 53(4):432–447.

Williams, David R. 2018. "Stress and the Mental Health of Populations of Color: Advancing Our Understanding of Race-Related Stressors." *Journal of Health and Social Behavior* 59(4):466–485.

Yang, Tse-Chuan, I-Chien Chen, Seung-won Choi, and Aysenur Kurtulus. 2018. "Linking Perceived Discrimination During Adolescence to Health During Mid-Adulthood: Self-Esteem and Risk Behavior Mechanisms." *Social Science and Medicine.* Retrieved May 5, 2019 (https://doi.org/10.1016/j.socscimed.2018.06.012).

Yang, Yang C., Courtney Boen, Karen Gerkin, Ting Li, Kristen Schorpp, and Kathleen M. Harris. 2016. "Social Relationships and Physiological Determinants of Longevity across the Human Life Span." *Proceedings of the National Academy of Sciences* 113:578–583.

CHAPTER 6

Health Behavior

Learning Objectives

- Identify and define the key dimensions of "health."
- Identify and distinguish between the four dimensions of health behavior—prevention, detection, promotion, and protection.
- Explain the difference between a "macro" and a "micro" approach to understand participation in health behaviors. Discuss these factors as they relate to engaging in adequate physical exercise or smoking cigarettes.
- Distinguish between the *health belief model* and the *theory of reasoned action* in terms of the factors emphasized as being important influences on participation in health behavior.

In the last few decades, medical sociology, like the medical profession and society generally, has focused more attention on health and health-related behaviors. This has produced some important questions. What does it mean to be "healthy" or "well"? To what extent do people engage in behaviors that will promote health or prevent disease—or at least not engage in health-damaging behaviors? What are the strongest influences on participation in these positive and negative health behaviors? How do society and culture encourage people to live a healthy or non-healthy lifestyle? To what extent should public policy attempt to regulate health-enhancing and health-harming behaviors?

THE CONCEPT OF HEALTH

Health is a broad-based concept comprising several dimensions. John Ware (1986) identified six primary orientations (or dimensions) used by researchers in defining health:

1. *Physical functioning.* The physical ability to take care of oneself, being mobile and participating in physical activities, ability to perform everyday activities, and limiting the number of days confined to bed.
2. *Mental health.* Positive emotional health, psychological well-being, control of emotions and behaviors, and limiting feelings of anxiety and depression.
3. *Social well-being.* Ability to visit or speak with friends and family, and having close friends and acquaintances.
4. *Role functioning.* Freedom of limitations in discharging usual role activities, such as work or school.
5. *General health perceptions.* A positive self-assessment of current health status, and on limiting the amount of pain experienced.
6. *Symptoms.* Limiting the number of physical and psychophysiological symptoms.

The Biomedical Focus

The traditional **biomedical definition of health** focuses solely on an individual's physiological state and the presence or absence of symptoms of sickness. **Health** is defined simply as the absence of disease or physiological malfunction.

It is not a positive state but rather the absence of a negative state—if you're not sick, you're well. According to Wolinsky (1988), the biomedical model makes four primary assumptions that limit its utility for completely understanding health and illness:

1. The presence of disease and its diagnosis and treatment are all completely objective phenomena—symptoms provide accurate information from which valid diagnosis can unfailingly be made. In reality, individuals' cultural background affects not only their reaction to symptoms but also how these symptoms are reported to physicians, and the presentation of symptoms can influence diagnosis.
2. Only medical professionals are capable of defining health and illness. In reality, both the patient and his or her significant others—in addition to the physician—are involved.
3. Health and illness should be defined solely in terms of physiological malfunction. In reality, people are not merely biological beings; they are also psychological and social creatures, and health is affected by all three aspects.
4. Health is defined as merely the absence of disease. This focuses attention on the malfunctioning part of the organism but excludes the positively functioning being. Much may be learned about disease, but little is known about health.

The Sociological (Sociocultural) Definition of Health

Sociologists typically consider all six dimensions in defining health and emphasize the social and cultural aspects of health and illness. This approach focuses on an individual's capacity to perform roles and tasks of everyday living and acknowledges social differences in defining health.

Capacity to Perform Roles and Tasks. Objecting to the biomedical definition, Talcott Parsons suggested that health is the ability to comply with social norms. In a **sociological definition of health**, he defined health as "the state of optimum capacity of an individual for the effective performance of the roles and tasks for which he has been socialized" (Parsons, 1972:173). This is contrary to the biomedical approach—no assumption is made that disease can be objectified, the focus is much broader (and more socially relevant) than mere physiological malfunctioning, the individual's own definition of his or her health is central (rather than the physician's), and the definition is stated in positive terms. In this approach, health is not just the lack of something but it is a positive capacity to fulfill one's roles; it is not just a physiological condition but it includes all the dimensions of individuals that affect social participation.

Social Differences in Defining Health. Twaddle (1974) also defines health more by social than by physical criteria. He views health and illness as a continuum between the perfect state of health and the perfect state of illness (death). While "normal" health and illness fall somewhere between the two extremes, a healthy state for one person may be considered unhealthy by another. Perception of health is relative to one's culture (e.g., being 10 pounds overweight is suggestive of ill health in some cultures but is socially approved in others) and one's position in the social structure (e.g., back pain that may cause a salaried worker to miss a day of work might be ignored by an hourly wage worker), and is influenced by social criteria.

Research demonstrates that social factors do influence how individuals define personal health status. For example, data from the Health and Lifestyle Survey, a national survey of men and women in England, Wales, and Scotland, show that personal definitions of health vary by age, gender, and perceived level of health (Blaxter,

2010). Young men conceptualize health in terms of physical strength and fitness, whereas women focus more on energy, vitality, and the ability to cope. Older men and women consider health in terms of ability to function as well as a state of contentment and happiness. Women of all ages often include social relationships in their definitions, whereas men rarely do.

The World Health Organization Definition

The World Health Organization takes an inclusive approach by defining health as a state of complete physical, social, and mental well-being, and not merely the absence of disease or infirmity. This definition suggests that health relates to one's ability to participate in everyday activities and to function fully—physically, socially, and emotionally. In this sense, health is a resource for everyday life. It is a positive concept that emphasizes social and personal resources as well as physical capacities (World Health Organization, 2016).

HEALTH BEHAVIOR

Sociologists include four types of activities in their understanding of the term **health behavior** (Alonzo, 1993):

1. *Prevention* refers to activities designed to prevent or minimize disease, injury, and disability.
2. *Detection* involves activities to detect disease, injury, or disability before symptoms appear, and includes medical examinations (e.g., taking blood pressure) or screenings for specific diseases.
3. Health *promotion* activities consist of efforts to encourage and persuade individuals to engage in a healthy lifestyle and to avoid or disengage from health-harming behaviors.
4. Health *protection* activities occur at the societal rather than the individual level and include

efforts to make the environment in which people live as healthy as possible. This involves monitoring the physical and social environments in which people live and work, physical structures and infrastructures, systems of transportation, and available food, air, and water, and developing social and economic policies that permit and encourage good health.

DESCRIBING INDIVIDUAL HEALTH BEHAVIORS

Prevention

Health-protective behaviors (HPBs) are individual actions taken to enhance health. These may be prescriptive (e.g., eating a nutritious diet, wearing a seat belt when in a car, and getting adequate exercise) or proscriptive (e.g., avoiding unsafe driving, not smoking, and avoiding excessive alcohol consumption).

Today, the primary gauge of participation in healthy lifestyles is the **Behavioral Risk Factor Surveillance System (BRFSS)**, a survey conducted by the Centers for Disease Control and Prevention in conjunction with the states and territories. The survey consists of more than 400,000 annual household telephone interviews conducted by state health departments and is the largest continually conducted health survey system in the world. Participation in several key health-related behaviors is presented in Table 6.1.

The summary picture of participation in healthy lifestyles for American adults is very poor. Most Americans eat a poor diet (high in sugar, salt, and trans fats, and low in fruits and vegetables), engage in too little physical exercise, and almost 1 in 7 smokes cigarettes (the single most health-harmful behavior). Poor diet and inadequate exercise combined lead to obesity (the second most dangerous lifestyle pattern). Excessive alcohol consumption contributes to the third-largest number of deaths in the United

TABLE 6.1 The 2000 and 2017 Behavioral Risk Factor Surveillance System for 50 States and DC

Behavioral Risk	Percentage Participating	
	2000	2017
Current smoker	20.0	14.0
Overweight/obese	61.6	71.6 (2016)
Consume too few fruits and vegetables	76.9	90.0
Too little physical exercise	78.2	80.0
Binge drink	N/A	16.7

Source: Centers for Disease Control and Prevention. 2019a. *Behavioral Risk Factor Surveillance System Survey Data.* Retrieved January 29, 2019 (www.cdc.gov/brfss/).

States. Unlike the percentage of smokers (which is declining) or the percentage of people who are obese (which is increasing), the percentage of people who drink excessively has remained at about the same level for at least the last decade.

The Multidimensional Basis of HPBs. Surprisingly, engaging in one particular HPB (e.g., drinking only in moderation) does not automatically mean (or increase the chances of) engaging in another HPB (e.g., engaging in adequate exercise). Men are much more likely than women *both* to exercise more and to drink immoderately (perhaps reflecting a traditional masculine ethic).

Nevertheless, some consistent relationships between HPBs do exist. For example, while level of exercise is highly dependent on age, in general those who eat nutritiously are more likely to exercise than those who have a poor diet. In fact, among those over 60 years of age, smokers and drinkers with a good diet are more than twice as likely to exercise vigorously as non-smokers and non-drinkers with a poor diet.

Correlates of Participation in HPBs. Participation in many HPBs is related to sociodemographic characteristics like age, gender, race,

level of education, and income. Three of these factors are discussed here. First, studies have consistently found that women are more likely than men to engage in a healthy lifestyle. Women are more likely to wear seat belts, less likely to smoke cigarettes and be heavy smokers, and less likely to drink alcohol excessively (men are three to four times more likely to be classified as a problem drinker). Women are also much more likely than men to wash their hands after coughing, sneezing, handling money, and especially after using a public restroom (88 percent of women do so, compared with only 67 percent of men). However, a much higher percentage of men than women exercise adequately. Overall, though, women—especially young women—are much more likely to lead a healthy lifestyle.

Second, people with more education lead healthier lifestyles than those with less education. They are less likely to smoke, more likely to exercise, have better nutrition, drink in moderation, use seat belts, and obtain preventive health care. This effect is most dramatic when we compare individuals with a college degree to those with less education. This strong relationship between college degree and living healthily is partly a reflection of differences that exist prior to college entrance (e.g., family income, high self-rated health) but is also a product of the education itself (Lawrence, 2017). Embedded within college education are factors such as knowledge, guidance, greater employment potential, and enhanced psychosocial resources that promote healthier living.

Third, financial resources affect engaging in healthy behaviors. This is illustrated in the case of birth control. Research has found that a key reason why the teen birth rate is much higher in the United States than in other developed countries is that the United States provides less comprehensive sex education starting at an early age and less access to contraceptives, especially those that are most effective in preventing pregnancy. A study published in the *New England*

Journal of Medicine in 2014 found that when adolescent girls were given free birth control and encouraged to use the most effective methods of pregnancy prevention (long-acting reversible methods such as IUDs and implants rather than birth control pills and condoms), the rates of pregnancy, abortion, and births all declined dramatically. When given information about effectiveness and free access, 72 percent of adolescent girls selected IUDs or implants, whereas only 5 percent in a comparative group in the population did so (Secura et al., 2014).

The accompanying box, "Binge Drinking on College Campuses," addresses an important behavioral phenomenon among college students.

IN THE FIELD

BINGE DRINKING ON COLLEGE CAMPUSES

In response to several binge drinking–related deaths among college students in the early 1990s, the Harvard School of Public Health conducted a national survey in 1993 to determine the prevalence of binge drinking on campuses. They defined binge drinking as the consumption of at least five drinks in a row for men or four drinks in a row for women during the 2 weeks prior to the survey. Based on this definition, 44 percent of students were binge drinkers.

Prompted by the publicity surrounding the deaths and the widely disseminated findings of the study, many institutions challenged the traditional notion that binge drinking is simply part of the college experience. They developed drinking awareness and education courses, employed alcohol counselors, and established more stringent rules for drinking on campus. However, follow-up surveys conducted throughout the mid- and late 1990s and in the first two decades of the 2000s have found that the percentage of binge drinkers on campus has remained essentially unchanged. Why didn't the interventions not make a dent in rates of binge drinking?

Close analysis of the data did reveal two significant changes. Reflecting increasing polarization on campus, both the rate of abstention (which is about 20 percent) and the rate of *frequent* binge drinking increased—three or more binges in the previous 2 weeks (which is over 20 percent). Furthermore, whereas binge drinking among dormitory residents actually declined, it increased among students living off campus, especially among those living in fraternity and sorority houses. Thus the gaps between non-drinkers/light drinkers and intensive drinkers, and between Greeks and non-Greeks, widened. The study found that while binging occurs among all campus subgroups, the rate is especially high among white fraternity members (Caudill et al., 2006).

To what extent are students aware of binge drinking on their campus? The Harvard survey discovered that around 50 percent of students underestimated the binge drinking rate on their campus (29 percent *overestimated* it, and only 13 percent were on target). Binge drinkers were especially likely to overestimate the campus rate. Researchers found little evidence of a healthy alcohol-related social norm among fraternity members. Many view their consumption level as similar to their close friends (positive reinforcement), and they do not regard binging as a negative health behavior (Keeling, 2002).

Recently, many institutions have conducted research to test the effectiveness of various types of interventions. Very popular has been a *social norms approach to binge drinking*. The underlying theory of this approach is based on evidence that students generally misperceive the frequency with which their peers engage in unhealthy behaviors, and that their own behavior is influenced by this misperception. Students who overestimate the percentage of binge drinkers—that is, who think binging is very common—on their campus are most likely to become binge drinkers themselves (Martens et al., 2006). Thus institutions have sought to create a more accurate impression among students about the actual percentage of binge drinkers on campus. One study of more than 4,000 students at one university found that those who had read materials disseminated in a social norms marketing campaign developed more accurate perceptions of peer alcohol use, which, in turn, was associated with fewer drinks per sitting (Su et al., 2018).

Students who anticipate positive outcomes (e.g., socially or sexually) from binging are also more likely to binge drink than students who have observed or recall negative outcomes (McBride et al., 2014). In response, many colleges are attempting to educate students about

the link between binging and a variety of negative outcomes, including suicide, violence, alcohol poisoning, and sexual assault.

It is not yet clear if these programs will be successful. On the one hand, the percentage of students who binge remains steady at around 40 percent. About 150,000 college students each year develop an alcohol problem. The National Institute on Alcohol Abuse and Alcoholism (2019) reports that among 18- to 24-year-olds, each year more than 1,800 die from alcohol-related unintentional injuries (especially in motor vehicle accidents), almost 700,000 are assaulted and 97,000 are sexually assaulted or date raped by a student who has been drinking.

On the other hand, some limited experiments have found that participation in programs that emphasize the non-drinking or non-binging segment of students or emphasize more explicit discussion of the negative outcomes of binging could reduce the likelihood of problem and binge drinking.

Detection

Today, many health-screening procedures are available, including periodic physical examinations, eye and dental examinations, blood pressure and cholesterol readings, and prenatal and well-baby care. These procedures are designed to identify and monitor health problems. Much research has demonstrated considerable health and cost benefits of participation in these services.

Correlates of Participation in Detection Services. Because detection services are so effective, the question arises as to why some people do not use them. One important reason is that the cost of some services discourages participation of people with low incomes and inadequate or no health insurance. Individuals who do not incur any expense are much more likely than those who pay out of pocket to receive

preventive health care services. A good illustration is the fact that an annual wellness visit at no charge to the patient is provided by Medicare. For all Medicare enrollees and especially for

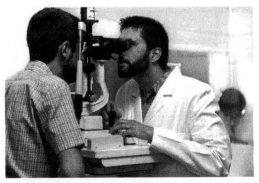

Stress can have a powerful impact on the organs throughout the body

those who were not insurance-covered prior to Medicare enrollment, the percentage receiving an annual exam increases dramatically.

Cost of services can also be calculated with reference to other factors. Not having access to a physician, not being able to get off work (without loss of wages) to visit a physician, and ultimately, becoming accustomed to going without care can play a part. When funds are unavailable or physicians are inaccessible, some families forgo detection services in the hope that they will be able to stay well without them.

Many poor parents forgo medical care for themselves so that available money can be used for their children. Research on families who receive services at free health clinics—where services are typically offered at no charge by volunteer physicians and dentists—has found that many parents bring their children to the clinic for preventive or therapeutic care, but do not ask to be seen themselves. Often, when staff inquire about this, the parent acknowledges having medical problems that could be addressed by clinic staff. However, the parent has become so accustomed to doing without medical care that no request for care is made (Weiss, 2006).

Healthy People 2020 and 2030

Since 1979, the Department of Health and Human Services has published a document every 10 years identifying broad national health goals and specific targeted health objectives for the following decade. *Healthy People 2030* was published in2020 and, like previous editions, is based on the latest scientific knowledge and comments from health experts and laypersons. It is designed to assist the construction of similar plans in communities and states across the country.

The overarching goals of *Healthy People 2030* (HealthyPeople, 2019) are:

- Attain healthy, thriving lives and well-being, free of preventable disease, disability, injury and premature death.

- Eliminate health disparities, achieve health equity, and attain health literacy to improve the health and well-being of all.
- Create social, physical, and economic environments that promote attaining full potential for health and well-being for all.
- Promote healthy development, healthy behaviors and well-being across all life stages.
- Engage leadership, key constituents, and the public across multiple sectors to take action and design policies that improve the health and well-being of all.

Other countries also set target population health goals and initiate programs to help achieve them and monitor their effectiveness. The accompanying box, "Providing Prenatal Care in Western Europe," illustrates one such public health initiative in Western European countries.

EXPLAINING HEALTH BEHAVIOR

In the late nineteenth century, Max Weber identified both *macro* factors (social-structural conditions) and *micro* factors (personal choices) as important influences on lifestyle. He called social-structural conditions and the opportunities afforded in life "life chances" and personal choices "life conduct," and he argued that they are interlinked (Weber, 1922/1978). This interdependence of life chances and life conduct can be particularly helpful in understanding health and illness. After all, certain life chances (e.g., socioeconomic status) can influence individual health behaviors (e.g., getting an annual medical checkup), and certain behaviors (e.g., excessive alcohol consumption) can be health damaging and negatively affect one's life chances. In the United States, much more attention has been directed to examining participation in health behaviors from the micro perspective. This section of the chapter reviews contributions from both approaches.

IN COMPARATIVE FOCUS

PROVIDING PRENATAL CARE IN WESTERN EUROPE

Many countries in the world have a lower infant mortality rate than the United States. Part of the explanation is that a higher percentage of babies born in the United States have low birth weight. Epidemiologists state that the most effective means of reducing the number of low-birth-weight babies is increasing access to prenatal care for all pregnant women. In 2016, 4 percent of non-Hispanic white women received late or no prenatal care, as did 6 percent of Asian/Pacific Islander women, 10 percent of non-Hispanic black women, and 12 percent of American Indian/Alaska native women. In the same year, 26 percent of births to girls younger than age 15 and 11 percent of births to those between 15 and 19 involved late or no prenatal care (Child Trends, 2018).

Why do other countries fare better than the United States? McQuide, Delvaux, and Buekens (2000) examined 17 Western European nations and determined that all of them provide comprehensive and accessible prenatal care at no charge to all women. In contrast to the United States, no woman is ever turned aside due to inability to pay or lack of available services. All of these countries offer universal coverage for health services, readily available

prenatal clinics, and special outreach programs for high-risk pregnant women and postpartum care. Some countries offer pregnancy (financial) allowances and the provision of prenatal care at work sites.

How do these countries afford this? The irony is that they actually save money by guaranteeing prenatal care to all women. In the United States, the average hospital delivery charge is almost twice as much for women who have not received prenatal care as for those who have (because of the greater likelihood of problem births), and there are significantly higher expenses through childhood and adolescence. Those who advocate guaranteed prenatal care in the United States cite economic as well as moral reasons for their rationale.

If the United States guaranteed accessible prenatal care, would the infant mortality differential between the poor and the non-poor disappear? Much of it would, but probably not all of it. Continuing differences in nutrition, general health of the mother, and health knowledge may mean that some differential would remain (as it has in other countries), but the social class difference is much smaller in other countries than in the United States.

The Macro Approach to Health Behavior

Medical sociologists have criticized the almost exclusive focus by policy makers and the general public on personal choices and individual behaviors in considering health behavior. The late Irving Zola creatively captured this criticism in an oft-quoted metaphor:

> You know, sometimes it feels like this. There I am standing by the shore of a swiftly flowing river and I hear the cry of a drowning man. So I jump

into the river, put my arms around him, pull him to shore and apply artificial respiration. Just when he begins to breathe, there is another cry for help. So I jump into the river, reach him, pull him to shore, apply artificial respiration, and then just as he begins to breathe, another cry for help. So back in the river again, reaching, pulling, applying, breathing and then another yell. Again and again, without end, goes the sequence. You know, I am so busy jumping in, pulling them to shore, applying artificial respiration, that I have *no* time to see who the hell is upstream pushing them all in.

(Zola in McKinlay, 1974:502–503)

What are the upstream factors? Cohen, Scribner, and Farley (2000) identify four health-related macro-level factors that have a direct impact on individual behaviors. These include:

1. *The availability of protective or harmful consumer products* (e.g., tobacco, high-fat foods, sterile needles, condoms, alcohol—both price-wise and geographic convenience).
2. *Physical structures/physical characteristics of products* (e.g., childproof medical containers, seat belts, well-lit neighborhood streets, nearby parks).
3. *Social structures and policies* (e.g., enforcement of fines for selling tobacco to underage persons, provision of community day care services).
4. *Media and cultural messages* (e.g., advertisements for alcohol products).

John McKinlay (1974) cogently argues that with regard to preventive health actions, we have spent most of our time downstream being preoccupied with encouraging people to avoid risky behaviors while we have neglected the consumer products, physical structures, social structures, and media messages upstream that create and promote risky behaviors. He states that a significantly greater impact on health is achieved by legislative acts that raise taxes or restrict advertising on cigarette manufacturers than by a multitude of efforts to persuade individual smokers to quit. Yet most efforts are directed downstream at individual smokers rather than upstream at the tobacco industry.

In concurring with McKinlay, Nancy Milio (1981) states that the paramount factor in shaping the overall health status of society is the *range* of available health choices, rather than the personal choices made by individuals. Moreover, the range of choices is largely shaped by policy decisions in both government and private organizations. Real impact on the health of the people, she argues, requires erecting national-level policy. An example is the increase in the percentage of drivers using a seat belt. After several years of "Buckle Up" campaigns stimulated only a slight increase in the number of seal belt users, states began in the mid-1980s to require seat belt use with a fine added for non-compliance. Immediately, there was a huge increase in seat-belt usage. The state legislative acts had far more effect on seat-belt use than all the public education "Buckle Up" campaigns combined.

The accompanying box, "Syringe Services (Needle Exchange) Programs," describes an interesting but controversial policy choice.

The Macro Approach and Cigarette Smoking. The use of tobacco kills more than 400,000 Americans each year and is predicted to lead to the deaths of 1 billion people worldwide in the twenty-first century. For decades, efforts in the United States focused downstream on encouraging individual smokers to quit. However, these efforts occurred against a backdrop of formal and informal (upstream) social policies that subsidized the tobacco industry, prevented measures that would discourage tobacco use, and allowed marketing campaigns that even the tobacco industry now acknowledges were dishonest.

In the last few years, several upstream, "macro" social policies have attempted to reduce the number of smokers and the social costs and health damages due to smoking. These include:

1. *Ending agricultural subsidies to tobacco farmers.* Beginning in the 1930s, the government offered a program to stabilize the price of tobacco and encourage small farmers to stick with tobacco as their primary crop. In 2004, legislation was signed to end this program (over a 10-year period). Part of the program termination is a US$10.1 billion payout to tobacco farmers to ease the loss of the annual subsidies.
2. *Taxing tobacco products at a higher level.* Until recently, the federal government and most

IN THE FIELD

SYRINGE SERVICES (NEEDLE EXCHANGE) PROGRAMS

One of the most common methods of transmission of HIV and hepatitis C is sharing contaminated needles. The percentage of AIDS cases traced to injectable drug use varies widely from state to state, but ranges from under 10 percent to almost 50 percent, with most states in the teens. A particularly dramatic example of disease transmission occurred in 2015 in and near a small town (with a population of 4,200) in Indiana. Over a period of a few months, 181 new cases of HIV were diagnosed. Most were caused by sharing contaminated needles used to inject the powerful painkiller Opana. The number of cases gave this small community an HIV incidence rate higher than that in any country of sub-Saharan Africa.

Public health officials and medical societies have for years been urging states to allow over-the-counter sale of syringes in pharmacies and/or allow drug users to exchange used needles for sterile ones in the hope of preventing disease. They have also lobbied the federal government to subsidize these programs.

States that offer syringe services programs have reported considerable success in reducing the percentage of AIDS and hepatitis C cases caused by infected needles. The programs have been called an excellent example of an evidence-based approach to reducing the risk of AIDS. By 2010, all states allowed either over-the-counter sales of syringes or had exchange programs, or both.

In the case described here, Indiana passed a state law allowing needle exchanges in communities experiencing a disease outbreak, although the money can be used only for education, substance abuse programs, referrals to medical providers, and support services. Local governments or non-profit organizations must buy the needles. In the ensuing 2 months, needle sharing in the community dropped by 85 percent. The ban on federal funding was also lifted, so programs had a reasonable chance of success.

These programs do not have unanimous support. Many Republicans, some Democrats, and many in the law enforcement and drug control communities have opposed them for being an implicit endorsement of the use of injectable drugs. They argue that the emphasis should be on treatment for drug abuse rather than reducing its dangers. However, at this point in time, the public health orientation focused on prevention of harms is prevailing.

state governments continued to tax tobacco products at a low level—especially relative to other countries like the United Kingdom, Canada, Norway, and Denmark, where the cigarette tax was several times higher per pack. Substantial research shows that as the price of cigarettes increases, the number of people, especially teenagers, who are able and willing to purchase them decreases.

In the last 10–15 years, the federal government and many state governments aggressively increased the tax on cigarettes. As of 2018,

New York and Connecticut added $4.35 per pack and Rhode Island $4.25 per pack. On the other end, Missouri added only 17 cents per pack, Virginia 30 cents, Georgia 37 cents, and North Dakota 44 cents).

3. *Developing creative anti-smoking campaigns.* Tobacco companies are fully aware that 90 percent of all smokers begin smoking during their teenage years. Their strategy was often to target adolescents because they are very susceptible to marketing techniques, and once hooked, it may be difficult for them

to stop smoking. For years, these marketing campaigns went largely unchallenged. Now public health departments, schools, and others have created their own marketing campaigns to discourage smoking. While some appear on television, anti-smoking campaigns increasingly appear on social media as well.

4. *Creating and enforcing strict smoking bans.* Since the Surgeon General reported "massive and conclusive scientific evidence" in 2006 that breathing in the smoke of other smokers can lead to significant health problems (an estimated 50,000 people die each year from breathing secondhand smoke), significant action has been taken to eliminate smoking in restaurants, bars, office buildings, apartments and condos, workplaces, and other buildings. In 2014, CVS Health, which operates nearly 8,000 stores and pharmacies, voluntarily stopped selling cigarettes, cigars, and other tobacco products—a loss of US$2 billion in annual revenue. Other efforts are underway to raise the legal smoking age. Four states have raised the age to 19 years, and Hawaii, California, and about 100 local jurisdictions have raised the age to 21 years. Studies in the United States and abroad have found that this increased minimum age leads to a significant decrease in the number of adult smokers.

5. *Holding the tobacco industry financially responsible for health damages resulting from their false claims.* In 1998, 46 states reached a joint settlement with the four largest tobacco manufacturers for tobacco-related health care costs annually and in perpetuity. (The other four states had reached individual agreements.) The settlement is estimated to be worth US$246 billion in the first 25 years. The states agreed to spend a significant portion of the settlement funds on tobacco education programs for children, smoking cessation programs, and health care. However, there is some controversy about the legitimacy of the ways in which some states are spending their settlement funds.

6. *Closely regulating the tobacco industry.* In 2009, President Obama signed legislation to give the US Food and Drug Administration (FDA) authority to regulate tobacco products and their marketing. Long a priority of the public health community, the law includes such components as banning outdoor tobacco advertising near schools and playgrounds, tobacco brand sponsorship of sports teams, free giveaways of non-tobacco items with tobacco purchases, and the sale of cigarettes and smokeless tobacco from vending machines. Penalties were increased for retailers who sell tobacco products to minors. It bans tobacco products from using terms found to be misleading, such as "light" and "low tar," and allows the FDA to monitor other tobacco company claims.

In the mid-1960s, about 40 percent of American adults smoked cigarettes. By 2006, the figure was only 20.6 percent. According to the most recent estimates from the National Health Interview Survey, only 13.8 percent of American adults smoked in 2018 (National Center for Health Statistics, 2019). These figures demonstrate the effectiveness of the "macro" policies outlined here.

The tobacco industry and members of national, state, and local legislatures who support them and their interests have certainly not surrendered efforts to convince the public—especially teenagers—to smoke cigarettes. Before such promotions were banned, Camel cigarettes sometimes offered giveaways such as berry-flavored lip balm, cell phone jewelry, purses, and wristbands. They developed new cigarette brands with a variety of exotic flavors that appeal to adolescents. (The FDA immediately banned the sale of candy-, fruit-, and clove-flavored cigarettes, but menthol-flavored cigarettes, which are especially popular among some teens, remain on the market.) When significant tax increases went into effect for roll-your-own tobacco, companies began marketing it as pipe tobacco (even though it would still be used for cigarettes) to avoid the tax. Two of the nation's largest cigarette makers— R. J. Reynolds Tobacco Company and Lorillard Tobacco Company—and several smaller manufacturers and retailers filed a lawsuit against the marketing restrictions. One means of bypassing these regulations in the United States has been to increase markets overseas—especially in less developed countries—a concern to the global health community (Gostin, 2007). A second means is described in the accompanying box, "The Emerging E-cigarette Industry."

IN THE FIELD

THE EMERGING E-CIGARETTE INDUSTRY

In the last several years, the tobacco industry has created a large e-cigarette (electronic nicotine delivery systems) market. E-cigarettes are typically battery-operated, cigarette-shaped (or shaped like a cigar or pen) devices that hold a cartridge of a liquid usually containing nicotine and other chemicals. The battery powers an atomizer that vaporizes the liquid for the user to inhale. Sweet flavorings can be added; these are especially popular with younger people. By 2018, e-cigarettes were a $10 billion industry globally, a figure estimated to rise to $60 billion by 2025.

In the United States, young people are more likely than older persons to use e-cigarettes. In 2018, less than 3 percent of adults "vaped," while 6.1 percent of 8th graders, 16.1 percent of 10th graders, and 20.9 percent of 12th graders had done so in the previous month (National Institute on Drug Abuse, 2018). The percentage of people who vape continues to climb rapidly.

Proponents claim that e-cigarettes are less harmful than tobacco and can be used to curb reliance on tobacco smoking. High satisfaction rates are reported by users, and some studies have found users reporting a decreased desire to smoke cigarettes. The percentage of high school students who smoke cigarettes has decreased as use of e-cigarettes has increased. Because they do not burn tobacco, they do not produce carbon monoxide (which can lead to heart disease) or tar (which can clog the lungs).

However, most e-cigarettes contain nicotine, which is very addictive, can have a negative effect on the heart, and can interfere with fetal development. Large doses can be especially harmful to children. E-cigarettes also contain a variety of other chemicals that can cause respiratory and nervous system problems. There are also dangers from secondhand smoke. Recent research reviews of 38 studies (Kalkhoran and Glantz, 2016) and 20 studies (Sutfin et al., 2015) found that trying e-cigarettes did not deter people from cigarette smoking (about 75 percent of smokers use both), and that the odds of quitting smoking were actually 28 percent lower for those using e-cigarettes. Young non-smokers may be more likely to initiate cigarette smoking by starting with e-cigarettes due to their non-harmful reputation.

The World Health Organization and various US groups and agencies have encouraged establishing of tight regulations for the industry, including a ban on indoor use, restrictions on advertising, and strong penalties for selling to minors. In 2015, the Center for Health and the Environment (CHE) chastised the tobacco industry for attempting to weaken and circumvent various laws. CHE sued 19 e-cigarette companies for failing to warn consumers about the reproductive health threats from nicotine in their products. Later that year, CHE filed legal actions against more than 60 companies for failing to warn consumers about exposure to nicotine and/or one or both of two cancer-causing

(Continued)

(Continued)

Vapour enthusiasts inhaling from their e-cigarettes as thousands of vapourists attend the 2nd annual Vapour Festival in 2014

chemicals, formaldehyde and acetaldehyde, from e-cigarettes, as required by California law (Cox, 2015).

In 2016, the Food and Drug Administration was given responsibility for regulating all aspects of e-cigarettes, including ingredients, warning labels, and health risks. The FDA's focus has been on reducing youth access, curbing marketing directed at young people, and educating adolescents about the dangers of all tobacco products (Ribisi et al., 2017). In 2018, the FDA asked the five largest e-cigarette manufacturers to develop robust plans to reduce widespread use of their products by minors.

The industry has also created "front groups"—seemingly independent groups that support industry claims and promote industry positions. Among others, in 1994, R. J. Reynolds created the "Get Government Off Our Back" group, but kept its own involvement secret. The group appeared to outsiders as a group of disaffected citizens who supported the tobacco industry against external criticism rather than what it actually was—an industry interest group (Apollonio and Bero, 2007). The industry has attempted to prevent policy-relevant research from being conducted by bringing lawsuits against researchers testing for the damage caused by tobacco, and has attempted to use its influence to stop anti-tobacco media campaigns.

The Macro Approach and Obesity. In the United States, 72 percent of adults are at least 10 pounds over their recommended body weight (compared with only 25 percent in 1960). Recent statistics show that 36 percent of adults are *overweight* (i.e., from 10 to 30 pounds over a healthy weight) and 36 percent of adults are *obese* (i.e., more than 30 pounds over a healthy weight). Of the total population, just over 6 percent are *extremely obese* (more than 100 pounds over a healthy weight). About 32 percent of kids are overweight or obese. Obesity is a problem for both women and men, and for whites, blacks, Hispanics, and Asian Americans.

On average, individual weight in the United States has increased by 1 to 2 pounds per year for the last 25 years. Between 1986 and 2000, there was a 216 percent increase in the number of obese individuals and a 389 percent increase in the number of extremely obese individuals. The World Health Organization emphasizes that exploding rates of obesity are a worldwide problem (there are almost 2 billion overweight people in the world), but the United States has the largest percentage of obese people. Obesity increases dramatically in the late teens and twenties, but an alarmingly high percentage of children and adolescents are overweight. The percentage of obese 12- to 19-year-olds more than tripled between 1976 and 2000, and overweight children are likely to become overweight adults. After years of increases, it appears that these percentages are beginning to level off at these extremely high levels.

The consequences of this are clear. Obesity increases the likelihood of premature death, heart disease, diabetes, cancer, high blood pressure, arthritis, depression, Alzheimer's disease, injury, and days lost from work, and leads to significantly greater lifetime medical costs. Estimates are that overweight non-smokers lose 3 years of life, obese non-smokers lose 7 years, and obese smokers lose 13 years.

What has caused this dramatic shift toward weight gain? There is some genetic predisposition to obesity (e.g., genes that influence appetite

control and faulty versions of a particular gene that cause food to be stored as fat rather than burned), and there are physiological influences on hunger. For some individuals, these factors are the primary culprit. However, these factors have not changed over time and do not explain the escalating figures for the population. Instead, many social scientists and many in the public health community point to the fact that we have evolved into an **obesogenic culture** filled with influences that push people toward health-harming behaviors such as unhealthy eating and absence of a physically active lifestyle. This characterization is consistent with a macro approach to understanding health behaviors.

The signs of this obesogenic culture are evident in Americans' dietary habits. Whereas dining in a restaurant was once the exception, it is now a common pattern for many families. Restaurants often prepare foods in ways that provide a very high number of calories and saturated fats. Portion size has become a major marketing technique, and many restaurants provide meals that are double, triple, or more the recommended portion size. Research shows that the more we are served, the more we eat. Fast-food restaurants—perhaps by far the biggest culprit—are enormously popular. People who eat in fast-food restaurants at least twice a week are about 50 percent more likely to be obese. Many of the "most bang for the buck" foods available in grocery stores are notoriously unhealthy. The average adult American ate an estimated 140 more pounds of food in the year 2000 than in 1990.

For young people, eating nutritiously may be even more of a challenge. The nutritional quality of lunches served at schools has long been criticized, and many schools have snack vending machines that offer sugary soft drinks, candy, cookies, regular potato chips, and other unhealthy foods. On school days many students get a substantial percentage of their calories from these foods. It is only recently that serious, critical attention has been given to these issues. In 2010,

Congress passed the *Healthy, Hunger-Free Kids Act* with strengthened nutrition guidelines and provision for free lunches for children who could not afford to pay.

Fast-food restaurants are often located near schools, and many students eat meals or snacks there. Students whose school is within half a mile of a fast-food restaurant consume more soft drinks, eat fewer fruits and vegetables, and are more likely to be overweight (Davis and Carpenter, 2009). Whether the restaurant sells fast food or not, the children's menu at many restaurants is packed with calories, and some dishes offer as many calories as a child needs in an entire day.

Advertisers target children and adolescents with heavy campaigns involving food-related messages, with almost all of these ads featuring junk food. In one study, 34 percent of the ads intended for children were for candy and snacks, 29 percent for sugary cereals, 10 percent for beverages, 10 percent for fast food, 4 percent for dairy products, 4 percent for prepared foods, and the rest for breads, pastries, and dine-in restaurants (Kaiser Family Foundation, 2007). The CDC has reported that an overwhelming percentage of commercials in TV shows aimed at kids under 12 years of age are for products containing too much sugar, too much saturated fat, and too much sodium (Schermbeck and Powell, 2015).

In addition, parents are increasingly likely to view their overweight sons and daughters as being of appropriate weight. Because parents who recognize that their children are overweight are more likely to try to help their youngsters slim down, this misperception means that early weight gains are often ignored (Duncan et al., 2015).

The twin cause of the shift toward an overweight and obese population is the decrease in the number of people getting adequate physical exercise. According to most surveys, only about 20 percent of American adults engage in the recommended levels of physical activity—that is, at least 30 minutes of moderate-intensity physical

activity for a minimum of 5 days per week, or at least 30 minutes of high-intensity physical activity for a minimum of 3 days per week. About 40 percent of adults get no physical exercise. For young people, levels of physical activity drop markedly between the ages of 9 years (about 3 hours daily of physical activity) and 15 years (about 50 minutes of daily physical activity), and then drop again with the start of college. The feared "freshman 15" (pounds of weight gain) is in actuality a typical gain of 6 to 9 pounds for first-year college students. The most common reasons are a dramatic increase in beer drinking and a further significant decrease in physical activity.

What would be some possible "macro-level" solutions to combat unhealthy eating?

1. A requirement that restaurants post calorie information on menus. Now implemented in New York City for chain restaurants, and being studied in other cities, research shows that such information does influence selection and intake. If a substantial number of diners selected lower-calorie options, restaurants might offer more of them. Some restaurants—including fast-food restaurants—have added nutritional options to their menus.

2. A requirement that schools offer nutritious lunches. Have you ever wondered why school lunches are often based around cheeseburgers, roast beef with gravy, and sausage pizza? It is due to the Farm Bill legislation that requires the US Department of Agriculture to purchase commodity foods such as meat and dairy products—but rarely fruits and vegetables—in order to bolster agricultural businesses by buying their surpluses and ensuring that prices remain at a certain level. These surplus commodity foods are then given to schools for their lunch programs. As a result, many of the foods served are not the healthiest choices. Although the Obama administration made some necessary changes to this program, more recently, the Trump administration has scaled

back these efforts, citing increased economic costs for schools. Finally, some soft drink manufacturers are pulling out of schools.

3. Regulation of food advertising directed at children and adolescents, with some limits or required balance with healthy food products.

4. A tax on sugary beverages and sugary foods to discourage their purchase and generate money to assist healthy eating programs. In 2016, following the success of taxes on tobacco, the World Health Organization recommended that governments tax sugary drinks and other unhealthy products. Excessive sugar consumption increases risk for cardiovascular disease, obesity, type 2 diabetes, cancer, and dental caries. Sugary beverages are the main source of added sugar in the American diet. Among the early adopters, both New Mexico and the city of Berkeley, California (which started in 2015), reported declines in purchase of sugar-sweetened beverages. Several other municipalities—including San Francisco, Philadelphia, Albany, Oakland, Chicago, and Boulder, Colorado—followed suit. Soda companies created heavily funded opposition campaigns (and succeeded in getting Chicago's tax overturned) (Gostin, 2017). There was a very significant 25 percent decrease in non-diet soda consumption in the United States between 2000 and 2015.

5. Government legislation that requires the food industry to produce healthier foods. For example, in 2015 the Food and Drug Administration enacted a policy that gave food manufacturers 3 years to remove trans fats from their products. Research has clearly demonstrated that no amount of trans fats is safe for human consumption.

Some macro-level solutions to deal with the lack of physical exercise are:

1. A dedicated effort to construct "built" environments that encourage rather than discourage physical exercise. Many more people engage in physical exercise when they have safe, appropriate facilities in which to do so. Communities could start building "complete roads" (that provide space for cars, bikes, and pedestrians to use safely), sidewalks for safe walking or jogging, urban parks for recreational use, greenways (walking paths), community recreation centers, and better-lit neighborhoods (Orstad et al., 2018).

2. Commitment to genuine physical education classes in schools, with an emphasis on activities that students can incorporate throughout their life (i.e., more emphasis on walking, strength training, or aerobics than on dodgeball). Research confirms that school-based programming can increase young persons' enjoyment of physical activity.

3. Community-wide weight reduction efforts with strong social support and incentives.

4. Systematic development of employee wellness programs that emphasize physical exercise.

Reasons for Lack of Attention to Macro Factors. Why is so little attention devoted to macro-level factors? At least three reasons seem important. First, using social policy and the force of laws to regulate individual behavior is viewed by some as contradicting the cultural value of individualism. Alonzo (1993) points out that people are willing to cede prevention activities that they cannot undertake themselves to the government—for example, inspecting the safety of each bridge. However, people are more reluctant to empower the government to protect them from their own behaviors. Many believe that allowing the government to go too far upstream oversteps its legitimate role in a free society. The accompanying box, "The Controversy Regarding the Human Papillomavirus (HPV) Vaccination," illustrates this point.

Second, the value of individualism carries over into the political economy. Donahue and McGuire (1995) use the term *marketplace strategy* to describe the view that the government's

IN THE FIELD

THE CONTROVERSY REGARDING THE HUMAN PAPILLOMAVIRUS (HPV) VACCINATION

It is not uncommon for public health and individual choice to come into conflict. On the one hand, when the public health community is convinced that a particular action is clearly in the public interest, they may seek to have the service made widely available and even mandated. At the same time, people who are unconvinced of the value of the action or who in principle oppose government mandates on individual behavior object to such plans. These conflicts are especially complex in two circumstances—when the action involves children and adolescents and when failure to take the action could jeopardize the health of others.

An example relates to the development of a vaccine to protect against the human papillomavirus (HPV). HPV is a virus (actually, about 100 strains of a virus) that causes infection on the skin or in mucous membranes (the moist lining of body cavities such as the mouth and nose that connect with the outside of the body). HPV is spread through skin-to-skin contact with an infected person—either through a cut, abrasion or small tear in the skin or through vaginal, anal, or oral sex. Some HPV infections that result in oral or upper respiratory lesions are contracted through oral sex. HPV infection is one of the most common sexually transmitted infections (STIs). The CDC estimates that about 80 million Americans currently have the HPV virus, and about 14 million more contract it each year. At least 70 percent of sexually active men and women in the United States will have at least one HPV infection in their lifetime.

Most HPV infections go unnoticed. They may not show any symptoms (the virus can stay in the body for the rest of a person's life without showing symptoms), and often they will go away on their own. In other cases, HPV can lead to warts on the genitals, hands or feet, or on the face and neck. The most serious outcomes occur when HPV leads to cervical cancer (about 90 percent of cervical cancer is caused by HPV) or cancer of the vulva, penis, or anus, or cancer on the mouth, tonsils, back of the throat, or in the upper respiratory tract. In the United States, approximately 20,000 women and 12,000 men are affected by a cancer caused by HPV every year. About 60 percent of these women are diagnosed with cervical cancer, and more than 4,000 women die annually from cervical cancer.

There is no blood test to determine if one has HPV, and there is no treatment. There is now an HPV cervical screening procedure that many believe is superior to the traditional Pap Smear. The test involves looking on the cervix for the HPV strains linked to cervical cancer. Some women find out they have HPV only when they have an abnormal cervical screening finding, and others find out only when they develop cervical cancer. There is no procedure to detect HPV in males.

Since 2006, there have been three effective HPV vaccines. The HPV vaccination typically requires two shots (three if the recipient is older than 14). While these vaccines are very effective in providing protection against the types of HPV they cover, they do not provide 100 percent protection against HPV because they do not cover all possible strains.

The CDC recommends that all boys and girls ages 11 and 12 get vaccinated. Catch-up vaccines are recommended for boys and men through age 21 and for girls and women through age 26, if they did not get vaccinated when they were younger. Routine cervical cancer screening for women aged 21 to 65 years old is also highly recommended (Centers for Disease Control and Prevention, 2019b). The scientific community has endorsed the vaccine as a safe and effective public health intervention.

Within a year of the vaccine's development, legislators in almost half of the states introduced mandatory vaccination bills with parental opt-out provisions. Support was strong among both Democrats and Republicans. Then opponents became more vocal. Opposition was based on perceived interference with parental rights, a belief that the vaccination mandate seemed to encourage sexual promiscuity for very young girls, and was unnecessary for those who were not sexually active, and a concern that the drug had not been sufficiently tested and was dangerous. Research has found that girls who receive the vaccine do not become more promiscuous, and research has determined the vaccine is not dangerous (Rothman and Rothman, 2009).

Many countries around the world use the vaccine, and it is free for women in the target age group. In 2007, Australia was the first to initiate a national publicly funded HPV vaccination program for girls, and in 2013 expanded it to include boys. Given high utilization rates, researchers estimate that Australia could effectively eliminate cervical cancer within the next 20 years (Hall et al., 2019). However, in the United States, only Rhode Island has mandatory HPV vaccination for girls and boys (Virginia and Washington, DC, require for girls only), although it is available in all states. The vaccine is expensive (US$390–$500 for the three-shot protocol), but the vaccination is covered by insurance programs. However, as of 2016, only 43 percent of girls and boys age 13 to 17 had completed their HPV shots and only 16 percent had done so by the CDC-recommended 13th birthday (Bednarczyk, Ellingson, and Omer, 2019).

primary obligation is to stay out of the marketplace so that individual consumers can exercise their own judgment about what to purchase and how to live. Of course, the view that the medical marketplace is completely open is inaccurate. Corporations and the government itself have a strong influence on health (e.g., through the location of toxic dumps), and corporations contribute sizable amounts of money to political candidates each year hoping to influence the political process. In recent years the tobacco industry contributed millions of dollars each year to members of Congress. Whether these contributions influenced the reluctance of Congress to increase the cigarette tax—a measure with broad public support—can only be surmised, but the more money a member has received, the less likely he or she has been to support control legislation (Moore et al., 1994).

Third, the absence of attention to macro-level factors enables society to forgo dealing with the research that establishes a direct relationship between individuals' social and physical environment and their health status. Studies show that even a small increase in years of education for an individual—or in average years of education for a population—has a greater impact on health status than the available quantity of health resources. However, by focusing on the individual, and solely affixing responsibility for health behavior at that level, the important effects of poverty and unemployment, racism, and lack of educational opportunity can be ignored (Becker, 1993).

The Micro Approach to Health Behavior

The importance of macro-level factors does not negate the importance of understanding factors that influence individual health behaviors. Several micro-level theories attempt to explain health behavior. This section describes two theories that have received significant attention.

The Health Belief Model. The **health belief model (HBM)** provides a paradigm for understanding why some individuals engage in HPBs, while others behave in knowingly unhealthy ways. The model recognizes that, in making health decisions, individuals consider both health-related and non-health-related consequences of behavior.

Development of the HBM (Becker, 1974) was sparked by the concern of many public health researchers in the 1950s and 1960s that few people were altering their behavior (e.g., ceasing to smoke) *despite* public health warnings. Developed by a group of social psychologists, the basic premise of the HBM is that the likelihood of engaging in positive health behavior is influenced by certain beliefs about a given condition (such as developing cancer) rather than by objective facts.

According to the HBM, individuals will take preventive health action only when the following four conditions exist:

1. The individual feels susceptible or vulnerable to a certain disease or condition.
2. The individual feels that contracting the disease would have serious consequences.
3. The individual believes that taking the preventive action would effectively reduce susceptibility to the disease (or at least reduce its seriousness if contracted). Individuals who have an **internal health locus-of-control** (those who believe they have control over their own health) are more likely to engage in HPBs than those who feel powerless to control their own health and who believe health to be determined by luck, chance, or fate (an **external health locus-of-control**).
4. The individual does not face serious barriers (e.g., inconvenience, expense, pain, or trauma) in engaging in the healthy behavior.

In addition, the individual typically needs some cue or stimulus to act (e.g., media attention, or a friend contracting a disease), and confidence that they can succeed in performing the behavior (this is referred to as self-efficacy).

These beliefs can be influenced by several other factors, including demographic (age, gender, socioeconomic status, and race/ethnicity),

sociopsychological (personality, peer, and reference group pressure), and structural (knowledge about the disease, prior contact with the disease).

The HBM has been shown to be an effective predictor of preventive health action in studies focusing on such behaviors as breast self-examination, patient adherence to regimens, getting an influenza vaccination, seeking dental care, dietary compliance among obese children, keeping follow-up appointments, use of sunscreen, cigarette smoking cessation, and vaccinating one's child against HPV. These studies show that taking preventive health action is more likely when perceived vulnerability to a serious disease or illness is high and when a preventive health action is perceived to be effective in avoiding a negative outcome. These studies generally report that the HBM is applicable across population subgroups.

However, the HBM also has limitations. A key limitation is that the model focuses on preventive health action relative to a particular disease or illness. To use the model, one must assess perceptions of a particular disease and perceptions of the efficacy of taking action to prevent that disease. Although the model has been helpful in examining these disease-specific behaviors, it is less applicable to understanding preventive health actions unrelated to fear of a particular disease.

The Health Belief Model and Sexually Transmitted Infections Among Young People. The HBM has been used to explain why some young people, but not others, voluntarily protect themselves against sexually transmitted infections. More than half of all children in the United States engage in some kind of sexual behavior before the age of 13 years, and more than 75 percent have engaged in sexual intercourse by the age of 19. Teen pregnancy in the United States—more than 300,000 pregnancies per year—has been decreasing sharply in recent years (although it is still one of the highest rates in the world). About 75 percent of these are unplanned. Combined with very high rates of sexually transmitted infections, (especially gonor-rhea, syphilis, and chlamydia) among the young (about half of the 20 million new cases of STIs each year occur among individuals aged 15 to 24 years), the widespread lack of safe sex practices is still clear.

According to the HBM, individuals have different perceptions of their susceptibility to infection as well as the seriousness of these infections. For example, a gay man may feel particularly vulnerable due to the high incidence of HIV in this group and may recognize its seriousness if he has witnessed the illness of friends. These perceptions must be complemented by information about the methods of transmission and the precautions that must be taken to avoid transmission.

However, individuals may still fail to take precautions. Some trust that medical technology will find a solution to the problem (which may be a reflection of incorrect information as well as a form of denial of individual risk), others may not have been exposed to a triggering event (e.g., the death of a friend), and some may calculate that perceived barriers (e.g., sacrificing sexual pleasure) outweigh the perceived benefits of preventive action. Individuals must also feel capable of making the recommended behavioral changes and believe that those changes will actually make a difference. In high-prevalence areas, some may continue to engage in unsafe practices because they believe they are already exposed.

A study of more than 300 introductory psychology students in California postulated that three factors (perceptions of personal vulnerability, sexual behavior history, and homophobia) would predict levels of worry about contracting an STI, and in turn that worry would predict behavioral change to safer sex practices. These predictions were supported by the research, although somewhat different patterns were found for women and men. For both, worry was a strong predictor of risk reduction behaviors. However, only women students were influenced by sexual behavior history (e.g., number of partners and having had an STI), and only men students were influenced by perceived vulnerability and homophobia. Thus gender was identified as a key influence on the processes within the HBM (Cochran and Peplau, 1991).

A more recent study of 245 undergraduate students examined the sexual history and risk beliefs of students relative to the likelihood of accepting various hypothetical HIV vaccines. Students who were most accepting of the vaccines were those with the greatest behavioral risks and highest perceived susceptibility to HIV accompanied by the lowest personal invulnerability beliefs—all consistent with the HBM model (Ravert and Zimet, 2009).

The Theory of Reasoned Action. Developed by Ajzen and Fishbein (1973), the central premise of the **theory of reasoned action (TRA)** is that intention to perform a behavior precedes actual performance of the behavior. The intention to behave in a particular way is influenced by attitude toward the behavior (how enjoyable or unenjoyable is this behavior?), social norms (is this an expected behavior in society?), messages conveyed by significant others (do others want me to engage in this behavior?), and the importance to the individual of complying with the relevant social norms and wishes of others.

Actual participation in a preventive health action would be preceded by beliefs, attitudes, and norms that encourage the action and an intention to engage in it. Similar to the HBM, background characteristics of the individual and certain personality and other social-psychological traits can be important influences. Unlike the HBM, the TRA is almost entirely rational and does not include a significant emotional component (like perceived susceptibility to disease). In addition, the TRA includes more explicit consideration of social influences by incorporating the wishes of significant others for the individual and the desire of the individual to comply with these wishes. Vanlandingham et al. (1995) determined that the TRA was a better predictor than the HBM of using safe sex practices precisely because it places more emphasis on peer group influence.

The Theory of Reasoned Action and the Cessation of Smoking.

Although the TRA has not in general been as successful as the HBM in predicting preventive health actions, it has been more effective in predicting smokers who attempt to stop smoking. One study determined that behavioral intention was a critical precursor to actual attempts to cease smoking and was a more powerful predictor than any of the individual items in the HBM (which was also tested). Although the researchers preferred the HBM for other reasons, they concluded that the intention to engage in a preventive health action is an important influence of the action (Mullen, Hersey, and Iverson, 1987).

Although not specifically testing the TRA, Christakis and Fowler (2008) examined the extent to which groups of people quit smoking together. They studied a densely interconnected group of more than 12,000 people who were repeatedly assessed over a 32-year period. Within the group, they found discernible clusters of smokers and non-smokers. During the study period, whole groups of smokers ceased smoking at the same time. Smoking cessation by a spouse, a sibling, a friend, or a coworker in a small firm all increased the likelihood of an individual stopping smoking. Moreover, smokers were increasingly moved to the periphery of the network. All these patterns are consistent with the importance of social norms and social influences. Additional research has pointed to increased stigma being attached to cigarette

Fitness centers have become increasingly popular in communities and on college campuses. They enable vigorous exercise throughout the year and can add a social dimension to physical conditioning.

smoking—another form of social influence (Stuber, Galea, and Link, 2008).

Several studies have documented the influence of significant others and of ongoing personal relationships on practicing healthy behaviors. Among adults, this often occurs as significant others attempt to influence and persuade the individual to practice a healthy lifestyle. Relatives, friends, and co-workers often play an important part in promoting changed behavior and maintaining changes that are made. This pattern of influence also occurs within marriages, although wives are more likely to try to influence their husband's behavior than the other way around. This may help explain why there is a significant health benefit when men get married, although not when women do. Broman (1993) has further established this relationship in his research

showing that disengagement from social relationships is often accompanied by an increase in health-harming behaviors.

The influence of others is particularly strong among adolescents. Research has identified both perceived peer and parental approval of alcohol use to be important determinants of drinking behavior among teenagers. Adolescents who reported high parental approval of alcohol use also reported high levels of alcohol use by their friends. In a study of health care practices during the first 3 years of college, both parents and peers were found to have a significant influence on students' alcohol consumption, diet, exercise, and seat-belt use. The researchers concluded that the direct modeling of behavior was the most important avenue of influence by both parents and peers (Lau, Quadrel, and Hartman, 1990).

SUMMARY

The World Health Organization defines health as a state of complete physical, social, and mental well-being. Sociological approaches to understanding health emphasize the social and cultural aspects of health and illness and an ability to function in various social roles.

In general, the lifestyle of Americans includes many health-harming aspects. About 14 percent of adults continue to smoke cigarettes (the most health-harming behavior), more than two-thirds are overweight or obese due to poor diet and lack of physical exercise, and about 5 percent are heavy drinkers. Binge drinking occurs in all population subgroups but continues to be a particular problem among college students. Because preventive

health care often involves direct or indirect costs, people on a low income have been much less likely to receive it.

Explanations for participation in healthy lifestyles adopt both a macro and micro approach. Macro approaches focus on the important influence of social structure (including poverty, unemployment, and racism) on ill health, and on the potential of social policy to influence participation in HPBs. Micro approaches, like the HBM and the TRA, focus on individual decision making and the process of determining whether or not to participate in specific preventive health actions. Both perspectives are important in understanding health behavior.

HEALTH ON THE INTERNET

In the last several years increasingly contentious debate has occurred in the United States regarding the issue of mandated childhood vaccinations. On one side are those who support mandated

vaccinations for highly contagious diseases. They contend that governments have a responsibility to protect children from potentially serious and even fatal diseases when it is possible to do so, and to protect all members of a community from an unnecessary disease epidemic. On the other side are those who believe that children's health is a parental responsibility rather than that of the government and that there are sound personal, philosophical, and medical reasons for rejecting some or even all vaccinations.

A recent case in point exists with measles, a disease once thought under control in the United States. Measles is a very contagious disease caused by a virus and spread through the air when an infected person coughs or sneezes. It is said that if you are in a room with an infected person, there is a 90 percent change you will get the disease. It typically starts with a fever, then a cough, runny nose, and red eyes, and finally a rash of tiny red spots on the head and the rest of the body. Prior to the measles vaccination program, which started in 1963, an estimated 3 to 4 million people got measles each year in the United States. Of these, approximately 500,000 cases were reported to CDC; of these, 400 to 500 died, 48,000 were hospitalized, and 1,000 developed encephalitis (brain swelling). Although most victims get well, even in the United States, measles presents a risk of death.

Measles can be prevented with the MMR vaccine, which protects against measles, mumps, and rubella. CDC recommends children get two doses of MMR vaccine, a first dose at 12 through 15 months of age and a second dose at 4 through 6 years of age. Teens and adults should also be up to date on their MMR vaccination. In 2017, about 92 percent of individuals between the ages of 12 and 23 had received the recommended vaccinations.

The MMR vaccine is very safe and effective. Two doses of MMR vaccine are about 97 percent effective at preventing measles; one dose is about 93 percent effective. Since 1963, widespread use of measles vaccine has led to a greater than 99 percent reduction in measles cases compared with the pre-vaccine era. However, measles is still common in other countries. Unvaccinated people continue to get measles while abroad and bring the disease into the United States and spread it to others (Centers for Disease Control and Prevention, 2019c).

However, in recent years a growing anti-vaccination movement has developed in the United States. Despite overwhelming scientific evidence regarding the safety of vaccines, opponents contend that it might be a cause of a variety of diseases including autism, epilepsy, allergies, multiple sclerosis, diabetes, and HIV. Some express concern about "vaccine overload"—possible negative effects of too many vaccines at once. For others, it is a matter of individual liberty and that governments should not infringe on an individual's freedom to make medical decisions for themselves or their children. Some argue from a religious perspective that vaccines may interfere with God's plan to have certain individuals contract a disease. Some do not trust pharmaceutical companies.

The anti-vaccination position has especially caught on among certain groups of people and people in certain areas of the country. For example, the Amish and Orthodox Jewish communities object to vaccination, and the movement has become popular in niches in the states of Oregon and Washington, particularly those with higher education and income (Reich, 2016). For these groups and in these areas, the percentage of children receiving their recommended vaccinations has decreased. In 2018, the number of measles cases increased significantly, and in early 2019 (at the time this new edition is being written), outbreaks of measles were occurring in Washington, Colorado, and New York. One anti-vaccination hot spot is Clark County, Washington—the site of 73 cases within a couple months. In 2005, 96 percent of school children there got their shots; in 2019, it was 78 percent. In some private schools, only 20 to 30 percent of the students had received the MMR. After just a few months, the outbreak had cost public health departments $1.6 million (enough to have paid for 40,000 inoculations).

Proponents and opponents of mandated vaccinations often contend in state legislatures where vaccination laws are determined. Currently, all 50 states and Washington, DC, require vaccinations, but 47 states allow parents to opt out their children for religious reasons and 17 allow opt-out for personal/philosophical reasons. Vaccination proponents argue that refusing the vaccines puts children at unnecessary risk and threatens harm to the rest of the community (because the vaccine is less than 100 percent effective, some vaccinated children could still get the disease). Vaccination opponents argue that the opt-out clauses protect their individual liberty and protect their children from having to receive a vaccine to which they object.

Recently, Jennifer Reich, a sociologist at the University of Colorado, Denver was interviewed on National Public Radio about her book *Calling the Shots: Why Parents Reject Vaccines*. Go to www.npr.org/2019/04/29/718165015/ why-arent-parents-getting-their-kids-vaccinated and listen to the interview or read the transcript. Then answer the following questions: How do you think this issue should be handled? What arguments do you think are most important? Would you support a no-exceptions mandate on the MMR vaccine for children? Banning any unvaccinated person under 18 from schools and/ or from other public places such as shopping centers, restaurants, and places of worship? Or would you support altogether removing mandates on childhood vaccines? Keeping the mandate but making it easier for parents to exempt their children?

DISCUSSION CASES

Case 1

In recent years, epidemiologists have carefully examined the consequences of being distracted while driving. Although there are many sources of distraction, primary attention has been focused on talking on a cell phone or texting while driving. One study found that talking on a cell phone while driving increased the risk of an accident by four times—making it approximately the same risk as driving while intoxicated (Strayer, Drews, and Crouch, 2006). A second study found that the likelihood of a collision while texting during driving was 23 times greater than when undistracted (Virginia Tech Transportation Institute, 2009). The National Safety Council reports that 28 percent of all automobile crashes are caused by drivers talking on a cell phone or texting while driving (Ship, 2010).

People in all age groups engage in distracted driving, although the percentages are highest in adults aged 18 to 29 years. About 75 percent of people in this age group talk on a cell phone while driving, 68 percent text while driving, and 48 percent access the Internet on their phone while driving. The Department of Transportation reports that in 2017, 3,166 people were killed and approximately 400,000 were injured in accidents caused by drivers who were texting or using their cell phones. In recent years the number of deaths of teenage drivers has sharply increased. Currently, 47 states and the District of Columbia (not Montana, Arizona, or Missouri, although the latter two have a ban for novice drivers) ban texting while driving, and 16 states plus DC ban the use of handheld cell phones while driving. Studies show that an overwhelming percentage of teenagers believe that texting while driving will eventually lead to an accident or even being killed, but few have abandoned the practice.

Recent studies have also shown increased dangers for distracted pedestrians. Pedestrians who are using cell phones show the same reduced situation awareness, distracted attention, and unsafe behavior as drivers do (Nasar and Troyer, 2013). The number of pedestrian deaths in the United states—about 6,000 per year—has increased significantly in the last decade and pedestrian distraction is the number one reason.

Given what you have read in this chapter and other knowledge about the topic you have, answer the following questions: (1) Given the evidence on danger, why do so many adults of all ages—but especially younger drivers—continue to talk on their cell phone, text, and access the

Internet while driving? (2) Would you support a National Transportation Safety Board (NTSB) recommendation to ban all use of portable electronic devices while driving? (3) What, if anything, would you propose in addition to or instead of this recommendation to reduce the negative consequences of distracted driving?

Case 2

Since 1984, the national minimum legal age for drinking alcohol has been 21 years. In 2009, a group of 135 college and university presidents endorsed the *Amethyst Initiative*—an advocacy proposal that comments on the failure of current policies to socialize young people to handle alcohol responsibly, and that encourages study and public debate about finding better ideas. Included among the ideas for debate was lowering the legal drinking age for all alcohol to 18 years. Estimates are that each year about 5,000 people under the age of 21 years die as a result of underage drinking (from motor vehicle crashes, homicides, suicides, etc.).

Proponents argue that the current drinking age has not stopped excessive alcohol consumption, but it has pushed it out of the open to places where it cannot be monitored. Rather than reducing driving after drinking, it may actually be leading to an increase as parties move from on campus to off campus. Opponents of lowering the drinking age argue that it would simply push the dangers of excessive alcohol consumption to a younger age and that it might lead to an increase in driving after drinking among this age group.

What would you identify as being the likely consequences—positive and/or negative—of lowering the drinking age to 18 years? As a social scientist, how could you study this issue? What are the key arguments on both sides of the issue?

GLOSSARY

Behavioral Risk Factor Surveillance System (BRFSS)
biomedical definition of health
external health locus-of-control
health
health behavior

health belief model (HBM)
health-protective behaviors (HPBs)
internal health locus-of-control
obesogenic culture
sociological definition of health
theory of reasoned action (TRA)

REFERENCES

Ajzen, Icek, and Martin Fishbein. 1973. *Belief, Attitude, Intention, and Behavior.* Reading, MA: Addison-Wesley.

Alonzo, Angelo A. 1993. "Health Behavior: Issues, Contradictions, and Dilemmas." *Social Science and Medicine* 37(8):1019–1034.

Apollonio, Dorie E., and Lisa Ann Bero. 2007. "Creating Industry Front Groups: The Tobacco Industry and 'Get Government off Our Back.'" *American Journal of Public Health* 97(3):419–427.

Becker, Marshall H. (ed.). 1974. *The Health Belief Model and Personal Health Behavior.* San Francisco, CA: Society for Public Health Education, Inc.

———. 1993. "A Medical Sociologist Looks at Health Promotion." *Journal of Health and Social Behavior* 34(1):1–6.

Bednarczyk, Robert A., Mallory K. Ellingson, and Saad B. Omer. 2019. "Human Papillomavirus Vaccination Before 13 and 15 Years of Age: Analysis of National Immunization Survey Teen Data." *The Journal of Infectious Diseases* (https://doi.org/10.1093/infdis/jiy682).

Blaxter, Mildred. 2010. *Health* (2nd ed.). Cambridge: Polity Press.

Broman, Clifford L. 1993. "Social Relationships and Health-Related Behavior." *Journal of Behavioral Medicine* 16(4):335–350.

Caudill, Barry D., Scott B. Crosse, Bernadette Campbell, Jan Howard, Bill Luckey, and Howard T. Blane. 2006. "High-Risk Drinking Among College Fraternity Members: A National Perspective." *Journal of American College Health* 55(3):141–155.

Centers for Disease Control and Prevention. 2019a. "Behavioral Risk Factor Surveillance System." Retrieved March 6, 2019 (www.cdc.gov/brfss/).

———. 2019b. "Human Papillomarvirus." Retrieved March 6, 2019 (www.cdc.gov/hpv/index.html).

———. 2019c. "Measles Vaccination." Retrieved March 6, 2019 (www.cdc.gov/measles/vaccination.html).

ChildTrends. 2018. "Late or no Prenatal Care." Retrieved (www.childtrends.org/indicators/late-or-no-prenatal-care).

Christakis, Nicholas A., and James H. Fowler. 2008. "The Collective Dynamics of Smoking in a Large Social Network." *The New England Journal of Medicine* 358(21):2249–2258.

Cochran, Susan D., and Letitia A. Peplau. 1991. "Sexual Risk Reduction Behaviors Among Young Heterosexual Adults." *Social Science and Medicine* 33(1):25–36.

Cohen, Deborah A., Richard A. Scribner, and Thomas A. Farley. 2000. "A Structural Model of Health Behavior: A Pragmatic Approach to Explain and Influence Health Behaviors at the Population Level." *Preventive Medicine* 30(2):146–154.

Cox, Caroline. 2015. *A Smoking Gun: Cancer-Causing Chemicals in E-Cigarettes.* Oakland, CA: Center for Environmental Health.

Davis, Brennan, and Christopher Carpenter. 2009. "Proximity of Fast-Food Restaurants to Schools and Adolescent Obesity." *American Journal of Public Health* 99(3):505–510.

Donahue, John M., and Meredith B. McGuire. 1995. "The Political Economy of Responsibility in Health and Illness." *Social Science and Medicine* 40(1):47–53.

Duncan, Dustin T., Andrew R. Hansen, Wei Wang, Fei Yan, and Jian Zhang. 2015. "Change in Misperception of Child's Body Weight among Parents of American Preschool Children." *Childhood Obesity* 11(4):384–393.

Gostin, Lawrence O. 2007. "The 'Tobacco Wars'— Global Litigation Strategies." *Journal of the American Medical Association* 298(21):2537–2539.

———. 2017. "2016: The Year of the Soda Tax." *Milbank Quarterly* 95(1):19–23.

Hall, Michaela T., Kate T. Simms, Jie-Bin Lew, Megan A. Smith, Julia ML Brotherton, Marion Saville, Ian H. Frazer, and Karen Canfell. 2019. "The Projected Timeframe until Cervical Cancer Elimination in Australia: A Modelling Study." *The Lancet Public Health* 4(1):19–27.

HealthyPeople.gov. 2019. "Healthy People 2030 Framework." Retrieved (www.healthypeople.gov/2020/About-Healthy-People/Development-Healthy-People-2030/Framework).

Kaiser Family Foundation. 2007. "New Study Finds That Food is the Top Product Seen by Children." *Kaiser Family Foundation.* Retrieved March 10, 2019 (www.kff.org/other/event/new-study-finds-that-food-is-the/).

Kalkhoran, S., and Stanton A. Glantz. 2016. "E-cigarettes and Smoking Cessation in Real-World and Clinical Settings: A Systematic Review and Meta-Analysis." *The Lancet Respiratory Medicine* 4(2):116–128.

Keeling, Richard P. 2002. "Binge Drinking and the College Environment." *Journal of American College Health* 50(5):197–201.

Lau, Richard R., Marilyn J. Quadrel, and Karen A. Hartman. 1990. "Development and Change of Young Adults' Preventive Health Beliefs and Behavior: Influence from Parents and Peers." *Journal of Health and Social Behavior* 31(3):240–259.

Lawrence, Elizabeth M. 2017. "Why Do College Graduates Behave More Healthfully Than Those Who Are Less Educated?" *Journal of Health and Social Behavior* 58(3):291–306.

Martens, Matthew P., Jennifer C. Page, Emily S. Lowry, Krista M. Damann, Kari K. Taylor, and M. Delores Cimini. 2006. "Differences between Actual and Perceived Student Norms: An Examination of Alcohol Use, Drug Use, and Sexual Behavior." *Journal of American College Health* 54(5):295–300.

McBride, Nicole M., Blake Barrett, Kathleen A. Moore, and Lawrence Schonfeld. 2014. "The Role of Positive Alcohol Expectancies in Underage Binge Drinking among College Students." *Journal of American College Health* 62(6):370–379.

McKinlay, John B. 1974. "A Case for Refocusing Upstream: The Political Economy of Illness." Pp. 502–516 in *Sociology of Health and Illness: Critical Perspectives,* edited by Peter Conrad and Rochelle Kern. New York: St. Martin's Press.

McQuide, Pamela A., Therese Delvaux, and Pierre Buekens. 2000. "Prenatal Care Incentives in Europe." *Journal of Public Health Policy* 19(3):331–349.

Milio, Nancy. 1981. *Promoting Health Through Public Policy.* Philadelphia, PA: F.A. Davis.

Moore, Stephen, Sidney M. Wolfe, Deborah Lindes, and Clifford E. Douglas. 1994. "Epidemiology of Failed Tobacco Control Legislation." *Journal of the American Medical Association* 272(15):1171–1175.

Mullen, Patricia D., James C. Hersey, and Donald C. Iverson. 1987. "Health Behavior Models Compared." *Social Science and Medicine* 24(11):973–981.

Nasar, Jack L., and Derek Troyer. 2013. "Pedestrian Injuries Due to Mobile Phone Use in Public Places." *Accident Analysis and Prevention* 57(C):91–95.

National Center for Health Statistics. 2019. "Early Release of Selected Estimates Based on Data from the 2018 National Health Interview Survey." Retrieved March 12, 2019 (www.cdc.gov/nchs/nhis/releases/released201905.htm#8).

National Institute on Alcohol Abuse and Alcoholism. 2019. "College Drinking." Retrieved March 12, 2019 (https://pubs.niaaa.nih.gov/publications/CollegeFactSheet/CollegeFactSheet.pdf).

National Institute on Drug Abuse. 2018. "Teens Using Vaping Devices in Record Numbers." Retrieved March 12, 2019 (www.drugabuse.gov/news-events/news-releases/2018/12/teens-using-vaping-devices-in-record-numbers).

Orstad, Stephanie L., Meghan H. McDonough, Peter James, David B. Klenosky, Francine Laden, Marifran Mattson, and Philip J. Troped. 2018. "Neighborhood Walkability and Physical Activity Among Older Women: Tests of Mediation by Environmental Perceptions and Moderation by Depressive Symptoms." *Preventive Medicine* 116(1):60–67.

Parsons, Talcott. 1972. "Definitions of Health and Illness in Light of American Values and Social Structure." Pp. 165–187 in *Patients, Physicians and Illness* (2nd ed.), edited by E. Gartly Jaco. New York: Free Press.

Ravert, Russell D., and Gregory D. Zimet. 2009. "College Student Invulnerability Beliefs and HIV Vaccine Acceptability." *American Journal of Health Behavior* 33(4):391–399.

Reich, Jennifer A. 2016. *Calling the Shots: Why Parents Reject Vaccines.* New York: NYU Press.

Ribisi, Kurt M., Heather D'Angelo, Ashley L. Feld, Nina C. Schleicher, Shelley D. Golden, Douglas A. Luke, and Lisa Henrikson. 2017. "Disparities in Tobacco Marketing and Product Availability at the Point of Sale: Results of a National Study." *Preventive Medicine* 105(1):381–388.

Rothman, Sheila M., and David J. Rothman. 2009. "Marketing HPV Vaccine: Implications for Adolescent Health and Medical Professionalism." *Journal of the American Medical Association* 302(7):781–786.

Schermbeck, Rebecca M., and Lisa M. Powell. 2015. "Nutrition Recommendations and the Children's Food and Beverage Advertising Initiative's 2014 Approved Food and Beverage Product List." *Preventing Chronic Disease* 12(1):140–472.

Secura, Gina M., Tessa Madden, Colleen McNicholas, Jennifer Mullersman, Christina M. Buckel, Qiuhong Zhao, and Jeffrey F. Peipert. 2014. "Provision of No-Cost, Long-Acting Contraception and Teenage Pregnancy." *New England Journal of Medicine* 371(14):1316–1323.

Ship, Amy N. 2010. "The Most Primary of Care—Talking About Driving and Distraction." *New England Journal of Medicine* 362(23):2145–2147.

Strayer, David L., Frank A. Drews, and Dennis J. Crouch. 2006. "A Comparison of the Cell Phone Driver and the Drunk Driver." *Human Factors* 48(2):381–391.

Stuber, Jennifer, Sandro Galea, and Bruce G. Link. 2008. "Smoking and the Emergence of a Stigmatized Social Status." *Social Science and Medicine* 67(3):420–430.

Su, Jinni, Linda Hancock, Amanda W. McGann, Mariam Alshagra, Rhianna Ericson, Zackaria Niazi, Danielle M. Dick, and Amy Adkins. 2018. "Evaluating the Effect of a Campus-Wide Social Norms Marketing Intervention on Alcohol-Use Perceptions, Consumption, and Blackouts." *Journal of American College Health* 66(3):219–224.

Sutfin, Erin L., Beth A. Reboussin, Beata Debinski, Kimberly G. Wagoner, John Spangler, and Mark Wolfson. 2015. "The Impact of Trying Electronic Cigarettes on Cigarette Smoking by College Students: A Prospective Analysis." *American Journal of Public Health* 105(8):e83–e89.

Twaddle, Andrew. 1974. "The Concept of Health Status." *Social Science and Medicine* 8(1):29–38.

Vanlandingham, Mark J., Somboon Suprasert, Nancy Grandjean, and Werasit Sittitrai. 1995. "Two Views of Risky Sexual Practices Among Northern Thai Males: The Health Belief Model and the Theory of Reasoned Action." *Journal of Health and Social Behavior* 36(2):195–212.

Virginia Tech Transportation Institute. 2009. "New Data from VTTI Provides Insight into Cell Phone Use and Driving Distraction." Retrieved January 12, 2013 (www.vtti.vt.edu/featured/052913-cellphone.html).

Ware, John E. 1986. "The Assessment of Health Status." Pp. 204–228 in *Applications of Social Science to Clinical Medicine and Health Policy*, edited by Linda H. Aiken and David Mechanic. New Brunswick, NJ: Rutgers University Press.

Weber, Max. 1922/1978. *Economy and Society: An Outline of Interpretive Society.* Berkeley, CA: University of California Press.

Weiss, Gregory L. 2006. *Grass Roots Medicine: The Story of America's Free Health Clinics.* Lanham, MD: Rowman-Littlefield.

Wolinsky, Fredric D. 1988. *The Sociology of Health—Principles, Practitioners, and Issues* (2nd ed.). Belmont, CA: Wadsworth Publishing Company.

World Health Organization. 2016. "World Health Organization Constitution." Retrieved March 9, 2019 (www.who.int/governance/eb/constitution/en/).

CHAPTER 7

Experiencing Illness and Disability

Learning Objectives

- Identify and discuss Suchman's stages of illness experience.
- Identify and discuss the most important factors that influence the assessment of disease/illness symptoms.
- Explain the concepts of "medicalization" and "demedicalization" and the factors that impact them.

- Identify and discuss the key social influences on the decision to seek professional medical care.
- Identify and describe the primary effects of living with a chronic illness or disability.

Medical sociologists have a natural interest in how people respond to illness. The concept of **illness behavior** refers to how "symptoms are perceived, evaluated, and acted upon by a person who recognizes some pain, discomfort or other signs of organic malfunction" (Mechanic and Volkart, 1961:52). It may seem that the nature and severity of an illness would be the sole determinants of an individual's response, and for very severe illnesses this is often true. However, many people either fail to see a physician or go very late in the disease process despite the presence of serious symptoms, while many others see physicians routinely for minor complaints. These patterns suggest that illness behavior is influenced by social and cultural factors in addition to (and sometimes instead of) physiological condition.

STAGES OF ILLNESS EXPERIENCE

Edward Suchman (1965) devised an orderly approach for studying illness behavior with his elaboration of five key **stages of illness experience:** (1) symptom experience, (2) assumption of the sick role, (3) medical care contact, (4) dependent-patient role, and (5) recovery and rehabilitation (see Figure 7.1). Each stage involves major decisions that must be made by the individual, which determine whether the sequence of stages continues or the process is discontinued. We use Suchman's schema to organize our discussion at the beginning of the chapter and then elaborate on his model in the section of the chapter on living with **chronic illness** and disability.

Figure 7.1 Condensed Version of Suchman's Stages of Illness Experience

I Symptom Experience	II Assumption of the Sick Role	III Medical Care Contact
The feeling that something is wrong; the individual may self-treat (or try to ignore the problem).	The individual may surrender typical responsibilities and take on "sick role" responsibilities of trying to get better (or still be in denial).	The individual makes contact with a medical provider acknowledging that expertise is necessary and seeking illness legitimation (but may still be in denial and may get a second opinion).

IV Dependent-Patient Role	V Recovery and Rehabilitation
The individual agrees to undergo medical therapy administered by professionals (but may or may not follow medical advice).	If recovery occurs, the individual leaves the sick role and returns to customary responsibilities and activities associated with the well role (although some individuals may enjoy the benefits of the sick role and linger in that stage).

STAGE 1: SYMPTOM EXPERIENCE

The illness experience is initiated when an individual first senses something is wrong—a perception of pain, discomfort, general unease, or some disruption in bodily functioning. Suchman states that three distinct processes occur at this time: (1) the physical pain or discomfort, (2) the cognitive recognition that physical symptoms of an illness are present, and (3) an emotional response of concern about the social implications of the illness, including a possible disruption in ability to function.

Assessment of Symptoms

David Mechanic (1968) developed a **theory of help–seeking behavior** to facilitate an understanding of this assessment process and how individuals act prior to (or instead of) seeking a health care provider. Mechanic traces the extreme variations in how people respond to illness to differences in how they define the illness situation and in their ability to cope with it. The process of definition and the ability to cope are both culturally and socially determined. As individuals mature through life stages, they are socialized within families and within communities to respond to illness in particular ways. Part of this socialization involves observing how others within the group respond to illness and noting the positive or negative reaction their behaviors elicit. Among the factors that Mechanic identifies as determining how individuals respond to illness are the following:

1. Perception and interpretation of symptoms: the visibility, recognizability, perceived seriousness, amount of disruption caused, and persistence of symptoms.

2. The tolerance threshold (e.g., tolerance to pain) and perceived fear of the illness by the individual.
3. Knowledge and available information about the illness.
4. Availability and accessibility of treatment resources, the cost of taking action, and competing needs for attention and resources.

Which of these factors most influences one's perception of their health? Stewart et al. (2008) found the amount of pain being experienced, limitations on ability to perform normal social roles, and feelings of having little or no energy mattered most.

The Importance of Pain as a Symptom

Although the importance of pain as a medical symptom may seem obvious, research on pain and its treatment has greatly increased only in the last 10 to 20 years. This research has found that pain is more common in the general population than was previously thought. Over 20 percent of US adults experienced chronic pain (defined as pain on most days or every day in the past 6 months) in 2016, and 8 percent had high-impact chronic pain (defined as chronic pain that interferes with work or life on most days or every day in the past 6 months). Both chronic and high-impact chronic pain are more common among older people, women, those below or near poverty, and those who worked previously but were not currently employed, while rates are lower among those with a bachelor's degree or higher (Dahlhamer et al., 2018). In 2016, 15.5 percent of adults reported experiencing migraines, 28.4 percent reported low back pain, and 15 percent had neck pain (National Center for Health Statistics, 2018).

Although many physicians say that most pain can be safely and effectively controlled, only in recent years has **palliative care**—treating the pain and suffering of seriously ill patients— become widespread. Palliative care programs have reached a general level of acceptance for terminally ill patients—the United States now has more than 1,700 hospital-based palliative care programs and 4,382 Medicare-certified hospice programs that deal with people in the last 6 months of their life (Center to Advance Palliative Care, 2019; National Hospice and Palliative Care Organization, 2018). These programs have achieved significant success in relieving pain. However, palliative care is still in its relative infancy for treating people with serious chronic (but not terminal) illnesses, who take curative medicines at the same time as pain relief medicines. Palliative care programs for non-terminally ill people are increasing in physicians' offices and hospitals, and these programs are expected to become a more significant component of the health care system.

There are four major obstacles to the use of pain relief medicine for more patients. (1) Few physicians have training in pain management, and they are ill-informed about opioids, synthetic versions of morphine, the most potent oral painkillers. (2) Insurance companies inadequately compensate physicians who spend large amounts of time with patients in pain. (3) The Drug Enforcement Agency has actively prosecuted physicians for a variety of offenses related to the prescription of narcotic pain relief medications. (4) Many patients are fearful that narcotic drugs will be addictive or have significant negative side effects. Several pain relief medications have been pulled from the market. Oxycontin led to addiction and abuse, and its manufacturer was found to have lied about these risks. Vioxx, which was used to control pain for many users, doubled the risk of heart attack and stroke. Celebrex was even more likely to lead to heart problems than Vioxx. However, complicating the situation is the fact that higher risks were observed only in long-term users of high doses of the drug. Some patients said they would willingly take the risks in order to effectively control their pain. Nevertheless, prescription drug overdoses have increased markedly in the United States. See the accompanying box, "America's Opioid Crisis."

Fed Up! (a coalition calling for an end to the epidemic of opioid addiction and overdose deaths) marches in Washington, DC.

Research on Symptom Assessment

Significant social and cultural influences affect how people interpret and respond to medical symptoms such as pain. For example, variations in response to pain are based on level of pain tolerance, which is culturally prescribed in different ways for women and men and for members of different ethnic groups.

Zborowski (1969) found that Protestants of British descent tended to respond in a matter-of-fact way to pain, which enabled them to adapt to illness more quickly than other groups. Patients of Irish heritage often repressed their suffering and tended to deny pain. Both Jewish and Italian patients responded to pain with more open emotionality. However, Jewish patients were primarily concerned about the long-term consequences of their illness and were not much comforted by the administration of pain-killing medication, whereas Italian patients were more oriented to current pain and were at least somewhat satisfied when the pain was relieved.

Research on perceived pain when getting one's ears pierced also found significant ethnic differences. Testing both men and women volunteers between the ages of 15 and 25 years, Thomas and Rose (1991) found that Afro-West Indians reported significantly less pain than Anglo-Saxons, who reported significantly less pain than Asians—all for the same procedure.

What causes these patterns? Both role modeling within families and social conditioning are important influences. Growing up within a particular family provides countless opportunities to observe family members' reactions to pain. Children's anxiety about receiving painful medical

IN THE FIELD

AMERICA'S OPIOID CRISIS

More than 50 million American adults experience chronic pain (Dahlhamer et al., 2018). In some cases, pain is of mild or moderate intensity, but many people suffer from extremely painful back problems, joint problems, osteoarthritis, and other conditions. Not surprisingly, these individuals have worse overall health, use more health care resources, and have more disabilities.

In the last 25 years, pharmaceutical companies have manufactured more powerful and highly addictive opioid prescription pain medications, such as oxycodone (Vicodin), hydrocodone (Percocet), and morphine, and significantly increased their marketing to physicians and patients. By 2015, the amount of opioids prescribed in the United States was three times the amount prescribed in 1999 (Guy et al., 2017). The annual opioid prescription rate increased from 72.4 prescriptions per 100 persons in 2006 to a peak of 81.3 in 2012. Rates have declined since then to 58.7 in 2017, although rates vary widely by location (Centers for Disease Control and Prevention, 2018b).

Many take prescription opioids inappropriately. They may take a drug prescribed for someone else, take more than the prescribed dosage, or take the drug for a recreational high rather than pain relief. This has frequently led to or contributed to substance abuse disorders, emergency hospitalizations, and overdose deaths. Between 1999 and 2017, the rate of overdose deaths from opioids increased from approximately 1 death per 100,000 population to over 5 (See Figure 7.3). In 2017, there were 70,237 drug overdose deaths in the United States, and 67.8 percent involved opioids (Scholl et al., 2019).

How did the prescription opioid epidemic materialize in the 1990s and grow into such a widespread problem in the next two decades? Before the 1990s, opioid pain medications were used to provide significant relief from pain from injury or after surgery as the body heals. They are also useful for controlling pain at the end of life. However, because they carry a high risk of overdose or addiction, they were rarely used for treating chronic pain. In the 1990s, several groups campaigned for providers to take chronic pain more seriously. Pharmaceutical companies pushed for greater use of opioids, often through educational programs for providers. Direct marketing strategies to patients also helped build demand. Many addiction treatment providers believe pharmaceutical companies overstated the effectiveness of the drugs and their safety and understated the risk of addiction (Jaret, 2015). A broad analysis of pharmaceutical companies is included in Chapter 14.

In an effort to curb the growing crisis, in March 2016, the Centers for Disease Control and Prevention issued its voluntary "Guidelines for Prescribing Opioids for Chronic Pain." Aimed at primary care physicians, the guidelines seek to reduce rates of opioid use disorders and overdose by helping physicians determine appropriate dose levels. Included are recommendations to use non-pharmacological modes of pain management (physical therapy, chiropractic, etc.) in addition to, or as a replacement for, prescription opioids, and to prescribe the lowest effective dose for the shortest possible time.

Beyond prescription opioids, the use of heroin and synthetic opioids have also contributed to the epidemic of opioid-related deaths. Because heroin is pharmacologically similar to prescription opioids, recreational use of prescription opioids is a risk factor for heroin use. The development of chemical tolerance to opioids, the greater ease of obtaining heroin in some communities, and the higher price of opioids compared with heroin have led to increased rates of heroin use (Compton, Jones, and Baldwin, 2016). The number of heroin deaths increased from less than 1 per 100,000 in 2010 to nearly 5 per 100,000 in 2017 (see Figure 7.2).

(Continued)

(Continued)

Figure 7.2   Waves of the Rise in Opioid Overdose Deaths

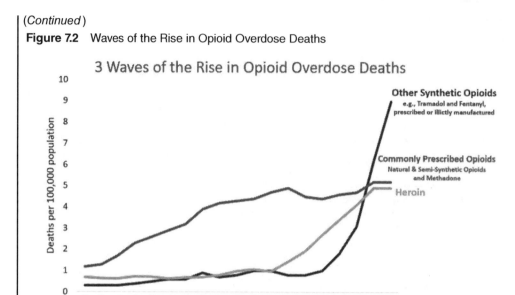

Source: www.cdc.gov/drugoverdose/images/epidemic/3WavesOfTheRiseInOpioidOverdoseDeaths.png

The availability of highly potent synthetic opioids (other than methadone), especially fentanyl, has worsened the situation. The rise in opioid-related deaths since 2013 is driven largely by the increase in fentanyl-related deaths. In the span of a single year, from 2016 to 2017, the death rate from synthetic opioids increased 45.2 percent (Scholl et al., 2019).

Clearly, the use and abuse of prescription opioids for pain management and the increased use of heroin and synthetic opioids are inter-related. Collectively, they constitute a major public health crisis that will likely persist into the next decade.

treatment has been shown to be strongly correlated with parental anxiety.

In response to the assessment of symptoms, an individual may decide to deny that the symptoms need attention, delay making a decision until symptoms become more obvious, or acknowledge the presence of an illness, and enter stage 2—the sick role.

STAGE 2: ASSUMPTION OF THE SICK ROLE—ILLNESS AS DEVIANCE

If an individual accepts that symptoms are a sign of illness and are sufficiently worrisome, they transition to the sick role, at which time the individual begins to relinquish some or all of their normal social roles.

Background of the Sick Role Concept

The **sick role**, one of the most fundamental concepts in medical sociology, was first introduced by Talcott Parsons in a 1948 journal article, but was elaborated upon in his 1951 book, *The Social System*. Parsons emphasized that illness is not simply a biological or psychological condition, and it is not simply an unstructured state free of social norms and regulation. When one is ill, one does not simply exit normal social roles to enter a type of social vacuum. Rather, one substitutes a new role—the sick role—for the relinquished, normal roles. The sick role is "also a social role, characterized by certain exemptions, rights, and obligations, and shaped by the society, groups, and cultural tradition to which the sick person belongs" (Fox, 1989:17).

Parsons and other functionalists viewed sickness as a type of deviant behavior because it is a violation of role expectations. Sickness is dysfunctional for the family because when one member is sick and relinquishes normal responsibilities, other members are required to pick up the slack and may become overburdened in doing so. In addition, sickness is dysfunctional for society. The equilibrium that society maintains can be disrupted when individual members, due to sickness, fail to fulfill routine responsibilities. The "lure" of sickness—the attraction of escaping responsibilities—requires society to exercise some control over the sick person and the sick role to minimize disruption.

However, sickness is a special form of deviant behavior; it is not equivalent to other forms of deviance such as crime or sin. Institutions (e.g., law and medicine) are created in society to deal with both behaviors, but whereas criminals are punished, the sick are provided with therapeutic care so they become well and return to their normal roles.

Within the context of the social control responsibilities of medicine, society not only allows two explicit behavioral exemptions for the sick person, but also imposes two explicit behavioral requirements. The exemptions are as follows:

1. The sick person is temporarily excused from normal social roles. Depending on the nature and severity of the illness, a physician can legitimize the sick role status and permit the patient to forgo normal responsibilities. The physician's endorsement is required so that society can maintain some control and prevent people from lingering in the sick role.
2. The sick person is not held responsible for the illness. Society accepts that cure will require more than the best efforts of the patient, and permits the patient to be "taken care of" by health care professionals and others.

In order to be granted these role exemptions, however, the patient must be willing to accept the following two obligations:

1. The sick person must want to get well. The previous two elements of the legitimized sick role are conditional on this requirement. The patient must not get so accustomed to the sick role or so enjoy the lifting of responsibilities that motivation to get well is surrendered.
2. The sick person is expected to seek medical advice and cooperate with medical experts. This requirement introduces another means of social control. The patient who refuses to see a health care professional creates suspicion that the illness is not legitimate. Such a refusal inevitably reduces the patience and sympathy of society and those surrounding the patient.

Criticisms of the Sick Role

Sociologists today are divided on the sick role's current value as an explanatory concept. The four main criticisms of the concept are:

1. The sick role does not account for the considerable variability in behavior among sick

people. Variation occurs not only by age, gender, and ethnicity but also by the certainty and severity of prognosis.

2. The sick role is applicable when describing patient experience with acute illnesses only and is less appropriate when describing people with chronic illnesses who may not have easily recognizable symptoms (e.g., a build-up of plaque in the coronary arteries) and may not get well no matter how much they want to and how vigilant they are in following the physician's instructions.

3. The sick role does not adequately account for the variety of settings in which physicians and patients interact. It is most applicable to a physician–patient relationship that occurs in the physician's office.

4. The sick role is more applicable to middle-class patients and middle-class values than it is to people in lower socioeconomic groups. Not everyone can follow this pathway—for example, lower-income persons have less freedom to curtail their normal responsibilities, especially their jobs, and thus have a more difficult time complying with the model.

Rebuttal to Sick Role Criticism

Talcott Parsons, in a 1975 journal article (he died in 1978), and others have suggested that critics failed to capture nuances in the sick role concept and see its flexibility (Fox, 1989). For example, Parsons argued that the sick role can pertain to persons with chronic illness—even though they are not "curable," their condition is often "manageable," and they are able to return to many of their pre-illness role responsibilities—and that, as an ideal type, it is unnecessary for the concept to account for all variations.

Medicalization

While Parsons described the role of medicine as an instrument of social control, many believe that the powers of the medical institution have now expanded far beyond areas of genuine expertise. This has led to **medicalization**, a concept that has two primary meanings. First, an increasing number of behaviors and conditions once thought of as normal life problems (e.g., alcoholism and obesity) have come to be interpreted in medical terms, giving the medical profession increased powers in determining what is normal and desirable behavior. Second, medical practice is understood to be the proper mechanism for controlling, modifying, and eliminating these "undesirable" behaviors.

When sociologists began focusing attention on medicalization in the 1970s, it seemed clear that the medical profession was the primary force behind these efforts, although interest groups and social movements (e.g., the effort to define alcoholism as a medical problem) often played an important role. Conrad (2005) adds three other agents: (1) biotechnology (e.g., the pharmaceutical industry promoting medical definitions for conditions such as male erectile dysfunction in order to create a market for their drugs). The concept of **pharmaceuticalization**—"the process by which social, behavioral, or bodily conditions are treated, or deemed to be in need of treatment/intervention with pharmaceuticals by doctors, patients, or both" (Abraham, 2010)—overlaps with medicalization, but is separate in that not all medicalized conditions require drug therapy; (2) consumers (e.g., seeking to receive accommodations in school for learning disabilities); and (3) managed care (acting either as an incentive or constraint for certain medical procedures based on its willingness to pay for them). Other examples illustrating medicalization include the increasing numbers of psychiatric diagnoses, menopause, obesity, baldness, anorexia, post-traumatic stress disorder, social anxiety disorder, and sleep disorders. The point is not that these are unimportant conditions. It is that medical categories and their consequent treatment have expanded to bring more individuals and life conditions into the medical realm (Conrad and Slodden, 2013).

Freund and McGuire (1999) argue that in contemporary society the power of religious definitions of deviance has declined. Such definitions appear to lack rationality and society-wide acceptance in a religiously pluralistic country. In addition, the force of legal definitions of deviance has declined, even though they appear more rational; they often ultimately come down to the subjective decisions of a small number of people on a jury. In their place, society has turned to medical definitions of deviance that appear rational, scientifically based, and dependent upon technical expertise rather than human judgment. People may be comforted by the knowledge that "undesirable" behaviors have a nice neat medical explanation and can be eradicated when sufficient scientific knowledge is accumulated.

The consequences of this medicalization can be interpreted in various ways. Fox (1989) points out that labeling additional behaviors as sickness and extending sick role exemptions to more people may be less stigmatizing and less punitive than relying on religious definitions of sin or legal definitions of crime. Bringing behaviors such as alcoholism, drug addiction, and compulsive overeating under a medical rubric introduces a "quality of therapeutic mercy into the way that they are handled" (Fox, 1989:29).

Others argue that defining someone as being sick is ultimately a moral decision in that it requires definition of what is normal or desirable (Freidson, 1988). Medicalizing behaviors leads inevitably to social stigmatization, which has occurred today with conditions such as AIDS, pelvic inflammatory disease, and cirrhosis of the liver (Freund and McGuire, 1999). According to this view, rather than being benevolent, the process of medicalization places a societally endorsed stamp of disapproval upon certain behaviors and extends the power of the medical profession over people's lives. An example follows.

Attention Deficit Hyperactivity Disorder (ADHD). In 1975, Peter Conrad described the medicalization of deviant behavior as it pertained to hyperkinesis (a concept that has evolved today to attention deficit hyperactivity disorder or ADHD). The term refers to a condition that has long been observed in children (about four times more common in males) and is characterized by hyperactivity, short attention span, restlessness, impulsivity, and mood swings—all typically defined as violations of social norms. Prompted by pharmaceutical developments (such as the development and marketing of Ritalin, a drug that has a depressing effect on those with ADHD) and by parents' groups (who sought medical solutions), the medicalization of ADHD occurred. Today, ADHD is the most commonly diagnosed childhood psychiatric disorder—about 9 percent of children and teens have been diagnosed, and the number diagnosed each year is rapidly escalating. About 5.2 percent of children and teens were taking ADHD medications in 2017 (Centers for Disease Control and Prevention, 2018a).

In the 1990s, ADHD was redefined as an adult disease. Adults who had never been diagnosed as children learned about ADHD from the media or when their own child was diagnosed, self-diagnosed, and sought pharmaceutical treatment from physicians (Conrad, 2007). Today, as much as 5 percent of the adult population has been diagnosed with ADHD, and more than 4 million adults use medication for it. Estimates are that ADHD medications globally may now be upwards of US$200 billion.

Conrad (1975) articulated the "up" side of this transition. Hyperactive children are considered to have an illness rather than to be "bad" kids (research has discovered some biochemical differences in the brains of people with ADHD), there is less condemnation of them (it is not their fault) and less social stigma, and medical treatment may be a more humanitarian form of control than the criminal justice system. In addition, proper diagnosis increases the likelihood that ADHD kids will have access to appropriately focused educational programs.

On the "down" side, however, identifying the behavior in medical terms takes it out of the public domain where ordinary people can discuss and attempt to understand it, enables the introduction and use of new and powerful drugs (alternatives to Ritalin that have fewer negative side effects are now available and becoming more common); contributes to an "individualization of social problems" by focusing on the symptoms of the child and diverting attention from family, school, and other aspects of the social structure that may be facilitating the problem; and depoliticizes deviant behavior—encouraging the view that deviant behaviors are individual problems rather than results of or challenges to the social system (Conrad, 1975).

Demedicalization

Concerned that the medical profession's powers of social control have become too extensive, a countermovement toward **demedicalization** has occurred. It includes such elements as the removal of certain behaviors (e.g., homosexuality) from the American Psychiatric Association's list of mental disorders and the deinstitutionalization of mental health patients (mental patients who can survive outside an institution and are not dangerous are mainstreamed into society). Ironically, both medicalization and demedicalization can occur simultaneously in society. Nevertheless, the dominant trend has been toward greater medicalization rather than demedicalization.

Biomedicalization

In the last few years, medical sociologists identified a new pattern referred to as **biomedicalization**. They use this term to refer to large technoscientific innovations occurring in molecular biology, biotechnologies, genomization, transplant medicine, and other new twenty-first-century medical technologies. This is considered a continuation of medicalization, but in a much more intense way that involves highly sophisticated computer and information technologies. Examples are new clinical innovations such as improved diagnostic images and telemedicine; increased requirements for electronic patient records; networked or integrated systems of hospitals, clinics, group practices, and insurance organizations; the bioscientific and medical technology and supplies industries; and the government. One aspect of this process is an expectation that patients will accept more responsibility for knowing how to use these new technologies (Bell and Figert, 2015; Clarke et al., 2003).

Symbolic Interactionism: The Labeling Approach to Illness

Whereas the biomedical approach assumes illness to be an objective state, labeling theory considers the definition of illness to be a subjective matter worked out in particular cultural contexts and within particular physician–patient encounters. Sociologists refer to this definitional process as the **social construction of illness** (Conrad and Barker, 2010).

Every society has its own particular norms for identifying the behaviors and conditions that are defined and treated as illnesses. These definitions are not objective and are not permanently fixed in two important ways. First, definitions differ from culture to culture and change over time within cultures. In the United States, alcoholism was once considered a voluntary, criminal act; it is now considered a medically treatable illness. Homosexuality used to be considered an illness; now it is often considered one of any number of acceptable sexual lifestyles.

Second, applications of the illness label are influenced by social position. Many people might be considered mentally ill for engaging in the same kinds of behaviors for which college professors are labeled "eccentric." Cocaine addicts, alcoholics, and people who abuse Valium are all medically defined in different ways even though all of them may be experiencing chemical substance abuse. Stigma (or lack of it) is certainly influenced by social standing.

Application of the illness label is especially important because labels influence how a person is treated. Individuals who have received mental health care may always be viewed somewhat differently to people who have not received such care, even after treatment ends and mental health is restored. Likewise, someone who is diagnosed with cancer may forever be considered fragile even if the cancer is successfully combated.

The Work of Eliot Freidson

Eliot Freidson (1988) devised a scheme to illustrate (1) that variations in the sick role do exist depending on one's illness, (2) that how sick people are treated depends upon the imputed seriousness of their disease and whether or not it is stigmatized within the society, and (3) that the illness label is not objective but rather a reflection of societal norms and cultural traditions. Freidson asserts that certain conditions are typically considered the responsibility of the sick person, and that society often responds negatively to these individuals, much as they would respond to one who has broken the law. Examples of these conditions include AIDS and other sexually transmitted infections, alcohol–related diseases, and increasingly, smoking-related diseases.

In part, the likelihood of stigma relates to the perceived seriousness of the disease—that is, the extent to which it deviates from normality. The consequent stigma results from societal definition; diseases that are stigmatized in one society may be relatively accepted in others (e.g., leprosy is highly stigmatized in India but much less so in Sri Lanka and Nigeria) (Freund and McGuire, 1999). A person with a socially stigmatized disease is much more likely to be looked down upon or victimized by discrimination than a person with a disease not so labeled.

Freidson's typology (see Table 7.1) considers both the extent of deviation from normality created by a disease (its "imputed seriousness") and the extent of stigmatization of persons with the disease (its "imputed legitimacy"). Illness states produce one of three types of legitimacy:

1. *Illegitimate (or stigmatized illegitimacy)* provides some exemption from role responsibilities but few additional privileges, and may carry social stigmatization. Freidson considers stammering (Cell 1) to be a minor deviation from social norms and epilepsy (Cell 4) to be a serious deviation. Because of the stigma attached, both present challenges to people with either of the conditions. See the accompanying box, "Labeling Theory and Stuttering."

2. *Conditional legitimacy* provides temporary exemption from role responsibilities with some new privileges—provided that the individual seeks to get well. A cold (Cell 2) and pneumonia (Cell 5) are Freidson's examples of a minor deviation and a serious deviation, respectively, from social norms, and ones that are considered legitimate.

3. *Unconditional legitimacy* provides permanent and unconditional exemption from role responsibilities due to the hopelessness of the condition. Pockmarks (Cell 3) are an example of a minor deviation, and cancer (Cell 6) exemplifies a serious deviation.

TABLE 7.1   Freidson's Model of Types of Illness (Deviance) for Which the Individual Is Not Held Responsible

Imputed Seriousness	Illegitimate (Stigmatized)	Conditionally Legitimate	Unconditionally Legitimate
Minor deviation	**Cell 1** "Stammer" Partial suspension of some ordinary obligations; few or no new privileges; adoption of a few new obligations.	**Cell 2** "A cold" Temporary suspension of a few ordinary obligations; temporary enhancement of ordinary privileges. Obligation to get well.	**Cell 3** "Pockmarks" No special change in obligations or privileges.
Serious deviation	**Cell 4** "Epilepsy" Suspension of some ordinary obligations; adoption of new obligations; few or no new privileges	**Cell 5** "Pneumonia" Temporary release from ordinary obligations; addition to ordinary privileges. Obligation to cooperate and seek help in treatment.	**Cell 6** "Cancer" Permanent suspension of many ordinary obligations; marked addition to privileges.

Source: Eliot Freidson. 1988. *The Profession of Medicine: A Study in the Sociology of Applied Knowledge.* Chicago: University of Chicago Press.

 IN THE FIELD

LABELING THEORY AND STUTTERING

Since childhood, I have had a stutter that makes a regular appearance in my oral interactions and, at one time or another, has affected nearly all facets of my life. My frustrated parents and I tried in vain to locate a solution, they hoping that years of speech therapy would pay off, me dreaming for a miracle cure that could instantly remove this painfully humiliating trait. . . . At the end of one school year, some of the other children in my therapy group received certificates of accomplishment. When I questioned the therapist as to why I didn't get one, she explained that, unlike me, the other children had achieved the goal of fluency and were therefore being rewarded. Most likely, she used this as a means of encouraging those of us who "failed" to try harder to succeed the next year, but to me this seemed a direct indication that my stutter was *my* fault, and that I was a less adequate person because of it. . . . When one is being told repeatedly that stuttering is bad and that one should attempt to eliminate it, any instance of dysfluency will contribute to the individual's sense of despair and hopelessness. . . . The definitive labels I received from myself and others only served to more deeply ingrain me in the role of a "stutterer" (Hottle, 1996).

STAGE 3: MEDICAL CARE CONTACT/ SELF-CARE

The third stage of Suchman's "stages of illness experience" was originally labeled as "medical care contact," but medical sociologists now include a wider variety of options, such as **self-care**, for people who have entered the sick role.

How do people decide how to behave in response to being sick? Borrowing from *rational choice theory*, one common approach has been to view sick individuals as people who have preferences and goals in life and who often meet constraints in satisfying these preferences. The rational individual will identify possible options, determine the advantages and disadvantages of each, and then select the option that will maximize the opportunity to satisfy preferences. A sick individual might consider the cost, availability, and convenience of seeing a medical doctor and recall the satisfaction or dissatisfaction produced in a prior visit.

Pescosolido (1992) believes that this approach focuses on the individual too much, and that it fails to include the important influence of social relationships. She advocates for a **social organization strategy (SOS)** that emphasizes that the process of definition and the ability to cope are both culturally and socially determined. In this perspective, responding to an illness is a *process*— rather than making a single choice, sick people talk with others, solicit advice, and possibly use a variety of professional, semiprofessional, and lay advisors until the matter is resolved or until the options are exhausted. Table 7.2, condensed from Pescosolido, identifies some of the many medical care options.

TABLE 7.2   The Range of Choices for Medical Care and Advice

Option	Advisor	Examples
Modern medical practitioners	MDs, osteopaths (general practitioners; specialists), and allied health professionals	Physicians, psychiatrists, podiatrists, optometrists, nurses, midwives, opticians, psychologists, druggists, technicians, and aides
Alternative medical practitioners	"Traditional" healers	Faith healers, spiritualists, shamans, curanderos, diviners, herbalists, acupuncturists, bonesetters, and granny midwives
	"Modern" healers	Homeopaths, chiropractors, naturopaths, nutritional consultants, and holistic practitioners
Non-medical Professionals	Social workers Legal agents Clergymen Supervisors	Police and lawyers Bosses and teachers
Lay advisors	Family Neighbors Friends Coworkers and classmates	Spouse and parents
Other	Self-care	Non-prescription medicines, self-examination procedures, folk remedies, and health foods
None		

Source: Bernice Pescosolido. 1992. "Beyond Rational Choice: The Social Dynamics of How People Seek Help." *American Journal of Sociology* 97(4):1096–1138.

Drawing on conversations with patients in internal medicine clinics, disabilities clinics, and HIV counseling and testing sites, Maynard (2006) found strong evidence for the importance of social relationships in assessing the meaning of particular diagnoses. Frequently, the physician or the patient or a family member/significant other of the patient suggest what the diagnosis means for the patient. Then one of the other participants either accepts or rejects that meaning and extends the discussion. All of the participants work toward alignment—that is, agreement about the short- and long-term effects on the patient.

Emotional responses can be exhibited throughout this discussion, and these can cover a wide range including shock, anger, sadness, threat of loss, and uncertainty. It is said that some people lose their faith and others find it. Some focus more on short-term pain and others on fear of death. Patients who have gone through this process urge that it is important to allow these emotional responses and then move attention as soon as is practicable to specific responses—learning more about the condition, considering possible treatments, contacting appropriate medical providers and other resources, and taking care of daily-life considerations such as job and family responsibilities. These responses often occur within social relationships.

Hunt, Jordan, and Irwin (1989) conducted extensive interviews with 23 women about their illness experiences just before seeing a physician and at 2, 6, 10, and 15 weeks post-consultation, and also interviewed their physicians and collected information from their charts. All the women in the sample reported at least two non-specific symptoms, such as dizziness and fatigue.

How did these women's understanding of their illnesses evolve? The researchers discovered that each woman brought several sources of information into the process, including previous medical history, ongoing experiences, and interaction with others. Each woman had evaluated her problems prior to seeing the physician and, in part, interpreted the physician's diagnosis in light of these prior understandings and thoughts.

In almost all cases, the physician's diagnosis was not simply accepted or rejected by patients; rather, it was transformed and incorporated into the understanding of the illness they had prior to the consultation. The diagnoses were also filtered through previous and current observations of others, and comments and advice offered by those in the patient's social world. Over the 4-month period, the patients continually adjusted and reworked the construction of their illnesses.

The next two sections in this chapter examine two of the many options for responding to illness—seeking professional medical care and self-care.

The Decision to Seek Professional Care

In Chapter 6, we emphasized the importance of considering both macro (social-structural) and micro (individual decision-making) factors as influences on participation in health behaviors. Both factors are also important influences on the decision about seeking professional medical care. Ronald Andersen and Lu Ann Aday, whose work significantly guides sociological thinking about the use of medical services, developed a framework for examining access to care that includes both structural and individual factors.

They posit that access to care can best be understood by considering (1) the general physical, political, and economic environment, (2) characteristics of the health care system, including health care policy and the organization and availability of services, and (3) characteristics of the population including those that may *predispose* one to use services (age, gender, and attitudes about health care), those that *enable* one to use health services (income and health insurance coverage), and the *need* for health services (Andersen, Aday, and Lytle, 1987; Andersen, 1995, 2008).

Patients, and the friends and family members accompanying them, wait to be called into a medical examination room. The decision to seek formal medical care is shaped by many factors, including the patient's age and gender, the perception of the illness, and the social situation.

The ability of this model to predict use of services has been affirmed in much research. McEwen (2000) used data from a national health survey to determine the predictive ability of the model with respect to both the postponement of needed medical care and the presence of unmet medical need. The best prediction of these dependent measures occurred when all three of the predisposing, enabling, and need factors were considered.

Concentrating more on the individual level, DiMatteo and Friedman (1982) specified three factors that influence the decision to seek care:

1. *The background of the patient.* Propensity to see a physician is influenced by such factors as age, gender, race and ethnicity, and social class. For example, men are often more reluctant than women to see a physician, and many married men schedule an appointment only when pressured by their wives to do so (estimates are that women make 70 percent of all health care decisions). Many (especially older) men prefer to "tough it out" and are embarrassed to discuss such matters as sexual dysfunction, prostate enlargement, and depression.

2. *The patient's perception of the illness.* Zola (1973:677–689) identified five social triggers that influence one's judgment about which symptoms need professional attention: (1) perceived interference with vocational or physical activity, especially work-related activity; (2) perceived interference with social or personal relations; (3) an interpersonal crisis; (4) a **temporalizing of symptomatology** (setting a deadline—if I'm not better by Monday, I'll call the doctor); and (5) pressure from family and friends.

3. *The social situation.* Even for pain that may relate to a serious condition, situational factors matter. Symptoms that begin during the week, rather than on the weekend, are more likely to motivate prompt contact with a physician, as are symptoms that appear at work and when other people are present (DiMatteo and Friedman, 1982).

Use of Medical Care Services

Americans on average have about five or six physician contacts each year. However, this average camouflages significant differences among population subgroups. Overall, the number of contacts increases significantly with age, is higher for women than men, and is highest among people in the lowest income category.

The following section describes patterns in the utilization of health services among several important population subgroups.

The Poor and the Medically Indigent. People below the poverty level and those just above it often have difficulty gaining access to quality medical care. Since the late 1960s (and largely as a result of Medicaid and Medicare), the poor have averaged as many or more physician contacts each year as the non-poor. However, relative to their greater medical need, the poor continue to have lower access. In fact, those just above the poverty level have the lowest utilization rates relative to need. These individuals—often called the *medically indigent* or *working poor*—earn just enough money to fail to qualify for Medicaid, but not enough to afford private medical care. In 2016, 16.3 percent of adults with family incomes just above the poverty level delayed or forewent needed medical care due to cost (National Center for Health Statistics, 2018).

In the past, most of the medically indigent lacked any form of health insurance (about 47 million Americans lacked health care coverage in 2010). Most were in households with a wage earner who worked in a job that did not offer health insurance as a benefit. Others most likely to be uninsured were the unemployed, and those with major health problems who could not afford individual insurance (or had been denied insurance due to their condition). These patterns have changed somewhat with the passage of the Affordable Care Act (ACA) in 2010 and implementation of key pieces in 2014. The ACA is discussed at length in Chapter 14.

Even after passage of the ACA, use of health care services by the poor differs from that by the non-poor in three other important respects. First,

the poor are much less likely to have a regular source of care—that is, a physician they routinely see for health care problems. In 2016–2017, among children and teens under 18 years, 7 percent of those with family incomes below poverty had no regular source of care, compared to less than 2 percent of those with family incomes over 400 percent of the poverty level (National Center for Health Statistics, 2018).

Second (as a consequence of the first), the poor are more likely to use a hospital emergency room (ER) or outpatient department as a routine care site. While this is not an efficient use of services (care in the ER is more expensive) and may be resented by hospital staff, these may be the only available and convenient facilities. Public hospitals and clinics tend to be larger, busier, colder, and more impersonal than medical offices. The waiting time to see a physician may be very long—sometimes most of a day. Staff members are often fiercely overworked and have little time for patients. The actual physician–patient encounter may be hurried and abrupt, with little warmth and little investigation of the patient's psychosocial concerns. Often this encounter is not a satisfying experience for either the patient or the physician. This "health care system barrier" reduces the likelihood of the poor receiving medical services.

Third (partially as a consequence of the first two), low-income persons are much sicker when they are admitted to a hospital and require longer hospital stays. Due to the higher rates of disease and illness in poor communities, the lack of access to outpatient care, and the inability to pay for hospital costs, the poor often become very sick before admission occurs. This often leads to longer stays and less successful outcomes.

The inability to obtain needed services occurs throughout health care. Low-income persons often forgo needed dental services (which are not covered in the ACA and only rarely in health insurance plans). They do not schedule regular check-ups or get severe and painful conditions treated. In 2017, 12.7 percent of adult women and 8.8 percent of adult men reported needing, but not getting, dental care in the past year because they could not afford it (Centers for Disease Control and Prevention, 2019).

For an international comparison, see the accompanying box, "Disparities in Primary Care Experiences by Income."

The Homeless. The homeless population in the United States rarely receives needed physical or mental health services. Estimates of the prevalence of psychiatric disorders among the homeless range from 25 to 50 percent, and estimates of previous psychiatric hospitalization range from 15 to 42 percent. Research has consistently found very high levels of need for

physical and mental health services, but very few services received (Wood et al., 2010).

Racial and Ethnic Minorities. In recent years, the black–white disparity in both utilization of health care services and having a regular source of health care have almost disappeared (National Center for Health Statistics, 2018). However, significant differences remain in other aspects of use patterns. Blacks are more likely than whites to secure care in hospital emergency departments and have slightly higher rates of forgoing needed prescription drugs due to cost (National Center for Health Statistics, 2018). Racial and ethnic minorities experience more difficulty getting initial and follow-up appointments with a physician and wait longer during an appointment.

IN COMPARATIVE FOCUS

DISPARITIES IN PRIMARY CARE EXPERIENCES BY INCOME

In 2006, the Commonwealth Fund, a respected private foundation that seeks to improve the health care system, reported on a 2004 study of the use of primary care by adults in five countries—the United States, Australia, Canada, the United Kingdom, and New Zealand. The report authors summarized as follows:

> Given the strong correlation worldwide between low income and poor health—including disability, chronic disease, and acute illness—it is especially critical for people with limited incomes to have ready access to medical care. Inequities in access can contribute to and exacerbate existing disparities in health and quality of life, creating barriers to a strong and productive life (p. xiii).

How did the United States fare in the comparison?

> Overall, the report finds a health care divide separating the United States from the other four countries.

The United States stands out for income-based disparities in patient experiences—particularly for more negative primary care experiences for adults with below-average income (p. xiii).

On 16 of the 30 specific measures of primary care experience for below-average income patients, the United States ranked last. Patients in the United States were most likely to go without care because of costs, most likely to have difficulty getting care at night, during weekends, or on holidays without going to the emergency room, most likely to report duplication of medical services (due to lack of coordination of care), and most likely to rate their encounter with the physician as being only fair or poor. The gap between above-average-income patients and below-average-income patients was by far the largest in the United States (Huynh et al., 2006).

In addition to economic reasons, another factor accounting for these patterns is the lack of services in black communities in inner-city areas of large metropolitan cities and in rural areas, especially in the Southeast. These are the two areas of the country most underserved by physicians. This shortage makes it difficult for physicians located in these areas and complicates patients' efforts to find a physician with whom to establish a continuing relationship. Since patients with a regular source of care tend to be more satisfied with their physician, other benefits accrue, including higher adherence rates.

Despite high levels of morbidity, Hispanics have the lowest rate of utilization of medical services of any racial or ethnic group in the United States (National Center for Health Statistics, 2018). Hispanics are more likely than non-Hispanic whites to have no regular source of medical care, they are twice as likely to use a hospital ER as a regular source of care, they are much more likely to be admitted to a hospital through an ER, and they are likely to be much sicker at the point of admission (indicating delay in seeking services), resulting in longer and more expensive hospital stays. Hispanics are much less likely to initiate prenatal care in the recommended first trimester, and are three times less likely to receive any prenatal care whatsoever.

Several factors are responsible for these differential utilization patterns, including lower family incomes and a lack of accessible health care services for Mexican American farmworkers and those who live in inner-city areas of large cities. Even when services are available, communication difficulties due to the absence of an interpreter and cultural differences from providers often represent important barriers.

Age. Older people are consistently the heaviest users of health care services. Persons over 65 years of age receive more preventive care than do younger people and visit physicians more frequently in response to medical need. In 2014, people over age 65 years made up about 15 percent of the US population but accounted for over one-third of all personal health care expenditures (Centers for Medicare and Medicaid Services, 2019).

Gender. There are consistent differences between women and men in utilization of health care services. Women use more physician services, are more likely to have a regular source of care, receive significantly more preventive care, take more medications, are more likely to visit outpatient clinics, and are more likely to be hospitalized. On the other hand, men are more likely to use ER services.

Why do women and men have such different utilization patterns? The most obvious reason—the extra use of services by women for reproductive care—explains only part of the difference (reproduction accounts for only about 20 percent of women's physician contacts). More important factors are the greater number of illnesses reported by women (need for care being an important predictor of use) and the greater willingness of women to seek professional health care.

Gender roles are clearly implicated with the latter reason. Women are socialized to be more sensitive to medical symptoms, and once symptoms are perceived, to take them more seriously. Once this evaluation has occurred, women find it easier to seek medical assistance; therefore, they show a higher utilization rate. On the other hand, men often exhibit a reluctance to get check-ups, required screening tests, and medical attention for problems as diverse as depression, substance abuse, physical disability, and stress (Galdas, Cheater, and Marshall, 2005). Recent research has traced at least some of this pattern to the traditional gender role of men—a sense of immunity and immortality, difficulty relinquishing control, and a reluctance to seek help (Springer and Mouzon, 2011). See the accompanying box, "Gender and the Use of Medical Services in Rural India."

IN COMPARATIVE FOCUS

GENDER AND THE USE OF MEDICAL SERVICES IN RURAL INDIA

While certain cultural norms in the United States discourage men from seeking professional medical care, the opposite pattern is evident in some parts of rural India. Even in areas where health services are readily available, certain cultural values related to gender ideology and gender-based behavior influence women to underuse medical care. To better understand this pattern, Kumar (1995) spent 9 months in a rural village in northern India conducting a general household survey and open-ended interviews with married women.

Married women in the village observe *ghungat* (veiling), which includes covering the face with a veil and complying with a set of restrictions on speech, mobility, and social relationships. The female body is associated with shame for reasons that relate to ideas about cleanliness (menstruation and childbirth add even further restrictions, due to the powerful meaning ascribed to blood as a particularly dirty substance), the necessity of maintaining pure patrilineage, and fear of uncontrolled

sexuality. Women are financially dependent on men, although men are dependent on women to manage the home and raise the children. *Ghungat* is viewed as a practice that honors both men and women because it is a visual expression of the acceptance of the greater power of men and their control over women.

When married women are sick, their access to medical care is limited by the necessity of having their husband's approval to seek care, by not having direct access to financial resources, and by the difficulty of taking time off from household chores. Limitations in movement throughout the village and a requirement not to visit the health center alone are further discouragements, as is the perceived inappropriateness of having a man physician "look at" parts of the woman's unclothed body. These cultural restraints explain the less frequent use of medical services by women than by men, and the fact that women are sometimes not seen until they have reached an advanced stage of illness.

The Concept of Self-Care

Self-care describes the broad range of behaviors initiated by individuals to promote optimal health, prevent illness, detect symptoms of ill health, heal acute illness, and manage chronic conditions. It includes obtaining information about health and illness, doing self-screening exams, managing one's own illness (including self-medication), and formulating clear goals and preferences with regard to end-of-life treatment decisions. Although the term "self-care" implies an individual behavior, these practices occur within a social network and are influenced by family, friends, and cultural norms.

Reliance on self-care is not new. Since the earliest civilizations, people have taken personal measures to protect their safety and well-being and deal with illnesses. However, the advent of modern scientific medicine shifted primary responsibility for managing health and illness from the individual and family to the physician.

Nevertheless, self-care remains a vitally important element in health care. One national study found that more than 5 in 6 people aged 55 years or older had experienced at least one illness symptom in the previous 6 months for which they relied exclusively on self-care (Kart and Engler, 1994). Studies indicate that people who use self-care practices reduce both the number of visits to physicians and the number of days in the hospital, and that the commonplace use of self-selected over-the-counter drugs saves the nation millions of dollars each year in physicians' fees.

Self-Help and Health Social Movements. The concept of self-help is related to, yet distinct from, self-care. Self-care is often practiced alone or within a family and does not require a more formally organized group. **Self-help** groups consist of individuals who experience a common problem and come together to share personal stories, knowledge, and social support. While taking an over-the-counter pain medication (whether on one's own or at a family member's insistence) is a form of self-care, a group of migraine sufferers coming together to share their experiences and offer mutual support constitutes self-help. The knowledge and support gained from participation in a self-help group can lead to members' adoption of more effective self-care practices but may also lead to larger structural changes (Chesney and Chesler, 1993).

The roots of self-help can be traced to the mutual aid and friendly societies of the colonial period, which provided financial and social assistance to members in times of need. As trade unions, scientific medicine, social service agencies and private insurance grew, these groups assumed many of the functions fulfilled by friendly societies. Modern self-help groups emerged in the 1960s as an outgrowth of the women's health movement, which criticized the medical monopoly on women's health (including, but not limited to, reproductive health) and sought to empower women to become active agents in their own care.

Today, groups are organized around almost every conceivable disease, addiction, and disability. See the accompanying box, "Selected Self-Help Groups." An estimated 10 to 15 million people participate in the nation's half million plus self-help groups annually, and more than 30 million people have participated at some time. Self-help groups may be formally organized nonprofits (or their local chapters) such as Alcoholics Anonymous, but they may also be unaffiliated and informal local groups. Self-help groups are increasingly virtual, using online discussion boards, Facebook groups, and e-mail lists to offer the same mutual support as more traditional face-to-face groups.

IN THE FIELD

SELECTED SELF-HELP GROUPS

Alcoholics Anonymous
Alliance for the Mentally Ill
CHADD (Children and Adults with Attention-Deficit/Hyperactivity Disorder)
Co-dependents Anonymous
Compassionate Friends (Bereaved Parents)
Concerned United Birthparents
Crohn's and Colitis Foundation of America
Exceptional Cancer Patients
Fathers United Inc.
Gamblers Anonymous
Gilda's Club (cancer support)

Gluten Intolerance Group of North America
La Leche League (breastfeeding support)
Narcotics Anonymous
Overeaters Anonymous
Parents of Children with Asthma
Parents without Partners
Resolve (infertility)
Sex Addicts Anonymous
Shhh (hard-of-hearing)
Step-Family Association of America
Suddenly Single
Veterans Outreach Program

Taylor (1996) identified four characteristics common to modern self-help groups: (1) mobilization around a common experience (e.g., having a particular disease), (2) a focus on experiential knowledge (e.g., prioritizing personal experience over scientific knowledge), (3) embrace of mutual support, and (4) an emphasis on societal change. For example, members of celiac disease support groups forge a common identity around celiac and the need to follow a gluten-free diet, often question scientific understandings of celiac based on their collective experience, rely on members for dietary support, and advocate for gluten-free menu offerings in schools and restaurants, thus effecting larger structural change (Copelton, 2011).

Because of their role as agents of social change, self-help groups are an important component of **health social movements (HSMs)**, defined as "collective challenges to medical policy and politics, belief systems, research and practice" (Brown et al., 2004:52). HSMs have improved patient access to care, led to more effective treatment options, and strengthened laws and regulations governing occupational safety and accommodations for disabilities.

The growing interest in both self-care and self-help is also part of a larger cultural emphasis on shifting at least some responsibility for managing health care from medical professionals back to individuals. This shift is facilitated by the increased availability of health-related information online and the growing number of people who use this information either in conjunction with, or as a substitute for, professional care. The expansion of alternative medical philosophies and clinical approaches that place primary responsibility for health on the individual—including behavioral approaches, concepts of holistic health, and therapies derived from Eastern philosophies (e.g., yoga, meditation, and biofeedback)—is another important factor (discussed more in Chapter 12). Finally, greater recognition by individuals, governments, and insurance companies of the need to reduce health care spending also plays a role.

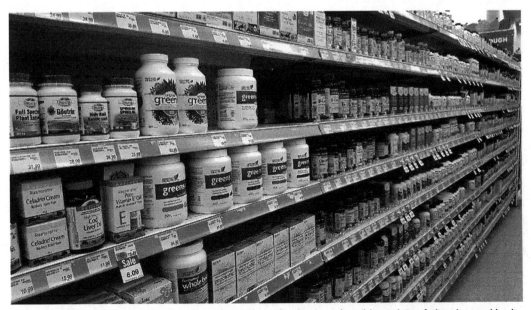

An important part of the self-help movement is the self-selection of a wide variety of vitamins and herbs that are now readily available in natural food stores, grocery stores, drug stores, and other outlets.

STAGE 4: DEPENDENT–PATIENT ROLE

The patient enters the fourth stage, the dependent-patient role, when a recommendation of the health care provider for treatment is accepted. This creates new role expectations that include increased contact with the provider and altered personal relationships. The patient is expected to make every effort to get well. Nevertheless, as we explore in greater detail in Chapter 12, entering the dependent–patient role does not necessarily mean that patients follow doctors' orders steadfastly. Although patients may accept diagnosis and treatment recommendations, many do not fully adhere to the treatment program prescribed. Some don't take medications or don't take them as prescribed, and many more selectively implement recommended behavior or lifestyle changes (e.g., getting more rest, changing their diet).

Some people, of course, enjoy the benefits of the dependent–patient role (increased attention, escape from work responsibilities, etc.) and attempt to malinger. Eventually, however, the acute patient will either get well and move on to stage 5 or terminate the treatment (and perhaps seek alternative treatment).

STAGE 5: RECOVERY AND REHABILITATION

The final stage of Suchman's schema for patients with most acute illnesses occurs as the treatment succeeds and recovery occurs. As that happens, the patient is expected to relinquish the sick role and move back to normal role obligations. For chronic patients, the extent to which previous role obligations may be resumed ranges from those who forsake the sick role altogether to those who will never be able to leave it.

An interesting subfield of sociology that has developed in recent years is animals and society. The accompanying box, "The Role of Animals

---

IN THE FIELD

THE ROLE OF ANIMALS IN HUMAN THERAPY

Research has documented the health benefits for humans who interact positively with animals. Interaction with animals has been shown to have (1) *preventive benefits for health* (reduced stress, lower blood pressure, and greater happiness); (2) *therapeutic benefits* (riding horses is helpful in the physical rehabilitation of the developmentally disabled, animals assist with emotional recovery of battered women and their children, animals reduce levels of loneliness among the elderly, and animals assist recovery for stroke victims and those with orthopaedic problems); and (3) *recovery and rehabilitation benefits* (one major study examined the influence of hundreds of physical, social, and economic factors on the long-term survival of patients released from a hospital coronary care unit—the most important influence was the extent of the damage to the heart tissue itself, but the second largest influence was living with a pet. Less than half the patients had a pet, but those who did were four times less likely to die). In addition, service dogs and guide dogs are trained to help individuals who require physical assistance maintain an independent life.

Why do these benefits occur? Companion animals help fulfill (1) *social-psychological needs* such as contact, comfort, a feeling of being needed, unconditional love, empathy, patience, relaxation, and coping with stress; (2) *physical needs* such as more exercise (dog owners walk much more); and (3) *help with child socialization* in that children raised with an animal are more nurturing, have a greater sense of responsibility, and have more social and less self-absorbed behavior. (Based on material from *Kindred Spirits* by Allen M. Schoen, D.V.M., M.S., copyright 2001 by Allen M. Schoen. Used with permission of Broadway Books, a division of Random House, Inc.)

in Human Therapy," describes how the animal–human bond has important implications for health and rehabilitation.

EXPERIENCING CHRONIC ILLNESS AND DISABILITY

While patients usually survive and recover from acute illnesses, other conditions continue over time. A chronic illness is one that is ongoing or recurrent and that typically persists for as long as the person lives. Type 1 diabetes is an example of a chronic illness. While it can be treated with insulin, there is no cure, and it never disappears. As defined in Chapter 3, a **disability** includes *impairments* (a problem in body function or structure), *activity limitations* (a difficulty in executing a task or action), and *participation restrictions* (a problem experienced in involvement in life situations). Disability is a complex phenomenon, reflecting an interaction between features of a person's body and features of the society in which he or she lives.

Relationship Between Chronic Illness and Disability

Often, chronic illnesses have an insidious onset (e.g., cancer and coronary heart disease) and are characterized early on by symptoms that are not immediately detectable. Eventually, most chronic illnesses can be identified by diagnostic laboratory procedures. On the other hand, disability is more of a relational concept—it is rarely entirely present or absent in any individual; rather, its presence is often a matter of degree. It is a more subjective term that can only be understood by considering an individual within the cultural context. Moreover, some individuals with chronic illness become disabled, but some do not, and disabilities may result from chronic illness but they also may be traced to trauma, accidents, injuries, and genetic disorders.

Living With Chronic Illness and Disability

Experiencing chronic illness and/or disability typically involves a period of assessment, emotional adjustment, and mental and physical accommodation. Research has identified five

Animals now assist in a variety of therapeutic procedures, and positive interaction with animals has important benefits for human health.

very important concerns shared by many chronically ill and disabled people:

1. *Impairment of personal cognitive functioning.* Patients may be concerned that their illness will progress to a point where their cognitive functioning may be impaired, or that medications will have a dulling effect on their memory, reasoning ability, and capacity for communication.
2. *Loss of personal independence.* Many people deeply value their independence and appreciate it even more when it is threatened. Reliance on others may be a devastating thought because of the inconvenience and the idea of becoming a burden on others.
3. *Changes in body image.* For patients whose illness creates any dramatic alteration in physical image, a major readjustment may be needed. Many people view themselves as physical beings as much as or more than mental beings; any change in body image is significant.
4. *Withdrawal from key social roles.* Because so many people derive their identity from their work, any disruption in work pattern or work accomplishment is very threatening. If remuneration is affected, an extra emotional burden is created. Withdrawal from key family responsibilities may be of paramount concern, along with anxiety about creating more work for other family members. Withdrawal and related concern can jeopardize family cohesiveness.
5. *The future.* Any chronic or disabling condition raises questions about the patient's future and the extent to which there will be further incapacitation or physical or mental limitations, as well as questions about financial indebtedness and permanent losses in daily activities.

The extent of these concerns and the ability to adjust, adapt, and even resolve them occur within a social environment. A study of women living with HIV found that those with greater social capital (e.g., adequate financial resources, a stable housing situation, access to health care) were better able to manage the demands of their condition. They practiced better daily health habits, had greater social support, and were better able to accept the chronic nature of HIV (Webel et al., 2013).

The Impact on Sense of Self

Having a chronic illness or disability challenges the individual's sense of self. Patients may have to get accustomed to significant changes in their body, their lifestyle, and interactions, and to prolonged regimens of medication, continuing bureaucratic hassles with the medical care system, and in some cases disabling pain.

Based on more than 100 interviews with 55 people, Charmaz (1991) described how experiencing a progressively deteriorating chronic illness can reshape a person's life and sense of self. People experience chronic illness in three ways— as an *interruption in life*, as an *intrusive illness*, and as an *immersion in illness*.

At first, a person with a chronic illness may notice the disruption in life. There is time spent hoping for the best and trying to convince oneself that things will work out. Difficult times lower hopes and increase fears that important life events will need to be sacrificed. A bargaining process may occur when the person promises to do whatever can be done to feel better. Not fully comprehending chronicity, ill people seek recovery and, in doing so, maintain the same image of self and keep the illness external, not allowing it to become an essential part of their being. Only through time and the words and actions of others do the meanings of disability, dysfunction, and impairment become real.

Chronic illness becomes intrusive when it demands continuous attention, more and more time, and significant accommodations. Intrusion happens when the illness is recognized as a permanent part of life—when symptoms and treatments are expected and planned around. The ill person loses some control over life, but may work to maintain some control and to boost their self-esteem. Limits may be placed on the illness— for example, allowing oneself a certain number of bad days. Efforts are made to prevent the illness from occupying more and more of one's time and being.

Immersion occurs as the illness begins to dominate life. Responsibilities are surrendered, and days are dominated by dealing with the illness. "No longer can people add illness to the structure of their lives; instead, they must reconstruct their lives upon illness" (Charmaz, 1991:76). They face physical and perhaps social and economic dependencies, their social world shrinks, and more and more of each day is ordered by the routines demanded by the illness. People turn inward, become more socially isolated, and begin challenging their own identity ("How can I continue to be myself while having relentless illness?") (Charmaz, 1991:101).

The trajectory of self-image for those with traumatic but stable disabilities may differ in some ways. In a study of 35 adults with traumatic spinal cord injury, Yoshiba (1993) found that patients actively sought to "reconstruct" the self, and this process swung back and forth like a pendulum between the non-disabled and the disabled aspects of self. At any one time, these adults had a "predominant identity view" that at one extreme emphasized the former non-injured self and at the other extreme emphasized the disabled identity as the total self. Between the extremes were several gradations based primarily on the extent of dependence on others. Yoshiba discovered that the primary identity is dynamic and shifting and can be very fluid from one day to another and/or from one situation to another.

Moreover, with the possible exception of the disabled identity as the total self, Yoshiba's respondents contradicted the popular perception that having a disability is a totally negative experience. Some shared examples of activities

for which they had never previously had time, and several spoke of their personal maturation in dealing with the situation. These experiences are akin to observations of chronically ill and disabled patients made by Lindsay (1996). She noted a constant striving for "health within illness" among her respondents, as many sought to identify or achieve positives from their condition.

Further confirmation of this perspective comes from research by Pudrovska (2010). She compared the trajectory of personal growth among those who had had cancer and those who had not for three age cohorts (those born in the 1940s, 1950s, and 1960s, those born in the 1930s, and those born in the 1920s). For those in the oldest cohort, cancer did accelerate decline in personal growth (an impairment trajectory). However, dealing with cancer neither accelerated nor decelerated decline in personal growth for those in the middle group (a resilient trajectory), and dealing with cancer actually slowed decline in personal growth for those in the youngest age cohort (a thriving trajectory). Pudrovska referred to this as psychological growth in response to an adverse event.

The Role of Social Stigma

The adjustment of people with a chronic illness or disability is influenced by the manner in which they are treated by others. When others view an illness or disability in a demeaning manner, they impose a **stigma** or deeply discrediting label on the individual. The stigmatizing attitudes of others can have a pronounced effect on an individual's sense of self.

In a study comparing perceived stigma attached to cancer patients and HIV/AIDS patients, Fife and Wright (2000) identified four dimensions of perceived stigma:

1. *Social rejection.* Feelings of being discriminated against at work and in society, including a perception that others do not respect them,

want to avoid them, and feel awkward in their presence.

2. *Financial insecurity.* Inadequate job security and income that result from workplace discrimination.

3. *Internalized shame.* Feelings of being set apart from others who are well, blaming oneself for the illness, and feeling a need to maintain secrecy about the illness.

4. *Social isolation.* Feelings of loneliness, inequality with others, uselessness, and detachment.

Fife and Wright found that while stigma was a central force in the lives of both sets of patients, the HIV/AIDS patients perceived greater stigma on all four dimensions. The more negative self-perception held by both sets of patients came more from the perceived stigma attached to the disease than from the disease itself. For example,

both cancer and HIV/AIDS patients had reduced self-esteem. However, this stemmed not from having the disease but from the negative stigma that had been attached to them because of the disease.

Wingood et al. (2007) found that HIV-infected women who had perceived discrimination were more likely to report high stress levels than those who had not and had more symptoms of depression, lower self-esteem, a greater likelihood of considering suicide, and a greater likelihood of not seeking or continuing with medical care. Other research (Turner-Cobb et al., 2002) has confirmed that HIV/AIDS patients who are more satisfied with their relationships and are more securely engaged with others make a better adjustment. These findings illustrate well the dramatic effect of societal response on sense of self.

SUMMARY

Illness behavior refers to activity undertaken by a person who feels ill in order to define the illness and seek relief from it. As outlined by Edward Suchman, the illness experience consists of five stages: (1) symptom experience, (2) assumption of the sick role, (3) medical care contact, (4) dependent–patient role, and (5) recovery and rehabilitation. Decisions that are made during these five stages and the behaviors exhibited are culturally and socially determined.

The symptom experience stage occurs in response to physical pain or discomfort and includes cognitive reflection and emotional response. Individuals use many types of cues to determine whether to seek help. If they decide to relinquish normal social roles in response to illness, they enter a sick role. This involves giving up normal roles and the responsibility of caring for oneself, but only if the individual wants to get well and takes action to do so. Labeling theorists emphasize that the definition of illness

is a subjective phenomenon that is socially constructed within society and within particular physician–patient encounters.

Medicine's license to legitimize illness has extended more widely than originally envisioned—a process termed "medicalization." An increasing number of behaviors (e.g., alcoholism and infertility) have come under medicine's domain, and physicians and other health care providers are sought for guidance.

The use of professional medical services in times of illness varies among population groups. Response to symptoms is affected greatly by socioeconomic, cultural, and structural variables. Access to quality medical care is still a problem for a number of disadvantaged population groups, especially people with low income and many racial and ethnic minority groups.

Self-care is an extremely common practice that involves a number of behaviors related to promoting health, preventing illness, and restoring health if illness occurs. Millions of people are helped annually through self-help groups.

Those who experience progressively deteriorating chronic illnesses and those who experience traumatic but stable disabilities undergo transformations in self-image and sometimes experience stigmatization. While the former gradually become "immersed" in the disease, the latter often shift back and forth between a disabled and non-disabled identity.

HEALTH ON THE INTERNET

1. To learn more about the role of palliative care for the treatment of chronic pain, go to the following website:

   https://getpalliativecare.org/podcasts/

   Listen to (or read the transcript for) one of the palliative care podcasts posted there. What features of the illness experience does the story highlight? Explain how Charmaz's distinction between chronic illness as an interruption, intrusion, or immersion does or does not apply to the patient portrayed in the podcast. To what extent did palliative care help the patient featured in the story maintain his or her sense of self?

DISCUSSION QUESTIONS

1. In 1997, the case of Casey Martin received considerable national publicity. Martin was a young golfer who had had some success on the professional golf tour. However, he suffered from Klippel–Trenaunay–Weber syndrome, a rare and painful circulatory disorder that affected his lower right leg (his right leg has only half the girth of his left) and severely limited his ability to walk a golf course.

   The Professional Golf Association (PGA) mandates that participants in its tournaments walk the golf course, although they hire others to carry their golf bag. Martin requested an exemption to this rule and asked to be allowed to use a golf cart (the kind most recreational golfers use) to get around the course. The PGA refused on the grounds that walking the course is an integral part of the game.

   Martin sued the PGA under the Americans with Disabilities Act (ADA). The ADA, which was passed in 1990, prohibits discrimination on the basis of disability in jobs, housing, and places of public accommodation. The law requires businesses to make reasonable modifications for people with disabilities, unless doing so would fundamentally alter the nature of the activity in question. Martin contended his being allowed to ride in a cart would not constitute such a fundamental change, but the PGA argued that it would.

   The case ultimately wound its way to the US Supreme Court. In May 2001, by a 7 to 2 vote, the Court ruled that walking was, at most, peripheral to the game of golf and that Martin's use of a cart would not fundamentally alter the activity. Justices Scalia and Thomas, in dissent, argued that the ruling would doom all sports at all levels because anyone with any disability could insist on having the rules of a game changed to accommodate a disability. ADA advocates insisted that the "fundamental change" stipulation would prevent such interpretation.

   In your judgment, did the Supreme Court rule properly or improperly in the Casey Martin case? What implications did the decision have for people with disabilities?

The case of Casey Martin (a young professional golfer with a rare circulatory disease in his right leg) raised significant questions about treatment of individuals with limiting medical conditions. Ultimately, and despite their opposition, the PGA was required by courts to allow him to use a golf cart in professional tournaments.

(As an aside, Martin gave up tournament golf in 2006, but qualified for and played in the US Open in 2012. In 2013, while riding in his cart as a spectator at a US Junior Amateur tournament (he is currently golf coach at the University of Oregon), the US Golf Association (USGA) pulled him off the course and told him that spectators could not ride in a cart. Despite the Supreme Court decision and despite having been given permission by the tournament chairman and rules director, the USGA disallowed him use of the cart.)

2. In June 2013, the American Medical Association formally declared obesity a disease. The decision was hailed by some as a long overdue action that would improve medicine's ability to treat obesity but was denounced by others who believe it will increase the stigma experienced by obese people. Having read about medicalization issues in this chapter, identify the various ways in which this declaration may affect obese people.

GLOSSARY

biomedicalization
chronic illness
demedicalization
disability
health social movements (HSM)
illness behavior
medicalization
palliative care
pharmaceuticalization
self-care

self-help
sick role
social capital
social construction of illness
social organization strategy (SOS)
stages of illness experience
stigma
temporalizing of symptomatology
theory of help-seeking behavior

REFERENCES

Abraham, John. 2010. "The Sociological Concomitants of the Pharmaceutical Industry and Medications." Pp. 290–308 in *Handbook of Medical Sociology* (6th ed.), edited by Chloe E. Bird, Peter Conrad, Allen M. Fremont, and Stefan Timmermans. Nashville, TN: Vanderbilt University Press.

Andersen, Ronald M. 1995. "Revisiting the Behavioral Model and Access to Medical Care: Does It Matter?" *Journal of Health and Social Behavior* 36(1):1–10.

———. 2008. "National Health Surveys and the Behavioral Model of Health Services Use." *Medical Care* 46(7):647–653.

Andersen, Ronald M., Lu Ann Aday, and C.S. Lytle. 1987. *Ambulatory Care and Insurance Coverage in an Era of Constraint*. Chicago, IL: Pluribus.

Bell, Susan E., and Anne E. Figert. 2015. *Reimagining (Bio)Medicalization, Pharmaceuticals and Genetics*. New York: Routledge.

Brown, Phil, Stephen Zavestoski, Sabrina McCormick, Brian Mayer, Rachel Morello-Frosch, and Rebecca Gasior Altman. 2004. "Embodied Health Movements: New Approaches to Social Movements in Health." *Sociology of Health & Illness* 26(1):50–80.

Center to Advance Palliative Care. 2019. *Palliative Care Facts and Stats*. New York: Center to Advance Palliative Care.

Centers for Disease Control and Prevention. 2018a. "Data and Statistics About ADHD." Retrieved June 26, 2019 (www.cdc.gov/ncbddd/adhd/data.html).

———. 2018b. "U.S. Opioid Prescribing Rate Maps." Retrieved June 26, 2019 (www.cdc.gov/drugoverdose/maps/rxrate-maps.html).

———. 2019. "QuickStats: Age-Adjusted Percentage of Adults Aged ≥18 Years Who Reported That They Needed Dental Care During the Past 12 Months but Didn't Get It Because They Couldn't Afford It." *Morbidity and Mortality Weekly Report* 68(11):273.

Centers for Medicare and Medicaid Services. 2019. "NHE Fact Sheet." Retrieved June 26, 2019 (www.cms.gov/Research-Statistics-Data-and-Systems/Statistics-Trends-and-Reports/NationalHealthExpendData/NHE-Fact-Sheet.html).

Charmaz, Kathy. 1991. *Good Days, Bad Days: The Self in Chronic Illness and Time*. New Brunswick, NJ: Rutgers University Press.

Chesney, Barbara K., and Mark A. Chesler. 1993. "Activism through Self-Help Group Membership." *Small Group Research* 24(2):258–273.

Clarke, Adele E., Janet K. Shim, Laura Mamo, Jennifer R. Fosket, and Jennifer R. Fishman. 2003. "Biomedicalization: Technoscientific Transformations of Health, Illness, and U.S. Biomedicine." *American Sociological Review* 68(2):161–194.

Compton, Wilson M., Christopher M. Jones, and Grant T. Baldwin. 2016. "Relationship between Nonmedical Prescription-Opioid Use and Heroin Use." *New England Journal of Medicine* 374(2):154–163.

Conrad, Peter. 1975. "The Discovery of Hyperkinesis: Notes on the Medicalization of Deviant Behavior." *Social Problems* 23(1):12–21.

———. 2005. "The Shifting Engines of Medicalization." *Journal of Health and Social Behavior* 46(1):3–14.

———. 2007. *The Medicalization of Society*. Baltimore, MD: Johns Hopkins University Press.

Conrad, Peter, and Kristin K. Barker. 2010. "The Social Construction of Illness: Key Insights and Policy Implications." *Journal of Health and Social Behavior* 51(1):S67–S79.

Conrad, Peter, and Caitlin Slodden. 2013. "The Medicalization of Mental Disorder." Pp. 61–173 in *Handbook of the Sociology of Mental Health* (2nd ed.), edited by Carol S. Aneshensel, Jo C. Phelan, and Alex Bierman. New York: Springer.

Copelton, Denise. 2011. "Advocacy and Everyday Health Activism among Persons with Celiac Disease: A Comparison of Eager, Reluctant, and Non-Activists." Pp. 561–575 in *Taking Food Public: Redefining Foodways in a Changing World*, edited by Carole Counihan and Psyche Williams-Forson. New York: Routledge.

Dahlhamer, James, Jacqueline Lucas, Carla Zelaya, Richard Nahin, Sean Mackey, Lynn DeBar, Robert Kerns, Michael Von Korff, Linda Porter, and Charles Helmick. 2018. "Prevalence of Chronic Pain and High-Impact Chronic Pain Among Adults—United States, 2016." *Morbidity and Mortality Weekly Report* 67(36):1001–1006.

DiMatteo, M. Robin, and Howard S. Friedman. 1982. *Social Psychology and Medicine*. Cambridge, MA: Oelgeschlager, Gunn, & Hain.

Fife, Betsy L., and Eric R. Wright. 2000. "The Dimensionality of Stigma: A Comparison of its Impact on the Self of Persons with HIV/AIDS and Cancer." *Journal of Health and Social Behavior* 41(1):50–67.

Fox, Renee. 1989. *The Sociology of Medicine*. Upper Saddle River, NJ: Prentice Hall.

Freidson, Eliot. 1988. *The Profession of Medicine: A Study in the Sociology of Applied Knowledge*. Chicago, IL: University of Chicago Press.

Freund, Peter E.S., and Meredith McGuire. 1999. *Health, Illness, and the Social Body* (3rd ed.). Upper Saddle River, NJ: Prentice Hall.

Galdas, Paul M., Francine Cheater, and Paul Marshall. 2005. "Men and Health Help-Seeking Behaviours: Literature Review." *Journal of Advanced Nursing* 49(6):616–623.

Guy, Gery P., Kun Zhang, Michele K. Bohm, Jan Losby, Brian Lewis, Randall Young, Louise B. Murphy, and Deborah Dowell. 2017. "Vital Signs: Changes in Opioid Prescribing in the United States, 2006–2015." *Morbidity and Mortality Weekly Report* 66(26):697–704.

Hottle, Elizabeth. 1996. "Making Myself Understood: The Labeling Theory of Deviance Applied to Stuttering." *Virginia Social Science Journal* 31(1):78–85.

Hunt, Linda M., Brigitte Jordan, and Susan Irwin. 1989. "Views of What's Wrong: Diagnosis and Patients' Concepts of Illness." *Social Science and Medicine* 28(9):945–956.

Huynh, Phuong T., Cathy Schoen, Robin Osborn, and Alyssa L. Holmgren. 2006. *The U.S. Health Care Divide: Disparities in Primary Care Experiences by Income.* New York: The Commonwealth Fund.

Jaret, Peter. 2015. "Forty-Six Americans Die Each Day from Painkiller ODs." *AARP Bulletin* September:6–8.

Kart, Cary S., and Carol A. Engler. 1994. "Predisposition to Self-Help Care: Who Does What for Themselves and Why?" *Journal of Gerontology* 49(6):S301–S308.

Kumar, Anuradha. 1995. "Gender and Health: Theoretical Versus Practical Accessibility of Health Care for Women in North India." Pp. 16–32 in *Global Perspectives on Health Care,* edited by Eugene B. Gallagher and Janardan Subedi. Upper Saddle River, NJ: Prentice Hall.

Lindsay, Elizabeth. 1996. "Health Within Illness: Experiences of Chronically Ill/Disabled People." *Journal of Advanced Nursing* 24(3):465–472.

Maynard, Douglas. 2006. "'Does It Mean I'm Gonna Die?': On Meaning Assessment in the Delivery of Diagnostic News." *Social Science and Medicine* 62(8):1902–1916.

McEwen, Kellie J. 2000. "The Behavioral Model Applied to the Postponement of Needed Healthcare and Unmet Healthcare Need." Paper presented at the annual meeting of the Southern Sociological Society, April 2000.

Mechanic, David. 1968. *Medical Sociology.* New York: The Free Press.

Mechanic, David, and Edmund H. Volkart. 1961. "Stress, Illness Behavior and the Sick Role." *American Sociological Review* 26(1):51–58.

National Center for Health Statistics. 2018. *Health, United States, 2017, With Special Feature on Mortality.* Hyattsville, MD: National Center for Health Statistics.

National Hospice and Palliative Care Organization. 2018. *NHPCO Facts and Figures: Hospice Care in America* (Rev. ed.) Alexandria, VA: National Hospice and Palliative Care Organization.

Parsons, Talcott. 1951. *The Social System.* Glencoe, IL: The Free Press.

———. 1975. "The Sick Role and Role of the Physician Reconsidered." *Milbank Memorial Fund Quarterly* 53(3):257–278.

Pescosolido, Bernice A. 1992. "Beyond Rational Choice: The Social Dynamics of How People Seek Help." *American Journal of Sociology* 97(4):1096–1138.

Pudrovska, Tetyana. 2010. "What Makes You Stronger: Age and Cohort Differences in Personal Growth after Cancer." *Journal of Health and Social Behavior* 51(3):260–273.

Schoen, Allen M. 2001 *Kindred Spirits.* New York: Broadway Books.

Scholl, Lawrence, Puja Seth, Mbabazi Kariisa, Nana Wilson, and Grant Baldwin. 2019. "Drug and Opioid-Involved Overdose Deaths—United States, 2013–2017." *Morbidity and Mortality Weekly Report* 67(5152):1419–1427.

Springer, Kristen W., and Dawne M. Mouzon. 2011. "'Macho Men' and Preventive Health Care: Implications for Older Men in Different Social Classes." *Journal of Health and Social Behavior* 52(2):212–227.

Stewart, Susan T., Rebecca M. Woodward, Allison B. Rosen, and David M. Cutler. 2008. "The Impact of Symptoms and Impairments on Overall Health in U.S. National Health Data." *Medical Care* 46(9):954–962.

Suchman, Edward A. 1965. "Stages of Illness and Medical Care." *Journal of Health and Social Behavior* 6(3):114–128.

Taylor, Verta. 1996. *Rock-A-By Baby: Feminism, Self-Help, and Postpartum Depression.* New York: Routledge.

Thomas, Villani J., and F.D. Rose. 1991. "Ethnic Differences in the Experience of Pain." *Social Science and Medicine* 32(9):1063–1066.

Turner-Cobb, Julie M., Cheryl Gore-Felton, Feyza Marouf, Cheryl Koopman, Peea Kim, Dennis Israelski, and David Spigel. 2002. "Coping, Social Support, and Attachment Style as Psychosocial Correlates of Adjustment in Men and Women with HIV/AIDS." *Journal of Behavioral Medicine* 25(4):337–353.

Webel, Allison R., Yvette Cuca, Jennifer G. Okonsky, Alice K. Asher, Alphoncina Kaihura, and Robert A.

Salata. 2013. "The Impact of Social Context on Self-Management in Women Living with HIV." *Social Science and Medicine* 87(June):147–154.

Wingood, Gina M., Ralph J. DiClemente, Isis Mikhail, Donna H. McCree, Susan L. Davies, James W. Hardin, Shani H. Peterson, Edward W. Hook, and Mike Saag. 2007. "HIV Discrimination and the Health of Women Living with HIV." *Women and Health* 46:99–112.

Wood, Michelle, Lauren Dunton, Brooke Spellman, Michelle Abbenante, and John Griffith. 2010. *Homelessness Data in Health and Human Services Mainstream Programs.* Washington, DC: U.S. Department of Health and Human Services.

Yoshiba, Karen K. 1993. "Reshaping of Self: A Pendular Reconstruction of Self and Identity Among Adults with Traumatic Spinal Cord Injury." *Sociology of Health and Illness* 15:217–245.

Zborowski, Mark. 1969. *People in Pain.* San Francisco, CA: Jossey-Bass.

Zola, Irving K. 1973. "Pathways to the Doctor: From Person to Patient." *Social Science and Medicine* 7(9):677–689.

CHAPTER 8

Physicians and the Profession of Medicine

Learning Objectives

- Define the concept of "professional dominance." Identify and explain key ways in which the dominance of physicians within medicine has declined.

- Identify the key internal control mechanisms in medicine, and assess their effectiveness.

- Describe how the medical malpractice system in the United States works, and

identify and describe key weaknesses of the system.

- Identify and discuss key concerns related to the number, composition, and distribution of physicians in the United States.

- Identify and discuss key differences in the practice of medicine based on physician gender. Describe the practice of sexual harassment in medicine.

Being a physician in America in the eighteenth and nineteenth centuries was not highly regarded. Medical "knowledge" was often inaccurate and sometimes dangerous, credentials were easy to acquire or non-existent, and there was little prestige associated with the field.

Families (typically the wife and mother) were the primary locus of healing services, and information was secured from newspapers, almanacs, and domestic guides that discouraged the use of physicians. Apothecaries dispensed medical preparations, sometimes provided medical advice, and even performed amputations, midwives commonly assisted in the birthing process, and black slaves were primary healers on Southern plantations.

Furthermore, many countercultural health movements flourished. Most sought to disempower the dangerous techniques of the regular physicians and promoted the improved conditions

already brought about by better nutrition and hygiene. "Every man his own doctor" was one of the slogans of the time, and the "regular" doctors were attacked as members of the "parasitic, nonproducing classes" (Ehrenreich and English, 1973).

However, by the early 1900s, medical doctors had secured virtually total domination of the health care field. They had largely eliminated many of their competitors (e.g., some of the countercultural movements), had subordinated others (e.g., women in nursing), and had obtained state-endorsed legitimation to control medical education and medical licensure. Few occupations in any country have ever enjoyed such a swift transformation or such extreme dominance as was captured by professional medicine in the United States in the early twentieth century—a dominance that peaked in the 1950s, 1960s, and 1970s.

THE PROFESSION OF MEDICINE

Characteristics of Professions

There have been many efforts to define the essential traits of **professions**. A classic formulation by William Goode can be organized around the three common denominators of autonomy, rigorous standards, and prestige and identification (see the accompanying box, "Essential Traits of a Profession").

The Dominance of the Medical Profession

In 1970, Eliot Freidson published two books, *Professional Dominance* (1970a) and *Profession of Medicine* (1970b), which contributed significantly to subsequent thinking about the medical profession. He defined a profession as "an occupation which has assumed a dominant position in a division of labor, so that it gains control over the determination of the substance of its own work" (1970a:xvii). This right is given with three understandings: (1) the profession is based on technical knowledge that is not accessible to the layperson, (2) the profession commits to a service orientation in which it puts the interests of those whom it serves before its own interests, and (3) the profession will conscientiously regulate itself (Freidson, 1970b). At some point, the public generally accepts that it can be trusted to regulate itself.

Freidson identified medicine as the epitome of professions, and introduced the term **professional dominance** to refer to the extensive control held by the medical profession over the organization, laws, training, clinical practice, and financing of medical care, and to its ability to promote its own autonomy, prestige, and income. It meant, according to Navarro (1988:59), that the medical profession was *the* "dominant force in medicine."

IN THE FIELD

ESSENTIAL TRAITS OF A PROFESSION

The term "profession" is used to describe occupations that have certain special traits and characteristics. Generally, professions are considered vocations—that is, occupations to which an individual is specially drawn and conform to her or his talents and interests. Three traits of professions are especially noteworthy.

1. *Rigorous standards*. Professions carry special responsibilities, so those entering the profession must undergo a rigorous formal and informal educational and training process and must comply with stringent practice norms.

2. *Significant autonomy*. Professions provide significant autonomy to members and freedom from lay control. Each profession maintains self-regulation—that is, it determines and enforces standards of education, licensure, and quality of practice, and it has control over other workers in the same domain.

3. *Considerable prestige and identification with the profession*. In part due to the first two characteristics, professions generally are accompanied by high levels of income and prestige. Members tend to identify strongly with the profession and remain in it for their entire career (Goode, 1960).

Medical credentials help to convey the amount of training and rigorous standards required to earn a medical degree

 IN THE FIELD

OATH TAKING IN MEDICAL SCHOOL CEREMONIES

Medical schools typically have students recite an oath either at the start of medical school or, more commonly, at commencement, or both. Historically, it was common to recite the Hippocratic Oath (or a variation of it) or the Oath of Geneva (written by the World Medical Association after World War II and modified most recently in 2017), or the Modern Physician's Oath (written in 1964 by Louis Lasagna, Dean of the Tufts University School of Medicine).

In the last few decades, however, more than half of medical schools have adopted use of an oath unique to that school or one written by that particular medical school class. This has led to less uniformity in recited oaths. A recent study (Scheinman, Fleming, and Niotis, 2018) found that only three elements were present in as many as 80 percent of current commencement oaths. What promises appeared most frequently? Respecting confidentiality. Avoiding harm. Upholding the profession's integrity.

The Decline of Professional Dominance

Has the medical profession sustained this position of professional dominance in the medical field? Over the last several decades, countless challenges to medicine's dominance have occurred, including the massive growth of corporate (for-profit) medical companies, the increasing governmental role in medicine, and movements promoting more responsibility for self-care, for patients (consumers), and for women's health.

Has the collective weight of these and other challenges reduced the professional dominance of medicine? Is the profession now being controlled by forces outside medicine—in much the same manner as occupations experience outside controls? Two major perspectives have suggested that significant change has occurred.

Deprofessionalization. Primarily developed by Marie Haug of Case Western Reserve University, the **deprofessionalization** theory contends that, over time, patients have become increasingly well informed about health and illness and increasingly assertive about controlling their own health. Coupled with some loss of confidence in the service orientation of the medical profession, patients have sought more egalitarian relationships in medicine—more participation in decision making about their own medical treatment, and a less authoritarian demeanor in their physician. The emergence of medical information online has led to a reduction in the medical profession's monopoly over medical knowledge, a reduction in the domination of physicians over patients, and a decrease in physician autonomy—all elements of reduced professional dominance (Haug, 1973, 1988; Haug and Lavin, 1983).

Proletarianization. John McKinlay and others concur that there has been a reduction in professional dominance, but they trace the stimulus to changes within the health care system. For many years during the middle and latter parts of the 1900s, professional medicine was largely concerned about losing its autonomy to encroachment by the federal government. The American Medical Association (AMA) consistently opposed public health–related government programs due to fear that they would allow the government to increase its authority over medicine. Efforts to legislate some form of national health insurance were heatedly opposed by the AMA.

Some analysts believe that the attention of organized medicine was so strongly focused on minimizing government's involvement in health care that the increasing corporate presence in medicine was largely ignored, and its potential for reducing medical dominance underestimated.

By the 1980s, however, **corporatization**—an increasing amount of corporate control of medicine—had clearly occurred as more and more businesses became active in medicine. Once corporations were allowed into the medical field—in hospital construction and ownership, pharmaceuticals, medical equipment supply, laboratories, and insurance companies—it was only a matter of time until they assumed greater control of medical practice itself. Their control was enhanced by other developments within medicine, such as increasingly sophisticated technologies that required more organizational complexity, more money, and more managers to run the operation (Light and Levine, 1988).

This large-scale entrance of corporations into medicine created a "clash of two cultures," according to McArthur and Moore (1997). They foresaw danger as medicine's commitment to the patient was replaced by a commercial ethic that sought profit from the clinical care of the sick. Corporatized medicine contains the paradox that physicians increasingly rely on corporate organization and finances while simultaneously realizing that these forces intrude on their work and reduce their autonomy (Light and Levine, 1988).

For some, this corporatization has led to a **proletarianization** of medicine—that physicians, like other workers in capitalist economies, eventually have their autonomy and self-control stripped away and replaced with control by corporate owners and managers. New medical technologies reduce the need for certain traditional skills (including diagnosis), make work more routinized (more like a trade than a profession), and create needs for capital and bureaucracy (with the potential for control by those with capital). As an example, workers within insurance companies often make decisions about paying for services that exerts extensive influence on clinical decision making.

An Alternative Theory: Countervailing Power. Donald Light and others have offered an alternative perspective from which to consider professional dominance—the theory of **countervailing power**. Light (1991) agrees that professional dominance was won by medicine decades ago, but he does not believe its dominance was ever fully entrenched. His position is that when any profession gains extraordinary dominance, it stimulates countervailing powers—that is, efforts by other agents to balance its power.

According to Light, the relationship between a profession and related institutions within a society is in a constant state of flux—sometimes an imbalance of power occurs, with one side or the other clearly gaining a dominant position. Professional dominance describes the time when the powers of the profession are great—even though that circumstance initiates efforts that will eventually diminish the profession's dominant position. In medicine, many factors, including evidence of the use of unnecessary procedures, the unexplained large variations in clinical practice from physician to physician, and the lack of technological self-restraint inevitably led to increased efforts by countervailing agents.

For medicine today, countervailing powers include the government, other providers of health care services, consumers in the form of advocacy groups such as AARP, large employers ("corporate purchasers") who purchase health care for their employees, and "corporate sellers" of health care services (e.g., insurance companies). Each of these agents seeks to exercise influence on health care, and thus exists in a constant interplay with the medical profession (Hafferty and Light, 1995).

Does this mean that physicians today have been converted into corporatized workers and are no longer a profession? According to Light the answer is no. Relations between physicians and the corporate sector are very complex. Physicians sometimes own hospitals, facilities and laboratories, and thus are owners as well as workers. Employers, management companies, and insurance companies enter into contractual arrangements with physicians who sometimes have a voice in the companies. However, it does mean that complete physician control over any aspect of medical practice no longer exists (Light, 2000).

In addition, many sociologists and other scholars have questioned the extent to which the medical profession has maintained sufficient devotion to its service orientation to patients or whether it now so colludes with business interests that financial gain has become a significant focus (Light, 2010).

> In the current climate of escalating costs, widespread variation in the quality of available care, a growing uninsured population, and medical errors, observers raise doubts about the physician as business entrepreneur pursuing economic opportunities at the expense of patients' best interests. At stake is whether the influx of money in health care has corrupted a professional mandate to take care of clients.
>
> (Timmermans and Oh, 2010:S95)

Numerous studies have focused on the relationships among physicians and industry and whether these relationships impact patient care. In 2009, one national survey of **primary care** physicians and specialists found that 83.8 percent of physicians had some financial relationship with the medical industry during the previous year. About two-thirds had received drug samples, more than 70 percent received food and beverages in their workplaces, almost 1 in 5 received reimbursements for costs associated with attending professional meetings or programs to obtain continuing education credits, and about 1 in 7 received payments for professional services (consulting, speaking, or enrolling patients in clinical trials) (Campbell et al., 2010).

A second line of research investigates whether these financial incentives affect patient outcomes and health care costs. One review of dozens of empirical studies focused on (1) physicians' role in self-referring (referring patients to another medical service—such as an imaging center—in which the physician has a financial interest), (2) insurance reimbursement schemes that create incentives for certain clinical choices over others, and (3) financial relationships between physicians and the pharmaceutical industry. Researchers found that financial incentives and conflicts of interest do sometimes have an impact on clinical decisions (Robertson, Rose, and Kesselheim, 2012).

In light of studies such as this, recent efforts have been initiated to reduce or even eliminate certain types of physician–industry relationships (especially with pharmaceutical and medical equipment supply companies). The Physician Payments Sunshine Act of 2010 seeks greater transparency by requiring manufacturers of drugs and medical supplies covered by federal programs to track and report all financial relationships with physicians. The intention is to uncover conflicts of interest. In the first 1½ year data collection period, industry paid physicians $4.7 billion for research and development activities, nearly $100 million for educational materials, and more than $50 million for speaker compensation (Agrawal and Brown, 2016).

The American Medical Association

The American Medical Association (AMA) was established as a national society in 1847 "to promote the science and art of medicine and the betterment of public health." It eventually sought control over the profession by determining who entered it, how they were trained, and how they practiced medicine, and it hoped to elevate the public's opinion of the profession by driving out untrained practitioners. Although the AMA initially had little power, it gained significant status in the early 1900s as a result of the power bestowed upon it by the federal government to oversee standards for medical education and medical licensure. Over the next few decades, the AMA grew into the most powerful health care lobbying group in the United States.

The American Medical Association is the largest professional association of physicians in the United States, although most physicians join a specialty organization instead. The AMA's main office, shown here, is located in Chicago.

Today, although the AMA retains considerable power and prestige (it is one of the most well-organized, best funded, and most effective lobbying agents in Washington), its influence has declined. Almost 80 percent of licensed physicians were members in 1963, whereas only 15 percent of practicing US physicians were members in 2016. In 2016, the association had approximately 240,000 members, including practicing physicians, medical students, and residents. Recent aggressive membership recruiting campaigns have largely failed to boost membership.

Some of the decline in membership can be attributed to more physicians opting to join societies within their specialty (e.g., the American College of Surgery), or a medical society based on gender (e.g., the American Medical Women's Association for women physicians) or race (e.g., the National Medical Association for black physicians) rather than the national organization.

THE SOCIAL CONTROL OF MEDICINE

Sociologically, the term **social control** refers both to the ability of individuals and groups to regulate themselves (internal control) and to measures taken by outsiders to regulate an individual or group (external control). One expression of the autonomy that professional groups earnestly desire is the freedom to be self-regulatory and to be allowed to rely solely on internal control mechanisms. Perhaps more than any other profession in the United States, physicians have emphasized their autonomy and their disapproval of outside efforts at control.

This section offers a brief review of control mechanisms within medicine and an important external control mechanism—medical malpractice litigation. Of course, in the last few decades, medicine has had to contend with two other powerful external agents—the federal government and the corporate sector. Medicine's relationship with these agents is touched upon throughout this book but is examined in detail in Chapters 14 and 15.

Internal Control Mechanisms

The three key types of internal controls are peer review, hospital review committees, and the board of medicine in each state.

Peer Review. The most basic and potentially most pervasive type of control mechanism is **peer review**—the comments, questions, suggestions, and personal conversations that occur on a daily basis as physicians work with or near each other. Obviously, this does not occur for physicians working independently and with little interaction, but most physicians now work in some type of group setting and encounter other physicians while attending patients at the hospital.

Is the peer review process an effective internal control mechanism? What typically happens when one physician oversees an error or problematic behavior in a colleague? Based both on surveys of physicians and on dozens of insider accounts, the answer is clear that physicians often do not report it. An Institute of Medicine survey found that almost all physicians thought that they *should* report impaired or incompetent physicians or situations involving medical errors, but only about half actually did so (Campbell et al., 2007). Physicians express considerable reluctance about making public judgments about colleagues and provoking a hostile response. In situations like these, physicians often consider that medicine is an "art" rather than a "science," and they feel uncomfortable suggesting that they know better than the colleague being observed. Even if an obvious error occurs, many physicians express the view that everyone is fallible ("There, but for the grace of God, go I").

If physicians observe a colleague making repeated errors, a personal chat may take place, patient referrals might be avoided, and a system of "grayzoning" (overseeing the physician's patient care) may be created, but there is a strong unwritten code of not making an official report. This code explains situations sometimes reported in the media of a physician practicing blatantly incompetent or negligent medicine over a period of years—with the full knowledge of others—but never being reported. Some years ago, a California physician admitted in court that he needlessly maimed at least 30 surgical patients over a period of 7 years, and had performed many unnecessary procedures simply for financial gain. Despite the fact that others were aware of the situation, he was never once challenged by any other staff member.

Hospital Review Committees. A more formal mechanism occurs with a variety of review committees that now exist in all hospitals. Some of these *hospital review committees* are mandated by the federal government or other regulatory groups, and some have been created by hospital initiative. They include credentials committees (especially for new hospital employees), internal quality control committees (usually to guard against overprescribing medication or unnecessary procedures), mortality review committees (for any patient who dies in the hospital), and peer review organizations (PROs) (established to ensure that Medicare patients receive high-quality care).

Are these effective agents against poor clinical practice? Sometimes they are, but at other times not. For example, most states require all health care facilities to report to the State Board of Medicine any instance when they question the competence of a physician. However, hospitals are reluctant to do this and often do not report such cases. Imagine the terrible publicity a hospital would receive if it became known that it was questioning the performance of its own physicians. In addition, most states require that the board be advised whenever a physician loses hospital privileges (this automatically becomes public knowledge in some states). In an attempt

to avoid the negative publicity, the hospital may pressure the offending physician to leave on his or her own accord. No formal action is taken, the physician often moves to another community or state, and a possibly dangerous physician is not stopped. One review of the performance of PROs determined that the committee missed two-thirds of the cases that were judged by an independent panel of physicians to have involved substandard care (Rubin et al., 1992).

A particularly egregious example occurred in 2010 when a Delaware pediatrician was charged with 471 counts of sexually abusing children over a 13-year period. It was learned that a nurse had filed a complaint against him in 1996 for inappropriately touching young girls in his care, but he was cleared. While the city police were investigating several similar complaints in 2005, the hospital was given a subpoena seeking any complaints or disciplinary actions against the physician. Because he was cleared, the hospital was not obligated to report the 1996 complaint, and they did not do so. Another police investigation in 2008 also led to no charges.

State Boards of Medicine. Ultimately, the most severe form of internal control is enacted when a physician is reported to the *state board of medicine*. The primary mission of state boards of medicine is to protect public and patient safety by ensuring that only competent and conscientious individuals are allowed to practice medicine. Although states have organized these boards in different fashions, they typically consist of several health care practitioners (sometimes also even a consumer or two) with an investigative staff who can conduct informal or formal hearings on charges against physicians. In most states the charges can be brought by anyone—the courts, hospitals, physicians, and patients. The board can levy various sanctions, including reprimands, continuing education, fines, probation, suspension, and license revocation. Since 2000, every disciplinary action taken by a state medical board is automatically communicated to the medical board in all other states.

These boards work well in some states, not very well in others, and pursue wrongdoers with widely divergent levels of effort. The total number of actions taken by state medical boards is small—in 2018, about 8,800 disciplinary actions involving a punitive measure such as loss of license, limitations on the license, and probation against physicians were taken. The number of such actions has increased somewhat in the last 5 years. Generally, physicians who have committed insurance fraud, abused substances, or engaged in prescribing violations receive light sanctions, whereas physicians convicted of violent crimes such as rape or assault receive very heavy sanctions. (Want to know how *Consumer Reports* rates the state medical board in your state? Check out: https://advocacy.consumerreports.org/wp-content/uploads/2016/03/Chart-website-review-CR-blobs-all-states-FINAL-4.pdf).

Most agree that the number of physicians sanctioned represents only a small fraction of those guilty of wrongdoing. As an example, about 5 percent of the nation's physicians account for more than half of medical malpractice suits. Of those physicians who have paid out more than five malpractice claims, only about 1 in 7 has ever been professionally disciplined. Common problems among the boards are too few investigators (producing huge backlogs and long delays), failure to make actions public (in some states), and an unwillingness to impose and/or maintain penalties. Not surprisingly, therefore, there is a high recidivism rate among physicians who have been disciplined by their state medical board (Grant and Alfred, 2007). As an example, see the accompanying box, "The Slow Disciplinary Process."

The National Practitioner Data Bank. The *National Practitioner Data Bank (NPDB)* was created in September 1990 as a federal repository for specific information on all health care practitioners. Reports of malpractice payments and adverse licensure actions must be reported to the NPDB within 30 days of final action. All health care institutions that grant clinical privileges and medical staff appointments must request information from the data bank. Ironically, the NPDB is not available to the public. In 2000, an effort in Congress to open it up so that patients could check the records of physicians received little support.

On the other hand, more than 30 states now publish lists of physicians who have been disciplined or who have been convicted of medical malpractice, and some have begun to use the Internet to post this information. National repositories of information on physicians are springing up, although some of these are available only for payment.

Medical Errors: The Failure of Internal Control Mechanisms. The dominance that the medical profession has held carries with it the presumption that physicians will conscientiously monitor the practice of medicine. It is the most dependable method of ensuring consistently high quality of care and avoiding harmful medical errors. The sometimes failure of peer review, hospital review committees, and state medical boards to carefully protect patients from incompetent and negligent physicians and from medical facilities with inadequate quality controls is an indictment of the extent to which responsibilities have been carried out.

This failure makes likely the possibility that serious and repeated medical errors can occur, and considerable research has shown medical errors to be common and devastating. In 1998, the Institute of Medicine issued a report that caught national attention. The report estimated that medical errors are responsible for the deaths of between 44,000 and 98,000 hospital patients in the United States each year.

Two types of errors were discussed. Front-line errors include such problems as failure to promptly and correctly diagnose an illness (there

IN THE FIELD

THE SLOW DISCIPLINARY PROCESS

The following is an actual account of a particular case handled before a state board of medicine:

April 26, Year 1: Board of Medicine informs Dr. S that it will hold a hearing on charges that he knowingly, intentionally, and unlawfully did indiscriminately prescribe amphetamines.

June 26, Year 1: Board committee concludes that Dr. S was extremely careless in the excessive prescription of amphetamine drugs and issues a reprimand, warning Dr. S not to do so in the future.

May 30, Year 2: Board committee sets up a hearing to investigate whether Dr. S has continued to improperly prescribe amphetamines.

June 11, Year 2: Committee concludes that Dr. S was extremely careless in excessive prescribing of amphetamine drugs, and restricts Dr. S's ability to prescribe controlled drugs.

April 22, Year 5: Dr. S's local medical society writes to the state board expressing concern about Dr. S's handling of two cases, indicating that Dr. S is a long-standing problem in the community and needs investigation.

May 2, Year 6: The president of the local medical society again writes to the board about Dr. S, expressing fear for the safety of the general population.

May 11, Year 6: The board tells the local medical society that Dr. S is being investigated and that the investigation will be completed in the near future.

November 26, Year 7: The board informs Dr. S that it has scheduled a formal hearing to decide whether Dr. S failed to diagnose or improperly treated 18 patients, including an 11-year-old boy who died of asthma.

January 15, Year 8: The formal hearing for Dr. S is postponed due to legal maneuvering by his attorneys.

May 27, Year 8: Dr. S's attorneys and the state's attorney general's office in consultation with a few board members reach a compromise settlement the day before the formal hearing is scheduled. Dr. S's license is suspended, and he is ordered to take continuing education courses and work under the supervision of another physician.

November 14, Year 8: The board returns Dr. S's license and puts him on probation for 2 years. He is to continue taking education courses, and his practice is monitored by a team of physicians.

August 31, Year 12: The board informs Dr. S that it will hold a formal hearing on charges that Dr. S illegally sold and prescribed weight control drugs, and failed to maintain proper records for drugs kept in his office. Dr. S retires before the hearing is held (Hite and Pardue, 1984).

are an estimated 12 million diagnostic errors each year—about 5 percent of adults who seek outpatient care—leading to 10 percent of all patient deaths), the administration of substandard or faulty treatment (leading to thousands of deaths each year), and the administration of the wrong medication or the wrong dosage of the correct medication (estimates are that 1.5 million medication errors occur in hospitals each year). Such common and obvious problems as the poor handwriting of physicians (with the result that pharmacists misread important information) and the failure of health workers to wash their hands between patients contribute to these errors. Second-line (less conspicuous) errors are those that are removed from the physician or nurse and include inadequate staffing to offer proper care, shortcomings in practitioner licensing and credentialing, a faulty medical malpractice system, fragmented delivery systems, and a failure to implement new technologies to help physicians to avoid making errors. The *Journal of the American Medical Association* describes these medical errors as being real and common. (Medical errors are discussed in Chapter 15.)

External Control: Medical Malpractice

Patients may attempt to exert several kinds of control over the practice of medicine. If they are sufficiently assertive and are working with a communicative physician, they may discuss desired parameters of their interaction, including the amount of communication, the right to ask questions and receive understandable answers, and how truthful they want the physician to be. If this communication does not occur or the physician is not responsive to requests, the patient may "doctor-shop" (i.e., search for a more compatible physician). Patients are always free to encourage others to see or to avoid any physician. In cases where wrongdoing is perceived, a complaint may be filed with the state board of medicine. In cases where an adverse event occurs as a result of physician error or negligence, the patient may file a medical malpractice legal suit. The following section of the chapter focuses on trends in the process and use of malpractice, and examines the medical malpractice system in the United States.

The Malpractice Concept. The underlying concept of legal **medical malpractice** is straightforward. Malpractice litigation is intended to compensate patients whose harm by the actions (or inactions) of a physician could have been prevented, and to discourage such harms from occurring. The injured patient (the plaintiff) must prove that (1) she or he was injured or damaged, (2) the health care provider (the defendant) was negligent (i.e., failed to meet a standard of care expected in the community), and (3) the negligence caused or contributed to the injury or damage.

If convicted of the malpractice, the defendant is supposed to pay the plaintiff a sum of money determined by a judge or jury. In reality, however, almost all providers carry malpractice insurance, so the insurance company is the payer in successful suits.

Malpractice Versus Actual Negligence. The malpractice system functions best when those who are injured through negligence file and win suits, and those who receive no injury or who are injured but not through negligence do not file suits and do not win if they do file. This acknowledges that some injuries occur but are not caused by negligence, and some negligence occurs but does not lead to injury. It is the negligence-caused injury that is the proper object of malpractice. See Figure 8.1.

The *Harvard Medical Practice Study* of malpractice claims and medical records of 31,429 patients hospitalized in New York State in 1984 is the most thorough study conducted on malpractice. The study identified patients who filed a malpractice claim against physicians and/or hospitals, and also examined their medical records to determine the incidence of injuries caused by medical negligence (Localio et al., 1991).

While patients filed a total of 51 malpractice claims, the audit of medical records revealed 280 actual cases of injury caused by negligence. Were the 51 part of the 280? Not for the most part. Only 8 of the 280 cases filed a malpractice claim; 272 had a legitimate claim but did not file, and 43 did not have a legitimate claim but did file. Thus most actual cases of negligence-caused injury do not get filed, and a large percentage of those that are filed are not justified—the opposite of the way the system is designed to work (Localio et al., 1991). This pattern was affirmed in a similar type of study in Utah and Colorado in the early 1990s (Studdert et al., 2000).

The Incidence and Severity of Malpractice. After decades of an increasing number of malpractice suits being filed, and increasingly large

Figure 8.1 The Malpractice System as Designed and as Actually Occurs

The malpractice tort system is designed to compensate victims of cases in which a medical provider's negligence causes a patient injury. Provider negligence without patient injury and patient injury without medical negligence are not situations of medical malpractice. The injury must be linked to the negligence. In the figure below, only the shaded area is medical malpractice.

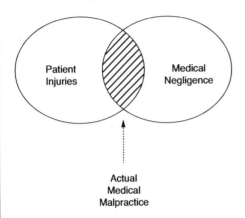

Actual
Medical
Malpractice

Unfortunately, studies show that the system does not work effectively in two ways: (1) patients who are injured by medical negligence often never file a medical malpractice suit (and therefore do not receive the compensation they are due), and (2) patients who are not actually injured or patients who are injured but not through provider negligence sometimes do file a medical malpractice suit (seeking money that they are not due). In the figure above, the sections without diagonal lines are not legitimate cases of medical malpractice, but they represent a large number of malpractice lawsuits.

mid-1980s, and back down to 5 to 7 in recent years. About 60 percent of physicians are sued for malpractice at least once in their career. The most common reasons for malpractice suits are delayed/incorrect diagnosis, prescription medication errors, and mistakes during childbirth. Typically, the types of physicians most likely to be sued are ob-gyns, surgeons, and anesthesiologists.

Of the lawsuits filed, around 4 in 5 are dismissed, dropped, or settled before actually going to court. Of those going to court, physicians win the case about 80 percent of the time. These statistics are consistent with the picture painted by the *Harvard Medical Practice Study*.

Total malpractice payout rates per year have also increased, peaked, and are now decreasing. Payouts increased from less than US$3 billion in 1992 to US$4.8 billion in 2003, and now range between $3 and $4 billion per year. Malpractice suits are most likely in Louisiana, Oklahoma, and Delaware and least likely in Hawaii, North Carolina, and Georgia. Due to the declining number of suits and declining payouts, the premiums insurance companies charge to medical providers have been declining.

Consequences of the Malpractice Crisis. The intended consequences of the medical malpractice system represent only the tip of the iceberg with regard to realized effects. Many patients who have sustained injury through medical negligence have secured compensatory damages, and many physicians who committed injuries by negligence have been found guilty. However, the health care system has been affected in other ways.

1. The AMA and individual physicians acknowledge the common practice of **defensive medicine**, whereby physicians prescribe every imaginable test for patients in order to protect themselves from liability in the case of a negative patient outcome. A study based on a survey of Massachusetts physicians found that 83 percent of physicians reported practicing

awards being given to successful plaintiffs, and significantly larger premiums being paid by physicians for malpractice insurance, patterns have reversed in the last decade. Currently, there are about 20,000 medical malpractice suits filed each year in the United States. Measurement of malpractice is typically expressed in terms of the number of claims filed per 100 physicians. This ratio increased from only 1 per 100 physicians in 1960 to a peak of 17 per 100 physicians in the defensive medicine, and that 18 to 28 percent of tests, procedures, referrals, and consultations and 13 percent of hospitalizations were ordered for defensive reasons (Sethi and Aseltine, 2008). Estimates are that US$60 billion a year is spent for defensive medicine.

2. The premiums physicians pay to insurance companies also add to the nation's total health care bill. Ultimately, of course, physicians pass these costs on to patients, further driving up health care costs. On average, physicians pay about 3 or 4 percent of their revenue for malpractice insurance (as compared with about 12 percent for staff salaries, 12 percent for office expenses, and 2 percent for equipment). However, the premium varies widely by specialty, and obstetricians at about 7 percent pay the most. Prices tend to be higher in some states and areas than others. Rates are highest in Florida, especially southern Florida, which is sometimes called the medical malpractice capital of the United States.

3. The malpractice crisis has embittered many physicians, who may come to see every patient as a potential lawsuit, thus creating strain in the relationship. Many physicians believe that their profession has been subjected to criticism beyond what is justified. Many decry the fact that there is often negative public attention when a suit is filed but little public exoneration when the complaint is unproven. Many physicians who have been charged but not convicted of malpractice are among the most bitter because of the trauma created by the experience, as are many physicians who "settle" the case for economic reasons while perceiving themselves not to be liable (Peeples, Harris, and Metzloff, 2000).

4. The malpractice crisis has increased acrimony between the medical and legal professions, each of which accuses the other of being the root cause of the crisis. Lawyers argue that malpractice cases are caused by medical errors that physicians commit, and that the way to reduce malpractice cases is to reduce malpractice. Physicians argue that malpractice lawyers encourage patients to file suits and seek large rewards because the lawyer gets a percentage of the award. Doctors believe that the large number of cases is primarily due to attorney behavior. Some physicians have gone so far as to stop offering services to lawyers and spouses of lawyers.

Efforts to Reduce the Malpractice Crisis. Efforts to improve the malpractice system have followed two main approaches: efforts to improve the physician–patient relationship and efforts to alter the system.

Research shows that negligence in physician behavior often results from a poor physician–patient relationship. Patients filing suits often charge that the physician did not provide sufficient information or did not clarify the risks of treatment. Patients who have rapport with a physician are much less likely to file a malpractice claim than those in a more distant relationship. Given these findings, many physicians have enrolled in workshops and seminars to learn how to better "manage" relationships with patients. To the extent that these classes are directed at making substantive improvements, real progress may occur; to the extent that these classes are cynical efforts at manipulation, the problems are not likely to be effectively redressed.

Some states have developed *communication and resolution programs* in which medical providers discuss adverse events with patients, explain what happened, offer an apology, and possibly offer compensation. Some states have implemented *apology laws* that encourage providers to express regret or convey an apology by prohibiting those statements from being used in a malpractice case. Some states now use *dispute resolution* or *mediation* to resolve cases without a lawsuit (Mello, Studdert, and Kachalia, 2014). Studies show that when physicians actively and genuinely engage patients who have been victims of a medical error, patients are more likely to forgive the error and less likely to seek legal assistance (Hannawa, Shigemoto, and Little, 2016). Other states have adopted *no-fault insurance systems*. In this system, providers are not required to make an admission of guilt, and cases are settled more quickly with the patient receiving compensation.

Finally, more than 30 states have modified the malpractice system by placing a maximum cap on the dollar value of awards for "pain and suffering" and punitive damages (meaning that insurance companies would pay out less when suits are won and would therefore charge physicians lower premiums, resulting in cost savings that could be passed on to patients). The typical cap amount is US$250,000. Physicians and insurance companies strongly endorse this approach, but lawyers and patients who have been victimized strongly oppose it. Some states have set a cap at a substantially higher level, but it covers medical expenses, lost income, and pain and suffering. This creates the possibility that not even all of a victim's costs are covered. Research has found that damage caps of US$250,000 do lead to reduced average payments, while a US$500,000 cap does not (Seabury, Helland, and Jena, 2014). Alternatively, some states have considered restricting the amount of money that lawyers can earn from successful malpractice

suits. Typically, they receive 30 or 40 percent of the judgment in successful suits.

THE NUMBER, COMPOSITION, AND DISTRIBUTION OF PHYSICIANS IN THE UNITED STATES

Many scholars focus their attention on the number of physicians within a country (do we have enough physicians to meet the need?), the composition of the physicians (what is the representation of women and racial and ethnic minorities in medicine?), and their distribution (are physicians sufficiently dispersed geographically and by specialty?).

The Number of Physicians

In 2015, there were almost 1.1 million medical doctors in the United States (although just 871,000 were active and 827,000 were providing patient care). This number includes both "allopathic" physicians, who earned an MD degree, and osteopathic physicians, who earned a D.O. degree. This is an increase in the overall number of about 100,000 since 2010 (see Table 8.1). Growth in the number of physicians in the last 50 years has been about four times faster than growth of the population. In 1960, there were

TABLE 8.1   Number of Physicians in the United States, 1970, 1990, 2010, and 2015

Category	1970	1990	2010	2015
Total	334,028	615,421	985,375	1,085,783
Men	92.4%	83.1%	67.6%	66.0%
Women	7.6%	16.9%	32.4%	34.0%
In primary care	44.2%	43.6%	42.6%	43.3%
Graduate of US med school	81.0%	77.2%	72.6%	75.7%

Source: Data from the American Medical Association, Department of Physician Data Sources, Division of Survey and Data Resources, *Physician Characteristics and Distribution in the United States* (Chicago, IL: AMA, 2012) and Statista: The Statistics Portal, Retrieved November 19, 2019 (www.statista.com/topics/1244/physicians/).

703 persons per physician, compared with 294 persons per physician in 2015.

The Training of Physicians. A key point to remember is that students who fill medical residencies in the United States (and go on into medical practice) come from three sources: domestic allopathic medical schools, domestic osteopathic medical schools, and foreign medical school. A popular misperception is that almost of our nation's physicians come from domestic medical schools. This is false. The country also depends heavily on international medical school graduates.

For example, in 2018, of the 2,814 applicants to ob–gyn residencies in the United States, a little over two-thirds had graduated from a domestic medical school, and about one-third had graduated from a foreign medical school. In internal medicine, only about 45 percent had graduated from a domestic medical school.

This is especially significant because experts anticipate a coming physician shortage. According to the Association of American Medical Colleges (2019), the United States will have a shortage of between 40,800 and 104,900 physicians by the year 2030. This forecast is made even after counting all of the new physicians who will have been trained in any of the four categories. If any of these categories even modestly diminished, the expected shortage would be much greater. This is the reason that many health care experts expressed strong reservations about more rigid immigration policies (Pinsky, 2018).

Why is the supply of physicians not keeping up with demand? The primary factors driving demand are continuing increases in population growth (expected to grow by 12 percent by 2030), continuing increases in the number of older Americans (73 percent more people 75 and older by 2030) because they use more medical services, and the anticipated retirement of many of today's physicians (more than one-third of all active physicians will be 65 or older in the next 10 years). Should the United States ever guarantee access to services for all persons—as occurs in all other democracies in the world—the physician need would significantly increase (Mann, 2017).

These patterns also demonstrate increased acceptance of osteopathic medicine. While osteopathic medicine retains its focus on the whole person and some focus on the manipulation of joints and bones, the standard training is very similar to that of allopathic physicians. Osteopathic doctors use conventional methods of diagnosis and treatment, can practice the full scope of medicine, and are now often integrated into medical offices with MDs. About 1 in 5 medical students today, and an anticipated 1 in 4 by 2025, is enrolled in an osteopathic medical school.

The Composition of Physicians

By Gender. The total number of women physicians in the United States increased from around 54,000 in 1980 to about 294,000 in 2010—an increase of more than 500 percent. Women accounted for only 11.6 percent of all physicians in 1980 but 34 percent in 2015. Significant increases in medical school applications, matriculants, and graduates in the last two decades are reflected in the age distribution of men and women physicians. Older physicians in the United States are predominantly men; younger physicians are about evenly divided.

By Race and Ethnicity. Due to extensive recruiting efforts, the number of under-represented racial and ethnic minority students in medical school increased in the 1990s, but has now leveled off or even slightly declined.

Their proportion remains low among practicing physicians and medical students. While African Americans, Hispanics, Native Americans, Alaskan and Hawaiian natives, and other Pacific Islanders constitute 35 percent of the US population, they represent only about 7 percent

Women now account for about one-third of all physicians, but are approximately 50 percent of today's medical graduates.

of practicing physicians. The medical education of individuals from these groups is particularly important because they are more likely than white physicians to practice in medically underserved areas and provide medical care for underserved black, Hispanic, and Native American patients, and it is a measure of social justice (Merchant and Omary, 2010).

By Geography. Despite the significant growth in overall physician supply, millions of Americans have inadequate access to health care—there are simply not enough medical providers near their home to handle the need for services. In 2018, there were more than 79 million people living in mostly rural and inner-city areas designated as primary care **health professional shortage areas** (7,000+ areas in 2018), dental care (5,800+ areas), or mental health care (5,100+ areas) and millions more living in **medically underserved areas** (which are defined by the number of physicians available, the infant mortality rate, the number of people below poverty, and the number of people aged 65 years or older) (Bureau of Health Workforce, 2018).

The number of practicing physicians per resident is more than twice as high in urban as in rural areas. Between 20 and 25 percent of the US

population—and one-third of the elderly—live in rural areas, but only 12 percent of active physicians practice there (and many of these are nearing retirement). More than half of people living in health professional shortage areas and medically underserved areas live in rural areas.

Recruitment and Retention of Rural Physicians. Why are rural areas so undersupplied? There are three key factors:

1. *Personal factors.* Preference for practice location appears to be dependent on personal desire for rural or urban living, rather than on characteristics of specific settings. Considerations include opportunity for personal time, employment opportunities for their partner, quality educational opportunities for children, and the availability of social and cultural activities.
2. *Professional considerations.* Preference for settings with access to professional colleagues for consultation, medical libraries, and continuing education opportunities.
3. *Economic factors.* Preference for higher-paying jobs to help erase student loans. The widespread poverty in most rural areas (and the greater number of uninsured and the lower availability of Medicaid) results in lower salaries.

Have the medical profession, medical schools, and governing bodies noticed the physician shortage in rural areas? Yes. Some medical schools have begun recruiting more in rural areas because students from rural areas are more likely to return there to practice medicine and enjoy the rural community life. Some states and localities have devised strategies to boost recruitment of physicians in underserved areas. Other factors that foster interest in rural practice are financial incentives, partner receptivity to rural living, anticipation of good work-life balance, and endorsement by medical school faculties (Parlier et al., 2018). Thus medical schools can encourage subsequent location in rural areas both through the admissions process and through training programs with positive messages.

In addition, the National Health Service Corps (NHSC) was created in 1972 to provide financial assistance to medical students in return for a commitment to practice in an assigned, underserved area for a specified number of years. Physicians sponsored by this program have made significant contributions to rural health care, although some studies have discovered that many were unhappy with the area where they were assigned and with the work conditions in isolated areas. These programs notwithstanding, rural and inner-city areas continue to lack adequate medical resources, and significantly greater effort will be needed to correct the inequity.

International diversity of physicians in the United States has increased in recent decades, although the percentage of African American, Hispanic, and Native American doctors continues to lag behind their population percentage.

By Specialty.   During medical school, students decide upon an area of specialization. While their choice may later change, students apply for residencies in a particular specialty. Specialization choice has been an important issue in the United States, as a large percentage of American physicians have opted for a specialty area (e.g., surgery, cardiology, and dermatology) rather than entering a primary care field (family practice, internal medicine, and pediatrics—which are specialties themselves).

This pattern is important for two related reasons. First, primary care physicians are the logical entry point into the health care system. If primary care is unavailable, patients are forced to go to a less appropriate first stop—a specialist. Second, the cost of care from a specialist is higher than the cost of primary care, both in terms of standard fees and because of the greater number of more expensive tests conducted by specialists.

Early in the twentieth century, the vast majority of physicians worked in primary care, but by 2000 almost 80 percent were specialists. The percentage of medical school graduates going into primary care was low in the late 1980s and early 1990s, increased slightly in the late 1990s, and has now dropped again in the 2000s (between 1997 and 2010 the percentage of American medical school graduates going into primary care dropped by more than 50 percent).

What factors have contributed to this declining interest in primary care? Faculty in many medical schools openly encourage students to pursue specialization and explicitly discourage them from choosing primary care. Why? The specialties offer more prestige, higher incomes, less frantic work schedules, more research opportunities, and more opportunities to work with high-tech medicine (see the box "Disparities in Physician Income.").

As fewer physicians opt for primary care, a vicious cycle is created. There are more patients for fewer doctors, thus creating more time pressure and less time for each patient. The opportunity

IN THE FIELD

DISPARITIES IN PHYSICIAN INCOME

A critical issue within the health care field is the wide variation in physician salaries. The key pattern is that specialist physicians earn considerably more than primary care physicians. Some justify this pattern because it recognizes the longer period of training required in many of the specialties, and the greater expertise required with high-technology care. Others oppose this pattern because it is based on a compensation system that rewards procedures (which specialists often provide) much more than time and consultation (which are central in primary care). Divergent salaries are also an incentive for medical school graduates to enter higher-paying specialties to help pay off their debt, rather than primary care where the need is much greater. The following table is an example of salary divergences based on the median of several physician salary surveys in 2017.

Orthopedic surgery	$586,000
Gastroenterology	$496,000
Plastic surgery	$496,000
Radiology	$476,000
Cardiology	$474,000
Dermatology	$457,000
Oncology	$434,000
Anesthesiology	$427,000
General surgery	$415,000
Emergency medicine	$353,000
Obstetrics/gynecology	$332,000
Neurology	$302,000
Internal medicine	$258,000
Family medicine	$241,000
Pediatrics	$235,000

Source: Data from Modern Healthcare, "2017 Physician Compensation Survey," *Modern Healthcare*, July 23, 2018.

---

to engage in a thorough conversation with a patient—something that once attracted physicians to primary care—is reduced. This leads even fewer physicians to choose primary care. Despite the recognized need for primary care physicians, most students find compelling reasons for opting for a specialty area. The shortage of primary care physicians is expected to grow significantly in the coming years—it is one of the key problems in the American health care system.

WOMEN PHYSICIANS

With the increased percentage of women medical students, many researchers have focused on identifying and explaining differences between women and men physicians. Four consistent differences between women and men physicians

have been detected: (1) they tend to enter different specialties, (2) they have different practice patterns, (3) they interact somewhat differently with patients, and (4) sexual harassment—especially of women medical students and physicians—continues at a high level. The first two differences are examined here, the third is covered in Chapter 12, and the fourth is covered in the accompanying box, "Sexual Harassment of Women in Medicine."

Different Specializations

Women and men fourth-year medical students offer similar reasons for selecting a particular specialty area—opportunities for self-fulfillment, positive clinical experiences, and the intellectual challenge of the field. The only key differences are that financial advantage is somewhat

IN THE FIELD

SEXUAL HARASSMENT OF WOMEN IN MEDICINE

Does equity now exist between men and women in medicine? No. Are there still considerable problems with discrimination and sexual harassment in medicine? Yes.

In 2018, three prestigious professional societies—the National Academy of Sciences, the National Academy of Engineering, and the National Academy of Medicine—published a consensus report entitled *Sexual Harassment of Women: Climate, Culture, and Consequences in Academic Sciences, Engineering, and Medicine* (2018). The Report Introduction states:

> As women increasingly enter [these] fields, they face biases and barriers that impede participation and career advancement in science, engineering, and medicine. As in other historically male-dominated fields, whether in academia or not, sexual harassment is one of the most pervasive of these barriers. Sexual harassment is a form of discrimination that includes gender harassment (verbal and nonverbal behaviors that convey hostility to, objectification of, exclusion of, or second-class status about members of one gender), unwanted sexual attention (verbally or physically unwelcome sexual advances, which can include assault), and sexual coercion (when favorable professional or educational treatment is conditioned on sexual activity). Over the past 30 years, the incidence of sexual harassment in different industries has held steady, yet now more women are in the workforce and in academia, and in the fields of science, engineering, and medicine (as students and faculty), and so more women are experiencing sexual harassment as they work and learn.

The reports of sexual harassment that have dominated news headlines have illustrated just how pervasive this discriminatory behavior is in our society. Women who have remained silent for years are now coming forward and sharing their experiences with sexual harassment that include lewd or denigrating comments, hostile or demeaning jokes, professional sabotage, repeated unwelcome sexual advances, groping, demands for sexual favors, and other offensive and discriminatory actions or language. Sexually harassing behavior can be either *direct* (targeted at an individual) or *ambient* (a general level of sexual harassment in an environment).

The report concluded that sexual harassment remains a persistent problem in the workplace. Gender harassment (e.g., behaviors that communicate that women do not belong or do not merit respect) is by far the most common type of sexual harassment. When an environment is pervaded by gender harassment, unwanted sexual attention and sexual coercion are more likely—in part because they are almost never experienced by women without simultaneously experiencing gender harassment. The report stated that women of color experience more harassment (sexual, racial/ethnic, or combination of the two) than do white women, white men, or men of color. Sexual- and gender-minority people experience more sexual harassment than heterosexuals.

Sexual harassment is especially likely where (1) men are more common (especially in leadership positions) and (2) an organizational climate communicates tolerance of sexual harassment (e.g., leadership that fails to take complaints seriously, fails to sanction perpetrators, or fails to protect complainants from retaliation). Organizational climate is by far the greater predictor of sexual harassment.

Sexual harassment within medicine occurs as women are systematically encouraged to pursue specialties with shorter training time and lower salaries, and are selected less for research grants, research awards, and research recognition; for publication in prestigious journals, for promotion to higher ranks; for selection for leadership positions; and for salary increases. This occurs within medical schools, hospitals, health insurers, and other medical organizations.

What effects does sexual harassment have on women faculty, physicians, and other workers? Effects include decline in job satisfaction, distancing oneself from the work either physically or mentally or even quitting, feelings of disillusionment, anger, and job stress; and declines in productivity or performance. When students experience sexual harassment, they may experience a decline in motivation to attend class, pay less attention in class, receive lower grades, change advisors and majors, and transfer to another educational institution or drop out. The more frequent and intense the sexual harassment, the more women report symptoms of depression, stress, and anxiety, and generally negative effects on psychological well-being. For women of color, when sexual harassment occurs simultaneously with other types of harassment (i.e., racial harassment), the experiences have even more severe consequences. The cumulative effect is significant damage to each woman and a significant loss of talent in academic science, engineering, and medicine.

Can anything be done to address this problem? Yes, a lot. In their report, the three academies delivered 15 specific recommendations. These included efforts to create diverse, inclusionary, and respectful academic and workplace environments; taking legislative action and creating specific programs to change the culture; incentivizing change; making settings less hierarchical; conducting research on the matter; and being as transparent as possible.

more important to men, and type of patient is somewhat more important to women. Despite the similarity in motivation, they systematically choose different specializations.

The clearest difference is that women are much more likely than men to train in primary care and in conditions affecting children and older adults, while men are more likely than women to train in all surgical specialties. In addition to primary care, women physicians have become especially common in obstetrics and gynecology, psychiatry, and dermatology. Also, women physicians are less likely than their men counterparts to become board certified (i.e., to receive certification from a board overseeing each specialty). Over the last few decades, however, specialty choices for women and men have started to converge. For example, internal medicine, general and family practice, and pediatrics (although in different order) are now the most common areas of medical specialization for both men and women.

Different Practice Patterns

Women and men physicians differ in several significant ways in their practice of medicine:

1. Women are much more likely than men to work in salaried positions in institutional settings (e.g., teaching in medical school) and are more likely to practice in urban areas. They are less likely to have an office-based practice.
2. Women work fewer hours per week than men and earn less money. While differences in both dimensions are narrowing, overall, men physicians still work about 7 to 10 more hours per week than women physicians, and men earn considerably more in salary (not all of which can be explained by the difference in the number of working hours). The convergence of number of hours worked per week is occurring not because women are working more, but because men are working fewer hours (a reduction of about 10 percent in the last

15 years). Both women and men physicians are increasingly interested in part-time work.

3. Women are more likely than men to see younger patients and women and minority patients.

Reasons for the Different Specializations and Practice Patterns. The differences between women and men physicians have two primary underlying causes—differential expectations regarding child-rearing and differential professional socialization by faculty and colleagues.

The difference in the number of hours worked per week by men and women physicians occurs almost entirely among physicians who are parents—the difference among non-parents is insignificant. At older ages, when family responsibilities have largely been completed, women work about the same number of hours as men—and are even more likely to be working full-time at the age of 60 years (Zimmerman, 2000). This pattern reflects different societal expectations for family responsibilities for men and women. Traditionally, few would have thought about men physicians altering their work hours upon the birth of a child, but that expectation is often communicated to women physicians.

In dual-career families with a woman physician, as in other dual-career families, the man's career is often prioritized. In addition to her career obligations, the woman typically still has primary responsibility for family life and child-rearing (Ly, Seabury, and Jena, 2018). Many women physicians find full dedication to their career incompatible with full dedication to family, and compromise by temporarily dropping out of the labor force or reducing the number of working hours—in essence, sacrificing career advancement for time to raise the children.

Some analysts have suggested an alternative interpretation of this circumstance. Some research indicates that childcare responsibilities account for only a small part of the working hours' differential. Since most women physicians (about 70 percent) are married to a professional, and about 50 percent are married to a physician, they do not have financial pressures to continue working after the birth of a child. So, after childbirth, women physicians reduce their workload to the level they most desire. However, this explanation does not explain why physician-mothers desire a smaller workload than physician-fathers nor why physician-mothers are more likely to reduce working hours after a birth. Whichever explanation prevails, the woman's career is more likely to be put on hold after the birth of a child.

Part of the differences between men and women physicians is traceable to socialization processes in medical school and during residency. Some women students are discouraged by men faculty members from entering certain specialties because they require so much time and would conflict with parental responsibility. Men students do not receive the same message. The problem is exacerbated by the fact that women are still under-represented in leadership positions in academic medicine and are therefore less available for role modeling and mentoring.

An interesting cross-cultural example is provided in the accompanying box, "Women Physicians in Mexico."

CHANGES WITHIN THE PHYSICIAN'S WORKPLACE

As the medical institution undergoes change, so does the work experience of the physician. Changes in three significant aspects of physician work experience are already underway:

1. The organizational setting and structure of the workplace. Currently, there is widespread

IN COMPARATIVE FOCUS

WOMEN PHYSICIANS IN MEXICO

Since the 1970s, social scientists have conducted a considerable amount of research on the role of women in economic, social, and political development in developing countries. However, little of this research has focused on the small number of well-educated, middle-class professional women in these countries.

Increased access to medical education has provided many women in Mexico with the opportunity to be physicians. Today, women make up approximately 30 percent of physicians and 50 percent of medical graduates in Mexico—both figures being about the same as in the United States. However, given the strong emphasis in Mexican culture on family and women's central role within family life, the question emerges about the practice patterns of women physicians. Harrison (1998) focused on the extent to which women physicians were as able as men physicians to migrate within

Mexico, especially to areas underserved by physicians. Would women physicians be more influenced by professional opportunities and responsibilities, or by expectations of responsibilities to family and home life?

Using both personal interviews and analyses of secondary data sources, Harrison found that women physicians tend to live and work in their native or adopted state (often the city in which their medical school is located) in order to be close to family and friends. This is partially influenced by constraints in the health care system, such as availability of specialist training and the medical labor market. However, at virtually every point in the life course, family and household demands strongly influence specialist choice, career development, and migration patterns. Career decisions are subordinate to those of the husband, thus conforming to traditional Mexican sociocultural values.

---

movement from physicians practicing in small groups with several physicians to practicing in large groups with sometimes 100 or more physicians. Because large group practices are typically owned by a physician collective or a hospital, the professional autonomy of individual physicians is lower. Recently, the percentage of physicians with ownership in their practice dropped below 50 percent for the first time ever.

2. Reimbursement models for physician care. Traditionally, payments to physicians came directly from patients, insurance companies, or the government and were based on a fee-for-service model—that is, they were paid for the specific services that they provided. Now, increasingly, alternative models are being tested with reimbursement based on factors such as the value of rendered services in terms

of patient outcomes. In part, this is being driven by a desire to limit the financial incentive to do more and more costly procedures (Mendelson et al., 2017).

3. The expansion of new information technologies. Physicians now spend an increasing amount of their time on the computer practicing medicine electronically rather than in personal interaction with patients. This is discussed more fully in Chapter 16.

PHYSICIAN SATISFACTION AND PHYSICIAN IMPAIRMENT

Physician Satisfaction

Are today's physicians satisfied with their careers? Research has found generally positive feelings: between 80 and 85 percent of physicians express career satisfaction. The most cited factors are both intrinsic (feeling a 'calling' to medicine, relationships with patients, intellectual stimulation, and contributions to a genuine need) and extrinsic (financial rewards and the prestige of the position) (Tak, Curlin, and Yoon, 2017; Statista, 2019). The intrinsic factors are especially related to job satisfaction, commitment to the position, and finding the work to be personally meaningful. Physicians who work with children and those who work with the elderly report the highest satisfaction levels. Younger physicians tend to be more satisfied than older physicians, and greater satisfaction is also associated with lower educational debt at graduation.

However, based on surveys, professional reports, and anecdotes, there is growing concern about physician well-being—that is, the ability to maintain good physical and mental health within the career context. Problems such as stress, burnout, and suicide ideation convey that many physicians go through difficult periods in their career. This is troubling for the physician personally and for its effect on quality of patient care.

Physician Dissatisfaction

The major source of physician dissatisfaction is frustration with the expansion of bureaucratic and institutional controls that restrict physician autonomy and overly influence patient care decisions. These regulations typically come from employers (as more physicians work for someone else) and insurance companies (that make decisions on what services will or will not be reimbursed). These frustrations are combined with high amounts of paperwork now required and especially to requirements to maintain **electronic health records (EHRs)** (which require a large amount of time).

Studies show that physicians' time each day is almost evenly divided between direct patient care and "desktop medicine"—that is, the time spent on activities such as communicating with patients through a secure patient portal, responding to patients' requests for prescription refills and medical advice, ordering tests, sending messages to staff, and reviewing test results (Tai-Seale et al., 2017). These tasks create a feeling of loss of control over one's own work and an interference with determining what is in patients' best interest. Physicians are also frustrated by declining incomes relative to purchasing power and possible loss in prestige. Many physicians are disturbed that the mission of medicine seems to have changed from one of service to patients to one of compliance with corporate policies.

Physician Stress

Many people consider that physicians "have it made." They are bright, well-educated, wealthy, prestigious members of the community who typically live in exceptional houses in exceptional neighborhoods with an exceptional number of personal possessions. The image contains some truth—but it misses another side to the career in medicine. Being a physician can be an extremely stressful responsibility, and physicians frequently suffer from the accumulation of stressors.

Cultural expectations for physicians are certainly high. Physicians are expected not only to be medical experts but also to exercise this expertise without error. Every physician is expected to function at a maximum level of competence all the time. Few patients would be very understanding about a misdiagnosis that occurs because a physician's mind is temporarily diverted. Yet physicians as people experience the same personal traumas as everyone else, and sometimes find it difficult to block personal concerns from professional activity.

Traditionally, physicians have been expected to be assertive decision makers on the job. They have wanted and have been given tremendous authority. They are often treated with considerable deference. While these qualities may or may not be beneficial in a health care setting, they can be devastating within family relationships. (Many medical spouses swear that physicians believe that the MD degree stands for "medical deity.") When physicians carry their authoritarian persona home, family relationships can suffer. Moreover, many physicians—especially those in primary care specialties and obstetrics/gynecology—are rarely off the job. Knowing that they are only a beep or telephone call away from going back to work, they find it difficult to relax.

Physician Burnout

The feeling of overwork combined with loss of control over clinical decision making, and a perceived inability to always provide optimal care for patients, often lead to **physician burnout**. Burnout is typically considered a state of emotional and physical exhaustion, with an accompanying decrease in job identification, job satisfaction, and confidence in work ability. In 2011, research found a high rate of physician dissatisfaction with work–life balance, and 45 percent of physicians felt burned out. When the study was repeated in 2014, satisfaction with work–life balance declined further and the burnout rate increased to 54 percent—that is, more than half of practicing physicians were experiencing emotional and physical exhaustion (Shanafelt et al., 2015). These findings are alarming given that research has found that the quality of patient care and patient satisfaction decrease when physicians experience burnout.

Physician Impairment

Experiencing significant stress, frustration, and burnout can take a serious toll and sometimes lead to an **impaired physician**—one who is unable to practice medicine with reasonable skill and safety due to physical or mental illness, including loss of a motor skill due to aging or to excessive use or abuse of drugs, including alcohol. An estimated 15 percent of physicians will be impaired at some point in their career due to alcoholism, drug dependency, or mental illness—about the same as or a slightly higher percentage than the general population. The incidence of depression is higher among physicians than members of similarly educated groups. Physicians end their own lives with greater frequency (two to three times more likely) and earlier in life than other professionals or members of the general population. Suicide rates for women physicians are especially high relative to other occupational groupings.

Recognizing the problem, the AMA has instituted "physician health programs" that encourage physicians to report colleagues in trouble and urge state and local medical societies to initiate treatment programs. These programs are designed to provide treatment for substance abuse and other problems while protecting confidentiality and reducing the likelihood of punitive sanctions against the impaired physician. A total of 47 states now have programs in place. Although there is limited evidence about the success of these programs, the general feeling is that they are working well and have increased the willingness of physicians to report a colleague demonstrating worrying signs of substance abuse (Farber et al., 2005).

In addition, in 2016, chief executives from ten major health organizations gathered to discuss strategies to combat physician burnout, and in 2018, the National Academy of Medicine, the Association of American Medical Colleges, and the Accreditation Council for Graduate Medical Education launched a major national program on *Clinician Well-Being and Resilience* (Dzau, Kirch, and Nasca, 2018).

One novel response by some primary care physicians is described in the accompanying box, "Concierge Care and Direct Practice Care for the Public."

IN THE FIELD

CONCIERGE CARE AND DIRECT PRACTICE CARE FOR THE PUBLIC

In the last two decades, a small number of **concierge care** practices have developed in the United States. These practices typically involve a physician bypassing the health insurance system (and its requirements and paperwork) and offering direct, personalized care to patients who enroll with the physician by paying a flat monthly or annual fee. Patients then receive comprehensive primary care, including consultations, basic medications, and lab tests, and an assurance of having a physician always on call. In the early years, concierge doctors targeted wealthy patients and charged thousands of dollars a year for their retainers. These exclusive arrangements were sometimes called "health care for billionaires." Patients often liked having a physician directly available. Enrollees were those who did not have to worry about the price.

In the last few years, some physicians (an estimated 6,000 in 2016) have begun offering a type of this structure called **direct practice care**. These arrangements require payment of a low, flat-rate fee (concierge practices require a slightly higher retainer but guarantee more time with the physician). Physicians in both types of arrangements spend more time on patient care and keep costs down. Direct practice care physicians average about 600 patients, compared to the 2,500 or so patients of a typical primary care physician. Patients benefit by having close access to the physician for (often) lower cost than health insurance. Patients do still need insurance policies for specialist care, emergency care, and catastrophic expenses.

It is too soon to determine whether this model of care would work for larger populations, but several employers are now experimenting with or monitoring the arrangement. Several of the most acclaimed health systems in the country have recently established concierge practices in which patients (for an annual retainer of $2,500 to $6,000 in addition to normal fees) are guaranteed same-day appointments, immediate text responses, and day or night service.

SUMMARY

The medical profession in the United States evolved from a poorly regarded, poorly paid, disorganized occupation in the eighteenth and nineteenth centuries to a position of professional dominance by the mid-twentieth century. Scientific developments gave the public more confidence in medicine, and the government extended legal autonomy—the right of self-control.

However, the medical profession's dominance has waned since then and is being replaced by agents such as corporations, the federal government, and consumers. The theory of countervailing power posits that any profession's dominance is only a temporary phenomenon, existing only until other forces increase their power.

Social control of medicine refers to forces inside and outside medicine that can regulate medical practice. Internal control mechanisms have a mixed record of effectiveness, although patients exercise some external control through such means as malpractice litigation. While injured patients may be compensated through lawsuits, the American system has numerous problems, including many victims of malpractice who are not compensated and many non-victims who file suits.

The number of physicians in the United States is inadequate despite increases in the number of osteopathic physicians and the number of international students. Moreover, too few physicians have been entering primary care or choosing to practice in medically underserved areas.

Women and men physicians practice medicine somewhat differently: women are more likely to go into primary care, while men are more likely to enter surgical specialties; when children are present, women work fewer hours than men and make lower salaries despite the number of hours worked; and women are more likely to see women and racial and ethnic minority patients. Due to continuing sexual discrimination and harassment, women are often held down within medicine. Despite an overall high level of satisfaction, research has identified high levels of physician stress, burnout, and impairment.

HEALTH ON THE INTERNET

Many health care providers now send surveys to patients to ask about recent care experiences, and several independent health care ratings companies have created online evaluations to provide ratings of individual physicians and hospitals. Each is set up slightly differently, but may provide background information, public liability records, and patient ratings of individual physicians.

Physicians and patients tend to regard these employer-sent and online rating sites very differently. Physicians judge the employer-sent ratings and accompanying narratives to be more accurate than the independent rating sites. Patients are just the opposite—putting more trust in the ratings and comments from the independent sites (Holliday et al., 2017). About 6 in 10 Americans believe the information provided is very or somewhat helpful in selecting a physician. You can check out the following:

www.healthgrades.com
www.drscore.com
www.ratemds.com

What kind of information can you obtain at each of these sites? Why can't you get even more detailed information? More than 1,000 physicians are so unhappy with these sites (especially with those that allow patients to add personal comments) that they now ask their patients to sign a legal form that promises they will not post unfavorable information about the physician or care received.

How do you think the presence of Internet sites such as these will affect the practice of medicine? What advantages can you identify? What disadvantages can you identify? Why do you believe physicians and patients rate the two different kinds of ratings/comments differently?

DISCUSSION CASE

Drawn from: Herbert J. Keating and Terrence F. Ackerman. 1991 "When the Doctor Is On Drugs." *Hastings Center Report*, Vol. 21 (September–October), 29.

You are both personal physician and friend to another physician. Lately, he has seemed withdrawn, irritable, and distracted. You have heard rumors that not long ago he made a serious error in calculating a medication dosage but that the error was caught by the pharmacist before the drug was dispensed. He surprised you yesterday during a routine office visit with you that he had been using cocaine daily, but he says he is now drug-free. You have doubts about that because his behavior seems different. When you directly confront him with your suspicions, he cuts off all further contact with you.

You are uncertain how to proceed. You believe you should at least raise your concerns to the hospital, to the state medical society, or the state licensing board. (According to American Medical Association guidelines, physicians have an ethical obligation to report impaired, incompetent, and/ or unethical colleagues in accordance with the legal requirements in each state.)

Are you justified in reporting your friend on the basis of your current information? Won't he just deny everything? You realize you have no proof that thus far he has harmed any patient. What if you are wrong and he is no longer using drugs? Being irritable is not a crime. If you intervene, there is a real chance that his reputation and career will be harmed. What are your duties to him as a friend, physician, and colleague, and what are your duties to society?

GLOSSARY

American Medical Association (AMA)
concierge care
corporatization
countervailing power
defensive medicine
deprofessionalization
direct practice care
electronic health records (EHRs)
health professional shortage area
health rating scales

impaired physician
medical malpractice
medically underserved area
peer review
physician burnout
primary care
professional dominance
professions
proletarianization
social control

REFERENCES

Agrawal, Shantanu, and Douglas Brown. 2016. "The Physician Payments Sunshine Act—Two Years of the Open Payment Program." *New England Journal of Medicine* 374(10):906–909.

American Medical Association, Department of Physician Data Sources, Division of Survey and Data Resources. 2012. *Physician Characteristics and Distribution in the United States.* Chicago, IL: American Medical Association.

Association of American Medical Colleges. 2019. "FACTS: Applicants, Matriculants, Enrollment, Graduates, MD-PHD, and Residency Applicants Data." Retrieved March 11, 2019 (www.aamc.org/data/databook/).

Bureau of Health Workforce. Health Resources and Service Administration. 2018. *Designated Health Professional Shortage Areas Statistics.* Washington, DC: US Department of Health & Human Services.

Campbell, Eric G., Sowmya R. Rao, Catherine M. DesRoches, Lisa I. Iezzoni, Christine Vogeli, Dragana Bolcic-Jankovic, and Paola D. Miralles. 2010.

"Physician Professionalism and Changes in Physician-Industry Relationships from 2004 to 2009." *Archives of Internal Medicine* 170(20):1820–1826.

Campbell, Eric G., Susan Regan, Russell L. Gruen, Timothy G. Ferris, Sowmya R. Rao, Paul D. Cleary, and David Blumenthal. 2007. "Professionalism in Medicine: Results of a National Survey of Physicians." *Annals of Internal Medicine* 147(11):795–802.

Dzau, Victor J., Darrell C. Kirch, and Thomas J. Nasca. 2018. "To Care Is Human—Collectively Confronting the Clinician-Burnout Crisis." *New England Journal of Medicine* 378(4):312–314.

Ehrenreich, Barbara, and Deirdre English. 1973. *Witches, Midwives, and Nurses—A History of Women Healers.* Old Westbury, NY: The Feminist Press.

Farber, Neil J., Stephanie G. Gilbert, Brian M. Aboff, Virginia U. Collier, Joan Weiner, and E. Gil Boyer. 2005. "Physicians' Willingness to Report Impaired Colleagues." *Social Science and Medicine* 61(8):1772–1775.

Freidson, Eliot. 1970a. *Profession of Medicine: A Study in the Sociology of Applied Knowledge.* New York: Dodd, Mead.

———. 1970b. *Professional Dominance: The Social Structure of Medical Care.* New York: Atherton Press.

Goode, William J. 1960. "Encroachment, Charlatanism, and the Emerging Profession: Psychology, Sociology, and Medicine." *American Sociological Review* 25(4):902–914.

Grant, Darren, and Kelly C. Alfred. 2007. "Sanctions and Recidivism: An Evaluation of Physician Discipline by State Medical Boards." *Journal of Health Politics, Policy, and Law* 32(5):867–885.

Hafferty, Frederic W., and Donald W. Light. 1995. "Professional Dynamics and the Changing Nature of Medical Work." *Journal of Health and Social Behavior* 35(Extra Issue):132–153.

Hannawa, Annegret F., Yuki Shigemoto, and Todd D. Little. 2016. "Medical Errors: Disclosure Styles, Interpersonal Forgiveness, and Outcomes." *Social Science and Medicine* 156(May):29–38.

Harrison, Margaret E. 1998. "Female Physicians in Mexico: Migration and Mobility in the Lifecourse." *Social Science and Medicine* 47(4):455–468.

Haug, Marie. 1973. "Deprofessionalization: An Alternate Hypothesis for the Future." *Sociological Review Monograph* 20(S1):195–211.

———. 1988. "A Re-examination of the Hypothesis of Physician Deprofessionalization." *Milbank Quarterly* 66(S2):48–56.

Haug, Marie, and Bebe Lavin. 1983. *Consumerism in Medicine: Challenging Physician Authority.* Beverly Hills, CA: Sage.

Hite, Chuck, and Douglas Pardue. 1984. "Despite 'Ignorance, Carelessness,' Doctor Regains License to Practice." *Roanoke Times and World News*, October 7, pp. A1, A14.

Holliday, Allison M., Allen Kachalia, Gregg S. Meyer, and Thomas D. Sequist. 2017. "Physician and Patient Views on Public Physician Rating Websites: A Cross-Sectional Study." *Journal of General Internal Medicine* 32(6):626–631.

Keating, Herbert J., and Terrence F. Ackerman. 1991. "When the Doctor Is on Drugs." *Hastings Center Report* 21(5):29.

Light, Donald W. 1991. "Professionalism as a Countervailing Power." *Journal of Health Politics, Policy, and Law* 16(3):499–506.

———. 2000. "The Medical Profession and Organizational Change: From Professional Dominance to Countervailing Power." Pp. 201–216 in *Handbook of Medical Sociology* (5th ed.), edited by Chloe E.

Bird, Peter Conrad, and Allen M. Fremont. Upper Saddle River, NJ: Prentice Hall.

———. 2010. "Health Care Professionals, Markets, and Countervailing Powers." Pp. 270–289 in *Handbook of Medical Sociology* (6th ed.), edited by Chloe E. Bird, Peter Conrad, Allen M. Fremont, and Stefan Timmermans. Nashville, TN: Vanderbilt University Press.

Light, Donald W., and Sol Levine. 1988. "The Changing Character of the Medical Profession: A Theoretical Overview." *The Milbank Quarterly* 66(S2):10–32.

Localio, A. Russell, Ann G. Lawthers, Troyen A. Brennan, Nan M. Laird, Liesi E. Hebert, Lynn M. Peterson, Joseph P. Newhouse, Paul C. Weiler, and Howard H. Hiatt. 1991. "Relation between Malpractice Claims and Adverse Events Due to Negligence." *New England Journal of Medicine* 325(4):245–251.

Ly, Dan P., Seth A. Seabury, and Anupant B. Jena. 2018. "Characteristics of U.S. Physician Marriages, 2000–2015: An Analysis of Data from a U.S. Census Survey." *Annals of Internal Medicine* 168(5):375–376.

Mann, Sarah. 2017. "Research Shows Shortage of More than 100,000 Doctors by 2030." *Medical Education.* Retrieved November 7, 2019 (https://news.aamc.org/medical-education/article/new-aamc-research-reaffirms-looming-physician-shor/).

McArthur, John H., and Francis D. Moore. 1997. "The Two Cultures and the Health Care Revolution." *Journal of the American Medical Association* 277(12)985–989.

Mello, Michelle M., David M. Studdert, and Allen Kachalia. 2014. "The Medical Liability Climate and Prospects for Reform." *Journal of the American Medical Association* 312(20):2146–2155.

Mendelson, Aaron, Karli K. Kondo, Cheryl L. Damberg, Allison Low, Makalapua Matupuaka, Michele Freeman, Maya O'Neill, Rose Relevo, and Devan Kansagara. 2017. "The Effects of Pay-for-Performance Programs on Health, Health Care Use, and Processes of Care: A Systematic Review." *Annals of Internal Medicine* 166(5):341–353.

Merchant, Juanita, and M. Bishr Omary. 2010. "Clogged Up: Efforts to Train More Minority Doctors Stalled as Population Diversifies." *Modern Healthcare* (February 22):24.

Modern Healthcare. 2018. "Physician Compensation Survey." *Modern Healthcare* (July 23):20–24.

National Academies of Science, Engineering, and Medicine. 2018. *Sexual Harassment of Women: Climate, Culture and Consequences in Academic Sciences, Engineering, and Medicine.* Washington, DC: The

National Academies Press. Retrieved March 11, 2019 (https://doi: 10.17226/24994).

Navarro, Vicente. 1988. "Professional Dominance or Proletarianization? Neither." *The Milbank Quarterly* 66(S2):57–75.

Parlier, Anna B., Shelley L. Galvin, Sarah Thach, David Kruidenier, and Ernest B. Fagan. 2018. "The Road to Rural Primary Care: A Narrative Review of Factors That Help Develop, Recruit, and Retain Rural Primary Care Physicians." *Academic Medicine* 93(1):130–140.

Peeples, Ralph, Catherine T. Harris, and Thomas A. Metzloff. 2000. "Settlement Has Many Faces: Physicians, Attorneys, and Medical Malpractice." *Journal of Health and Social Behavior* 41(3):333–346.

Pinsky, William W. 2018. "Immigration Policies Likely to Have Unintended Consequences for Healthcare Access in U.S." *Modern Healthcare* (September 10):27.

Robertson, Christopher, Susannah Rose, and Aaron S. Kesselheim. 2012. "Effect of Financial Relationships on the Behaviors of Health Care Professionals: A Review of the Evidence." *Journal of Law, Medicine, and Ethics* 40(3):452–466.

Rubin, Haya, William H. Rogers, Katherine L. Kahn, Lisa V. Rubenstein, and Robert H. Brook. 1992. "Watching the Doctor-Watchers: How Well Do Peer Review Organization Methods Detect Hospital Care Quality Problems?" *Journal of the American Medical Association* 267(17):2349–2354.

Scheinman, Steven J., Patrick Fleming, and Kellyann Niotis. 2018. "Oath Taking at U.S. and Canadian Medical School Ceremonies: Historical Perspectives, Current Practices, and Future Considerations." *Academic Medicine* 93(9):1301–1306.

Seabury, Seth A., Eric Helland, and Anupam B. Jena. 2014. "Medical Malpractice Reform: Noneconomic Damages Caps Reduced Payments 15 Percent, With Varied Effects by Specialty." *Health Affairs* 33(11):2048–2056.

Sethi, Manesh K., and Robert Aseltine. 2008. "The Investigation of Defensive Medicine in Massachusetts: Extent and Cost of Defensive Medicine." Results released at the Medical Society's Interim Meeting of House of Delegates, Waltham, MA, November 14–15. Retrieved January 7, 2016 (www.massmed.org).

Shanafelt, Tait D., Omar Hasan, Lotte N. Dyrbye, Christine Sinsky, Daniel Sarele, Jeff Sloan, and Colin P. West. 2015. "Changes in Burnout and Satisfaction with Work-Life Balance in Physicians and the General US Working Population Between 2011 and 2014." *Mayo Clinic Proceedings* 90(12):1600–1613.

Statista. 2019. "Distribution of U.S. Physicians' Opinions About Most Satisfying Factors in Medical Practice from 2008 to 2018." *Statista.* Retrieved January 5, 2019 (www.statista.com/statistics/416007/most-satisfying-factors-in-medical-practice-by-us-physicians/).

Studdert, David M., Eric J. Thomas, Helen R. Burstin, Brett W. Zbar, E. John Orav, and Troyen A. Brennan. 2000. "Negligent Care and Malpractice Claiming Behavior in Utah and Colorado." *Medical Care* 38(3):250–260.

Tai-Seale, Ming, Cliff W. Olson, Jinnan Li, Albert S. Chan, Criss Morikawa, Meg Durbin, Wei Wang, and Harold S. Luft. 2017. "Electronic Health Records Logs Indicate That Physicians Split Time Evenly Between Seeing Patients and Desktop Medicine." *Health Affairs* 36(4):655–662.

Tak, Hyo J., Farr A. Curlin, and John D. Yoon. 2017. "Association of Intrinsic Motivating Factors and Markers of Physician Well-Being: A National Physician Survey." *Journal of General Internal Medicine* 32(7):739–746.

Timmermans, Stefan, and Hyeyoung Oh. 2010. "The Continued Social Transformation of the Medical Profession." *Journal of Health and Social Behavior* 51(S1):94–106.

Zimmerman, Mary K. 2000. "Women's Health and Gender Bias in Medical Education." Pp. 121–138 in *Research in the Sociology of Health Care, 2000,* edited by Jennie J. Kronenfeld. Stamford, CT: JAI Press.

CHAPTER 9

Medical Education and the Socialization of Physicians

Learning Objectives

- Describe the Flexner Report and identify specific ways it altered medical education.
- Identify and discuss criticisms of today's medical school curriculum, and describe specific ways in which the curriculum is changing.
- Describe the value orientations "tolerance for uncertainty" and "detached concern,"

and explain the reasons why they are viewed as important for medical students.

- Identify and describe the primary sources of stress for medical students.
- Identify and describe the impact of medical school on the career practice patterns of students.

Socialization is the process by which a person becomes a member of a group or society and acquires values, attitudes, beliefs, behavior patterns, and a sense of social identity. It is a lifelong process; as each new role is added, one integrates new expectations with previous behavior.

Physicians undergo both formal and informal socialization into the medical role. The medical school experience is structured to impart not only knowledge and technique but also certain attitudes and values. Through the process, medical students are consciously and subconsciously converted from laypeople to health care professionals. This chapter traces the development and organization of the formal educational system for physicians and describes the socialization processes that occur.

THE HISTORY OF MEDICAL EDUCATION

Early Medical Education

During the colonial period, the primary mode of medical instruction was the apprenticeship

system, but the quality of these apprenticeships varied enormously. A few preceptors provided meaningful experiences in active practice and close supervision of their students, but many others made little effort to provide any systematic instruction. Although a 3-year apprenticeship was considered standard, in reality a certificate was routinely issued to any student who merely registered with a physician.

By the year 1800, three formal medical schools (the University of Pennsylvania, Harvard, and King's College) had been established. These schools were eventually joined by an increasing number of for-profit medical schools, which became the dominant vehicle of medical education by the mid-nineteenth century. Ability to pay the fees was the only entrance requirement for white men, and few applicants had any college preparation. In fact, most students had completed elementary school only, and many were illiterate (Ludmerer, 1985).

Two 4-month terms of lectures made up the standard course of instruction. The curriculum focused on subjects of "practical" value, with little attention to scientific subjects. Written examinations were not required in order to graduate, but the diploma "licensed" the young physician to practice medicine anywhere in the country. Some students opted to supplement their medical education by serving as a "house pupil" in a hospital. These pupils, selected by a competitive examination, would reside in a hospital and assume responsibility for managing cases, much as medical students and house officers do today (Ludmerer, 1985).

An alternative to an apprenticeship or American medical school was European study—most often in France. Between 1820 and 1861, nearly 700 Americans studied medicine in Paris. However, few aspiring doctors had the financial means to study abroad (Ludmerer, 1985).

Medical Education for Women.   Whereas the standards for admission were very lax for white men, women faced significant obstacles. By 1880, only a handful of medical schools accepted women on a regular basis. Although Elizabeth Blackwell (1821–1910) earned an MD degree from the Geneva College of Medicine in upstate New York in 1849 (becoming the first woman in the country to do so), most women were forced to attend independent medical schools created expressly for their training. During the second half of the nineteenth century, 14 of these women's medical colleges were established in the United States.

Some of this bias receded during the latter part of the nineteenth century and the first two decades of the twentieth, and numerous medical societies began admitting women. By 1900, women accounted for more than 10 percent of enrollment at almost 20 medical schools, and 12 of the women's colleges had closed or merged. However, beginning around 1920, a reversal occurred as acceptance of women into professional medicine declined.

Medical Education for Blacks.   Medical education was formally denied to blacks throughout the United States prior to the Civil War. After emancipation, would-be black physicians turned to missionary or for-profit medical schools in the South—schools expressly created to train black physicians to serve the black population.

Howard University, the most prestigious black medical college, opened in 1869, and it remained the primary source for medical education of blacks for the next century. As late as 1890, however, blacks made up less than 1 percent of physicians in the United States. The schools for women and the schools for blacks constantly struggled to survive.

Early Reform Efforts

Early efforts to reform medical education included raising standards for admission, lengthening the training process, revising the curriculum, and adding clinical instruction. One obstacle to reform was the dependence of medical professors on student fees—thus mandating that students not be discouraged from applying or persisting once admitted. In addition, American physicians distrusted the laboratory and lacked respect for experimental science, and few medical educators had any interest in research (Ludmerer, 1985).

However, by the mid-1880s, many medical schools themselves had initiated reform. The length of training expanded—eventually to 4 years—and entrance requirements were strengthened. Curricula were revised to emphasize scientific subjects, and laboratory experiences were included whenever possible. Although these changes were not instituted uniformly, and hence the quality of medical education varied greatly, momentum for reform was high (Ludmerer, 1985).

The Flexner Report.   Capitalizing on this desire for improvement, the American Medical

Association (AMA) made reform of medical schools a top priority in 1904 by establishing a Council on Medical Education. The council determined premedical education requirements, developed a standard training period, and constructed a licensing test. In addition, the quality of medical schools was evaluated, and many schools were judged to be inferior. The report was distributed to medical schools but was never published because it was considered politically risky for a medical organization to criticize medical schools publicly.

Instead, the council commissioned the Carnegie Foundation for the Advancement of Teaching to conduct a similar study, to be headed by Abraham Flexner, a respected educator. As discussed in Chapter 2, Flexner's study recognized the diversity of the American medical scene, which included some of the best and some of the worst medical schools in the world. His 1910 report, *Medical Education in the United States and Canada,* strongly attacked the weakest schools, especially the for-profits. "The result was a classic piece of muckraking journalism that deserves to rank with the other great muckraking treatises of the era. He provided a wealth of details, named names, and devastated the bad schools with humiliating public exposure" (Ludmerer, 1985:179).

The **Flexner Report** accomplished its purpose as it aligned medical educators and the public against for-profit schools and in favor of a homogeneous, university-based system of education focused on scientific medicine and formation of a professional identity (Irby, Cooke, and O'Brien, 2010). The AMA worked closely with philanthropic foundations to provide financial assistance to help embed this model on a national level. Numerous colleges were forced to close, including 5 of the 7 black medical schools and all but one of the women's colleges. As a result, the total number of medical graduates, and especially the number of women and black graduates, declined.

MODERN MEDICAL EDUCATION

The Foundation of a New Curriculum

By the 1920s, a new type of medical education was in place. Advocated by Flexner and embraced by the AMA and the nation's top medical schools, a revised medical school curriculum (sometimes referred to as the Johns Hopkins model) was implemented. Despite some later innovations, the basic principles of the new curriculum remain in place today. They include:

1. A clear separation between the basic sciences (taught in the first 2 years) and the clinical sciences (taught in the third and fourth years).
2. A heavy reliance on lectures to large classes (especially in teaching the basic sciences) and utilizing the instructor as expert (as opposed to personal investigation).
3. Relatively independent and often uncoordinated courses taught by full-time faculty in many different departments.
4. The clerkship years (often relying on residents as instructors) as an integral part of medical education.

Academic Health Centers and Medical Schools Today

As of 2019, there were 141 fully accredited allopathic (MD) medical schools and 35 osteopathic (D.O.) medical schools in the United States (with more in process). The number of medical schools in the United States represents a significant increase in just the last 20 years—a response to the perceived need for more physicians. This is a major development, as no new allopathic medical schools opened in the 1980s or 1990s. Medical schools employ more than 175,000 full-time faculty (only 16,000 in 1966) for 91,000 medical students and 110,000 medical residents.

Each medical school is part of a large configuration of programs and services called an **academic health center (AHC)**. AHCs have a three-pronged mission—to provide cutting-edge clinical care, to conduct clinical research, and to play a key role in medical education. These centers typically consist of one or more hospitals with comprehensive medical specialties, the latest and most advanced medical technology, and sophisticated research laboratories. Often they are a dominant part of the university in which they are located, and they may be the institution's largest securer of grant money and its most prestigious component. In many cases the health centers have such extensive facilities and generate so much money that they are largely independent of university control.

Medical Students

The number of applicants to US medical schools varies from year to year. There were about 47,000 individual applicants in 1996, only 33,600 in 2002, and steadily increasing numbers since then to 52,777 discrete applicants in 2018 (see Table 9.1). These applicants submitted more than 781,000 applications to medical schools—an average of about 15 each. Several medical schools are currently in the

TABLE 9.1   Applications to US Medical Schools Over a 40-Year Period

Academic Year	Number of Applicants	First-Year Enrollment
1979–1980	36,141	17,014
1989–1990	26,915	16,749
1999–2000	38,529	16,856
2009–2010	42,269	18,390
2018–2019	52,777	21,662

Source: Data from Association of American Medical Colleges. 2019a. US Medical School Applications and Matriculants by School, State of Legal Residence, and Sex, 2018–2019. Retrieved January 25, 2019 (www.aamc.org/download/321442/data/factstablea1.pdf).

process of increasing their enrollment. The mean grade point average for matriculants in 2018 was 3.57. Once admitted, almost all students earn their degree (the attrition rate is only about 1 percent).

Women Medical Students.   In recent years, the number of medical school applicants has been about evenly divided between women and men (women were 50.9 percent of 2018 applicants,

After two decades without the creation of any new allopathic medical schools, several new schools have been accredited in the last few years, and several more are in various stages of establishment.

Source: Photo courtesy of Janet Jonas.

and men 49.1 percent). Women now represent slightly more than half of first-year students each year (51.6 percent in 2018), but the percentage of women admitted by school varies widely (more than 60 percent in 15 schools, less than 45 percent in 15 schools). Given that women account for about 56 percent of all baccalaureate graduates, they are still under-represented in medical school. In 2018, men matriculants had very slightly higher Medical College Admission Test (MCAT) scores, and women matriculants had very slightly higher grade point averages. Check out the recent rapid changes in Table 9.2.

Racial and Ethnic Minority Medical Students. In 2018, just about half (49.9 percent) of medical school matriculants were white. Other racial and ethnic groups with the highest percentage of first-year medical students were Asian American (22.1 percent), students of mixed race (9.5 percent), African American (7.1 percent), and Hispanics (6.2 percent) (see Table 9.3).

TABLE 9.2 Women in US Medical Schools Over a 40-Year Period

Academic Year	Number (%) of Women Applicants	Number (%) of Entering Women	Number (%) of Graduates
1979–1980	10,222 (28.3)	4,748 (27.9)	3,497 (23.1)
1989–1990	10,546 (39.2)	6,404 (38.2)	5,197 (33.9)
1999–2000	17,433 (45.2)	7,725 (45.8)	6,712 (42.4)
2009–2010	20,252 (49.9)	8,817 (47.9)	8,035 (48.8)
2018–2019	26,882 (50.9)	11,160 (51.6)	8,907 (47.6)

Source: Data from Association of American Medical Colleges, 2019b. Applicants, First-Time Applicants, Acceptees, and Matriculants to US Medical Schools by Sex, 2009–2010 through 2018–2019. Retrieved January 25, 2019 (www.aamc.org/download/492954/data/factstablea7_2.pdf).

TABLE 9.3 Race and Ethnic Background of Medical School Matriculants, 2018

Background	Applicants	First-Year Enrollment
White only	24,680 (46.8%)	10,780 (49.9%)
Asian only	11,216 (21.3%)	4,786 (22.1%)
Mixed race	4,852 (9.2%)	2,044 (9.5%)
African American only	4,430 (8.4%)	1,540 (7.1%)
Hispanic, Latino only	3,296 (6.2%)	1,349 (6.2%)
Non-US	1,947 (4.0%)	280 (1.3%)
Other	1,166 (2.2%)	380 (1.8%)
Unknown	1,008 (1.9%)	393 (1.8%)
Native American/Alaskan Native only	109 (0.2%)	39 (0.2%)
Native Hawaiian/Pacific Islander only	53 (0.1%)	23 (0.1%)
Total	52,757	21,614

Source: Data from Association of American Medical Colleges. 2019c. Applicants to US Medical Schools by Selected Combinations of Race/Ethnicity and Sex, 2015–2016 through 2018–2019. Retrieved January 25, 2019 (www.aamc.org/download/321472/data/factstablea8.pdf) and 2019d.

Matriculants to US Medical Schools by Race, Selected Combinations of Race/Ethnicity and Sex, 2015–2016 through 2018–2019. Retrieved January 25, 2019 (www.aamc.org/download/321474/data/factstablea9.pdf).

The landmark Civil Rights court decisions and legislation of the 1950s and 1960s opened the doors of all medical schools to minority candidates. In 1969, the AAMC established an Office of Minority Affairs in an attempt to encourage more minority students to pursue medical education. The AAMC established the goal of proportional representation in medicine for all groups, and pays special attention to minorities that have been under-represented. For example, in 2018, blacks were 13.2 percent of the population but only 7.1 percent of first-year medical students, so a sizable gap still exists.

The scaling back of affirmative action programs in the late 1990s and early 2000s led to a significant decrease in minority applicants, but numbers in 2018 approached or exceeded earlier numbers. Two reasons these numbers are important are that black physicians are more likely than their white counterparts to enter primary care and to practice in inner-city areas (both significant national needs) and the larger number of minority students, the greater the opportunity for white students to interact with diverse peoples. This interaction increases white students' confidence treating diverse populations (Saha et al., 2008).

The Medical Education Curriculum

Years 1 and 2. Most medical schools offer a similar curriculum. The first 2 years are devoted to the basic sciences (e.g., anatomy, biochemistry, microbiology, pathology, pharmacology, and physiology). Largely taught through the traditional lecture format, students are often overwhelmed by the amount of information presented.

The units are highly compact and very intense; students soon realize that they cannot possibly learn everything, so they quickly search for memorization aids. Classes are often quite large, and medical faculty tend to be impersonal (a significant change and major disappointment for many students). Most schools require that students take and pass Part I of the US Medical Licensing Examination (USMLE) (on basic science knowledge) after the second year.

Years 3 and 4. During the third and fourth years—the clinical years—students learn to use

Although large lecture classes continue to be prevalent in the first 2 years of medical school, an increasing number of schools are adopting small groups as a preferred mode of teaching.

their basic medical science to solve actual clinical problems by working with patients (almost always in hospitals). During these 2 years, students rotate through several (typically about nine) clerkships to learn specialized applications of medical knowledge. They spend an average of about 6 weeks in family practice, 12 weeks in internal medicine, 8 weeks in general surgery, 8 weeks in pediatrics, 7 weeks in obstetrics and gynecology, and 7 weeks in psychiatry. Students often make rounds during these years—accompanied by impersonal faculty and intensive oral exams. Most schools require students to pass the two parts of Part II (on clinical knowledge and clinical skills) of the USMLE exam after the fourth year. Students are ultimately required to pass a third part (on application of clinical knowledge and patient management) in order to receive a medical license in the United States.

The Residency. After the fourth year, most students enter a medical residency (except for those who intend to do research or work outside medicine). A computerized matching process is used to pair residents looking for a teaching hospital with particular traits (e.g., specialization or location) and for hospitals attempting to secure the best possible residents. The number of years required in residency depends upon the specialty interests of the resident—3 years is common, but several specialties require longer. The resident (the first year of the residency is still sometimes referred to as the internship) is legally able to practice medicine under the supervision of a licensed physician.

Significant role identity change from student to physician occurs during these years. The resident has much more authority than the fourth-year student, and that often comes across in relationships with patients and ancillary staff. This is a learning period for residents, and they often search for—and are most excited to work with—intriguing cases. On the other hand, medical residents are a primary source of cheap labor

for hospitals, and they are expected to handle many routine responsibilities. The hours assigned are typically very long, exhaustion is not uncommon (due to medical school debts, many residents even moonlight, taking on additional paid medical responsibilities in the few off-hours they have), and it is often a frustrating and disillusioning time.

The accompanying box, "Medical Education in China," discusses a system of medical education found to be appropriate for a developing country.

Criticisms of the Medical Education Curriculum

The traditional medical school curriculum has faced considerable criticism for many years. At least four important issues have been raised (Braunwald, 2006; Cooke et al., 2006).

First, medical faculty are hired and promoted based on their record and interest in research, obtaining grants, and clinical practice. They give too little attention to teaching and working with medical students (Regan-Smith, 1998).

Second, extensive department and research specialization prevents integration of the curriculum, and leads to uncoordinated coursework. Departments (referred to as "fiefdoms" by many faculty) are locked into continuous competition for prestige and for internal and external funding (e.g., basic science and clinical departments often struggle for power) (Ludmerer, 1985).

Third, medical curricula overly focus on presentation of and ability to memorize facts and too little on developing analytic and problem-solving skills, especially in the first 2 years. Crucial aspects of the actual practice of medicine—like understanding the importance of sociocultural influences, interpersonal skills, developing rapport with patients, and reflection on ethical issues—are given too little attention.

Finally, today's medical school curriculum is out of step with current realities, such as changes

IN COMPARATIVE FOCUS

MEDICAL EDUCATION IN CHINA

China faces the challenge of serving the world's largest population, one that is very rural. To prepare an adequate number of health care providers, China relies on a model based partly on Western-style medicine and partly on its own cultures, and includes three levels of education for physicians:

Assistant doctors are trained for 2 or more years to be able to provide basic primary care in mostly rural villages.

Medical doctors are trained either at Level 1 (a 3-year program that includes condensed basic sciences and clinical subjects in the first 2 years and hospital practice in the third year, and prepares doctors to work in rural communities) or at Level 2 (a 5-year curriculum that includes all the basic sciences in the first 3 years, general medicine and surgery in the fourth year, and hospital practice in the fifth year, and prepares doctors to work in urban areas).

Specialists undergo 7 or 8 years of training, and essentially receive the same training as Level 2 doctors plus additional training in specialty areas. They typically work in urban areas and provide specialty care and complex surgeries.

Graduates must work as a resident physician for a few years to be eligible to take the National Medical Licensing Examination (NMLE) for physician certification. This examination is conducted by the National Medical Examination Center (NMEC).

Medical education in China includes both a Western-style, scientifically based curriculum (including anatomy and physiology), and education in traditional Chinese healing theory and practice. Some schools focus more on Western medicine, others more on traditional medicine. We explore traditional Chinese medicine more in Chapter 11.

The Chinese system for medical education acknowledges that China does not have a sufficient number of fully trained physicians to meet the needs of the total population. By requiring fewer years of preparation for those who will solely provide basic primary care, more individuals can be medically trained and the needs of both the urban and rural populations can be addressed. In addition, health care providers can focus their education on traditional or Western medicine, thus making both approaches available to patients (Lassey, Lassey, and Jinks, 1997).

---

in disease patterns and changes in the financing of health care. Despite the fact that chronic disease accounts for approximately 75 percent of deaths in the United States, medical education continues to focus heavily on acute health problems and late-intervention therapies, and largely ignores the importance of lifestyle education, preventive health care, and the influence of social factors on disease and illness.

Curricular Reform

During the last few decades, at least five significant types of curricular change have begun.

1. *Problem-based learning (PBL)* was developed at McMaster and Michigan State Universities in the 1970s to overcome the traditional fact-based, large-lecture teaching style. PBL is based more on active learning and team-based

activities that occur outside the classroom. Factual material is conveyed through modest-sized study assignments, and students learn the material and apply it in a series of problem-solving exercises.

This approach usually includes the presentation of an applied problem to a small group of students who engage in discussion over several sessions to explain the problem. A facilitator (who is not an answer expert) provides supportive guidance for the students. As students discover the limits of their knowledge, they identify questions that need to be answered. Between meetings of the group, learners research these questions and share results at the next meeting. PBL learners are also likely to have actual patient contact from the beginning of medical school, and to work routinely with patient case studies and simulated patients.

Is this an effective teaching strategy? Research indicates that it is. Several studies have found that students using PBL outperform those using lecture-based learning on tasks such as ability to take a history and perform a physical exam, deriving a diagnosis, and organizing and expressing information (Hoffman et al., 2006). Medical school faculty who have worked with PBL rate it very highly in the areas of clinical preparation, medical reasoning, and student interest, but less highly in teaching factual knowledge and efficiency of learning. Faculty most involved with PBL rate it most highly (Vernon and Hosokawa, 1996).

2. *Teaching professional skills and perspectives* has recently begun to be incorporated into the curriculum at many medical schools. Although still offered only as electives, courses in physician–patient communication, health promotion and disease prevention, public health, working with diverse populations, medical ethics, and medical sociology are now more widely available in medical schools, and are increasingly recognized as essential for comprehensive training. Several schools have implemented efforts to give students a better idea of the overall health care system and health care reform.

3. *Community-based medical education* involves the shifting of clinical training from hospital wards to outpatient settings such as physicians' offices and community health centers. While this shift may reduce the number of opportunities medical students have to perform certain procedures (e.g., insertion of a nasogastric tube), it creates many more opportunities to interact with patients in the type of setting in which most physician–patient interaction actually occurs.

4. *Evidence-based medicine (EBM)* has become much more common in medicine and in medical schools. EBM emphasizes that physicians should recommend medical therapies less on intuition and anecdotal evidence and more on findings of scientific research. It has evolved now to a point at which physicians are asked to integrate evidentiary knowledge with clinical experience and patient preferences. Research has found that students learn well when being taught with an EBM approach (West and McDonald, 2008).

5. *Incorporation of Competency-Based Standards.* Within all of education today, there is a major shift occurring toward use of competency-based systems for developing instruction and measuring achievement (Englander et al., 2015). As of 2014, all medical schools must have a competency-based program in effect in order to be reaccredited.

Each medical school is required to have a list of defined competencies. The common list used contains competency in (1) patient care, (2) knowledge for practice, (3) practice-based learning and improvement, (4) interpersonal and communication skills, (5) professionalism, (6) systems-based practice, (7) interprofessional collaboration, and (8) personal and professional development. Each medical school must determine what a student or resident must be able to do to demonstrate competency in each of these areas and how it will measure that. A program of continuous evaluation must be in place.

Recent Developments in Medical Education Reform

Recently, five additional innovations in medical education have been developed. These include taking a more holistic approach in admissions decisions, revising the Medical College Admissions Test (MCAT), emphasizing social determinants of health, emphasizing working with diverse populations, and further revising the medical school curriculum.

A More Holistic Admissions Process. Since the 1910 Flexner Report, the biological and physical sciences have been at the core of the medical school admissions process. Medical school admissions committees typically focused on student grades in the sciences and their performance on the science sections of the Medical College Admissions Test (MCAT). Data show that these two measures predict success in medical school science courses and on Part I of the USMLE Licensing Examination. However, they are not predictors of character, behavior, interaction skills, sensitivity to patients, and values that are important ingredients of a good physician (Witzburg and Sondheimer, 2013).

The Association of American Medical Colleges (AAMC) now encourages medical schools to expand their admissions criteria. The Supreme Court has endorsed "highly individualized, holistic review of each applicant's file, giving serious consideration to all the ways that an applicant might contribute to a diverse educational environment," allowing each school to "seriously consider each applicant's promise of making a notable contribution to the class by way of a particular strength, attainment, or characteristic— e.g., an unusual intellectual achievement, employment experience, nonacademic performance, or personal background" (Schwartzenstein, 2015).

The rationale is that this more holistic review allows medical schools to tap into a variety of backgrounds, experiences, and interests that might contribute to becoming an excellent physician. "To the extent that these approaches attempt to determine whether applicants have a strong understanding of ethical issues, concern for underserved populations, and appropriate communication skills, they are held out as significant steps toward graduating doctors who can relate to patients" (Schwartzenstein, 2015).

A Revised MCAT. In 2011, the AAMC issued a report that emphasized the importance of the behavioral and social sciences in medical education. The next year, it announced that the MCAT, a prerequisite for admission to almost all US medical schools, would undergo significant revision in 2015. The re-formulated test now consists of four sections: (1) Biological and Biochemical Foundations of Living Systems; (2) Chemical and Physical Foundations of Biological Systems; (3) Psychological, Social, and Biological Foundations of Behavior (a completely new section); and (4) Critical Analysis and Reasoning Skills.

The new Psychological, Social, and Biological Foundations of Behavior section reflects the recognition that behavioral and social factors influence health and illness and interact with biological factors to influence health outcomes. Other topics of particular interest include knowledge of the changing health care system, health care inequalities, how we think about ourselves and others, and physician stress and burnout. Fundamental knowledge about behavioral and social sciences is acknowledged to be critical to the practice of medicine (Kaplan, Satterfield, and Kington, 2012). In addition, medical school applicants are encouraged to take more social sciences and humanities courses as undergraduates. (About 35 percent of medical school applicants have majored in something other than biology, chemistry, or another physical science, and they are just as successful or even slightly more likely to be admitted to medical school.)

Assuming that medical schools make effective use of this new section, its inclusion on the MCAT will necessarily increase the exposure of premedical students to the behavioral and social sciences, and hopefully will pave the way for additional attention to these areas in medical school.

Emphasis on the Social Determinants of Health

> Social scientists know a lot about the root causes of so much of the ill-health in our society, yet health-care systems have rarely acted on that knowledge. That's finally starting to change.
>
> (Goozner, 2018)

In Chapter 4, the concept of "social determinants of health" was introduced. Although Rudolph Virchow (see Chapter 2) and others in the mid-nineteenth century emphasized that social determinants and disparities are major influences on health and disease, only recently has medicine begun to reflect this importance. Now, there is rapidly spreading recognition that factors such as gender, race, ethnicity, sexual orientation, gender identity, income, education, neighborhood characteristics, quality of housing, nutrition, and social support are essential to our understanding of disease and illness, and that our ability to improve population health is tied closely to addressing their influence. For example, research shows that 60 percent of the factors leading to premature death in the United States are due to a combination of social and environmental issues and behavior.

To reduce premature death, medicine must deal with these factors.

Some medical schools are beginning to develop programs to teach students more about the social determinants of health within the curriculum in the first 4 years (for example, courses in which fourth-year students serve as apprentices to community health workers and creation of structured opportunities to volunteer in free health clinics). Some residency programs are creating courses in which students learn about population health within their community.

Emphasis on Working With Diverse Populations.   Research with medical students continues to underscore the need for more training in working with diverse populations. Depending on the population composition of one's community, neighborhood, and school system, medical students may or may not have spent any considerable amount of time with members of diverse groups. Depending on their undergraduate coursework and experiences, they may or may not have ever studied diverse people. Yet, now more than ever, medical schools are recognizing the importance of communication and interaction between medical providers and patients.

We have discussed this diversity in most chapters of this book. Here, to illustrate the importance of medical education's increasing awareness, two examples are cited: better understanding of people with disabilities and better understanding of sexual minority group members.

People with a disability are under-represented in medicine. Approximately 20 percent of Americans have a disability, and many experience disparities in the health care they receive. However, many health care providers lack a genuine understanding about disability. This may be due to the small number of disabled persons who become physicians (and thus are not present to share their insights with peers) and to the lack of disability-related training in the medical school curriculum (Meeks, Herzer, and Jain, 2018).

Three ways that medical schools can show commitment to people with disabilities is through hiring faculty and other employees who have a disability, making appropriate accommodations for students with disabilities, and offering curricular exposure to treating disabled patients. Today, however, only about 1 percent of physicians and between 0.3 percent and 2.7 percent of medical students have a disability. Many medical schools do not provide reasonable accommodations for students with disabilities as intended by the Americans with Disabilities Act (Zazove et al., 2016). Moreover, few medical schools offer curricular exposure to disability and working with people with disabilities, and those that do often focus on disability as an impairment rather than as a condition for which appropriate accommodations can enable people to meet the same standards as the non-disabled (Sarmiento et al., 2016). The good news is that several medical schools are in the process of developing programs to help students' understanding of disability and working with disabled patients (Liasidou and Mavrou, 2017).

Lesbian, gay, bisexual, transgender, and queer patients face many of the same issues and often even more discrimination. Approximately 4 percent of Americans are a sexual minority, and many have faced discrimination and harassment as a result of that. As recently as the 1990s, nearly one-fifth of physicians in a California survey endorsed homophobic viewpoints, and 18 percent reported feeling uncomfortable treating gay or lesbian patients (Smith and Mathews, 2007). Because of prior experiences of bias or the expectation of poor treatment, many LGBTQ+ patients report reluctance to reveal their sexual orientation or gender identity to their providers.

This is concerning because as discussed in Chapter 3, LGBTQ+ status can affect health in particular ways. For example, lesbian and bisexual women have higher rates of heart disease, asthma, and chronic obstructive pulmonary disease. Gay and bisexual men have increased risk for cardiovascular disease. Transgender and nonbinary individuals have worse self-reported physical and mental health. LGBTQ+ youth have higher rates of alcohol, smoking, and other drug use and are 2 to 3 times more likely to attempt suicide. Knowledge of one's gender identity and sexual orientation can improve physicians' ability to treat these patients.

Medical schools have traditionally provided little, if any, education regarding LGBTQ+ health. A 2011 survey of medical schools in the United States and Canada found that most curricula taught students to ask if patients have sex with men, women, or both, but rarely went beyond this to address issues of identity (Obedin-Maliver et al., 2011). No wonder that in one study of medical oncology physicians, 87 percent said they felt comfortable treating transgender individuals, but only 37 percent reported feeling that they knew enough to do so (Schabath et al., 2019). Medical students often report this lack of training as a reason they are particularly uncomfortable asking about a patient's sexual orientation or gender identity (Stott, 2013).

As with education regarding people with disabilities, some changes can be seen in medical training to treat sexual minorities. Founded in 1981 but growing in size ever since, the GLMA: Health Professionals Advancing LGBTQ Equality is an international organization of about 1,000 lesbian, gay, bisexual, transgender, and queer health care professionals and students attempting to ensure health equity for all sexual minority individuals. Although the Accreditation Council for Graduate Medical Education has not developed any requirements for medical schools regarding LGBTQ+ health, in 2014 the Association of American Medical Colleges did issue recommendations for inclusion of LGBTQ matters in the curriculum, and the American Academy of Family Physicians has done the same for family medicine residency programs. Systematic research on sexual minority health is now appearing regularly in medical journals (e.g., Streed et al., 2019).

Further Revision of the Medical School Curriculum. In the last decade, several medical schools have designed and implemented other important curricular innovations including developing programs or courses in cultural competency, medical ethics, end-of-life care, health care leadership, health care delivery systems, global health, and public health. Some schools are studying the possibility of shifting to a 3-year curriculum, and three already have for students interested in primary care.

In 2013, the American Medical Association enacted a new program, "Accelerating Change in Medical Education," to promote meaningful change (American Medical Association, 2016). The program gave 11 medical schools (80 applied) US$1 million each to pursue a 5-year plan to support their work on transformative medical education projects. The goals chosen included finding better ways of measuring physician competency, improving patient safety, promoting patient-centered team care, improving the understanding of the health care system, and optimizing the medical school learning environment. School representatives meet periodically to share their ideas and stimulate new ones. Twenty-one more schools joined the consortium in 2016 with each receiving US$75,000 over 3 years for curricular reform projects, and five more were added in 2019. The ultimate goals are to create the medical school of the future and transform physician training. You can learn about each school's work at www.ama-assn.org/ama/pub/about-ama/strategic-focus/accelerating-change-in-medical-education/schools (Skochelak and Stack, 2017).

THE MEDICAL SCHOOL EXPERIENCE: ATTITUDE AND VALUE ACQUISITION

The medical school experience has a profound socializing influence on medical students. The length of time in medical training, the intensity of the experience, and formal and informal interaction with faculty, fellow students, other health care workers, and patients help to shape important attitudes and values of the physician-to-be. This section of the chapter examines two of these important attitude and value changes—a "tolerance for uncertainty" and "detached concern."

Tolerance for Uncertainty

For several decades, medical schools have explicitly or implicitly socialized students to have a "tolerance for uncertainty." Renée Fox (1957) identified three kinds of uncertainty that confront students as they progress through medical school. Early in the first year, a type of uncertainty is created when students become aware that they cannot possibly master all the concepts and facts covered in their classes and textbooks. For students accustomed to mastery of course materials, the enormity of the field of medicine can be a very threatening and disheartening realization.

> In college, I didn't always do all the work, but I was good at managing my time, and I was happy with the work I was doing and satisfied with what I was achieving. But somehow here, it's Pass/Fail . . . it should be easy, [but] the pressure is so much greater . . . I think part of it is the sense that what you learn now may make the difference in someone's life. The material begins to impress you over and over again; this is serious. You need to know it to treat people.
>
> (Good and Good, 1989:304)

Second, and more gradually, students become aware that the knowledge base of medicine is incomplete. There is much about the human being that is yet to be fully understood, and important gaps in understanding disease and illness remain. Students come to realize that, even if they could somehow know all that is known within medicine, there would still be much they would not know.

The third type of uncertainty is created when students attempt to distinguish between the first two types. When they run into a question in the process of making a patient diagnosis, students need to determine whether it is a limitation in their own knowledge or something not yet known in medicine. As clinical work increases, they are often concerned that their own lack of knowledge might jeopardize a patient's health or recovery.

> Uncertainty is interwoven in daily life and in virtually all clinical situations experienced by patients and health professionals. Uncertainty in healthcare pertains to numerous unknowns: whether a patient has or will develop a particular condition; how that condition will evolve; to what extent a particular treatment is beneficial; and whether a patient is receiving the right care, in the right place, at the right time, from the right people. The sheer number and variety of these unknowns make uncertainty a ubiquitous problem in health care.
>
> (Hillen et al., 2017:62)

Aware of this rite of passage, medical faculties and upper-level students socialize newer students to accept that some uncertainty is inevitable in medicine, that it has some fortunate consequences (e.g., stimulating new medical knowledge), and that it is best dealt with by openly acknowledging its existence (Fox, 1989).

However, students also realize the dysfunctions of being too candid about their own uncertainties. Desiring to come across as knowledgeable and competent future physicians, and not wishing to jeopardize patient or instructor confidence in them, they often present themselves as more certain about a matter than they really are. Light (1979) suggests that the real socialization that occurs is "training for control." This is accomplished not only through mastery of course materials and clinical experience, but also through "psyching out instructors" (e.g., finding out what instructors want and giving it to them, and using impression management techniques) and becoming more authoritarian with patients. Katz (1984) has referred to this process not as tolerating uncertainty but as "disregarding" it.

Do these efforts to control uncertainty continue into clinical practice? Many believe that some of the excessive diagnostic testing that occurs today is due to physicians seeking diagnostic certainty and pursuing every test that might offer it. When diagnostic certainty cannot be attained, however, physicians often portray themselves to patients as being supremely confident about their conclusions ("micro-certainty")—even when there is considerable dissent with other health care professionals about the diagnosis ("macro-uncertainty") (Baumann, Deber, and Thompson, 1991).

Detached Concern

Concern for one's patients is certainly an accepted ideal in medical education, but students are encouraged to develop **detached concern**— that is, concern about the patient without excessive emotional involvement or overidentification. It is a "supple balance" of "objectivity and empathy" and "equanimity and compassion" that are combined to enable the "delivery of competent, sagacious, and humane patient care" (Fox, 1989:85). The danger of becoming too emotionally involved with a patient is that diagnostic proficiency or treatment recommendations might be compromised by personal involvement. The death of a patient is often difficult for physicians, but if there is extensive emotional involvement, the death may so affect the physician that the care of other patients is compromised—not a desirable circumstance. For these reasons, many physicians prefer not to treat family members.

Students learn specific techniques to facilitate this detachment. They learn to "intellectualize" and "technicalize" the cadavers they work with in anatomy laboratory and engage in "gallows humor" as a means of venting personal emotions. In their clinical years, they repeatedly perform certain tests (e.g., urinalyses) so that they become accustomed to them and feel less awkward about doing them. As actual patient care begins, many students feel uncomfortable about asking certain questions (e.g., about sexual history) and certain procedures that must be performed (e.g., rectal examination). Students are often still thinking of the patient as an individual person—making these tasks more difficult. Often they consciously seek more detachment (Fox, 1989).

At some point during the third year, many students become aware that their efforts to detach have been too successful. They have made a transition by depersonalizing the patient and by focusing on diseases, procedures, and tasks that have become second nature rather than focusing on the person. Some refer to this as a type of "emotional numbness" (Fox, 1989). Rather than learning to walk the fine line between concern and detachment, students often master detachment at the expense of genuine concern, become increasingly doctor centered and less patient centered (Haidet et al., 2002), and sometimes develop disinterested or even hostile attitudes toward patients.

Curing Rather Than Caring. Critics charge that these attitudes are more than an unfortunate by-product of learning to maintain objectivity. Rather, it is posited that medical schools are so devoted to teaching students how to "cure" patients that they offer little guidance, training, or encouragement in ways to "care" for patients. Conrad (1988) analyzed four separate book-length accounts ("insider reports") of the medical school years written by medical students. The accounts portrayed an educational experience clearly oriented toward curing—understanding disease, technical procedures, and high-tech medicine—with little attempt to focus on caring for patients. An "ideology of caring" was sometimes voiced but not often demonstrated.

> Perhaps the most consistent theme that recurred in these accounts was the scarcity of humane and caring encounters between doctors and patients. . . . Doctors' clinical perspectives focused almost entirely on the disease rather than on the illness. Virtually all teaching emphasized the technical aspects of doctoring: diagnosis, treatment,

and intervention. Too often this approach caused patients to become the disease: "the lymphoma in Room 304." A fascination with technological intervention pervades medicine, from neonatal intensive care to neurosurgery to cardiac catheterization. These are the frontiers of medicine . . . and are seductive to medical students.

(Conrad, 1988:328)

The physician–patient interaction that is observed often devalues caring behaviors. During rounds in a hospital, physicians often talk to residents or medical students about a patient as if the patient is not even present. When talking to the patient, many doctors do not make eye contact, are not attentive, and are very abrupt—these are the behaviors that students observe.

Renée Anspach (1988) also investigated the way physicians talk to each other about patients. She conducted a 16-month field study of life-and-death decision making in two newborn intensive care units, and spent an additional 3 months in a hospital obstetrics and gynecology department. She closely studied "case presentations"—formal and informal case histories presented at formal conferences, during daily rounds, in consultations with specialists, and at various points on the case record—made by interns, residents, and fellows. She observed that the terminology used often "depersonalized" the patient (e.g., using a very impersonal vocabulary), that the passive voice was used to omit reference to the physician, nurse, or other health care workers who attended the patient or that a technology was identified as the agent (e.g., "the arteriogram showed"), and that skepticism was often expressed about patients' self-reports.

Medical students have also developed special terms they use among themselves to identify patients whom they perceive as undesirable, such as "gomers" ("get out of my emergency room"—often used to describe patients with poor hygiene, incontinence, habitual malingering, and a tendency to pull out intravenous lines), "crocks," "dirtballs," and "brain stem preparations" (Liederman and Grisso, 1985). It is little wonder that when medical students begin their own interaction with patients, they are often ill-equipped to offer a caring manner. Many have yet to develop a comfort level with patients. They do not introduce themselves or do anything to try to make the patient feel more at ease. They may be very self-conscious, thinking more about how they are coming across than about the patient's pain, discomfort, or unease.

Much of this research on detached concern and curing versus caring was conducted in the 1980s, 1990s, and early 2000s. Have things changed since then? Yes, in part. While medical students continue to learn the benefits of detached concern, greater emphasis is now placed on the importance of empathy. For example, in a search of medical databases, Underman and Hirshfield (2016) found that in 1985 only 43 articles had the word "empathy" as a keyword in the journal article abstract, but the number rose to 172 in 1995 and to 442 in 2005.

This increased emphasis is reflected in three very important ways. First, the aforementioned addition to the MCAT exam for medical school applicants on the psychological and social foundations of medicine conveys increased importance to empathy. Second, more courses on the physician–patient relationship are being taught in medical schools, and these courses typically include attention to empathy. Finally, students are now tested on their ability to act empathetically with patients in a section of the USMLE (which must be passed in order to be licensed) (Underman and Hirshfield, 2016).

THE MEDICAL SCHOOL EXPERIENCE: STRESS

Without question, the 4 years of medical school and the 3 or more years of residency are an extremely stressful time. Some have chosen to regard this stress as simply a rite of passage. Recently, more concerned attention has been given to this issue.

Indicators of Stress in Medical School and During the Residency

Many observers of medical education and graduate medical education believe that high levels of stress often lead to critically poor mental health among students. Surveys of US medical students (Jackson et al., 2016) and medical residents (Slavin and Chibnall, 2016) have found high levels of burnout, depression, fatigue, suicide ideation, and alcohol abuse and dependence (Jackson et al., 2016). Some studies have found that about one-third of students and residents experience depressive symptoms or full-blown depression at some point in their training (Mata et al., 2015).

Stressors in the First Four Years

Three primary types of stressors occur during the four medical school years (Carmel and Bernstein, 1987): (1) academic stressors—including examinations and the large number of hours required for study, (2) anticipated medical career stressors—including passing the national examinations, selecting a specialty field, securing a desired residency, making errors in patient care, and aspects of patient contact; and (3) social stressors—especially the limited amount of time for relationships with family and friends including pressures on one's marriage.

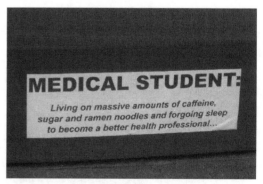

This is a light-hearted look at the life of medical students and residents, but the gruelling schedule can be extremely stressful.

Stressors During the Medical Residency

The issues that surface during the medical school years often appear to an even more significant level during the residency years—a subject that has received considerable study. These stresses occur at a time in life when other stressors may be happening—marriage and children, altered relationships with parents, financial worries, and post-school emotional letdown. Piled onto these activities are responsibilities that are often physically and emotionally draining. Among the biggest stressors are:

1. *The grueling schedule.* Prior to 2003 (1989 in some states), there were no mandated limits on the number of hours that a resident could work in a week. The traditional setup often required extended work shifts (often 36 consecutive hours on) with work weeks of 100 hours or more. The long shifts included some time for sleep (in the hospital), but the resident remained on call and could conceivably not get any sleep during this time. The long hours were justified in various ways—as important socialization for the long hours that physicians work, an opportunity to learn more, and a way to staff hospitals—but the dangers of sleep deprivation on the safety of patient care were also well known. For example, a person who has not slept for 24 hours has about the same cognitive skill as one with a blood alcohol level of .10. Most of the medical residents studied in the 1990s reported that sleep deprivation was a problem, 10 percent said that it was almost a daily problem, and 70 percent reported having observed a colleague working in an impaired state (with sleep deprivation being the most common cause) (Daugherty, Baldwin, and Rowley, 1998).

   These dangers were dramatized in the 1984 hospital death of Libby Zion—an 18-year-old woman brought to the emergency room of New York Hospital at 11:30 p.m. and died

(needlessly) 7 hours later of bilateral bronchopneumonia. Although no criminal indictments were ever handed down, Zion was treated only by an intern and a junior resident, each of whom had been at work for 18 hours. The grand jury criticized five specific aspects of the care Zion received as contributing to her death. Its report was viewed as an indictment of the traditional system of graduate medical education.

In 2003 the Accreditation Council for Graduate Medical Education approved national limits on the number of hours medical residents can work. These were revised in 2011 and 2017. As of 2017, the duty hour limits allow a full 24-hour shift followed by up to 4 hours for activities related to patient safety, education, and effective transitions. No allowance is made for "strategic napping." All residents are limited to 80-hour work weeks, averaged over 4 weeks.

These limits have been controversial. After reducing the allowable length of shifts in earlier revisions, the 2017 changes actually increased the allowable shift length for first-year residents from 16 to 28 hours. Proponents contend that the longer shifts give students an opportunity to show their dedication to medicine, give them practice should they ever have to work such long hours in the future, and are an important part of resident culture, and that hospitals cannot afford to hire replacements for the hours lost. However, many believe that the number of permitted hours increases the risk of medical errors.

2. *Worries about medical school debts.* Although medical school tuition constitutes a very small percentage of the medical school budget (4 to 5 percent on average), it has been increasing rapidly in both private and public medical schools. Approximately 90 percent of medical students receive financial assistance, but increasingly this is in the form of loans (now about 87 percent is loan assistance).

Today, about 75 percent of graduating medical students have accrued some debt—the average per graduate is $195,000 (plus about a $25,000 debt carried over from undergraduate school). Relative to other financial indicators, medical school is less affordable now than it has ever been. Research indicates that some qualified students forgo a career in medicine due to the anticipated level of debt. More than half of all medical students come from the richest 20 percent of American families, only about 5 percent from the poorest 20 percent. Repayment of the loan is a major worry for many medical students, and often colors their perception of the entire medical school experience.

3. *Feelings of mistreatment.* Many medical students experience feelings of being abused by the medical school process. Both empirical research and widely shared personal anecdotes portray the extent of these feelings. A study of 431 medical school students discovered that almost 50 percent felt that they had received some abuse in medical school, and by the fourth year more than 80 percent reported personal abuse. The kinds of abuse reported included verbal abuse (insulting, humiliating, unjust statements), academic abuse (excessive workload, unnecessary scut work, unfair grade), sexual abuse (solicitation, harassment, sexism, discrimination), physical abuse (threatened or actual), and intentional neglect or lack of communication. Who did the abusing? For freshmen, PhD faculty were cited most often, whereas for juniors and seniors, physician clinical faculty were most often cited (Silver and Glicken, 1990)—in both cases, the medical school faculty with whom they had the most interaction.

Although Title IX, the federal law prohibiting sexual harassment in educational institutions, was enacted in 1972, reports show sexual harassment in medical schools continues to be a problem. Although both women and men in these institutions convey increased intolerance for harassing behavior, it is not uncommon for those being harassed to fail to report such behavior. The typical reason for nonreporting is fear of retaliation—both overt and covert—from the person being harassed and concern that the accuser's own career will be harmed (Binder et al., 2018).

All this comes as no surprise to Howard Stein (1990), a leading critic of medical education. According to Stein, students often arrive at medical school with idealism, a concern for others, and general communication skills but leave narrowly focused on biological factors and without the desire and ability to listen to and talk with others.

Medical students often use *excremental symbolism* to describe themselves, their work, their status, their clinical experiences, and their patients. They feel treated like "shit," they are often asked to do "shit work," they learn who is entitled to "shit on" whom, and one learns how much "shit" one must take and for how long. In effect, "one learns how to be a physician and how to occupy one of the highest of American social statuses by beginning as one of the lowest of the low" (Stein, 1990:201).

Recognizing the significance of the problem, several medical schools are now initiating programs that attempt either to reduce the stressfulness of medical education and/or to assist students in their coping skills with the stress (Krug et al., 2017).

THE MEDICAL SCHOOL EXPERIENCE: CAREER CHOICES

During medical school, students make several important decisions about their medical career, including the size and type of community in which to practice, the specific type of setting desired, and the field in which to specialize.

Research has attempted to understand factors that influence these choices, and especially if student preferences change (they do for most students).

Research has shown that many students begin medical school with an interest in practicing in a small town or community, in an office-based setting, and in a primary care field. However, by graduation, they opt for a specialty located in a large city and/or connected to an academic medical center (in all cases, away from areas that are more needed to areas where physicians are well supplied). What motivates these interest changes? Exposure to (and being intrigued by) the research careers of faculty members, exposure to (and appreciation of) high-tech medicine, and the opportunity for larger salaries all play an influential role.

REASONS FOR SPECIALTY CHOICE

Several factors influence the selection of a particular specialty. These include the content of the specialty, having a role model in a particular specialty, and the prestige, opportunities for cognitive performance, and future financial remuneration of the specialty. In the last 20 years, medical students have begun to assign much more importance to a concept called **controllable lifestyle (CL)**—the extent to which one's specialty allows for greater control over the hours worked.

CHOOSING PRIMARY CARE

What motivates a medical student to select a career in primary care rather than a high-tech specialty? Generally, a strong dedication to providing patient care, a desire to establish long-term relationships with patients, and the opportunity to be involved in the social-psychological aspects of medical care. The opportunity to do research and to perform procedures, as well as a desire

for a higher income and a favorable lifestyle, are more important factors in the decisions those who select high-tech specialties.

Interestingly, most of these factors are discernable at the point of school admission. Applicants who have a high *service index* reflective of a strong orientation to community service, who have taken a generous number of non-science courses as an undergraduate, and who come from a lower socioeconomic family background and rural areas are most likely to pursue a career in primary care later on (Xu et al., 1999).

Can medical schools impact this choice? Yes. Medical schools with a mission that emphasizes community service, that offer a primary care–focused curriculum, have physician role models in primary care, and promote a favorable primary care culture do influence students to pursue primary care training (Erikson et al., 2013).

FUTURE DIRECTIONS IN MEDICAL EDUCATION IN THE UNITED STATES

One of the most respected voices in medical education is Ezekiel "Zeke" Emanuel, a prominent American oncologist, bioethicist, and administrator. He believes that medical education still needs to respond to four current trends in medical care:

1. A greater focus on caring for chronic medical conditions. Chronic conditions now represent 7 of the 10 leading causes of death in the United States, nearly two-thirds of all deaths, and an estimated 84 percent of all health care spending. Medical education must shift its focus from acute to chronic diseases and focus more on lifestyle changes and compliance with medications. Physicians need more training in the social sciences.
2. Delivery of most medical care services outside the hospital. Twentieth-century medicine was largely hospital based, but hospital admissions peaked in 1981. There are now approximately

35 million hospital admissions each year but nearly 1 billion outpatient visits. Physicians need more training in working with interdisciplinary teams and in care coordination.

3. Increased attention to the delivery of higher value and lower cost medical care. Pressure to deliver consistently high-value care is increasing. Future physicians will need training in areas such as intervention evaluation and operations management.

4. An increase in medical information and patient data. Science is doubling in size every 10 to 15 years. Future medical care will be more information-driven, and physicians will need more training in the retrieval, management, and critical evaluation of relevant medical information (Emanuel, 2017).

For the prospective medical student, Emanuel believes this means more courses in the social sciences, humanities, and statistics but not in physics, organic chemistry, or calculus (whose subject areas should be eliminated from the MCAT).

For medical students, what is now the first two preclinical years should be no longer than 15 months. Less clinical training should occur in the hospital and more in outpatient settings shadowing talented clinicians. Medical training should be reduced to 3 years or include more of the key areas identified earlier.

Finally, Edmund Pellegrino (1987), a distinguished university and health center administrator, has long encouraged medical education to follow a path of medical humanism by emphasizing humanitarianism—that is, humaneness and sensitivity to the patient's needs as a person. While it is possible to heal in the strictest sense without compassion, he views healing as being more complex than simply applying the correct medical method. This is true because illness and disease affect the whole life of a person and because effective clinical decisions should be "morally good" as well as technically correct. This requires the physician to have some sense of what the illness means for the life of a patient. Many recent curricular reforms are grounded in this orientation.

SUMMARY

Until the early 1900s, medical education in the United States was often poorly organized, lacking in academic rigor, and discriminatory against women and racial and ethnic minorities. The Flexner Report issued in 1910 strongly recommended a science-focused, university-based curriculum with significant clinical practice. Although several schools have been and are experimenting with important innovations, the model that Flexner advocated continues to dominate medical education. However, critics contend that significant reform is needed in medical education.

Applications to medical schools are on a significant upswing. Women now account for about 50 percent of medical students, although the percentage of black students still falls far short of their population percentage.

For the last few decades, medical education has been sharply criticized—very often by medical school faculty and students. The concerns include faculty being focused on their own careers to the exclusion of teaching, curricula that have failed to keep pace with changes in medicine, and a lack of innovative teaching styles. In response, many schools have now incorporated techniques such as problem-based learning, competency-based standards, and evidence-based medicine. Very recently, schools have begun providing greater emphasis on the social determinants of health and have modified admissions standards, the MCAT, and the curriculum to convey that.

Among the most important value orientations to which students are socialized are a tolerance for uncertainty (learning to identify and accept what they do not know and what science does not know—and to distinguish between the two) and detached concern (learning to be concerned about the patient without being overly involved emotionally). Critics believe that formal and informal socialization has often led students to depersonalize and dehumanize patients, a problem increasingly being addressed with greater emphasis on empathy.

The medical school years have a profound influence on students. They are a very stressful period in which students' attitudes, values, and career choices are developed.

HEALTH ON THE INTERNET

To find out what is happening in medical education or to learn about a particular medical school, you can gather information at the website of the American Association of Medical Colleges (AAMC) at

www.aamc.org

Medical students are often a very active agent in promoting change within the profession of medicine and within the health care system. For insight into what medical students are focusing on today, go to the American Medical Students Association (AMSA) at

www.amsa.org

Click on "Get Involved" in the top menu to identify the issues on which this group is focusing. Focus especially on "Campaigns and Initiatives." If you were a medical student and a member of the AMSA, which one of these campaigns would you be most interested in joining? Why?

DISCUSSION CASE

In August 2018, New York University's School of Medicine announced that it would immediately begin covering tuition (about $55,000 annually) for all its current and future students. (The plan does not cover room and board or fees—an additional $27,000 per year, on average.) With 93 first-year students, and another 350 students who have up to 3 years left before obtaining their degrees, the program will be costly—about $600 million. Currently, about 62 percent of graduates leave with some debt; the average debt incurred by members of the class of 2017 was $184,000. NYU said that it had already raised more than $450 million in private donations for the program. The school expressed a firm position that the cost of medical education and the amount of student loans had reached unacceptable levels, so it committed to becoming the first medical school to go tuition-free.

At a recent (hypothetical) meeting in your state, government leaders expressed concern about the large debts most medical students incur and the consequent pressure to enter specialties and move to locations where their earning capacity would be greatest rather than where needs are greatest. Concern was also expressed about the lack of access many people have to health care.

One of the leaders at the meeting proposed an idea to try to resolve both problems. Beginning in the next academic year, the state would initiate a mandatory program—it would pay the complete education costs for all students attending one of the state's medical schools. In return, students would be obligated to spend the first 4 years of their career in a location assigned by the state—presumably an inner-city or rural area in need of physicians. The idea is similar to the

National Health Service Corps (an underfunded federal government program) and the Armed Forces Health Professions Scholarships, but differs in that it is a mandatory program.

If a state referendum were to be held on this proposal, how would you vote? Is this a creative response to the problems of large debts of medical students and the lack of health care services in certain areas? Or is the mandatory nature of the program unfair to medical students? Does the government have a right to dictate practice site to physicians even if it does pay their medical education expenses? Might other students (e.g., in law, engineering, business, education, and sociology) demand a comparable program? The state government could not afford all these programs. Is medical education and the delivery of care qualitatively different?

GLOSSARY

academic health center (AHC)
competency-based standards
controllable lifestyle (CL)
detached concern
evidence-based medicine (EBM)

Flexner Report
problem-based learning (PBL)
socialization
tolerance for uncertainty

REFERENCES

American Medical Association. 2016. "Accelerating Change in Medical Education." Retrieved January 15, 2019 (www.ama-assn.org/ama/pub/about-ama/strategic-focus/accelerating-change-in-medical-education/schools).

Anspach, Renée. 1988. "Notes on the Sociology of Medical Discourse: The Language of Case Presentation." *Journal of Health and Social Behavior* 29(4):357–375.

Association of American Medical Colleges. 2019a. "US Medical School Applications and Matriculants by School, State of Legal Residence, and Sex, 2018–2019." Retrieved April 2, 2019 (www.aamc.org/download/321442/data/factstablea1.pdf).

————. 2019b. "Applicants, First-Time Applicants, Acceptees, and Matriculants to US Medical Schools by Sex, 2009–2010 through 2018–2019." Retrieved April 2, 2019 (www.aamc.org/download/492954/data/factstablea7_2.pdf).

————. 2019c. "Applicants to US Medical Schools by Selected Combinations of Race/Ethnicity and Sex, 2015–2016 through 2018–2019." Retrieved April 2, 2019 (www.aamc.org/download/321472/data/factstablea8.pdf).

————. 2019d. "Matriculants to US Medical Schools by Race, Selected Combinations of Race/Ethnicity and Sex, 2015–2016 through 2018–2019." Retrieved April 2, 2019 (www.aamc.org/download/321474/data/factstablea9.pdf).

Baumann, Andrea O., Raisa B. Deber, and Gail G. Thompson. 1991. "Overconfidence Among Physicians and Nurses: The 'Micro-Certainty, Macro-Uncertainty' Phenomenon." *Social Science and Medicine* 32(2):167–174.

Binder, Renee, Paul Garcia, Bonnie Johnson, and Elena Fuentes-Afflick. 2018. "Sexual Harassment in Medical Schools: The Challenge of Covert Retaliation as a Barrier to Reporting." *Academic Medicine* 93(12):1770–1773.

Braunwald, Eugene. 2006. "Departments, Divisions and Centers in the Evolution of Medical Schools." *The American Journal of Medicine* 119(6):457–462.

Carmel, Sara, and Judith Bernstein. 1987. "Perceptions of Medical School Stressors: Their Relationship to Age, Year of Study, and Trait Anxiety." *Journal of Human Stress* 13(1):39–44.

Conrad, Peter. 1988. "Learning to Doctor: Reflections on Recent Accounts of the Medical School Years." *Journal of Health and Social Behavior* 29(4):323–332.

Cooke, Molly, David M. Irby, William Sullivan, and Kenneth M. Ludmerer. 2006. "American Medical

Education 100 Years After the Flexner Report." *New England Journal of Medicine* 355(13):1339–1344.

Daugherty, Steven R., DeWitt C. Baldwin, and Beverley D. Rowley. 1998. "Learning, Satisfaction, and Mistreatment during Medical Internship." *Journal of the American Medical Association* 279(15):1194–1199.

Emanuel, Ezekiel J. 2017. "Reforming American Medical Education." *Milbank Quarterly* 95(4):692–697.

Englander, Robert, Terri Cameron, Amy Addams, Jan Bull, and Joshua Jacobs. 2015. "Understanding Competency-Based Medical Education." *Academic Medicine* 90(5):19.

Erikson, Cleese E., Sana Danish, Karen C. Jones, Shana F. Sanberg, and Adam C. Carle. 2013. "The Role of Medical School Culture in Primary Care Career Choice." *Academic Medicine* 88(12):1919–1926.

Flexner, Abraham. 1910. *Medical Education in the United States and Canada: A Report to the Carnegie Foundation for the Advancement of Teaching. New York*: The Carnegie Foundation for the Advancement in Teaching.

Fox, Renée C. 1957. "Training for Uncertainty." Pp. 207–241 in *The Student-Physician*, edited by, Robert K. Merton, George G. Reader, and Patricia Kendall. Cambridge, MA: Harvard University Press.

———. 1989. The Sociology of Medicine: A *Participant Observer's View*. Upper Saddle River, NJ: Prentice Hall.

Good, Mary-Jo D., and Byron J. Good. 1989(2). "Disabling Practitioners: Hazards of Learning to be a Doctor in American Medical Education." *American Journal of Orthopsychiatry* 59:303–309.

Goozner, M. 2018. "Anchors Away on Tackling the Social Determinants of Health." *Modern Healthcare* (May 19):26.

Haidet, Paul, Joyce E. Dains, Debora A. Paterniti, Laura Hechtel, Tai Chang, Ellen Tseng, and John C. Rogers. 2002. "Medical Student Attitudes toward the Doctor-Patient Relationship." *Medical Education* 36(6):568–574.

Hillen, Marij A., Caitlin M. Gutheil, Tania D. Strout, Ellen M.A. Smets, and Paul K.J. Han. 2017. "Tolerance of Uncertainty: Conceptual Analysis, Integrative Model, and Implications for Healthcare." *Social Science and Medicine* 180(May):62–75.

Hoffman, Kimberly, Michael Hosokawa, Robert Blake, Linda Headrick, and Gina Johnson. 2006. "Problem-Based Learning Outcomes: Ten Years of Experience at the University of Missouri-Coulmbia School of Medicine." *Academic Medicine* 81(7):617–625.

Irby, David M., Molly Cooke, and Bridget C. O'Brien. 2010. "Calls for Reform of Medical Education by the Carnegie Foundation for the Advancement of Teaching: 1910 and 2010." *Academic Medicine* 85(2):220–227.

Jackson, Eric R., Tait D. Shanafelt, Omar Hasan, Daniel V. Satele, and Liselotte N. Dyrbye. 2016. "Burnout and Alcohol Abuse/Dependence among U.S. Medical Students." *Academic Medicine* 91(9):1251–1256.

Kaplan, Robert M., Jason M. Satterfield, and Raynard S. Kington. 2012. "Building A Better Physician— The Case for the New MCAT." *New England Journal of Medicine* 366(14):1265–1268.

Katz, Jay. 1984. *The Silent World of Doctor and Patient*. New York: The Free Press.

Krug, Michael F., Anna L. Golob, Pandora L. Wander, and Joyce E. Wipf. 2017. "Changes in Resident Well-Being at One Institution Across a Decade of Progressive Work Hours Limitations." *Academic Medicine* 92(10):1480–1484.

Lassey, Marie L., William R. Lassey, and Martin J. Jinks. 1997. *Health Care Systems Around the World*. Upper Saddle River, NJ: Prentice Hall.

Liasidou, Anastasia, and Katerina Mavrou. 2017. "Disability Rights in Higher Education Programs: The Case of Medical Schools and Other Health-Related Disciplines." *Social Science and Medicine* 191(October):143–150.

Liederman, Deborah B., and Jean-Anne Grisso. 1985. "The Gomer Phenomenon." *Journal of Health and Social Behavior* 26(3):222–232.

Light, Donald W. 1979. "Uncertainty and Control in Professional Training." *Journal of Health and Social Behavior* 20(4):310–322.

Ludmerer, Kenneth M. 1985. *Learning to Heal: The Development of American Medical Education*. New York: Basic Books, Inc.

Mata, Douglas A., Marco A. Ramos, Narinder Bansal, Rida Khan, Constance Guille, Emanuele Di Angelantonio, and Srijan Sen. 2015. "Prevalence of Depression and Depressive Symptoms among Resident Physicians: A Systematic Review and Meta-analysis." *Journal of the American Medical Association* 314(22):2373–2383.

Meeks, Lisa M., Kurt Herzer, and Neera R. Jain. 2018. "Removing Barriers and Facilitating Access: Increasing the Number of Physicians with Disabilities." *Academic Medicine* 93(4):540–543.

Obedin-Maliver Juno, Elizabeth S. Goldsmith, Leslie Stewart, William White, Eric Tran, Stephanie Brenman, Maggie Wells, David M. Fetterman, Gabriel Garcia, and Mitchell P. Lunn. 2011. "Lesbian, Gay, Bisexual and Transgender Content in Undergraduate Medical Education." *Journal of the American Medical Association* 306(9):971–977.

Pellegrino, Edmund D. 1987. "The Reconciliation of Technology and Humanism: A Flexnerian Task 75 Years Later." Pp. 77–111 in *Flexner: 75 Years Later: Current Commentary on Medical Education*, edited by Charles Vevier. Lanham, MD: University Press of America.

Regan-Smith, Martha G. 1998. "Reform without Change: Update, 1998." *Academic Medicine* 73(5):505–507.

Saha, Somnath, Gretchen Guiton, Paul F. Wimmers, and LuAnn Wilkerson. 2008. "Student Body Racial and Ethnic Composition and Diversity-Related Outcomes in U.S. Medical Schools." *Journal of the American Medical Association* 300(10):1135–1145.

Sarmiento, Christina, Sonya R. Miller, Eleanor Change, Philip Zazove, and Arno K. Kumagai. 2016. "From Impairment to Empowerment: A Longitudinal Medical School Curriculum on Disabilities." *Academic Medicine* 91(7):954–957.

Schabath, Matthew B., Catherine A. Blackburn, Megan E. Sutter, Peter A. Kanetsky, Susan T. Vadaparampil, Vani N. Simmons, Julian A. Sanchez, Steven K. Sutton, and Gwendolyn P. Quinn. 2019. "National Survey of Oncologists at National Cancer Institute–Designated Comprehensive Cancer Centers: Attitudes, Knowledge, and Practice Behaviors About LGBTQ Patients with Cancer." *Journal of Clinical Oncology* 37(7):547–558.

Schwartzenstein, Richard M. 2015. "Getting the Right Medical Students—Nature Versus Nurture." *New England Journal of Medicine* 372(17):1586–1587.

Silver, Henry K., and Anita D. Glicken. 1990. "Medical Student Abuse: Incidence, Severity, and Significance." *Journal of the American Medical Association* 263(4):527–532.

Skochelak, Susan E., and Steven J. Stack. 2017. "Creating the Medical Schools of the Future." *Academic Medicine* 92(1):16–19.

Slavin, Stuart J., and John T. Chibnall. 2016. "Finding the Why, Changing the How: Improving the Mental Health of Medical Students, Residents, and Physicians." *Academic Medicine* 91(9):1194–1196.

Smith, Davey M., and W. Christopher Mathews. 2007. "Physicians' Attitudes Toward Homosexuality and HIV: Survey of a California Medical Society." *Journal of Homosexuality* 52(3–4):1–9.

Stein, Howard F. 1990. *American Medicine as Culture*. Boulder, CO: Westview Press.

Stott Don B. 2013. "The Training Needs of General Practitioners in the Exploration of Sexual Health Matters and Providing Sexual Healthcare to Lesbian, Gay and Bisexual Patients." *Medical Teacher* 35(9):752–759.

Streed, Carl G., Helen F. Hedian, Amanda Bertram, and Stephen D. Sisson. 2019. "Assessment of Internal Medicine Resident Preparedness to Care for Lesbian, Gay, Bisexual, Transgender, and Queer/ Questioning Patients." *Journal of General Internal Medicine* 34(6):893–898.

Underman, Kelly, and Laura E. Hirshfield. 2016. "Detached Concern? Emotional Socialization in Twenty-First Century Medical Education." *Social Science and Medicine* 160(July):94–101.

Vernon, David T.A., and Michael C. Hosokawa. 1996. "Faculty Attitudes and Opinions About Problem-Based Learning." *Academic Medicine* 71(11):1233–1238.

West, Colin P., and Furman S. McDonald. 2008. "Evaluation of a Longitudinal Medical School Evidence-Based Medicine Curriculum: A Pilot Study." *Journal of General Internal Medicine* 23(7):1057–1059.

Witzburg, Robert A., and Henry M. Sondheimer. 2013. "Holistic Review—Shaping the Medical Profession One Applicant at a Time." *New England Journal of Medicine* 368(17):1565–1567.

Xu, Gang, Mohammadreza Hojat, Timothy P. Brigham, and J. Jon Veloski. 1999. "Factors Associated with Changing Levels of Interest in Primary Care during Medical School." *Academic Medicine* 74(9):1011–1015.

Zazove, Philip, Benjamin Case, Christopher Moreland, Melissa A. Plegue, Anne Hoekstra, Alicia Ouelette, Amanda Sen, and Michael D. Fetters. 2016. "U.S. Medical Schools Compliance with the Americans for Disabilities Act: Findings from a National Study." *Academic Medicine* 91(7):979–986.

CHAPTER 10

Nurses, Advanced Practice Providers, and Allied Health Workers

Learning Objectives

- Describe the circumstances in which nursing and midwifery originated.
- Identify key orientations included in nursing socialization.
- Select any two of the key issues in nursing today and discuss the various sides of the issues.

- Compare and contrast the responsibilities of nurse practitioners and physician assistants. Discuss the extent to which they have earned patient satisfaction.
- Evaluate the extent to which physicians have positive working relationships with nurses and allied health workers.

The shift in dominance from acute to chronic conditions and the development of increasingly sophisticated medical technologies led to a growing array of specialized practitioners within health care. These practitioners play an indispensable role in the provision of health care services. This chapter focuses on nurses, advanced practice providers, and allied health personnel.

EVOLUTION OF NURSES, ADVANCED PRACTICE PROVIDERS, AND ALLIED HEALTH WORKERS

Early America

Families rather than physicians were the most important health care providers in colonial America. Most families relied on women members to provide health care, and when additional

help was necessary, they employed medically knowledgeable women from other families. The duties of these formally untrained, but typically wise and benevolent "nurses" generally focused on childcare, surrogate breastfeeding, birthing, and care of the ill (Starr, 1982).

Early Midwifery. Midwives were a vital source of care for women in colonial times. Most came from England, where the Church of England granted licenses to practice. They were generally held in high esteem and often paid for their services, even though they were sometimes suspected of practicing witchcraft (e.g., in the case of an impaired baby). Many midwives served on Southern plantations; some were slaves, others were white women who were paid in kind for their services. Although formal training was not available in the United States, some manuals were in print so that any woman who had borne children herself and assisted in a few births could be designated a midwife.

With the development of the obstetric forceps and subsequent acceptance of midwifery as a science, male physicians assumed greater responsibility for the birthing process. The belief that women were incapable of understanding and performing obstetric techniques enabled this transition. As formal medical education in the United States became available and was routinely restricted to men, physicians gained further advantage over women midwives and attempted to monopolize the birthing field.

Early Nursing. The increased dominance of men in the birthing process led many women to nursing. Many became private duty nurses whose responsibilities included tending the sick at their bedside and providing both caring and curing services. Although most nurses were relatively uneducated and lacked formal training, they provided a valuable service (Reverby, 1987).

Whereas private duty nursing was an acceptable occupation, hospital nursing—given the marginal nature of hospitals at this time—was perceived as less desirable. Many hospital nurses lived and worked in the hospital. Their qualifications and the quality of their work were uneven. The job entailed long hours, was physically demanding, and involved frequent friction with physicians and hospital managers over the content and pace of work.

The importance and visibility of nursing increased during the Civil War. Thousands of women on both sides of the conflict established hospitals and worked as volunteers and paid nurses. Many were working-class women who were accustomed to hard labor as domestics and nurses, although others were middle-class women who had not worked previously for wages outside the home. In addition, some worked through the Sanitary Commission, implementing innovative public health measures, while others attempted to create a role for women in the army's medical system.

Post–Civil War to 1920: Professional Medicine and Separate Domains

Growth of Health Care Institutions. The end of the Civil War and beginning of accelerated urbanization and industrialization separated many families geographically. Increasingly, non-family members were needed to provide care for the sick and injured outside the home. It was particularly important to the growing "middling class" that caretakers in institutions be as "reliable, respectable and clean (in all senses) as the mothers or sisters . . . formerly charged with the responsibility" (Baer, 1990:460).

As a result, a custodial role of "nurse" was established. Religious women of the Church managed Roman Catholic, Lutheran, and Episcopal hospitals. Community women worked for wages in hospitals for the working poor. In big city almshouses, "the progression from inmate to keeper to assistant nurse to nurse comprised a sort of job ladder" (Baer, 1990:461). None of these "nurses" had formal training.

Advent of Nursing Education. When hospitals demanded public assistance with caring for the ill, demands for formal training of nurses accelerated. Programs were developed around the philosophy of Florence Nightingale, an upper-class British reformer who believed that the proper moral, environmental, and physical order was necessary for the restoration of health. Known as the founder of modern nursing, she made significant contributions to nursing education, nursing care, nursing research, understandings of the importance of hygiene and sanitation, and hospital design (Lee, Clark, and Thompson, 2013). She accepted a gendered division of labor as given and believed that women's characteristics made them naturally suited to creating the conditions needed for care of the ill. As Cottingham (2014:135) explains, "Nightingale's efforts to professionalize nursing as a white, middle-class, and feminine occupation exaggerated the disconnect between 'caring' and 'curing' in order to mirror Victorian sex roles". Curing became the domain of men (as physicians), while caring was women's work (as nurses).

Although nursing was known for its drudgery, it attracted both white and black women who regarded it as a way to serve fellow human beings and an opportunity for personal autonomy and geographic mobility. However, employment opportunities for trained nurses were few. After completing training, the nurse often had neither a place in the hospital (which depended upon cheap student labor) nor a position in private duty (where cheaper, untrained nurses were typically used). Many physicians and families were unconvinced that the training offered any significant benefit (Reverby, 1987).

Maternity Care. By the late 1800s, the American medical profession had taken specific steps to ensure a place for obstetrics. In 1859, the American Medical Association (AMA) designated practical medicine and obstetrics as one of its four scientific sections, and in 1868, the *American Journal of Obstetrics* became the first specialized medical journal published in the United States. In 1876, the American Gynecological Society was formed, followed by the American Association of Obstetricians and Gynecologists in 1888.

Despite these developments, at least 50 percent of all births were still attended by midwives at the beginning of the twentieth century. Midwives were especially important for Southern black families, immigrant families, and families in rural areas. Middle- and upper-class women were more likely to have physician-assisted deliveries. There was a general belief, however, that lack of adequate maternity care was a problem.

Home Nursing Care. Agencies that provided home nursing care were an important source of employment for nurses at the turn of the century. These agencies were primarily located in northeastern cities, which had large concentrations of immigrants and were characterized by poverty, disease, and unsanitary conditions. In the beginning, a few wealthy women hired nurses to visit the poor sick in their homes, but visiting nurses soon became popular in other settings. All types of groups began hiring these public health nurses, including Metropolitan Life, which discovered it could reduce the number of death benefits it paid by offering home nursing service to policyholders.

The 1920s to the 1950s: The Advent of Scientific Medicine

Midwifery. Debate concerning the regulation of midwifery reached its height between 1910 and 1920. In 1921, the Sheppard-Tower Maternity and Infancy Protection Act provided funds in several states for midwife education and registration. By 1930, all but ten states required midwives to be registered. These regulations were partly responsible for the decline in midwifery, but other factors such as declining birth rates, restricted immigration, the increased number of hospital beds available for maternity cases, and a growing anxiety about the dangers of birth also contributed to the decline. However, midwifery was sustained by the needs of the urban and rural poor (DeVries, 1985).

The first *nurse-midwives* to practice in the United States were brought from England in 1925 by Mary Breckinridge as part of her plan to provide health care for rural people in Kentucky. As a consequence of these midwives' services, comprehensive health care became available to the rural population and the maternal death rate declined dramatically. Eventually several states passed laws granting legal recognition to midwives, and several midwifery schools were established.

Emergence of Staff Nursing. During the Depression years, the emphasis on nursing shifted from private duty nursing back to hospital staffing. While there was an oversupply of nurses in the 1920s and 1930s, a shortage developed during World War II, due in part to the fact that women had opportunities for better-paying jobs in war-related industries. The shortage led to the creation of "practical nurses" and nursing assistants. Although these new occupations initially provided a temporary solution to a short-term problem, their contributions to health care were evident, and they eventually became permanent health care occupations.

The New Allied Health Workers. The emergence of **allied health workers** (health care workers such as physical therapists and medical technologists whose work supports that of the physician) occurred during the second quarter of the twentieth century. The development of these positions was encouraged by the complexity of new methods of diagnosis and treatment that required a specialist, and by the fact that there were not enough primary care physicians to handle the additional workload.

Beginning in the 1930s and continuing into the 1940s, the Committee on Allied Health Education and Accreditation (CAHEA) (now CAA-HEP, as described later in the chapter), sponsored by the AMA, began to accredit a variety of allied health occupations. "Essentials" (nationally accepted minimum standards for an educational program) were first adopted for occupational therapy programs in 1935 and for most other allied health fields in the late 1930s and 1940s.

Nursing Moves Away From Patient Care. During World War II and its aftermath, nursing moved away from direct patient care. Other than distributing medication, nurses spent much of the war years in the nurses' station, coordinating other staff, making notes on charts, and keeping records. In response, new categories of nurse-related workers emerged to provide direct patient care—the licensed practical nurse (LPN)

or vocational nurse, and the nurse's aide (Reverby, 1987).

Meanwhile, nurse-midwifery struggled to establish standards for education, legal recognition, and professional identity. In 1955, the American College of Nurse-Midwifery was founded; it subsequently joined the Kentucky-based American Association of Nurse-Midwives in 1969 and formed the American College of Nurse-Midwives. However, legal recognition continued to be a problem. By 1959, only two states, New Mexico and New York, formally recognized nurse-midwives, despite the positive impact of nurse-midwifery on maternal and infant mortality rates.

CONTEMPORARY NURSES AND THE FIELD OF NURSING

Overview

The nursing profession today constitutes the largest segment of the US health care workforce with over 3 million members (three times the number of physicians) (Bakhamis et al., 2019; Institute of Medicine, 2011). Approximately 85 percent of nurses with active licenses are working, and two-thirds are working full-time (Smiley et al., 2018). Regulation of nursing is a state responsibility. Under a state board of nursing, each state licenses nurses and defines the boundaries of the practice. All states require that prospective nurses attend an approved training program and take a national licensing examination. Certification in various specialty areas is administered by the American Nurses Credentialing Center, a subsidiary of the American Nurses Association (ANA).

Types of Nurses. There are three main types of nurses:

1. *Licensed practical nurses* typically are high school graduates who have completed an additional 1-year vocational program and have passed

an examination leading to the LPN certification. There were approximately 724,500
LPNs employed in the United States in 2018,
and employment opportunities for LPNs are
expected to grow faster than the national
average through 2026 (US Bureau of Labor
Statistics, 2019). Only 6 percent of nurses
practicing in 2017 initially entered the field
via a vocational training program (Smiley et
al., 2018).

2. *Registered nurses (RNs)* have obtained a
diploma or degree in nursing and are distinguished by the type of nursing education they
have completed. In 2018 there were approximately 2.9 million registered nurses employed
in the United States, and employment opportunities are expected to increase by 15 percent
through 2026 (US Bureau of Labor Statistics,
2019).

   a. *Diploma nurses* have completed a 3-year
   program in a hospital-based school of nursing and earned a nursing license. Until the
   early 1970s, this was the dominant form of
   nursing education, although only 12 percent of practicing RNs in 2017 entered the
   field via this route (Smiley et al., 2018).

   b. *Associate degree nurses* have completed a 2-
   to 3-year program consisting of both academic and nursing courses in a community
   college or junior college, and earned an
   associate degree and nursing license. These
   programs primarily offer a vocational orientation to nursing. About 36 percent of
   practicing RNs in 2017 entered the field
   with an associate's degree (Smiley et al.,
   2018).

   c. *Baccalaureate nurses* have completed an
   undergraduate curriculum of academic
   courses, usually with a nursing major, and
   have earned a bachelor of science in nursing (BSN) degree. With a greater emphasis on theory and broad-based knowledge,
   these programs offer more of a professional
   orientation to nursing. Generally, more

highly educated nurses enjoy higher status and pay. Approximately 42 percent of
RNs practicing in 2017 first entered the
field with a BSN, an increase of 6 percentage points since 2013 (Smiley et al., 2018).
In addition, many colleges already offering
the BSN degree have begun offering "RN
to BSN" programs allowing nurses with an
associate degree to add courses to earn the
BSN, and "BS/BA to RN" programs for
those with a baccalaureate degree in a field
other than nursing.

3. *Advanced practice registered nurses (APRNs)* are
registered nurses who have acquired a master's
or post-master's degree and additional certification in one or more of about 20 nursing
specialties. In 2017, 10 percent of RNs held
an APRN degree, a slight increase since 2015
(Smiley et al., 2018). The largest categories of
APRNs are nurse practitioners (NPs), clinical
nurse specialists, nurse-anesthetists, and nurse-
midwives. These nurses often have a master's
degree. They must pass a certifying examination, and they take on many responsibilities
traditionally handled by physicians. There
are now more than 250,000 APRNs in the
United States—a number expected to grow
significantly (Institute of Medicine, 2011).

In 2004, the member schools affiliated with
the American Association of Colleges of Nursing
endorsed moving the current level of preparation
necessary for advanced nursing practice from the
master's degree to the doctorate level (a doctor
of nursing practice degree or DNP) by 2015.
One of the rationales was that the course credit
requirements for APRNs were already equivalent
to that for doctoral degrees in many other fields.
The focus of the DNP curriculum is evidence-
based practice, quality improvement, and systems
leadership, among other key areas. There are now
nearly 350 DNP programs that operate in all 50
states and the District of Columbia, with nearly
100 more in development. In fact, the growth

rate for DNP programs now outpaces the more traditional research-based nursing PhD programs (AACN, 2019b).

Key Roles of Nurses. McClure (1991) identifies the two key roles held by nurses today as those of caregiver and integrator. As a caregiver, the nurse functions to meet patients' needs—dependency (hygiene, nutrition, safety, etc.), comfort (physical and psychological), therapy (medications and other treatments), monitoring (collecting, interpreting, and acting on patient data), and education. As an integrator, the nurse coordinates the contributions of separate medical units in the hospital or clinic to provide total and effective patient treatment and care.

Viewed from another perspective, Chambliss (1996) identifies three difficult and sometimes contradictory roles that hospital nurses must fulfill. First, nurses must be caring individuals who interact directly with patients and work with them as "whole people." Second, nurses are professionals who have an important job that requires special competence and deserves special status and respect. Finally, within the hospital hierarchy, nurses are subordinate workers who are often under the direction of physicians. The contrasting expectations created by these disparate roles place nurses in an awkward position where the practical requirements of the job may conflict with the moral expectations of the professional role.

Nurse Supply and Demand

In the last few decades of the twentieth century, continuing into the 2010s, the demand for nurses outpaced the supply, creating a significant shortage of nurses throughout the United States. Hospitals—where 55 percent of registered nurses work (Smiley et al., 2018)—reported a nurse vacancy rate of 8 percent in 2019, and many nursing positions in physician offices and community-based facilities (such as nursing homes) have gone unfilled (Nursing Solutions, 2019).

What created this vast nursing shortage? Many factors were responsible, including both demand- and supply-side factors. Demand-side factors include the increased number of elderly people seeking care, the heavy time demands of patients with chronic diseases, delays in seeking treatment by the medically uninsured, thereby increasing the severity of illness, the expansion of home health care, an expansion of school nursing, increased use of a wide variety of health care technologies (for which nurses must have at least sufficient knowledge to coordinate care), and the ability of more individuals to seek medical care due to the Affordable Care Act. Supply-side factors include the aging of the nurse population (with retirements exacerbating the shortage), and a shortage of nursing faculty, which limited significant expansion of nursing school classes.

Hospitals addressed the nurse shortage by attempting to reduce demand and increase supply. To reduce demand, some hospitals reorganized staff responsibilities by hiring less well-educated individuals to do traditional nursing tasks in order to downsize the number of nurses needed. This effort is a contentious issue in medicine and is discussed in more detail later in this chapter.

Hospitals and other medical providers also tried to expand the supply of nurses by increasing nurse salaries to attract more people to the field, and increasing recruitment of nurses from other countries. The first approach was long overdue. Nursing has been traditionally undersalaried, but measurable progress has been made. In 2018, the median salary was approximately US$46,000 for licensed practical nurses and just over US$71,000 for registered nurses (Bureau of Labor Statistics, 2019). The second approach, however, raises serious ethical concerns. Efforts to recruit nurses from other countries, especially developing countries, were accompanied by concerns about the health care systems in sending countries and the quality of care in the United States. These concerns are addressed in the accompanying box, "Recruiting Nurses From Abroad."

IN THE FIELD

RECRUITING NURSES FROM ABROAD

Faced with a sizable and chronic shortage of nurses, hospitals and health care systems in the United States began recruiting nurses from other countries. Hospitals employed recruiting companies (paying as much as US$15,000–20,000 per hire) to secure foreign-educated nurses (FENs). In 2004, the National Council of State Boards of Nursing began offering the mandatory US licensing nursing exam in other countries to make it easier for foreign nurses to become licensed in the United States.

The interest of nurses in other countries—especially very poor ones—is understandable. The average monthly take-home salary for nurses in the United States is significantly higher than in other countries, especially developing ones. However, there can be drastic consequences for the health care system in the countries from which FENs are recruited.

> There are legal, economic, cultural, social, educational, and other ramifications to be considered as the greater health care workforce, and nursing in particular, evolves globally. For example, nurses may leave their home countries because of poor working or living conditions or to provide support and resources to their families. This creates a "domino" effect in which the population health needs in one country may be negatively impacted, whereas those in another country may benefit.
>
> (Jones and Sherwood, 2014:59–60)

Joyce Thompson (2003), a professor of community health nursing at Western Michigan University, says that the practice is "clearly devastating the health care infrastructure" in several of these countries, which have been forced to close hospitals due to a lack of nurses (1,000 hospitals in the Philippines alone have been forced to close). Thompson personally witnessed the exodus of nurses from Africa during her work on a program promoting women's health in Uganda and Malawi. Her reaction was that "it's always difficult (to see) a resource-rich country that hasn't planned appropriately depend on lesser-developed countries to meet their needs" (Thompson, 2003:20).

A second concern with recruiting FENs is the potential negative impact on quality of care in the United States. One early study found higher mortality rates in hospitals that employed higher proportions of FENs and had poor nurse-to-patient ratios (Neff et al., 2013). Patient satisfaction rates also decrease as the proportion of FENs increases (Germack et al., 2017).

FENs constitute a very small proportion (about 5 percent) of the US nursing workforce, and this percentage has stopped growing (Smiley et al., 2018). As enrollment in US nursing schools has surged in recent years, reliance on foreign-educated recruits has slowed.

Nursing schools responded to the shortage by expanding recruitment efforts (discussed more in the next section) and enrolling more students. Following an enrollment decline in the late 1990s, enrollments increased in the early 2000s, and are continuing to increase today, although at a slower rate (AACN, 2019a). The number of students nursing schools can accommodate is limited by a shortage of clinical placements

and nursing faculty. Nursing schools report that 8 percent of full-time nursing faculty positions in 2018–2019 remained vacant (an average of two per school), mostly due to non–competitive salaries and lack of doctorally prepared nurses (Li, Turinetti and Fang, 2019). Because 30 percent of nursing faculty in 2015 were aged 60 years or over, impending faculty retirements will exacerbate the faculty shortage (Fang and

Kesten, 2017). Consequently, US nursing schools rejected an estimated 75,000 qualified applicants to baccalaureate and graduate nursing programs in 2018 (AACN, 2019a).

Have these combined efforts ended the nursing shortage? For now, yes. The situation has improved and the United States now enjoys a relative balance in supply and demand. The economic downturn of 2008–2009 assisted the above efforts, as job losses in other economic sectors increased interest in nursing and older nurses postponed retirement (Auerbach, Buerhaus, and Staiger, 2011). However, nursing shortages tend to be cyclical and demand for nurses is projected to grow as baby boomers age, the size of the insured population increases, nursing retirements accelerate (the median age of RNs in 2017 was 53), and a shortage of primary care physicians intensifies reliance on APRNs (Buerhaus et al., 2017). If these projections prove accurate, and/or if the recent upsurge of interest in nursing subsides, the country may again experience a severe nurse shortage (Staiger, Auerbach, and Buerhaus, 2012).

Demographics of Nurses

The nursing workforce does not adequately mirror the diversity of the US patient population, particularly in terms of gender and race. The Institute of Medicine's 2011 landmark report, *The Future of Nursing*, cited nursing's lack of diversity as an even greater challenge facing the profession than the projected nursing shortage. A diverse nursing workforce, it argued, is essential for the delivery of high-quality culturally appropriate care. Here, we examine the demographic characteristics of nurses and recent efforts to diversify the nursing workforce.

Gender. Although men historically served as nurses in monasteries and military orders, after the Nightingale reforms of the nineteenth century, modern nursing became defined as women's work. Evans (2004:323) notes that "the belief that nursing was an extension of women's domestic roles was instrumental in establishing nursing as not only a woman's occupation, but one that was unskilled and of low value in comparison with men's occupations, particularly medicine".

Striking nurses march in a Detroit Labor Day parade.

Nursing's lower status and pay relative to that of physicians, and stereotypes of men nurses as effeminate or gay deterred men from pursuing nursing careers. Men interested in health care occupations were tracked into medicine instead, and many nursing schools refused to admit men.

Today, nursing remains a woman-dominated occupation—90.9 percent of RNs and 92.3 percent of LPN/LVNs were women in 2017 (Smiley et al., 2018). Recruiting men into the profession offers opportunities both to address the nursing shortage and to diversify nursing's ranks. In recent years, nursing associations, hospitals, and schools have actively sought to recruit men.

Cottingham (2014) analyzed recruiting materials aimed at men, showing how these mobilize masculine ideals. Twenty-two percent of the materials analyzed associated nursing with traditionally masculine traits (i.e., rational/technical skills, strength, autonomy, income). These often showed men playing competitive sports, riding motorcycles, or engaging in other stereotypically masculine activities. Fifty-three percent emphasized both masculine and feminine traits of nursing, but highlighted their contrasting rather than complementary qualities. One such ad aimed to reassure men that, contrary to expectations, financial rewards and helping people can co-occur: "You really do make a difference every day you work as a nurse helping people, but it's also financially rewarding as well" (Cottingham, 2014:146). Just one-quarter of materials featured alternative conceptions of manhood that emphasized caring, making a difference, or working with a team, absent of more traditional masculine characteristics.

Between 2013 and 2017, the number of male nurses increased by 2.5 percentage points (Smiley et al., 2018), although it is unclear if this was due to recruiting efforts or other factors. Regardless, men still constitute less than 13 percent of RN and baccalaureate nursing students combined, and just 12 percent of master's level students in 2018 (AACN, 2019a).

Despite their minority status, men enjoy subtle advantages in nursing that propel them into leadership positions (e.g., nurse managers) and higher paying specialties (e.g., nurse anesthetists) at higher rates than women. These hidden advantages include preferential treatment in hiring and promotions and positive relationships with supervisors and coworkers. These advantages are termed the glass escalator effect because, as if on an invisible escalator, men effortlessly ride these advantages to higher status positions within nursing considered more appropriately masculine (Williams, 1992).

Race and Ethnicity.   Nurses also remain overwhelmingly white (81 percent in 2017), with people of color making up just 19 percent of RNs. Although they were 13 percent of the US population in 2017, African Americans accounted for only 6 percent of RNs (Smiley et al., 2018). Among students, 34 percent of those enrolled in entry-level baccalaureate nursing programs in 2018 were students of color (up from 26 percent in 2009) and 32 percent graduating from such programs in 2018 were non-white (up from 24 percent in 2009) (AACN, 2019c).

Compared to RNs, a higher proportion of LPN/LVNs are people of color (19 percent versus 29 percent, respectively) (Smiley et al., 2018). Efforts to make the BSN the minimum requirement to enter nursing (discussed later in the chapter) may reinforce both class and racial-ethnic disparities by closing off the more common educational pathway for nurses of color (Glazer, 1991).

Unlike men in nursing, whose minority status elevates them into higher status positions, people of color and men of color, in particular, do not receive these same advantages. Wingfield (2009) shows that men nurses of color often do not have collegial relationships with supervisors or coworkers like white men nurses do; and, unlike white men nurses, whose male privilege leads others to assume they possess superior skills

Efforts to diversify the nursing workforce include recruiting more men and people of color.

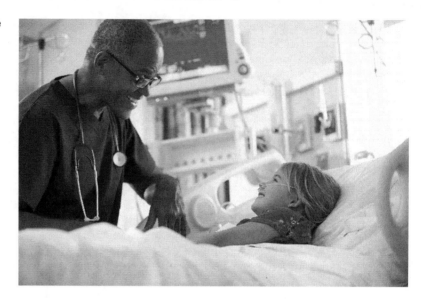

and are well suited for and desire managerial positions, men of color find their abilities questioned. Unlike white men nurses, who are often mistaken for doctors, black men nurses are more often mistaken for janitors or other lower-skilled service workers. Wingfield (2009:19) concludes that "race and gender intersect to determine which men [namely, white men] will ride the glass escalator."

Socialization of Nurses

The socialization of nursing students has received less systematic study than that of medical students. Fred Davis (1972) studied a West Coast nursing school, discovering a 6-step socialization experience not unlike that experienced by medical students.

Students enter nursing school with an *initial innocence*, seeking to become mother surrogates by engaging in nurturant and helping behaviors. The failure of nursing instructors to endorse or model this image, however, creates frustration and anxiety. Students spend time learning technical and seemingly inconsequential skills. Later during the first semester, students enter a *labeled*

recognition of incongruity stage. This includes open statements of disillusionment and despair over the incongruity between their anticipated view of nursing school and their actual experience. Many question their career choice and drop out of nursing school during this time.

Students who remain enter a *psyching out the faculty* stage (just as medical students do, as described in Chapter 9). They attempt to determine what part of the course materials and training faculty think is most important, so they can concentrate on that. Typically, they realize that faculty place high value on professionalism, and students collectively begin to mold their behavior in that direction. This is the *role simulation stage*, which usually occurs around the end of the first year. As their behaviors become more convincing, the students gain confidence in themselves.

During the second half of training (the *provisional internalization* and *stable internalization* stages), students increasingly accept a professional identity and become accustomed to it until, by graduation, it is typically fully accepted and internalized. However, even by the end of nursing school, substantial value differences may exist between students and nursing instructors. Eddy et al. (1994) discovered that faculty placed significantly more value than students on freedom (e.g., honoring patients' right to refuse treatment), equality (basing care on patients' needs, not their background characteristics), and human dignity (e.g., maintaining confidentiality), whereas students placed more emphasis than faculty on aesthetics (creating a pleasing environment for patients and pleasant work environment for themselves and others). The study authors suggested that these responses reflected students' idealism about work settings and their lack of experience in actual settings.

Occupational Status

Although common to speak of "the nursing profession," many nursing responsibilities fall under the direction of physicians, and this external control is a primary barrier to a genuinely professional status. Nevertheless, nurses have gained greater autonomy in recent years because of the professionalization of nursing and strengthening of nursing education. Nurses both desire more independence in patient care and increasingly exercise such independence.

In addition, nursing associations and unions have developed a larger advocacy voice. Service Employees International Union (SEIU) Healthcare is the largest healthcare union in North America, with more than 1.1 million members. In addition to nurses, its members include physicians, home care and nursing home workers, laboratory technicians, environmental service workers, and dietary aides. The National Union of Healthcare Workers, with over 15,000 members, broke away from the SEIU in 2009 over differences in organizational structure. National Nurses United (NNU), with more than 150,000 members, is the largest union and professional association of registered nurses. Affiliated with the AFL-CIO and comprising largely of direct care RNs, NNU has adopted an aggressive strategy to promote its causes. Its approaches include extensive lobbying, marches, and demonstrations in Washington and around the country. In April 2020, NNU organized a protest outside the White House to call attention to the large number of healthcare workers who had contracted COVID-19 or died from it due to a lack of personal protective equipment (Rodriguez and Reyes, 2020).

The most prominent nursing associations are the American Nurses Association (ANA) and the National League for Nursing (NLN). The majority of ANA members are registered nurses with practice-related concerns. The ANA has experienced considerable tension in recent years over the best way to lobby for a nursing role in the changing health care system. NLN membership consists mainly of nursing educators and agencies associated with nursing education. Their primary goal is to promote quality standards for nursing education.

Issues in Nursing Today

Education and Image. Throughout its history, nursing has struggled internally to define its primary goals and purposes. One faction has attempted to maintain an image of a nurturer/caregiver, while another faction has worked to professionalize nursing by emphasizing education and a scientifically based nursing curriculum.

This controversy over image centers on educational preparation. At one time, most practicing nurses were diploma trained, and they actively resisted increased emphasis on training in academic institutions and curricular changes making science rather than technique the primary focus of nursing education. Today, however, despite this resistance, nearly all training occurs in academic institutions, with science increasingly at the core of the curriculum.

Some friction remains between graduates of associate–degree and 4-year programs. Because both programs prepare students for the same state licensing examination, many assume they can perform at the same skill level. Advocates of bachelor-level programs are concerned that 2-year programs do not adequately prepare students for the rapid changes in modern technology nurses now encounter. Advocates of associate-level programs dismiss the need for an undergraduate degree and prefer the technique-focused curriculum. Because hospitals do not typically differentiate between training backgrounds when determining salary and responsibilities, advocates of baccalaureate training feel the bachelor's degree is devalued.

Since 1965, the ANA has tried unsuccessfully to make a bachelor's degree the minimum educational requirement for licensure of registered nurses. In 1985, the ANA revised its stance to recommend two levels of nursing based on educational preparation—the professional nurse with a baccalaureate degree, and the technical nurse with an associate degree.

This is consistent with the concept of a **differentiated practice model**, which bases the roles and functions of registered nurses on education, experience, and competence. It clarifies which type of registered nurse is appropriately accountable for which aspects of nursing by separating technical and professional practice. Proponents of the model believe it will lead to more effective and efficient patient care, increased job satisfaction, and greater organizational viability. A sizable number of hospitals across the nation now use some type of differentiated practice model.

In 2010, the Institute of Medicine (IOM) recommended increasing the percentage of nurses with a baccalaureate degree to 80 percent. Their rationale for the recommendation rested on the fact that the nation desperately needs more nurse practitioners and other advanced practice nurses and that baccalaureate nurses are much more likely than associate degree or diploma nurses to eventually pursue an advanced practice degree (Aiken, 2011).

Overall, nursing enjoys a very positive image. A 2018 Gallup Poll found that nursing ranked as the "most honest and ethical" occupation—an honor it has received for 17 consecutive years (see Table 10.1).

TABLE 10.1   Ten Highest Ranking Occupations for Honesty and Ethical Standards, 2018

Occupation/Career	Percentage Ranking Very High or High (percent)
Nurses	84 (highest overall ranking)
Medical doctors	67
Pharmacists	66
High school teachers	60
Police officers	54
Accountants	42
Funeral directors	39
Clergy	37
Journalists	33
Building contractors	29

Source: Brenan, Megan. 2018. "Nurses Again Outpace Other Professions for Honesty, Ethics." Retrieved June 12, 2019 (https://news.gallup.com/poll/245597/nurses-again-outpace-professions-honesty-ethics.aspx).

Specific Job Responsibilities. Nurses have assumed additional responsibilities in recent years, some that involve direct patient care and others that simply comply with bureaucratic requirements. In contrast to 20 or more years ago, nurses are now involved in assessing patients, reading tests and lab results, inserting intravenous lines, checking for abnormalities, and monitoring blood pressure. They work with electronic health records, manage chronic illness cases, transition patients to hospitals, provide health education, and work on quality improvement.

Downsizing Nursing Staffs. In the mid-1990s, responding to pressures to become more cost-effective, hospitals cut back on nurses and reassigned some job responsibilities to a new category of health care workers, variously referred to as "nurses' aides," "patient care technicians," "unlicensed assistive personnel," and "care associates." These workers, who sometimes receive 2 months or less of training, help with such tasks as changing linen, bathing patients, and assisting physicians with routine procedures, but they are also involved in EKG testing, drawing blood, and respiratory therapy (Norrish and Rundall, 2001). An ad posted on commuter trains and bus-stop shelters in New York City, and printed in *New York* magazine, read: "BABY CARE TECHNICIAN WANTED—Work with newborns and preemies in NY hospitals. Regulate incubators, draw blood, insert feeding tubes, give medications. On-the-job training. NO EXPERIENCE NECESSARY/NO EDUCATION NECESSARY" (Moore, 1995:3).

The ANA and other groups charged that this "reconfiguration" threatened quality patient care. An impressive array of studies found that hospitals with lower RN-to-patient ratios have higher patient mortality rates, longer hospital stays, higher rates of adverse outcomes, and higher readmission rates. To make up for staffing cuts, hospitals often require nurses to work extra or extended shifts (sometimes 12 hours or more). The risk of medical error increases when nurses work long hours (Griffiths et al., 2014).

Nurse Burnout. Just as physicians may experience burnout on the job (see Chapter 8), nurses too may become emotionally and physically exhausted and suffer decreased job identification, job satisfaction, and self-confidence. Hospital nurses, who often work in high-stress situations with life and death consequences, are especially prone to burnout. In a recent review of the literature, Bakhamis et al. (2019) identified the following as important causal factors in nurse burnout:

Management characteristics, including lack of appropriate supervision, lack of resources offered, mandatory overtime, and extended work hours.

Organizational characteristics, including excessive workloads, staff shortages, and low nurse-to-patient ratios.

Work characteristics, including a poor working environment and ineffective team relationships.

The accompanying box, "Discontent Among Nurses: A Report on Hospital Care in Five Countries," describes common correlates of work dissatisfaction that can impact nurse burnout. The consequences of nurse burnout can be severe and include high turnover rates, poor patient care, patient dissatisfaction, and higher rates of medical error, infection, and mortality.

Political Activism. The frustrations many nurses feel about their working conditions have fostered increased political activism, and in recent years, union organizing has been especially fervent among nurses and other non-physician health care workers. A prime objective has been to get state legislatures to adopt nurse-staffing laws that require hospitals to maintain a minimum ratio of nurses to patients. California was the first state to pass such legislation. California nurses recommended a minimum ratio of 1 nurse per 3 patients, while California hospitals recommended 1 nurse per 10 patients. Minimums were eventually set at 1 nurse per 6 patients in medical-surgical units, 1 nurse per 4 patients in pediatric wards, and 1 nurse per 2 patients in intensive care. These efforts received a boost in 2010 with the publication of a major study on the effect of nurse–patient ratios comparing California (with minimum ratios) with Pennsylvania and New Jersey (without minimum ratios). Researchers found that the ratios required in California enabled nurses to spend more time with patients, monitor patient condition more accurately, inspire more confidence in patients and their families, lower patient mortality, and reduce nurse burnout (Aiken et al., 2010).

IN COMPARATIVE FOCUS

DISCONTENT AMONG NURSES: A REPORT ON HOSPITAL CARE IN FIVE COUNTRIES

A 2001 survey by Aiken and colleagues of more than 43,000 nurses in 711 hospitals in the United States, Canada, Germany, England, and Scotland found widespread discontent. Although these countries have different health care systems, nurses reported similar shortcomings in their work environment and the quality of hospital care. Five sources of discontent emerged:

1. A large majority of nurses in all five countries indicated that there were not enough registered nurses in their hospital to provide high-quality care, there were not enough support staff, and hospital management was nonresponsive to their needs.
2. Nurses in most countries reported that their workload increased in the last year, while nursing managerial staff were eliminated or decreased.
3. Nurses in the United States, Canada, and Germany reported that they often spent considerable time on non-nursing-skill duties (e.g., cleaning rooms and transporting food trays), while many tasks that are markers of good patient care (e.g., oral hygiene and skin care) were left undone.
4. Nurses reported concerns about the quality of patient care. Only 1 in 9 nurses in Germany, and 1 in 3 in other countries, rated the quality of nursing care on their unit as excellent. Nurses in the United States and Canada were most likely to report that the quality of care provided deteriorated in the last year.
5. Many nurses were dissatisfied, experienced burnout, and were intent on leaving nursing.

Interestingly, nurses reported positive feelings about the quality of physicians and nurses with whom they worked, and about physician–nurse interactions. Their complaints focused on problematic working conditions and their negative effects on quality of patient care.

ADVANCED PRACTICE PROVIDERS

Two key problems in health care today are very high health care costs and a critical shortage of primary care physicians, especially in rural and inner-city areas. One response to both problems was the creation of several **advanced practice providers (APPs)**. These positions include several advanced practice nursing positions—the **nurse practitioner (NP)**, the **certified nurse-midwife (CNM)**, and the **certified registered nurse-anesthetist (CRNA)**—and the **physician assistant (PA)**. APPs offer several benefits to the health care system. They provide many direct care services to patients (and are critically important in areas with physician shortages), they enable physicians with whom they work to see from 20 to 50 percent more patients, they are cost-efficient because they charge less than physicians, and many research studies have found that they offer high-quality services that are appreciated by patients.

Advanced Practice Registered Nurses

Nurse Practitioners. A nurse practitioner (NP) is a registered nurse with a graduate degree in advanced practice nursing. All NPs must complete a master's degree beyond the RN, and some obtain additional degrees (e.g., DNP or PhD). NPs undertake about 70–80 percent of the basic primary and preventive care offered by physicians. They conduct physical examinations, order and interpret diagnostic tests, and diagnose and treat acute and chronic conditions. They also provide patient counseling and health education (American Association of Nurse Practitioners, 2019). In 2018 there were more than 179,000 NPs employed in the United States, and slightly more than 50 percent of them were working in primary care (most often in hospital inpatient and outpatient settings, private practice, primary care settings, and school settings). The number of NPs is expected to increase rapidly in the future. In 2018, the median salary of NPs was approximately US$110,030 (US Bureau of Labor Statistics, 2019).

NPs are licensed by the state in which they practice, are governed by state nurse practice acts, and must pass a national certification exam. State policies vary, but in 22 states and Washington, DC, NPs can practice without physician supervision. The remaining states limit NP practice by restricting practice settings and/or requiring NPs to be managed by or collaborate with a physician in order for the NP to provide patient care (American Association of Nurse Practitioners, 2019). All states give NPs some prescriptive privileges, although several states require that a physician cosign or approve NP prescriptions.

Professional associations of NPs, including the American Association of Nurse Practitioners (AANP), advocate for fewer practice restrictions and more consistent practice regulations across states. The American Medical Association and the professional associations for several medical specialties have taken the position that NPs should not be permitted to practice independently, and that physician supervision is an important quality control.

Multiple studies demonstrate that NPs provide care equivalent to that provided by physicians. In a recent review of ten studies using random assignment of patients to either NPs or physicians in a primary care setting, Swan and colleagues (2015) concluded that NPs perform as well or better than physicians in terms of clinical outcomes and patient satisfaction, and that NPs spend more time with patients. Moreover,

because NPs in primary care settings are more likely than primary care physicians to work in traditionally underserved urban and rural areas and to treat Medicaid patients and other vulnerable populations, increasing the number of NPs is likely to increase access to primary health care for underserved populations (Buerhaus et al., 2015).

Certified Nurse-Midwives. A certified nurse-midwife (CNM) is a registered nurse who has additional nationally accredited training (usually 18 months to 2 years) in midwifery (all programs are located in a college or university), and who possesses certification by the American College of Nurse-Midwives. A national certification exam must be completed. A CNM degree is typically at the master's level. CNMs receive extensive training in gynecological care, taking histories, performing physical examinations, and monitoring care, especially as it relates to pregnancy and childbirth. Restrictive practice acts limit autonomous CNM practice in some states, but all 50 states and Washington, DC provide at least some statutory prescriptive authority for CNMs. Most states now require private health insurers to reimburse nurse-midwives, and all states provide reimbursement for treating Medicaid patients.

Approximately 6,250 CNMs were employed in the United States in 2018 in hospitals, physician offices, managed care networks, or private (including group) practice. The median annual salary of CNMs was US$106,910 (US Bureau of Labor Statistics, 2019).

Despite considerable disagreement between lay-midwives and nurse-midwives, and debate over home versus hospital deliveries, nurse-midwifery has experienced significant growth since the 1980s. In 1985, the Institute of Medicine recommended that programs serving high-risk mothers use more certified nurse-midwives, and that state laws support nurse-midwifery practice.

In 1986 the Congressional Office of Technology Assessment concluded that CNMs manage routine pregnancies safely, noting that CNMs are more likely than physicians to test for urinary tract infections and diabetes, but less inclined to prescribe drugs; that CNMs are less likely to rely on technology, but communicate and interact more with their patients; and that patients of CNMs spend less time waiting for visits, have shorter hospitalizations and are more likely to feel satisfied with their care.

(Rooks, 1990:34)

Despite serving higher-risk mothers (i.e., those more likely to be young, unmarried, foreign-born, and non-white, and less likely to receive adequate prenatal care), midwife-attended births have better-than-average outcomes (Gabay and Wolfe, 1997) and higher patient satisfaction rates (Sutcliffe et al., 2012). CNMs delivered 9 percent of babies born in the United States in 2017 (Martin et al., 2018). Worldwide, midwives deliver about 70 percent of all births.

Certified Registered Nurse–Anesthetists. Nurses have a long history of providing anesthesia to patients in the United States prior to the establishment of anesthesiology as a medical specialty. In the Civil War and World War I, nurses, not doctors, provided the bulk of anesthesia services to soldiers in need. The first nurse anesthetist school offering a master's degree was established in 1909 in Portland, Oregon, and in 1931, the first professional association—since renamed the American Association of Nurse Anesthetists or AANA—was formed (Matsusaki and Sakai, 2011).

Today's certified registered nurse-anesthetists (CRNAs) are registered nurses with a master's degree from an accredited program (taking 2–3 years) who have passed a national certification exam. They are fully qualified to perform anesthesiology in all 50 states, and frequently work as licensed independent practitioners (AANA, 2019).

Federal law requires physician supervision of CRNAs unless a state submits a written letter by the governor to opt out of the requirement in the best interest of state citizens. To date 17 states have opted out, and others are considering doing so. Some states, such as California and Missouri, have passed legislation specifically stating that supervision is not required, but physician associations are seeking to overturn these laws. No state requires supervision specifically by an anesthesiologist (AANA, 2019). Studies have not detected any harm to patients when CNRAs work without physician supervision (Dulisse and Cromwell, 2010).

CRNAs administer more than 45 million anesthetics in the United States each year, are the only providers in rural hospitals in some states, and are the primary providers in many military situations (AANA, 2019). Studies fail to demonstrate any significant differences in patient outcomes for CRNAs versus medical anesthesiologists, but CRNAs are more cost-effective (Hogan et al., 2010).

As of 2018, there were 43,500 CRNAs in the United States with a median salary of US$167,950 (US Department of Labor Statistics, 2019), making nurse-anesthesiology the highest paid nursing specialty. It also has the highest proportion of men of any nursing specialty (41 percent of CRNAs in 2017 were men) (Smiley et al., 2018), providing further evidence of the glass escalator.

Physician Assistants. Under the direct or indirect supervision of a physician, a physician assistant (PA) can offer most of the basic care provided by physicians, including performing physical examinations, monitoring and treating minor ailments, counseling, and prescribing some medications. PAs act under laws within their state of practice, but all must pass a national certification exam. PAs must have a formal relationship with a collaborative physician supervisor. The physician supervisor must also be licensed in the state in which the PA is working, but physician supervision can be done in person, by telecommunication, or simply by being available for consultation.

PAs and PA programs of study were created by physicians in the 1960s as a competency-based program emphasizing proficiency in clinical skills as the entrance criteria, rather than a minimum degree (i.e., a baccalaureate or master's). Their goal was twofold—to offer a shorter, more efficient route to practice than that of MDs in order to fulfill primary care needs of underserved populations in rural and urban areas, and to free up physician's time for complicated patient care by having PAs handle routine patient care (Cawley, 2007).

Despite their initial competency-based focus, most PAs programs today require a baccalaureate degree for admission and award the master's degree, which has become the most common degree for new PAs entering practice (Jones, 2007; US Bureau of Labor Statistics, 2019). Programs of study are typically 2 years, and a national certification exam is required for licensure.

There were 114,710 PAs employed in the United States in 2018, and employment prospects are expected to increase significantly in the coming years. PAs work in all medical specialties, including primary care, surgery, anesthesiology, pathology, orthopedics, and radiology. Although nurse practitioners are primarily women, about 33 percent of PAs are men (Coplan, Smith, and Cawley, 2017). The median salary of PAs in 2018 was US$108,610 (US Bureau of Labor Statistics, 2019).

The professional autonomy of PAs is more limited than that of NPs. All states and Washington, DC, allow PAs to provide medical services, but only under physician supervision. PAs may prescribe medications in all 50 states and Washington, DC, although some states limit what drugs they may prescribe (Kaiser Family Foundation, 2015). All government insurance programs and most private insurers pay for PA services.

Analysts have concluded that PAs are competent in taking social and medical histories and in performing physical examinations, and that quality of care is not decreased when they provide these services. Several studies have found high levels of satisfaction with the care offered by PAs. With the average cost of PA care ranging from one-quarter to one-half

There are over 100,000 physician assistants in the United States. They work under the supervision of a physician, but are able to provide most primary care services.

that of physicians, there is obvious potential for expanding PA care within the health care system (Jones, 2007).

ALLIED HEALTH WORKERS

A majority of the health care workforce are allied health personnel. Although there is some controversy about this specific term, it includes a wide variety of non-physician and non-nursing health care workers. These providers work in all types of care and in all settings, including physicians' and dentists' offices, HMOs, laboratories, clinics, ambulance services, home care, and hospitals. Depending on the particular field, allied health practitioners require varying amounts of education and training, and they work with widely differing degrees of autonomy, dependence on technology, and regulation.

Table 10.2 lists the allied health fields accredited by the Commission on Accreditation of Allied Health Education Programs (CAAHEP). Many of these occupations have several levels of certification, so the prerequisites and length of training vary considerably even within fields.

Many other health fields have developed around particular technologies or techniques that require specialized knowledge and training. These include positions related to physical therapy, occupational therapy, radiological therapy, speech therapy, and diagnostic imaging fields such as nuclear medicine technology (NMT), magnetic resonance imaging (MRI), computed axial tomography (CAT), and medical laboratory technology. Although physicians continue to do some of these procedures, it is more efficient to employ specialized workers. Many of these workers (e.g., nuclear medicine technologists) perform diagnostic tests, which are then interpreted by physicians.

TABLE 10.2   Commission on Accreditation of Allied Health Education Programs (CAAHEP) Health Science Fields

Fields

Advanced cardiovascular sonography	Anesthesia technology
Anesthesiologist assistant	Art therapy
Assistive technology	Cardiovascular technology
Clinical research	Cytotechnology
Diagnostic medical sonography	Emergency medical services—paramedic
Exercise physiology	Exercise science
Intraoperative neurophysiological monitoring	Kinesiotherapy
Lactation consultant	Medical assisting
Medical illustration	Medical scribe specialist
Neurodiagnostic technology	Orthoptics
Orthotic and prosthetic technician	Orthotic/prosthetic assistant
Orthotist/Prosthetist	Pedorthist
Perfusion	Personal fitness training
Polysomnographic technology	Recreational therapy
Rehabilitation disability studies	Specialist blood bank technology/transfusion
Surgical assisting	Surgical technology

Source: Commission on Accreditation of Allied Health Education Programs, Profession Description and Certification Information. 2019. Retrieved June 30, 2019 (www.caahep.org/Students/Program-Info.aspx).

THE HEALTH CARE TEAM

The Concept of a Health Care Team

During the last few decades, the **health care team** approach has become commonplace in health care institutions. In practice, the concept of "team" is used in many different ways: (1) to describe a group of highly competent technical specialists, subspecialists, and supporting personnel who work together to execute some dramatic, intense, and usually short-term activity (e.g., a neurosurgery team); (2) to refer to the cooperation of technically oriented providers (e.g., physician specialists) with socially and/or behaviorally oriented providers (e.g., social workers); and (3) to simply refer to a less hierarchical and more egalitarian mode of health care organization and decision making (especially among physician and non-physician providers).

The primary objectives of team care are to avoid duplication and fragmentation of services and develop better and more comprehensive health plans by including more perspectives. Ideally, this occurs through a group process involving cooperation and coordination. Research shows the existence of a "teamwork culture" in a hospital is related to greater feelings of patient satisfaction (Meterko, Mohr, and Young, 2004).

Perceptions of the Team Approach

The team approach developed in earnest in medicine in the last 20 years.

> Health care has not always been recognized as a team sport, as we have recently come to think of it. In the "good old days," people were cared for by one all-knowing doctor who lived in the community, visited the home, and was available to attend to needs at any time of day or night. If nursing care was needed, it was often provided by family members, or in the case of a family of means, by a private-duty nurse who "lived in." Although this conveyed elements of teamwork, health care has changed enormously since then and the pace has quickened even more dramatically in the past 20 years. The rapidity of change will continue to accelerate as both clinicians and patients integrate new technologies into their management of wellness, illness, and complicated aging. The clinician operating in isolation is now seen as undesirable in health care—a lone ranger, a cowboy, an individual who works long and hard to provide the care needed, but whose dependence on solitary resources and perspective may put the patient at risk.
> (Mitchell et al., 2012:1–2)

Enthusiasm for the team approach remains high among many—though not all—health care workers and patients. Temkin-Greener conducted interviews with 12 department heads in a large medical center and teaching hospital to explore how leaders in nursing and medicine understand and define the team concept, its purposes, and its goals. Physicians and nurses differed in their views of health care teams. Physicians often viewed teamwork as "a nursing concept, beneficial primarily to nursing and used to 'usurp' the traditional authority of medicine" (Temkin-Greener, 1983:647), whereas nurses imputed considerable value to the team approach but believed medicine was closed to the concept unless it was imposed from outside (e.g., by the Joint Commission for Accreditation of Hospitals).

Tempkin-Greener interprets these divergent attitudes as evidence of two cultures. Medicine "emphasizes the status quo of its traditional authority and inherently hierarchical mode of organization and function," while nursing "stresses a more egalitarian vision of power relations with collaboration and peer cooperation as prerequisites for team care provision" (Temkin-Greener, 1983:647). Although the team approach is likely to remain part of health care delivery, these varying perceptions indicate that the approach is still evolving and difficulties remain.

Nuclear medicine is one of several high-technology imaging fields that offer enhanced diagnostic abilities. This patient is working with a cardiac nuclear technologist.

Source: Photo by Gregory Weiss.

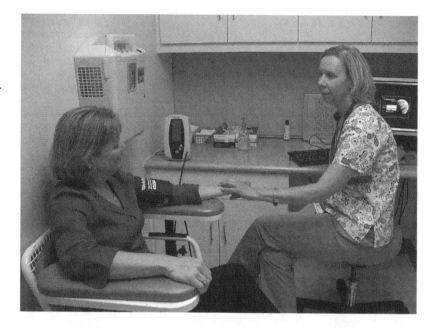

In many health care settings, a "team" of health care professionals works together to offer comprehensive care. "Medical homes" that are structured around physician-led teams are becoming increasingly popular.

The "Medical Home"

One popular approach to providing comprehensive "team-based" medical care is the **medical home** or patient-centered medical home. A medical home is a physician-led team that includes nurses, nurse practitioners, physician assistants, health educators, and others working together to provide comprehensive primary care. The model aims to provide better coordinated care that is more family centered and accessible.

Ideally, patients receive more time with team members than they would with just a primary care physician, with interaction focusing on prevention and education as well as diagnosis and treatment. The medical home philosophy also emphasizes that patients be treated with respect, dignity, and compassion, and that strong and trusting relationships be developed between providers and patients.

Although the concept dates back to 1967, a variety of professional physician associations issued a report in 2007 that advanced a vision of the medical home for reforming primary care. Since then, the popularity of medical homes has increased rapidly. By 2017, nearly half of family physicians were in a practice recognized as a medical home and another 5 percent were in practices seeking medical home status. Early assessment of clinical outcomes, costs, and patient satisfaction is favorable (Patient-Centered Primary Care Collaborative, 2018). The Affordable Care Act provided funding for pilot programs for several medical home configurations. With the current shortage of primary care physicians, the medical home may have added utility.

Accountable Care Organizations

The Affordable Care Act also encouraged the formation of accountable care organizations (ACOs), similar to medical homes. ACOs involve a variety of medical providers coming together to offer well-coordinated and high-quality care and to lower costs by reducing unnecessary tests and treatment. This is accomplished by changing the method of provider compensation. Rather than being paid for each office visit, test, and procedure—as in most of the current system—an ACO is rewarded for keeping patients healthy and working with patients to avoid unnecessary services. This gives medical providers and patients an incentive to be cost-conscious. By 2017, 32 million Americans received care through an ACO (Patient-Centered Primary Care Collaborative, 2018).

RELATIONSHIPS AMONG HEALTH CARE WORKERS

The delivery of health care services involves an extensive and interdependent network of personnel. Each position carries certain expectations for practitioners as well as for those with whom they interact. These positions typically are arranged in a hierarchy of status based on prestige and power, and these status arrangements significantly affect the dynamics of interaction among personnel throughout health care. The following section examines the relationship among physicians and other medical providers discussed in this chapter.

Physician-Nurse Relationships

Of all the interactions among health care workers, the relationship between nurses and physicians has received the most attention (Gordon, 2005). To understand this relationship historically, Keddy et al. (1986) interviewed 34 older nurses who had worked and/or trained in the 1920s and 1930s about their interactions with physicians. They recalled that 50 years prior, physicians were primarily in control of nursing education, giving many of the lectures and examinations, serving on registration boards, and controlling the hiring of nurses. The role of the nurse was defined in terms of efficient compliance with the physician's orders rather than patient care responsibilities. Early in training, student nurses were taught the hierarchy of hospital personnel and proper conduct in the presence of physicians. They were expected to show respect to physicians by standing at attention when physicians were present, and were taught never to make direct recommendations regarding patient care and never to suggest diagnoses to the physician. Although nurses had ideas, they did not voice them. For carrying out this role, these nurses believed that the doctors admired and respected them.

These dynamics persisted, and in 1967, Leonard Stein coined the phrase "the doctor–nurse game" to describe these relationships. According to this game, physicians and nurses agree that their relationship is hierarchical, that physicians are superordinate, and that this structure must be maintained. While nurses can make recommendations to physicians, their suggestions must appear to be initiated by the physician, and open disagreements must be avoided at all costs.

These norms governing doctor–nurse interactions are strikingly similar to gendered roles within traditional marriage, and are linked historically to the gendered hierarchy Nightingale advocated in the Victorian era. According to Hughes (2017:8), gender is "both a resource and liability for nursing; it justifies the occupation's claims to jurisdiction over caring work but consigns it to a subordinate position *vis-à-vis* medicine."

In 1990, Stein and colleagues revisited the doctor–nurse game. They described a changing milieu that encouraged a new type of physician–nurse relationship, including a decline in public esteem for physicians, increased questioning of the profession's devotion to altruistic concerns, and a greater recognition of physicians' fallibility. By 1990, physicians were increasingly likely to be women, and although women physicians are trained to play the same game as men, "the elements of the game that reflect stereotypical roles of male dominance and female submissiveness are missing" (Stein, Watts, and Howell, 1990:546). The nursing shortage at the time also restructured nurse–physician interaction by focusing attention on the value of nurses, especially as they became more highly trained and specialized. The study authors speculated that feelings of colleagueship might replace the typical hierarchical relationship between superior and subordinate.

For these reasons, and partly in response to the women's movement, nurses now seek greater equality with physicians and autonomy in defining their own roles. In addition, nursing education, which is increasingly located in academic settings, is socializing nursing students to relate to physicians differently than in the past. Most nurses are no longer willing to stand aside as subordinates.

This has provoked mixed reactions among physicians—while some physicians are supportive of nurses' attempts to become more professional and autonomous, others believe nurses are no longer doing their jobs. For example, in response to the "Revisited" piece, the editorial section of the *New England Journal of Medicine* published several letters from physicians defending an ongoing status differential between themselves and nurses (Lewis, 1990). Physicians argued that nurses are not equal partners with physicians because they are not as highly educated, are less technically proficient, and are not autonomous since they lack ultimate responsibility for patient treatment.

Campbell-Heider and Pollock (1987:423) caution that nurses' expectations that their status will be enhanced through increased knowledge and skills fail to consider the deeply rooted gender hierarchy in medical care: "It is clear that the social control of nurses (and women) has enabled physicians to increase their own status and that the maintenance of female stereotypes has increased the power differentials between gender groups."

Prescott and Bowen (1985) conducted an extensive study of dynamics within the physician–nurse relationship. In contrast to studies documenting problems in physician–nurse relationships, they found considerable satisfaction among both groups (69 percent of nurses and 70 percent of physicians described their relationships as positive), although each differed in their descriptions of the elements of and factors contributing to good relationships. Nurses emphasized mutual respect and trust as the most important elements of a good relationship, and considered it important that physicians regard them as intelligent resources who should be involved in planning and decision making related to patient care. For physicians, the most important elements of a good relationship with nurses were how well the nurse communicated with the physician, the nurse's willingness to help the physician, and the nurse's competency.

They also examined areas of disagreement between physicians and nurses. Nurses disagreed most often with physicians about the general plan of care, specific orders, and patient movement (from unit to unit, and the timing of discharge). Physicians were concerned about nurses taking actions they considered to be outside nurses' domain, making poor clinical decisions, and not following specific physician orders. Approximately half of the physicians and one-third of the nurses reported that disagreements were handled through the medical chain of command, but final authority almost always rested with the physician.

More recently, McGrail et al. (2009) found that physicians and nurses, especially novices in both fields, often entered a care episode feeling worried, inadequate, or uncertain. Such feelings often triggered greater physician–nurse collaboration, which led to feelings of satisfaction, being understood, and appreciation for their colleagues. These experiences helped physicians and nurses alike to gain "collaborative competence"—skills interacting with and relating to others. This suggests that the kinds of orientations and demeanors that have been off-putting in physician–nurse collaboration might be at least somewhat amenable to education and training.

Despite the benefits of meaningful collaboration among physicians and nurses, Leape et al. (2012) remain skeptical about the potential for change in physician–nurse relationships. Despite its negative effect on patient care, they describe the existence of a dysfunctional medical culture in which physicians act disrespectfully toward nurses, residents, and students. They attribute this culture to physicians' belief in individual privilege and their own autonomy. Such a culture impairs open communication with nurses and other members of the care team and creates

distance from patients. It also helps explain physician resistance to following safety protocols.

The Relationship Between Physicians and Advanced Practice Providers

Physicians and advanced practice providers work cooperatively and with mutual respect in many (but not all) situations. In general, physicians are most comfortable with practitioners who clearly supplement their own work and are restricted from practicing without physician supervision. For this reason, physicians have more amicable relationships with physician assistants (who typically work for physicians and under their supervision) than with nurse practitioners (who are sometimes seen as competitors for patients seeking primary care), CRNAs and CNMs (who work independently and are reimbursed directly).

The most heated point of contention is the extent to which APRNs should be able to practice independently. For years, nurse practitioners have played an increasing role in the health care system. Many states have passed legislation to enable NPs to assume an even larger share of primary care responsibilities. Nurses' associations contend that the 2 to 4 years of training beyond the nurses' degree should qualify APRNs to serve as primary care providers without physician supervision. In addition, nursing associations believe that, where necessary, state laws should be changed to enable APRNs to receive direct reimbursement from public and private insurance and have extensive—if not complete—legal authority to write prescriptions.

The AMA vehemently opposes these changes. It contends that the additional training required of physicians makes them the most effective providers of health care services, and the only group sufficiently knowledgeable about pharmacology to have full prescription-writing authority. An AMA report issued in late 1993 stated that "substitution for, rather than extension of, physician care by non-physicians raises questions of patient safety, competence of therapeutic decision, fragmentation of care and delays to patients in need of medical care" (Burda, 1993:6).

Several studies have documented communication problems between physicians and advanced practice providers. One intriguing study analyzed interaction patterns of resident physicians and CNMs working in an obstetrical training program at a major medical center (Graham, 1991). The faculty and administration envisioned two separate but equal services, with CNMs responsible for low-risk patients and normal vaginal deliveries and residents responsible for high-risk patients and difficult labors and deliveries. In fact, what emerged were competing and often conflicting systems that potentially jeopardized patient care. Because 70 percent of the residents and all the CNMs were women, Graham concluded that gender differences did not account for the friction. Instead, the primary problems were the absence of a formally articulated structure for interaction and differing perceptions of group status. CNMs saw themselves as professionals who had completed their training and acquired many years of experience. They

regarded residents as inexperienced apprentices. However, residents regarded themselves as "doctors" and the midwives as "nurses," stressing their own extended training, abilities to perform procedures that the CNMs could not, and longer working hours. Differing treatment philosophies also contributed to the problem. The midwives considered their emphasis on the individual and the use of noninterventionism superior to what they regarded as the impersonal, interventionist philosophy of residents.

THE CHANGING ENVIRONMENT AMONG HEALTH CARE WORKERS

Relationships among physicians, nurses, advanced practice providers, and allied health personnel must be viewed as a constantly evolving and dynamic process. This process is governed not only by factors internal to each field—such as changing education requirements and a search for autonomy—but also by changes in the wider health care system (such as the Affordable Care Act), the economy, and society (Hartley, 1999).

SUMMARY

The numbers and types of health care workers in the United States have changed significantly in the past 200 years. With these changes has come a complex bureaucracy to regulate and control millions of providers working in numerous health care settings.

The field of nursing is undergoing significant change. No longer content to be silent and obedient assistants to physicians, nurses have sought to professionalize the field through increased educational requirements and greater assertiveness. While in most cases nursing does not offer genuine autonomy—an important prerequisite for a profession—the field does have much in common with professions. Nurses have become

more centrally involved in the direct provision of health care.

Advanced practice providers—nurse practitioners, certified nurse-midwives, certified registered nurse-anesthetists, and physician assistants—occupy important roles in the health care system. While their ability to practice independent of physician supervision varies, all perform services once provided by physicians, and at lower cost. These practitioners deliver high-quality services and earn high patient satisfaction ratings. Relationships with physicians vary, but physicians' attitudes are more positive when advanced practice providers have less autonomy.

Scientific and technological advancements led to the development of a wide variety of allied health positions that have become essential parts of the overall health care system. These personnel perform diagnostic work that is interpreted by physicians, and provide some therapeutic modalities and rehabilitative care.

HEALTH ON THE INTERNET

What is it really like to be a hospital nurse? While this chapter provides insight into the nursing profession as whole, interviews with nurses can reveal much about the day-to-day experience of being a nurse. CNBC recently ran an interview with nurse Victoria Pasha of New York-Presbyterian Hospital in New York City. Watch the short video of the interview (or read the transcript):

www.cnbc.com/2019/04/02/a-day-in-the-life-of-a-registered-nurse-at-newyork-presbyterian.html

What features of nursing discussed in the chapter can you identify in Pasha's story? Identify and describe at least four similarities between issues discussed in the text and Pasha's interview. Did anything about Pasha's experience surprise you?

DISCUSSION QUESTION

As described in this chapter, some health care workers (most often nurses and allied health workers) have unionized. Ostensibly, unions are a bargaining force for increased salaries and benefits, job security, and greater say in management decisions. However, these unions very often threaten to strike or go on strike regarding patient safety and quality of patient care issues. Unions derive much of their power from the willingness of members to strike if they feel they have not been treated fairly by management.

Suppose you heard that all the hospital-based nurses in your community presented a list of grievances (lower-than-average salaries, inadequate benefits, little workplace autonomy, reduction in staff, and patient care being compromised) to the administrative officers of the hospitals, who refused to consider them. In response, nurses are forming a union to establish stronger bargaining power. The nurses have indicated that they will consider a general strike if their requests (demands?) are not met.

Should health care workers have the same rights as other workers to unionize, and, if they deem it necessary, to strike? Are health care occupations qualitatively "different" from other occupations because of their role working in life-and-death situations? If nurses cannot unionize or strike, what options do they have in terms of bargaining for better conditions?

Is your position the same or different with regard to the right of physicians to unionize, to collectively bargain, and if deemed necessary, to strike? Under what conditions, if any, do you think a physicians' strike would be justifiable?

GLOSSARY

advanced practice providers (APPs)
advanced practice registered nurses (APRNs)

allied health workers
certified nurse-midwife (CNM)

certified registered nurse-anesthetist (CRNA)
differentiated practice
glass escalator
health care team
licensed practical nurse (LPN)

medical home
nurse practitioner (NP)
physician assistant (PA)
registered nurse (RN)

REFERENCES

Aiken, Linda H. 2011. "Nurses for the Future." *New England Journal of Medicine* 364(3):196–198.

Aiken, Linda H., Sean P. Clarke, Douglas M. Sloane, Julie A. Stochalski, Reinhard Busse, Heath Clarke, Phyllis Giovannetti, Jennifer Hunt, Anne Marie Rafferty, and Judith Shamian. 2001. "Nurses' Reports on Hospital Care in Five Countries." *Health Affairs* 20(3):43–53.

Aiken, Linda H., Douglas M. Sloane, Jeannie P. Cimiotti, Sean P. Clarke, Linda Flynn, Jean A. Seago, Joanne Spetz, and Herbert L. Smith. 2010. "Implications of the California Nurse Staffing Mandate for Other States." *Health Services Research* 45(4):904–921.

American Association of Colleges of Nursing. 2019a. *2018–2019 Enrollment and Graduations in Baccalaureate and Graduate Programs in Nursing.* Washington, DC: American Association of Colleges of Nursing.

———. 2019b. "DNP Fact Sheet." Retrieved June 12, 2019 (www.aacnnursing.org/News-Information/Fact-Sheets/DNP-Fact-Sheet).

———. 2019c. "Latest Data on Race and Ethnicity." Retrieved June 12, 2019 (www.aacnnursing.org/News-Information/Research-Data).

American Association of Nurse Anesthetists. 2019. "CRNA Fact Sheet." Retrieved June 16, 2019 (www.aana.com/membership/become-a-crna/crna-fact-sheet).

American Association of Nurse Practitioners. 2019. "Practice Information by State." Retrieved June 16, 2019 (www.aanp.org/practice/practice-information-by-state).

Auerbach, David I., Peter I. Buerhaus, and Douglas O. Staiger. 2011. "Registered Nurse Supply Grows Faster Than Projected Amid Surge in New Entrants Ages 23–26." *Health Affairs* 30(12):2286–2292.

Baer, Ellen D. 1990. "Nurses." Pp. 459–475 in *Women, Health, and Medicine in America: A Historical Handbook*, edited by Rima D. Apple. New York: Garland Publishing, Inc.

Bakhamis, Lama, David Paul, Harlan Smith, and Alberto Coustasse. 2019. "Still an Epidemic: The Burnout Syndrome in Hospital Registered Nurses." *The Health Care Manager* 38(1):3–10.

Brenan, Megan. 2018. "Nurses Again Outpace Other Professions for Honesty, Ethics." Retrieved June 12, 2019 (https://news.gallup.com/poll/245597/nurses-again-outpace-professions-honesty-ethics.aspx).

Buerhaus, Peter I., Catherine M. DesRoches, Robert Dittus, and Karen Donelan. 2015. "Practice Characteristics of Primary Care Nurse Practitioners and Physicians." *Nursing Outlook* 63(2):144–153.

Buerhaus, Peter I., Lucy E. Skinner, David I. Auerbach, and Douglas O. Staiger. 2017. "Four Challenges Facing the Nursing Workforce in the United States." *Journal of Nursing Regulation* 8(2):40–46.

Burda, David. 1993. "AMA Report Slams Practice of Using Nurses, Not Doctors, as Primary Care Providers." *Modern Healthcare* 23:6.

Bureau of Labor Statistics, United States Department of Labor. 2019. "Occupational Outlook Handbook." Retrieved June 12, 2019 (www.bls.gov/ooh/home.htm).

Campbell-Heider, Nancy, and Donald Pollock. 1987. "Barriers to Physician-Nurse Collegiality: An Anthropological Perspective." *Social Science and Medicine* 25(5):421–425.

Cawley, James F. 2007. "Physician Assistant Education: An Abbreviated History." *Journal of Physician Assistant Education* 18(3):6–15.

Chambliss, Daniel. 1996. *Beyond Caring: Hospitals, Nurses, and the Social Organization of Ethics.* Chicago, IL: University of Chicago Press.

Commission on Accreditation of Allied Health Education Programs. 2019. "Profession Description and Certification Information." Retrieved June 30, 2019 (www.caahep.org/Students/Program-Info.aspx).

Coplan, Bettie, Noel Smith, and James F. Cawley. 2017. "PAs in Primary Care: Current Status and Workforce Implications." *Journal of the American Academy of PAs* 30(9):35–42.

Cottingham, Marci. 2014. "Recruiting Men, Constructing Manhood: How Health Care Organizations Mobilize Masculinities as Nursing Recruitment Strategy." *Gender & Society* 28(1):133–156.

Davis, Fred. 1972. *Illness, Interaction, and the Self.* Belmont, CA: Wadsworth.

DeVries, Raymond G. 1985. *Regulating Birth: Midwives, Medicine, and the Law.* Philadelphia, PA: Temple University Press.

Dulisse, Brian, and Jerry Cromwell. 2010. "No Harm Found When Nurse Anesthetists Work without Supervision by Physicians." *Health Affairs* 29(8):1469–1475.

Eddy, Diane M., Victoria Elfrink, Darlene Weis, and Mary J. Schank. 1994. "Importance of Professional Nursing Values: A National Study of Baccalaureate Programs." *Journal of Nursing Education* 33(6):257–262.

Evans, Joan. 2004. "Men Nurses: A Historical and Feminist Perspective." *Journal of Advanced Nursing* 47(3):321–328.

Fang, Di, and Karen Kesten. 2017. "Retirements and Succession of Nursing Faculty in 2016–2025." *Nursing Outlook* 65(5):633–642.

Gabay, Mary, and Sidney M. Wolfe. 1997. "Nurse-Midwifery: The Beneficial Alternative." *Public Health Reports* 112(5):386–394.

Germack, Hayley D., Matthew D. McHugh, Douglas M. Sloane, and Linda H. Aiken. 2017. "U.S. Hospital Employment of Foreign-Educated Nurses and Patient Experience: A Cross-Sectional Study." *Journal of Nursing Regulation* 8(3):26–35.

Glazer, Nona Y. 1991. "'Between a Rock and a Hard Place': Women's Professional Organizations in Nursing and Class, Racial, and Ethnic Inequalities." *Gender and Society* 5(3):351–372.

Gordon, Suzanne. 2005. *Nursing Against the Odds: How Health Care Cost Cutting, Media Stereotypes, and Medical Hubris Undermine Nurses and Patient Care.* Ithaca, NY: Cornell University Press.

Graham, Susan B. 1991. "A Structural Analysis of Physician-Midwife Interaction in an Obstetrical Training Program." *Social Science and Medicine* 32(8):931–942.

Griffiths, Peter, Chiara Dall'Ora, Michael Simon, Jane Ball, Rikard Lindqvist, Anne-Marie Rafferty, Lisette Schoonhoven, Carol Tishelman, and Linda H. Aiken. 2014. "Nurses' Shift Length and Overtime Working in 12 European Countries: The Association with Perceived Quality of Care and Patient Safety." *Medical Care* 52(11):975–981.

Hartley, Heather. 1999. "The Influence of Managed Care on Supply of Certified Nurse-Midwives: An Evaluation of the Physician Dominance Thesis." *Journal of Health and Social Behavior* 40(1):87–101.

Hogan, Paul F., Rita Furst Seifert, Carol S. Moore, and Brian E. Simonson. 2010. "Cost Effectiveness Analysis of Anesthesia Providers." *Nursing Economics* 28(3):159–169.

Hughes, David. 2017. "Nursing and the Division of Labour: Sociological Perspectives." Pp. 1–22 in *Nursing and the Division of Labour in Healthcare,* edited by Davina Allen and David Hughes. New York: Palgrave Macmillan.

Institute of Medicine. 2011. *The Future of Nursing: Leading Change, Advancing Health.* Washington, DC: National Academy of Sciences.

Jones, Cheryl B., and Gwen Sherwood. 2014. "The Globalization of the Nursing Workforce: Pulling the Pieces Together." *Nursing Outlook* 62(1):59–63.

Jones, Eugene P. 2007. "Physician Assistant Education in the United States." *Academic Medicine* 82(9):882.

Kaiser Family Foundation. 2015. "Physician Assistant Scope of Practice Laws." Retrieved June 17, 2019 (www.kff.org/other/state-indicator/physician-assistant-scope-of-practice-laws/).

Keddy, Barbara, Margaret J. Gillis, Pat Jacobs, Heather Burton, and Maureen Rogers. 1986. "The Doctor-Nurse Relationship: An Historical Perspective." *Journal of Advanced Nursing* 11(6):745–753.

Leape, Lucian L., Miles F. Shore, Jules L. Dienstag, Robert J. Mayer, Susan Edgman-Levitan, Gregg S. Meyer, and Gerald B. Healy. 2012. "Perspective: A Culture of Respect, Part I: The Nature and Causes of Disrespectful Behavior by Physicians." *Academic Medicine* 87(7):845–852.

Lee, Geraldine, Alexander M. Clark, and David R. Thompson. 2013. "Florence Nightingale—Never More Relevant Than Today." *Journal of Advanced Nursing* 69(2):245–246.

Lewis, Mary Ann. 1990. "Correspondence: The Doctor-Nurse Game Revisited." *New England Journal of Medicine* 323(3):201–203.

Li, Yan, Michael Turinetti, and Di Fang. 2019. "Special Survey on Vacant Faculty Positions for Academic Year 2018–2019." *American Association of Colleges of Nursing.* Retrieved June 13, 2019 (www.aacnnursing.org/News-Information/Fact-Sheets/Nursing-Faculty-Shortage).

Martin, Joyce A., Brady E. Hamilton, Michelle J.K. Osterman, Anne K. Driscoll, and Patrick Drake. 2018. "Births: Final Data for 2017." *National Vital Statistics Reports* 67(8):1–50.

Matsusaki, Takashi, and Tetsuro Sakai. 2011. "The Role of Certified Registered Nurse Anesthetists in the United States." *Journal of Anesthesia* 25(5):734–740.

McClure, Margaret L. 1991. "Differentiated Nursing Practice: Concepts and Considerations." *Nursing Outlook* 39(3):106–110.

McGrail, Kathleen A., Diane S. Morse, Theresa Glessner, and Kathryn Gardner. 2009. "'What is Found There': Qualitative Analysis of Physician-Nurse Collaboration Stories." *Journal of General Internal Medicine* 24(2):198–204.

Meterko, Mark, David C. Mohr, and Gary J. Young. 2004. "Teamwork Culture and Patient Satisfaction in Hospitals." *Medical Care* 42(5):492–498.

Mitchell, Pamela, Matthew Wynia, Robyn Golden, Bob McNellis, Sally Okun, C. Edwin Webb, Valerie Rohrbach, and Isabelle V. Kohorn. 2012. *Core Principles and Values of Effective Team-Based Health Care.* Washington, DC: Institute of Medicine. Retrieved June 30, 2019 (https://nam.edu/wp-content/uploads/2015/06/VSRT-Team-Based-Care-Principles-Values.pdf).

Moore, Duncan J. 1995. "Nurses Nationwide Air Gripes Against Hospitals." *Modern Healthcare* 25(15):3.

Neff, Donna Felber, Jeannie Cimiotti, Douglas M. Sloane, and Linda H. Aiken. 2013. "Utilization of Non-US Educated Nurses in US Hospitals: Implications for Hospital Mortality." *International Journal for Quality in Health Care* 25(4):366–372.

Norrish, Barbara R., and Thomas G. Rundall. 2001. "Hospital Restructuring and the Work of Registered Nurses." *The Milbank Quarterly* 79(1):55–79.

Nursing Solutions, Inc. 2019. "2019 National Health Care Retention & RN Staffing Report." Retrieved June 13, 2019 (www.nsinursingsolutions.com).

Patient-Centered Primary Care Collaborative. 2018. "Executive Summary, Advanced Primary Care: A Key Contributor to Successful ACOs." Retrieved June 17, 2019 (www.pcpcc.org/results-evidence).

Prescott, Patricia A., and Sally A. Bowen. 1985. "Physician-Nurse Relationships." *Annals of Internal Medicine* 103(1):127–133.

Reverby, Susan M. 1987. *Ordered to Care: The Dilemma of American Nursing, 1850–1945.* Cambridge: Cambridge University Press.

Rodriguez, Adrianna, and Lorenzo Reyes. 2020. "Nurses Read Names of Colleagues Who Died of COVID-19 in Protest Outside White House." *USA TODAY.* Retrieved April 25, 2020 (https://www.usatoday.com/story/news/nation/2020/04/21/us-nurses-who-died-coronavirus-honored-white-house-protest/2996839001/).

Rooks, Judith P. 1990. "Nurse-Midwifery: The Window is Wide Open." *American Journal of Nursing* 90(12):30–36.

Smiley, Richard A., Pamela Lauer, Cynthia Bienemy, Judith G. Berg, Emilie Shireman, Kyrani A. Reneau, and Maryann Alexander. 2018. "The 2017 National Nursing Workforce." *Journal of Nursing Regulation* 9(3):S1–54.

Staiger, David O., David I. Auerbach, and Peter I. Buerhaus. 2012. "Registered Nurse Labor Supply and the Recession—Are We in a Bubble?" *New England Journal of Medicine* 366(16):1463–1465.

Starr, Paul. 1982. *The Social Transformation of American Medicine.* New York: Basic Books.

Stein, Leonard I. 1967. "The Doctor-Nurse Game." *Archives of General Psychiatry* 16(6):699–703.

Stein, Leonard I., David T. Watts, and Timothy Howell. 1990. "The Doctor-Nurse Game Revisited." *New England Journal of Medicine* 322(8):546–549.

Sutcliffe, Katy, Jenny Caird, Josephine Kavanagh, Rebecca Rees, Kathryn Oliver, Kelly Dickson, Jenny Woodman, Elaine Barnett-Paige, and James Thomas. 2012. "Comparing Midwife-Led and Doctor-Led Maternity Care: A Systematic Review of Reviews." *Journal of Advanced Nursing* 68(11):2376–2386.

Swan, Melanie, Sacha Ferguson, Alice Chang, Elaine Larson, and Arlene Smaldone. 2015. "Quality of Primary Care by Advanced Practice Nurses: A Systematic Review." *International Journal for Quality in Health Care* 27(5):396–404.

Temkin-Greener, Helena. 1983. "Interprofessional Perspectives on Teamwork in Health Care: A Case Study." *Milbank Memorial Fund Quarterly* 61(4):641–657.

Thompson, Joyce. 2003. "Quoted in Patrick Reilly, 'Importing Controversy'." *Modern Healthcare* 33:20–24.

Williams, Christine L. 1992. "The Glass Escalator: Hidden Advantages for Men in the 'Female' Professions." *Social Problems* 39(3):253–267.

Wingfield, Adia Harvey. 2009. "Racializing the Glass Escalator: Reconsidering Men's Experiences with Women's Work." *Gender & Society* 23(1):5–26.

CHAPTER 11

Complementary and Alternative Medicine

Learning Objectives

- Define "complementary and alternative medicine," and identify and describe the key characteristics they have in common.

- Discuss the extent to which CAM has become institutionalized in the United States.

- Compare and contrast the origins and historical development of the four CAM approaches examined in this chapter.

- Compare and contrast the relationship with organized medicine of the four CAM approaches examined in this chapter.

Through much of the twentieth century, the scientific medicine paradigm (as described in Chapter 2) was so dominant in the United States that it was referred to as *orthodox* or *conventional* medicine. While alternatives to medical doctors—everything from home remedies to prayer to chiropractors—were used, they were considered unorthodox or unconventional medicine. Scientific medicine has been taught almost exclusively in health courses in schools, has been the subject of public health campaigns, and has been the dominant perspective in the medical school curriculum.

THE MEANING OF COMPLEMENTARY AND ALTERNATIVE MEDICINE (CAM)

Because of scientific medicine's broad societal endorsement, it is rather remarkable that *complementary and alternative medicine (CAM)*—"health care approaches that are not typically part of conventional medical care or that may have origins outside of usual Western practice"

(National Center for Complementary and Integrative Health [NCCIH], 2019b:3)—has flourished and is now more popular than ever. The NCCIH (2019b) makes the following distinctions between key terms:

1. *Complementary medicine* is a non-mainstream practice that is used *together with* conventional medicine.
2. *Alternative medicine* is a non-mainstream practice that is used *instead of* conventional medicine.
3. *Integrative medicine* consists of practices that attempt to *integrate* mainstream and non-mainstream approaches in medicine.

Generally, CAM techniques fall into one of two categories:

1. Natural products including herbs, vitamins and minerals, and probiotics [foods or supplements that contain living microorganisms such as yogurt that can change the bacterial balance in the human body]. They are widely

marketed, readily available to consumers, and often sold as dietary supplements.
2. Mind and body practices, including acupuncture, massage therapy, meditation, movement therapies, relaxation techniques, chiropractic and osteopathic manipulation, and yoga.

In addition to these two categories, there are some whole medical systems that would be complementary or alternative to conventional American medicine. These "whole systems" include traditional Chinese healing, Ayurveda (an Indian approach emphasizing herbal medicines, mediation, and yoga), folk healing, homeopathy, and naturopathy.

Goldstein (1999) has extracted five core elements from this wide variety of CAM healing practices:

1. *Holism.* This practice involves treating the patient holistically—that is, considering the entire physical, mental, spiritual, and social makeup of the patient when diagnosing illness and providing therapeutic care.
2. *The interpenetration of mind, body, and spirit.* While most physicians today recognize the importance of the mind-body connection, CAM places great emphasis on their relationship, and generally never treats one without the other.
3. *The possibility of high-level wellness.* Health is viewed as a positive physical-emotional state, not just the absence of symptoms or clinical disease.
4. *Vitalism: life suffused by the flow of energy.* Life is viewed as a type of ecosystem in which various elements of mind, body, and spirit are united by a force or flow of energy throughout the body. (An amusing overview of the evolution of CAM is provided in the accompanying box, "A Short History of Medicine.")
5. *The healing process.* In most forms of CAM, unlike much of conventional medicine, healing is viewed as a cooperative, active process involving both healer and patient. The healer is caring and nurturant and works "with" instead of "on" patients.

Given the disdain that organized medicine has historically had for CAM (and in many cases the disdain that CAM has had for scientific medicine), the popularity of alternatives makes an important statement about many people's understanding of health and healing. In fact, Goldner (1999) argues that one reason that many patients choose a CAM technique is precisely because they feel alienated from the impersonality of conventional medicine, and they prefer a more holistic approach.

IN THE FIELD

A SHORT HISTORY OF MEDICINE

"Doctor, I have an earache."

2000 BC	"Here, eat this root."
1000 BC	"That root is heathen, say this prayer."
AD 1850	"That prayer is superstition, drink this potion."
AD 1940	"That potion is snake oil, swallow this pill."
AD 1985	"That pill is ineffective, take this antibiotic."
AD 2000	"That antibiotic is artificial. Here, eat this root."

SCIENTIFIC MEDICINE AND ALTERNATIVE HEALING

Orthodox Medicine's View of Alternative Healers

Historically, physicians justified their opposition to complementary and alternative healing practices in two ways. First, many medical doctors considered any form of "non-scientific" healing to be quackery or a danger to public health (if a harmful substance is administered or if people delay seeking conventional care). Their criticism of CAM was justified as being part of their duty to protect the public's health. Physician-critics acknowledge that some alternative healers seem to have a professional manner and appear to base their practice on well-articulated (although non-scientific) principles. However, by offering a healing practice that has not undergone rigorous scientific testing, physicians viewed alternative healers as deluding the public and risking people's health (Angell and Kassirer, 1998).

Second, physicians have expressed concern that some people are fooled into believing the claims of CAM healers. Whether due to effective advertising or to appeals made to people who have not been helped by orthodox medicine, physicians sometimes view CAM users as unable to distinguish between legitimate and illegitimate medical care (Beyerstein, 2001).

An alternative view is that organized medicine's opposition to CAM healers has been based on perceived self-interest. By persuading the public and politicians that scientific medicine is the only legitimate healing practice, its cultural authority (as described in Chapter 2) is protected. This in turn restricts competition for patients and for private and public money spent on health care. How has this been done?

One way to do so was through an educational campaign, using the vast public relations resources of the AMA [the American Medical Association] and other organizations to expose the dangers and errors of these cults. Another approach was to employ political leverage and legal muscle. Organized medicine excluded from its ranks those who espoused such systems; denied such practitioners the privilege of consultation; refused to see patients when such healers were assisting in the case; prevented such practitioners from working in or otherwise using public hospitals; went to court to prosecute them for violating existing medical practice acts; and actively opposed legislative protection for them or, when that failed, opposed allowing them any additional privileges.

(Gevitz, 1988:16–17)

This outright condemnation characterized orthodox medicine's response to CAM throughout the 1960s and early 1970s, when the profession's cultural authority was strongest. But organized medicine's response to CAM has changed in response to different social and political circumstances.

Based on an analysis of articles published in top medical journals, Winnick (2005) documented how the medical profession's response to CAM shifted away from condemnation to a period of reassessment in the late 1970s and 1980s, as medicine's cultural authority waned. As patients increasingly turned to alternative therapies, medical practitioners began to reexamine their own practices and to recognize the limitations of modern medicine and growing patient dissatisfaction with conventional therapies. Ultimately, in the 1990s, after this cultural and medical reckoning, the medical profession entered a period of integration and began evaluating and testing CAM therapies on conventional medicine's own terms, incorporating those practices with demonstrated effectiveness into scientific medicine and discrediting and eliminating ineffective ones.

Aided by the larger shift toward evidence-based medicine (discussed in Chapters 9 and 10), this new approach of integration gave medical scientists control over testing and gave CAM a veneer of social legitimacy, even if clinical trials showed some forms of CAM ineffective. In 1992, the US Senate established the Office of Alternative Medicine (OAM) within the National Institutes of Health, with a budget of US$2 million to evaluate the effectiveness of unconventional medical practices. The budget for the now-renamed National Center for Complementary and Integrative Health in 2019 was US$146.5 million, with the bulk allocated to research on various practices and to public education.

Many hospitals now offer select CAM techniques such as massage therapy and acupuncture. Health insurance policies increasingly cover care from at least some types of alternative healers, although levels of coverage vary. For example, among adults seeking acupuncture, only one-quarter had insurance that covered it and less than 10 percent had full coverage. Among adults seeking chiropractic services, 60 percent had insurance that covered the visit, with under 20 percent enjoying full coverage. And among adults seeing a massage therapist, only 15 percent had insurance that would cover it either in full or partially (Nahin, Barnes, and Stussman, 2016b).

Additionally, many medical schools have started or are developing courses on complementary and alternative therapies. A recent analysis of course offerings at US allopathic medical schools conferring the MD degree revealed that out of the 125 schools with accessible data (representing 96.2 percent of such schools), just over half (52.8 percent) offered at least one course with CAM-related content. The majority offered a single course, and only five schools required a CAM course (Cowen and Cyr, 2015). In fact, fewer allopathic medical schools are offering CAM instruction now than previous reports from the late 1990s and

early 2000s indicated, suggesting either that earlier figures were overstated or schools have reduced CAM offerings (Cowen and Cyr, 2015).

Nevertheless, the general attitude of medical doctors toward CAM has certainly softened. While some remain skeptical about approaches that have not undergone rigorous scientific testing, many now accept the value of at least some practices and routinely refer patients whom they are unable to help to CAM practitioners. Efforts are also underway to better disseminate to physicians the results of clinical trials of CAM healing practices (Tilburt et al., 2009).

CAM's View of Conventional Healers

Many practitioners and proponents of complementary and alternative healing share a similar goal with conventional medicine—to offer effective healing therapies. Their belief is that orthodox medicine has helped some people but has failed to help many others and often harms them (e.g., negative drug reactions or drug dependency).

CAM healers contend that the many people who have been helped by their practices, the high levels of patient satisfaction, and the high percentage of people who see them on a continuing basis testify to the efficacy of their treatments. They believe patients should have an unencumbered right to choose a healing practice from a variety of options, just as they have a right to choose their religion. If a particular type of healing practice is worthless, patients will soon discover that, and demand for that service will diminish. CAM healers have often asked for the right to practice without attack from organized medicine. See the box "The Ability of Teenagers to Choose a CAM."

IN THE FIELD

THE ABILITY OF TEENAGERS TO CHOOSE A CAM

In 2005, a 15-year-old Virginia teenager, Abraham Cherrix, underwent 3 months of chemotherapy for Hodgkin's disease, a type of cancer. The treatment left him so weak and so nauseated that at times he had to be carried by his father because he couldn't walk. In February 2006, when he learned that the cancer had become active once again, he refused to undergo another round of chemotherapy and radiation. He said that he did not think he could live through it. Hodgkin's is generally considered a treatable condition, and has a 5-year survival rate of about 80 percent. Due to the recurrence, Abraham's survival probability was estimated at 50 percent.

Instead, after doing significant reading, he chose a sugar-free organic diet that included large amounts of fruits and vegetables, herbs, and visits to a clinic in Mexico. This raised the issue of the age at which an individual is able to make lawful decisions for him- or herself. Abraham's parents supported his choice, saying that they believed he was a mature and thoughtful young man. In May, a judge found Abraham's parents neglectful for supporting his choice. They were ordered to give partial custody of Abraham to the County Department of Social Services, so his chemotherapy and radiation could resume. If his parents refused to comply, they would lose custody of Abraham.

In August 2006, a circuit court judge cleared the family of all charges of medical neglect and allowed them to follow their treatment choice as long as Abraham would be periodically examined by a specific board-certified oncologist in Mississippi who was experienced in alternative cancer treatments—a resolution Abraham and his parents found acceptable.

Ironically, nearly a decade after the court decision giving him the legal right to refuse conventional treatment, Abraham's recurring bouts of cancer led him to embrace conventional medical treatment and ultimately to undergo a stem-cell transplant. In 2017, he explained his decision to a reporter: "These days I have a different thinking about alternative therapies." He added, "Honestly, if I had not done this, I would have died" (Simpson, 2017). Although Abraham ultimately changed his views on the use of alternative therapies, a significant and controversial outcome of his legal battles was Virginia's passage of Abraham's law, which gives teens aged 14 and over and their parents the right to refuse medical treatments.

The case of Abraham Cherrix—shown here—raised the important question of whether mature individuals under the age of consent may choose to follow CAM rather than conventional medicine

COMPLEMENTARY AND ALTERNATIVE HEALERS

Use of Complementary and Alternative Healers

Millions of people use complementary and alternative healers every year. According to the NCCIH, more than 30 percent of American adults and about 12 percent of American children use at least one form of complementary and alternative medicine. When broader definitions of CAM are used, about half of all Americans use it. Total out-of-pocket expenditures on CAM were $30.2 billion in 2012, with visits to CAM practitioners constituting the largest expenditure ($14.7 billion), followed by natural product supplements ($12.8 billion) (Nahin, Barnes, and Stussman, 2016a). When Oxford Health Plans included use of CAM in its benefit package, between 40 and 50 percent of members saw a CAM provider in the first year (Kilgore, 1998).

Table 11.1 shows that CAM use is common across all major demographic groups. However, women are slightly more likely to use it than men, non-Hispanic whites are somewhat more likely to use CAM than non-Hispanic blacks (although use by "other" non-Hispanics is also high), and middle-aged persons are more likely to use it than other age groups. CAM use also rises with higher educational attainment. A recent study of more than 2,500 undergraduate and graduate students at Columbia University found that nearly 82 percent reported using at least one form of CAM in the last 12 months. Among the commonly used practices were non-vitamin, non-mineral products (green tea, herbal tea, aloe, ginger, and chamomile), yoga, deep breathing exercises, massage therapy, and meditation (Versnik et al., 2015).

According to Table 11.2, "Natural products," specifically nonvitamin, nonmineral dietary supplements, constitute the most common CAM therapy, used by 17.7 percent of US adults in 2012. Had vitamin and mineral supplements

TABLE 11.1   CAM Use Among Various Demographic Groups, 2012

Gender	Used CAM in Last Year (%)
Men	28.9
Women	37.4
Age	
18–44	32.2
45–64	36.8
65 and over	29.4
Education	
Less than high school	15.6
High school only	24.4
Some college	36.5
College degree or higher	42.6
Race	
Non-Hispanic white	37.9
Non-Hispanic black	19.3
Hispanic	22.0
Other Non-Hispanic	37.3

Source: Tainya C. Clarke, Lindsey I. Black, Barbara Stussman, Patricia M. Barnes, and Richard L. Nahin. 2015. "Trends in the Use of Complementary Health Approaches Among Adults: United States, 2002–2012" *National Health Statistics Report,* Number 79. Hyattsville, MD: National Center for Health Statistics.

TABLE 11.2   The Ten Most Common CAM Therapies Used by Adults, 2012

Therapy	Used in the Last Year (%)
Natural products	17.7
Deep breathing	10.9
Yoga, Tai Chi, Qi Gong	10.1
Chiropractic/osteopathy	8.4
Meditation	8.0
Massage	6.9
Diet-based therapies	3.0
Homeopathy	2.2
Progressive relaxation	2.1
Guided imagery	1.7

Source: Tainya C. Clarke et al. 2015. "Trends in the Use of Complementary Health Approaches Among Adults: United States, 2002–2012," *National Health Statistics Report,* Number 79. Hyattsville, MD: National Center for Health Statistics.

been included in the question, the proportion of adults using such products would have been well over 50 percent (Nestle, 2013). What exactly is a dietary supplement, and how does a supplement differ from a drug? Put simply, drugs and dietary supplements are defined and regulated differently by the Food and Drug Administration (FDA). The FDA treats supplements as a subcategory of food. Specifically, supplements are a dietary substance (e.g., vitamins, minerals, herbs, amino acids or the constituents or extracts of any of these) used to supplement the diet by increasing total dietary intake. According to the FDA, "Unlike drugs, supplements are not intended to treat, diagnose, prevent, or cure diseases. That means supplements should not make claims, such as 'reduces pain' or 'treats heart disease.' Claims like these can only legitimately be made for drugs, not dietary supplements." (USFDA, 2019). This is because drug manufacturers, but not supplement manufacturers, "must demonstrate through controlled scientific and clinical studies that the products not only are safe for human consumption but also are more effective as remedies than placebos or comparable drugs" (Nestle, 2013:222). However, manufacturers can label supplements with statements of nutritional support or structure/function claims such as 'helps maintain a healthy immune system,' 'supports heart health,' or 'promotes healthy

TABLE 11.3   The Ten Most Common Dietary Supplements Used by Adults, 2012

Supplement	Used in the Past 30 Days (%)
Fish oil/omega 3	7.8
Glucosamine or chondroitin	2.6
Probiotics or prebiotics	1.6
Melatonin	1.3
Coenzyme Q-10	1.3
Echinacea	0.9
Cranberry (pills/capsules)	0.8
Garlic supplements	0.8
Ginseng	0.7
Ginkgo biloba	0.7

Source: Tainya C. Clarke et al. 2015. "Trends in the Use of Complementary Health Approaches Among Adults: United States, 2002–2012," *National Health Statistics Report,* Number 79. Hyattsville, MD: National Center for Health Statistics.

joints.' These statements are often accompanied by the disclaimer, 'the Food and Drug Association has not evaluated these statements.' Table 11.3 lists the most commonly used dietary supplements.

What motivates people to use alternative therapies, either in conjunction with or as a replacement for conventional medicine? Common reasons include a belief that products obtained from nature are purer or safer than prescription medicines, appreciation of the more

Yoga classes are increasingly popular and expose participants to holistic philosophies that may serve as an entry point into other, less common forms of CAM.

holistic approach taken by many CAM providers, and dissatisfaction with conventional medicine. Additionally, some of the more common forms of CAM such as yoga (practiced by nearly 10 percent of the US adult population in 2012) may serve as an entry point to other less common forms such as Reiki and reflexology. A recent study of long-term yoga participants in Florida found that most began practicing yoga to address physical or mental health issues, such as alleviating back problems or depression. The longer they practiced yoga, the more likely they were to try other CAM modalities. Thus, exposure to yoga and the holistic philosophy it promotes may encourage use of other CAM techniques, demonstrating the progressive nature of CAM use over time (Sivén and Mishtal, 2012).

The Dual Model of Care

Are all or most people who use CAM completely dissatisfied with conventional medicine? No. Research shows that many people follow a "dual model of medical care," making use of an alternative healer at the same time as they receive care from a medical doctor.

While some become disillusioned with conventional care and make a cognitive commitment to complementary and alternative practices, the more common pattern is that individuals use different healers for different problems. For example, many patients consult chiropractors for chronic low back pain but continue to rely on medical doctors for other problems. Their selection of a healer is pragmatic. They continue to see medical doctors for most ailments because that has been helpful before, but if their back pain has received little relief from the family doctor, they will seek relief from a chiropractor. If that works, they maintain allegiance to both practitioners—each in a specified domain (Kronenfeld and Wasner, 1982; Shim, Schneider, and Curlin, 2014).

However, most people who follow the dual model of care do not inform their medical doctor that they are also seeing a CAM healer, even if it is for the same complaint. An analysis of National Health Interview Survey data from 2012 found that 42.3 percent of CAM users did not discuss their use of CAM with their primary care physician (Jou and Johnson, 2016). A recent study of doctor–patient communication about patient CAM use in the American Southwest, where rates of CAM (especially traditional practices such as curanderismo and Native American healing discussed later in this chapter) are fairly common, found that patients were more likely to tell their doctor about CAM treatments if the doctor directly asked about their use and if patients perceived doctors as nonjudgmental. However, time constraints often prevented doctors from asking about CAM use during clinical encounters. When doctors did ask about other treatments, patients did not always interpret their questions as inquiries about CAM, believing instead that doctors were asking about other prescription or over-the-counter medications (Shelley et al., 2009).

Similar patterns of nondisclosure have been observed with dietary supplements. Although over 17 percent of US adults take dietary supplements, only one-third share this information with their physician (Asher, Corbett, and Hawke, 2017; Clarke et al., 2015). This can be particularly problematic with certain supplements that interfere with standard drug treatments. One example is the herbal supplement St. John's wort, which has many documented interaction effects with both prescription and over-the-counter medications. Used most commonly for depression, St. John's wort can weaken the effect of other medications by speeding up the body's metabolism of conventional drugs.

Finally, when CAM is combined with orthodox medical treatments it becomes difficult to attribute definitively any improvement in patient symptoms to CAM. Did the patient improve because of the CAM treatment or because of the orthodox treatment? There is simply no way to tell, bringing us to the larger issue of the efficacy of CAM.

The Efficacy of Complementary and Alternative Healers

Is the popularity of CAM a valid and reliable indication that at least some CAM healers offer efficacious treatment? Possibly, but not necessarily. Determining the efficacy of any medical treatment—conventional or unconventional—is more complicated than it might seem. Rodney-Coe (1970) identified three reasons why use of magic in primitive medicine is (or seems to be) effective. These can be generalized to any form of medical treatment, whatever a society's level of scientific sophistication.

First, in all societies, most patients most of the time will recover regardless of the form of treatment received or even whether any treatment is provided. The amazing recuperative powers of the human body are only now being recognized. The same point is made by the old adage about seeing a physician for a cold—if you do, you'll be well in a week; if you don't, it will take 7 days. Thus, whether one receives muscle relaxants from a medical doctor or spinal manipulation from a chiropractor, one's back pain will usually diminish eventually. Typically, we give credit to whatever treatment was received, although we would often have healed without treatment.

Second, when patients believe strongly in the medical care they receive, it has great psychotherapeutic value, whatever its direct effects. The determination to get well and the confidence that recovery will occur are relevant factors in the healing process. Believing in the cure offered by your family physician can contribute to its success, just as believing in the efficacy of being needled by an acupuncturist or sharing prayer with a Christian Science practitioner can.

Finally, some CAM practices are scientifically correct, even though the rationale for the practice is unscientific. Coe uses the example of a medicine man treating a snakebite victim. He might open the wound further and suck out the evil spirit that had entered. In so doing, he is actually sucking out the poisonous venom from the wound, thus accomplishing what orthodox medicine would recommend, but basing it on an entirely different underlying theory.

Furthermore, every medical treatment must be considered within the context of the practitioner–patient relationship. The quality of this relationship may influence the course of treatment and the healing process. Treatments offered by alternative healers are enhanced by the greater rapport they develop with patients. Alternative healers are often more sympathetic than medical doctors to minor but nagging conditions that trouble an individual. Most alternative healing practices involve more talking and more touching—both tremendously reassuring processes—than are often involved in treatment by a medical doctor. Alternative healers also spend more time with patients (more than four times as much as MDs), do a better job of avoiding medical jargon, and provide warmer, more relaxed treatment settings. One study found that individuals who use CAM are more likely than those who do not to report their own health as excellent and their health to have improved in the last year (although the study could not determine causality) (Nguyen et al., 2011).

All this is not to say that we do not make individual judgments about the efficacy of medical care received. We do. And it is not to say that patterns of efficacy cannot be studied. They can. But it is to say that drawing firm conclusions about the efficacy of any form of medical care must be done very carefully.

In the remaining sections of this chapter, we examine four CAM practices—chiropractic, acupuncture, religious healing, and ethnic folk healing.

CHIROPRACTIC

Chiropractic contains many contradictions. Millions of people in the United States enthusiastically support chiropractic, while many see it as nothing more than successful quackery. (A former president of the American Chiropractic Association was fond of saying "People either swear by us or at us.") Nearly one-quarter of the adult population has used chiropractic services and an estimated 19.1 million people sought chiropractic services in 2012 (Adams et al., 2017). Without altering its basic philosophy or practice, chiropractic has achieved increased acceptance by many MDs, yet is condemned by others. There is even dissensus among chiropractors themselves on the appropriate boundaries of the field.

Nevertheless, certain facts are clear. Chiropractic is a licensed health profession in all 50 states, and chiropractors are recognized and reimbursed by federal, state, and most commercial insurance companies. According to the U.S. Bureau of Labor Statistics (2020), there were 50,300 working chiropractors in 2018, with a median income of $70,340 a year. The field of chiropractic is projected to grow by about 7 percent through the year 2028 due to the expanding elderly population, which experiences more neuromusculoskeletal and joint problems. According to the American Chiropractic Association (2019), there are more than 80,000 licensed doctors of chiropractic in the United States and currently about 10,000 students in nationally accredited chiropractic schools. Doctors of chiropractic (D.C.s) must complete a 4-year doctoral graduate school program in a curriculum that includes a minimum of 4,200 hours of classroom, laboratory, and clinical internship (which is equivalent to MD and D.O. schools).

Origin

The field of chiropractic was founded by Daniel David Palmer (1845–1913), a healer living in Davenport, Iowa. Palmer credited his vision of the field to two successful experiences he had in 1895. By realigning displaced vertebrae, he restored hearing to one man who had become deaf 17 years earlier when something had "given way" in his back, and he relieved another patient's heart problems. He reasoned that if two such disparate conditions could be treated through manipulation of the vertebrae, potential existed for curing all ailments in this fashion. His research findings, published in 1910, served as the foundation for chiropractic and for a chiropractic school, which he established in 1897 (Wardwell, 1992).

Basic Principles

The National Center for Complementary and Integrative Health (2019a) identifies three basic tenets of chiropractic:

1. The body has a powerful self-healing ability. Illness results from a failure to maintain homeostasis—the positive bodily drive toward health. Maintenance of homeostasis occurs through good nutrition, good posture, exercise, stress management, creative meditation, and natural (non-pharmacological) healing. Serious disease is viewed as the end result of a process that could have been avoided through this holistic approach.

2. The body's structure (primarily that of the spine) and its function are closely related, and this relationship affects health. Vital energy flows throughout the body's nerves during a homeostatic state. However, this energy can be blocked by subtle malalignments of the vertebrae called subluxations. These subluxations are the origin of most human illness.

3. Therapy aims to normalize this relationship between structure and function and assists the body as it heals. By correcting the spinal malfunction, the chiropractor expects the specific problem to disappear and the patient's general health to improve.

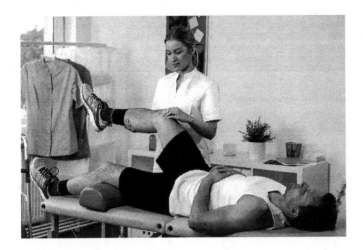

Chiropractors believe that health problems are expressions of underlying problems, including blockages of the flow of vital energy caused by malalignments of the vertebrae.

Caplan (1984) explicates the three main ways in which this philosophy of healing contrasts with orthodox medicine:

1. Medical doctors typically equate symptoms with particular diseases and often identify health as the absence of symptoms. Disease is discovered when symptoms appear and is usually judged to have ended when symptoms disappear. Chiropractic does not make this equation.
2. Orthodox medicine considers it scientifically proven that germs are the underlying cause of many disorders, and disdains any healing philosophy that does not subscribe to this view. Chiropractic's belief that subluxations are an important cause of disease is in seeming contradiction to scientific medicine.
3. While chiropractors see themselves as holistic healers specializing in preventive care, some physicians believe the field should be restricted to musculoskeletal conditions or eliminated altogether.

Historical Developments

Early in its history, chiropractic split into camps. The first camp, which included many MDs who were also chiropractors, maintained that chiropractors should offer a variety of treatment techniques in addition to spinal adjustment. This group created a national association—the American Chiropractors Association (ACA)—in 1922, and is today the far larger of the groups. An alternative philosophy—that chiropractic was not the practice of medicine and ought to offer solely spinal adjustment as a therapeutic modality—emerged, and in 1938 created the International Chiropractic Association (ICA).

Chiropractic struggled through its early years. The Flexner Report of 1910 condemned existing chiropractic schools for failure to develop ties with universities and for the absence of demanding training programs. The Great Depression significantly reduced philanthropic contributions and applications for schooling decreased.

The most important early objective for chiropractic was to gain state-sanctioned licensure. It was not an easy battle, as chiropractors were often jailed for practicing medicine without a license. Ultimately, being jailed became a successful strategy used to win public support for the field as a reaction to its persecution. Kansas passed the first chiropractic licensing law in 1913, 39 states gave some form of legal recognition by 1931, and in 1974, when Louisiana began licensure for chiropractors, acceptance was won in every state.

Wardwell (1992) has suggested that 1974 was the turning point for chiropractic. In addition to Louisiana's accepting licensure, the US Office of Education gave the Chiropractic Commission on Education the right to accredit schools of chiropractic, the federal government determined that chiropractors' fees were reimbursable under Medicare, and Congress authorized the spending of US$2 million on a study of the merits and efficacy of chiropractic treatment by the National Institute of Neurological Disorders and Stroke (NINDS) of the National Institutes of Health. The NINDS conference concluded that spinal manipulation does provide relief from pain, particularly back pain, and sometimes even cures.

Organized Medicine and Chiropractic

For decades, the American Medical Association attempted to drive chiropractic out of existence. As early as 1922, AMA officials adopted the slogan "Chiropractic Must Die" (Reed, 1932). In 1963, the AMA's Committee on Quackery referred to the elimination of chiropractic as its ultimate mission, and engaged in such activities as "producing and distributing anti-chiropractic literature, communicating with medical boards and other medical associations, fighting chiropractic-sponsored legislation, and seeking to discourage colleges, universities, and faculty members from cooperating with chiropractic schools" (Gevitz, 1989:292).

In 1965, the AMA declared it a violation of medical ethics for MDs to have any professional association with chiropractors. This included making or accepting referrals of patients, providing diagnostic, laboratory, or radiology services, teaching in chiropractic schools, and practicing jointly in any form.

What was the motivation for such strong action? Organized medicine defended its actions on the grounds that it was attempting to eliminate a practice it considered to be detrimental to patient welfare. Believing the vertebral

subluxation concept to be grossly inaccurate and denigrating the low standards of chiropractic education, orthodox medicine defined chiropractic as having little or no therapeutic value and as being potentially dangerous.

On the other hand, chiropractic contended that the AMA's actions were motivated by professional elitism (i.e., not wanting to share the prestige of the medical profession) and an effort to restrict economic competition. These contentions became part of a lawsuit brought by chiropractors in 1976 against the AMA for violating the Sherman Antitrust Act. During the decade that the case was bogged down in court, the AMA relaxed its opposition to chiropractic.

Nevertheless, in August 1987, District Judge Susan Getzendanner found the AMA, the American College of Radiology, and the American College of Surgeons guilty of violating the Sherman Antitrust Act. She judged that the three associations acted conspiratorially in instituting a boycott of chiropractic, had failed to justify their actions through their "patient care defense," and required the actions to cease.

Current and Future Status

Chiropractic clearly has established an important place in the health care system. The educational preparation for chiropractors has continued to be upgraded. The curriculum is now comparable to that in medical schools with respect to study of the basic sciences. The major difference is that chiropractic students take courses in spinal analysis and manipulation and nutrition rather than in surgery and pharmacology (chiropractors are prohibited from performing surgery or prescribing drugs). Chiropractors must pass a national examination administered by the National Board of Chiropractic Examiners and must be licensed by a state board. Unlike many medical doctors, chiropractors are required to continue their education in order to retain their license (Wardwell, 1992). Both the ACA and the ICA promote the field of chiropractic and view the field as being patient oriented and wellness focused.

Unquestionably, many people believe strongly in the value of chiropractic. Based on data from the 2012 National Health Interview Survey, 64.5 percent of respondents who had used chiropractic services reported that it helped a great deal with the particular issue for which they sought treatment, and just under half (47.9 percent) said chiropractic care was very important for maintaining overall health and well-being (Adams et al., 2017). Numerous other studies confirm that an increasing percentage and genuine cross section of the population visits chiropractors, that levels of patient satisfaction are quite high, and that the general prestige of the field is on the upswing (Meeker and Haldeman, 2002).

ACUPUNCTURE

Chinese understanding of health and illness has evolved over nearly 3,000 years and is recorded in more than 6,000 texts. Traditional Chinese medicine is a holistic system that understands health in the context of the relationship between the human body and nature.

Medical theory rests on the belief that each object in nature is both a unified whole and a whole comprising two parts with opposing qualities—*yin* and *yang*—that are constantly in a dynamic interplay, shifting from being opposites to becoming each other. Yin represents the cold, slow, and passive principle, while yang represents the hot, excited, and active principle. Health is achieved and preserved by maintaining a balanced state within the body, and disease occurs when the yin and yang forces become imbalanced (National Center for Complementary and Integrative Health, 2017).

An imbalance leads to a blockage that disrupts the flow of *chi* (vital energy) within the body. Chi is considered the primary force of nourishment and bodily protection. Although there is nothing exactly comparable in Western thought,

it is sometimes viewed as the "will to live." Chi flows through the body through 12 (or 14 or 20; sources vary) main channels (or meridians), activating energy in the circulatory system as it flows. The exact location of these channels has been charted and diagrammed, and each is thought to represent and be connected with an internal organ. Exercise, especially the martial arts, stimulates the flow of this vital energy in the channels.

The harmony and balance within the body may be disrupted either by endogenous factors, which originate from some serious internal imbalance, or by exogenous factors, which come from the external environment and may be physical (e.g., climatic conditions) or biological (e.g., bacteria and viruses). In performing diagnosis, traditional Chinese medicine follows the principle that "anything inside is bound to manifest outwardly." An implication of this principle is that even localized symptoms (e.g., a headache) are not viewed as local disturbances but rather as a sign of abnormality within bodily organs and the body's channel system. Therefore, a headache does not necessarily mean an imbalance in or near the head.

The primary goal of Chinese medicine is to restore the internal balance of the body and the harmony between the environment and the human being. Since the body's internal balance is fluctuating constantly, specific treatment must be tailored to the situation at the time.

While much of Western attention has focused on acupuncture as a treatment technique, it is actually only one of many options in traditional Chinese medicine. Other important treatment techniques include acupressure (significant pressure applied to the body via the fingertips), herbology (the use of natural herbs), moxibustion (placing ignited moxa wool on certain points of the body to create heat), various breathing exercises, physical activity, massage, and cupping (placing a small jar with a partial vacuum created by a flame over a selected part of the body producing an inflammatory response). Due to acupuncture's unique history in the United States, this section will focus on it as a healing practice.

Origin of Acupuncture in the United States

Even though it has been long used in China and was practiced by Chinese immigrants in the states, acupuncture gained broad popular attention in the United States only in the early 1970s. This "discovery" of acupuncture can be traced to two events that occurred in 1971: first, the opening of political relations with China, and second, an attack of appendicitis suffered by famed *New York Times* columnist James Reston while visiting China—acupuncture was used the day after surgery to eliminate significant pain. Reston wrote of his experience in the *Times*, attracting widespread interest in the subject. A group of American physicians (including a delegation from the AMA) visited China in the ensuing months, and their glowing reports of the efficacy of acupuncture ensured further popular and professional attention (Wolpe, 1985).

Basic Principles

Acupuncture is the insertion of fine needles into one or more acupuncture "points" on the body. To date, more than 700 points have been identified, although only 40 or 50 are commonly used. The needles vary in length, width, and type of metal, and treatments vary with regard to the depth to which needles are inserted, the duration of insertion, and needle rotation. The insertion of needles stimulates chi in the body and redirects it to correct imbalances. The needles are inserted in those points that correspond to the particular internal organs where the imbalance exists.

Historical Developments

Although American physicians largely focused on the anesthetic value of acupuncture, ignoring its therapeutic utility, the popular press offered vivid descriptions of acupuncture as a miracle process. The federal government encouraged research into acupuncture, and scientific journals published scores of articles. The Internal Revenue Service decided that payments for acupuncture service qualified as a medical expense, and the Food and Drug Administration developed quality control regulations for acupuncture needles. An American Society of Chinese Medicine was formed (Wolpe, 1985).

In July 1972, the first acupuncture clinic opened in New York City. When it was shut down a week later for practicing medicine without a license, it had already served 500 patients and was booked solid for several months. Acupuncture had captured America by storm. Although the manner in which it would be incorporated remained to be determined, acupuncture seemed on the verge of becoming a major healing practice in the United States.

Organized Medicine and Acupuncture

The medical establishment quickly reined in the enthusiasm. One can understand the professional embarrassment caused by a healing practice based on a theory that seemed completely contradictory to "scientific" medicine.

> Physicians had no expertise in acupuncture and no knowledge of physiological mechanisms that could account for it. Indeed, it seemed to violate laws of anatomy and neurophysiology. Acupuncture was an alien treatment with an alien philosophical basis imported as a package from the East; it was not an indigenous alternative modality that reacted to (and thus was informed by) the biomedical model.
>
> (Wolpe, 1985:413)

Negative and hostile physician reactions escalated. The therapeutic effects of acupuncture were dismissed as nothing more than placebo, and its effectiveness as an anesthetic was dismissed as a type of hypnosis or form of suggestibility. It was even suggested that "Chinese stoicism" or patriotic zeal enabled patients to undergo excruciatingly painful surgery without other anesthetics (Wolpe, 1985). One physician referred to acupuncturists as "nonscientific weirdos" and attempted to portray the entire practice as modern-day quackery (Goldstein, 1972).

To protect its cultural authority over medicine, the medical establishment employed two additional strategies. The first was to sponsor and conduct research that would explain acupuncture in terms of the traditional biomedical model (Wolpe, 1985). While Chinese practitioners strongly believe the practice cannot be separated from its underlying theory, and therefore cannot be studied by traditional scientific methods, much research has been conducted to find a conventional explanation for its anesthetic effects.

For example, Melzack and Wall (1965) developed the "gate control theory" based on research showing that the insertion of needles excites nerve fibers that enter the spinal column and inhibit the transmission of pain to the brain. Stimulating these nerve fibers effectively "closes the gate" to pain. An alternative theory, also consistent with traditional neurophysiology, is that the needle insertion stimulates the release of certain pain-reducing hormones (endorphins and enkephalins), which create the anesthetic or analgesic effects. Some recent research has found that needle insertion reduces the flow of blood to the areas of the brain that control pain.

The second strategy was to place acupuncture under the jurisdiction of medical doctors (Wolpe, 1985). After all, if acupuncture was beneficial only for pain relief, and if the explanation for it could be provided in conventional terms, then it could be argued that Oriental practitioners were not as able as Western practitioners to provide safe and effective treatment. Regulations governing the practice of acupuncture were quickly established in many states (either by the legislature or by the state medical board).

Current and Future Status

There were 57 accredited or pre-accredited schools of Oriental Medicine in the United States, and more than 33,000 licensed (by the National Certification Commission for Acupuncture and Oriental Medicine, or NCCAOM) practitioners in 2019. The NCCAOM offers certification in oriental medicine, acupuncture, Chinese herbology, and Asian bodywork therapy. The additional designation of licensed acupuncturist (L.Ac.) is awarded by a state regulatory board. Currently, 47 states plus the District of Columbia require NCCAOM certification or passing NCCAOM examinations as a requirement for licensure. According to the 2012 National Health Interview Survey, approximately 1.5 percent of the adult population used acupuncture in the 12 months preceding the survey (Clarke et al., 2015). Many private insurers and state Medicaid programs now cover the cost of acupuncture treatment.

Is acupuncture an effective anesthetic or therapeutic healing practice? Considerable research reports favorable findings. In late 1997, a panel of scientists at the National Institutes of Health (including some who practice acupuncture and some skeptics) concluded that acupuncture is effective in treating many conditions, including nausea and vomiting after chemotherapy and surgery, the nausea of pregnancy, and postoperative dental pain. Although fewer data were available, they concluded that acupuncture may help stroke rehabilitation and relieve addictions, headaches, menstrual cramps, a variety of muscle pains, carpal tunnel syndrome, insomnia, arthritis, and asthma. Moreoever, acupuncture has fewer side effects and is less invasive than many conventional treatments. The World Health Organization now recognizes more than 43 conditions as effectively treatable by acupuncture.

The accompanying box, "Medical Marijuana and Marijuana Derivatives," discusses two related CAM techniques in the news.

Most states require traditional Chinese medicine practitioners to have a master of acupuncture or Oriental medicine degree or its equivalent, and national certification.

Source: Photo by Gregory Weiss.

IN THE FIELD

MEDICAL MARIJUANA AND MARIJUANA DERIVATIVES

In 1996, California voters approved Proposition 215, which permitted physicians to *recommend* marijuana for their patients. Because it would violate federal law, physicians were prohibited from *prescribing* it. In 1997, the *New England Journal of Medicine* endorsed the legalization of medical marijuana, arguing that it has clearly brought relief from pain for many people. Later that year, the AMA, although rejecting endorsement of legalization, called for the right of physicians to discuss any treatment alternatives with patients without possibility of criminal sanction.

Despite legalization in some states, in May 2001, the US Supreme Court ruled that the federal law prohibiting the manufacture and distribution of marijuana meant that it could not be sold or used for medicinal purposes. The Justice Department indicated that it would use its authority under the Controlled Substances Act to revoke the license to prescribe drugs of any physician who even *recommended* marijuana to a patient.

Although medical marijuana users were typically not prosecuted, they were in the awkward position of engaging in a behavior that has been expressly approved by their state but disapproved by the federal government. Only in 2009 did then Attorney General of the United States Eric Holder announce that raids would be stopped on state-approved marijuana dispensaries. However, the federal government still has not recognized or approved marijuana as medicine.

By 2019, only Idaho, Nebraska, and South Dakota still prohibited the cultivation and sale of marijuana for medical purposes, although some states only permit medicinal use of low-THC cannabidiol. Additionally, ten states and the District of Columbia have legalized the adult *recreational use* of marijuana and several others are considering it.

Can marijuana be medicinal? Yes. Research shows four beneficial medical effects: (1) It reduces the nausea associated with cancer chemotherapy. (2) It reduces "wasting

Patient identification card that can be used to legally obtain marijuana through the Arizona Medical Marijuana Program.

syndrome"—the deadly loss of appetite and consequent weight loss that many AIDS patients feel near the end of life. (3) It reduces the painful muscle spasms and tremors experienced by many people with spinal cord injuries and multiple sclerosis. (4) It reduces pressure inside the eye for people with glaucoma (although another drug is now more effective). There is experimental evidence that it may also be helpful in treating other conditions such as depression, Crohn's disease, and hepatitis C.

Are there any demonstrated negative side effects of marijuana use? Yes. Two such effects are (1) that it impairs cognitive functioning, negatively affecting coordination and short-term memory (studies have been inconsistent on whether there is any long-term cognitive impairment), and (2) that it leads to respiratory damage (studies have found that smoking marijuana is even more harmful to the lungs than smoking tobacco).

Proponents of medical marijuana argue that individuals should have the right to decide for themselves whether the benefits outweigh the harms. Because many of the users are and would be light users, and would be using it temporarily, they argue that harms are overstated. Besides, it is well known that many people with cancer or AIDS have long been using marijuana for relief, but have been forced to do so surreptitiously. Opponents argue that liberalizing use of the drug for medical purposes might lead to increased recreational use of marijuana and/or other drugs, and that the harms of the drug justify its continued ban. In addition, pharmaceutical companies, anticipating the possibility of patenting (potentially very profitable) drugs that include tetrahydrocannabinol (THC), which is the active ingredient of marijuana, have opposed legalization of medical marijuana.

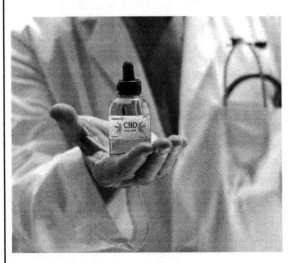

CBD advocates maintain that it promotes overall wellness and eases symptoms associated with several illnesses.

(Continued)

(Continued)

More recently, the marijuana-derivative cannabidiol has become popular. Commonly known as CBD and frequently sold in the form of CBD oil, advocates claim it can potentially treat anxiety, post-traumatic stress disorder (PTSD), and sleep disorders, and has a host of other benefits. Unlike medical marijuana, CBD does not produce the cognitive impairment or "high" associated with marijuana. CBD can be derived from marijuana or hemp, a type of cannabis with extremely low (less than 0.3 percent) concentrations of THC. The Agriculture Improvement Act of 2018 (aka the "Farm Bill") officially removed hemp from the Controlled Substances Act, which some CBD advocates interpret as evidence that CBD products derived from hemp are legal under federal law. However, the issue is far more complicated.

In 2018, the FDA approved Epidiolex, a prescription-based CBD treatment for two severe seizure disorders (Lennox-Gastaut syndrome and Dravet syndrome). As the first approved drug containing the active ingredient CBD, Epidiolex is the lone CBD product that can make therapeutic or treatment claims or be legally prescribed. Because Epidiolex was already on the market when the 2018 Agriculture Improvement Act went into effect, the FDA considers CBD a *drug ingredient* and maintains that it cannot legally be marketed as a dietary supplement or added to foods intended for interstate commerce.

Although the FDA does not consider CBD a dietary supplement, it has much in common with other supplements. First, very few scientific studies have tested the voluminous health claims made by CBD proponents (due largely to its nebulous legal status), making it difficult to determine the efficacy of CBD for uses other than the treatment of seizure disorders. Second, CBD products available over-the-counter are largely unregulated, making it difficult for consumers to know exactly what they are buying or how much to take. One recent study of 84 CBD products purchased online (including oils, tinctures, and vaporization liquids) found that 43 percent contained more, and 26 percent contained less, CBD than listed on the label (Bonn-Miller et al., 2017). Finally, like dietary supplements, many people take CBD to promote general wellness rather than to treat a given medical condition (some even give CBD to their pets).

Despite its murky legal status, CBD products are widely available, and restaurants have begun selling CBD-infused food and drinks. In 2015, the FDA began sending letters to companies marketing CBD products, warning them that they are violating both Federal Trade Commission (which regulates advertising) and FDA policies, and threatening legal action. In recent years, some states and cities have also begun cracking down on CBD sales. In February 2019, the New York City Department of Health announced that it would begin fining restaurants selling CBD-infused products (such as coffee and baked goods), citing FDA regulations that CBD is not among those food additives generally regarded as safe (commonly referred to as GRAS).

While the movement to legalize medical marijuana is well underway, the jury is still out on the legal status of CBD, especially for non-medical and non-prescriptive uses. In the ten states (plus Washington, DC) with legalized *recreational* marijuana, CBD is also likely to be legal. Yet, even in those select states, CBD may come under federal and state scrutiny if advertised for therapeutic purposes, as a dietary supplement, or a food additive.

SPIRITUAL HEALING AND CHRISTIAN SCIENCE

Belief in "psychic healing" has been present in both early and modern times and in both Western and non-Western cultures. Psychic healing "refers to the beneficial influence of a person on another living thing by mechanisms which are beyond those recognized by conventional medicine. These mechanisms may include focused wishes, meditation, prayers, ritual practices, and the laying-on-of-hands" (Benor, 1984:166).

Psychic healers use one of four approaches: (1) activating innate recuperative forces within the patient; (2) transferring their own healing energy to the patient; (3) serving as a conduit through which universally available cosmic energy is transferred to the patient; or (4) serving as a conduit through which the healing powers of spirits or God are transferred to the patient. The final channel is also referred to as **spiritual healing** or "faith healing" (Benor, 1984). Spiritual healers do not claim any personal ability to heal but rather an ability to convey the power of some transcendent being to the sick. Spiritual healers may or may not be affiliated with a particular church and may or may not be full-time healers.

Efficacy of Spiritual Healing

Determining the efficacy of spiritual healing is difficult. Most evidence supporting positive effects is anecdotal and comes from people strongly predisposed to its benefits. Other more systematic research has been conducted, but in ways that allow alternative explanations of the findings.

Many people accept that there are at least some cases where a subject's health status has improved following a spiritual healing encounter. These cases are interpreted in different ways. Those involved in the healing process typically contend that God intervened in a miraculous way to effect a cure. Others believe the health improvement or cure occurred through psychological processes—for example, marshaling the patient's mental powers and determination to combat the ailment and/or convincing the patient that a cure will occur (akin to the placebo effect).

In the largest study ever undertaken on the topic, researchers from six hospitals throughout the United States examined the effects of intercessory prayer—that is, someone praying for therapeutic improvement for another (Benson et al., 2006). Previous well-controlled clinical tests had not supported such benefits, but they had not addressed whether any outcomes were due to prayer itself or to the knowledge that prayer was being offered. Patients in the study were all undergoing coronary bypass surgery. They were randomly divided into three groups. In the first two groups, patients were told they may or may not receive intercessory prayer. The first group did receive it, while the second did not. Patients in the third group were informed they would receive prayer and did. The researchers focused on rates of complications following the surgery. Overall, they concluded that intercessory prayer had no effect on complication rates post-surgery among the first two groups (who were uncertain whether or not they had received prayer). Surprisingly, the third group—who had received prayer and knew it—actually had a higher rate of complications than the first group—who also received prayer but did not know this for certain.

Public Perceptions of Spiritual Healing

Many people do relate religion and illness experience. The perception that disease and illness are caused by God declined through the 1900s but has increased in the last two decades. Many people continue to rely on religion as a coping mechanism when they are sick.

One study of older adults discovered many who were unclear about God's role in health and illness but nevertheless turned to prayer when sick. For most of these illnesses, care had also been sought from a medical doctor. Rather than viewing prayer and conventional medical treatment as mutually exclusive, most of these respondents saw them as complementary (Bearon and Koenig, 1990).

Most of the increasing numbers of studies that are being conducted have found that religion has a positive influence on health. Compelling evidence has accumulated that individuals who attend religious services on a regular basis have a longer life expectancy than non-churchgoers.

Other research has found that regular church-goers on average have lower blood pressure and cope better with illness. The findings may be interpreted in different ways. One national survey found that about one-third of Americans use prayer for health concerns, and that about 7 in 10 of these individuals considered it very helpful (McCaffrey et al., 2004).

Several studies have found that individuals who regularly attend church are less likely to engage in unhealthy lifestyles. Some research has found that prayer or meditation has a calming effect on individuals, which would help explain patterns such as lower blood pressure (Koenig, McCullough, and Larson, 2001). Many analysts are concerned that these studies might be misinterpreted as providing evidence that faith-based practices may be used in lieu of medical treatment. All agree that more research is needed to understand the basis for these patterns.

The high level of religious commitment among many patients and the potentially positive effects of religious participation on health are acknowledged by most physicians. Even physicians who are themselves religiously skeptical must walk a thin line on this issue for fear of alienating devout patients. Koenig, Bearon, and Dayringer (1989) found that about two-thirds of a sample of family physicians and general practitioners believe that strong religious beliefs and frequent involvement in religious activities have a positive impact on mental health, and 4 in 10 believe there is a positive effect on physical health. Many physicians were unclear about the extent to which they should become involved in religious discussions with patients. Most would in some circumstances, but few preferred this as a standard course of action. Almost 25 percent expressed a belief that faith healers can divinely heal some people whom physicians cannot help.

However, skepticism about spiritual healing remains high. Spiritual healers have no licensure or formal professional associations and may be arrested for practicing medicine without a license. Even though it is careful in its language, the AMA is disdainful of spiritual healing and sees it as an attempt to take advantage of vulnerable people.

Christian Science as an Example of Spiritual Healing

Of the specific spiritual healing philosophies, **Christian Science** has received the most professional study.

Origin. The founder of Christian Science, Mary Baker Eddy (1821–1910), suffered frequent bouts of illness during her youth that prompted her devotion to find a cure for disease. Failing to be helped by medical doctors, she experimented with a variety of alternative healing philosophies.

At the age of 45 years, Mary slipped on an icy street, causing very painful head, neck, and back problems. When she received little help from local physicians, she turned to the Bible for comfort. While reading the account of the healings of Jesus, she discovered the "Healing Truth" and experienced a complete recovery. She initiated work as a healer, and in 1875 wrote *Science and Health,* which became the textbook of Christian Science.

The next few years were not easy. While alternately gaining followers and losing them (because of charges of temper tantrums, love of money, and hypocrisy), Mary Baker, her third husband, Asa Eddy, and a small group of devotees moved to Boston and founded the First Church of Christ, Scientist, in 1879. Although criticized by some, the church grew rapidly, branching out to additional churches, local societies, and schools. However, concerned about the bureaucratization of the church, Mary dismantled much of its organizational structure and substituted a highly centralized structure with herself and the mother church in key positions.

Basic Principles. The basic principle of Christian Science is that illness and pain are not real but only illusions of the mind. Since people are reflections of God, and God cannot be sick, people cannot be sick. A person feels ill only when the underlying spiritual condition is in disrepair. This causes the mind to think illness is present (Gottschalk, 1988). The only appropriate curative techniques are prayer and spiritual rediscovery, through which a deeper understanding of one's own spirituality is achieved. Christian Scientists believe that they have the power within to heal themselves, although the assistance of a Christian Science practitioner is frequently used. Christian Scientists believe their approach is incompatible with orthodox medicine. They view medical doctors as adding pain and illness to the world as a consequence of their lack of understanding of the role of the mind. In fact, even obtaining a medical diagnosis is thought to worsen any condition.

Historical Developments. The key issues in the last century have pertained to the standardization of Scientist-healing practices and external negotiation regarding their legality. Issues such as the appropriateness of Christian Science healing for emotional disorders and the extent to which Scientists should be commanded to live a "healthy lifestyle" have been debated.

Organized Medicine and Christian Science. Two chief points of contention exist between the medical establishment and Christian Scientists. The first is the extent to which Christian Science healing should be acknowledged by the government and commercial health insurance companies as a legitimate form of health care. Christian Science has largely prevailed on this issue as several states have written legislation that provides recognition for Christian Science healing as the equivalent of conventional medical care (e.g., Christian Science practitioners can sign certificates for sick leave and disability claims). Hundreds of commercial insurance companies reimburse charges for Christian Science

practitioners as they would for medical doctors. Christian Science prayer treatment is typically covered by insurance plans for government employees, and through Medicaid and Medicare.

The second issue pertains to the status of **religious exemption laws**, which permit legal violation of other laws based on religious grounds. Some states have religious exemptions for premarital blood tests for adults, prophylactic eye drops for newborns, required physical examinations for schoolchildren, and instruction about diseases and health in school. Some provide for exemption from required immunizations such as that for measles.

Following a widely reported case in Massachusetts in 1967, in which a Christian Scientist was convicted of manslaughter after her 5-year-old daughter died of medically untreated pneumonia, Christian Scientists have conducted a massive—and mostly successful—lobbying campaign for exemption from child neglect laws. Still in dispute, however, is whether these laws extend to situations where forgoing likely effective orthodox medical treatment results in the death of a child.

Christian Scientists argue that religious exemption laws are necessary to enable adherents to practice their religion. What meaning is there in "freedom of religion," they ask, if society compels its members to violate important tenets of their faith? Christian Science healing "is part of a whole religious way of life and is, in fact, the natural outcome of the theology that underlies it. This theology . . . is both biblically based and deeply reasoned" (Talbot, 1983:1641).

A second line of reasoning argues that Christian Science treatment is at least as efficacious as orthodox medicine. In a widely quoted passage, Nathan Talbot, a senior official in the First Church of Christ, Scientist, said:

> Christian Scientists are caring and responsible people who love their children and want only the best possible care for them. They would not have relied on Christian Science for healing—some times over

four and even five generations in the same family—if this healing were only a myth.

(Talbot, 1983:1641)

The church now disseminates data from its own research to demonstrate that Christian Science children are healthier than their peers and that there are lifetime health benefits in relying solely on Christian Science treatment. This line of reasoning is incorporated in statutes in some states that permit exemption for healing practices with a proven record of success.

Opponents of religious exemption laws cite three concerns. First, they contend that the laws violate the First Amendment's prohibition against special privileges for any religious group. For instance, in several states, Christian Science nursing homes do not have to meet required minimum standards for staffing or daily care provided to patients. Second, the religious exemptions to health laws can have harmful public health consequences (e.g., disease epidemics that traced to religious groups that received exemption from health immunizations or examinations). Third, health care provided for children can be compromised. They argue that children are unable to make fully informed and competent decisions about their religious preference and should not be placed in a life-threatening situation by the religious beliefs of their parents. An analogy often cited is the medical treatment given to Jehovah's Witness children. While most courts today routinely allow adult Jehovah's Witnesses to forgo blood transfusions (an important proscription of the faith), children are routinely transfused despite their parents' wishes. Only at the age of competence does the scale tip in favor of the patient's wishes.

Current and Future Status. The number of Christian Scientists in the United States reached a peak of 270,000 in the 1930s, dwindled to 106,000 in 1990, and is estimated to have decreased since then. There were more than 9,700 Christian Science churches in the 1930s, but only 943 in 2019 (Christian Science Journal Directory, 2019). There were just under 1,000 Christian Science practitioners in 2016 and, according to the Christian Science directory, 372 nurses.

Specialized training for Christian Science practitioners remains minimal. Typically, people who have demonstrated special interest and knowledge in Christian Science healing are selected for training. The primary course lasts only about 2 weeks, and focuses on Christian Science theology. At the conclusion of the class, one is listed as a practitioner in the *Christian Science Journal*. After 3 years of full-time successful healing, practitioners may apply to the board of education to take a 6-day course. Graduates of the class are given a CSB (bachelor of Christian science) degree.

Is Christian Science healing effective? Apart from the highly favorable data published by the church itself, two scientific studies by researchers outside the church have been conducted. An early study (based on data from 1935 to 1955 in the state of Washington) found lower life expectancy among Christian Scientists, a much higher than average rate of cancer, and about 6 percent of deaths that would have been medically preventable (Skolnick, 1990). A second study (Simpson, 1989), which compared the longevity of graduates of a Christian Science college with those of a neighboring university, found a much higher death rate among Christian Scientists. This pattern was discovered despite the fact that Christian Scientists neither smoke nor drink—factors that should have prompted a lower death rate.

ETHNIC FOLK HEALING

Folk understandings of disease and illness are typically interwoven into the beliefs and practices of cultural groups. In the United States, folk understandings of the causes and cures of disease occur most often in low-income racial and ethnic minority groups. Snow (1993) identified some common denominators in folk healing systems in her studies of black folk healers and their patients in Chicago. She found that her subjects' views of disease and illness were part and parcel of their religious beliefs—that illness may result from natural factors but might also be the result of sorcery, a temptation from Satan, or a punishment from God. Although traditional herbal remedies and prayer might be sufficient for some conditions, others were perceived to be beyond the scope of either self-care or care by medical doctors, and required a special healer from within the group. The folk healers practiced holistic medicine, treating the whole person rather than just the particular malady, and were more concerned about the cause of the illness than its symptoms.

These patterns also appear in the two most widely studied systems of folk healing—curanderismo (the Mexican and Mexican American form of folk healing) and traditional Native American folk healing, covered in this section.

Curanderismo

Although many use the term **curanderismo** to refer only to Mexican American folk healing, the term is used throughout the Hispanic world (especially in Mexico, Latin America, and the Southwestern United States) to describe a unique system of health care beliefs and practices that differ significantly from modern scientific medicine.

Origin and Historical Developments. Curanderismo developed from three primary sources: (1) the theory of bodily humors; (2) herbal medicine as practiced by the Aztecs, Mayans, and other Native American groups; and (3) religious belief systems, including both Spanish Catholicism and various witchcraft belief systems (Kiev, 1968). Over time in Hispanic communities, curanderismo has taken on

important cultural meaning above and beyond its therapeutic value.

Basic Principles. First, good health is associated with "a strong body, the ability to maintain a high level of normal physical activity, and the absence of persistent pain and discomfort" (Krajewski-Jaime, 1991:160–161). Good health is viewed as a reward for those who have kept God's commandments:

> Even when a curandero uncovers specific causes of illness, he is still likely to focus on sin and the will of God as critical factors affecting the susceptibility of the patient and predisposing him to illness. When illness occurs in a religious and pious person, it is rationalized by the belief that God allows men to suffer in order to learn.
>
> (Kiev, 1968:34)

Second, diseases are classified according to their underlying cause. Krajewski-Jaime (1991) traces disease etiology along three lines: (1) natural and supernatural forces (diseases believed to be caused by natural forces, such as moonlight, eclipses, cold, heat, air, wind, sun, and water, or traced to the supernatural and magic); (2) imbalances of heat and cold (drawing directly from the ancient humoral theory, which identified positive health as occurring when the hot and cold forces within the body are in balance); and (3) emotion-based diseases (often resulting from a frightening or traumatic experience).

Third, like all other healing systems, curanderismo healing logically follows the nature of disease etiology. Because disease is traced through several lines, the curandero (or curandera) must have several types of healing treatments available, including prayer, herbal medicine, healing rituals, spiritualism, massage, and psychic healing. Two examples (the first pertaining to hot–cold diseases and the second to emotion-based diseases) illustrate this. First:

> Some diseases are hot and some are cold. Foods and herbs are also classified into hot or cold for

treatments. Sickness that enhances the cold within the body requires a hot treatment to restore the balance, and vice versa. To avoid a hot sickness, the person must not become cold; therefore, the individual must not walk barefoot on cold tiles for fear of catching tonsillitis. . . . People are given chili, a hot food, or chicken soup, for a cold disease such as pneumonia or a common cold, and lard, having cold properties, is used on burns.

(Krajewski-Jaime, 1991:162)

The second example is a healing treatment used for a person suffering from *espanto*—a form of fright thought to be caused by the spirit being so frightened that it leaves the body:

Treatment by the folk healer includes having the patient lie down on the floor with arms outstretched in the position of a cross. Sweeping the body with branches, herbs, and prayers, she coaxes the lost spirit to re-enter the victim's body.

(Krajewski-Jaime, 1991:162)

Finally, the curandero–patient relationship is very close. Curanderos typically live in the same community as their patients, share the same basic values, and recognize the importance of personal involvement and rapport. Patients expect, and receive, extensive time with the curandero. The culture within which this relationship occurs supports the therapeutic value of the curandero's healing practices.

Organized Medicine and Curanderismo. Due to the cultural importance of folk healing in the Chicano community, the extent to which it is intertwined with religious beliefs, and its location primarily in just one region of the United States (although it exists in Hispanic communities around the country), organized medicine has been reluctant to aggressively comment on or act against curanderos. Research indicates that they are paid very little (sometimes with food or other goods) and are not viewed as representing a generalized or serious threat to the medical establishment. While there is evidence that use of curanderos has declined during the last few

decades, curanderismo remains an important part of many Hispanic communities.

Current and Future Status. Many Hispanic people follow a "dual model of medical care" in that they seek care from both medical doctors and curanderos. Padilla et al. (2001) found that almost all the Hispanic patients receiving conventional care at a public hospital in Denver knew what a curandero is, and 29 percent had been to a curandero at some time in their life. Visits were most common for treatment for Mexican folk illnesses such as espanto and *empacho* (gastrointestinal obstruction). Research on Hispanic patients with diabetes found two-thirds who used some form of alternative medicine (mostly herbs and prayer), but none who used a curandero (Hunt, Arar, and Akana, 2000).

Native American Healing

Traditional Native American healing remains common among the 5 million Native Americans and Alaskan natives in the United States. While all Native American peoples share a general understanding of the causes of health and illness and of healing practices, there are in effect as many different healing systems as there are tribes. This section focuses on healers and healing among the Dineh, part of the Navajo people. The Navajo are the second-largest Native American group (after the Cherokee), with just over 332,000 members, according to the 2010 US Census.

Origin and Historical Developments. Navajo healing practices can only be appreciated within the context of Navajo culture. Understandings of disease and illness emanate from and are consistent with Navajo beliefs about the creation of earth and how the Navajo people came to be located where they are—on Dinetah (mostly northern Arizona).

Navajo healing is completely intermeshed with the religious belief system. Many of the

Navajo religious rituals are focused on maintaining good health—on wellness—and eliminating the root causes of illness. To maintain good health, one must live according to prescribed lifeways identified at the time of creation.

Basic Principles. Navajo philosophy is based on the belief that "everything in the world has life; all things breathe and live and have a spirit and power . . . all of these beings are interrelated and influence the workings of the universe; each has a role and responsibility for maintaining order in the universe" (Avery, 1991:2271). This philosophy contributes to a love and respect for "Mother Earth" and "Father Sky" and the wonders of the natural environment, and a feeling of "oneness" with animals. Navajos do not attempt to "master" nature but to be one with it.

Wellness exists when this harmony is achieved. Ursula Knoki-Wilson, a Navajo nurse-midwife, interpreter, and teacher, defines health holistically as "the synergistic interaction of all the dimensions (physical, mental, and spiritual) of a person at full potential," and wellness as the "way that positive thought influences feeling so that the nature of a person's life experience includes growth, renewal, and miracles" (Knoki-Wilson, 1992).

Second, when imbalances or disharmony develop, illness results. Illness occurs "when the free flow of spiritual energy to the mind, body, and soul is decreased by factors inside or outside the person" (Knoki-Wilson, 1992). Internal factors include such things as violence, destructiveness, anger, stubbornness, guilt, shame, and participation in any Navajo taboos (e.g., wasting natural resources). External factors include being a victim of witchcraft, disease, or object intrusion (i.e., invasion of the body by a worm, snake, or insect) and soul loss (which usually occurs during a dream when the soul departs the body). All these occurrences may have a supernatural origin (Knoki-Wilson, 1983).

Third, restoration to health occurs when the disharmony or imbalances are resolved or

eliminated. Healing is enacted in physical, mental, and spiritual dimensions. Practitioners of Western medicine often emphasize the mental and spiritual dimensions of Navajo healing, but only because these are often given so little prominence in their own techniques. Navajos emphasize that healing can only occur when all three dimensions are involved. The ultimate goal of the healing practice is a return to oneness or harmony with nature. Figure 11.1 summarizes the ingredients necessary for successful Navajo healing.

Finally, at least four separate medical persons (all of whom can be female or male) are used in Navajo healing. One sees a *diagnostician* to learn the cause of illness and to obtain a prescription for the appropriate healing practice. The diagnostician, who is believed to have a special gift, may be a hand trembler (who diagnoses by passing their hands over the patient's body and receiving messages from the spirits), a stargazer (who reads messages in the stars), or a crystal gazer (who looks through crystals to "X-ray" the body in order to locate problems).

The primary healer is called a *medicine person* or *singer* and has received a divine calling as someone with special qualities through whom the spirits can work: "Medicine persons are gifted with extrasensory perception that allows them to make mythological associations and identify the causes and remedies for illnesses" (Knoki-Wilson, 1983:279). Healing practices include prayer, participation in rituals, use of herbal medicines, chants, physical manipulations, and ceremonial

Figure 11.1 Ingredients of Navajo Healing

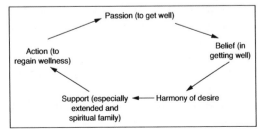

observances (Avery, 1991). Elaborate ceremonies lasting from a few hours to 9 days (with only brief respites) (e.g., the Yeibeichei Dance) are used to effect cures. Because the ceremonies are very structured and elaborate and must be followed precisely, medicine persons often study and apprentice for years in order to be able to conduct just one or two types.

The *herbalist* has practical knowledge about treatment of minor illnesses and has expertise in the preparation and use of herbal remedies.

Rather than utilizing the complex traditional healing ceremonies, some Navajos will use religious rituals of the Native American Church and practitioners known as *roadmen*. These ceremonies typically use peyote as the healing herb and last only a single night, but they combine elements of the philosophy of the Navajos, the Plains Indians, and Christianity.

Organized Medicine and Native American Healing.   Today, scientific medicine and Native American healing practices largely coexist peacefully on the Navajo reservation. Although scientific medicine is practiced in the hospitals and clinics of the Indian Health Service, provisions are made within hospitals for patients to bring in medicine persons, and space is provided for traditional healing ceremonies. Many Navajos, including those who live on the reservation and those who live in urban areas, use both conventional and traditional types of medicine (Buchwald, Beals, and Manson, 2000; Kim and Kwok, 1998). Navajos often use scientific medicine to treat the symptoms of illness but rely on traditional healing practices to treat the cause. This enables access to modern medical knowledge and technology without sacrificing the benefits of the holistic approach and community support provided by traditional healing practices.

Current and Future Status.   The beauty of the Navajo culture and the benefits of traditional Native American healing practices will be preserved if young Navajo women and men who have been called to be healers and are willing to make the commitment to learn the healing ceremonies. This remains a major challenge.

SUMMARY

Although scientific medicine is firmly established in the United States, millions of people use, are satisfied with, and even prefer complementary, alternative, and integrative healing practices. Organized medicine has traditionally expressed opposition to many CAM practices for being ineffective and potentially harmful to patients. CAM healers have argued that, like conventional healers, they seek to provide effective care, and they counter that orthodox healing practices have proved ineffective or even harmful for some. In recent years, antagonism has diminished and cooperative relationships have grown. Many people follow a "dual model of medical care," using both orthodox and CAM healers.

Chiropractic has gained significant legitimacy. It is licensed in all 50 states, accepted by insurance companies, and is increasingly accepted by many medical doctors.

In the early 1970s, acupuncture took America by storm. Although it quickly became popular with patients, orthodox medicine did not accept its theoretical foundation and acted to restrict its practice. Recently, however, there has been substantial scientific endorsement of acupuncture and its use has become more common.

Many physicians and laypeople perceive religious practices to have beneficial effects on health, but much skepticism exists about the general efficacy of spiritual healing. While the relative health of the Christian Science population is in dispute, Christian Scientists have achieved much recent success in having their healers recognized as legitimate and in getting religious exemption laws passed in states.

Curanderismo and Native American healing represent two types of folk healing practices.

Both are very much a part of their respective cultures and religious belief systems. Although there are differences between the systems, both are more holistic than orthodox medicine and more concerned with the causes of illness than with merely treating symptoms.

HEALTH ON THE INTERNET

1. You can learn more about complementary and alternative medicine by visiting the website of the National Center for Complementary and Integrative Health at

   www.nccih.nih.gov

   What is the purpose of this site? Click on "Health Info" and then click on "What is Complimentary, Alternative, and Integrative Health?" Read through all the information provided. How many of the CAM practices identified here have been used by you, members of your family, or your friends?

   To find out about two other popular CAM healing practices, visit

   www.homeopathic.org (National Center for Homeopathy) to learn about homeopathy

   and www.naturopathic.org (American Association of Naturopathic Physicians) to learn about naturopathy. How are these two practices alike, and how are they different?

2. To learn more about CBD oil, listen to the podcast, "CBD: Weed Wonder Drug?" from *Science Vs.* at

   https://gimletmedia.com/shows/science-vs/wbhj24/cbd-weed-wonder-drug

   How did CBD oil progress so quickly from being a potential treatment for certain types of seizure disorders to the newest health fad? What health benefits do regular users attribute to CBD oil? In your opinion, is enthusiasm for the therapeutic effects of CBD oil justified?

DISCUSSION CASE

In June 1990, David and Ginger Twitchell were tried for negligent homicide (involuntary manslaughter) of their 2½-year-old son Robyn, who had died of an untreated bowel obstruction. The parents had contacted a Christian Science practitioner but not a medical doctor. Massachusetts law does recognize spiritual healing as a form of medicine, but it requires parents to seek orthodox medical care for seriously ill children.

Testimony at their trial revealed that Robyn had suffered excruciating pain during the last 5 days of his life. A large section of his colon,

scrotum, and other tissues had become necrotic, and even the pressure of a diaper on his abdomen caused him to scream in pain. Before becoming comatose, he began vomiting fecal material. The Twitchells consulted a Christian Science practitioner and nurse whose treatment consisted of "heartfelt yet disciplined prayer." The Twitchells' defense was that they were within their First Amendment rights to treat their son's illness with prayer, and that Massachusetts had recognized this right in an exemption to the statute outlawing child neglect.

The jury was said to be affected by testimony that, while forbidding medical care for children with critical illnesses, Christian Science does permit orthodox obstetric care (Mrs. Twitchell had received anesthesia when Robyn was born) and orthodox dental care (Mr. Twitchell had received treatment from a dentist for a root canal and impacted wisdom teeth).

What should be the legal responsibility of parents with critically ill children? Should society legally obligate all parents, regardless of their religious convictions, to utilize orthodox medical care? Would this, as Christian Scientists claim, interfere with the First Amendment right to religious freedom? Do judges and juries have a right to state that prayer is inadequate medical treatment? Based on the histories of alternative healing practices presented in this chapter, what dangers would there be from this type of regulation?

On the other hand, there are many laws in the United States governing parental behavior toward children and prohibiting child abuse and neglect. Shouldn't the failure to obtain medical care that would probably have eliminated their son's pain and saved his life be considered the ultimate act of child abuse? Even if adults have a right to use whatever type of healing practice they choose, shouldn't society require orthodox medical care for children (after all, wasn't Robyn too young to adopt Christian Science as his own religious philosophy)?

In this particular case, the Twitchells were convicted of involuntary manslaughter. They were sentenced to 10 years' probation and required to take their remaining children for regular visits to a pediatrician. In 1993, the conviction was overturned on a legal technicality. However, a spokesperson for the prosecutor's office stated that the law now clearly stated that parents could not sacrifice the lives of their children in the name of religious freedom.

GLOSSARY

acupuncture
alternative medicine
chiropractic
Christian Science healing
complementary medicine

curanderismo
dual model of care
integrative medicine
religious exemption laws
spiritual healing

REFERENCES

Adams, Jon, Wenbo Peng, Holger Cramer, Tobias Sundberg, Craig Moore, Lyndon Amorin-Woods, David Sibbritt, and Romy Lauche. 2017. "The Prevalence, Patterns, and Predictors of Chiropractic Use Among US Adults: Results from the 2012 National Health Interview Survey." *Spine* 42(23):1810–1816.

American Chiropractic Association. 2019. "Key Facts and Figures About the Chiropractic Profession." Retrieved May 30, 2019 (www.acatoday.org/Patients/Why-Choose-Chiropractic/Key-Facts).

Angell, Marcia, and Jerome P. Kassirer. 1998. "Alternative Medicine: The Risks of Untested and Unregulated Remedies." *New England Journal of Medicine* 339(12):839–841.

Asher, Gary N., Amanda H. Corbett, and Roy L. Hawke. 2017. "Common Herbal Dietary Supplement–Drug Interactions." *American Family Physician* 96(2):101–107.

Avery, Charlene. 1991. "Native American Medicine: Traditional Healing." *Journal of the American Medical Association* 265(17):2271, 2273.

Bearon, Lucille B., and Harold G. Koenig. 1990. "Religious Cognitions and Use of Prayer in Health and Illness." *The Gerontologist* 30(2):249–253.

Benor, Daniel J. 1984 "Psychic Healing." Pp. 165–190 in *Alternative Medicines: Popular and Policy Perspectives*, edited by J. Warren Salmon. New York: Tavistock.

Benson, Herbert, Jeffery A. Dusek, Jane B. Sherwood, Peter Lam, Charles F. Bethea, William Carpenter, Sidney Levitsky, Peter C. Hill, Donald W. Clem, Manoj K. Jain, David Drumel, Stephen L. Kopecky, Paul S. Mueller, Dean Marek, Sue Rollins, and Patricia L. Hibberd. 2006. "Study of the Therapeutic Effects of Intercessory Prayer (STEP) in Cardiac Bypass Patients: A Multicenter Randomized Trial of Uncertainty and Certainty of Receiving Intercessory Prayer." *American Heart Journal* 151(4):934–942.

Beyerstein, Barry L. 2001. "Alternative Medicine and Common Errors of Reasoning." *Academic Medicine* 76(3):230–237.

Bonn-Miller, Marcel O., Mallory J.E. Loflin, Brian F. Thomas, Jahan P. Marcu, Travis Hyke, and Ryan Vandrey. 2017. "Labeling Accuracy of Cannabidiol Extracts Sold Online." *Journal of the American Medical Association* 318(17):1708–1709.

Buchwald, Dedra, Janette Beals, and Spero M. Manson. 2000. "Use of Traditional Health Practices among Native Americans in a Primary Care Setting." *Medical Care* 38(12):1191–1199.

Caplan, Ronald L. 1984. "Chiropractic." Pp. 80–113 in *Alternative Medicines: Popular and Policy Perspectives*, edited by J. Warren Salmon. New York: Tavistock.

Christian Science Journal Directory, Professional Services and Church Information. 2019. Retrieved May 31, 2019 (https://directory.christianscience.com/).

Clarke, Tainya C., Lindsey I. Black, Barbara J. Stussman, Patricia M. Barnes, and Richard L. Nahin. 2015. *Trends in the Use of Complementary Health Approaches among Adults: United States, 2002–2012*. National Health Statistics Reports, Number 79. Hyattsville, MD: National Center for Health Statistics.

Coe, Rodney M. 1970. *Sociology of Medicine*. New York: McGraw-Hill.

Cowen, Virginia S., and Vicki Cyr. 2015. "Complementary and Alternative Medicine in US Medical Schools." *Advances in Medical Education and Practice* 6:113–117 (https://doi.org/10.2147/AMEP.S69761)

Gevitz, Norman. 1988. *Other Healers: Unorthodox Medicine in America*. Baltimore, MD: The Johns Hopkins University Press.

———. 1989. "The Chiropractors and the AMA: Reflections on the History of the Consultation Clause." *Perspectives in Biology and Medicine* 32(2): 281–299.

Goldner, Melinda. 1999. "How Alternative Medicine is Changing the Way Consumers and Practitioners Look at Quality, Planning of Services, and Access in the United States." *Research in the Sociology of Health Care* 16:55–74.

Goldstein, David N. 1972. "The Cult of Acupuncture." *Wisconsin Medical Journal* 71(10):14–16.

Goldstein, Michael S. 1999. *Alternative Health Care*. Philadelphia, PA: Temple University Press.

Gottschalk, Stephen. 1988. "Spiritual Healing on Trial: A Christian Scientist Reports." *The Christian Century* 105:602–605.

Hunt, Linda M., Nedal H. Arar, and Laurie L. Akana. 2000. "Herbs, Prayer, and Insulin: Use of Medical and Alternative Treatments by a Group of Mexican American Diabetes Patients." *Journal of Family Practice* 49(3):216–223.

Jou, Judy and Pamela Jo Johnson. 2016. "Nondisclosure of Complementary and Alternative Medicine Use to Primary Care Physicians: Findings from the 2012 National Health Interview Survey." *JAMA Internal Medicine* 176(4):545–546.

Kiev, Ari. 1968. *Curanderismo: Mexican-American Folk Psychiatry*. New York: Free Press.

Kilgore, Christine. 1998. "Alternative Medicine: Probing Its Core." *Health Measures* 3:26–30.

Kim, Catherine, and Yeong Kwok. 1998. "Navajo Use of Native Healers." *Archives of Internal Medicine* 158(20):2245–249.

Knoki-Wilson, Ursula M. 1983. "Nursing Care of American Indian Patients." Pp. 271–295 in *Ethnic Nursing Care*, edited by Modesta S. Orque, Bobbie Bloch, and Lidia S. Monroy. St. Louis, MO: Mosby.

———. 1992. "Lecture: 'Navajo Traditional Healing'." Chinle, AZ, June 23.

Koenig, Harold G., Lucille B. Bearon, and Richard Dayringer. 1989. "Physician Perspectives on the Role of Religion in the Physician-Older Patient Relationship." *Journal of Family Practice* 28(4):441–448.

Koenig, Harold G., Michael E. McCullough, and David B. Larson. 2001. *Handbook of Religion and Health*. New York: Oxford University Press.

Krajewski-Jaime, Elvia R. 1991. "Folk-Healing Among Mexican American Families as a Consideration in the Delivery of Child Welfare and Child Health Care Services." *Child Welfare* 70(2):157–167.

Kronenfeld, Jennie J., and Cody Wasner. 1982. "The Use of Unorthodox Therapies and Marginal Practitioners." *Social Science and Medicine* 16(11):1119–1125.

McCaffrey, Anne M., David M. Eisenberg, Anna T.R. Legedza, Roger B. Davis, and Russell S. Phillips. 2004. "Prayer for Health Concerns." *Archives of Internal Medicine* 164(8):858–862.

Meeker, William C., and Scott Haldeman. 2002. "Chiropractic: A Profession at the Crossroads of Mainstream and Alternative Medicine." *Annals of Internal Medicine* 136(3):216–227.

Melzack, Ronald, and Patrick Wall. 1965. "Pain Mechanisms: A New Theory." *Science* 150(3699):971–979.

Nahin, Richard L., Patricia M. Barnes, and Barbara J. Stussman. 2016a. "Expenditures on Complementary Health Approaches: United States, 2012." *National Health Statistics Reports* 95:12.

———. 2016b. "Insurance Coverage for Complementary Health Approaches Among Adult Users: United States, 2002 and 2012." *NCHS Data Brief* 235:8.

National Center for Complementary and Integrative Health. 2017. "Acupuncture." Retrieved June 19, 2019 (https://nccih.nih.gov/health/acupuncture/introduction).

———. 2019a. "Chiropractic." Retrieved June 19, 2019 (https://nccih.nih.gov/health/chiropractic).

———. 2019b. "Complementary, Alternative, or Integrative Health: What's in a Name?" Retrieved June 19, 2019 (https://nccih.nih.gov/health/integrative-health).

Nestle, Marion. 2013. *Food Politics: How the Food Industry Influences Nutrition and Health* (Revised & Expanded 10th Anniversary ed.). Berkeley, CA: University of California.

Nguyen, Long T, Roger B. Davis, Ted J. Kaptchuk, and Russell S. Phillips. 2011. "Use of Complementary and Alternative Medicine and Self-Rated Health Status: Results from a National Survey." *Journal of General Internal Medicine* 26(4):399–404.

Padilla, Ricardo, Veronica Gomez, Stacy L. Biggerstaff, and Phillip S. Mehler. 2001. "Use of Curanderismo in a Public Health Care System." *Archives of Internal Medicine* 161(10):1336–1340.

Reed, Louis. 1932. *The Healing Cults.* Chicago, IL: University of Chicago Press.

Shelley, Brian M., Andrew L. Sussman, Robert L. Williams, Alissa R. Segal, Benjamin F. Crabtree, and on behalf of the Rios Net Clinicians. 2009. "'They Don't Ask Me So I Don't Tell Them': Patient-Clinician Communication About Traditional, Complementary, and Alternative Medicine." *The Annals of Family Medicine* 7(2):139–147.

Shim, Jae-Mahn, John Schneider, and Farr A. Curlin. 2014. "Patterns of User Disclosure of Complementary and Alternative Medicine (CAM) Use." *Medical Care* 52(8):704–708.

Simpson, Elizabeth. 2017. "A Decade after Being in the Spotlight, Virginia Man Turned to Stem Cells to Treat Cancer. They Saved His Life." *The Virginian-Pilot*, July 27. Retrieved June 19, 2019 (https://pilotonline.com/news/local/health/honestly-if-i-had-not-done-this-i-would-have/article_cda34761-8278-53bf-8dfd-eb4f27571b61.html).

Simpson, William F. 1989. "Comparative Longevity in a College Cohort of Christian Scientists." *Journal of the American Medical Association* 262(12):1657–1658.

Sivén, Jacqueline M., and Joanna Mishtal. 2012. "Yoga as Entrée to Complementary and Alternative Medicine and Medically Pluralistic Practices." *Human Organization* 71(4):348–357.

Skolnick, Andrew. 1990. "Christian Scientists Claim Healing Efficacy Equal if Not Superior to That of Medicine." *Journal of the American Medical Association* 264(11):1379–1381.

Snow, Loudell F. 1993. *Walkin' Over Medicine: Traditional Health Practices in African-American Life.* Boulder, CO: Westview Press.

Talbot, Nathan A. 1983. "The Position of the Christian Science Church." *New England Journal of Medicine* 309(26):1641–1644.

Tilburt, Jon C., Farr A. Curlin, Ted J. Kaptchuk, Brian Clarridge, Dragana Blocic-Jankovic, Ezekiel J. Emanuel, and Franklin G. Miller. 2009. "Alternative Medicine Research in Clinical Practice." *Archives of Internal Medicine* 169(7):670–677.

US Bureau of Labor Statistics. 2020. "Chiropractors." *Occupational Outlook Handbook.* Retrieved April 24, 2020 (www.bls.gov/ooh/healthcare/chiropractors.htm).

US Food & Drug Administration. 2019. "Dietary Supplement Products & Ingredients." Retrieved May 29, 2019 (www.fda.gov/food/dietary-supplements/dietary-supplement-products-ingredients).

Versnik Nowak, Amy L., Joe DeGise, Amanda Daugherty, Richard O'Keefe, Samuel Sweard, Suma Setty, and Fanny Tang. 2015. "Prevalence and Predictors of Complementary and Alternative Medicine (CAM) Use among Ivy League College Students: Implications for Student Health Services." *Journal of American College Health* 63(6):362–372.

Wardwell, Walter I. 1992. *Chiropractic: History and Evolution of a New Profession.* St. Louis, MO: Mosby Year Book.

Winnick, Terri. 2005. "From Quackery to 'Complementary' Medicine: The American Medical Profession Confronts Alternative Therapies." *Social Problems* 52(1):38–61.

Wolpe, Paul R. 1985. "The Maintenance of Professional Authority: Acupuncture and the American Physician." *Social Problems* 32(5):409–424.

CHAPTER 12

The Physician–Patient Relationship: Background and Models

Learning Objectives

- Identify and explain each of the three key dimensions of the physician–patient relationship.

- Discuss the extent to which patients want to be informed fully about their health and be active participants in their health care. Identify and discuss the key reasons why patient expectations are often not met.

- Discuss the impact of race on physician attitudes and patient care.

- Identify and discuss ways in which the gender of the physician and gender of the patient influence patient care.

- Discuss the issue of patient adherence to medical regimens from a sociological perspective.

Despite the increasing complexity of the health care system, the actual encounter between physician and patient remains a key element. In the United States, patients make about 1 billion visits to physicians' offices each year. Many people have an idealized picture of this relationship—a sick patient places trust in and seeks comfort from a caring physician, and both do whatever is necessary to restore health to the patient.

In fact, neither patients nor physicians are so uncomplicated or behave in such a uniform manner, and the relationship between the two can be an elusive phenomenon to diagram. Sociologists attempt to clarify the relationships that actually develop between physicians and patients and to identify important influences on the relationship.

MODELS OF THE PHYSICIAN–PATIENT RELATIONSHIP

The Parsonian Model

Nature of the Relationship. Within sociology, Talcott Parsons (1951) pioneered efforts at explaining the physician–patient relationship as a subsystem of the larger social system. The key values in this subsystem reflected key values in society, and they were shared by physicians and patients as they entered a relationship. According to Parsons, the physician–patient relationship is inevitably (and fortunately) asymmetrical. Parsons believed that three circumstances dictated that physicians play the key, powerful role within the dyad and govern the relationship with patients.

1. *Professional prestige.* It is the physician who has medical expertise, years of training, and

societal legitimation as the ultimate authority on health matters.

2. *Situational authority.* It is the physician who has established the medical practice and is offering her or his services to patients who have admitted their own inadequacies by soliciting the physician.

3. *Situational dependency.* It is the patient who has assumed the role of supplicant by scheduling an appointment, often waiting past the scheduled time, answering the physician's questions, and allowing an examination to occur.

Throughout each encounter, the "competency gap" between physician and patient is highlighted as the patient is dependent on the physician and the resources of the physician's office. However, Parsons expected that physicians would use their power wisely in promoting patients' best interests, and that patients would accept this arrangement as the most efficient means to enact cure.

Freidson's Criticisms of the Parsonian Model.   Perhaps the most important criticism of Parsons' model is that it overstates the "mutuality of interests" between physician and patient and does not provide for the considerable variation that now exists in physician–patient encounters. Conflict theorists dispute the notion that physicians and patients interact harmoniously and develop mutually satisfactory relationships through cooperation and consensus. Eliot Freidson (1970) was a leading critic of the Parsonian model and an advocate for a conflict approach. He contended that conflict and dissensus are inevitable in any relationship in which parties have such different backgrounds and power is so unequally distributed.

The Szasz–Hollender Model

An early (and now classic) effort to modify the Parsonian model was developed by two MDs, Thomas Szasz and Marc Hollender (1956).

Arguing that Parsons paid too little attention to the important influence of physiological symptoms, they developed their own typology of the physician–patient relationship, which includes three models.

The Activity–Passivity Model.   This model closely parallels Parsons' asymmetrical relationship. The physician represents medical expertise, controls the communication flow between the two parties, and makes all important decisions. The patient is lacking in important information and must rely on the knowledge and judgment of the physician. The relationship is akin to that of a parent and infant, in which the parent takes actions without need of explanation.

The Guidance–Cooperation Model.   Szasz and Hollender view this form of interaction as typical of most medical encounters. The patient is acknowledged to have feelings, may be alarmed by the medical problem, and has certain hopes and aspirations for the outcome. Compared with the activity–passivity model, the patient has increased involvement in providing information and making decisions with regard to treatment. While the physician is still in charge and has responsibility for guiding the encounter, the cooperation of the patient is sought. The physician is less autocratic in the sense that some explanation is provided to the patient, and the patient's assent to decisions is desired, but the physician retains the dominant position. Szasz and Hollender describe this relationship as similar to that between a parent and an adolescent.

The Mutual Participation Model.   Based on a view that egalitarian relationships are to be preferred in medicine, this model elevates the patient to the level of full participant. In this case, both physician and patient acknowledge that the patient must be a central player for the medical encounter to be successful. The patient knows more about her or his own situation—medical history, symptoms, and other relevant events—than does the physician. While the physician attempts to ask the proper questions to elicit key information, it is assumed that the patient also has an obligation to ensure that relevant information is disclosed.

In order for this type of relationship to work, Szasz and Hollender stipulate that both participants must have approximately equal power (similar to a relationship between two adults), there must be some feeling of mutual interdependence, and the interaction must in some ways be satisfying to both parties.

Because this model "requires" more from the patient, Szasz and Hollender suggest that it may be less appropriate for children or those who are mentally deficient, poorly educated, or very immature. On the other hand, those who are more intelligent or sophisticated, who have broader experiences, and who are more eager to take care of themselves may find this to be the only satisfying relationship.

KEY DIMENSIONS OF THE PHYSICIAN–PATIENT RELATIONSHIP

An appropriate model of the physician–patient relationship must acknowledge the considerable differences that exist among physicians and patients about what should occur within the relationship. The following three dimensions of the relationship are key:

1. The appropriate model of health (a belief in the biomedical or biopsychosocial model of health) as viewed by physician and patient.
2. The primary ethical obligation of the physician (patient autonomy or beneficence) as viewed by physician and patient.
3. The extent of commitment to and realization of genuine therapeutic communication.

The actual relationship that develops between a given physician and patient is determined by the orientations held by both. This is not to deny that the physician is in a very powerful position. For the reasons enumerated by Parsons and elaborated upon by many others, physicians have the potential to command the decisive voice. However, many physicians now reject this position, and many patients have been socialized not to let them assume it.

The Appropriate Model of Health

The Biomedical Model. As scientific discoveries produced meaningful explanations of diseases and effective medical treatments, **the biomedical model** of health became the dominant therapeutic orientation—a position it held for much of the twentieth century. Biomedical medicine is disease or illness oriented rather than patient oriented. The key to effective medical care is believed to be correct diagnosis of some physiological aberration followed by proper application of the cure. Physicians seek to learn all they can about symptoms and abnormalities so they can provide the appropriate "magic bullet."

Consideration of social, psychological, and behavioral dimensions of illness has little place in this framework because they appear unnecessary. Engel (1977:129) cited one health authority speaking at a Rockefeller Foundation seminar who urged that "medicine concentrate on the 'real' diseases and not get lost in the psychosociological underbrush. The physician should not be saddled with problems that have arisen from the abdication of the theologian and the philosopher." Another speaker advocated "a disentanglement of the organic elements of disease from the psychosocial elements of human malfunction."

This biomedical focus has been the cornerstone of medical education, which surely helped to sustain it. Both coursework and clinical experience emphasized the biological basis of disease and illness, while psychological and social factors received little attention.

The Biopsychosocial Model. While some individuals have always lobbied for a broader approach to health care, it was not until the 1970s that the campaign flourished. A key figure, George Engel, a professor of psychiatry and medicine at the University of Rochester Medical School, argued that a broader approach could be incorporated without sacrificing attention to biomedical matters, and that both are needed to provide optimal care. He emphasized that a full understanding of disease and illness and the formulation of proper treatment must include consideration of the patient, the social context in which he or she lives, and the health care system. This requires a **biopsychosocial model** (Engel, 1977:132).

Well-respected physician and author Timothy Quill (1982) has suggested the following four principles distinguish the biopsychosocial approach to patient care:

1. The patient is addressed as a whole person, whether or not he or she has a disease.
2. The doctor–patient relationship is continuous, at all stages of the patient's life, through sickness and health, until either the physician or the patient dies, moves, or terminates the relationship.
3. The physician utilizes both biotechnical skills and interpersonal skills to help the patient.
4. Both the patient and the physician make explicit, and then negotiate, their respective needs and expectations.

Current Assessment. The extent to which physicians employ the biomedical or biopsychosocial approach is determined by their efforts to identify psychosocial concerns of patients. Three empirical questions can be posed. First, do many patients have specific psychosocial concerns? Do patients want their physicians to consider these concerns? Do physicians attempt to do so?

Many researchers have formulated a specific list of social or psychological matters that may affect health status and then have interviewed physicians and patients to determine the extent to which

these are actually discussed in the medical encounter. These matters pertain to family circumstances, personal relationships, income concerns, work environment and activities, sexual activity, nutritional patterns, and self-care practices—all topics that may influence health, but that many physicians have not routinely discussed. Interestingly, research shows that many primary care patients do not have a serious physical ailment, but as many as half do have psychosocial concerns. These may include matters related to social stress and emotional distress (e.g., normal anxiety, grief, frustration, and fear), social isolation (people seeking advice, human interaction, social support, and information), and need for reassurance.

Are patients genuinely interested in discussing these psychosocial concerns with their physician? Do these discussions actually occur? A study involving 23 primary care practices found that more than 70 percent of the patients believed it was appropriate to seek help from primary care physicians for psychosocial problems, but less than one-third of those who had experienced such problems had discussed them with their physician. Providers frequently failed to recognize emotional distress and family difficulties (Good, Good, and Cleary, 1987). Several studies find that family physicians are unaware of most of what is happening in their patients' lives, and that less than 10 percent of the conversation during average medical visits centers on patient psychosocial concerns (Roter, Hall, and Katz, 1988).

Why don't more physicians give attention to psychosocial concerns? Traditionally, many physicians felt that they were poorly trained to do so, that these issues were beyond their expertise, and/or that patients may consider it an invasion of privacy. But, in the last decade, important changes have begun to occur as medical schools focus more on social determinants of health and illness, and more physicians have patients complete social histories, which are then followed up on in discussion. Still, there is much room for progress.

Primary Ethical Obligation

Perhaps the most important ethical orientation of physicians relative to patient care is whether they give priority to the principle of patient autonomy or the principle of beneficence.

The Principle of Autonomy. Autonomy is a term derived from the Greek words for "self" and "rule, governance, or law," and refers to self-determination. Autonomous individuals are able to make their own choices and decisions and have them respected by others. The concept of autonomy makes three key assumptions:

1. An autonomous person is able to make rational and competent decisions following contemplative thought. People who are incapable of acting autonomously may include those who are too young, who have some significant mental disability, or are coerced or unduly pressured into a decision by physicians or other health care professionals—or, more commonly, by family members ("You have the surgery or the kids and I are leaving").

2. A second assumption is that an action does not cause harm to others. The freedom of any individual to act stops short of causing harm to another; a decision to harm another incurs no obligation of respect.

3. Patients do not have the right to demand that physicians or other health care professionals violate a personal or professional moral code. For example, patients cannot make an unrestricted claim on some scarce resource (e.g., by demanding a liver transplant). This assumption was clearly expressed in the Elizabeth Bouvia case described in the accompanying box, "The Case of Elizabeth Bouvia."

The principle of autonomy requires that physicians enable patients to make fully informed decisions and then respect the decisions patients make. This does not limit professional expertise in diagnosis, developing a prognosis, making recommendations for treatment, or carrying out agreed–upon treatment. However, it does prevent physicians from acting without the patient's fully informed consent.

IN THE FIELD

THE CASE OF ELIZABETH BOUVIA

In the summer of 1983, Elizabeth Bouvia, a 26-year-old woman with physically incapacitating cerebral palsy, checked into Riverside (California) Hospital and stated her intention to starve herself to death. She said that her deteriorating condition (an inability to feed or care for herself in any way, increasingly painful arthritis, and physical incontinence) made life not worth living. She was physically unable to take her own life and wished the hospital to provide hygienic care and pain relief while she starved herself to death.

The hospital refused her request and made plans to force-feed her should she not eat of her own volition. The chief of psychiatry at the hospital was quoted as saying, "The court cannot order me to be a murderer nor to conspire with my staff and employees to murder Elizabeth." The story became public, and the American Civil Liberties Union decided to represent Elizabeth's wishes in court.

The initial court ruled against Elizabeth. The judge acknowledged prior court decisions (and the ethical principle) that competent,

(Continued)

(Continued)

informed patients have the right to refuse medical care, even if their refusal contradicts medical advice or might shorten their life. However, he concluded that Elizabeth's plan not to take food and water in the hospital involved more than a refusal of treatment. Because she desired care while she died of malnutrition and dehydration, she was, in essence, asking hospital staff to assist in a suicide or direct killing that was morally and professionally unacceptable to them.

While the *Bouvia* decision carried several ramifications, and was later overturned, it has been interpreted as supporting the principle that neither physicians nor hospital staff may be forced to act in ways they interpret as violating a professional or personal moral code.

Informed Consent. Legally and ethically, patients who are able to exercise autonomy must be given all relevant information regarding their condition and alternative treatments, including the possible benefits, risks, costs, and other consequences and implications. This is the meaning of **informed consent**. A genuine informed consent exists only when the patient is competent, is given all of the information that might affect decision making, comprehends this information, and makes a voluntary choice. For surgery, other invasive procedures, or procedures with any significant risk, patients are typically required to sign an official informed consent form. However, the spirit of informed consent is no less applicable—although often less followed—in the medical office.

Recently, some have suggested that physicians may have a responsibility to share information with patients beyond that that which affects them directly. For example, do physicians have an obligation to discuss with patients the fact that many commonly used medical tests are often not necessary yet add significant dollars to the nation's overall health bill? In 2012, the American Board of Internal Medicine Foundation created a "Choosing Wisely" program to inform physicians and patients about the cost of medically unnecessary tests (Sawicki, 2017).

The Principle of Beneficence. An alternative guiding ethical principle for physicians is **beneficence**—doing good for the patient. While the general meaning of the concept is to promote goodness, kindness, or charity, in the medical context it refers to physicians taking whatever actions (e.g., surgery or prescribing a medication) are considered in the patient's best interest.

Prioritizing Autonomy and Beneficence. An ethical dilemma arises when doing good for the patient (beneficence) conflicts with an informed patient's wishes (patient autonomy). It sometimes occurs that a rational and competent patient chooses an action that a physician believes is not in her or his best interest. Physicians must then decide whether it is more important to protect patient autonomy or do what is perceived to be in the patient's best interest. A physician exhibits **paternalism** when she or he overrides a patient's wishes and takes action presumed to be in the patient's best interest but is unwanted by the patient.

This situation also creates a choice for the patient. If a patient desires self-determination, and the physician refuses to grant it, the patient can try to be persuasive, can accede to the physician's wishes, or can shop for another physician. Of course, if full information is not given, the patient may not be aware that their choice is being limited.

The accompanying box, "Autonomy and Paternalism in Israel," describes how the tension between these orientations is worked out in another country.

IN COMPARATIVE FOCUS

AUTONOMY AND PATERNALISM IN ISRAEL

In 1991, the US Congress passed the Patient Self-Determination Act (PSDA) as a means to protect and highlight patient autonomy. The PSDA requires hospitals and other institutional providers to inform patients that they have a legal right to make their own health care decisions (through the process of informed consent), to prepare an advance directive to indicate how they would like to be treated if they are unable to make their own decisions at some future time, and to refuse unwanted medical treatment. It is a clear expression of the importance of patient autonomy in the United States.

In 1996, Israel passed the Israeli Patient Rights Act (IPRA) to address some of the same issues. The IPRA guarantees that Israel will provide universal health care coverage (which, of course, is not provided in the United States) and embraces the concept of informed consent. However, Israelis were not provided with a right to refuse unwanted medical treatment, and physicians were not obligated to respect the wishes of any patient making an informed refusal of treatment. In those cases, the matter is submitted to an ethics committee, which typically requires that the treatment be given as long as it is expected to help the patient's condition, and there is some expectation that the patient will give consent *after* the procedure.

US law is rooted in the importance of the individual and in the principle of autonomy. Israel is a communitarian society with a high level of collective consciousness, mutual concern, and interdependence. In communitarian societies, individual rights are often subservient to collectively defined ideals and goals. Ensuring that health care is available to all citizens is one aspect of the collective ideal, and ensuring that individuals receive life-saving treatment, with or without their consent, is another aspect (Gross, 1999).

Current Assessment. Historically, most physicians prioritized beneficence and automatically made decisions for patients, and neither physicians nor patients gave much thought to the importance of patient self-determination. However, in the last 50 years, the principle of autonomy has become the dominant ethical orientation. Now, most physicians support patient participation in medical decision making, although many still see themselves as the ultimate decision maker.

Research examining patients' desire to participate in medical decision making and their desire to make their own decisions shows that patients overwhelmingly want as much information as possible. However, there is some ambivalence among patients regarding the proper decision maker. While few patients want to make their own decisions without help from the physician, many believe that it should be a shared process, and many others are most comfortable with the physician being the ultimate decision maker.

The desire to participate in medical decision making was examined in a study of more than 600 patients at a Boston hospital. Based on responses to a series of questions, the authors placed each patient in one of four categories: (1) pre–contemplation (do not participate and do not intend to), 17.2 percent of patients; (2) contemplation (do not participate but contemplating doing so), 6.9 percent of patients; (3) preparation (participate to some degree), 36.1 percent of patients; and (4) action (participate fully), 39.8 percent of patients. What predicted the patients' desired level of participation? Patients who were older, less educated, had greater severity of illness, and were most trusting of physicians had the lowest level of participation and the least interest in participating. Younger patients, the well-educated, those with less severe illnesses, and those with the most confidence in their own decision making wanted to be and were the most involved (Arora, Ayanian, and Guadagnoli, 2005).

When patients do fully participate, it is often because they are assertive and demand participation. For example, a study of women receiving care in an ultrasound clinic for reasons other than pregnancy found that those who were more assertive—repeating information when they thought the physician had not heard them, asking the physician to clarify information they did not understand, and reminding the physician about screening tests—were more likely to receive a mammogram than patients who were less assertive (Andersen, Abullarade, and Urban, 2005).

Moreover, even on occasions when it may appear that physicians are seeking to promote autonomy and involve the patient in decision making, they sometimes offer patients only an illusion of choice. In these situations, physicians have essentially predetermined a course of action and then presented the options in such a way as to steer the patient toward the physician's preferred course (Zussman, 1992).

Establishment of Therapeutic Communication

It may seem obvious that good communication between physician and patient is desirable. However, this commonsense understanding understates the therapeutic importance of communication as it has been linked to improved health outcomes, increased patient adherence to instructions, and greater patient and physician satisfaction. It is a wonder that for so long it was not a point of emphasis in medical education. This section addresses four questions: (1) What is meant by "therapeutic communication?" (2) Does it routinely develop? (3) What barriers prevent it

from developing more often? (4) How can it be facilitated?

Therapeutic Communication. There are three components of **therapeutic communication**: (1) The physician engages in full and open communication with the patient and feels free to ask questions about psychosocial as well as physical conditions. (2) The patient provides full and open information to the physician and feels free to ask questions and seek clarifications. (3) A genuine rapport develops between physician and patient.

The Frequent Absence of Therapeutic Communication. Although many physicians place a high value on developing therapeutic communication with patients, and routinely do so, therapeutic communication does not exist in many physician–patient dyads. This may occur when physicians do not invite it and/or conduct themselves in such a way to encourage it and when patients do not feel comfortable with the physician, do not feel free to talk openly about their worries and concerns, have questions that go unasked or unanswered, and do not understand information that is provided. These are not satisfying encounters for most patients.

Providing ample time for patients, engaging in full and open communication, and establishing rapport are all ways that physicians encourage therapeutic communication

Barriers to Therapeutic Communication. Development of genuine therapeutic communication requires considerable effort, even for those committed to it as an ideal. This is due to several inherent obstacles to open communication in the medical setting.

1. *Setting of the medical encounter.* Most physician–patient contacts occur in the physician's office or a hospital—settings that do not put most people at ease. The unpleasant odors, the many sick people who seem to be invading each other's space, and the paperwork requirements all contribute to discomfort. There are few ways to relax except by reading current editions of esoteric magazines or newsmagazines that were timely in some previous year.

2. *Length of the medical encounter.* Genuine therapeutic communication cannot be developed in brief time segments. The average length of an office visit with a primary care physician is 13 to 16 minutes. Because some patients require more than that, others receive less time. Of course, only a fraction of this time is spent discussing the patient's illness.

3. *The mental state of the patient.* It would be a rare person who could communicate best when feeling worst. Most patients are feeling ill, are uncomfortable, may be anxious about their health and fearful of what will be learned, and are in awe of the physician. Not surprisingly, many do not think, speak, or hear clearly.

4. *Mismatched expectations of physicians and patients.* Patients go to a physician with symptoms, feelings of discomfort, and an inability to carry on normal activities. They seek clarification and want to know what to do to get better. Physicians, on the other hand, have been trained to convert patient complaints into medical diagnoses. They may evade discussions of anxieties and fears, and focus on the "medical facts." What the patient may need most is what the physician is least prepared to offer. These contrary expectations make therapeutic communication unlikely. One recent study found that physician and patient priorities in an encounter were aligned 69 percent of the time. Although this is a high figure, there were only partially aligned priorities in 19 percent of cases and totally unaligned priorities in 12 percent of cases (Tomsik et al., 2014).

5. *Language barriers.* The increasing diversity of the population means more patients have limited proficiency in the English language. In 2016, 21.6 percent of Americans spoke a language other than English at home, and many understood little or no English. Although an increasing number of health care sites offer interpreters in Spanish or whatever language is most familiar to their patients, many other sites do not. In these cases, genuine therapeutic communication is unlikely.

6. *Physician communication style.* Several decades of research on physician–patient communication has demonstrated remarkable consistency on two key patterns. First, physicians often "talk down" to patients, are abrupt with them, and discourage open communication. Some physicians offer little greeting to patients as they enter the room. Going after "just the facts," they provide no opening for patients to talk about their concerns or how they perceive current problems relate to other events in their life. These physicians may interrupt patients or otherwise signal a lack of interest in what is being said. They maintain spatial distance when not conducting a physical examination, and do everything possible to reinforce social distance.

Buller and Buller (1987) refer to this as the *control* style of communication, and the net result is predictable—almost no therapeutic communication occurs. Often physicians who adopt this style do not even allow patients to complete their opening statement (recent research has found that on average physicians interrupt patients' opening comments after 11 seconds), do not invite questions, and do not respond directly to patient questions. No wonder that many patients see their physician as being authoritarian and they feel discouraged from participating in their own care. The alternative style, *affiliation*, includes such behaviors as friendliness, empathy, candor, genuineness, openness to conversation, and a non-judgmental attitude, and is designed to establish a positive relationship with the patient.

Second, patients often do not understand the terminology used by physicians. People who have learned the jargon of a particular subject often forget that most others have not. Even terms that are familiar to most college students, such as "eating disorder" and "depression," are not understood by many patients. These are commonly used terms in the medical setting, yet when they are used, many patients misunderstand the message. Not surprisingly, many physicians underestimate their own use of medical jargon.

THE CURRENT MOVE TO PATIENT-CENTERED CARE

In the last several years, clinicians have initiated a major move toward **patient–centered care**—that is, respectful care that is responsive to individual patient preferences, needs, and values. This statement addresses all three principal components of the physician–patient relationship: it endorses a biopsychosocial model of medicine that values patient autonomy and the development of therapeutic communication. It is designed to move health care delivery to fully consider the patient's cultural traditions, personal values, family situation, and social circumstances. The emphasis is on providing ready access to coordinated care for all, treating the whole person, developing effective communication, empowering patients, and collaborating with them. The intent is to shift health care's orientation from the physician as centerpiece to the patient as centerpiece.

A core element of patient-centered care is **shared decision making**, defined by the Office of the National Coordinator for Health

Information Technology as "a process in which clinicians and patients work together to make decisions and select tests, treatments and care plans based on clinical evidence that balances risks and expected outcomes with patient preferences and values" (quoted in Heath, 2017).

> We've learned, for instance, that providing patients with information or evidence alone isn't sufficient to support patients who are making a decision. An initial assumption in shared decision making was that if the technical information of medicine were available in a patient-friendly format, then patients would have the necessary resources to come to decisions. When we summarized the evidence on each medication option for patients with type 2 diabetes, we found this did little to help them make decisions. When we changed the focus to how patients and clinicians talked through this decision and organized evidence according to how each medication affected the issues that matter to patients (e.g., weight gain or loss and the manner of administration), patients were able to draw on the evidence to ask questions in conversation and come to decisions that made good sense for them. . . . The real challenge is how to use evidence to discover what's best for the particular patient in light of his or her circumstances and values. The medium in which this happens is patient-clinician conversation.
> (Hargraves et al., 2016)

The two keys to enhancing patient participation and shared decision making are **health literacy** and **patient activation**. **Health literacy** is the degree to which individuals have the capacity to obtain, process, and understand basic health information and services needed to make appropriate health decisions. To be health literate, one must be able to navigate the health care system, including filling out complex forms and locating providers and services; share personal information, such as health history, with providers; engage in self-care and chronic-disease management; and understand mathematical concepts such as probability and risk.

Typical estimates are that only 12 or 13 percent of adults in the United States are at a proficient health literacy level, and more than a third have difficulty with tasks such as understanding patient handouts, following medication instructions, or reading nutrition labels. To have patients be able to competently engage in shared decision making, health literacy levels must be increased.

Patient activation describes "the skills and confidence that equip patients to become actively engaged in their health care" (Hibbard and Greene, 2013:207). This entails having individuals assume greater responsibility for managing their own health and their own health care. It includes making good decisions about lifestyle—for example, about diet, exercise, and tobacco use—and knowledgeably using health care resources available to them. It requires a cultural shift toward individuals being more responsible for their own health, but also a shift in creating environments in which positive and appropriate health actions are encouraged.

The current push toward shared decision making, health literacy, and patient activation is due to accumulating research evidence that they lead to significant benefits to patients and to the health care system. Patients with lower levels of health literacy:

- Are more likely to report poor health status
- Are less likely to obtain preventive health services
- Are twice as likely to be hospitalized
- Remain in the hospital for more days during each admission
- Are less likely to comply with recommended treatment

- Are more likely to make medication errors
- Incur higher health care costs
- Are less likely to ask health care questions (Seubert, 2009).

Patients with lower patient activation levels:

- Are more likely to report unmet medical needs
- Are more likely to have unmet prescription drug needs
- Are more likely to delay care
- Have lower levels of preventive health behaviors and preventive care
- Are less likely to engage in self-management of health conditions
- Are less likely to seek and use health care information from available health sources
- Appear to get less support from their providers in managing their health
- Are less likely to report that their provider helped them to set goals and taught them how to self-manage their condition
- Are less likely to follow through on lifestyle changes and comply with treatment plans
- Are less likely to ask questions (Seubert, 2009).

Advocates for strengthening the emphasis on patient activation and health literacy believe they should become an organizational goal of all health care organizations (Koh et al., 2013).

IN THE FIELD

CHANGING THE PHYSICIAN–PATIENT RELATIONSHIP

In addition to "patient–centered care," at least four other developments are changing the physician–patient relationship:

1. The use of evidence-based medicine. Traditionally, health care providers used a variety of techniques—medical school

training, personal experiences, peer consultation, reading medical journals, personal intuition—to develop treatment recommendations. This resulted in considerable variation in treatment plans from physician to physician. As discussed in Chapter 8, physicians are increasingly using evidence-based

(Continued)

(*Continued*)

medicine—that is, research that directly compares the success of treatments. Many professional medical associations have issued and are encouraging physicians to follow consensus development statements that delineate standardized diagnosis and treatment protocols for various diseases based on careful examination of the scientific evidence.

2. The increased use of patient satisfaction surveys. Research increasingly finds that satisfied patients are more likely to maintain a continuing relationship with their provider and are more likely to adhere to medical instructions. Hospitals are looking more closely at patient satisfaction data in an effort to boost their reputation. Since 2013, part of physicians' reimbursement from Medicare is based on patient satisfaction data, thus giving physicians a financial incentive to establish more satisfied patients.

3. The increased public availability of health information. Through both the Internet and direct-to-consumer advertising, medical knowledge is increasingly available to the general public. The number of health-related apps is increasing every day, and they enable users to monitor their health in previously unavailable ways. Various consumer groups are encouraging individuals to procure and use this information to their health benefit. Although many physicians have yet to be convinced of the utility of all this information, it is highly improbable that it will decrease in popularity.

The fundamental change between past and present medicine is access to information. There used to be a significant inequality between doctor and patient. No longer. As people understand the risks as well as the benefits of modern medicine, we increasingly desire more information before we are willing to rely on trust to see us through. This need to be transparent about what doctors know (and what they do not), to engage in a consultation on closer to equal terms with patients, has changed the way medicine is practiced (Horton, 2003).

4. The increasing incorporation of and financial incentives to use electronic health records (EHRs). EHRs are an electronic version of a patient's medical record, including background information, medical history, medications, vital signs, immunizations, laboratory data, radiology reports, and billing information. EHRs are designed to eliminate the need to track down a patient's previous paper medical records, and hopefully assist in ensuring accurate and legible data. EHRs are increasingly used as part of the patient activation process. They can be useful in electronic messaging, facilitating patient access to personal medical records and test results, tracking chronic illness management, and providing health education (White and Danis, 2013).

THE INFLUENCE OF RACE, SEXUAL ORIENTATION, GENDER IDENTITY, AND GENDER ON THE PHYSICIAN–PATIENT RELATIONSHIP

Ideally, physicians offer their best professional efforts to every patient. This does not mean that every patient will be treated in exactly the same manner—that is unrealistic. College professors do not treat all students the same, clergy do not treat all parishioners the same, and physicians do not treat all patients the same. However, a reasonable objective is that physicians will impartially deliver their best efforts to every patient. Yet physicians have a more difficult time working with some patients than others. This causes less effective interactions with, for example, patients from lower socioeconomic groups, or patients with a specific gender or sexual identity, or patients who are of a different gender, race, or ethnic group to the medical provider.

The existence of cultural stereotypes, prejudice, and discrimination remains a powerful force in the United States. When explicit biases and personal discrimination are enacted, inequities in life circumstances result. When institutional discrimination (unjust treatment of members of a particular group by practices embedded in large organizations such as governments and corporations) exists, there are enormous oppressive forces on entire groups of people. These forces also exist in health care.

Recently, considerable attention in the provision of health care has focused on the concept of **implicit bias**. An implicit bias is one that may not be consciously endorsed, intended, or even recognized, but exists nevertheless. Research suggests that such implicit biases contribute to health care inequities by shaping provider behavior and generating differences in medical treatment based on socioeconomic status, gender, gender identity, and race. For example, physicians experience higher levels of anxiety and frustration when working with lower-class patients, are less interested in the patient encounter, and spend less time with the patient. Because implicit biases are unrecognized, they can be especially difficult to monitor and control, but they can exert a very strong influence on behavior (Chapman, Kaatz, and Carnes, 2013; Hall et al., 2015).

Why does this discomfort or anxiety exist in some provider–patient relationships? Shim has proposed that these patterns are grounded in the perceived **cultural health capital** of the patient. Following the work of French sociologist, anthropologist, and philosopher Pierre Bourdieu, she conceives of cultural capital as the "repertoire of cultural skills, verbal and nonverbal competencies, attitudes and behaviors, and interactional styles" that people have to one degree or another and that may be prized or not at certain historical moments. Shim (2010:4), like Bourdieu, sees

cultural capital as being context specific, so she uses the term "cultural health capital" to denote:

- Knowledge of medical topics and vocabulary, which in turn depends upon an understanding of scientific rationality and health literacy
- Knowledge of what information is relevant to health care personnel
- The skills to communicate health-related information to providers in a medically intelligible and efficient manner
- An enterprising disposition and proactive stance toward health, both of which presuppose a sense of mastery and self-efficacy
- The ability to take an instrumental attitude toward one's body
- Belief in the value of, and the resources to practice, self-discipline
- An orientation toward the future and its control through calculation and action
- A sensitivity to interpersonal dynamics and the ability to adapt one's interactional styles
- The ability to communicate social privilege and resources that can act as cues of favorable social and economic status and consumer savvy.

These traits are especially valued in American culture, and are embodied by many medical providers. They have become especially important at this juncture of history.

Over the course of the past four decades, the shifting health care landscape has intensified the demands placed on patients to be knowledgeable about how to maneuver through the health care bureaucracy and to be self-directive about their own care in a time of shortened appointments and heightened gate-keeping. . . . Patients who possess or acquire and display an enterprising and proactive disposition, a fluency in biomedical concepts and language, bureaucratic know-how, and an interactional agility with authoritative experts are more able to successfully navigate such organizational complexity. The cultural expectations and responsibilities of contemporary patienthood—in terms of self-knowledge, self-surveillance, health promotion, disease management, and the like—have also escalated, at least in the United States.

(Shim, 2010:6)

Thus provider–patient interactions are shaped in part by the cultural health capital brought to an interaction by patients and in part by the receptiveness of providers and their willingness to work with patients to develop cultural health capital. This is very much a micro perspective. However, Shim also advocates for understanding how broader social forces—including explicit biases and personal and institutional discrimination—confer advantages of social status, education, and power on some rather than others, and thus enable some to develop more cultural health capital. This adds a macro-institutional perspective to her analysis.

Race

People of color in the United States experience disparities across the health care system (Feagin and Bennefield, 2014). They have less access to health care, less satisfactory interactions with medical providers, slower and fewer referrals to a variety of medical procedures, and worse health outcomes. An increasing number of studies have found that many white physicians feel some discomfort working with black patients. Hall et al. (2015) examined 15 studies of health care bias that met methodologically rigid criteria. Fourteen of the studies found low to moderate levels of implicit racial and ethnic bias among health care professionals. Most of the providers held implicit bias toward black, Hispanic, Latinx, and dark-skinned people, at about the same level found in the general population.

According to many studies, this implicit bias negatively affects provider–patient interaction (Chapman, Kaatz, and Carnes, 2013). Black patients have lower levels of trust in their physician, rate their visits to physicians as less participatory, and wait longer for medical care.

Several studies report evidence of disparities in treatment for heart disease received by blacks and whites. Data from the National Hospital Discharge Survey showed that blacks were less likely than whites to receive cardiac catheterization, coronary angioplasty, and coronary artery bypass surgery even after controlling for age, health insurance, hospital, and condition. The authors concluded that the race of the patient influenced the likelihood of receiving these procedures (Giles et al., 1995). In a study of more than 5,000 Medicare recipients, Epstein et al. (2003) found whites were more likely than blacks to receive clinically indicated revascularization procedures, and that the underuse by black patients was linked to higher mortality rates. Key documents published by the Institute of Medicine in 2003 and within the American Sociological Association's Series on How Race and Ethnicity Matter (Spalter-Roth, Lowenthal, and Rubio, 2005) concluded that systematic racial bias in the provision of health care contributes to the unequal health outcomes among racial and ethnic groups.

IN COMPARATIVE FOCUS

CLINICIANS' BIASES IN THE UNITED STATES AND FRANCE

Much can be learned about the effects of American physicians' negative racial attitudes toward black patients by using a comparative focus. For example, Khosla et al. (2018) studied racial attitudes of physicians in both the United States and France (both majority-white Western nations). Physicians in both countries were asked to report their impressions of an identical black or white man patient based on a physician's notes. Specifically, the study focused on clinicians' expectations of anticipated patient improvement, adherence to treatment instructions, and perceptions about how personally responsible the patient was for his health for both the black and white patients.

French clinicians did not exhibit any significant racial differences on any of the three examined attitudes. On the other hand, American physicians rated hypothetical white patients, compared to identical black patients, as significantly more likely to improve, to adhere to treatments, and to be personally responsible for his own health. Results indicated that the personal responsibility item was key for American physicians and influenced the other two attitudes. Due to the large differences, the authors concluded that the formation of racial attitudes is country-specific and thus possibly culturally rooted. If American physicians were reflecting racial attitudes that they themselves had learned, they may in fact be unaware of them—that is, an implicit bias.

Moreover, much research (Shelton and Richeson, 2015; Penner et al., 2017) has discovered that attitudes and beliefs brought by black patients to medical interactions with white providers also influence the orientation of both participants. In Penner's study of racially discordant oncology interactions, perceived previous discrimination, mistrust of physicians, and an expectation of mistreatment by black patients influenced provider behavior in a negative way. Thus predispositions of both provider and patient influenced the quality of interaction.

Gender and Sexual Minorities

Research demonstrates significant health disparities between transgender and gender non-binary (TGGNB) persons compared to cisgender persons. These disparities arise from several factors, including negative health experiences. Findings from the US Transgender Survey (James et al., 2016) show that one-third of TGGNB persons have experienced a negative interaction with a health care provider related to their gender, and that anticipated or experienced discrimination has discouraged as many as 1 in 3 from seeking care. In turn, lack of care-seeking negatively affects the mental and physical health of TGGNB individuals (Cruz, 2014).

Attempting to learn more about what TGGNB individuals want and don't want in their health care encounters, Baldwin et al. (2018) studied descriptions of positive and negative experiences from 119 TGGNB individuals. The things most desired are:

1. Use of language that respects gender diversity
2. Being knowledgeable and experienced with TGGNB health issues
3. Receiving disclosure of identity in a routine, non-judgmental way.

Characteristics of negative experiences are:

1. Misgendering (not recognizing/understanding one's identity; not knowing what pronoun to use); Paine (2018) referred to this as a process of "embodied disruption" that occurs when providers are not able to think beyond dominant binary terms in dealing with sex/gender/sexuality—a process that can stigmatize the patient and disrupt the medical interaction;
2. Lack of information and experience with TGGNB health issues;
3. Transphobia (providers showing discomfort or negative attitudes about identity; denial of care).

These negative experiences are often rooted in the explicit and implicit biases of providers. In a study that lasted from 2006 to 2012 and included more than 2,300 medical doctors, 5,300 nurses, 8,500 mental health providers, and 2,700 other treatment providers, heterosexual providers had implicit preferences for treating heterosexuals over lesbian and gay people. Heterosexual nurses—both men and women—had the strongest implicit preference for treating heterosexual men as opposed to gay men. Among all groups of providers, implicit preferences were stronger than explicit preferences (Sabin, Riskind, and Nosek, 2015).

On the positive side, the amount of research on the health care needs and experiences of LGBTQ+ individuals has increased significantly in recent years, and these issues are beginning to receive more attention in medical schools.

Cisgender

Considerable research has focused on the role of gender (using the cisgender binary categories of men and women) in the physician–patient relationship. This section focuses on both gender of the physician and gender of the patient.

Gender of the Physician. Weisman and Teitelbaum (1985) suggest that physician gender could influence the physician-patient relationship in three ways:

1. *Systematic differences in the socialization of men and women physicians may lead to differences in personality, attitudes, or interpersonal skills.* For example, early gender-role socialization might result in women physicians being more nurturant and expressive with patients and better able to develop empathic relationships.
2. *Systematic differences in expectations that patients bring to the encounter based on physician gender. For example, whatever the actual practice style, patients might expect women physicians to be*

more nurturant and empathic and relate to them on that basis.
3. *Alteration of the relationship based on the congruence or lack of congruence in gender of physician and patient.* For example, women patients seeing a woman physician are more likely to feel comfortable than when seeing men physicians.

Systematic Differences Between Women and Men Physicians. In many respects, physician practice style is unaffected by gender of the physician. Women and men physicians evaluate common medical problems in a similar manner, and there are few differences in diagnoses, prescriptions of medications, or frequency in hospitalizing patients. These similar practice styles are influenced primarily by the professional socialization process that occurs in medical schools and during residency.

However, some consistent and important differences between women and men physicians have been documented. Research has found that that women physicians are more likely than their men counterparts to adhere to clinical guidelines (using evidence-based medicine), provide preventive care, and provide more psychosocial counseling to their patients (Tsugawa et al., 2017). Several studies (e.g., Hall, Blanch-Hartigan, and Roter, 2011) have reported that women physicians demonstrate superior communication skills. Debra Roter, a professor of health, behavior, and society at Johns Hopkins Bloomberg School of Public Health and a leading expert in this field, stated:

> The work that my colleagues and I have done has demonstrated that there are very distinct gender-linked patterns of communication among male and female doctors. . . . Female physicians typically conduct longer patient visits than male physicians. They tend to ask more questions to elicit patients' opinions and check for mutual understanding. They provide more counseling on psychosocial issues related to lifestyle, daily living activities, social relationships, coping strategies, and stress. They're also more emotionally responsive. They're

more likely to express empathy, legitimation, concern, and reassurance when patients express the need for that, and they're also much more positive in the words that they use and the voice tone that they use.

   While these average differences are statistically significant, that doesn't mean that all female doctors are better than all male doctors. The overlap in the normal curve is much greater than the non-overlap.
   (quoted in Cruickshank, 2018)

Do patients notice these differences in communication style? Yes, at least subconsciously. Roter points out that both women and men patients talk more when with women physicians than men physicians, and they disclose more information that has medical relevance—both psychosocial information (such as lifestyle and coping) but also specific information about their medical condition (such as problems they are having with medications) (Cruickshank, 2018).

Several studies have found that women's strongest preference for a woman physician is in relation to women's health problems, including cervical screening, breast screening by physical examination, breast screening by mammography, and instruction in breast self-examination. While women physicians spend more time than men physicians with each patient, the greatest differential is in obstetrics and gynecology—the field in which the superior communication skills of women physicians are especially noted (Christen, Alder, and Bitzer, 2008).

Do these differences in practice style affect health outcomes? Yes, they can. Recently, Tsugawa and colleagues (2017) conducted a massive study of 58,344 general internists (32.1 percent women) who had treated at least one Medicare beneficiary who was hospitalized with a medical condition during a 4-year study period. More than 1.5 million hospitalization episodes were examined. They investigated the association between physician gender and 30-day mortality and readmission rates, standardized by all potentially influential patient, physician, and hospital characteristics.

Patients treated by women internists had lower 30-day mortality rates and fewer hospital readmissions compared with patients cared for by men internists. Were the differences large? No and yes. The differences were statistically significant but very modest (about half a percentage point). However, they did occur in all eight of the medical conditions on which researchers focused and occurred at all levels of illness severity. Had men physicians had the same outcomes as women physicians, there would have been 32,000 fewer deaths in the Medicare population in this 4-year period. These findings suggest that differences in practice patterns between men and women physicians may have important clinical implications for patient outcomes.

Gender of the Patient.   Although there is considerable anecdotal evidence of gender stereotyping among physicians, the extent to which gender stereotyping of patients still occurs is unclear. Traditionally, many medical providers held the view that women's complaints were often related to emotional instability, that women exaggerate claims of the severity of medical symptoms, and that women are more demanding patients. Research has found that these views are still held by some physicians.

Does gender stereotyping lead to differential treatment? Research has produced mixed findings. In one widely cited study from the late 1970s, the answer was yes. Five medical complaints (back pain, headache, dizziness, chest pain, and fatigue) were studied in married couples who had been seen for at least 5 years by one or more men family practice physicians. The researchers found that the physicians conducted more extensive workups for the men patients, and concluded that gender stereotyping affected care (Armitage, Schneiderman, and Bass, 1979).

However, some studies from that same period failed to detect treatment differences. Greer et al. (1986) attempted to replicate the Armitage study (using the same five medical complaints) when examining the medical charts of 100 married couples seen for a minimum of 2 years by one or more of 20 physicians (10 men and 10 women). They found no significant differences in the extent of the workup based on gender of the patient.

Waitzkin (1984) attempted to identify biases that occur in the actual communication process between women patients and their physicians. Using audiotapes of 336 interactions between men internists and their patients, Waitzkin sought to determine if the men internists withheld information from or talked down to women patients more often than with men patients. Contrary to expectations, women patients received more physician time, asked more questions, and received more technical explanations and clarifications.

On the other hand, there is conclusive research evidence that gender bias does exist in the management of coronary heart disease. Chakkalakal et al. (2013) studied the application of five specific aspects of the physical examination given by medical residents to patients presenting with chest pains. The residents were more likely to perform correctly each of the five aspects of the examination on men patients than on women patients.

A separate study of adults presenting to an emergency room with acute chest pain found that women patients were less likely to be admitted to the hospital, undergo a stress test in the next month, and undergo cardiac catheterization, even after controlling for clinical and non-clinical factors (Johnson et al., 1996). Other studies have found that women receive less aggressive treatment than men following a heart attack, even after controlling for relevant factors.

In attempting to explain exactly how this happens, researchers have sought explanations beyond gender stereotyping and discrimination. Welch et al. (2012) have found that physicians tend to treat heart disease symptoms less aggressively— that is, they order fewer diagnostic tests and delay prescribing appropriate medication—when they are uncertain about the diagnosis. Because so much heart disease research has been conducted on men, and because the prevailing understanding is that women are more likely to have atypical heart disease symptoms, physicians have greater diagnostic uncertainty when considering heart disease for women patients. This is one possible explanation, but much more needs to be learned about gender differences in clinical decision making, especially regarding heart disease.

Cultural Competency

In recent years, efforts have begun to produce "culturally competent" physicians. **Cultural competence** is an ability to work effectively with members of different cultures. It includes awareness of one's own cultural background, knowledge about other cultures, an openness to working with diverse individuals, and effective communication skills to do so (Office of Minority Health, 2016). The Affordable Care Act requires that health care providers be capable of practicing in a multicultural society. They must be aware of their own biases and stereotypes and also of different cultural, racial/ethnic, and linguistic factors that form barriers to patients' understanding of and adherence to prescribed regimens and to optimal health outcomes. Academic accreditation agencies now mandate that health-related professions include cultural competence in the list of competencies students should demonstrate by graduation.

These initiatives are beginning to show some success, as patients from all cultural groups report improved interaction with and positive feelings about the physicians undergoing this training. Studies have found that positive physician affect, rapport-building behaviors, and longer visits have reduced racial disparities in level of physician trust for minority patients (Martin et al., 2013). However, for programs aimed at reducing racial disparities to be genuinely effective, Malat (2013) cautions that they must go beyond efforts to understand "cultural differences" and squarely address the existence and effects of the racial bias and discrimination discussed earlier in this chapter.

PATIENT SATISFACTION WITH PHYSICIANS

Even if there was no instrumental value attached to patient satisfaction, it would be a highly desirable end product of the physician–patient encounter. However, research has confirmed that patient satisfaction is linked to several other desirable outcomes. Satisfied patients are more likely to adhere fully to medical regimens, more likely to return for scheduled follow-up visits and to maintain continuity of care, more likely to seek physician care when sick, and less likely to initiate a medical malpractice suit. There is increasing recognition that positive health outcomes are more likely to occur when the patient is satisfied with the care received.

Level of Satisfaction

Are most patients satisfied with the primary health care they receive from a physician? The answer is yes. Research shows a consistent pattern— patients have significant misgivings about the health care system in general (in 2018, only 34 percent of the general public expressed a positive view of the health care industry; in 1975, it was 75 percent) and about physicians in general, but they are very satisfied with their own physician (McCarthy, 2018). On most surveys, satisfaction level is quite high, although not as high as in many other countries.

Factors Related to Patient Satisfaction

Based on dozens of studies, four conclusions can be drawn about factors that influence patient satisfaction:

1. Patient background characteristics have little effect on satisfaction. As discussed earlier, race

is a clear exception. In a systematic review of the literature on this subject, Malat (2001a) concluded that satisfaction with medical care is lower among blacks than among whites, and identified both structural factors (e.g., lower incomes, less likelihood of health insurance, and less likelihood of continuity of care) and microlevel factors (e.g., racial discrimination and social distance) as contributing to the pattern.

Several studies have found that, among all racial and ethnic groups, patient satisfaction is higher when the race of the provider and the patient is the same (LaVeist and Nuru-Jeter, 2002). Audiotaped physician–patient encounters document that race-concordant visits are longer and are characterized by more positive patient affect (Cooper et al., 2003), and that African American patients perceive that they are treated more respectfully by black than by white physicians (Malat, 2001b). However, few studies have found clear clinical benefits from race-concordant relationships.

However, a 2016 study (which used data collected in 2009–2010) of the Hospital Consumer Assessment of Health Care Providers and Systems compared responses of black and white patients on measures of overall hospital rating, communication, clinical processes, and hospital environment. They found no substantive differences. Blacks were less likely to recommend hospitals but reported more positive experiences than whites. They rated hospitals serving mostly minority patients as lower in quality, but within any given hospital, black patients reported better experience than whites (Figueroa et al., 2016). Does this study portend broader change or is it an aberration? Additional research will need to address this point.

2. Most patients feel ill-equipped to assess the technical competence of their physician. Typically, patients simply assume that the physician is competent and base their evaluation on

other factors such as interaction skills. However, patients are now more knowledgeable than ever before about health matters, and many actively solicit second opinions. This may provide patients with more information with which to make informed assessments of the technical competence of their physician.

3. The level of satisfaction or dissatisfaction patients have with their health care is significantly influenced by the quality of the communication process that occurs. Patients are much more likely to be satisfied with their health care when they establish an ongoing relationship with a physician, when they establish rapport with the physician, when the physician conveys empathy, when they are given (and retain) more information about their symptoms and participate more in possible treatments, and when they are able to ask questions and discuss their ideas and those of the physician. Not surprisingly, patient satisfaction is lower when there are language differences between physician and patient.

4. Patient satisfaction is positively affected when physicians discuss psychosocial concerns and preventive health care. Despite the reluctance of some physicians to delve into these areas, or their belief that patients might prefer not to talk about them, patients want these matters discussed and are more satisfied with the care received when they are.

PATIENT ADHERENCE TO MEDICAL REGIMENS

Adherence to medical regimens (often formerly called "compliance") refers to the extent to which patients adhere to instructions communicated in the medical encounter. Instructions may include a request for follow-up visits, taking medications, and changes in lifestyle—either temporary (e.g., get plenty of rest this week) or long term (e.g., stop smoking cigarettes). Research shows that about 25 percent of prescriptions are never filled, and half of all patients fail to take their medications as instructed and fail to adhere with other regimens. Understanding the reasons for non-adherence is important because it is associated with worse patient outcomes, more hospital visits, and higher out-of-pocket expenses (Roebuck et al., 2011).

Research indicates that patients want and appreciate physicians who take time with them and establish genuine rapport.

Source: Photo by Janet Jonas.

When research on adherence began in the 1970s, studies showed that most physicians underestimated the proportion of patients who did not adhere to their instructions. Physicians believed that they provided sufficient information and rationale for patients to adhere fully, and they regarded non-adherence as an irrational response by the patient. Accounts of non-adherence pointed to factors such as individual personality characteristics (e.g., having uncooperative personalities), unpleasant drug side effects, not understanding physicians' instructions, and a lack of motivation (Spencer, 2018).

Factors Related to Adherence

Considerable research on patient non-adherence has led to five specific findings:

1. Sociodemographic characteristics of patients such as age, gender, level of education, and income are not reliable predictors of adherence behavior.
2. Patient knowledge of the disease or illness does not accurately predict adherence. For many years, clinicians and social scientists believed that adherence rates could be increased by creating more knowledgeable patients. However, many non-adherers are very knowledgeable about their condition but still choose not to follow instructions.
3. The seriousness of the patient's disease or illness is not strongly related to adherence—that is, more seriously ill patients are not more likely to be adherers. Even having had a heart attack does not make a patient more likely to give up smoking.
4. The complexity of the medical regimen does influence adherence behavior. More complex regimens (e.g., medications that must be taken several times per day in restricted situations for a long period of time) are less likely to be followed than simpler, short-term medication orders.
5. The most important factor affecting adherence is the extent of change required in the patient's life. Regimens that require significant life change (e.g., a major change in diet, a significant increase in exercise, or elimination of tobacco products)—especially those that require giving something up as opposed to adding something—are least likely to be followed.

Sociological Explanations for Adherence Behavior

Sociological research offers an alternative way of thinking about non-adherence: there may be logical explanations for patient decisions not to follow instructions. These include difficulties navigating the medical system, economic limitations, constraints arising from relationships with family members, and problems integrating some regimens into life demands. Spencer (2018) identifies three ways that these factors fit better with today's health care system in which physician authority has declined and biomedicalization and patient involvement have increased:

1. Biomedicalization now generates more possible pathways for care, and medical directives are less forceful, directional, and clear-cut than their 1970s counterparts.
2. Examining adherence now must take into account how the regimen was created and communicated and the extent of acceptance by the patient.
3. The greater number of options for health decision making requires a shift in thinking from "patient refusal to follow regimens" to "patient actively determining the course of treatment."

Peter Conrad (1987) suggests that non-adherence should be regarded as a matter of patient self-regulation. Rather than viewing non-adherence as a matter of deviance needing correction, he sees non-adherence as a matter of patients tailoring their medical regimens to their lifestyles and life responsibilities. This may include factors such as beliefs of the patient about potential consequences of a disease and the extent of life-style disruption created by certain regimens.

One in-depth study of 19 women given one or more regimens found that they assigned greater priority to normal life routines, and modified treatment regimens to fit into their pre-existing lifestyles. Rather than seeing themselves as non-adherent, they perceived that they were adhering as much as possible, given their other life responsibilities (Hunt et al., 1989).

SUMMARY

Talcott Parsons laid the foundation for understanding physician–patient interaction. Writing in the mid-twentieth century, he perceived the physician–patient relationship as asymmetrical, with power residing in the physician. He believed this asymmetry was inherent in the relationship due to the professional prestige and situational authority of the physician, and the situational dependency of the patient. Physician–patient relationships are now much more complex.

Three key dimensions define the physician-patient relationship—the patient treatment approach (biomedical or biopsychosocial), the primary ethical obligation of physicians (patient autonomy or beneficence), and the extent to which genuine therapeutic communication develops within the relationship. Patients do go to physicians with many psychosocial concerns that they want the physicians to address, but many physicians do not do this. Patients want to be well informed, but many still prefer the physician to be the chief decision maker. Research shows that many physicians talk down to patients and use terminology with which patients are unfamiliar.

Many physicians have difficulty communicating with patients whose background is different than their own. This difficulty can negatively impact patient care and health outcomes. However, there is increased emphasis today on patient-centered care, developing greater health literacy in patients, and encouraging patient activation. Despite many similarities between women and men physicians, women physicians demonstrate some important practice differences including many elements of superior communication skills.

Patients in the United States generally rate highly their encounters with physicians. The quality of communication between physician and patient and the physician's interest in patient psychosocial concerns are among the major determinants of patient satisfaction level.

About 50 percent of all patients fail to adhere to medical regimens. The more complex the regimen and the more invasive its effect on the patient's lifestyle, the lower the likelihood of adherence. Sociologists urge that we move beyond the traditional idea of patients complying or not complying with a physician's instructions and view instructions as something developed by physicians and patients together that patients then integrate into their life as well as possible.

HEALTH ON THE INTERNET

An interesting medical school–based website that deals with issues in the physician–patient relationship is sponsored by the University of Washington. Connect to this site at

https://depts.washington.edu/bhdept/ethics-medicine

What kinds of topics are covered? Click on "The Physician-Patient Relationship." Which of the three key dimensions in the physician-patient relationship—the patient treatment approach (biomedical or biopsychosocial), the primary ethical obligation of physicians (patient autonomy or beneficence), and the extent to which genuine therapeutic communication develops within the relationship—are encouraged in these sections? Click on Case #1. How would you respond in this circumstance? What values would underlie your responses?

DISCUSSION CASE

A complex situation occurs in medicine when a patient's religious beliefs dictate a medical decision that could be life-threatening. Attending physicians can be caught between respect for the patient's personal religious values and the First Amendment right to privacy on the one hand and their commitment to engaging in all reasonable efforts to save the patient's life on the other.

A specific illustration of this dilemma occurs when a member of the Jehovah's Witnesses sect needs a blood transfusion in order to survive. Jehovah's Witnesses adamantly refuse this procedure based on their interpretation of biblical scripture forbidding the "eating" or "taking in" of blood. They believe that voluntary or involuntary receipt of blood results in the loss of eternal life, and reject blood transfusions for adults and children. For discussion purposes, three cases involving Jehovah's Witnesses (modified from Tierney et al., 1984) are presented here.

Scenario 1: A 45-year-old bachelor visits his private physician after regurgitating large quantities of blood in the preceding 2 hours. He is taken to the hospital where examination reveals a continued slow oozing of blood in the patient's stomach. He is fully alert and informs his physician that, as a Jehovah's Witness, he will not accept a blood transfusion. His condition worsens, and the physician determines that a transfusion may be necessary to save his life.

Scenario 2: A 26-year-old married woman with two small children is involved in an automobile accident. Immediate removal of her spleen and a blood transfusion are necessary to save her life. The woman protests that she is a devout Jehovah's Witness and would sacrifice the chance to be with her family for eternity if she is transfused.

Scenario 3: An otherwise healthy infant is suffering and in need of an immediate life-saving blood transfusion. However, the parents are Jehovah's Witnesses and refuse transfusion of any blood products to their child. The parents state that they would rather have their child die (and be granted eternal life) than be transfused and continue life on earth but sacrifice eternal life.

What should be done in each of these situations? Should the blood transfusions be given? What are the implications of your position for the medical profession and for the rights of patients?

GLOSSARY

autonomy
beneficence
biomedical model
biopsychosocial model
cultural competence
cultural health capital
health literacy

implicit bias
informed consent
paternalism
patient activation
patient-centered care
shared decision making
therapeutic communication

REFERENCES

Andersen, Robyn M., Janne Abullarade, and Nicole Urban. 2005. "Assertiveness with Physicians is Related to Women's Perceived Roles in the Medical Encounter." *Women and Health* 42(2):15–33.

Armitage, Karen J., Lawrence J. Schneiderman, and Robert A. Bass. 1979. "Response of Physicians to Medical Complaints in Men and Women." *Journal of the American Medical Association* 241(20):2186–2187.

Arora, Neeraj, John Z. Ayanian, and Edward Guadagnoli. 2005. "Examining the Relationship of Patients' Attitudes and Beliefs with Their Self -Reported Level of Participation in Medical Decision-Making." *Medical Care* 43(9):865–872.

Baldwin, Aleta, Brian Dodge, Vanessa R. Schick, Brenda Light, Phillip W, Schnarrs, Debby Herbenick, and J. Dennis Fortenberry. 2018. "Transgender and Genderqueer Individuals' Experiences with Health Care Providers." *Journal of Health Care for the Poor and Underserved* 29(4):1300–1318.

Buller, Mary K., and David B. Buller. 1987. "Physicians' Communication Style and Patient Satisfaction." *Journal of Health and Social Behavior* 28(4):375–388.

Chakkalakal, Rosette J., Stacy M. Higgins, Lisa B. Bernstein, Kristina L. Lundberg, Victor Wu, Jacqueline Green, Qi Long, and Joyce P. Doyle. 2013. "Does Patient Gender Impact Resident Physicians' Approach to the Cardiac Exam?" *Journal of General Internal Medicine* 28(4):561–566.

Chapman, Elizabeth N., Anna Kaatz, and Molly Carnes. 2013. "Physicians and Implicit Bias: How Doctors May Unwittingly Perpetuate Health Care Disparities." *Journal of General Internal Medicine* 28(11):1504–1510.

Christen, Regula N., Judith Alder, and Johannes Bitzer. 2008. "Gender Differences in Physicians' Communicative Skills and Their Influence on Patient Satisfaction in Gynaecological Outpatient Consultations." *Social Science and Medicine* 66(1):1474–1483.

Conrad, Peter. 1987. "The Noncompliant Patient in Search of Autonomy." *Hastings Center Report* 17(4):15–17.

Cooper, Lisa A., Debra L. Roter, Rachel L. Johnson, Daniel E. Ford, Donald M. Steinwachs, and Neil R. Powe. 2003. "Patient -Centered Communication, Ratings of Care, and Concordance of Patient and Physician Race." *Annals of Internal Medicine* 139(11):907–915.

Cruickshank, Heather. 2018. "Are Women Better Doctors Than Men?" *Healthline*. Retrieved November 29, 2018 (www.healthline.com/health-news/women-doctors-better-patient-interactions#1).

Cruz, Taylor M. 2014. "Assessing Access to Care for Transgender and Gender Nonconforming People: A Consideration of Diversity in Combating Discrimination." *Social Science and Medicine* 110(June):65–73.

Engel, George L. 1977. "The Need for a New Medical Model: A Challenge for Biomedicine." *Science* 196(4286):129–136.

Epstein, Arnold M., Joel S. Weissman, Eric C. Schneider, Constantine Gatsonis, Lucian L. Leape, and Robert N. Piana. 2003. "Race and Gender Disparities in Rates of Cardiac Revascularization." *Medical Care* 41(11):1240–1255.

Feagin, Joe, and Zinobia Bennefield. 2014. "Systematic Racism and U.S. Health Care." *Social Science and Medicine* 103(February):7–14.

Figueroa, Jose F., Jie Zheng, John E. Orav, and Ashish K. Jha. 2016. "Across US Hospitals, Black Patients Report Comparable or Better Experiences Than White Patients." *Health Affair* 35(8):1391–1398.

Freidson, Eliot. 1970. *Professional Dominance: The Social Structure of Medical Care*. New York: Atherton Press.

Giles, Wayne H., Robert F. Anda, Michele L. Casper, Luis G. Escobedo, and Herman A. Taylor. 1995. "Race and Sex Differences in Rates of Invasive Cardiac Procedures in United States Hospitals." *Archives of Internal Medicine* 155(3):318–324.

Good, Mary-Jo D., Byron J. Good, and Paul D. Cleary. 1987. "Do Patient Attitudes Influence Physician Recognition of Psychosocial Problems in Primary Care?" *Journal of Family Practice* 25(1):53–59.

Greer, Steven, Vivian Dickerson, Lawrence J. Schneiderman, Cathie Atkins, and Robert Bass. 1986. "Responses of Male and Female Physicians to Medical Complaints in Male and Female Patients." *Journal of Family Practice* 23(1):49–53.

Gross, Michael L. 1999. "Autonomy and Paternalism in Communitarian Society: Patient Rights in Israel." *Hastings Center Report* 29(4):13–20.

Hall, Judith A., Danielle Blanch-Hartigan, and Debra L. Roter. 2011. "Patients' Satisfaction with Male versus Female Physicians: A Meta -Analysis." *Medical Care* 49(7):611–617.

Hall, William J., Mimi V. Chapman, Kent M. Lee, Yesenia M. Merino, Tainayah W. Thomas, B. Keith Payne, Eugenia Eng, Steven H. Day, and Tamera Coyne-Beasley. 2015. "Implicit Racial/Ethnic Bias among Health Care Professionals and Its Influence on Health Care Outcomes: A Systematic Review." *American Journal of Public Health* 105(12):e60–e76.

Hargraves, Ian, Annie LeBlanc, Nilay D. Shah, and Victor M. Montori. 2016. "Shared Decision Making: The Need for Patient-Clinician Conversation, Not Just Information." *Health Affairs* 35(4):627–629.

Heath, Sara. 2017. "Three Best Practices for Shared Decision-Making in Healthcare." *Patient Engagement Hit.* Retrieved November 29, 2018 (https://patientengagementhit.com/news/3-best-practices-for-shared-decision-making-in-healthcare).

Hibbard, Judith H., and Jessica Greene. 2013. "What the Evidence Shows About Patient Activation: Better Health Outcomes and Care Experiences: Fewer Data on Costs." *Health Affairs* 32(2):207–214.

Horton, Richard. 2003. *Second Opinion: Doctors, Diseases and Decisions in Modern Medicine.* London: Granta Books.

Hunt, Linda M., Brigitte Jordan, Susan Irwin, and C.H. Browner. 1989. "Compliance and the Patient's Perspective: Controlling Symptoms in Everyday Life." *Culture, Medicine and Psychiatry* 13(3):315–334.

James, Sandy E., Jody L. Herman, Susan. Rankin, Mara Keisling, Lisa Mottet, and Ma'Ayan Anafi. 2016. *The Report of the 2015 U.S. Transgender Survey.* Washington, DC: National Center for Transgender Equality. Retrieved March 8, 2019 (www.transequality.org/sites/default/files/docs/USTS-Full-Report-FINAL.PDF).

Johnson, Paula A., Lee Goldman, E. John Orav, Li Zhou, Tomas Garcia, Steven D. Pearson, and Thomas H. Lee. 1996. "Gender Differences in the Management of Acute Chest Pain." *Journal of General Internal Medicine* 11(4):209–217.

Khosla, Natalia N., Sylvia P. Perry, Corinne A. Moss-Racusin, Sara E. Burke, and John F. Dovidio. 2018. "A Comparison of Clinicians' Racial Biases in the United States and France." *Social Science and Medicine* 206(June):31–37.

Koh, Howard K., Cindy Brach, Linda M. Harris, and Michael L. Parchman. 2013. "A Proposed 'Health Literate Care Model' Would Constitute a Systems Approach to Improving Patients' Engagement in Care." *Health Affairs* 32(2):357–367.

LaVeist, Thomas A., and Amani Nuru-Jeter. 2002. "Is Doctor-Patient Race Concordance Associated with Greater Satisfaction with Care?" *Journal of Health and Social Behavior* 43(3):296–306.

Malat, Jennifer. 2001a. "Race and Satisfaction with Medical Care: What Do We Know?" Paper presented at the Annual Meeting of the Southern Sociological Society, Atlanta, GA.

———. 2001b. "Social Distance and Patients' Rating of Healthcare Providers." *Journal of Health and Social Behavior* 42(4):360–372.

———. 2013. "The Appeal and Problems of a Cultural Competence Approach to Reducing Racial Disparities." *Journal of General Internal Medicine* 28(5):605–607.

Martin, Kimberly D., Debra L. Roter, Mary C. Beach, Kathryn A. Carson, and Lisa A. Cooper. 2013. "Physician Communication Behaviors and Trust among Black and White Patients with Hypertension." *Medical Care* 51(2):151–157.

McCarthy, Kevin. 2018. "Bipartisan Negativity in View of the Health Care System." Retrieved February 17, 2019 (https://news.gallup.com/poll/242168/bipartisan-negativity-views-healthcare-industry.aspx).

Office of Minority Health. 2016. "Cultural Competency." Retrieved January 20, 2019 (https://minorityhealth.hhs.gov/omh/content.aspx?ID=2804).

Paine, Emily A. 2018. "Embodied Disruption: 'Sorting Out' Gender and Nonconformity in the Doctor's Office." *Social Science and Medicine* 211(August):352–358.

Parsons, Talcott. 1951. *The Social System.* Glencoe, IL: Free Press.

Penner, Louis A., Felicity W.K. Harper, John F. Dovidio, Terrance L. Albreacht, Lauren M. Hamel, Nicole Senft, and Susan Eggly. 2017. "The Impact of Black Cancer Patients' Race-Related Beliefs and Attitudes on Racially Discordant Oncology Interactions: A Field Study." *Social Science and Medicine* 191(October):99–108.

Quill, Timothy E. 1982. "How Special Is Medicine's Nonspecialty?" *The Pharos* 45(1):25–30.

Roebuck, M. Christopher, Joshua N. Liberman, Marin Gemmill-Toyama, and Troyen A. Brennan. 2011. "Medication Adherence Leads to Lower Health Care Use and Costs Despite Drug Spending." *Health Affairs* 30(1):91–99.

Roter, Debra L., Judith K. Hall, and Nancy R. Katz. 1988. "Patient-Physician Communication: A Descriptive Summary of the Literature." *Patient Education and Counseling* 12(2):99–119.

Sabin, Janice A., Rachel G. Riskind, and Brian A. Nosek. 2015. "Health Care Providers' Implicit and Explicit Attitudes Toward Lesbian Women and Gay Men." *American Journal of Public Health* 105(9):1831–1841.

Sawicki, Nadia N. 2017. "Informed Consent as Societal Stewardship." *Journal of Law, Medicine and Ethics* 45(1):41–50.

Seubert, Doug. 2009. *The Connection between Health Literacy and Patient Activation.* Marshfield, WI: Marshfield Clinic. Retrieved February 12, 2016 (www.wisconsin-literacy.org/documents/Health Literacy_Patient-Activation.pdf).

Shelton, J. Nicole, and Jennifer A. Richeson. 2015. "Interacting Across Racial Lines." In *APA Handbook of Personality and Social Psychology. Volume: Group Processes*, edited by Mario Mikulincer and Philip R. Shaver. Washington, DC: American Psychological Association.

Shim, Janet K. 2010. "Cultural Health Capital: A Theoretical Approach to Understanding Health Care Interactions and the Dynamics of Unequal Treatment." *Journal of Health and Social Behavior* 51(1):1–15.

Spalter-Roth, Roberta, Terri A. Lowenthal, and Mercedes Rubio. 2005. *Race, Ethnicity, and the Health of Americans*. ASA Series on How Race and Ethnicity Matter. Washington, DC: American Sociological Association.

Spencer, Karen L. 2018. "Transforming Patient Compliance Research in an Era of Biomedicalization." *Journal of Health and Social Behavior* 59(2):170–184.

Szasz, Thomas S., and Marc H. Hollender. 1956. "The Basic Models of the Doctor-Patient Relationship." *Archives of Internal Medicine* 97(5):585–592.

Tierney, William M., Morris Weinberger, James Y. Greene, and P. Albert Studdard. 1984. "Jehovah's Witnesses and Blood Transfusion: Physicians' Attitudes and Legal Precedents." *Southern Medical Journal* 77(4):473–478.

Tomsik, Philip E., Ann M. Witt, Michael L. Raddock, Peter DeGolia, James J. Werner, Stephen J. Zyzanski, Kurt C. Stange, Peter J. Lawson, Mary Jane Mason, Samantha Smith, and Susan A. Flocke. 2014. "How Well Do Physician and Patient Visit Priorities Align?" *Journal of Family Practice* 63(8):E8–E13.

Tsugawa, Yusuke, Anupam B. Jena, Jose F. Figueroa, E. John Orav Daniel M. Blumenthal, and Ashish K. Jha. 2017. "Comparison of Hospital Mortality and Readmission Rates for Medicare Patients Treated by Male vs Female Physicians." *JAMA Internal Medicine* 177(2):206–213.

Waitzkin, Howard. 1984. "Doctor—Patient Communication: Clinical Implications of Social Scientific Research." *Journal of the American Medical Association* 252(17):2441–2446.

Weisman, Carol S., and Martha A. Teitelbaum. 1985. "Physician Gender and the Physician -Patient Relationship: Recent Evidence and Relevant Questions." *Social Science and Medicine* 20(11): 1119–1127.

Welch, Lisa C., Karen E. Lutfey, Eric Gerstenberger, and Matthew Grace. 2012. "Gendered Uncertainty and Variation in Physicians' Decisions for Coronary Heart Disease: The Double-Edged Sword of 'Atypical Symptoms.'" *Journal of Health and Social Behavior* 53(3):313–328.

White, Amina, and Marion Danis. 2013. "Enhancing Patient -Centered Communication and Collaboration by Using the Electronic Health Record in the Examination Room." *Journal of the American Medical Association* 309(22):2327–2328.

Zussman, Robert. 1992. *Intensive Care: Medical Ethics and the Medical Profession*. Chicago, IL: The University of Chicago Press.

CHAPTER 13

Professional and Ethical Obligations of Physicians in the Physician–Patient Relationship

Learning Objectives

- Distinguish between principlism, casuistry, and the sociology of bio-knowledge as approaches for determining moral rules of behavior.

- Compare and contrast the relevant moral codes regarding physicians' obligations always to tell patients the truth, protect confidentiality, and treat patients who have highly contagious diseases.

- Identify and discuss the major arguments on both sides of the three issues discussed in this chapter.

- Discuss patient preferences regarding physician behavior relevant to these three issues.

- Discuss physician preferences and actual behavior relevant to these three issues.

One way to examine the dynamics of the physician–patient relationship is consideration of the "rights" of patients versus the professional obligations of physicians. Three such issues (truth-telling, confidentiality, and the obligation to treat patients with highly contagious diseases) are examined in this chapter.

For sociologists, these issues are important for many reasons. They are closely related to the nature of the medical profession, the status of patients, and interactions between physicians and patients; they are creating new role demands for physicians and patients; and they are now part of the formal and informal socialization process for health care professionals.

Moreover, the sociological perspective is essential for understanding the social context of

these issues. In the preface to *Bioethics and Society*, DeVries and Subedi (1998:xiv) articulate sociology's contribution to understanding these issues as "getting the whole picture," "looking beyond the taken for granted," scrutinizing "existing arrangements of power," and raising "questions about the social bases of morality"—all "classic sociological concerns."

THE APPROACH OF MEDICAL ETHICS

The term **ethics** is derived from the Greek word "ethos" (meaning "character") and the Latin word "mores" (meaning "customs"). Ethics is a field of study that helps to "define what is good for the individual and for society and establishes the nature of duties that people owe themselves and one another" (Legal Information Institute, 2016). As such, ethics leads us to rules of moral conduct. **Medical ethics** is one of many applied areas of ethics. It focuses on rules of moral conduct as they apply to the practice of medicine. While traditionally a branch of moral philosophy, medical ethics is most informative when it draws from history, sociology, anthropology, theology, philosophy, and the clinical sciences.

As described in Chapter 2, thinking about medical ethics began in ancient times and is most associated in early history with Hippocrates in the fourth and fifth centuries BC. But medical ethics blossomed as an academic discipline only in the 1960s and 1970s. The timing is due to discovery of the gruesome medical experiments conducted by clinicians and others in Nazi Germany without, of course, any consent from the subjects; magazine reports of so-called God Committees in Seattle in 1962 deciding who would and who would not receive kidney dialysis and a chance to live; reports (also in 1962) of seriously questionable medical research projects in the United States, and the first human heart transplant in 1967. The social activism of the 1960s and the emphases on civil rights for African Americans, Native Americans, women, and sexual minorities also contributed to greater consideration of the rights of patients.

Approaches to Determining Moral Rules of Conduct Relative to Medicine

Principlism. Stemming in part from criticism of the Nazi medical experiments, many medical ethicists, clinicians, and others adopted an approach called **principlism,** which based morality of conduct on its consistency with well-considered principles. This approach was given a substantial boost with the publication of Tom Beauchamp's and James Childress's *The Principles of Biomedical Ethics* in the late 1970s (as of 2012, it is its seventh edition). Beauchamp and Childress

thoroughly laid out four moral principles relevant to medicine:

- *Autonomy*: the right of competent individuals to be self-determining
- *Beneficence*: the commitment to doing good for others
- *Non-maleficence*: the commitment not to harm others
- *Justice*: fair distribution of social benefits and burdens.

Principlists believe that the appropriateness of each of these principles should be considered, and thought given to their relative priority. When a question of moral duty occurs in the medical field, one can determine the moral action by applying and following the principles.

Casuistry. Casuistry is an approach that emphasizes the value of beginning with analysis of particular cases, extracting moral rules from them, and applying these rules to new cases. It may be seen as a contrast to principlism, which starts with consideration of moral principles and then moves to particular cases. Casuistrists are more likely than principlists to consider specific aspects of cases in determining whether particular actions are moral.

A Sociology of Bio-Knowledge. Some critics of the emphasis on principlism and casuistry in medical ethics contend that a new approach that gives more attention to social context is needed. Alan Petersen, a medical sociologist at Monash University in Australia, commends the idea of developing a **sociology of bio-knowledge** that focuses on human rights in determining what is moral and what is not. He envisions contributions to this field from various fields of scholarship including the sociology of human rights, science and technology, feminist bioethics, and the work of Michel Foucault. Foucault was a French social theorist and social critic, philosopher, and historian of ideas whose intellectual contributions include efforts to understand the ideas that shape our present society and how power and knowledge exert social control. Petersen is especially interested in emerging biotechnologies and our need for more useful tools in considering them (Petersen, 2013).

As you read through the three issues in this chapter, think about both the moral principles involved in each and the influence of social context, social outcomes, and human rights in determining the professional and ethical obligations of physicians.

TRUTH-TELLING AS AN ISSUE

An important gauge of the relative status of patients in the physician–patient relationship is the discretion felt by physicians to lie to or in some manner intentionally deceive patients. This occurs in various ways, but is common when a physician learns some distressing news about a patient, such as a diagnosis of terminal cancer or some other life-threatening or chronic disease. The following brief case study illustrates one kind of situation in which the issue of truth-telling might arise:

> A physician determines that a patient is suffering from an advanced stage of lung cancer. It is too late for benefit from surgery, chemotherapy, or radiation. She feels that communicating this diagnosis to the patient will so depress and traumatize him that he will simply give up and die. In order to try to provide even a few weeks of additional time, she tells him the tests are inconclusive and asks him to return in a couple of weeks to repeat the tests.

Are Lying and Deception Acceptable Professional Behaviors?

Medical Codes. Historically, most codes of ethical behavior for physicians were silent about the issue of lying and deception. While the Hippocratic Oath includes numerous pledges

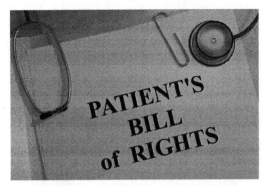

Many medical associations and organizations have now formally expressed the "rights" of patients in medical settings and in medical research

to patients, including confidentiality, nothing is said about truth-telling. There is no reference to truth-telling in the Declaration of Geneva, written in 1948 by the World Medical Association as a response to Nazi atrocities performed in World War II under the name of medical science, or in the AMA's Code of Ethics until 1980.

Other prominent ethical codes in medicine now make a strong case for truth-telling. Both the "Patient's Bill of Rights" and the AMA's Code of Medical Ethics (American Medical Association, 2016b) now clearly state that patients have a right to complete information regarding diagnosis, treatment options, and prognosis. Recent Presidential Commissions for the Study of Bioethical Issues have also support full disclosure of information to patients as a way of increasing patient participation in actual decision making. Coursework in medical schools is increasingly likely to include attention to physician communication to patients and especially to communication of negative prognoses (Sisk, 2016).

Arguments Used to Justify Lying and Deception. A common justification for lying and deception by physicians is **benevolent deception**. Traditionally, some physicians believed that they had a professional duty to lie to patients when it was perceived to be in the patient's best interest. Physicians contend that they are employed by patients to provide the best possible diagnosis and treatment. Since physicians are professionals and not automatons, they cannot and should not be expected simply to report the "facts." Instead, they should be able to make judgments about what information would benefit a patient and what information would harm them, and to act on these perceptions.

Guiora (1980) suggests that too much has been made of "freedom of information" while too little consideration has been given to "freedom from information."

> Information is medicine, very potent medicine indeed, that has to be titrated, properly dosed based on proper diagnosis. Diagnosis, of course, in this context means an assessment of how information will affect the course of illness, how much and what kind of information is the most therapeutic in the face of the patient's preferred modes of coping.
>
> (Guiora, 1980:32)

Second, some physicians believe that patients are typically unable to comprehend the "whole truth" of a matter, and physicians therefore should not be expected to try to provide it. This circumstance exists because some patients are believed to have limited medical knowledge and may incorrectly or incompletely interpret terminology used by the physician. Conveying a diagnosis of cancer exemplifies the point. Despite the tremendous progress made in the treatment of cancer and the steadily increasing rate of cure for many cancers, the "C" word continues to carry frightening implications. Since patients lack understanding of the disease and its treatment, the argument goes, it would make little sense to obligate physicians to communicate fully this diagnosis.

Finally, many physicians believe that some patients prefer not to be told the whole truth. Discounting surveys that show a large majority of patients want full information, some physicians believe patients subtly communicate otherwise to them. They contend that some patients explicitly state their desire to have the truth couched in gentle language or withheld altogether, and others communicate this preference implicitly through body language, tone of voice, or a message that requires the physician to "read between the lines." If this is the message being communicated, some physicians argue, it would be unethical for them to reveal the truth.

Arguments Used to Oppose Lying and Deception. An alternative view is that truth-telling is an unconditional duty of medical professionals—that physicians are morally required always to provide full information to patients and never to lie or attempt to deceive. Four primary arguments buttress this position. The first is that telling the truth is part of the respect owed to all people. To lie to or intentionally deceive another is to denigrate that person's worthiness and treat that person as undeserving of a full and honest account. The legal requirement for informed consent from patients or research subjects implies a decision maker who is fully informed and has complete access to the truth. A physician who fails to provide honest information to a patient has usurped the possibility that genuine informed consent can occur.

Second, veracity is consistent with the ideas of fidelity and keeping promises. When a patient solicits a physician, he or she is entering into an implied contract. In exchange for payment, the patient seeks the best possible diagnosis, recommendations for treatment, and (if agreed upon) the provision of treatment. Accordingly, any information learned by the physician about the patient should be provided to the patient. After all, who "owns" that information? Does the physician own it and have a right to parcel it out according to his or her discretion? Or does the patient own this information? Those arguing from this position believe that the contract established between the patient and physician requires a full and honest account.

A third argument is that lying or deception undermines a trusting relationship between patient and physician. If trust in a physician is a desirable goal, and trust facilitates a therapeutic relationship, then physicians must act to maintain trust. A patient who learns that he or she has been intentionally deceived by a physician may never again be able to trust that physician fully.

Finally, those taking this position claim that it offers clear benefits to the patient. No one, including the physician, knows a patient better than the patient himself or herself. For a physician to determine that a given patient would be better off being deceived than hearing the truth would, at the very least, require intimate familiarity with the patient's life history, important values, perceived obligations to self and significant others, and the decisions the patient would make in the light of truthful information. Rarely, if ever, could a physician claim to have access to such matters or to know more about patients than they know about themselves.

> The damages associated with the disclosure of sad news or risks are rarer than physicians believe; and the benefits which result from being informed are more substantial, even measurably so. Pain is tolerated more easily, recovery from surgery is quicker, and cooperation with therapy is greatly improved. The attitude that "what you don't know won't hurt you" is proving unrealistic; it is what patients do not know but vaguely suspect that causes them corrosive worry.
>
> (Bok, 1991:78)

A recent study of 590 terminally ill cancer patients (median survival time was just 5.4 months) revealed that 71 percent wanted to be told their life expectancy, but only 17.6 percent recalled a prognostic disclosure by their physician. Those who received a prognostic disclosure had a much more realistic idea of their likely life expectancy. Those who had an overly optimistic view about their survival chances were much more likely to choose aggressive therapies that made them sick but did not extend their life. Patients with realistic views

were more likely to opt for treatments designed simply to make them comfortable. Patients who were given an accurate prognostic disclosure did not experience more sadness, more anxiety, or a deterioration in the physician–patient relationship (Enzinger et al., 2015).

The Current Situation Regarding Truth-Telling

Do Patients Want to Know the Truth?. Social science surveys find that most persons express a desire for truthfulness from physicians. As early as 1950, 89 percent of cancer patients, 82 percent of patients without cancer, and 98 percent of patients participating in a cancer detection program expressed a desire for honesty in a cancer diagnosis (Kelly and Friesen, 1950). Surveys conducted since then have routinely found that 8 or 9 out of every 10 respondents want all of the available information about a medical condition and treatment, even if it is unfavorable. This preference for candor crosses all population subgroups—it is not specific to any age, gender, race, or socioeconomic group.

Are Physicians Truthful With Patients?. In the middle of the twentieth century, a large majority of physicians reported that they sometimes withheld the truth from patients. As attention to ethical issues in medicine increased in the 1960s and 1970s, more physicians adopted a truth-telling perspective. By the late twentieth and early twenty-first century, most physicians reported a propensity to tell the truth but also a continued willingness to deceive. Physicians typically acknowledge that most patients want accurate information about the diagnosis and prognosis, and that they typically provide it. However, they sometimes also indicate a reluctance to communicate as straightforwardly as possible with patients who have a negative prognosis. Many physicians place greater emphasis on the consequences (or outcomes) of a medical encounter than on adherence to a principle of unconditional truth-telling (Novack et al., 1989).

The most recent large-scale study of the propensity of physicians to give complete information to patients was conducted in 2003. This study of more than 1,000 practicing physicians found that 86 percent believed physicians are obligated to present all information and medical options to patients. However, there was a desire to retain some discretion, and 63 percent believed it ethically permissible to explain to patients their moral objections about certain possible courses of treatment. This research also identified what may be a developing trend. One physician in seven (14 percent) felt no obligation to present information about procedures about which they disagreed, or to refer patients to other physicians who did not have the same moral outlook as themselves. These physicians tended to be very religious and justified withholding medical options from patients based on their own religious beliefs (Curlin et al., 2007).

The findings of these studies are consistent with research conducted by Naoko Miyaji (1993), who discovered that American physicians seem to value ethical principles that support disclosure of information to patients—through both truth-telling and informed consent—and these physicians give the impression that patients have control over obtaining information. However, in reality, physicians continue to manage the information-giving process. They interpret the principle of disclosure selectively and in such a way that they share with patients only as much

information as they wish them to have. In the case of a patient with a newly diagnosed terminal illness, physicians emphasize possible treatments and decision-making options and give extensive information about them, but give much less information about and play down grim prognosis information, citing uncertainty and lack of relevance to future actions.

This communication pattern is justified by physicians as showing compassion and respect for the patient *and* the principle of disclosure while preserving as much hope as possible. These physicians could well respond to survey questions that they provide truthful diagnoses to patients; this may explain some of the very high percentage of physicians who now report themselves to be unconditional truth-tellers. However, on closer examination, it is clear that they still control the information-giving process and may not share complete information about the patient's condition. Miyaji concludes that this pattern

> shows the ambiguity and tension which define the doctor's new role as a partner of the patient. Preservation of their image (and self-image) as compassionate and caring physicians helps them to manage patient care in emotionally-laden situations like truth-telling as a healer. However, this humanistic model of the physician serves also to maintain the power of the profession, enhancing its "cultural authority" over patients.
>
> (Miyaji, 1993:250)

The manner in which medical truth-telling is handled in Japan is described in the accompanying box, "Truth-Telling and Cancer Patients in Japan."

IN COMPARATIVE FOCUS

TRUTH-TELLING AND CANCER PATIENTS IN JAPAN

Most countries in the world continue to struggle with the moral issues involved in disclosing or failing to disclose a terminal prognosis. In Japan, physicians have traditionally refused to disclose terminal illness. In the United States, the right of autonomous individuals to be informed is now commonly respected (at least to a degree). In Japan, however, individuals are viewed primarily as part of a family and a community. The Confucian emphases on *kyokan* (the feeling of togetherness) and *ningen* (the human person in relationship to others) are prioritized over individual autonomy.

Given these emphases, Japanese physicians have traditionally lied to or deceived patients who are terminally ill (e.g., pretending the cancer is just an ulcer) and instead revealed the prognosis to family members and consulted with them. Family members were strongly encouraged not to inform the patient of the truth. Consultation with members occurred both in face-to-face interaction and through written communication.

In recent years, the tradition has begun to give way to greater respect for the autonomy of the individual. While young people still respect the role of the family in decision making and medical care, there is now a greater call for open disclosure to the patient. While the likelihood of medical truth-telling in Japan is still less than in the United States, today more and more Japanese physicians are providing full disclosure of a terminal illness (Brannigan and Boss, 2001; Elwyn et al., 1998).

CONFIDENTIALITY AS AN ISSUE

The *Tarasoff* Case

On July 1, 1976, the California Supreme Court handed down a decision in the case of *Tarasoff v. Regents of the University of California*, one of the most important judicial cases to affect medical practice in our country's history. The facts of the case were basically undisputed. In 1969, a student at the University of California at Berkeley, Prosenjit Poddar, confided to his psychologist, Dr. Lawrence Moore, who was on the staff at Cowell Memorial Hospital on the Berkeley campus, that he intended to kill Tatiana Tarasoff, a young woman who lived in Berkeley but was at that time on a trip to Brazil.

Dr. Moore, with the concurrence of a colleague and the assistant director of the department of psychiatry, reported the threat to the campus police and asked them to detain Poddar and commit him to a mental hospital for observation. The campus police questioned Poddar, but they were satisfied that he was rational and accepted his promise to stay away from Tarasoff. They released him, and reported their action to Dr. Harvey Powelson, the director of the psychiatry department.

Dr. Powelson requested no further action to detain Poddar or to follow up on the threats. Two months later, shortly after Tarasoff returned from her Brazil visit, Poddar went to her home and killed her. Later, when Tatiana's parents learned that university officials had known about the threat to their daughter's life but had failed to detain Poddar or warn them or their daughter, they brought a negligence suit against the therapists involved, the campus police, and the university, and sought additional punitive damages.

The original court hearing of the case dismissed all charges against all defendants. However, on appeal, the California Supreme Court partially reversed the lower court's judgment when a majority ruled that general damages against the therapists and the university were in order for their failure to warn the girl or her family (punitive damages were dismissed) (Tobriner, 1976). (Due to a technical error, Poddar's second-degree murder conviction was overturned. Because more than 5 years had elapsed since the murder, he was not retried under an agreement that he would return to his native India, which he did.)

What are the implications of this ruling? Should the therapists have been morally and legally required to warn Tatiana Tarasoff? If so, what other circumstances would justify breaching confidentiality? Or should physicians maintain absolute confidentiality regarding information shared with them by all patients in all circumstances?

The Meaning of Confidentiality

The term **confidentiality** is often used interchangeably with "privacy" and with the concept of "privileged communication." However, the terms mean different things. **Privacy** refers to freedom from unauthorized intrusions into one's life. As applied to medical matters, it largely refers to the control that an individual has over information about himself or herself (Wasserstrom, 1986).

Clearly, there are some things—a person's thoughts, hopes, or fears—which no one else will know about unless that individual chooses to disclose them. As individuals, we are permitted to retain full custody of our private thoughts, and we cannot be compelled to compromise this sense of privacy. There are some occasions when we reveal our private thoughts to others but still hold dominion over them. For example, when we share information with certain professionals, such as physicians or the clergy, we do so with an understanding that this other person will respect our privacy and not reveal what has been said. This is the notion of "professional secrecy" (Wasserstrom, 1986).

Once information has been revealed to another person, it is never again as private. At this point, the individual must rely on the professionalism or goodwill of the other person not to reveal the information. This is the meaning of confidentiality. In the medical encounter, an individual patient who reveals information to a physician must rely on the physician not to share the information with others. Maintaining confidentiality means that the information goes no further.

The idea of **privileged communication** comes from the legal system, which operates on the basis of **testimonial compulsion**—that is, individuals with pertinent information can be required to present that information in a court of law. However, our legal system recognizes the value of professional secrecy. In order to foster a close and trusting relationship between individuals and selected professionals, information shared with these professionals may be exempt from testimonial compulsion. The information or communication is said to be "privileged" in this sense.

Medical Codes

The principle of confidentiality has been firmly rooted in codes of medical ethics. The classic reference to the importance of confidentiality occurs in the Hippocratic Oath (see Chapter 2): "What I may see or hear in the course of the treatment or even outside of the treatment in regard to the life of men, which on no account one must spread abroad, I will keep to myself holding such things shameful to be spoken about." This statement is credited with influencing all subsequent efforts regarding the ethical responsibilities of physicians. Today, the ethical code of nearly every medical group includes some reference to confidentiality.

The Laws Pertaining to Confidentiality

Contrary to common perception, there are no constitutional provisions covering confidentiality of information shared with a physician. Although the Fourth Amendment deals with the issue of privacy, its relevance to medical confidentiality has been left up to judicial interpretation. There is no common law that obliges physicians to hold confidential information shared by a patient. Such law does exist between lawyers and clients and between clergy and parishioners.

To fill this void, individual states developed privileged communication statutes. About two-thirds of states now have these statutes, which specify that physicians cannot be compelled to reveal in a court of law information received from a patient. However, states have also identified certain types of information that physicians are legally obligated to share with proper authorities. This includes certain health conditions (primarily communicable diseases such as tuberculosis and sexually transmitted infections), gunshot wounds, and suspected or clear physical or sexual abuse of children. Some states now require physicians to report patients who may be unfit drivers (e.g., older individuals with certain illnesses), and some states recently tried unsuccessfully to require physicians to notify authorities if they treat undocumented immigrants.

Does a patient who feels that her or his physician has wrongfully breached confidentiality have any recourse in the law? Yes. Physicians may be sued for malpractice for wrongfully disclosing patient information under one or more of three legal theories: (1) an unauthorized disclosure of confidential information, (2) an invasion of privacy, and (3) a violation of an implied contract between the physician and the patient.

The Health Insurance Portability and Accountability Act 1996 (HIPAA)

The most significant legislation ever passed in the United States regarding medical privacy and confidentiality is the **Health Insurance Portability and Accountability Act 1996 (HIPAA)**. This act was originally created to address the treatment of preexisting conditions in coverage for workers changing jobs. This requirement has now been superceded by parts of the Affordable Care Act. The HIPAA Privacy Rule was actually something of an afterthought when Congress decided it needed to address the increased sharing of electronic health records.

The Privacy Rule includes several measures to protect the privacy of patients and their medical records and to establish security of electronic health information. Most importantly, it grants individuals a right to access their own health records, it contains training requirements for those working with health care data, it prescribes standards for handling data and avoiding inappropriate access, and it requires notification of individuals when a serious security breach involving their health information occurs (Rothstein, 2016). This legislation has led to significant changes in protocol in medical facilities and with regard to sharing information about patients.

However, some experts have raised concerns that certain provisions in the Privacy Rule are unacceptably weak and do not provide as much

The most important bill ever passed in the United States regarding medical privacy was the Health Insurance Portability and Accountability Act 1996.

safety to patients as desired. For example, although there are standards for training those who work with health records, there are no penalties for businesses—health care or otherwise—that fail to meet these standards. This has led to underuse of strong training and to weakened safeguards for patient data (Agris and Spandorfer, 2016).

When Confidentiality Becomes an Issue

Today, medical confidentiality may become an issue in four kinds of situations. The first are accidental or not so accidental "slips of the tongue" that physicians commit when chatting with family, friends, or colleagues. Fortunately, most health care professionals are careful not to let patient information slip, although these "irresponsible" breaches do occur—often when inhibitions have been lowered by exhaustion or alcohol.

In addition, as the use of social networking sites such as Facebook and Twitter by the general population has increased, so has their use by medical professionals. Although there are restrictions on online behavior by medical professionals, there are also cases of communications that technically do not violate HIPAA but are ethically questionable. Often these are situations in which medical students reveal important details about a patient or medical situation without revealing the patient's name. The purpose may be benign (e.g., reflecting on a difficult situation or seeking out social support), but such cases could inadvertently disclose a patient's identity, violate a patient's desire for privacy, or undermine trust in the health care system (Wells, Lehavot, and Isaac, 2015).

The second type of situation results from the increasingly large number of people who have access to patient information and data. With the advent of **electronic health records (EHRs)**, more and more physicians, nurses, and allied health workers have access to patient records, and more and more agencies, including public health agencies, third-party payers, medical peer review committees, employers, credit investigation

agencies, social welfare agencies, and medical researchers have a legal right to obtain patient data. There are some legal restrictions. However, there are volumes of people even beyond the obvious who are legally able to view patient information. For example, when an individual applies for life insurance, disability insurance, or long-term care insurance, the insurance companies are legally permitted to hire specialty firms to analyze the applicant's medical records. Etzioni (1999) has referred to these breaches of confidentiality as "authorized abuse." They occur on a daily basis and are perfectly legal, but they raise serious ethical questions.

The third area of concern is the increasing level of cyberattacks against physicians, clinics, and hospitals in efforts to steal medical records and personal patient information. The sensitive data that are stolen can be used by identity thieves to facilitate such matters as taking out a loan, getting a passport, blackmail, and making fraudulent income tax returns. In 2015, Anthem, one of the nation's largest health insurance companies, announced that hackers had breached a database containing 80 million patient records (Gosk, 2015). Since then, an average of 1–2 medical record hackings have occurred each day with an average of about 25 million hacked medical records per year. About 1 in 4 data breaches are in the health care field. Cyberattacks now cost the health care system billions each year.

Finally, an intriguing set of ethical questions occurs in situations in which physicians must make a conscious decision about whether or not to violate confidentiality. Examples like the *Tarasoff* case dramatize the issue. The remainder of this section of the chapter focuses on this subject.

Justifications for the Principle of Confidentiality

Philosopher Sissela Bok (1989) summarizes four justifications for physicians to protect the privacy of information shared by patients: (1) protection of the patient's autonomy over personal information; (2) enhancement of the physician–patient relationship; (3) respect for the patient; and (4) the opportunity for individuals to communicate more freely with the physician.

This final rationale was used by the justices writing the dissenting opinion in the *Tarasoff* case. Writing for the minority, Justice William P. Clark (1976) described three specific reasons why confidentiality ought never be broken. First, individuals who need treatment will be more likely to seek help if they trust physician confidentiality. Second, individuals seeking assistance will be more likely to provide full disclosure. Third, trust in the psychotherapist will be enhanced. Although distressed by situations like the *Tarasoff* case, the justices contended that maintaining confidentiality, rather than breaking it, will minimize tragedies in the long run because those needing help will not be dissuaded from seeking it.

Grounds for Breaking Confidentiality

Few people would dismiss the importance of confidentiality. However, whereas some see confidentiality as an unconditional duty (never to be broken), others believe it to be a prima facie responsibility—that is, it can justifiably be broken if there are compelling reasons for doing so. Three such reasons are cited.

The first is benefit to the patient himself or herself—the principle of beneficence. An example would be a temporarily depressed or traumatized individual who threatens to commit suicide or engage in some disreputable, out-of-character behavior. In order to secure assistance to prevent the action, the physician may need to break confidentiality and disclose the person's stated intention. However, physicians must be sure that an action contemplated by a patient really is a product of an irrational mind. Many people are too quick to assume that any decision made by another that is inconsistent with one's own values is not a rational decision.

A second possible justification is that it may conflict with the rights of an innocent third party. As a society, we must determine whether we prefer that innocent third parties be warned of impending danger, even if that means a breach of confidentiality or that confidentiality not be broken. The *Tarasoff* case is an example of this justification, but it may occur in less extreme circumstances. For example, suppose that a physician has as a patient a young man engaged to be married. He knows that the young man is concealing his permanent impotence from his fiancée. The question arises as to whether the physician should break confidentiality with this young patient and reveal the information to the fiancée, or place priority on maintaining confidentiality and letting the chips fall where they may.

A third possible rationale is danger or threat to the rights or interests of society in general. As previously mentioned, various states require physicians to report certain specified diseases or conditions to proper authorities. However, not all such situations are governed by law. For example, how should a physician respond when he or she detects a serious medical problem in a patient whose occupation influences the safety or lives of countless other people? What should be done in the case of a railroad signaler who is discovered to have attacks of epilepsy, or an airline pilot with failing eyesight? Cases such as these force physicians to determine their primary obligation. Is it to protect the confidentiality of the diagnosis, recognizing all the accompanying benefits, or is there a greater obligation to the unknown others whose lives may be jeopardized by the patient's medical condition? (Allmark, 1995).

Right Versus Duty to Breach Confidentiality

If, in certain situations, society decides that physicians have a "right" to break confidentiality, would we ever say that they have a "duty" to do so? That is, does the physician who diagnoses the epileptic railroad signaler not only have a right to disclose the information but also have a moral responsibility to do so? Or a legal responsibility? Should society morally and legally insist that the proper authorities be notified?

When serious harm is likely to occur, Bok (1991) argues that the duty to warn is overriding. She contends that patients have no right to entrust information of this type to physicians and expect them to remain silent, and physicians have no right to promise confidentiality about such information. Of course, this is also the position taken by the majority in the *Tarasoff* case when the judges argued that the university psychotherapists had a duty to warn Tatiana of the threat made against her.

Others, including many psychotherapists, were unhappy (to say the least) with the *Tarasoff* decision. Even those who could abide the idea

that physicians *may* disclose a threat objected to the requirement that physicians *must* disclose it. For many, that compromised professional autonomy. The difficulties in determining which patients are serious about stated threats and questions about the required severity of threat (e.g., is a broken arm sufficiently serious?) make this requirement difficult to follow. Some research shows that predictions of danger are unreliable, and that mental health professionals are more likely to be incorrect than correct when making such predictions—usually erring on the side of over-predicting danger (Oppenheimer and Swanson, 1990).

The manner in which personal characteristics of the patient might influence physician behavior regarding confidentiality is addressed in the accompanying box, "The Influence of Patient Gender, Race, and Sexual Orientation on Maintenance of Confidentiality."

IN THE FIELD

THE INFLUENCE OF PATIENT GENDER, RACE, AND SEXUAL ORIENTATION ON MAINTENANCE OF CONFIDENTIALITY

Physicians may consider a variety of factors in determining whether to break a confidence with a patient. Schwartzbaum, Wheat, and Norton (1990) attempted to determine whether physician behavior was at all influenced by the gender, race, or sexual orientation of the patient—factors that would not seem relevant. A sample of white primary care physicians was given a case study in which an HIV-infected patient presented a risk to a third party. Eight different descriptions of the gender, race, and sexual orientation of the patient were distributed randomly among the physicians, one description to each of them. Each physician was asked to select his own likely behavior from a list of five choices reflecting a range of confidentiality breaches.

Findings showed that physician respondents were more likely to report black homosexual and heterosexual men to the health department and black heterosexual men to their partners than hypothetical patients in other categories. Were these physicians influenced by the greater use that blacks make of public health departments (so that informing the health department seemed logical)? Were they influenced by the perception that black HIV-positive men are more likely to be intravenous drug users and thus possibly less likely to be conscientious about informing their partners? Were these physicians reflecting an explicit or implicit racial bias that influenced behavior?

OBLIGATION TO TREAT PATIENTS WITH HIGHLY CONTAGIOUS DISEASES

Do medical professionals have a professional obligation to treat patients with contagious diseases? How we define professional certainly influences professional obligations, duty to individual patients and society, and duty to self? This issue has been raised recently by the emergence of viruses such as Ebola, MERS, SARS, HIV, and, obviously, the coronavirus, COVID-19. This section summarizes the key arguments in the debate about obligation to treat patients. It focuses on HIV/AIDS in the years before treatments were available because it is too early for scholarly research on COVID-19 to have been published. However, it is already apparent that health care professionals conducted themselves in extraordinarily heroic ways in providing care to COVID-19 patients, and they often did so without the personal protection equipment necessary to provide for their own safety. This section summarizes the key arguments in the debate about obligation to treat patients with highly contagious diseases by focusing mostly on HIV/AIDS in the years after it was discovered and before any treatments were available.

Historical Perspectives on the Obligation to Treat

Does history offer a clear picture of how physicians in earlier times viewed the issue of obligation to treat contagious diseases? Yes, but there was not a consistent tradition in earlier epidemics such as the Black Death (in Europe in the thirteenth century), the Great Plague (in London in the seventeenth century), and yellow fever (in the United States in the eighteenth century). During those epidemics, many physicians fled from patients with contagious disease and from cities with a large disease population, while many others, often at considerable personal risk, remained to care for patients (Zuger and Miles, 1987).

Laws Pertaining to the Obligation to Treat

Several legal principles pertain to the issue of treatment obligation. George Annas summarizes the basic concept of legal obligation to treat:

> American common law is firmly grounded on notions of individual liberty and economic freedom that support the proposition that absent some special relationship, no citizen owes any other citizen anything. As applied to the practice of medicine, the general rule, sometimes denoted the "no duty rule," is that a physician is not obligated to treat any particular patient in the absence of a consensual doctor-patient relationship [or a contractual obligation as through an insurance plan].
> (Annas, 1988:26)

Medical Codes

Hippocratic Oath. It is unclear as to whether the Hippocratic Oath specifies any legal obligation to treat. A line in the oath, "into whatsoever houses I enter, I will enter to help the sick," has been interpreted by many as stating a prescribed duty of physicians, one "neither abrogated or attenuated by incapacitating or terminal disease, nor by the assumption of personal risk" (Kim and Perfect, 1988:136). On the other hand, some contend that the line attaches only very loosely to "obligation to treat," and does not offer sufficient detail to clarify a complex matter such as treating AIDS patients.

The AMA's Code of Medical Ethics. The official position of the AMA on obligation to treat has evolved through the years and has undergone important transformations. In constructing its first code of medical ethics in 1847, the AMA broke from existing medical codes by establishing a duty to treat: "and when pestilence prevails, it is the [physician's] duty to face the danger, and to continue their labors for the alleviation of the suffering, even at the jeopardy of their own lives" (Jonsen, 1990:161). However, in 1912, as the AMA was ascending in power, it added the statement that "a physician shall, in the provision of appropriate patient care, except in emergencies, be free to choose whom to serve" (Judicial Council of the American Medical Association, 1986).

In the years since then, the AMA has revised the code several times, sometimes emphasizing the "duty to face danger" phrase and sometimes the "free to choose" phrase. A compromise attempt in 1986 both to reaffirm the longstanding duty to treat contagious patients while simultaneously offering physicians a way to opt out (e.g., if they did not think they were emotionally able to care for AIDS patients) satisfied some, but was widely criticized. The American College of Physicians and the Infectious Diseases Society of America issued a joint statement proclaiming that "denying appropriate care to sick and dying patients for any reason is unethical" (Health and Public Policy Committee of the American College of Physicians and the Infectious Diseases Society of America, 1986). Public opinion strongly supported the "duty to treat" position (Wallis, 2011).

A year later, in December 1987, the AMA issued another position paper, clearly shifting its emphasis toward the duty to treat as being most consistent with professional standards. On the other hand, AMA leaders made it clear that any physician who wished not to treat AIDS patients could opt out by claiming incompetence to treat (American Medical Association, 2016a). George Annas, a professor of health law, concluded that "in effect, this reduces the AMA's position to a statement that a doctor *must* treat an AIDS patient if the doctor *wants* to treat an AIDS patient" (Annas, 1988:S30).

Physicians' Perceptions Regarding the Obligation to Treat

In the decade after AIDS came to public attention, much research showed that a sizable percentage of physicians did not wish to treat AIDS patients and did not believe they had a professional obligation to do so. For example, in a study of New York City medical residents, Link et al. (1988) found that while only 11 percent of respondents were moderately or extremely resentful of having to care for AIDS patients, 25 percent stated that they would not continue to do so if given a choice. Moreover, 24 percent believed that refusing to care for AIDS patients was not unethical, 34 percent believed that house officers and 53 percent believed that medical students should be permitted to decide for themselves. In a national survey of family physicians, 62.9 percent stated that physicians have a right to refuse to care for a patient solely because he or she is infected with the AIDS virus (Bredfeldt et al., 1991).

Rationale for No Obligation to Treat

Many physicians at this time stated that the right to choose was an important part of their traditional autonomy and their choice was not to see AIDS patients. What reasons did they give for this position? Ezekiel Emanuel (1988), an MD in Harvard's Program in Ethics and the Professions, identified four factors cited by advocates of this position.

Excessive Risks. Many physicians considered the risk of contracting HIV to be too great. Studies in the 1980s routinely found that between one-third and one-half of medical residents reported moderate to major concern about treating HIV/AIDS patients. Almost half of the physicians surveyed by Taylor et al. (1990) said they were more frightened of contracting AIDS than any other disease. Those who perceived the greatest risk were most likely to believe in the no-obligation position.

These results assess subjective state—the fear of or concern about contracting AIDS. These perceptions are crucial because physicians, like others, behave on the basis of what they perceive to be real. Based on experimental studies, the Centers for Disease Control and Prevention estimated at the time that the risk of becoming infected with HIV and developing AIDS after a single accidental exposure (most likely through an accidental puncture wound) was 0.5 percent (1 in 200) or less.

Is this possibility sufficiently high to justify treatment refusal? Many suggest that physicians overreacted to the possible risk and should have recognized that their own behavior (e.g., extreme carefulness in avoiding punctures) would reduce the likelihood of transmission. However, a commentary in the *Journal of the American Medical Association* condemned efforts to reduce the significance of perceived risks of infection by emphasizing "low" transmission rates. Gerbert et al. (1988) asked what is meant by "low" when discussing a condition that (at that time) was always fatal, and one that could be contracted regardless of the physician's carefulness and other infection control measures. Among their recommendations for dealing with the fear felt by many health care professionals was acknowledgment that risk does exist and that concern is warranted.

Questionable Benefits. Some physicians pointed to the likely absence of long-term benefits as a no-duty rationale. ("After all, he (or she) is going to die anyway.") Physicians are not obligated to provide unnecessary or useless care, and not all medical procedures are ethically obligatory. (Recall that advances in drug therapy for those with HIV/AIDS did not begin until the very late 1990s and early 2000s.)

Obligations to Other Patients. Some physicians justified this position by emphasizing risk to other patients should the physician contract AIDS, or financial loss should other patients discontinue their relationship with the physician if they learned he or she was seeing AIDS patients. One survey reported that 40 percent of a sample of family practice physicians feared they would lose some patients if they found out that AIDS patients were also being seen in the office (Bredfeldt et al., 1991).

Obligations to Self and Family. Some physicians cited potential risk to their family through transmission to the spouse should the physician contract AIDS.

Unspoken Factors. Some critics suggested that the aforementioned reasons were bolstered by attitudes that devalued certain patients. Was the preference not to treat related to the fact that many of the HIV/AIDS patients were gay men and/or intravenous drug users? Some research suggested a relationship. A study of matriculating medical students in Chicago found 92 percent would welcome HIV patients into their practice, but homophobia and fear of infection were the most common explanations for those who would not (Carter, Lantos, and Hughes, 1996). A research study of preclinical medical students also found largely favorable attitudes toward treatment, but students who were uncomfortable with homosexual behavior and felt awkward about taking a sexual history from gay people were least willing to treat (McDaniel et al., 1995). Finally, a study comparing the attitudes of students in their fourth year of medical school and again as third-year residents found the strongest predictors of change in attitudes for those whose willingness to treat declined were homophobic attitudes and aversion to intravenous drug users (Yedidia, Berry, and Barr, 1996).

Rationale for Obligation to Treat

Countering the no-duty position, many medical practitioners, philosophers and ethicists, lawmakers, and social scientists reflected on the rationale for an obligation to treat. Three such reasons are described here.

The Nature of the Profession.   Perhaps the strongest supporting rationale relates to the inherent nature of the medical profession. Professions represent special statuses, they involve more training and greater commitment than other careers, and they are rooted in a special ideal of service to others.

> The objective of the medical profession is devotion to a moral ideal—in particular, healing the sick and rendering the ill healthy and well. The physician is committed to the help and betterment of other people—"selflessly caring for the sick," as the president of the American College of Physicians has put it. When a person joins the profession, he or she professes a commitment to these ideals and accepts the obligation to serve the sick. It is the profession that is chosen. The obligation is neither chosen nor transferable: it is constitutive of the professional activity.
> (Emanuel, 1988:1686)

According to this viewpoint, making distinctions among the sick based on the type or nature of the disease is contrary to the ideal of the profession. The noble dimension of this professional duty is treatment of all patients—especially the most vulnerable—without making these distinctions.

The Social Contract.   A second justification is the implicit *social contract* made between society and the medical profession. In exchange for professional control of the medical field, physicians have an obligation to treat the sick and vulnerable. Potential danger in doing so does not exempt the physician from fulfilling this obligation any more than it exempts a police officer or firefighter (Arras, 1988).

Fulfillment of this reciprocal obligation, however, can be viewed in two ways. One interpretation is that it creates an obligation on the part of each physician to treat those in medical need and not to shun those with particular diseases. Because all physicians benefit from control over medical practice, all physicians should be willing to provide needed care to those most in need. On the other hand, perhaps the obligation to care for the sick is attached to physicians in general, but not

necessarily to each individual physician. According to this view, the reciprocal obligation is fulfilled as long as there are a sufficient number of physicians to care for the sickest, even if not every individual physician participates (Arras, 1988). This latter interpretation is consistent with a voluntary system in which only willing physicians treat people with AIDS or other contagious diseases.

In some cases, the social contract may be explicit. For example, the Americans with Disabilities Act of 1990 prohibits denying an individual access to health care because of disability, unless the individual poses a direct threat or significant risk to the health and safety of others that cannot be eliminated by adequate precautions or reasonable modification. In a 1998 decision, the Supreme Court ruled that asymptomatic HIV infection is a disability and ruled against a dentist who refused to fill a cavity in his office. This decision made clear a health care provider's legal obligation to treat HIV-infected patients along with patients with other disabilities (Katz and Paul, 2019).

The Dependent Patient.   A third rationale is that there is a unique moral dimension in medicine, especially in cases of a "dependent" patient in need of the professional's services.

> The responsibility to treat those in need is a key component of medical professionalism. This ethical obligation holds in the face of greater than usual threats to their own safety, lives, or health.
> (Bostick, Levine, and Sade, 2008)

This responsibility is even more compelling given the physical and emotional suffering endured by AIDS patients. Peter Conrad (1990) and others have written about the "marginal" place in which society often places AIDS patients, and the severe stigma attached to the disease. Siegel and Krauss (1991) studied the major challenges of daily living experienced by 55 HIV-positive gay men. One of the three major adaptive challenges they reported was dealing with reactions to a stigmatizing illness. They talked openly in focused interviews of their feelings of shame based on the way that others interacted with them. Even deciding whom to tell of their infected status was a difficult decision, as they knew that many would respond negatively. Those who speak of a special relationship between physician and "dependent" patient find no better example than that of a physician working with AIDS patients.

SUMMARY

Much can be learned about the dynamics of the physician–patient relationship by examining the manner in which the issues of truth-telling, confidentiality, and the obligation to treat patients with highly contagious diseases are handled. Surveys consistently show that the vast majority of people want physicians to unconditionally tell the truth, but many physicians (although fewer than in the past) still use their discretion when deciding whether or not to tell the whole truth (including a clear statement of prognosis) to individual patients.

Those who support unconditional truth-telling justify their position by stating that only truth-telling displays real respect for the patient, that it is necessary to keep promises, that lying would undermine the patient's trust in the physician, and that patients need to know the truth in order to be able to make decisions on an informed basis. Those who believe that physicians should use their discretion argue that it might be in the patient's best interest, that it is impossible to communicate the "full truth" to a medical layperson, and that many patients really do not want to know the truth about a serious illness.

While most medical codes emphasize the importance of protecting confidentiality, some justify breaking confidentiality in order to protect the patient, an innocent third party (e.g., in the case of Tatiana Tarasoff), or society in general. Others believe that confidentiality should always be maintained in order to protect the patient's autonomy, legitimate secrets, keep faith with a patient, and encourage people who need help to feel free to seek it.

Research shows that in the early years of AIDS many physicians preferred not to treat HIV/AIDS patients. While neither history nor medical codes offer a decisive position on the existence of a "duty to treat," many physicians contend they should not have been compelled to offer care to AIDS patients due to: (1) excessive risk, (2) questionable benefits of treatment, (3) obligations to other patients, and (4) obligations to self and family.

Those who believe in the duty to treat cite three reasons: it is an inherent part of the nature of the profession, it is part of a social contract between society and medicine, and that the "special" physician–patient relationship calls for physicians to offer care to dependent patients.

HEALTH ON THE INTERNET

You can research the latest ethical policies of the AMA on issues covered in this chapter by accessing its code of medical ethics. Start at:

www.ama-assn.org/delivering-care/ethics/code-medical-ethics-overview.

What are the emphases of the preamble and these nine principles? What rights are patients given in these principles?

 Then, go to:

www.ama-assn.org/delivering-care/ethics/withholding-information-patients.

Read Code of Medical Ethics 2.1.3. What responsibilities are assigned to physicians within this section?

Finally, go to:

www.ama-assn.org/delivering-care/ethics/confidentiality.

Read Code of Medical Ethics 3.2.1. What responsibilities are assigned to physicians within this section?

DISCUSSION CASES

Case 1

Scenario 1: A 35-year-old woman who is unmarried and without children, but has parents and three sisters in a neighboring state, is diagnosed with cancer. By the time of diagnosis, the cancer has already spread throughout her body, and it is too late for any beneficial treatment. Patients diagnosed with cancer at this stage rarely live more than a year.

The physician knows that the patient has been working on her first novel for 2 years, that it should be completed in the next 3 months, and that it is her major life interest. The physician believes he can stall giving the correct diagnosis and prognosis, through deception and evasive answers, until the patient has completed her novel. He fears that providing the honest diagnosis at this point will so depress the patient that she will not be able to finish the book. The physician and patient have never discussed how a situation like this should be handled.

How would the physician–patient relationship be affected by a general expectation of unconditional truth-telling versus an expectation that physicians ought to use their discretion in revealing information to patients? How do these two expectations affect the physician's role in the encounter, and how do they affect the patient's role? In this case, do you believe the physician ought to provide this patient with the correct diagnosis and prognosis now or attempt to deceive her until her novel is completed?

Scenario 2: Alter the preceding scenario as follows. On the day before the patient is to return to the office to hear her test results, her parents call the physician long distance. They explain that they are calling out of love and concern for their daughter and due to a fear that she has cancer. If that is the case, they plead for the physician not to reveal the diagnosis. Their understanding of their daughter leads them to believe that hearing the correct diagnosis will so traumatize her that she would quickly give up the will to live.

Should the physician be influenced by the wishes of the family? What does his decision imply about the role of significant others in the care of patients?

Scenario 3: Add the following circumstance to scenario 1, and omit the information in scenario 2. On the day of her return visit, the patient initiates conversation with the physician. She expresses her fear that she has cancer. If that is the case, she says, she would rather not know it. She states that she would rather avoid hard-and-fast reality, believing that this would give her the best opportunity to complete her novel and carry on as normally as possible for as long as possible.

Should the physician be influenced by the wishes of the patient? Do patients have a right to make this request of physicians?

Case 2

The state medical board in your home state is considering a new regulation that would strictly forbid any physician to refuse to accept a patient or to refuse to continue seeing a patient (whom he or she is qualified to treat) solely on the basis that the patient has a highly contagious disease. Suspected violations of this policy would be investigated by the state medical board and a hearing would be held. If convicted of violating this regulation, a physician would lose his or her medical license for 6 months for a first offense, 1 year for a second offense, and permanently for a third offense.

Knowing that you have taken a course in medical sociology and have a keen interest in this subject, the board has called you to testify about this proposed regulation. Would you testify in favor of or against this proposal? What is the rationale for your testimony?

GLOSSARY

benevolent deception
casuistry
confidentiality
electronic health records
ethics
Health Insurance Portability and Accountability Act 1996 (HIPAA)

Hippocratic Oath
medical ethics
principlism
privacy
privileged communication
sociology of bio-knowledge

REFERENCES

Agris, Julie L., and John M. Spandorfer. 2016. "HIPAA Compliance and Training: A Perfect Storm for Professionalism Education?" *Journal of Law, Medicine and Ethics* 44(4):652–656.

Allmark, Peter. 1995. "HIV and the Bounds of Confidentiality." *Journal of Advanced Nursing* 21(1):158–163.

American Medical Association. 2016a. "Opinion 9.131: HIV-Infected Patients and Physicians." In *Code of Medical Ethics.* Chicago, IL: American Medical Association.

———. 2016b. "Opinion 8.082: Withholding Information from a Patient." In *Code of Medical Ethics.* Chicago, IL: American Medical Association.

Annas, George J. 1988. "Legal Risks and Responsibilities of Physicians in the AIDS Epidemic." *Hastings Center Report* 18(2)S26–S32.

Arras, John D. 1988. "The Fragile Web of Responsibility: AIDS and the Duty to Treat." *Hastings Center Report* 18(2):S10–S20.

Beauchamp, Tom L., and James F. Childress. 2012. *The Principles of Biomedical Ethics* (7th ed.). New York: Oxford University Press.

Bok, Sissela. 1989. *Secrets: On the Ethics of Concealment and Revelation.* New York: Vintage.

———. 1991. "Lies to the Sick and Dying." Pp. 74–81 in *Biomedical Ethics* (3rd ed.), edited by Thomas A. Mappes and Jane S. Zembaty. New York: McGraw-Hill.

Bostick, Nathan A., Mark A. Levine, and Robert M. Sade. 2008. "Ethical Obligations of Physicians Participating in Public Health and Quarantine Measures." *Public Health Reports* 123(1):3–8.

Brannigan, Michael C., and Judith A. Boss. 2001. *Healthcare Ethics in a Diverse Society.* Mountain View, CA: Mayfield Publishing Company.

Bredfeldt, Raymond C., Felicia M. Dardeau, Robert M. Wesley, Beth C. Vaughn-Wrobel, and Linda Markland. 1991. "AIDS: Family Physicians' Attitudes and Experiences." *The Journal of Family Practice* 32(1):71–75.

Carter, Darren, John Lantos, and J. Hughes. 1996. "Reassessing Medical Students' Willingness to Treat HIV-Infected Patients." *Academic Medicine* 71(11):1250–1252.

Clark, William P. 1976. "Dissenting Opinion in *Tarasoff v. Regents of the University of California.*" Pp. 160–162 in *Taking Sides: Clashing Views on Controversial Bioethical Issues* (2nd ed.), edited by Carol Levine. Guilford, CT: The Dushkin Publishing Group.

Conrad, Peter. 1990. "The Social Meaning of AIDS." Pp. 285–294 in *The Sociology of Health and Illness: Critical Perspectives* (3rd ed.), edited by Peter Conrad and Rochelle Kern. New York: St. Martin's Press.

Curlin, Farr A., Ryan E. Lawrence, Marshall H. Chin, and John D. Lantos. 2007. "Religion, Conscience, and Controversial Clinical Practices." *New England Journal of Medicine* 356(6):593–600.

DeVries, Raymond, and Janardan Subedi. 1998. *Bioethics and Society*. Upper Saddle River, NJ: Prentice Hall.

Elwyn, Todd S., Michael D. Fetters, Daniel W. Gorenflo, and Tsukasa Tsuda. 1998. "Cancer Disclosure in Japan: Historical Comparisons, Current Practices." *Social Science and Medicine* 46(9):1151–1163.

Emanuel, Ezekiel J. 1988. "Do Physicians Have an Obligation to Treat Patients with AIDS?" *New England Journal of Medicine* 318(25):1686–1690.

Enzinger, Andrea C., Baohui Zhang, Deborah Schrag, and Holly G. Prigerson. 2015. "Outcomes of Prognostic Disclosure: Associations with Prognostic Understanding, Distress, and Relationship with Physician among Patients with Advanced Cancer." *Journal of Clinical Oncology* 33(32):3809–3816.

Etzioni, Amitai. 1999. "Medical Records: Enhancing Privacy, Preserving the Common Good." *Hastings Center Report* 29(2):14–23.

Gerbert, Barbara, Bryan Maguire, Victor Badner, David Altman, and George Stone. 1988. "Why Fear Persists: Health Care Professionals and AIDS." *Journal of the American Medical Association* 260(23):3481–3483.

Gosk, Stephanie. 2015. "Electronic Medical Records Are Latest Target for Identity Thieves." Retrieved December 15, 2018 (www. nbcnews.com/us-news/electronic-medical-records-latest-target-identity-thieves-n365591).

Guiora, Alexander Z. 1980. "Freedom of Information Versus Freedom from Information." Pp. 31–34 in *Ethics, Humanism, and Medicine*, edited by Marc D. Basson. New York: Alan R. Liss.

Health and Public Policy Committee, American College of Physicians, and the Infectious Diseases Society of America. 1986. "Position Paper: Acquired Immunodeficiency Syndrome." *Annals of Internal Medicine* 104(4):575–581.

Jonsen, Albert R. 1990. "The Duty to Treat Patients with AIDS and HIV Infection." Pp. 155–168 in *AIDS and the Health Care System*, edited by Lawrence O. Gostin. New Haven, CT: Yale University Press.

Judicial Council of the American Medical Association. 1986. *Current Opinions—1986*. Chicago, IL: American Medical Association.

Katz, Laura L., and Marshall B. Paul. 2019. "When a Physician May Refuse to Treat a Patient." *Physicians News Digest*. Retrieved February 6, 2019 (https://physiciansnews.com/2002/02/14/when-a-physician-may-refuse-to-treat-a-patient/).

Kelly, William D., and Stanley R. Friesen. 1950. "Do Cancer Patients Want to Be Told?" *Surgery* 27(6):822–826.

Kim, Jerome H., and John R. Perfect. 1988. "To Help the Sick: An Historical and Ethical Essay Concerning the Refusal to Care for Patients with AIDS." *American Journal of Medicine* 84(1):135–137.

Legal Information Institute. 2016. *Ethics: An Overview*. Ithaca, NY: Legal Information Institute. Retrieved February 13, 2019 (www.law.cornell.edu/wex/ethics).

Link, Nathan R., Anat R. Feingold, Mitchell H. Charap, Katherine Freeman, and Steven P. Shelov. 1988. "Concerns of Medical and Pediatric House Officers about Acquiring AIDS from Their Patients." *American Journal of Public Health* 78(4):455–459.

McDaniel, J. Stephen, Lisa M. Carlson, Nancy J. Thompson, and David W. Purcell. 1995. "A Survey of Knowledge and Attitudes about HIV and AIDS among Medical Students." *Journal of American College Health* 44(1):11–14.

Miyaji, Naoko. 1993. "The Power of Compassion: Truth-Telling among American Doctors in the Care of Dying Patients." *Social Science and Medicine* 36(3):249–264.

Novack, Dennis H., Barbara J. Deterling, Robert Arnold, Lachlan Forrow, Morissa Ladinsky, and John C. Pezzullo. 1989. "Physicians' Attitudes Toward Using Deception to Resolve Difficult Problems." *Journal of the American Medical Association* 261(2):2980–2985.

Oppenheimer, Kim, and Greg Swanson. 1990. "Duty to Warn: When Should Confidentiality Be Breached?" *Journal of Family Practice* 30(2):179–184.

Petersen, Alan. 2013. "From Bioethics to a Sociology of Bio-Knowledge." *Social Science and Medicine* 98(December):264–270.

Rothstein, Mark A. 2016. "The End of HIPAA Privacy Rule?" *Journal of Law, Medicine, and Ethics* 44(2):352–358.

Schwartzbaum, Judith A., John R. Wheat, and Robert W. Norton. 1990. "Physician Breach of Patient Confidentiality Among Individuals with HIV Infection: Patterns of Decision." *American Journal of Public Health* 80(7):829–834.

Siegel, Karolynn, and Beatrice J. Krauss. 1991. "Living with HIV Infection: Adaptive Tasks of Seropositive Gay Men." *Journal of Health and Social Behavior* 32(1):17–32.

Sisk, Bryan. 2016. "The Truth about Truth-Telling in American Medicine: A Brief History." *The Permanente Journal* 20(3):215–219.

Taylor, Kathryn M., Joan M. Eakin, Harvey A. Skinner, Merrijoy Kelner, and Marla Shapiro. 1990. "Physicians' Perception of Personal Risk of HIV Infection and AIDS Through Occupational Exposure." *Canadian Medical Association Journal* 143(6):493–500.

Tobriner, Mathew O. 1976. "Majority Opinion in Tarasoff v. Regents of the University of California." Pp. 154–159 in *Taking Sides: Clashing Views on Controversial Bioethical Issues* (2nd ed.), edited by Carol Levine. Guilford, CT: The Dushkin Publishing Group.

Wallis, Patrick. 2011. "Debating a Duty to Treat: AIDS and the Professional Ethics of American Medicine." *Bulletin of the History of Medicine* 85(4):620–649.

Wasserstrom, Richard. 1986. "The Legal and Philosophical Foundations of the Right to Privacy."

Pp. 140–147 in *Biomedical Ethics* (2nd ed.), edited by Thomas A. Mappes and Jane S. Zembaty. New York: McGraw-Hill.

Wells, Deva M., Karen Lehavot, and Margaret L. Isaac. 2015. "Sounding Off on Social Media: The Ethics of Patient Storytelling in the Modern Era." *Academic Medicine* 90(8):1015–1019.

Yedidia, Michael J., Carolyn A. Berry, and Judith K. Barr. 1996. "Changes in Physicians' Attitudes toward AIDS During Residency Training: A Longitudinal Study of Medical School Graduates." *Journal of Health and Social Behavior* 37(2):179–191.

Zuger, Abigail, and Steven H. Miles. 1987. "Physicians, AIDS, and Occupational Risk: Historical Traditions and Ethical Obligations." *Journal of the American Medical Association* 258(14):1924–1928.

CHAPTER 14

The Health Care System of the United States

Learning Objectives

- Describe and discuss ratings of the health care system in the United States prior to the Patient Protection and Affordable Care Act (ACA).

- Describe the foundation and origin of the private nature of the health care system in the United States, and the entry of public programs such as Medicare and Medicaid.

- Describe and evaluate the managed care approach that was developed to control rapidly increasing health care costs.

- Identify and explain five key reasons for the high cost of health care in the United States.

- Describe the "uninsured" problem in the United States prior to the ACA, and the extent to which it has or has not improved. Discuss the problems associated with not having health insurance.

- Thoroughly analyze the ACA. Describe how it changes the US health care system, who benefits most from it, and political perspectives about the law.

America's health care system is undergoing one of the most significant transformations in its history. After extensive health care policy debates in the 1990s and 2000s, significant health care reform legislation—the Patient Protection and Affordable Care Act, now routinely identified as the Affordable Care Act (ACA) or Obamacare—was passed in 2010. Almost all of the legislation has survived ongoing constitutional challenges in the years since then, although Congressional Republicans are committed to "repeal and replace" it.

Prior to the ACA, the US health care system, at its best, was an innovative system that provided effective, high-technology care that was among the world's finest. At the same time, the health care system was recognized as extremely expensive, inefficient and wasteful, grounded in profit making, and leaving tens of millions of Americans

lacking the resources to obtain basic health care. This chapter describes the health care system of the United States up until reform legislation was passed in 2010, including the serious fiscal crisis of the system and its inability to provide care for all in need, and it examines passage of the ACA and its effects.

RATING THE HEALTH CARE SYSTEM OF THE UNITED STATES

Based on Systematic Analysis

In the first decade of the 2000s, the Commonwealth Fund (CF), a respected private nonpartisan foundation that seeks to promote a higher-quality medical care system, undertook a major research effort to systematically evaluate the overall quality of the US health care system (Schoen et al., 2006).

In 2006, the CF analyzed 37 important indicators of the functioning of the health care system, focusing on health outcomes, quality, access, efficiency, and equity. Some specific indicators included number of deaths from preventable disease, number of school days that children miss due to illness, life expectancy, and percentage of national health expenditures that go for administrative costs. Performance of the system was compared with benchmarks from within the country and with health care systems in other countries.

Based on a 100-point scale, the performance of the US health care system was calculated as 66 (by 2011—the last year a national score was calculated—the score had dropped to 64). On no indicator did the US system function as well as the top performers, and in some cases its performance was far behind that of the leaders. The CF determined that improvement on key indicators could annually save as many as 150,000 lives and up to US$100 billion. Study leaders summarized the situation as follows:

> The overall picture that emerges from the scorecard is one of missed opportunities and room for improvement. Despite high expenditures, the United States lags behind other countries on indicators of mortality and healthy life expectancy. Within the United States, there is often a substantial spread between the top and bottom groups of states, hospitals, or health plans as well as wide gaps between the national average and top rates. . . . On multiple indicators, the United States would need to improve its performance by 50 percent or more to reach benchmark countries, regions, states, hospitals, health plans, or targets.
>
> (Schoen et al., 2006:472)

In a longitudinal study comparing health care systems, the CF analyzed 72 indicators of health care quality, access, efficiency, equity, healthy lives, and health expenditures per capita in 11 wealthy nations: Australia, Canada, France, Germany, the Netherlands, New Zealand, Norway, Sweden, Switzerland, the United Kingdom, and the United States. How did the United States fare? In the first study in 2004, the United States finished last, and was last or nearly last in access, efficiency, and equity. The study was conducted again in 2006, 2007, 2010, and 2014. Last on each occasion. And in 2017, the most recent analysis? Still last (Schneider et al., 2018). Studies conducted by other respected organizations—such as the World Health Organization—affirm the low ranking of the United States among world health care systems.

Based on Consumer Attitudes

Over the years, many surveys on the attitude of Americans about the American health care system have been conducted. They have consistently pointed to satisfaction with the quality of health care personally received, but dissatisfaction, disappointment, and anger with the health care system.

In 2009, the year before the ACA passed, the Gallup Poll found 21 percent of Americans viewed the health care system as in a state of crisis, 50 percent believed it had major problems, 25 percent as having minor problems, and 2 percent as having no problems. Seventy-nine percent were dissatisfied with the cost of care, and only 17 percent rated the system as excellent (The Gallup Poll, 2019). Satisfaction with one's own health care system has been greater in all other high-income countries than in the United States for the last 30 years (Hero et al., 2016).

The question then is how and why the United States developed a health care system that is fundamentally different than those in all other countries, and that is by far the world's most expensive system, yet one that is both objectively and subjectively rated so unfavorably.

THE HEALTH CARE SYSTEM OF THE UNITED STATES

The Foundation of the Health Care System

The foundation of today's health care system largely originated in a series of events between 1850 and the early 1900s. Advances in the scientific understanding of disease and illness and in the effectiveness of medical procedures, the expansion and elaboration of hospitals, and the growth of commercial health insurance companies contributed to an increasingly complex system of health care delivery and financing. The professionalization of medicine, the establishment of high standards for medical education, and the institution of medical licensure contributed to significant autonomy for medical providers, increased medical fees, and greater difficulty for those with low income and no insurance to obtain needed care.

America's reliance on a "private market" approach for its health care system was established in these years. This means that the system is based on private decisions made by medical facilities, medical providers, and patients with minimal government involvement. The laws of supply and demand that function in other areas of the economy were considered appropriate for the health care system. The rationale for this approach is that competition for profit is the strongest possible motivator for individuals and companies to work their hardest and do their best.

This approach assumes that the most equitable means of allocating health care is through the private market. Health care is viewed as an economic good or a privilege that is most accessible to those with the greatest resources. Proponents contend that this competitive basis has stimulated the development of superior medical schools, new medical technologies, and the highest quality health care possible.

Early on, many countries around the world used a similar approach but later converted from it. While the United States maintained a strong belief in the principle of individualism, other countries showed a greater collective orientation and stronger commitment to the general welfare. Over time, other countries determined that a private market approach was unsuccessful with regard to health. They observed that the health care system did not follow basic rules of supply and demand, that many people were unable to access health care services, and that the health care system was not functioning as effectively or justly as was desirable.

In fact, every other modern country in the world today emphasizes a "social justice" approach to its health care system rather than a private market approach. Other countries identify health care as a "right" for all persons rather than an economic good or privilege. They believe that the government is more effective than the private market in allocating health care equitably and ensuring that no one goes without needed health care services.

The Development of Private Health Insurance

Private health insurance companies began appearing in the mid-1800s, and they became the cornerstone of health care financing in the United States by the early 1900s. Initially, they provided compensation for sick workers or those injured on the job. During the early 1900s—the time when medicine was professionalizing and hospital care was growing in importance—private insurers saw potential profit in selling health insurance policies. These quickly became a crucial element in paying for health care.

Today, there are almost 1,300 *private* (commercial) health insurance companies in the United States (although the largest 35 of these companies dominate the market). Some offer only health insurance while others also offer life, homeowners, automobile, and other types of insurance. These are profit-making companies whose intention is to set premiums at a level that will allow them to pay out all claims, pay for administrative, salary, and overhead expenses, and have money left over for profit for investors.

Health insurance policies are sold to individuals, families, and groups (usually businesses). It is often said that no two health insurance policies are exactly alike—they cover whatever the buyer negotiates. They may include basic health benefits, benefits for very large bills, income replacement during disability, and benefits for dental care, eye care, drugs, and so forth. In addition to the basic premium, policies usually have a *deductible* provision (the policy owner pays a set amount of money before the insurance kicks in) and *coinsurance* provision (the policy owner pays a set percentage of all costs beyond the deductible) and *co-payments* (specific fees paid out of pocket for particular services, such as US$20 for each visit to a primary care physician beyond what the insurance pays).

In time, health insurance became a benefit provided by employers for workers and their families. This arrangement was considered consistent with the private market approach. It gave individuals an additional incentive to have a job and work hard, and gave employers an extra mechanism for recruiting and retaining good workers. Because they represented large numbers of workers and families, employers could purchase sizable policies that gave them leverage to negotiate a good rate. Insurance companies competed with each other for sales, and this gave them an incentive to be efficient. In 2017, about 60 percent of non-elderly adults had health insurance through their employer (Kaiser Family Foundation, 2017).

Thus was the advent of a private-market, employer-based health insurance system. Individuals and families without employer-sponsored health insurance but with sufficient wealth could purchase their own policies. Those without health insurance coverage and without adequate financial resources could not afford to access the system, but this was seen as an acceptable result for people who had not successfully competed in the job world. Pharmaceutical companies, medical equipment companies, some hospitals, and a variety of other health services also became part of the private market designed to be profit making.

The Development of a Non-profit Health Insurance Alternative

By the late 1920s and the Depression, it was apparent that millions of individuals were not in the labor force through no fault of their own, and they certainly were unable to afford private health insurance. Their need for health care services was high, but they were unable to pay for the services. Hospitals sometimes provided care, but without getting paid. To offer a more affordable alternative than the for-profit companies, Blue Cross—later to become Blue Cross Blue Shield (BCBS)—a non-profit health insurance company, was created in 1929. In exchange for its non-profit status and exemption from paying taxes, the BCBS plans offered comprehensive policies to a wide range of individuals at prices often measurably below those of commercial companies. This approach was enormously successful, and throughout much of the twentieth century the health insurance field was dominated by BCBS. However, in the 1990s the "Blues" determined that their non-profit status did not serve them well in the changed health care system, and most BCBS plans (now with a variety of company names) converted to a for-profit basis.

The Entry of Public (Government-Sponsored) Health Insurance

In the 1960s, Americans experienced considerably heightened awareness about the extent of poverty and the fact that many individuals—adults and children alike—could not afford medical care. Many analysts believed that the private health care market failed to function effectively and advocated for increased public (government) involvement. They emphasized that public programs are often created to serve those whose needs are not being met by the private sector. Among the many health programs that were already supported by public dollars were those for members of the armed forces, veterans, mothers and children, Native Americans, and the disabled.

The two groups most unable to access services in the private market were (1) older people who were retired and trying to live on Social Security and perhaps a small pension and (2) people with a very low income, who frequently worked at jobs that did not offer employer-sponsored health insurance. Presidents Kennedy and Johnson formulated legislation that led to passage of Medicare (largely for those aged 65 years or older) and Medicaid (largely for those with a very low income) in 1965. These have become by far the largest government-sponsored health insurance programs.

Medicare.   **Medicare** is a federal insurance program originally designed to protect people aged 65 years or older from the rising costs of health care. In 1972, permanently disabled workers, their dependents, and people with endstage renal disease were added to the program.

The two key long-standing parts of the program are Part A (the hospital insurance program, which covers inpatient hospital services, skilled nursing services, home health services, and hospice care) and Part B (the physician services program, which covers physician services, outpatient hospital services, and therapy). All people aged 65 years or older are eligible for Part A simply by enrolling, although there are deductible and coinsurance provisions. A premium must be paid for participation in Part B, which also includes a deductible and coinsurance. Medicare is financed by a combination of general tax revenues, a specific Medicare payroll tax levied on employers and employees, and the enrollee payments.

Historically, Medicare did not contain any prescription drug coverage. That led many seniors (perhaps as many as 25 percent) to forgo needed prescriptions. As the price of medications skyrocketed, the problem became more severe. In 2003, Congress added a hotly debated and very narrowly passed prescription drug benefit (Part D) to Medicare. Using a complex formula, enrollees in Part D paid a monthly premium and deductible and had co-payments. Many Congressional Democrats believed the bill was inadequate and did nothing to control drug price increases. They wanted Medicare to be able to use its size to negotiate lower drug prices from pharmaceutical companies. Many Congressional Republicans opposed the bill for overly interfering with the private market and for being too expensive. While Medicare enrollees still must pay a substantial amount for their health care and for medications, almost all now agree that the program contributes significantly to the health care needs of those aged 65 years or older.

In 2018, Medicare covered 59.7 million people (more than 18 percent of the population) at a cost of US$704.6 billion. Medicare alone accounts for 20 percent of all health dollars spent in the United States and about 15 percent of the federal budget.

Medicaid.   **Medicaid** is a jointly funded federal-state program designed to make health care more available to the very poor. Eligibility requirements and program benefits vary from state to state, even though the federal government requires that people receiving certain types of public assistance (such as pregnant women, children under the age of 6, low-income Medicare enrollees, and recipients of foster care and adoption assistance not covered by other programs) be eligible for the program.

Federal and state funds paid through Medicaid for health care amounted to US$629.3 billion for 75.1 million recipients (about 22 percent of the population) in 2018. Medicaid accounts for 17 percent of all health dollars spent in the United States. (It is possible to receive Medicare and Medicaid simultaneously, so the total number of recipients is less than the combination of the two sets of enrollment.) Together, in 2018, Medicare and Medicaid paid for 37 percent of national spending on health care and generated more than 40 percent of hospital revenues.

The elderly, blind, and disabled account for more than 50 percent of Medicaid expenditures, even though they represent less than 25 percent of recipients. On the other hand, more than two-thirds of Medicaid recipients are members of a family receiving public assistance, but they receive only 32 percent of program benefits.

The Medicare and Medicaid programs are examples of "entitlement" programs. This means that people receive benefits automatically when they qualify for the programs (in the case of Medicare Part B, qualifying includes payment of a premium). The number of people covered is determined primarily by the number of people aged 65 years or older for Medicare and by the number of people below a designated income/assets line (which varies from state to state) for Medicaid. Because the government has little control over the number of participants, it has limited ways to control costs. Eligibility requirements for Medicaid can be tightened, but more than half of all people under the age of 65 years and below the poverty level are already ineligible for Medicaid. Benefits can be reduced, but they are already at very low levels. Reimbursement to providers can be reduced, but compensation from both programs has already been cut. Medicaid reimbursement for primary care physicians is now less than two-thirds of prevailing market rates. In addition, both Medicare and Medicaid are in some financial difficulty. Prior to the ACA, it was anticipated that Medicare would go bankrupt within a few years. Most states are having a difficult time balancing their budgets due in part to their Medicaid expenditures.

Children's Health Insurance Program (CHIP). A third large public program, although much smaller than Medicare and Medicaid, is the **Children's Health Insurance Program (CHIP**, formerly known as SCHIP). CHIP was created in 1997 with the objective of reducing the number of children without health insurance. CHIP serves uninsured children up to the age of 19 years in low-income families whose income is just high enough to disqualify them for Medicaid. States have broad discretion in setting their income eligibility standards, and eligibility varies greatly across states. The federal government gives grants to states that pay for about two-thirds of the program, and the state pays for the remainder. In the first 10 years of CHIP's existence, the percentage of children in the United States without any health insurance decreased from 23 percent to 15 percent, and by 2017 it was down to 5 percent (although the percentage has actually increased since then). However, the more successful the program is in covering children (more than 9 million children are now enrolled), the more the program costs (just over US$20 billion annually). Analyses of CHIP have uniformly found it to be very effective (Oberlander and Jones, 2015), and it enjoys widespread popular support. Nevertheless, it is a program that Congressional Republicans frequently attempt to scale back, and funding almost ended in late 2018.

Incentives to Overuse Services

The creation of the Medicare and Medicaid programs (and later CHIP) has been of tremendous help to those covered by them. In many cases the programs mean the difference between receiving and not receiving health care, and between life and death. They have also pumped billions of dollars into the health care system and ensured that many providers would be compensated for services delivered. However, the programs also highlighted a problem with the traditional way insurers compensated providers.

In the traditional reimbursement method, patients covered by any form of health insurance would see a medical provider and receive a set of medical services. The medical provider would determine the amount to be charged and send a bill to the insurance company, which would remit the amount of the charge. This system lacked cost control mechanisms, as no one had an incentive to be cost-conscious. Patients often paid nothing for services received and willingly accepted all of the suggested services. Physicians could charge whatever they wanted and receive full reimbursement. Insurers could pass on higher premiums to those they insured. After the passage of Medicare and Medicaid, both the number of people able to receive services and the number of services provided to each patient increased substantially and the charges for services rapidly escalated. This stimulated tremendous growth in the health care system.

Provision of Unnecessary Services. By the early 1980s, compelling evidence had been uncovered that the lack of cost-consciousness led to many unnecessary health care services. Researchers determined that as many as one-sixth to one-fifth of all surgical operations were unnecessary, that the annual cost for these unnecessary operations was in the billions of dollars, and that as many as 12,000 patients per year died in the course of an unnecessary procedure. Table 14.1 shows the increase in overall health expenditures since 1960.

The most intensive study of surgical necessity was conducted by the Rand Corporation,

a think tank in Santa Monica, California. In 1989, they developed a list of indicators of the need for four specific procedures and applied it to the records of 5,000 recent Medicare patients. They found that 65 percent of carotid endarterectomies (removal of blockages from one or both arteries carrying blood to the brain) were unnecessary, as were 17 percent of coronary angiographies (an X-ray technique in which dye is injected into the coronary arteries to diagnose blockages), 17 percent of upper gastrointestinal tract endoscopies (examination of the digestive organs with a fiber-optic tube), and 14 percent of coronary bypass surgeries (relieving or replacing blocked arteries by adding or rerouting other blood vessels). Other studies with other population groups found very high rates of unnecessary surgery for procedures such as cesarean section births, hysterectomies, laminectomies, tonsillectomies, colonoscopies, spinal fusion, prostate and gall bladder removal, and knee replacement (Brook et al., 1990).

In response, policy makers sought ways to restructure the health care system to discourage unnecessary procedures and create some cost control incentives. Cost containment strategies and the managed care approach were developed with this in mind.

TABLE 14.1 National Health Expenditures

Year	Total Amount (US$)	Domestic Product (%)	Amount per Capita (US$)
1960	26.9 billion	5.1	141
1970	73.2 billion	7.1	341
1980	247.2 billion	8.9	1,051
1990	699.5 billion	12.2	2,689
2000	1.3 trillion	13.3	4,670
2010	2.6 trillion	17.4	8,428
2016	3.3 trillion	17.9	10,348

Note: The average medical cost for a family of four in 2018 was US$28,166.

Source: National Center for Health Statistics: Faststats. *2019*. Gross Domestic Product, National Health Expenditures, Per Capita Amounts, Percent Distribution, and Average Annual Percent Change: United States, Selected Years 1960–2016. Retrieved March 4, 2019 (www.cdc.gov/nchs/data/hus/2017/093.pdf).

Cost Containment and the Development of Managed Care

Most **cost containment** strategies offer financial incentives to provide only necessary services and to do so in a cost-efficient manner. The most significant cost containment plan within health care financing in the last 30 years has been the movement toward **managed care**. The rationale underlying managed care is that these plans can control health care cost increases because they oversee and monitor patient behavior, provider behavior, and insurer behavior. Controls are designed to manage or guide the patient care process, attempting to ensure that appropriate and cost-efficient care is provided and that inappropriate and unnecessarily expensive care is not. Originally, managed care provisions were incorporated within traditional health insurance plans, but they have now almost completely replaced traditional plans. Table 14.2 shows the distribution of insured people across types of insurance plans in 1990,

2000, 2009 (the year prior to passage of the Affordable Care Act), and in 2016. Note the decline in conventional insurance, the increase and then decrease in preferred provider organizations (PPOs, discussed more later), and the recent growth in high-deductible plans (which is expected to continue).

There are three essential components of managed care. First, a **managed care organization (MCO)** (which is often owned by a traditional private health insurance company) recruits medical providers in an area to be part of the MCO. Typically, a physician who joins continues to practice in the same location but understands that some patients will now be insured by the MCO and that there will be special regulations when treating these patients. The physician must also agree to a lower-than-usual reimbursement amount. Why would physicians or hospitals sign up? The reason is because the MCO is promising large numbers of patients and warning that these patients will go elsewhere unless the provider agrees to join.

Second, the MCO recruits patients. Typically, this means contracting with local employers to cover all of their employees. If the employer signs on, patients will be given financial incentives to see only providers who are part of the MCO, and they also agree to abide by special regulations. Why would an employer contract with a particular MCO? The reason is because the MCO is guaranteeing a good deal—the most services covered for the least amount of money (because providers are accepting a lower reimbursement amount and patient behavior will be regulated).

Third, the MCO will construct a list of its providers, the cost per service, and the "special regulations." These regulations might include a requirement to see a primary care physician before a specialist for a care episode (because primary care physicians are less expensive), pre-admission review for all elective hospital admissions (because some may not be necessary),

TABLE 14.2   Distribution of Employees Across Health Benefit Plans

Type of Plan	1990 %	2000 %	2009 %	2016 %
Conventional	62	8	1	<1
Health maintenance organization	20	29	20	15
Preferred provider organization	13	42	60	48
Point of service	5	21	10	9
High deductible	0	0	8	29
Total managed care	**38**	**92**	**99**	**>99**

Source: Kaiser Family Foundation. 2018b. "Employer Health Benefits." Retrieved March 18, 2019 (https://kff.org/report-section/ehbs-2016-section-five-market-shares-of-health-plans/). Reprinted with permission from the Henry J. Kaiser Family Foundation, 2018. The Kaiser Family Foundation based in Menlo Park, California, is a nonprofit, private operating foundation focusing on the major health care issues facing the nation, and is not associated with Kaiser Permanente or Kaiser Industries.

mandatory second opinions before surgery (because less expensive options might be identified), continued review of patient care during hospital stays (to discharge the patient as early as possible), and alternative benefit coverage (e.g., outpatient surgery, home health care, and skilled nursing facility care). In the case of pre-admission and continued review of hospital stays, a physician (or their nurse or assistant) will call the MCO to have a nurse reviewer verify the admission and report the expectations (e.g., length of stay) of the insurance company. Failure of the physician or hospital to stay within the limits jeopardizes full reimbursement. Renegotiation can occur while the patient is in the hospital. In addition, almost every service covered will include a coinsurance or co-payment. This is to give patients an added incentive not to overuse services.

Types of Managed Care Organizations.
There are four main types of MCOs—health maintenance organizations (HMOs), preferred provider organizations (PPOs) (this includes exclusive provider organizations—EPOs), point-of-service plans (POS), and high deductible health plans (HPHPs).

Health maintenance organizations (HMOs) are *prepaid* plans in which a group of physicians and hospitals provide health care to enrolled persons in return for a fixed premium. HMOs must provide basic health care services (typically a minimum of ambulatory and hospital care, medications, and laboratory tests) that must be available 24 hours a day. Providers who have contracted with the HMO have agreed to accept a lower reimbursement level and some regulations in exchange for a promise of patients. Most HMOs are now owned by for-profit companies such as Cigna and Prudential.

HMOs differ from conventional insurance plans in three main ways. First, in a traditional plan, the provider is reimbursed on a fee-for-service basis after a service is provided. The more services provided, the more the provider makes.

In HMOs, physicians are typically compensated on a "capitation" basis—that is, based on the number of patients they have agreed to see and not on the number of services provided. So, there is no financial benefit in doing more tests and procedures. Theoretically, HMOs maximize profit by keeping people healthy and by discouraging inappropriate use of costly physician and hospital services.

Second, patients with traditional private health insurance can see any physician of their choosing in the community, while HMO enrollees must select from the list of providers who have contracted with the HMO. Third, both providers and patients agree to all of the HMO's regulations for each care episode.

While there are other differences, many HMO enrollees are willing to accept some limitations in physician choice and some regulations on care in order to pay lower costs. On average, HMOs do save patients approximately 10 to 20 percent in expenditures.

Do HMOs offer high-quality care? Are patients and physicians satisfied with their experiences? The answer to both questions is that it depends on the particular HMO. In general, HMO enrollees receive more preventive care, have the same or slightly more physician visits, receive fewer expensive tests and procedures, have lower hospital admission rates, have a shorter length of stay when hospitalized, receive less costly technology, and have mixed but generally better health outcomes. However, significant variations exist among HMOs.

The most heated controversy surrounds the issue of whether HMOs are apt to deny needed services in order to maximize short-term profit. Some HMOs have developed incentive systems that could easily discourage physicians from ordering services. For example, some HMOs have given telephone clerks (people typically with little or no medical training who answer phone calls from patients wanting to make an appointment) cash bonuses for keeping calls short and limiting the number of appointments they schedule. Many HMO enrollees have publicized cases in which they were denied care that they considered necessary.

In some HMOs, most patients express satisfaction with the care they receive, but in other HMOs most patients express dissatisfaction. Reported satisfaction levels range from as high as 75 percent to as low as 35 percent. These differences have led some of the best HMOs to adopt marketing plans that attempt to distinguish themselves from lower rated plans.

Preferred provider organizations (PPOs) are networks of physicians and hospitals that agree to give price discounts to groups who enroll in their program, use their services, and agree to follow specified regulations. Unlike HMOs, PPOs allow members to receive care outside the network, although the co-payments are higher. Although patients typically pay for care received on a fee-for-service basis, they pay lower fees than do other patients. In exchange for discounting fees, PPO providers are likely to see more patients. On average, cost savings for PPOs relative to conventional insurance are in the range of 5 to 15 percent. Most PPOs are owned by a commercial insurance company, and more than 80 percent of PPOs are run on a for-profit basis.

Over time, HMOs and PPOs have come to more closely resemble each other. The four key differences are that (1) HMOs do more regulation of patient care, (2) HMOs have smaller rosters of available medical providers from which to choose, (3) HMOs cost less than PPOs, and (4) providers are typically paid by the capitation method in HMOs but by discounted fees in PPOs. When given a choice between the two, patients decide whether to accept the greater restrictions and smaller roster of providers in HMOs in order to achieve greater cost savings, or to pay more for PPO membership to get fewer regulations and a larger list of providers from which to choose.

A variation of PPOs is the Exclusive Provider Organizations (EPOs). They are structured like PPOs, but do not pay anything for services received from an out-of-network provider.

Point-of-service (POS) plans are a hybrid of HMOs and PPOs. Typically, they offer more choice of providers (like PPOs) while retaining more care management regulations (like HMOs). Providers are reimbursed by the capitation method. Members are able to receive care from a provider outside the system by paying a higher premium or absorbing a larger share of the cost. Some have described POS plans as having the benefits of the network discount of PPOs and the gatekeeper process of HMOs, but with the possibility that the participant can receive partially subsidized care outside the network.

High Deductible Health Plans. An increasingly popular cost-containment approach is the *High Deductible Health Plan (HDHP)*—a type of health insurance plan that is somewhat less expensive but has a very high deductible. These plans are very popular among employers as they basically shift costs from the employer to the employee. Because insurance does not kick in until the covered person has paid a very high deductible amount, insurance companies can offer these policies to employers at a lower price. On the other hand, the insured must pay for 100 percent of medical costs until the deductible is reached. This may discourage use of medical services. If nothing catastrophic occurs during the year, the insurance company may not need to pay anything.

Many analysts believe these programs are unsuitable for low-income and middle-income individuals and families due to having to pay for all costs up to the deductible. Research shows that they reduce utilization of preventive services and even some needed services—that is, the very problem that insurance is supposed to alleviate. According to one study, nearly 30 percent of adults with deductibles of at least US$1,500 per person per year forgo needed medical care because they cannot afford it (Sutherly, 2015). In addition, the increasing use of these policies has created problems for hospitals as an increasing percentage of bills must be paid by patients (who may have difficulty paying) rather than insurance companies (which always pay).

THE FINANCING OF HEALTH CARE IN THE UNITED STATES

How Much Money Does the United States Spend on Health Care?

The United States has the most expensive health care system in the world (by far). During the last five decades, health care spending has grown more rapidly than any other sector of the economy. **National health expenditures (NHEs)**—that is, the total amount of spending for personal health care and for administration, construction, research, and other expenses not directly related to patient care—reached US$3.3 trillion (i.e., US$3,300 billion) in 2017—or more than 12 times the amount spent in 1980 and almost 5 times that spent in 1990. Notice the tremendous increase in all three items in Table 14.1. National health spending growth is anticipated to be about 5.5 percent annually in the next decade (NCHS, 2019).

Table 14.3 compares the role of health care within the gross domestic product and the percent of the population covered by health insurance. The 2017 figure accounts for almost 18 percent of the gross domestic product (GDP)—the nation's total economic output. This means that health care represents about 18 percent of the US economy, and about 1 out of every 6 dollars spent in the United States is spent on health care. This percentage is much higher than in any other developed country, even though they all provide universal health care coverage. Americans spent an average of US$10,348 per person on health care in 2017—more· than twice as much as people in any other country. By 2027, it is estimated that health care will be about 20

TABLE 14.3   Total Health Spending as Percentage of Gross Domestic Product and Percentage of Population with Health Insurance, 2016

Country	Percent of National GDP	Percentage of Population With Health Insurance
United States	17.8	90
Switzerland	12.4	100
Sweden	11.9	100
Germany	11.3	99.8
France	11.0	99.9
Japan	10.9	100
Denmark	10.8	100
Netherlands	10.5	99.9
Canada	10.3	100
United Kingdom	9.7	100
Australia	9.6	100

Source: *Irene Papanicolas, Liana R. Woskie*, and *Ashish K. Jha*. 2018. "Health Care Spending in the United States and Other High-Income Countries." *Journal of the American Medical Association*, 319(10):1024–1039.

percent of the US economy (Papanicolas, Woskie, and Jha, 2018).

Personal health expenditures (PHEs) focuses just on direct patient care items like physician care, hospital care, and medications, but not spending on things like medical research. It is by far the largest component (about 85 percent) of NHE. In 2017, PHE amounted to approximately US$3 trillion. The next section focuses on NHE.

Who Receives the Dollars Spent on Health?

Who receives the dollars spent by Americans on health? According to the CDC (2019), the five largest items (listed by dollars spent in 2017 and rounded off) are as follows:

1. *Hospital care* (38 percent of PHE). Hospitals remain the largest recipient of health care dollars, but this percentage is dropping as more services are utilized outside hospitals.

2. *Professional services* (27 percent of PHE) (Physicians = 24 percent, other professionals = 3 percent). Physicians are the second largest recipient of health care dollars, but this percentage has held steady or decreased in recent years due to more tightly controlled reimbursement levels used by the government and MCOs, and sharp increases in spending in other categories.

3. *Drugs and medical supplies* (14 percent of PHE) (Drugs = 10 percent, medical supplies = 4 percent). Prescription drugs and durable (e.g., wheelchairs, sleep-assistance machines) and nondurable (e.g., over-the-counter medications) medical products are the fastest increasing category of PHE. This category includes only those drugs purchased from retail outlets and excludes drugs dispensed in hospitals, nursing homes, and physicians' offices. If all drugs are included, the percentage spent on drugs increases to around 12 percent.

4. *Nursing home care and home health care* (9 percent of PHE) (Nursing homes = 6 percent, home care = 3 percent). While the growth rate for nursing home care is decelerating, the increasing number of elderly people and the high charges per day make this the fourth largest category of expenditures. The home health care industry continues to expand.

5. *Dental care* (4 percent of PHE). This is the fifth largest recipient of PHE, and the only other one over US$100 billion in 2017.

Other recipients combined receive approximately 8 percent.

Who Spends the Dollars for Personal Health Care?

How is money channeled into the health care system? Health care in the United States is financed by a complex mix of private purchasers (employers, families, and individuals) and public purchasers (the federal and state governments) who pay health care providers directly for services and products or channel payment through private or public health insurance.

Private Sources

In 2016, over half (55 percent) of all personal health care expenditures were paid for by private sources. The fact that this percentage is close to 50 reflects both the private market foundation of the health care system *and* the fact that the system has become more of a public-private mix. Most of the private payments—and the single largest source of payments for health care—came from private health insurance, and most of the remainder was paid out of pocket by individual patients and their families (see Table 14.4). Over the last 50 years, the relative contribution of private insurance within this category has increased while the relative contribution paid out of pocket has decreased (Centers for Disease Control and Prevention, 2019).

Payment for health insurance policies comes both from employers (who pay for all or part of a policy for employees and their families as a job benefit) and from individuals and families (who typically pay for part of the employer-provided policy or purchase a policy directly from a private health insurance company and must pay the entire premium).

Employers. Health insurance policies are expensive regardless of who pays. In 2018, employers paid about US$5,700 as their share for a policy to cover a single employee (and the employee contributed more than US$1,200). For family policies, employers on average contributed almost US$14,000 and individual employees about US$5,700. Businesses derive funds to pay for these policies largely by increasing the price of goods or services that they sell.

Rapid increases in insurance premiums in the last few decades have prodded many employers to require their employees to pay for a larger share

TABLE 14.4   Source of Payments for Health Services, 2016

Item	Amount (%) of Expenditures (in US$ billions) and Percent of Personal Health Expenditures
Personal health expenditures	2,834.0
Out-of-pocket	352.5 (12.4%)
Health insurance	2,243.9 (79.2%)
Private	993.8 (35.1%)
Medicare	625.3 (22.1%)
Medicaid	505.2 (17.8%)
CHIP + other	119.6 (4.2%)
Other	237.6 (8.4%)
Percentage paid from private dollars = 55%	
Percentage paid from public dollars = 45%	

Source: Centers for Medicare and Medicaid Services. 2019. National Health Expenditure Accounts. Retrieved March 23, 2019 (www.cdc.gov/nchs/data/hus/2017/fig17.pdf).

of their insurance cost. Four changes have been especially dramatic:

- Some small businesses (which are hardest hit by providing insurance) have discontinued employee coverage. Only about 3 in 5 workers today are covered by an employer-provided plan—the lowest percentage in several decades, and still decreasing. Just under half (47 percent) of firms with three to nine employees offered a health insurance benefit to employees, while virtually all businesses with 1,000 or more employees did so (Kaiser Family Foundation, 2018b).
- Most employers have increased the percentage of the health insurance plan that must be paid by employees. Whereas many companies formerly paid 100 percent of the costs, the average today has dropped to 82 percent for employees and 71 percent for their families.
- Employers have reduced the types and amount of health care covered by the policy.
- Policies have increased the deductible, increased the coinsurance, and increased the co-payment for those covered.

Individuals and Families. These changes in the provision of employer-provided health insurance mean that individuals and families pay for health care in a variety of ways: (1) by paying a portion of the cost of an employer-provided health insurance policy, or by paying the entire cost if the employer does not provide coverage; (2) by paying out-of-pocket health care expenses not covered by an insurance policy (deductibles, coinsurance, co-payments, and uncovered services), and (3) through various taxes such as the Medicare tax (employees pay 1.45 percent of salary or wages to subsidize Medicare; employers match this amount).

For many workers, these changes make paying for health care extremely difficult or impossible. In 2005, workers paid an average of US$584 for health care before insurance kicked in; in 2015, the figure was US$1,318. In 2005, only 55 percent of workers had a deductible on their plan; in 2015, 81 percent did so, and many of these were high-deductible plans (Brandeisky, 2015).

Public Sources (Government)

Over the last half century, payment for health care has shifted from a reliance on private sources to increased government funding. From 1960 to 2016, the government share of health care financing increased from 24.9 to 45 percent.

EXPLANATIONS FOR THE HIGH COST OF AMERICAN MEDICINE

How does the United States manage to spend more money and a higher percentage of its GDP on health care than any other developed country, while being the only one that fails to provide universal health care coverage? The high cost of health care can be traced to several complex changes in society and within the health care system. This section examines the most important factors.

The Aging of the Population

The most important factor *external* to the health care system (but *not* the largest overall factor) contributing to increases in health care costs is the aging of the population. Between 2000 and 2040, the number of people in the United States age 65 years or older will increase from 34.8 million to 81.0 million, and the number of people age 85 years or older will increase from 4.3 million to 14.6 million.

The increasing number of older Americans contributes to increased health care costs in several ways. As people age, they are more likely to experience one or more chronic degenerative diseases such as heart disease, cancer, and diabetes. These diseases are often manageable, but they are resource intensive in terms of the number of health care workers, health care facilities, and medications that are necessitated—all of which are very expensive. (An estimated 86 percent of all health care dollars are spent on chronic diseases.) The very high and rapidly increasing cost of drugs is especially problematic. These individuals may require home health care, assisted living, or nursing home care—all of which are very expensive. Health care costs escalate very rapidly after the age of 65 years. It is estimated that a 65-year-old couple who retired in 2019 will need US$285,000 of their own money for health care costs in their lifetime (O'Brien, 2019).

As one nears the end of life, extremely expensive high-technology care is often used to prolong life—sometimes for a matter of only days or weeks, and often in a painful or uncomfortable condition. Studies show that the last year of one's life tends to incur far more health care costs than any other year, and sometimes more than in the rest of one's whole lifetime.

Having an increasing number of older people in the population is certainly not unique to the United States. Most countries in the world are experiencing the same trend. What is different is

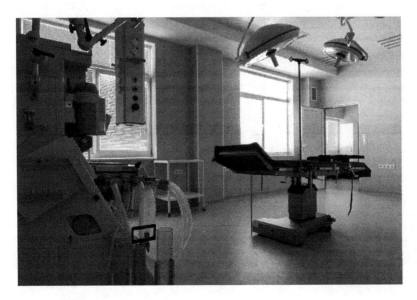

Advances in high-technology forms of medical diagnosis and treatment have improved patient treatments but have also driven up the cost of medical care

that medical services are far more expensive in the United States, and there is much greater propensity to use expensive, high technology care during the final days of life. At this stage, other countries put more emphasis on pain relief and allowing death to occur.

The High Cost of New Medical Technologies

Many experts believe that the most important factor driving up health care costs is expensive new medical technologies. There is more emphasis in the United States than in any other country on quickly incorporating new medical technologies. This occurs for several reasons. Medical providers want to offer the best possible care to patients, and high-technology innovations are often viewed as the highest-quality treatments. Hospitals often engage in fierce competition with each other and want to attract top physicians and other providers. Having the latest equipment (whether or not it substantially improves patient outcomes) can be an effective marketing device both to the community and to medical providers (Bodenheimer, 2005).

High-technology medical equipment comes with a very high price tag (e.g., most diagnostic cameras cost at least several hundred thousand dollars, plus the cost of maintaining the equipment and having people trained to use it). Once it has been purchased, hospitals and medical providers have a strong financial incentive to use the equipment to have it bring in revenue. Studies show that greater availability leads to greater per-capita use. Greater per-capita use leads to higher expenditure on these procedures, but rarely to lower expenditure on other procedures. The overall contribution to cost increases is substantial. For example, throughout the last decade of the twentieth century and the first decade of the twenty-first, the number of diagnostic imaging procedures (including MRIs, CTs, PETs, and nuclear medicine) increased dramatically every year, tripling or quadrupling over a 10-year

period. The number of CT scans increased from 3 million in 1980 to 85 million in 2015 (*Consumer Reports*, 2015).

Defensive Medicine. Two other factors related to technology contribute to increased health care costs, sometimes in situations where it is unnecessary. Chapter 8 reported that medical malpractice is much more common in the United States than in any other country. Most physicians readily admit to practicing **defensive medicine**—that is, ordering medical tests primarily to protect against a malpractice suit. Often these extra services are high-technology diagnostic services or surgical procedures. To the extent that they are motivated primarily or solely in order to protect against a lawsuit, unnecessary medical costs occur.

Physician Self-Referral. Physician self-referral—that is, physicians referring patients to other health care facilities in which the physician has a financial interest—became increasingly common and controversial in the 1980s and 1990. This was especially troublesome in Florida, where 40 percent of physicians had investments in medical businesses (e.g., clinical laboratories and diagnostic imaging centers) to which they could refer patients.

What is the problem? Hillman et al. (1990) studied the use of diagnostic imaging tests among primary physicians who performed the tests in their own office (with financial benefit) and counterparts who referred patients to radiologists (with no financial benefit). Based on analysis of more than 65,000 insurance claims for patients with a variety of medical conditions, they found self-referring physicians ordered 4 to 4.5 times more imaging examinations than the radiologist-referring physicians, and the charges were higher per examination.

Defenders of self-referring practices counter that these studies do not prove that the higher use of services is inappropriate. They argue that having physician-owned facilities increases the likelihood of needed services being available in communities, and that the ease of self-referring may enable physicians to get more appropriate tests performed for their patients. Nevertheless, the American Medical Association (AMA) has declared self-referring to be unethical and has encouraged physicians to abstain from it, and Congress passed sweeping new anti-self-referral legislation in 2009 that (with some exceptions) bans referral of Medicare and Medicaid patients to laboratories and facilities in which the referring physician has a financial stake.

Medical Entrepreneurialism

The Medical-Industrial Complex. In 1980, Arnold Relman, then editor of the *New England Journal of Medicine*, used the term **medical-industrial complex** to describe the huge and rapidly growing industry that supplied health care services for profit. It included

> proprietary hospitals and nursing homes, diagnostic laboratories, home care and emergency room services, renal dialysis units, and a wide variety of other medical care services that had formerly been provided largely by public or private not-for-profit community based institutions or by private physicians in their offices.
>
> (Relman, 1991:854)

He referred to this effort to invest in health as a means to profit as being **medical entrepreneurialism**.

What was the problem? Relman expressed concern that the marketing and advertising techniques of the companies and their drive for profit would encourage unnecessary use, inappropriate use, and overuse of health care resources that would push up health care costs; that expensive technologies and procedures would be preferred to less costly efforts; that attention would become riveted on patients able to pay, leaving the poor and uninsured to an overburdened not-for-profit sector; and that physicians' allegiance to patients would be usurped by their involvement in health-related profit-making ventures (Relman, 1980).

Four specific concerns about the medical-industrial complex are linked to the issue of high medical costs: (1) corporate profit, (2) high administrative costs, (3) exorbitant salaries and compensation packages for management, and (4) medical fraud.

Corporate Profit. The pharmaceutical industry has become a global force dominated by several huge multinational companies ("Big Pharma"). In 2018, it was a US$1.11 trillion-dollar industry. The largest companies in 2019 were Johnson & Johnson (US$81 billion in annual revenue); Roche (US$57 billion), Pfizer (US$53 billion), Novartis (US$52 billion), and Merck & Company (US$40 billion). All of these companies are highly commercial, have the highest (or among the highest) profit margins of any industry, and are major contributors to the economy of the nation in which they are based (most but not all are based in the United States). Even in down years, they tend to outperform the rest of the economy by a wide margin.

The pharmaceutical industry is solidly plugged in to the political arena. Hundreds of former Congressional staffers work for the pharmaceutical industry or one of their lobbying groups and spend considerable time lobbying their former co-workers. Executive staff at the companies often move into key positions in the government. It is not illegal, but there is oft-expressed concern that Big Pharma has such a close relationship with public officials.

The pharmaceutical industry was once a very widely respected industry, but it has been the subject of significant criticism in the last several years. These are nine of the most common criticisms:

- *The price of patent-covered medications is extremely high and increasing very rapidly.* Prescription drugs account for 10 percent of personal health care expenditures in the United States, more than that if drugs administered in hospitals and nursing homes are included, and even more if over-the-counter medications are counted. In most recent years, prescription drug payments have increased more than twice as fast as any other type of health expenditure, and sometimes much more than that. For example, in 2000 the average annual cost for cancer drugs was approximately US$18,000; in 2014, the average price was US$120,000. In 2018, two new cancer drugs were introduced, and both are more effective than their predecessors. The price for a single dose of the first drug is US$373,000; for the second it is US$475,000.

Diabetes I is a very serious disease. Without insulin, it is fatal. In 2016, Type I diabetics spent US$5,705 per person on insulin—double what it was just 4 years earlier. The product has not changed and diabetics are using the same amount of it, but prices have skyrocketed. The source of the price increase: increased profit for pharmaceutical companies and the supply chains that gets the insulin to the patient.

In 2015, Martin Shkreli, a "drug entrepreneur" and CEO of Turing Pharmaceuticals and Kalo-Bios Pharmaceuticals, purchased rights to a drug used to treat a parasitic disease that affects AIDS sufferers and others with weakened immune systems, such as organ transplant recipients. He immediately hiked the price from US$13.50 a pill to US$750 (a 5,000 percent increase), and wrote in a memo that almost all of the windfall (perhaps US$375 million in the first year) would be profit. He was called in to Congress to testify, but he refused to answer any questions, asserting his constitutional protection against self-incrimination. In 2018, Shkreli was charged in federal court, then convicted on two counts of securities fraud and one count of conspiring to commit securities fraud. He was fined US$7.4 million and is now serving a 7-year sentence in federal prison.

Moreover, the price of medications is currently increasing due to the emergence of new specialty drugs, which are in a class called biologics (Lotvin et al., 2014). Biologics, which may include vaccines, blood and blood components, somatic cells, gene therapy, tissues, and so forth, are complex medicines made from cultures of living cells—either human, animal, or microorganisms—and are produced by cutting-edge technologies. In contrast, most drugs are chemically synthesized.

Biologics are used to treat relatively uncommon and/or very serious chronic ailments, including some forms of cancer, rheumatoid arthritis, hepatitis C and multiple sclerosis. Research shows these drugs to be more effective than previous drugs and have fewer negative side effects. However, they are far more expensive than conventional medicines. On average, biologics cost about 20 times more, because they have little or no competition, they require special handling (e.g., refrigeration), and they often need to be administered intravenously.

More than half of the specialty drugs cost more than US$100,000 per year. For example, Spinraza, a new drug from Biogen and Ionis Pharmaceuticals, treats spinal muscular atrophy in children and young adults. The patient population for the drug in the United States is between 6,000 and 9,000. Early onset is usually fatal before age 2; later onset patients often die in early childhood. Spinraza has reduced first-year mortality from 43 percent to 23 percent. The development of Spinraza was funded by the Muscular Dystrophy Association and the National Institutes of Health, and is the first-ever treatment for this disease. It cost $750,000 in the first year for each patient, and then $375,000 in each subsequent year. In 2017—its first year on the market—Biogen recorded US$833 million in revenue from the drug (Goozner, 2018).

In 2017, specialty drugs represented only 1.9 percent of all prescribed medications, but nearly 40 percent of spending on pharmaceuticals and that should quickly climb to 50 percent. Some are approaching US$1 million per year (The IQVIA Institute for Human Data Science, 2018).

- *The price of generic medications is increasing rapidly.* Generic drugs are bioequivalent replicas of brand-name drugs. They have the same active ingredients and identical quality, safety, and effectiveness. They differ from brand-names only in their inactive ingredients such as coloring and flavoring. They can legally be produced by multiple manufacturers (because the original patent has expired), they are easy to bring to market, they already have users when they are introduced, and consequently they are lower priced. They account for nearly 90 percent of the drug market in the United States, although less in other countries.

Because they make less money for the drug manufacturers per dosage, some manufacturers are decreasing their production. This has reduced competition that has kept the price of generics lower, and has led to rapidly escalating prices. Data from 2014 show that if there is only one manufacturer of a generic, it costs 88 percent as much as a brand name. However, if there are nine manufacturers, the cost is only 15 percent as much (Modern Healthcare, 2019).

- *The price of drugs in the United States is much higher than in other countries.* All other developed countries exercise some control over drug prices. That can range from negotiation for lower prices to absolute limits on the rate of price increases. Unlike in the United States, pharmaceutical companies do not have unrestrained freedom to charge whatever they want. As a result, drug prices are lower in all of these countries. On average, Americans pay 3 to 16 times more per medication than individuals in other countries (Fralick, Avorn, and Kesselheim, 2017).

- *The justification that the high prices for drugs is necessary to support research and development is false.* The pharmaceutical industry spends much more on marketing (about 40 percent of budgets) than it does on research and development (about 20 percent of budgets). Much of the basic research and development (R&D) actually occurs in small companies that are then bought out by the large companies, and much of the R&D in the large companies is actually subsidized by the government. One senator pointed out in early 2019 that every one of the last 210 drugs to win Food and Drug Administration approval had been funded by the National Institutes of Health.

The pharmaceutical industry spends more than US$15 billion a year providing gifts, information, all-expenses-paid trips to plush resorts, samples, financial incentives for prescribing specified levels of certain drugs, honoraria, and other inducements like tickets to cultural and sporting events trying to persuade physicians to use their products rather than those of a competitor (Herman, 2015). In 2015, companies spent more than US$100 million to advertise each of 16 drugs, and US$357 million was spent on advertising just one drug—Humira (Robbins, 2016).

Some states have now banned these inducements to physicians or have mandated disclosure. Has this had any effect? Using a data set of 189 million prescriptions for psychotropic drugs, King and Bearman (2017) found that the prescribing of new, costly medications was 39 to 83 percent lower in states that regulated or banned these marketing practices.

- *Pharmaceutical companies routinely engage in fraudulent activities.* Pharmaceutical companies have frequently been charged with fraudulent activity. Among those paying settlements in recent years were Abbott Laboratories (US$421 million for knowingly reporting false and inflated prices for a variety of pharmaceutical products), Par Pharmaceuticals (US$154 million for overcharging Medicare and Medicaid), Watson Pharmaceuticals (US$79 million for defrauding Medicaid), and Serono Laboratories (US$44 million for illegal kickbacks to health care providers). GlaxoSmithKline pled guilty to three criminal counts plus civil charges and paid US$3 billion to the federal government and participating state governments; Johnson & Johnson paid US$2.2 billion to settle claims for promoting drugs for uses not approved by the FDA and for paying kickbacks to physicians; Ranbaxy pled guilty to seven felonies and paid $500 million in fines and settlements; and Eli Lilly & Company paid $1.415 billion to settle civil and criminal claims that it marketed an antipsychotic drug for uses not approved by the FDA. And so on.

• *Pharmaceutical companies routinely engage in unethical activities.* Three examples of unethical practice:

    1. Pharmaceutical companies have given money to "experts" who then promote their drugs. About 25 percent of biomedical researchers in the United States who study drugs and may speak favorably about them have financial ties to the companies whose products they are studying. This is not illegal, but it is a clear conflict of interest. Studies show that researchers receiving industry funding are more than 3.5 times more likely to report a result that is favorable to the company (Bekelman, Li, and Gross, 2003).

    2. Like many industries, drug manufacturers have created front groups—such as United Seniors Association and the Seniors Coalition—which ostensibly are groups of seniors advocating for health benefits, but are really just supporting drug company positions on issues. Virtually all of the funding of some of these groups has come from the pharmaceutical industry. A 2018 Senate report found that the five largest opioid manufacturers paid more than US$10 million between 2012 and 2017 to these "patient advocacy" groups and others that then strongly promoted use of the highly addictive drugs (US Senate Homeland Security and Government Affairs Committee, 2018).

    3. Pharmaceutical companies have made payments to individuals serving on FDA Advisory Committees for drug approvals. A study of the period between 1997 and 2011 found that FDA advisory board members with financial interests solely in one drug manufacturer were more likely to vote to approve their drugs than were members with ties to more than one manufacturer (Pham-Kanter, 2014).

• *The pharmaceutical industry has unnecessarily allowed shortages of certain drugs to occur.* In the last decade the medical care system has experienced frequent shortages of certain drugs, especially drugs that are effective against cancer and heart disease. Hospitals, physicians, medical professional associations, and the Food and Drug Administration have complained that treatment is being delayed for some patients. While the explanation for these shortages seems to be multifactorial, a key reason is that the involved drugs are generic, do not make as much money for pharmaceutical companies, and are not prioritized.

• *Pharmaceutical companies have strongly lobbied to prevent the importation of less expensive drugs from other countries.* Pharmaceutical companies have strongly lobbied to prevent the importation of drugs from other countries where they are less expensive. In Canada, one such country, drug prices are 50 to 80 percent lower than in the United States.

So why don't Americans just buy their drugs online from Canadian pharmacies? American pharmaceutical companies strongly oppose this, for fear that it would undercut their exorbitant prices. They have warned Canadian wholesalers and pharmacies not to do this or to risk losing their business. Through much of the first decade of the 2000s, the US government argued that Canadian drugs might be counterfeit or adulterated (despite the fact that this had never happened). Laws were passed to prevent Americans from engaging in large-scale drug buying from other countries, although several states and cities have ignored the warnings and established purchase arrangements (Kesselheim and Choudhry, 2008).

- *Pharmaceutical companies have taken advantage of people in developing countries.* Pharmaceutical companies have taken advantage of patients in developing countries in several ways. They test drugs on patients in developing countries because it is less expensive to do so there. This occurs even when the drug may be for a condition that is more likely to be found in developed countries. The drug companies do not focus research on or market drugs for conditions that are primarily found in developing countries, because the anticipated profits are less. The pharmaceutical industry has lobbied intensively to prevent poor countries from manufacturing their own generic equivalent of patented medicines. Big Pharma has pressured to levy trade sanctions on countries such as India and Egypt for producing generic drugs (Petryna, Lakoff, and Kleinman, 2006).

The pharmaceutical industry strongly defends its practices. The industry contends that its profit motivation is necessary to encourage investment in the companies and to attract top management. Significant price increases are justified by overall price inflation in society and by the costs involved in drug research. A high advertising budget and extensive marketing techniques are necessary to capture the attention of physicians and patients. They contend that they have a right to defend themselves and to conduct successful businesses.

However, Marcia Angell, a well-respected physician, former editor of the *New England Journal of Medicine*, and now a senior lecturer at Harvard University Medical School, wrote the following in the preface to her book, *The Truth About the Drug Companies: How They Deceive Us and What to Do About It*:

> Sadly, there is little sign that the pharmaceutical industry is responding to its current difficulties by changing its behavior. It continues . . . to use its massive marketing muscle to promote [non-innovative drugs] relentlessly, to charge prices as high as it can get away with, and to act as if it puts short-term profits ahead of everything. It doesn't have to be that way. Drug companies could be what they once were—businesses that were quite profitable, yes, but also sources of cutting edge research that produced real medical miracles.
>
> (Angell, 2005:xv)

Surveys of the American public demonstrate that many concur with Angell. The health care industry in general is one of the least well-regarded industries in the United States. In 2018, about one-third of Americans (34 percent) viewed the health care industry favorably, but almost half (48 percent) had an unfavorable view. The pharmaceutical industry is viewed even less favorably than health care overall. While 30 percent have a favorable view of the pharmaceutical industry, 53 percent view it somewhat or very negatively—its lowest mark ever (McCarthy, 2018).

High Administrative Costs. The United States spends a much greater percentage of its health care dollars on administrative costs than does any other country. Approximately 8 percent of overall health expenditures in the United States go for administration of the system; in other countries, the average is only 1 to 3 percent (Papanicolas, Woskie, and Jha, 2018). This is primarily due to the complexity of the health care system in the United States and to the failure to take efforts to simplify it.

These high administrative expenses occur throughout the health care system and are especially apparent with regard to hospitals. Woolhandler, Campbell, and Himmelstein (2003) examined 1999 fiscal expenses for 5,220 US hospitals. They determined that hospital administrative costs in the United States averaged 24.3 percent—almost double that in Canada (12.9 percent). While this comparison may be influenced by several variables, they concluded that if the United States trimmed its hospital bureaucracy to the Canadian level, tens of billions of dollars could be saved annually. A more recent study using data from 2010 and 2011 compared hospital administrative costs in the United States to costs in Canada, England, Scotland, Wales, France, Germany, and the Netherlands. It found that 25.3 percent of total US hospital costs went for administrative expenses—by far the highest amount (Himmelstein et al., 2014).

The complexity of the billing system in the United States is part of the problem. Consider the difference between a hospital located in a country where everyone has insurance, carries an identical health card, and is governed by the same regulations, and a hospital in the United States in which patients may or may not have insurance, and if they do, it could come from any one of several government programs or any of 1,300 private insurance companies, each of which has countless options and variations in each policy. A medium-sized hospital in most countries will have a couple of people who work in billing; in the United States, it would have dozens and

dozens of billing agents. No wonder that an estimated 1 in 5 medical bills contains at least one error.

This billing cost extends to physicians' offices. By one estimate, for every 10 physicians providing care, almost 7 additional people are engaged in billing-related activities (Sakowski et al., 2009). In addition, the AMA estimates that physicians spend an average of 17 hours per week on administrative duties—completing patient charts, ordering tests, justifying procedures to insurers, and seeking reimbursement.

Exorbitant CEO Salaries and Compensation Packages.   Extraordinarily large salaries and compensation packages occur throughout the nation's economy, but health care has the highest CEO total compensation packages of any industry (Associated Press, 2019). Corporate executives of health insurance companies, pharmaceutical companies, medical equipment companies, hospitals, and health associations who receive noticeably large salaries and total compensation have come under special criticism given that health care is so expensive. The top annual salaries of health care CEOs in 2018 were in the US$20 million to US$30 million range, while highest total compensation packages were in the US40 million to US$50 million range with a few even higher. Given all of the health care organizations in the country, compensation packages just for CEOs represent a sizable sum.

Medical Fraud.   There is a massive amount of **medical fraud** occurring on a regular basis in the United States. In just the last few years, the parent company of a chain of dental clinics agreed to a US$24 million settlement after insiders reported that they were performing medically unnecessary procedures on children to bilk Medicaid. A Miami physician cheated Medicare out of US$40 million by dishonestly describing home care patients as being blind and diabetic in order to bill for extra nursing visits. A Massachusetts dentist used paper clips instead of stainless steel posts inside the teeth of root canal patients and charged Medicaid for the more expensive parts.

A Missouri pharmacist diluted chemotherapy drugs given to thousands of cancer patients. Scam artists have sent bills to Medicare using the ID numbers of deceased physicians. In 2018, a sting caught 600 defendants in 58 federal districts allegedly participating in schemes involving approximately $2 billion in losses to vital health care programs. Of the subjects charged, 165 were medical professionals, including 32 doctors who were charged for their roles in prescribing and distributing opioids and other dangerous narcotics.

Conservative estimates are that medical fraud costs the United States about US$70 billion each year. Florida—with its very large number of Medicare beneficiaries—has consistently led the nation in its very high rates of medical fraud.

AMERICA'S UNINSURED POPULATION PRIOR TO THE ACA

While government programs have offered substantial help to millions of people, they have never become a comprehensive safety net. By 2010 (the year in which the ACA was passed), approximately 50 million Americans (about 15 percent of them under the age of 18 years) did not have any private *or* public health insurance for the entire year. Some estimates are smaller—in the range of 47 million. This equates to about 1 person in 6 in the United States (USDHHS, 2011). In addition, millions more Americans have been *underinsured*—they have an insurance policy that either contains major loopholes (important services that are not covered), requires large out-of-pocket payments for services, or both.

The Uninsured

Becoming uninsured is something that can happen to anyone. For example, most people who lack insurance are employed. In 2010, most of the uninsured were in families with a worker employed full-time year round, and many more were in families with a year-round part-time worker or a partial-year full-time worker. People of all ages can be uninsured. The uninsured includes people in the early years of their careers, just beginning to get financially settled and often still moving from job to job, as well as people throughout the age spectrum all the way up to the age of 65 years, when Medicare eligibility occurs. Although two-thirds of the uninsured were white, people of all races and nationalities can be. However, members of racial and ethnic groups are more likely than whites to be uncovered. About 30 percent of Hispanics were uninsured in 2010, as were just under 20 percent of blacks and Asians, and about 12 percent of whites.

People at almost any income level can be uninsured. Many are below the federally established poverty level. Others are just above the poverty level—often referred to as the *medically indigent* or the *working poor*—and are sometimes in greatest need of health care. The cost of purchasing health insurance had increasingly become a problem even for people in the middle class. The percentage of people earning incomes of US$50,000 or more who lacked insurance rose in the several year preceding the ACA, reflecting just how expensive policies had become. Many of these families had children to support, home mortgages to pay, and college loans to reimburse, in addition to other basic expenses. Many had been working only a few years and did not have large financial savings; and many were taking care of elderly relatives. In such circumstances, paying US$10,000 a year or more for a family health insurance policy is just not possible. While some argue that many uninsured persons can actually afford health insurance, much research has found this not to be true (Bernard, Banthin, and Encinosa, 2009).

The Role of the Employment-Based Health Insurance System

As described earlier, health insurance provision in the United States largely relies on voluntary, employer-provided programs. Most large businesses offer health insurance to their employees as a benefit of employment. Typically, the employer pays for most of the cost of the policy. Employees pay the remaining amount of the premium, pay attached deductibles, coinsurances, and co-payments, and pay for whatever services are not covered in the policy. This system worked well for many, but it was a complete failure for millions more. In 2010, 160 million Americans had health insurance through employer-provided policies, more than 100 million were covered by Medicare, Medicaid, and other public programs, 16 million purchased their own health insurance, and more than 47 million people (about 17 percent of the entire population) lacked any form of health insurance.

Prior to the ACA, at least seven primary groups (and their dependents) were least likely to have health insurance (Weiss, 2006):

1. *Individuals who were unemployed.* People without a job can purchase a health insurance policy directly from a health insurance company, but that can be nearly impossible for someone without a job. If an applicant had a serious pre-existing condition, insurance companies would typically refuse to sell them insurance at all.

2. *Individuals after retirement but before Medicare.* The years between retirement and the onset of Medicare can be an insurance wasteland. Some individuals have been fortunate to work for an employer who subsidized their health insurance even after retirement. However, few companies offer this benefit and most of those that do have raised the employee contribution to a very high level—sometimes 50 or 60 percent or more. For low-income retirees, who had just entered a time of significantly reduced income, increased expense for health insurance was a heavy burden.

3. *Individuals during any transition period from one job to another.* Millions of Americans change jobs each year. Until the 1980s, when an individual left a job, employer-provided health insurance ended completely, and coverage with the employer did not begin until 6 or more months on the job had been completed. This created a dangerous gap between coverage periods. In 1986, Congress passed the Consolidated Omnibus Budget Reconciliation Act (COBRA), which enabled specified workers who had lost their jobs to continue their health insurance coverage for themselves and their dependents for up to 18, and sometimes 36, months. However, COBRA required the displaced worker to pay the portion of the insurance cost that they were paying plus the amount paid by the employer plus an additional amount. This was often too expensive; on average, only 20 to 25 percent of those eligible to purchase insurance through COBRA did so.

4. *Individuals working part-time, including those who are working simultaneously at two or more part-time jobs.* Many workers are not able to secure a full-time position and work only part-time. Many even take on a second part-time job and together may work a total of more than 40 hours per week. However, employer-provided health insurance is typically a benefit given only to full-time workers. Therefore, even though an individual may be working at a combination of part-time positions that total more hours than many full-time positions, no health insurance is provided. Furthermore, some employers—fast-food restaurants are a

common example—intentionally hire workers at just under the number of hours per week that would make them full time, so they do not have to offer them health insurance coverage.

5. *Individuals who work for small businesses.* Small businesses are in a very difficult position with regard to health insurance, and employees of small businesses suffer the consequences. Large employers with many employees can negotiate for better rates. Insurance providers recognize that especially costly procedures received by one or a few individuals in a large employee group can be spread across the entire group. Because many will use few services, part of the difference can be used to cover the higher costs incurred for others. Small businesses do not have this luxury. If one or a small number of employees in a small business has exceptionally high costs, there are not enough fellow employees to cover it. Therefore, health insurance companies routinely charge higher fees for policies—an average of almost 20 percent more—for small businesses, and raise their rates more sharply when high expenses occur. The result is that small businesses are much less likely to provide health insurance for their employees.

6. *Individuals who cannot afford the employee share of employer-provided health insurance.* Few employers continue to pay for the total cost of a health insurance policy for employees. In 2010, only 2 percent of large companies, and virtually no small companies, were still paying the full health insurance premium for employees. Many employers had begun shifting costs to employees in ways previously described in this chapter, and many employees could not afford their share.

7. *Undocumented immigrants.* Approximately 11 million individuals in the United States have entered the country without proper authorization. Many employers knowingly hire these individuals because they are willing to do jobs that others will not do, and because they are willing to work for less than the minimum wage. Often they are paid under the table, so that their illegal status is not discovered. Typically, they are not provided with any health benefits. Working at a low wage and without health insurance means that it is very difficult for these people to afford medical care regardless of the seriousness of any disease or illness.

The Consequences of Being Uninsured

The lack of personal financial resources to pay for medical care and the lack of health insurance have a profound effect on the health of individuals and families. This was one of the driving forces that led to the ACA. Much research has shown that individuals without health insurance are less likely to seek preventive medical care such as medical checkups (especially Pap smears and mammograms for women, and prostate cancer screening for men) and immunizations; and less likely to see a medical provider when sick (or they wait until they are very sick when the benefits of early detection are lost). They are less likely to have a regular source of medical care and more likely to see a different provider on each visit. They are less likely to receive mental health care, dental care, eye care, and care from primary care physicians, and are especially unlikely to receive care from specialists (Freeman et al., 2008).

The uninsured are less likely to be admitted to a hospital but are more ill when they are admitted. They receive fewer expensive medical treatments while in the hospital and are often deprived of the benefits of medical technology (even when controlling for need, the uninsured are less likely to receive clearly beneficial procedures such as heart bypass surgery, cataract surgery, and treatment for depression). When they analyzed discharge abstracts for almost 600,000 patients who were hospitalized in 1987, Hadley, Steinberg, and Feder (1991) found that the uninsured had, at the time of admission, a 44 to 124 percent higher risk of in-hospital mortality and, after controlling for this difference, a 1.2 to 3.2 times greater likelihood of dying in the hospital.

These negative health patterns occur among children as well as adults. Uninsured children are only one-sixth as likely as insured children to have a usual site where they receive health care. Uninsured children are five times more likely as the insured to have at least one unmet medical need each year, more than three times more likely to forgo a needed prescription, and 70 percent more likely to go without needed medical care for childhood conditions such as sore throats, ear infections, and asthma.

Not surprisingly, people without health insurance end up in poorer health and with earlier death than those with insurance. In 2009, the Institute of Medicine determined that 18,000 deaths each year could be blamed on the lack of health insurance and the resulting absence of preventive services, timely diagnoses, and appropriate care (Institute of Medicine, 2009).

One's risk of a health care catastrophe does not end even when one is insured. As many as half of all Americans have trouble paying for medical care each year, and most of these people have some form of health insurance. Prior to the ACA, there were approximately 25 million underinsured people in the United States. Their insurance often did not cover the types of care that were needed, may have had a low limit on the total amount that would be paid, or had such high premiums, deductibles, and co-payments that care could not be afforded. Research found that many insured people went without needed medical treatment due to the cost. In 2008, 34 percent of Americans skipped dental care, 27 percent put off getting needed medical care, 23 percent skipped a recommended medical test, 21 percent failed to get a prescription filled, 15 percent cut their pills in half or skipped doses, and 7 percent had trouble getting mental health care (Kaiser Family Foundation, 2009).

HISTORICAL EFFORTS TO REFORM THE HEALTH CARE SYSTEM

Efforts to enact major health care reform began in 1926 when the privately funded Committee on the Costs of Medical Care (CCMC) considered policies to address the high cost of and inadequate access to health care services. The CCMC proposed that health care should be delivered primarily by physicians organized in group practices, and that funding should come from voluntary insurance plans and subsidies from local governments for low-income persons. However, the AMA and many other groups inside and outside medicine strongly opposed these ideas as threats to private practice and physician autonomy (Waitzkin, 1989).

The Roosevelt administration pushed for National Health Program (NHP) legislation in 1938, as did the Truman administration in 1945, but Congress supported neither. Despite widespread popular support, the AMA along with the American Hospital Association and the US Chamber of Commerce led campaigns against what they labeled "socialized medicine." Coupled with the general anticommunist sentiment of the 1950s, no proposal was ever passed (Waitzkin, 1989).

Enthusiasm for health care reform emerged again in the 1960s when Congress considered several proposals for a NHP, leading to the eventual establishment of Medicaid and Medicare in 1965. These programs significantly increased public funding for health care, but did not create a comprehensive program with universal coverage.

The 1990s and the Clinton Health Initiative

By the late 1980s and early 1990s, public sentiment seemed to be running strongly in favor of a national health program. A 1989 Harris poll of consumers in Great Britain, Canada, and the United States found that US consumers were the *least* satisfied with their own health care system. Only 10 percent of US respondents assessed the health system as working even fairly well, and 9 out of 10 respondents thought that the system needed fundamental change (Coddington et al., 1990). Several surveys found that a large plurality, or even a majority, of Americans preferred a Canadian-style single-payer system with universal coverage.

A broader cross-section of the population expressed support for health care reform at this time, and it included many business leaders and health care providers who had formerly been opposed. Popular support for a comprehensive program appeared to be so pervasive that a bipartisan effort in Congress seemed possible.

Against this backdrop, Bill Clinton made health care reform a major issue in the 1992 presidential campaign and, after his election, a major commitment of his administration. After many months of fact-finding and deliberation by a task force led by Hillary Clinton, the Clinton proposal—termed *managed competition*—was introduced in late 1993. This proposal was an attempt to create universal coverage in a way that would be politically acceptable to Congress, key health care constituencies, and the American people. Large health alliances (groups of employers) would be created to negotiate for the best financial arrangements with MCOs. The plan would largely be funded through taxes applied to employers, with small employers being subsidized. Other cost-control mechanisms, such as capping insurance premiums and malpractice reform, were included. The complete proposal—all 1,342 pages of it—contained an enormous amount of detail.

Opposition to the plan emerged within weeks. The Health Insurance Association of America (HIAA), an organization representing many small- and medium-sized insurance companies, led opposition efforts. Small business owners felt it would be too costly for them to provide health care coverage for their workers. Small insurance companies were alarmed that they would not survive in the new system. Liquor, beer, and cigarette companies decried the extra taxes that would be placed on their products to help to pay for the system. The AMA and the American Hospital Association opposed limits on physicians' fees and hospital charges. Drug companies opposed mandatory cost controls on drugs. Trial lawyers opposed malpractice reform. Many people expressed reservations about creating new forms of bureaucracy (e.g., the health alliances). Some analysts charged that the Clinton administration failed to work sufficiently closely with congressional leaders in developing the plan, while others cited the continual difficulty of passing any broad-based reforms within the American political system (Quadagno, 2005).

When the Congressional Budget Office (CBO) declared that the proposal would cost significantly more than Clinton had estimated, many middle-class families became frightened about possible tax increases. While public opinion polls continued to show support for guaranteeing health care for everyone, controlling costs had become a more important objective for most people than universal coverage. In September 1993, almost 6 in 10 Americans supported the proposal; by July 1994, almost 6 in 10 opposed it. By fall of 1994, it was clear that the proposal lacked majority support in either house of Congress, and it was dropped.

Health Care Reform at the State Level

While the executive and legislative branches of the federal government were debating health care reform, several individual states initiated a variety of innovative health care programs. These reforms were typically aimed at increasing the number of people covered by health insurance and to create effective cost-containment provisions.

The momentum began in Hawaii, where since 1974 all employers have been required to provide their employees with comprehensive health care benefits. Employees also make a contribution. Combined with Medicare and Medicaid (which is set at the most generous eligibility level in the country), 98 percent of Hawaiians have basic health care coverage. Between 1974 and 2010, more than half of the states considered legislation to make health insurance more affordable. Since then, some states, including Massachusetts (with mandated health insurance and near-universal coverage), New York and California (both looking into single payer systems), Maine (a statewide health care co-op), Maryland (global health care budgets), and several states examining a public option for health insurance have committed to going beyond the ACA. However, fiscal problems have curbed legislative enthusiasm and caused some to back off their stated goals. Although some states have been more committed than the federal government to insurance reform, there have been financial limits on what they could accomplish (McDonough, Miller, and Barber, 2008).

HEALTH CARE REFORM OF 2010: THE PATIENT PROTECTION AND AFFORDABLE CARE ACT

After the unsuccessful attempt of President Clinton to enact health care reform legislation in the early 1990s, the issue moved off the front burner of the national political arena. Although President George W. Bush supported the enactment of the very significant Part D of Medicare—the prescription drug benefit—he was not an advocate for sweeping health care reform. However, the presidential campaign of 2008 brought health care issues back to the surface. Both Senator Clinton and Senator Obama supported large-scale health care reform in the Democratic primary. With Senator Obama's nomination and eventual election, and seemingly widespread popular support for significant reform, the issue once again became front page news.

Positions on Health Care Reform

Within Congress as within the country, positions on health care reform cover a wide spectrum. In 2010, three broad approaches were apparent.

Advocates for a Private Market Approach. *Private market approaches* are based on preserving the largest possible role for the private sector and the smallest possible role for the federal government. This approach is favored by almost all Republican politicians and, in earlier debates on health care reform, by the health insurance, pharmaceutical, and other for-profit health care businesses. The US Chamber of Commerce is a strong supporter. These groups have consistently opposed any significant intervention by the federal government in health care.

Advocates for an Incremental Social Justice Approach. *Incremental social justice approaches* are based on the belief that the best or only way to achieve universal health care coverage is to make as many changes as possible on a one-at-a-time basis. For example, on an individual basis, they have promoted instituting a uniform insurance billing form, prohibiting the denial of insurance because of pre-existing conditions, and working to guarantee coverage for all children. Many Democrats and Independents had come to support this approach.

Advocates for a Social Justice Approach. Proponents of a *social justice approach* contended that significant health care reform was necessary, that the private market approach had failed, and that federal government intervention was essential. Some advocated for a single-payer system (as in Canada) with the government being the only payer for health care. Others advocated for a public-private mix (as in many European countries) in which both the government and a for-profit or not-for-profit private sector play a large role in financing health care. This approach was also favored by many Democrats and Independents, and won endorsement from groups such as the Institute of Medicine, the American Public Health Association, and the Catholic Health Association.

The Political Process of Reform

Within weeks of his election, President Obama engaged the country and both political parties with ideas for health care reform. The overarching goals were to guarantee coverage for most or all people and to do it in such a way as to contain costs—the two massive problems of the health care system. There seemed to be strong support, and there were reasonably cooperative relations between the political parties. Significant reform seemed possible.

Then things quickly began to fall apart. Some Republican politicians decided to test the commitment of Americans to health care reform. They called the plan "socialism" and "socialized medicine," and characterized it as a "government takeover" of health care. These arguments had always been successful in the past, and they took hold again. In July 2009, the cost of the proposed reform was estimated to be over US$1 trillion, and that also stirred much opposition. The Congressional Budget Office, a carefully non-partisan agency that attempts to base its conclusions only on available evidence, declared that the proposed legislation would not slow health care cost increases. Polls began to show declining support for reform, and Republicans, now encouraged that they could defeat the bill, became more forceful opponents.

The declaration of the CBO caused Democrats to revisit an idea for controlling costs that had been discussed earlier but not pursued—creation of a "public option." This involved creation of a public health insurance program like Medicare that would compete with private insurers and force them to better control costs and premiums. Two-thirds of the public expressed support, but health insurance companies argued that they would not be able to successfully compete. Republicans argued that the plan would force the private sector out of health care. It became obvious that health care reform was not close to smooth sailing.

During the next 9 months, an extraordinary amount of political wrangling occurred between Democrats and Republicans and even within each political party. Contentiousness among supporters and opponents became extremely high. Prospects for reform began to look dim.

But, the political maneuvering continued, and ultimately The Patient Protection and Affordable Care Act was passed on March 22, 2010. The final Senate vote was 56 to 43 in favor with all but three Democrats and no Republicans in support. The final House vote was 219–212 in favor with all but 34 Democrats and no Republicans in support. On March 23, President Obama signed the bill into law.

Was the battle over? It was not. Even before the bill was passed, some state legislatures in conservative states voted that their citizens could not be required to buy health insurance (one component of the bill—a so-called individual mandate—required everyone to have some form of health insurance). On the day of the signing, the attorney generals in 14 states (all conservative Republicans plus the conservative Democratic attorney general in Louisiana) filed legal challenges to the bill on this "no

On March 23, 2010, before a group of supporters, President Obama signed into law the Patient Protection and Affordable Care Act.

requirement to buy" rationale. Most legal scholars thought the lawsuits had little chance—that federal laws routinely trump state laws. However, when Republicans gained control of the House of Representatives in the November 2010 elections, they initiated immediate conversation about the possibility of repealing the entire health reform bill.

Basic Benefits of Health Care Reform

The health reform plan was designed to be implemented over a period of several years. Some provisions began as early as 2010, most were in place by 2014, and all others were in effect by 2019 (Barry, 2010). The basic benefits of health care reform were identified as follows:

1. Approximately 32 million additional Americans would receive health care insurance.
2. Everyone is required to have health insurance (the individual mandate). Subsidies to enable this purchase are provided for those with moderate or low income, and more people become eligible for Medicaid. Financial penalties are assessed to anyone not having health insurance.
3. States are encouraged to expand their Medicaid programs, and the federal government will pay all the costs for doing so in the first

few years and most of the costs in ensuing years.

4. Health insurance companies are prevented from denying insurance on the basis of any pre-existing conditions, or placing a lifetime maximum on insurance benefits.

5. Several new health insurance benefits are required to be provided, such as coverage for adult children until the age of 26 years, and required coverage for preventive services such as childhood immunizations, cancer screenings, and contraceptives.

6. State-run **health insurance exchanges** are created to offer a choice of private health insurance plans for people who are not covered by an employer. If a state chooses not to set up its own exchange, the federal government does so for it. (Since 2010, two additional options have been created. Both involve partnerships of the federal and state government.)

7. Employers with at least 50 employees are required to offer health insurance plan options to their employees.

8. Tax credits are offered to assist small businesses in buying insurance for their employees.

9. Several changes are made in Medicare to keep it financially sound, to guarantee basic benefits, to make most preventive care services free, and to make drug coverage more affordable.

10. Incentives—such as higher reimbursement levels—are offered to physicians to encourage them to go into primary care practice.

11. Plus, there are many additional provisions, such as:

   • Requiring members of Congress to buy plans through the exchanges
   • Taxing tanning salons
   • Providing new long-term care options
   • Increasing funding for community health centers
   • Providing bonus payments to primary care physicians practicing in underserved areas

   • Denying use of the health insurance exchanges or receipt of subsidies to undocumented immigrants.

Who Pays for Health Care Reform?

The health care reform plan was estimated to cost US$940 billion over its first 10 years, and was set up to be paid in the following ways:

1. An annual fee on health insurance companies of US$8 billion starting in 2014; the fee increased to US$11.3 billion in 2015, to US$13.9 billion in 2017, and to US$14.3 billion in 2018.

2. An annual fee on pharmaceutical manufacturers of US$2.5 billion starting in 2011; the fee increased to US$3 billion in 2012, US$3.5 billion in 2017 and to US$4.2 billion in 2018.

3. A Medicare tax rate increase from 1.45 to 2.35 percent on earnings over US$200,000 for an individual and over US$250,000 for a family, and a new Medicare tax imposed on unearned income for the same groups.

4. Penalty payments from those not obtaining health insurance and from businesses with at least 50 employees not offering health insurance benefit.

5. A tax on high-cost insurance plans (referred to as the "Cadillac" tax).

6. Premium, deductible, coinsurance, and co-payments for the ACA insurance plans.

7. Anticipated cost savings from efficiencies such as greater use of primary care physicians (with reduced reliance on more expensive specialists), more preventive care, fewer people using the emergency room for non-emergency care, and increased use of information technology.

Who Benefits the Most From Health Care Reform?

1. The uninsured, who will obtain health insurance through one provision or another. This will include the self-employed, unemployed, part-time employed, and people between jobs.

2. People with health problems, who will no longer be allowed to be rejected by insurance companies or have a lifetime maximum on benefits.
3. Young adults, who will be covered on family insurance plans until the age of 26 years.
4. Medicare beneficiaries, who will receive added services and more complete drug coverage.
5. People who already have good, employer-sponsored health insurance, who will be able to keep it and get some added benefits.
6. Private health insurance, pharmaceutical, and other for-profit companies, which will be part of the system, will continue to be run for profit, and will have additional members.
7. Primary care physicians, whose compensation levels will increase.

What Are the Key Criticisms of the Plan?

Conservative criticism of the plan centers on three key points:

- There is too much government involvement. As we have discussed in this chapter, Congressional Republicans prefer a private-market approach in all or almost all matters, and minimal involvement of government. Even when Medicare was passed in 1965, a majority of Senate Republicans voted against it. The ACA makes use of both the public and private sectors, but increases government responsibility for paying for increased access to health care.
- The plan costs too much. Proponents of the plan acknowledge the high cost but argue that new revenues and cost savings will largely pay for the program. Opponents argue that those approaches together will fall far short, and that middle-income taxpayers will be called upon to make up the difference. Ironically, the public option that conservatives forced out of the bill was a primary mechanism to control cost increases by health insurers.

- Medical malpractice reform is not addressed. Conservative critics (and some from the left) criticize the reform package for not addressing medical malpractice reform. To the extent that the practice of defensive medicine in response to the threat of lawsuits is a contributor to the high cost of care, the reform plan misses an opportunity to reduce these wasted dollars.

Liberal criticism of the plan centers on two key points:

- The plan does not provide health insurance coverage for everyone. There is continued strong interest among liberal and progressive politicians and members of the public in a plan that provides universal coverage.
- There is too much private, for-profit company involvement. If indeed the complexity of the plan and the retention of a strong private sector lead to or maintain high profit, administrative waste, exorbitant salaries, and continuing medical fraud, then an opportunity has been missed to make the system more efficient by spending fewer dollars on items other than health care.

What Was the Successful Strategy in Getting Health Care Reform Legislation Passed?

How did the situation change from the lack of success of the Clinton proposal to the enacted legislation in 2010? Some analysts have suggested that a key was that Obama's proposal leaders were more effective in dealing with key stakeholders in the reform debate. While political opposition from Republicans was intense, many stakeholders saw reasons to support in 2010 what they had opposed in 1993.

Physicians. While there were differences of opinion among physicians in 2010, surveys found that most physicians supported the reform proposal. For the first time, the AMA went on record in support. Many physicians expressed unhappiness about the lack of social justice in the health care system, and appreciated that many formerly uninsured patients would now have their medical bills paid. (Nursing groups were strong supporters both in 1993 and in 2010.)

Hospitals. Hospitals have been trapped between the demands of paying bills (and making a profit in for-profit hospitals) and providing charity care. The conversion of 32 million people to insured status would decrease the number of people unable to afford their hospital bills.

Health Insurers. The health insurance industry was divided about health care reform but ended up agreeing to support it. The insurance industry had feared that either for-profit insurance would be banned or that a competing public nonprofit option would be created. In return for allowing current companies to continue to dominate the market and creating the insurance mandate, they agreed to contribute funds annually to help support it, and not to strongly oppose it. America's Health Insurance Plans, a major insurer lobbyist, advocated for much of the plan.

Pharmaceutical Companies. Pharmaceutical companies had feared that caps would be placed on the cost of drugs, thus lowering profits. In return for not creating these caps, for further subsidizing the purchase of drugs for Medicare beneficiaries, and for not including provisions that would help generic drug makers, pharmaceutical companies agreed to help to fund health care reform and not to speak strongly against it.

Business Groups. Although many business owners continued to oppose health care reform, and the US Chamber of Commerce was a leading opponent, many large and small businesses supported reform and appreciated the subsidies that would help them offer health insurance to employees. (Most labor unions endorsed health care reform in 1993 and 2010.)

The support of these stakeholders was especially important because they have powerful lobbying voices and large amounts of money to support lobbying. In the 15 months immediately preceding the ACA vote, health care interests spent US$812 million lobbying Congress. Which groups spent the most? The US Chamber of Congress was by far the biggest spender, but the Pharmaceutical Research and Manufacturers of America, Pfizer, AARP, the AMA, the American Dental Association, Blue Cross Blue Shield, and the American Hospital Association were all very large spenders. Lobbying efforts can influence public opinion, but most funds are spent directly lobbying congressional members.

Constitutional Challenges

Opponents of the Affordable Care Act began almost immediately to attempt to overturn it, and their efforts have not ceased. Some Republican-controlled states announced that they would refuse to obey aspects of the law. Lawsuits were filed in circuit courts, with some courts ruling that the ACA was constitutional and some ruling that features of it were unconstitutional. One judge ruled that the entire act was unconstitutional. These conflicting decisions enabled both proponents and opponents to appeal to the US Supreme Court to decide on the constitutionality of the act.

The months leading up to the case and to its ultimate decision were filled with drama and conjecture about how individual justices would decide and how a majority of the court would rule. In March 2012 the judges heard 5½ hours of arguments—an unprecedented amount of time in recent history—in favor of and opposed to the constitutionality of the law. The most important issue was whether Congress had constitutional authority to require private citizens to purchase health insurance. Should the Court rule no on

Supporters of the Affordable Care Act cheer after the Supreme Court ruled that ACA tax credits can go to residents of any state—a major victory in 2015 for President Barack Obama's health care reforms.

this issue, many believed the entire act would collapse. The second most important issue was whether the law unconstitutionally coerced states into expanding their Medicaid programs. (The law required states to expand Medicaid or lose all federal funds for the program.)

On June 28, 2012, a highly divided court ruled 5 to 4 to uphold most of the features of the Affordable Care Act. The very conservative chief justice of the Court, John Roberts, surprisingly joined the court's four liberal justices in approving the constitutionality of the individual mandate. That decision meant that the ACA would go forward. However, the court also ruled that requiring Medicaid expansion was unconstitutional and would need to be changed or eliminated. The court's four other conservative justices voted to scrap the entire act.

In 2015, the US Supreme Court heard another case that could have had devastating effects on the ACA. This case challenged the constitutionality of granting insurance subsidies in the states with a federally run exchange. This time the Court voted 6 to 3 that the subsidies were constitutional, thus once again protecting the law and program.

By 2015, public support for the ACA had reached a high level. An overwhelming majority of Americans believe that access to health care is a moral issue, and that if other developed nations can afford to do it, so should the United States (87 percent of Democrats and 33 percent of Republicans support universal health care). Although slightly more than half disapprove of the individual coverage mandate, a substantial plurality support Medicaid expansion, and wide majorities support the employer mandate, guaranteed issuance of insurance, including to people with pre-existing conditions, keeping the exchanges, and keeping the subsidies for low-income people. Overall, 26 percent want to keep the ACA as it is, 30 percent want to keep the ACA but change some parts of it, and 33 percent want to repeal the ACA. Ten percent of

Democrats and 65 percent of Republicans favor repeal (Thompson, 2015).

Has the ACA Been Successful?

The ACA has led to many improved indicators of the quality of the health care system. For the first time in history, the percentage of Americans who are uninsured dropped below 10 percent. The number of adults in their early and mid-twenties with health insurance sharply increased. Much preventive care is now provided without charge, and more people are receiving preventive services. The cost of prescriptive medications for Medicare enrollees has declined. Individuals with pre-existing conditions are able to access health insurance. More low-income individuals and families have been accepted by Medicaid. Efforts to identify and stop medical fraud in relation to Medicare and Medicaid have significantly increased. Hospital readmissions have declined (Long et al., 2017).

Number of Uninsured. Has the ACA reduced the number of uninsured? Yes, but there are still many persons without insurance. The ACA intended to reduce the number of uninsured through two primary mechanisms: enrollment in the government created exchanges and the expansion of Medicaid. Both approaches have been successful, but not without ongoing clamor.

In the years between 2015 and 2019, approximately 12 million persons enrolled annually in one of the health exchanges. As of 2018, 12 states had created their own exchange, 6 states had created a partnership with the federal government exchange, and 33 states had opted directly or indirectly to use the federal exchange. About three-fourths of enrollees do so through the federal exchange. Most (but not all) states with Democratic-controlled legislatures have set up their own exchange or used the partnership model. Most (but not all) states with a Republican-controlled legislature have used the federal government exchange.

The key problem that the exchanges have had to deal with is a declining number of health insurance companies willing to offer insurance through an exchange. They have justified their non-participation by saying it is not financially worthwhile for them. This had led to reduced competition and consequent higher premiums and deductibles. In many areas of the country, only one insurance company is available for potential enrollees (Griffith, Jones, and Sommers, 2018). For example, in the area in North Carolina where one of the co-authors lives, a policy with a US$7,600 deductible costs more than $11,000 a year for persons in their early sixties.

Many low- and middle-income persons who do not come close to qualifying for Medicaid cannot afford this amount. There are government subsidies for which one can apply, but these are also problematic. In the aforementioned area, the qualifying threshold for a family of two persons in 2019 was about US$63,000 (400 percent of the poverty level). If the family made that amount or less, they would qualify for a subsidy of up to about US$10,000 annually. If the family made one dollar more, they would not qualify for any subsidy. These high rates and high deductibles have kept many persons from purchasing insurance through an exchange.

Medicaid expansion is also responsible for decreasing the number of uninsured. Most estimates are that about 14.5 million persons were added to Medicaid as a result of the ACA. All agree that most, though not all, were enabled by Medicaid expansion.

The key problem confronting Medicaid expansion is that many states have refused to participate. The ACA includes a commitment by the federal government to pay for all of the cost of Medicaid expansion for 3 years and 90 percent of the cost after that. As of 2019, 37 states plus Washington, DC, have accepted this offer. These states almost all have Democratic-controlled legislatures or a Republican governor who has supported Medicaid expansion. Research on its early experience has shown improved access to care, higher utilization of services, greater afford-ability, improved health outcomes, and reduced mortality for those newly covered. Few stud-ies have reported any negative consequences (Mazurenko et al., 2018). One study reported that between 2014 and 2016, infant mortality in expansion states declined but that it rose in non-expansion states (Bhatt and Beck-Sague, 2018).

However, 14 states—almost all Republican-controlled legislatures—have rejected Medicaid expansion. These include all of the Southeastern states except Louisiana (North Carolina, South Carolina, Georgia, Florida, Alabama, Mississippi, and Tennessee) plus Texas, Oklahoma, Kansas, Missouri, South Dakota, Wisconsin, and Wyo-ming. Had they expanded, an additional 4 million people would be covered by health insurance.

Table 14.5 focuses on the US population age 0 to 64—individuals whose health insurance sta-tus might have been affected by the ACA. Due to the continued presence of Medicare, people age 65 and older are not included. In 2013, the year before key passages in the ACA went into effect,

there were 44.4 million Americans age 0 to 64 who lacked health insurance—16.8 percent of this age group. This number and percentage quickly decreased with ACA implementation and was down to 26.7 million or 10.0 percent by 2016.

Research confirms multiple benefits for for-merly uninsured persons who are now covered through the ACA. They have fewer barriers to receiving care, increased use of physician and other provider services, and increased ability to obtain needed medications (Goldman et al., 2018). Under the ACA, the socioeconomic disparities in health care access, though not eliminated, have been measurably reduced. Moreover, the ACA has changed the way that people obtain health insur-ance. By decoupling insurance from employers, spouses, and children—pathways that most coun-tries abandoned years ago—the ACA has reduced health insurance inequalities across gender, race, income, and education groups (Gutierrez, 2018).

However, in 2017, the most recent data avail-able at the time of this writing, the number and percentage of uninsured reversed and showed a small uptick. This may be an aberration, but analysts are concerned that the constant criti-cism and oft-repeated desire to repeal the ACA by President Trump and additional unsuccessful efforts by the Republican majority in the Sen-ate to repeal it have done harm to the program. The budget for program advertising was sharply cut, subsidies to insurance companies to keep rates low were eliminated, the individual man-date was eliminated in 2019, the number of people employed to help enrollees navigate the system was deeply cut, and the sign-up period was shortened. These efforts have been openly undertaken to make the ACA less appealing and with the hope that it dies off (Luhby, 2018).

What individuals are now most likely to be uninsured? Individually, men aged 19 to 64, hav-ing a high school education or less and a low income are least likely to be insured. Region-ally, people in the Southeast (where Medicaid has not expanded) are much more likely than people

TABLE 14.5 Number and Percent of Americans Ages 0 to 64 Uninsured by Year

Year	Number Uninsured	Percent Uninsured
2013	44.4 million	16.8%
2014	35.9 million	13.5%
2015	29.1 million	10.9%
2016	26.7 million	10.0%
2017	27.4 million	10.2%

Source: Kaiser Family Foundation. 2018a. *American Community Survey*. Retrieved March 18, 2019

(www.kff.org/uninsured/fact-sheet/key-facts-about-the-uninsured-population/). The Kaiser Family Foundation, based in Menlo Park, California, is a nonprofit, private operating foundation focusing on the major health care issues facing the nation and is not associated with Kaiser Permanente or Kaiser Industries.

living in any other region to be uninsured. Lack of insurance is most apparent in two groups:

1. *The working poor.* These individuals either work for small businesses (which are still having difficulty providing health insurance for employees) or they have a job (in areas such as food service, construction, sales, cleaning and maintenance, office and administrative support, transportation, and personal care) but are classified either as part-time workers or as independent contractors, so their employers are not obligated to provide employer-sponsored health insurance. Many are medically indigent—earning slightly too much to qualify for Medicaid or for exchange subsidies but too little to afford health insurance. Surveys show that many do not understand the insurance exchange process or the available subsidies, and that a small number of these individuals are actually eligible for assistance.

2. *Undocumented immigrants.* Recall that the nation's approximately 11 million undocumented immigrants are excluded from the various health insurance programs. Advocates for providing health care benefits to them contend that reimbursement to physicians, hospitals, and other medical providers would improve, that the younger and healthier immigrants would lower insurance costs, and that the goal of everyone in the country having access to health care would be achieved. California, New York, Illinois, Massachusetts, and Washington, DC, have agreed to provide health care insurance for undocumented children up to the age of 19 years, and some states (e.g., California) are considering expanding coverage to adults. Opponents disapprove of granting any benefits to people who are in this country illegally, and of the increased health care costs for covering them.

The Tea Party Coalition protests Medicaid expansion in Tucson, Arizona.

Cost Containment.   Has the ACA affected the annual rate of health cost increases? Table 14.6 shows the annual rate of health care cost increases through several recent critical time periods including that since the ACA was passed in 2010. The data show a marked decline since 2010 with total cost increases of 4.3 percent—the lowest in the last 60 years. Coupled with the significant increase in the number of persons covered by health insurance and the increase in covered services by health insurance, and the other benefits of the ACA, this is a significant accomplishment. The slowed rate of increase occurred for physician costs, hospital costs, and even drug costs.

However, there are also continuing worries. Although the rate of increase has slowed, the cost for health insurance from employer-provided policies is the highest ever, and the move toward high-deductible policies is creating new problems for most employees, their families, and for persons purchasing policies through the ACA. About 1 American in 8 reports being in a family having trouble paying its medical bills. About 1 in 5 has some medical debt (Americans borrowed about US$88 billion in 2018 to pay for medical debt). More than 1 person in 3 is concerned or extremely concerned about paying for prescription drugs. About 1 in 4 skipped needed care in the last year because of costs (The Gallup Poll, 2019).

TABLE 14.6   Annual Health Care Cost Increases, 1960 to 2018

Time Period	Average Percent Annual Growth in Health Spending
1960 to 1965	8.9
1966 to 1974	11.9
1975 to 1982	14.1
1983 to 1992	9.9
1993 to 2009	6.4
2010 to 2018	4.3

Source: Kimberly Amadeo. 2019. "The Rising Cost of Health Care by Year and Its Causes." *The Balance.* Retrieved June 1, 1019 (www.thebalance.com/causes-of-rising-healthcare-costs-4064878).

Recent Efforts to Overturn the ACA

Republican efforts to repeal the law have persisted as the House of Representatives and Senate have voted almost 100 times on ACA repeal. President Trump and congressional Republicans spent all of 2017 and part of 2018 focused on "repealing and replacing" the ACA. Republican leaders identified overturning the ACA as their most important legislative initiative. Early in 2017, they unveiled the American Health Care Act (AHCA), initially also referred to as Trumpcare. It involved an almost complete dismantling of ACA: cutbacks would mean that 23 million people would lose their health insurance, Medicaid expansion would be undone, the exchanges eliminated, the individual mandate erased, those with pre-existing conditions could again be denied insurance, and public health initiatives would be dropped. Three groups especially hard hit would be children, the disabled, and the elderly poor.

By late March 2017, the proposed legislation was withdrawn. Multiple health groups—the AMA, other physician groups, the AHA, health insurance companies, disability-rights groups, groups representing senior citizens, patient advocate groups—all expressed vehement opposition. Polls showed that more than half of Americans supported the ACA; the percent favoring the AHCA was in the teens. All Democrats and many Republicans opposed it.

In early May, Republican leadership presented a plan that had been revised to win over more support. Though the medical community was still overwhelmingly opposed, the bill passed in the House of Representatives by 217 to 213. All those voting yes were Republicans; those voting no included all Democrats and 20 Republicans. In order to become law, Senate approval was necessary. Senate Republicans liked some of the new AHCA, disliked other parts, and set out to create their own version of the bill, the Better Care Reconciliation Act (BCRA). It was received with even less enthusiasm than the House version with sizable opposition and only 12 percent of the public voicing support. Even at that, it almost passed, but repeal had again lost.

Only 2 months later, congressional Republicans tried again. Four Senate Republicans attempted a new approach: giving the money budgeted for ACA to states in the form of block grants. This was intended to allow states to retain some form of the ACA or to completely eliminate it. An estimated 22 million would lose insurance. The bill failed 43 to 57 with nine Republicans joining Democrats in voting no. Shortly thereafter, Republicans introduced a "repeal without replace" bill, that is, overturning the ACA but not proposing anything with which to replace it. That lost 45 to 55 with seven Republicans joining Democrats in opposition. Shortly thereafter, Republicans introduced a new, "skinny repeal" bill that just isolated some features of the ACA to be eliminated. It was defeated by 49 to 51 with Republican Senator John McCain joining two other Republican Senators and all Democrats in voting no.

EFFORTS TO GO BEYOND THE ACA

Congressional Democrats are currently considering two broad approaches for altering the health care system. Most moderate members support retaining the ACA but making changes in it to expand coverage to more people and to develop stronger cost containment. Examples are adding more money to Medicaid and CHIP programs and developing the "public option" in which a government-run health insurance program would be created to compete with private insurers.

More liberal Democrats are rallying around the idea of providing a health care system that provides universal coverage and does so through a single-payer approach. There are many ways this could be done—as countries around the world demonstrate—but the approach receiving the most attention thus far is "Medicare for all." Even this idea comes in many versions, but the basis is that all Americans would be covered in a program very similar to today's Medicare. Private insurers would not be permitted to compete with the new program, although they could continue to provide coverage for treatments not included in Medicare—such as cosmetic surgery. Services—even those not covered today like dental, vision, mental health, and long-term care—would be covered. The program would be financed through increased taxes, especially on the very wealthy, on employers, and on investment income.

The estimated cost of such a program would be US$2.5 to US$3.5 trillion a year. Presumably there would be some expected savings from the current arrangement in areas such as administrative costs. (Commercial insurance companies spend about 12 percent of total costs on administration; Medicare spends 1.4 percent.)

Polls in 2018 and 2019 show support for a single-payer system in the 50 to 60 percent range and increasing. However, when details of the system are included—such as those currently with private insurance being converted to the new system—support drops to less than 50 percent. Many hospitals and physician groups have also expressed concern because they might receive lower reimbursement levels. They prefer the improvements to ACA approach. By 2018, two states—Colorado and Vermont—put the issue on their state ballot. It was defeated in both cases.

What actually occurs will be determined largely by the political party of the President and the majority party in the House and Senate. Even with control of all three, Republicans were unable to pass legislation to overturn the ACA. It is unclear whether Democrats would or would not have more success if they controlled all three. In situations in which the House and Senate are controlled by different parties, it seems unlikely that any major change will occur.

SUMMARY

Despite the fact that the US health care system has many positive qualities, it compares unfavorably to systems in other countries. The system has been inefficient, fragmented, and expensive, and has been inaccessible to many people, especially the uninsured and underinsured. America spent almost 18 percent of its GDP on health care in 2010—more than any other country in the world—yet had more than 47 million people without health insurance.

Health care financing occurs through a complex mix of employers, individuals and families, and the government. Over time, third-party payers have paid a greater share of health care costs. The implementation of Medicaid and Medicare made the federal government the largest single purchaser of health care services.

Several factors have contributed to the rapidly escalating costs of health care, including the aging of the population, expensive new medical technologies, and medical entrepreneurialism (including high profits, high administrative costs, exorbitant CEO salaries, and medical waste). In response, cost-containment strategies such as managed care were implemented.

Managed care organizations, such as HMOs and PPOs, combine health insurance and a health care delivery mechanism into a single package. They attempt to provide cost-efficient care by securing lower provider reimbursements, regulating patient care, and rewarding physicians for keeping patients healthy.

In 2010, after very contentious debate, the United States passed significant health care reform legislation—the Patient Protection and Affordable Care Act. This legislation brought health insurance to millions more people, helped reduce the rate of cost increases, and made several other system improvements. However, there are still some concerns about aspects of the system. Most Republicans continue to desire overturning the program, while many Democrats wish to adopt a more universal approach.

HEALTH ON THE INTERNET

1. The Centers for Medicare and Medicaid Services (CMS) is responsible for collecting data about Medicare, Medicaid, and other government-sponsored health care programs. Connect to the CMS website at:

   www.cms.gov

   By clicking on "Medicare" and "Medicaid," you can connect to links with information about each of these programs. How does Medicare work? What are the basic programs offered through Medicare? How does Medicaid work? What are the basic services offered through Medicaid?

2. The *Healthcare.gov* website is designed to help individuals and businesses find their way through ACA rules and regulations. For this exercise, say you are single, living alone, and making US$35,000 per year.

   a. Determine if you would be eligible for Medicaid in the state where you live. If not, how much less would your income have to be to qualify?

   b. Determine if you would be eligible for a subsidy to help you pay for the cost of health insurance purchased through a health insurance exchange within your state. If not, how much less would your income have to be to qualify?

DISCUSSION CASE

A continuing controversy pertaining to the ACA is the best way to handle coverage for contraceptive services. Most lists of basic preventive health services include contraception, and it has been required in insurance coverage by the Pregnancy Discrimination Act. The ACA mandates that policies include it. However, in accordance with the Religious Freedom Restoration Act (RFRA), the rule (a) completely exempts religious organizations and (b) provides an accommodation for plans sponsored by nonprofit organizations (like some educational institutions) that claim a religious affiliation. In these situations, the organization notifies the insurer that it does not wish to offer contraceptive services in its policy, and the insurer then provides coverage directly to employees outside the scope of the employer plan. This arrangement was created as a compromise so that both contraceptive coverage and employer's religious beliefs could be respected.

However, two kinds of objections have been raised to this arrangement. First, some religious employers of for-profit companies have complained the policy does not give them the right to exclude contraceptive coverage in their health insurance plans. One such company is Hobby Lobby, a craft store chain with more than 32,000 employees. It is owned by a family that seeks to operate the business in accordance with its Christian principles (e.g., it is closed on Sundays). The owners did not object to covering certain types of contraceptives for its employees, but objected to those that work by preventing implantation of a fertilized egg (believing this to be a type of abortion). Hobby Lobby and five other businesses took their consolidated case all the way to the US Supreme Court. In June 2014, the Court ruled 5 to 4 in favor of the stores. The justices in the majority argued that employers such as these should be able to participate in the "accommodation" process described earlier (Cohen, Lynch, and Curfman, 2014).

A second objection was then raised as some of the non-profit religious organizations who could participate in the "accommodation" process believed that even having to request an accommodation was unjust and would make them complicit in the act of contraception. Lower courts ruled against the organizations, and this case (*Zubik v. Burwell*) also ended up in the US Supreme Court (in 2016). The Court took the rare step of sending the case back to the lower courts with a specific instruction to find a compromise (Rosenbaum, 2017).

However, in 2017, President Trump issued new regulations that provided all religious organizations with a full exemption from covering anything that violated their core beliefs. A settlement of the case then followed that gave religious organizations the right to exclude any practices that are morally unacceptable to them. At the same time, the government was allowed to continue listing contraceptive services (with the exclusion) as a requirement in ACA policies.

How do you assess these decisions? Did they result in a compromise that respects the positions of both sides? Are employees of organizations who now exclude contraceptive services and must pay for themselves being treated fairly?

GLOSSARY

Children's Health Insurance Program (CHIP)
cost containment
defensive medicine

health insurance exchanges
health maintenance organizations (HMOs)
managed care

managed care organizations (MCOs)
Medicaid
medical entrepreneurialism
medical fraud
medical–industrial complex
Medicare
national health expenditures (NHEs)

Patient Protection and Affordable Care Act (ACA)
personal health expenditures (PHEs)
point-of-service (POS) plan
preferred provider organizations (PPOs)
physician self-referral
single-payer approach

REFERENCES

Amadeo, Kimberly. 2019. "The Rising Cost of Health Care by Year and Its Causes." *The Balance.* Retrieved June 1, 2019 (www.thebalance.com/causes-of-rising-healthcare-costs-4064878).

Angell, Marcia. 2005. *The Truth About the Drug Companies: How They Deceive Us and What to Do About It.* New York: Random House.

Associated Press. 2019. "Health Care CEOs Again Lead the Way in Pay." Retrieved June 1, 2019 (https://apnews.com/c3febcd7d7bc4d909db2dbd50604abd0).

Barry, Patricia. 2010. "Health Care Reform." *AARP Bulletin* (May):19–26.

Bekelman Justin E.,Y. Li, and Cary P. Gross. 2003. "Scope and Impact of Financial Conflicts of Interest in Biomedical Research: A Systematic Review." *Journal of the American Medical Association* 289(4):454–465.

Bernard, Didem M., Jessica S. Banthin, and William E. Encinosa. 2009. "Wealth, Income, and the Affordability of Health Insurance." *Health Affairs* 28(3):887–896.

Bhatt, Chintan B., and Consuelo M. Beck-Sague. 2018. "Medicaid Expansion and Infant Mortality in the United States." *American Journal of Public Health* 108(4):565–567.

Bodenheimer, Thomas. 2005. "High and Rising Health Care Costs: Part 2." *Annals of Internal Medicine* 142(11):932–937.

Brandeisky, Kara. 2015. "Here's How Much the Average American Worker Has to Pay for Health Care." *Time*, September 22. Retrieved March 7, 2019 (http://money.com/money/4044394/average-health-deductible-premium/).

Brook, Robert H., Rolla E. Park, Mark R. Chassin, David H. Solomon, Joan Kessey, Jacqueline Kosecoff. 1990. "Predicting the Appropriate Use of Carotid Endarterectomy, Upper Gastrointestinal Endoscopy, and Coronary Angiography." *New England Journal of Medicine* 323(17):1173–1177.

Centers for Disease Control and Prevention. 2019. "Personal Health Care Expenditures, by Source of Funds and Type of Expenditure: United States, 2006–2016." Retrieved March 8, 2019 (www.cdc.gov/nchs/data/hus/2017/fig17.pdf).

Centers for Medicare and Medicaid Services. 2019. "National Health Expenditure Accounts." Retrieved March 23, 2019 (www.cdc.gov/nchs/data/hus/2017/fig17.pdf).

Coddington, Dean C., David J. Keen, Keith D. Moore, and Richard L. Clarke. 1990. *The Crisis in Health Care: Costs, Choices, and Strategies.* San Francisco, CA: Jossey-Bass Publishers.

Cohen, Glenn I., Holly F. Lynch, and Gregory D. Curfman. 2014. "When Religious Freedom Clashes with Access to Care." *New England Journal of Medicine* 371(7):596–599.

Consumer Reports. 2015. "The Surprising Dangers of CT Scans and X-rays." January.

———. 2017. "The Price of Crossing the Border for Medications." *New England Journal of Medicine* 377(17):311–313.

Fralick, Michael, Jerry Avorn, and Aaron S. Kesselheim. 2017. "The Price of Crossing the Border for Medications." *New England Journal of Medicine* 377(4):311–313.

Freeman, Joseph D., Srikanth Kadiyala, Janice F. Bell, and Diane P. Martin. 2008. "The Causal Effect of Health Insurance on Utilization and Outcomes in Adults: A Systematic Review of U.S. Studies." *Medical Care* 46(10):1023–1032.

The Gallup Poll. 2019. "Health Systems." Retrieved March 11, 2019 (https://news.gallup.com/poll/4708/healthcare-system.aspx).

Goldman, Anna L., Danny McCormick, Jennifer S. Haas, and Benjamin D. Sommers. 2018. "Effects of the ACA's Health Insurance Marketplaces on the Previously Uninsured: A Quasi-Experimental Analysis." *Health Affairs* 37(4):591–599.

Goozner, Merrill. 2018. "How to End the Financial Toxicity of Specialty Drugs." *Modern Healthcare* (July):26.

Griffith, Kevin, David K. Jones, and Benjamin D. Sommers. 2018. "Diminishing Insurance Choices in the Affordable Care Act Marketplaces: A County-Based Analysis." *Health Affairs* 37(10):1678–1684.

Gutierrez, Carmen M. 2018. "The Institutional Determinants of Health Insurance: Moving Away from Labor Market, Marriage, and Family Attachments under the ACA." *American Sociological Review* 83(6):1144–1170.

Hadley, Jack, Earl P. Steinberg, and Judith Feder. 1991. "Comparison of Uninsured and Privately Insured Hospital Patients." *Journal of the American Medical Association* 265(3):374–379.

Herman, Bob. 2015. "Drugmakers Funnel Payments to High-Prescribing Doctors." *Modern Healthcare* 21:7.

Hero, Joachim O., Robert J. Blendon, Alan M. Zaslavsky, and Andrea L. Campbell. 2016. "Understanding What Makes Americans Dissatisfied with Their Health Care System: An International Comparison." *Health Affairs* 35(3):502–509.

Hillman, Bruce J., Catherine A. Joseph, Michael R. Mabry, Jonathan H. Sunshine, Stephen D. Kennedy, and Monica Noether. 1990. "Frequency and Costs of Diagnostic Imaging in Office Practice—A Comparison of Self-Referring and Radiologist-Referring Physicians." *New England Journal of Medicine* 323(23):1604–1608.

Himmelstein, David U., Miraya Jun, Reinhard Busse, Karine Chevreul, Alexander Geissler, Patrick Jeurissen, Sarah Thomson, Marie-Amelie Vinet, and Steffie Woolhandler. 2014. "A Comparison of Hospital Administrative Costs in Eight Nations: US Costs Exceed All Others by Far." *Health Affairs* 33(1):1586–1594.

Institute of Medicine. 2009. *America's Uninsured Crisis: Consequences for Health and Health Care.* Washington, DC: Institute of Medicine.

The IQVIA Institute for Human Data Science. 2018. "Medicine Use and Spending in the United States." Retrieved March 29, 2019 (www.iqvia.com/institute/reports/medicine-use-and-spending-in-the-us-review-of-2017-outlook-to-2022).

Kaiser Family Foundation. 2009. "Trends in Health Care Costs and Spending." Retrieved March 18, 2019 (www.kff.org/insurance//7692.cfm).

———. 2017. "Employer-Sponsored Coverage Rates for the Nonelderly by Age." Retrieved March 18, 2019 (www.kff.org/other/state-indicator/rate-by-age/?currentTimeframe=0&sortModel=%7B%22

colId%22:%22Location%22,%22sort%22:%22asc%22%7D).

———. 2018a. "American Community Survey." Retrieved March 18, 2019 (www.kff.org/uninsured/fact-sheet/key-facts-about-the-uninsured-population/).

———. 2018b. "Employer Health Benefits." Retrieved March 18, 2019 (https://kff.org/report-section/ehbs-2016-section-five-market-shares-of-health-plans/).

Kesselheim, Aaron S., and Niteesh K. Choudhry. 2008. "The International Pharmaceutical Market as a Source of Low-Cost Prescription Drugs for U.S. Patients." *Annals of Internal Medicine* 148(8):614–619.

King, Marissa, and Peter S. Bearman. 2017. "Gifts and Influence: Conflict of Interest Policies and Prescribing of Psychotropic Medications in the United States." *Social Science and Medicine* 172(January):153–162.

Long, Sharon K., Lea Bart, Michael Karpman, Adele Shartzer, and Stephen Zuckerman. 2017. "Sustained Gains in Coverage, Access, and Affordability Under the ACA: A 2017 Update." *Health Affairs* 36(9):1656–1662.

Lotvin, Alan M., William H. Shrank, Surya C. Singh, Benjamin P. Falit, and Troyen A. Brennan. 2014. "Specialty Medications: Traditional and Novel Tools Can Address Rising Spending on These Costly Drugs." *Health Affairs* 33(10):1736–1744.

Luhby, Tami. 2018. "Eight Ways Trump Hurt Obamacare in His First Year." Retrieved March 10, 2019 (https://money.cnn.com/2018/01/20/news/economy/obamacare-trump-year-one/index.html).

Mazurenko, Olena, Casey Balio, Rajender Agarwal, Aaron E. Campbell, and Nir Menachemi. 2018. "The Effects of Medicaid Expansion Under the ACA: A Systematic Review." *Health Affairs* 37(6):944–950.

McCarthy, Justin. 2018. "Bipartisan Negativity in Views of the Healthcare Industry." *The Gallup Poll.* Retrieved March 9, 2019 (https://news.gallup.com/poll/242168/bipartisan-negativity-views-healthcare-industry.aspx).

McDonough, John E., Michael Miller, and Christine Barber. 2008. "A Progress Report on State Health Access Reform." *Health Affairs* 27(1):105–115.

Modern Healthcare. January 19, 2019. "Data Points: Competition Holds Generic Drug Prices at Bay." Retrieved February 2, 2019 (https://www.modernhealthcare.com/article/20190119/NEWS/190119914/data-points-competition-holds-generic-drug-prices-at-bay).

National Center for Health Statistics: Faststats. 2019. "Gross Domestic Product, National Health Expenditures, Per Capita Amounts, Percent Distribution, and Average Annual Percent Change: United States, Selected Years 1960–2016." Retrieved March 4, 2019 (www.cdc.gov/nchs/data/hus/2017/093.pdf).

Oberlander, Jonathan, and David K. Jones. 2015. "The Children's Cliff—Extending CHIP." *New England Journal of Medicine* 372(21):1979–1981.

O'Brien, Sarah. 2019. "Health Care Costs for Retirees Climb to $285,000." *CNBC*. Retrieved March 28, 2019 (www.cnbc.com/2019/04/02/health-care-costs-for-retirees-climb-to-285000.html).

Papanicolas, Irene, Liana R. Woskie, and Ashish K. Jha. 2018. "Health Care Spending in the United States and Other High-Income Countries." *Journal of the American Medical Association* 319(10):1024–1039.

Petryna, Adriana, Andrew Lakoff, and Arthur *Kleinman*. *2006. Global Pharmaceuticals: Ethics, Markets, and Practices*. Durham, NC: Duke University Press.

Pham-Kanter, Genevieve. 2014. "Revisiting Financial Conflicts of Interest in FDA Advisory Committees." *Milbank Quarterly* 92(3):446–470.

Quadagno, Jill. 2005. *One Nation Insured: Why the U.S. Has No National Health Insurance*. New York: Oxford University Press.

Relman, Arnold S. 1980. "The New Medical–Industrial Complex." *New England Journal of Medicine* 303(17):963–970.

———. 1991. "The Health Care Industry: Where Is It Taking Us?" *New England Journal of Medicine* 325(12):854–859.

Robbins, Rebecca. 2016. "Drug Makers Now Spend $5 Billion a Year on Advertising. Here's What That Buys." *STAT*. Retrieved March 11, 2019 (www.statnews.com/2016/03/09/drug-industry-advertising/).

Rosenbaum, Sara. 2017. "Contraception as a Health Insurance Right: What Comes Next?" *Milbank Quarterly* 95(1):28–31.

Sakowski, Julie A., James G. Kahn, Richard G. Kronick, Jeffrey M. Newman, and Harold S. Luft. 2009. "Peering into the Black Box: Billing and Insurance Activities in a Medical Group." *Health Affairs* 28(S1):544–554.

Schneider, Eric C., Dana O. Sarnak, David Squires, Arnav Shah, and Michelle M. Doty. 2018. "Mirror, Mirror 2017: International Comparison Reflects Flaws and Opportunities for Better U.S. Health Care." *The Commonwealth Fund*. Retrieved March 10, 2019 (https://interactives.commonwealthfund.org/2017/july/mirror-mirror/).

Schoen, Cathy, Karen Davis, Sabrina K.H. How, and Stephen C. Schoenbaum. 2006. "U.S. Health System Performance: A National Scorecard." *Health Affairs* 25(S1):457–475.

Sutherly, Ben. 2015. "Pinched by Deductibles, Some Forgo Medical Care." *The Columbus Dispatch*, November 22. Retrieved February 16, 2016 (www.dispatch.com/content/stories/local/2015/11/22/pinched-by-deductibles-some-forgo-medical-care.html).

Thompson, Dennis. 2015. "Most Americans View Access to Health Care as a Moral Issue." *Health Day/Harris Poll*. Retrieved March 9, 2019 (www.healthday.com/press/healthday_harris_Sept_2015.htm).

US Department of Health and Human Services. 2011. "Overview of the Uninsured in the United States: A Summary of the 2011 Current population Survey." Retrieved March 29, 2019 (https://aspe.hhs.gov/basic-report/overview-uninsured-united-states-summary-2011-current-population-survey).

US Senate Homeland Security & Governmental Affairs Committee. 2018. "Fueling an Epidemic: Exposing the Financial Ties Between Opioid Manufacturers and Third-Party Advocacy Groups." Retrieved June 3, 2019 (www.hsdl.org/?view&did=808171).

Waitzkin, Howard. 1989. "Health Policy in the United States: Problems and Alternatives." Pp. 475–491 in *Handbook of Medical Sociology* (4th ed.), edited by Howard E. Freeman and Sol Levine. Upper Saddle River, NJ: Prentice Hall.

Weiss, Gregory L. 2006. *Grass Roots Medicine: The Story of America's Free Health Clinics*. Lanham, MD: Rowman and Littlefield.

Woolhandler, Steffie, Terry Campbell, and David U. Himmelstein. 2003. "Costs of Health Care Administration in the United States and Canada." *New England Journal of Medicine* 349(25):768–775.

CHAPTER 15

Health Care Delivery

Learning Objectives

- Describe the key events in the origin and development of hospitals.

- Discuss three important issues facing hospitals today.

- Discuss two of the freestanding ambulatory and surgical sites. Identify and describe key

reasons why non–hospital delivery sites have increased in importance.

- Describe what is meant by "hospice." Describe the primary benefits of hospice care and the primary concerns about its future.

- Compare and contrast informal and formal home health care.

Throughout much of the twentieth century, the private physician's office (for primary care) and the hospital (for emergency, life-threatening, and surgical care) were almost the only medical treatment sites. However, in the last few decades, the health care delivery system has undergone a significant transformation, and now a wide array of care sites is available. This chapter describes and analyzes changes in five important components of the health care delivery system: (1) hospitals; (2) freestanding primary care, urgent care, and surgical sites; (3) nursing homes; (4) hospices; and (5) home health care.

HOSPITALS

History

The first American "hospital" was founded by William Penn in Philadelphia in 1713 primarily as a shelter for the poor. The first hospital designed primarily to serve the sick was Pennsylvania Hospital, founded in Philadelphia in 1751 by Thomas Bond, a local physician, and Benjamin Franklin. The hospital began in a small rented

house that was capable of holding no more than 20 patients, but grew in stages until the early 1800s. The hospital was always crowded, as the average length of stay was weeks or months long, but its main problem was that many mentally ill people occupied most of the beds. These patients were eventually moved to a new facility in 1835.

Most of the general hospitals built in the late 1700s and the 1800s provided care primarily for people without family and without the financial means to acquire housing. Their care was financed by charitable contributions, and many physicians volunteered their time. A steward or matron generally controlled the small staff and the patients, and a small number of women, assisted by a few volunteers, performed "nursing" duties. Most of the care focused on making the patients comfortable and preparing them for death.

With advances in science and the development of medical technologies, hospitals underwent significant transformation. By 1900, hospitals mostly admitted only sick but curable patients, while other sites served the elderly and homeless. Religious appeals for funding gave way to a more secular approach that emphasized the value of hospitals in treating illness and protecting the community against epidemics. As a result, cities of all sizes began to build community hospitals.

By 1920, the hospital had become the primary center of acute care treatment. Surgery was the key to both the growth and increased status of hospitals, along with the development of a skilled nursing force and the introduction of ancillary services such as X-ray facilities and laboratories. As the size of the hospital and the scope of its services increased, administrators were added to coordinate this work, and the complex bureaucratic hospital of today emerged (Rosenberg, 1987). Expansion in the number of community hospitals was spurred by the Hill-Burton Hospital Construction Act of 1946. This massive program committed nearly US$4 billion of federal monies and over US$9 billion of state and local government monies for the construction of new hospitals and the renovation of existing ones.

During the middle years of the twentieth century, the hospital was the primary acute health care organization and the distribution center of modern medical technologies. Advances in life expectancy and shifts in morbidity patterns from acute infectious diseases to chronic degenerative diseases resulted in a greater number of older patients who were chronically ill. This led to an enlargement of diagnostic services, an increased number of surgical procedures, and the development of rehabilitation units. In the remaining part of this section of the chapter, we will discuss developments in hospitals in the last few decades and especially in the last few years.

Organizational Structure

Today's hospitals are highly bureaucratic and hierarchical social organizations that exemplify the key characteristics of bureaucracies explicated by Max Weber. They typically contain an authority hierarchy (although not pyramidal in shape), extensive rules and regulations, fixed areas of responsibility based on competence, recruitment based on merit, regular remuneration, promotion based on objective criteria, and separation between the power of a position and of the incumbent. Superimposed upon these bureaucratic traits are twin lines of authority that run throughout hospital decision making.

Dual Line of Authority.   These twin lines are referred to as the dual line of authority. Figure 15.1 provides one model of hospital organizational structure. Most hospital departments report either to the first line of authority, namely the hospital administrator (generally a person trained in hospital or health administration and with a strong background in business), or to the second line of authority, namely the medical director or other person who is medically trained. Both the hospital administrator and the medical director are ultimately responsible to the hospital's governing body—generally a board of trustees.

This dual system of authority frequently results in tension between the business orientation of the administrator and the clinical orientation of the medical director. Although both the administrative and medical staff share the primary goal of patient care, they do not always agree on related goals and the methods by which to achieve quality and efficient patient care. Fundamental to this conflict is that the administrator is responsible for the fiscal survival of the institution, and the medical staff is most concerned with clinical efficacy.

Related to this dispute is the struggle between professional autonomy and bureaucratic control. Given their medical expertise, physicians maintain that only they are competent to make decisions regarding patient care and to instruct medical staff. However, many issues related to patient care also involve administrative decisions, and thus physicians may perceive an impingement on their clinical autonomy.

Nurses and other ancillary health care providers can be placed in an awkward situation by this structure. They are expected to carry out physicians' orders at the same time that they

Figure 15.1 Typical Hospital Structure

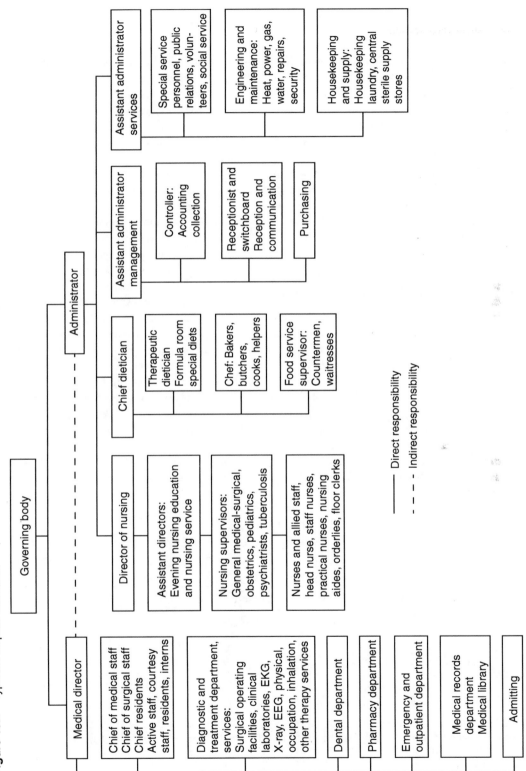

Source: Department of Labor, *Technology and Manpower in the Health Service Industry* (Washington, DC: Government Printing Office, 1967).

are obligated to follow hospital protocol. Being responsible to both can lead to stressful and conflicting responsibilities.

Relations among physicians and hospitals involve more tension today than perhaps ever before. The fact that many physicians are establishing freestanding sites that offer services once found only in the hospital and the fact that some hospitals have hired more physicians from the community to work on staff and have bought out local physician practices have led to some erosion of cooperation between the two groups (Berenson, Ginsburg, and May, 2007).

The Number of Hospitals and Hospital Beds

Ironically, as the American population continues to increase, the number of hospitals and hospital beds is decreasing. The number of hospitals increased each year from the mid-1940s to 1979, when the number began to decline, resulting in a total of 5,564 hospitals in 2015 (see Table 15.1). Of these, 4,862 are short-term general hospitals. Since 1980, the number of hospitals has declined by more than 20 percent due primarily to the closing of rural and inner-city facilities.

The total number of hospital beds began to decline earlier than the number of hospitals, peaking in the mid-1960s at about 1.7 million and declining to just under 900,000 in 2015. The total number of hospital admissions increased each year until the mid-1980s (nearly 40 million per year), but has since dropped to just over 35 million. However, given the increase in population in the last three decades, the likelihood of any one person being hospitalized has sharply declined.

Why are the number of hospitals and the number of hospital beds decreasing? There are two main answers—changing insurance reimbursement rates and an increase in the number of outpatient surgeries. Hospital care is the most expensive form of health care. In order to keep prices as low as possible, private insurance companies and managed care organizations have applied pressure, where feasible, to substitute other forms of care (e.g., outpatient care) for inpatient hospital care and to keep the number of days of hospitalization as low as possible. In addition, levels of reimbursement for hospitalized care, including that from Medicare and Medicaid, are being controlled more tightly. These efforts have led to a reduction in hospital admissions and a decline in average length of stay (from 1975 to 2015, the average length of hospital stay decreased from 11.4 days to 6.1). They have also led to an increase in the number of surgical settings outside the hospital. With demand down, fewer hospitals and fewer hospital beds are needed.

TABLE 15.1   Trends Among US Hospitals

Year	Hospitals	Beds (million)	Admissions (million)
1950	6,788	1.46	18.48
1960	6,876	1.66	25.03
1970	7,123	1.62	31.76
1980	6,965	1.37	38.89
1990	6,649	1.21	33.77
2000	5,810	0.98	34.89
2010	5,754	0.94	36.92
2015	5,564	0.90	35.06

Source: National Center for Health Statistics. 2018. *Health, United States, 2017*. Hyattsville, MD: US Department of Health and Human Services.

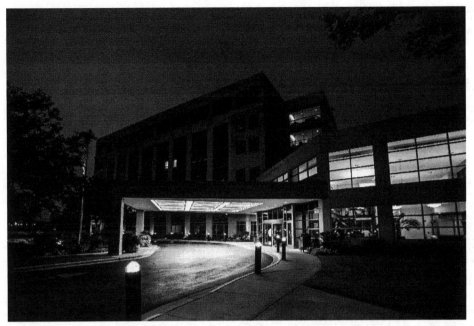

Despite continuing increases in the United States population, the number of hospitals and hospital beds has been declining for about 40 years.

Hospital Ownership

Each of the 4,862 short-term general hospitals in the United States is owned by one of three main entities:

1. *Non-profit (voluntary) hospitals* are the most common type of short-term general hospital. In 2015, there were 2,845 non-profit hospitals in the United States—59 percent of all short-term hospitals. Being non-profit, they answer to a board of directors comprised of community leaders, and end-of-year financial surpluses are reinvested in the hospital (as opposed to being paid to investors).

2. *For-profit (proprietary) hospitals* account for approximately 21 percent of all short-term hospitals. In 2015, there were 1,034 for-profit hospitals. These hospitals are created by individual or corporate entrepreneurs; they are sometimes "public" in the sense that shares in

the hospital (or controlling agent) are bought and sold on the stock market and are sometimes simply privately owned. These hospitals are expected to have greater revenues than expenses each year so that the difference can be returned to investors as profit.

3. *State and local government (public) hospitals* represent the third type of ownership. There were 983 public hospitals in 2015, about 20 percent of all short-term hospitals in that year. The number of public hospitals is declining sharply. Most state-funded hospitals are part of the mental health system, and most local hospitals are designed to serve the general population but end up being the primary care site for the poor and medically indigent. Public hospitals have charity caseloads about four times larger than those of other hospitals. All public hospitals rely on funding from the sponsoring government. Table 15.2 shows the changing number of hospitals from 1980 to 2015.

TABLE 15.2   Number of Community (Short-Term) Hospitals

Ownership Type	1980	1990	2000	2010	2015
Total	5,830	5,384	4,915	4,985	4,862
Non-profit	3,322	3,191	3,003	2,904	2,845
For-profit	730	749	749	1,013	1,034
Government	1,778	1,444	1,163	1,068	983

Source: National Center for Health Statistics. *Health, United States, 2017* (Hyattsville, MD: US Department of Health and Human Services, 2018).

Consolidation: Acquisitions, Mergers and Megamergers

The historical model of independent hospitals answerable only to its own administrative structure and board of directors is disappearing. Increasingly, hospitals are affiliating with each other through one of three methods:

1. Acquisitions, in which one hospital purchases control of another (usually smaller) one; typically, both hospitals continue to exist as separate entities.
2. Mergers, in which three or more hospitals agree to dissolve in order to form a new company with shared ownership, control, and profit.
3. Megamergers through the acquisition or merger of two large multi-hospital systems that creates control over a large share of the market. Megamergers are different than mergers due to their very large scale.

Hospital acquisitions and mergers have occurred on a small scale for decades, but a particularly important event occurred in 1968. That year, two men—one a physician and the other an entrepreneur—joined forces to create the Hospital Corporation of America (HCA) to provide funds for capital expansion for the physician's hospital and to acquire additional hospitals—thus, creating a major hospital chain. At that time, very few of the nation's short-term hospitals were part of a chain (Light, 1986). Over time, the pace of acquisitions and mergers increased, but the number has escalated very rapidly since 2010. In 2017 alone, there were 115 acquisitions and mergers (with total value of US$175 billion)—the largest number ever in a single year at that time.

Hospital megamergers began occurring frequently in the 1990s. For example, in 1993, the second largest chain, Columbia Healthcare (94 hospitals), acquired the largest chain, Hospital Corporation of America (96 hospitals), for US$5.7 billion, creating a gigantic Columbia/HCA Healthcare company (now titled just Health Corporation of America or HCA). Two months later, Healthtrust and Epic Holdings, two other large chains, merged to create a new company with 116 hospitals (a US$1 billion deal); this became the second largest chain. Tenet Healthcare Corporation was created from the merger of two other large firms—National Medical Enterprises and American Medical International.

As of 2016, HCA was the largest for-profit chain (with 169 hospitals and 116 freestanding surgery centers in 20 states and the United Kingdom, having 233,000 employees including 37,000 physicians), followed by Community Health Systems (159 hospitals in 20 states, having 123,000 employees including 20,000 physicians), and Tenet (79 hospitals, 20 short-stay surgical hospitals, and 470 outpatient centers, having 130,000 employees). Since then, Ascension Health has climbed into the top three with more than 2,600 care sites. These are gigantic firms.

The Drive to Consolidate. Joanne Kenen (2019), a health editor for a journal of the Association of Medical Journalists, poses several key questions about this consolidation activity. "Is this trend a wise and inevitable path to a more efficient health care system? Can big systems wring out waste and overlap and inefficiencies and better deploy data, telemedicine and EHRs [electronic health records]? Or are we just empowering bigger, more powerful hospital systems that will be able to demand higher prices from insurers and other payers as they come to dominate the market?

What are the intended benefits of this consolidation activity? Almost always, companies cite lower prices for patients as the primary motivating factor. Hospitals that are members of multihospital chains should have several advantages, including (1) economies of scale in purchasing (the chains buy more products and get a lower per-unit cost), (2) greater negotiating leverage with managed care networks and health insurance companies (due to the larger number of people being covered), (3) increased access to capital to replace aging infrastructure, (4) greater ability to share the costs of new technologies across many hospitals, and (5) elimination of some duplication of services.

In addition, since passage of the Affordable Care Act, both the federal government and private insurers have actively tried to change the way doctors and hospitals get paid by focusing more on quality of care provided than quantity of care. This model is referred to as **value-based care**. Because fees and payments are tied more closely to patient outcomes, health care providers are seeking ways to improve the value of care provided. Some believe consolidation can help hospitals work more closely together and better coordinate care.

What are the downsides to consolidation? Most important is that the primary benefit to patients—lower prices—rarely occurs. Barak Richman, a Duke University law professor and expert on hospital consolidation, states:

Reducing competition increases price. We know that, and we've known that for generations, as a matter of rudimentary economics, across markets of all kinds. What's remarkable, and unfortunate, is that we have been less demanding of competition in hospital markets. There seems to be a lingering belief that healthcare providers won't exploit pricing power the same way everyone else does. That belief is thoroughly refuted by research—recent findings indicate that a merger of two hospitals located near each other will increase prices an astounding 40%. . . . To date, there is very little evidence—I venture to say none—that the mergers over the past 20 years have generated any efficiencies.

(quoted in Kenen, 2019)

Vertical Integration of Health Services. Recently, there has been a flurry of acquisitions and mergers involving companies offering different kinds of health services. In these cases, rather than two hospitals or two groups of hospitals merging or two insurance companies or two groups of insurance companies merging, the new mergers involve combinations of hospitals, physicians, insurance companies, pharmaceutical companies, and so forth. These cases of vertical integration have also been justified by greater efficiency and integration of services and lower prices for patients. Like with other forms of consolidation, however, several studies have found that vertically integrated health care systems often raise their prices and do not demonstrate quality improvements (Berenson, 2017).

A recent example is the purchase of the large insurance company, Aetna (and its 39 million insurees), by CVS Health (including its in-store clinics, pharmacies, health products, prescription mail-order system, and 90 million members) for US$69 billion. In the deal, Aetna will retain its name but will be part of the CVS company. CVS and Aetna contend that this will lower medical costs for all involved, but cautious observers are watching carefully.

The Pressures on Independent Hospitals. Lacking the benefits of being in a network with other hospitals, independent hospitals have been squeezed. Especially hard hit have been black-owned hospitals and rural hospitals, both of which have sharply decreased in number. Today, there are only a few black-owned hospitals in the United States, and some of these are in serious financial condition. Because these hospitals often serve the uninsured who could not receive care elsewhere, their demise has left a significant gap in hospital services for the poor and medically indigent.

Similarly, many of the nation's rural hospitals have closed or are struggling to survive. Many are very small, but they are the only hospital and urgent care site within 100 miles. Admissions to many of these hospitals have declined in recent years—as they have in most hospitals—but the effect is more overwhelming for a small facility. The vast majority of these hospitals are in the South and in states that opted not to expand Medicaid under the Affordable Care Act.

Six Key Issues in Hospitals

The Relative Contributions of Not-For-Profit and For-Profit Hospitals.   Advocates of for-profit hospitals contend that the business approach they bring to health care leads to both the highest quality of care (because they must attract enough patients to earn a profit) and greater efficiencies (because eliminating waste maximizes profit). For-profit hospitals, like all profit-making companies, are required to pay federal, state, and local income taxes and property taxes. Proponents of the for-profit approach point out that these tax monies contribute in many ways to local community needs and represent a contribution to communities above and beyond delivery of health care services.

Advocates of not-for-profit hospitals believe it is inappropriate to make a profit from patients' ill health. They contend that managers in non-profit systems focus on meeting patient and community needs without having to consider the profitability of choices. Because they do not need to earn a profit, their fees reflect only enough money to cover all expenses plus the additional money necessary for capital and service improvements. Generally, non-profits are less expensive than for-profits.

Federal legislation provides a tax exemption for not-for-profit hospitals (that is, they do not pay any federal, state, or local taxes) in exchange for providing needed hospital care for community residents unable to pay. The exemption from taxation saves non-profit hospitals approximately US$25 billion each year. Since ACA was passed, non-profits are required to assess community health needs every 3 years and create a policy to address them.

The "uncompensated care" of non-profits is of three types: (1) charity care—the value of care provided to patients who have been deemed by the hospital to be unable to pay, (2) bad debt—the value of care provided to patients who are unable or unwilling to pay (but who have not requested charity care), and (3) payments from Medicaid (which typically reimburses hospitals somewhat less than the hospital's costs). The current total annual value of uncompensated hospital care is approximately US$40 billion. While for-profits do have some uncompensated care, it is far less than that of non-profits.

In the last several years, however, many government officials have expressed concern that some non-profit hospitals have failed to invest enough of the difference between their income and expenses to provide services for the community's indigent. For some non-profits, this margin has approximated that of for-profit hospitals. Some non-profits dedicate as much as 18 percent of their operating expenses to charity care, whereas for others the figure is less than 1 percent. The average is 7 to 8 percent (Young et al., 2018). Recently, as many as 7 of the 10 most profitable hospitals were not-for-profit (Bai and Anderson, 2016).

Community hospital administrators report that much of this money has been placed in reserve accounts that may be needed should an increasing number of people be unable to pay for care. However, the tax exemption for non-profit hospitals is in jeopardy in a few states. Both for-profits and not-for-profits are devising more sophisticated means of calculating the value of service rendered to the community.

Most for-profit hospitals severely limit the amount of charity care provided. One way they do this is by discouraging access by poor patients. For-profit hospitals are typically located only in affluent suburban areas where most patients have private insurance and where they can target marketing campaigns to these middle- and upper-class people (a process called cream skimming). In the first decade of the 2000s, there was a boom in hospital construction in the United States, and it largely consisted of new high-tech, high-amenities hospitals built in suburban areas to replace older downtown facilities.

A second method for discouraging poor patients is by conducting "wallet biopsies" in order to refuse uninsured patients access to the hospital. If a patient needs to be seen, the for-profit arranges for a transfer to a non-profit or public hospital, assuming it will accept the patient (a process called patient dumping), which some analysts believe happens frequently. Prompted by reports that hospitals sometimes turn away even emergency patients because they would be unable to pay for medical care, the federal government passed legislation in 1986 to stop patient dumping. The law requires hospitals to medically screen all emergency patients, and prohibits them from transferring patients with unstable medical conditions or women in labor to other facilities for economic reasons. The maximum penalty for each violation is US$50,000 and the possible loss of Medicare funding. Occasionally, however, patient dumping stories are still reported.

When for-profits do admit a charity care patient, they often have engaged in cost shifting to other payers—that is, charging more to those paying out-of-pocket or through health insurance to make up for their uncompensated care. In 2015, 50 hospitals (all but one of which were for-profit) charged uninsured patients more than ten times the actual cost of patient care (the all-hospital average is 3.4 times) (Bai and Anderson, 2015). The Affordable Care Act now makes it illegal to charge uninsured patients more than others, but there are reports of this still occurring.

Both for-profit and not-for-profit hospital administrators acknowledge that the large number of uninsured people unable to pay for hospital care is a significant problem. For example, in the late 1980s, a young man in Georgia, without medical insurance, suffered burns over 95 percent of his body and was taken to the closest medical center (which did not have a burn unit). The medical center contacted more than 40 for-profit and nonprofit hospitals with burn units—both within the state and in neighboring states—asking each to accept the patient. All of them refused, mainly due to the anticipated high costs associated with treatment and the likelihood of not being paid. Finally, a hospital in Baltimore, Maryland, accepted the patient, and he was flown there.

A case with some similarity occurred in 1998 at a California hospital. A woman who was having painful contractions and breathing problems due to asthma, and was about to give birth, requested an epidural (which blocks pain in the lower part of the body). The anesthesiologist demanded US$400 in cash on the spot, and refused the woman's offer of a credit card, check, or Western Union number for cash confirmation. The epidural was not given.

The Survival of Public Hospitals. Public hospitals are funded by local, state and federal funds. Typically, they are large hospitals, often in older buildings, with many beds. Limitations in available funds means they are often understaffed and have poor patient-to-doctor and patient-to-nurse ratios. Customarily, they have a difficult time competing for paying patients who prefer newer facilities located in the suburbs with more modern infrastructure. By law, public hospitals cannot turn anyone away even if the patient is unable to pay anything for his or her care, so they are a key element in serving the needs of the medically indigent. But fewer paying patients and more non-paying patients have placed many public hospitals in a desperate situation. They tend to do less well on quality assessment and have a more difficult time improving performance.

Many public hospitals lose money annually. Can this situation continue indefinitely? It cannot, and the survivability of public hospitals is at stake. The Affordable Care Act enabled more patients to become paying, but it is not a guarantee that they will use public hospitals. For a view of the role of public hospitals in a special situation, see the accompanying box, "Hurricane Katrina and the Resulting Health Care Crisis."

IN THE FIELD

HURRICANE KATRINA AND THE RESULTING HEALTH CARE CRISIS

On August 29, 2005, Hurricane Katrina landed in the Gulf Coast states and created massive destruction throughout the region. Louisiana, Mississippi, Alabama, and Florida experienced significant destruction. The city of New Orleans, long feared to be vulnerable should a hurricane strike, was especially hard hit. Two flood walls and a levee collapsed, unleashing torrents of water that covered 80 percent of the city. Residents of the city without the means to evacuate prior to the arrival of Katrina were housed at the Superdome. The city and rescue workers "faced oppressive heat, darkness from downed power lines, difficulties communicating by telephone, little fuel for their cars, and widespread devastation" (Wilson, 2006:153).

The human cost of Katrina: 1,836 lives lost, 780,000 people displaced, 850 schools damaged, 200,000 homes destroyed, 18,700 businesses destroyed, and 220,000 jobs lost. It was a public health emergency in the immediate aftermath of the hurricane and a long-term crisis. Threats existed in the mountainous debris; faulty sewage treatment; toxic chemical and oil spills; contaminated water; swirling dust; pesky insects and vermin; and mold, mold, and more mold (Wilson, 2006:153).

Moreover, New Orleans had one of the nation's highest rates of poverty and lack of health insurance. These residents bore the brunt of the hurricane damage. They relied on a system of state-run public hospitals and a network of more than 350 clinics that primarily served the poor and uninsured. Altogether, the city lost 7 of its 22 hospitals and more than 50 percent of its hospital beds. The Medical Center of Louisiana at New Orleans consisted of two hospitals that were the safety net for the uninsured. Both were severely damaged. An interim and much smaller version of University Hospital opened in 2006. Charity Hospital, which had been plagued by overcrowding, budget shortfalls, and an inconvenient location, but was the only option for many low-income residents, never reopened. Long-term care facilities and mental health services and emergency room resources were especially hard hit. Many health care providers who evacuated New Orleans just prior to the hurricane never returned after the disasters (Rudowitz, Rowland, and Shartzer, 2006).

Post-hurricane, some policy analysts hoped the catastrophe would be a stimulus to rebuild a stronger and more accessible health care system than existed prior to Katrina. And that is what has occurred. With a US$100 million grant from the federal government and additional support from the state government and foundations, a system of more than 60 community health centers based on the medical home model were established. Most of these centers have same-day appointments, and all serve everyone who comes in. The expanded use of electronic health records has been extremely helpful. Area medical schools and their faculty and students provided significant help. A US$1.1 billion medical center has opened. Although many challenges remain—especially in the city's mental health care system—some observers now call New Orleans' efforts a model for big city health care renewal (Todd, 2015). Lessons learned from Katrina have assisted many other cities in their disaster preparation (Todd, 2015).

The Shift From Inpatient to Outpatient Services. The economic marketplace for hospitals has undergone tremendous change. Today, hospitals are being pressured by the federal government and by health insurers to reduce hospital prices and offer services in the most economically efficient manner. To compete in the new environment, hospitals realize they need to become leaner, more efficient, and more diversified than they have been in the past. This is happening in two main ways.

First, most hospitals are attempting to reduce expenditures. They are doing this by eliminating inefficiencies (e.g., reusing supplies that formerly would have been discarded) and by trying to make more efficient use of staff. An example of the latter is the creation in recent years of a new medical specialist—the hospitalist. Hospitalists are physicians who work in and for a hospital and focus just on hospitalized patients. Most have a background in primary care. Currently, there are more than 50,000 hospitalists in the United States, and that number is increasing. Hospitals hope these specialists will help to manage closely the care of each hospitalized patient, improve patient outcomes, and be economically efficient. Importantly, they also release office-based physicians from the need to check in personally each day with their hospitalized patients—a benefit given the shortage of primary care physicians in the United States.

Second, many hospitals are diversifying patient care services. Prompted by the cost-containment environment and increased willingness of Medicare, Medicaid, and private insurance companies to pay for low-tech, out-of-hospital services, hospitals have diversified in two important ways:

1. They have shifted many former in-patient services—like many surgeries—to an outpatient basis. In 1980, only 16 percent of surgeries performed in hospitals were done on an outpatient basis, but by 2015, 66 percent were outpatient—a stunning change—and they accounted for 60 percent of total hospital revenues (the highest-ever percentage). In 2017 there were about 19 million outpatient surgeries (CDC, 2019).

2. They have become purchasers of or partners with freestanding urgent care centers and surgical centers. There are now more than 9,000 freestanding urgent care centers in the United States (with approximately 160 million annual patient visits), and more than 5,000 freestanding surgical centers (with more than 25 million annual surgeries). While the reimbursement for procedures performed outside the hospital is less, costs to the hospital are far lower, so the hospital profit margin is greater.

Data from the American Hospital Association (2019) show that in 2017 the net inpatient revenue for hospitals was US$498 billion, while net outpatient revenue was US$472 billion, reflecting a ratio of 95 percent—the highest ever (Bannow, 2019).

More Efficient Use of the Emergency Room. About 95 percent of acute care hospitals in the United States have emergency units open 24 hours a day. Although ERs are designed to provide care for acutely ill and injured patients, they serve as a family physician for many. In 2018, urgent care was not needed in more than half of the 144 million visits made to emergency rooms. Nearly as many patients complained of coughs and sore throats as complained of chest pain. Because ER visits now average about four to five times longer than visits to a primary care provider and cost about four times as much, they add significantly to health care costs.

What motivates so many individuals to seek primary care from the ER? Access is relatively easy because it does not depend on affiliation with a physician, an appointment, or time of day; the availability of advanced technology leads to a public perception of high-quality care; third-party payers have historically covered emergency room visits; and hospitals are obligated to provide emergency care even if the patient is not insured. Lack of access to primary care—either financially or in available hours—has been viewed as the main reason. Non-emergency visits to the ER are highest in areas where physicians are least willing to provide primary care to uninsured and Medicaid patients and where there are the fewest providers and facilities open outside regular work hours (O'Malley, 2013).

The expectation is that the Affordable Care Act will reduce use of the emergency room for individuals seeking non-emergency care. As more of the uninsured gain health care coverage, it seems reasonable to assume they will seek out primary care physicians in their offices. However, during the first few years of the ACA, use of the ER actually increased. This suggests that other factors are preventing access to private care, especially the difficulty for low-income families to access primary care physicians during daytime hours.

Reducing Medicare Patient Readmissions. In Chapter 14 we discussed the efforts of hospitals to save money by discharging Medicare patients as early as possible. Several years ago, this became a major firestorm as records indicated that many Medicare patients (more than 1 million per year) were quickly readmitted for the same or a related condition. Some of these cases were no doubt unforeseeable, but the concern was that hospitals were releasing patients before they were ready. The estimated total cost of these readmissions reached more than US$17 billion per year. Wide variations in readmission rates from hospital to hospital and from region to region of the country were also a concern.

To encourage hospitals not to release patients too early, in 2013, Medicare (through the Hospital Admissions Reduction Program) began levying heavy fines on hospitals that had too many readmissions. Almost immediately, fewer Medicare beneficiaries were readmitted. Just over US$2 billion was saved annually, even though in 2018, 81 percent of hospitals were still being penalized for excessive readmissions (the average penalty was US$217,000).

Research then uncovered another worrisome pattern. Wadhera and colleagues (2018) reported that deaths from heart failure and pneumonia (but not heart attacks) of Medicare patients within 30 days of discharge had risen since the program began. Critics charged that these deaths were attributable to patients not being readmitted even though they had significant need.

Medical Errors. Errors happen in medicine as they do everywhere. However, in the space of just a few months in 1995, an alarming and embarrassing series of very serious errors occurred in hospitals around the country. At one hospital in Tampa, Florida, in the space of 3 weeks, arthroscopic surgery was performed on the wrong knee of a woman, the wrong leg was amputated on a 51-year-old man, and a

77-year-old man died after a hospital employee mistakenly removed his respirator. Around the same time, the wrong breast was removed from a mastectomy patient in Michigan, the prostate gland was removed from the wrong patient in Maryland, a drug overdose killed an award-winning health columnist in Massachusetts, and oxygen was accidentally shut off to dozens of patients for up to 15 minutes in a Florida hospital.

IN THE FIELD

PROBLEMS IN THE MILITARY MEDICAL CARE SYSTEM

The Veterans Health Administration (VHA) is one of the largest single-target health care systems in the United States. In 2019, the VHA had a US$111 billion budget (provided by the federal government) to run 1,250 facilities (172 medical centers and 1,069 outpatient clinics). It has 306,000 employees and serves more than 9 million enrollees. About 14 million veterans opt not to receive their medical care from VA facilities.

Over the years, VA medical facilities have faced serious criticisms relating to quality of care, low accessibility (long patient wait times), and unnecessary inefficiencies. In 2014, these controversies became a major issue when it was discovered that the VA hospital in Phoenix, Arizona had average wait times for an appointment with a physician of nearly 4 months, and that schedulers were using a variety of subterfuges to conceal this fact from regulators. This information led investigators to expand their study, and they found similar problems in other facilities. Problems with safety measures and equipment and sterilization procedures were uncovered.

How could such devastating problems occur in the military medical care system? The VA claimed to be overrun with the high care needs of aging Vietnam War veterans and seriously wounded veterans—many with brain injuries and post-traumatic stress disorder—from the wars in Iraq and Afghanistan. Moreover, the VA facilities—like the nation as a whole—have a shortage of primary care physicians. They argue that more funds are needed to offer competitive salaries.

Legislation was passed in 2014 to provide additional funding. A new program that subsidizes care at private providers for veterans living more than 40 miles from a VA medical center was also implemented. The overall system average for wait times has been reduced to about 40 days—a significant improvement but still considerably more than the target goal of 30 days. Most analysts believe that an antiquated administrative structure in the VA has prevented more progress (Giroir and Wilensky, 2015).

In 2018, a major study compared how VA hospitals compared to other hospitals. The study produced the good news that death rates were lower and post-surgical complications were fewer in VA hospitals. However, nearly every VA hospital performed worse on patient satisfaction surveys, many had higher infection rates, and waiting times were still alarming. The 133 nursing homes run by the VA (with 46,000 residents) have received especially harsh criticism. Studies have found that residents are more likely to experience significant pain, more likely to get bed sores, more likely to get infections, lose daily living skills more quickly, and are more likely to be exposed to hazardous conditions. Veterans were being placed in "immediate jeopardy" at several of the homes, and "actual harm" to veterans was noted in more than half of the homes. Clearly, much more needs to be done (Slack and Estes, 2019; Wilensky, 2016).

The number and severity of these cases raised the issue of the adequacy of precautions and safeguards taken by hospitals to minimize the risk of error. Investigations promptly began. However, in early 1998, another flurry of reports was published. The Centers for Disease Control and Prevention reported that 2 million people each year contract an infection while in the hospital, and nearly 90,000 of them die from it. Several studies reported increasing evidence of drug errors in anesthesia and incorrect medications administered to patients.

In 1999, the Institute of Medicine published the first large-scale systematic study on medical errors. It reported that as many as 98,000 Americans die each year as a result of medical errors, and that millions more are injured. About one-third of these deaths occur in hospitals, and the remainder occur in physicians' offices, nursing homes, and other care sites. The study received massive publicity and renewed calls for steps to reduce the problem. In 2005, researchers at Harvard's School of Public Health repeated the study. They found that some hospitals and other providers had made significant improvements, but many had not. The number of fatalities annually was still about 98,000 (Leape and Berwick, 2005).

What have we learned since then? About 1,300 times each year, surgeons operate on the wrong person or the wrong body part. Once in every 5,000 surgeries, a medical instrument is left inside a patient's body. Medication errors are common and lead to an estimated 400,000 injuries each year. A study conducted in 2013–2014 by researchers in the anesthesiology department at Massachusetts General Hospital found about 50 percent of all surgeries involved some kind of medication error or unintended drug side effects, and that harm to the patient occurred in one-third of these cases (Nanji et al., 2016). About 650,000 patients a year contract an infection (e.g., pneumonia, or infections at the surgical site) while in a hospital, between 5 and 8 percent of intensive-care patients on ventilators

get pneumonia, and 100 patients a day wake during the middle of surgery. Studies have found that many hospitals are still reluctant to adopt all recommended safeguards due to the added cost. However, some of the checks require little time and no money. For example, studies continually show that medical providers do not always wash their hands between patients, and the lowest washing frequency is by physicians.

In 2016, researchers at Johns Hopkins Medical School reported that medical errors in hospitals and other health care facilities were still incredibly common, and claim 251,000 lives each year in the United States. This would make medical errors the third leading cause of death after heart disease and cancer. The estimate was based on an analysis of four impressive large studies conducted between 2000 and 2008 (Makary and Daniel, 2016).

Many analysts contend that the errors are a symptom of a larger systemic problem—medical culture. Lucian Leape, a pioneer in patient safety, says that the health care culture in almost all hospitals is incredibly dysfunctional. Hospitals remain very hierarchical, and those lower in the hierarchy are reluctant to call out those higher up. Thus, a nurse may observe a physician breaking protocol—for example, not washing his or her hands between patients—but not say anything for fear of personal consequences (Leape et al., 2012). Peter Pronovost and Eric Vohr (2010), co-authors of *Safe Patients, Smart Hospitals*, identify physician overconfidence and reluctance to admit errors or limitations as part of the culture that endangers patients. In order to put dollars behind the campaign to improve patient safety, some private insurers and Medicare now refuse to pay any costs associated with medical errors and/or hospital-acquired illnesses.

Has progress been made? Yes, but it is relatively modest. There has been reported progress in reducing certain types of medical errors, including hospital-acquired infections (an average annual decrease of 4.5 percent from 2010 to

2017), adverse drug events, and unnecessary use of antibiotics. But alarming reports persist. A study published in 2018 in the *American Journal of Infection Control* reported that 71 percent of reusable medical scopes deemed ready for use on patients tested positive for bacteria at three major US hospitals. These scopes were used in procedures such as colonoscopies, lung procedures, kidney stone removal, and other routine procedures. Despite much attention to the risks of contaminated instruments, the danger has not been eliminated.

FREESTANDING AMBULATORY AND SURGICAL SITES

Ambulatory care is personal health care provided to an individual who is not an inpatient in a health care facility. Ambulatory care services include preventive care, acute primary care, minor emergencies, and many surgical procedures, and they are provided today in an increasing variety of facilities.

The Traditional Setting

The traditional and still most common means of delivering ambulatory care is by a private physician in an office or clinic setting. About 9 in 10 active US physicians are involved in patient care, and 75 percent of these have an office-based practice (most of the others work in hospitals). However, today, only 42 percent of the more than 350 million annual visits for newly arising health problems are with patients' personal primary care physician. Visits to walk-in clinics, urgent care centers, outpatient departments, emergency rooms, and specialists are in aggregate more common (Pitts et al., 2010).

Freestanding Sites

The number of both independently owned and hospital-affiliated freestanding ambulatory care centers has increased dramatically in the last several years. Services offered in these settings include primary and urgent care, diagnostic imaging, rehabilitation, sports medicine, dialysis, and minor surgery. Some of the most important of these care sites are described in this section.

Walk-In Clinics. Walk-in-clinics are medical facilities that accept patients on a walk-in basis, with no appointment required. All types of walk-in clinics provide basic medical services, such as routine vaccinations, evaluation of cold and flu symptoms, and treatment for less severe physical injuries. Depending on the type of facility, the primary provider may be a physician, nurse practitioner, or physician assistant. Patients are attracted to walk-in clinics for several reasons: access to a professional medical provider, the convenience of seeing a provider without a long wait time for an appointment, the convenience of seeing a provider outside normal, weekday clinic hours, and the knowledge that most health insurance will cover such visits. The convenience and flexibility are important attractions for many millennials—a group that may not have a regular primary care provider and a group more likely to have acute, episodic problems rather than chronic health issues.

Some concerns about walk-in clinics have been expressed. There are many benefits of having a regular provider—something that does not occur in walk-in clinics. Access to patient records, which may assist in care, is often unavailable. When clinics are very busy, there may be a long wait time before seeing a provider.

Retail Store Clinics. In the first decade of the twenty-first century, a new treatment option emerged as many retail chain stores and pharmacies opened walk-in clinics. CVS and Walgreens were among the first to establish clinics, and Kroger and Walmart quickly followed. By 2018, there were approximately 2,800 retail clinics around the country (14 times more than a decade earlier).

The typical retail clinic is a small, thin-walled structure built into an existing store. Nurse practitioners and physician assistants rather than physicians are the providers. At first they offered a limited set of services, including screening tests, adult vaccinations, written prescriptions, and treatment for straightforward and simple medical problems such as sinusitis. However, almost all clinics now engage in diagnosis and treatment of patients for chronic conditions such as asthma, hypertension, diabetes, impaired kidney function, and high cholesterol.

Clinics emphasize their convenience to the many shoppers in these stores, that a patient can be seen without an appointment, that many are open in the evenings and on weekends when many physicians' offices are closed, the ease of filling a prescription at the care site, the availability of parking, and the lower charges for services (about one-third of that in a physician's office). Retail store clinics typically emphasize short waiting times for patients—often less than 20 minutes. Few primary care offices are able to do better (Levine and Linder, 2016). About half of the patients at retail clinics lack a regular source of care.

However, some physicians have raised concerns, such as the lack of continuity and comprehensiveness of care, and the fact that the clinics typically see only the uncomplicated and least intensive conditions, which puts more pressure on office and clinic physicians who also see more serious conditions.

In 2019, CVS announced it would test pilot a new concept to de-emphasize retail goods and convert more than 20 percent of its floor space to health treatments provided by nurse practitioners and supplemented by practitioners such as yoga instructors.

Urgent Care Clinics. Urgent care clinics provide services without an appointment and can treat more serious problems than walk-in clinics such as fractures, sprains, and wounds. They offer services such as blood tests, stitching, and X-rays—conditions that would not require an emergency room visit. Developed in the early 1980s to attract patients who need acute episodic care, they are now sometimes viewed as an alternative to the family physician because they offer a stable professional staff, and many are open for extended hours 7 days a week. In 2018, there were about 9,000 of these clinics, and they provided 160 million patient visits. About 50 percent are owned by physicians and about one-third by hospitals.

Ambulatory Surgical Centers (Surgicenters or ASCs). Surgicenters offer minor low-risk outpatient surgery. Today a dramatically increasing percentage of surgeries is performed on an outpatient basis, and much of it in facilities other than hospitals. Almost two-thirds of all surgical procedures are now performed on an outpatient basis, and two-thirds of these (more than 40 percent of all surgeries) are done in a freestanding facility. In 2018, there were more than 5,600 surgicenters in the United States—a 500 percent increase since 1990.

Outpatient surgery performed in offices and clinics and in freestanding facilities is typically less expensive and more convenient than that done in hospitals and takes place in an atmosphere where a higher priority may be given to the physician-patient relationship. The most common outpatient surgeries are cataract surgery, removal of benign tumors, gynecological diagnostic procedures, and minor ear, nose, and throat procedures.

The cost-efficiency of outpatient surgery is traceable to several factors. Hospital stays are extremely expensive. When recovery can occur at home or in a recovery center with minimal staff, less capital investment, and lower overheads, substantial savings result. Surgicenters can also be more cost-effective because they are designed to accommodate only less complex and lower-risk procedures, and thus need not purchase some of the most sophisticated and expensive equipment.

Moreover, ASCs operate with fewer legal regulations, thus eliminating associated costs.

However, hospital-affiliated services have a more readily available emergency backup system and, if necessary, easier transfer to an inpatient unit. An investigation by *Kaiser Health News* and *USA Today* found that surgicenters call 911 thousands of times each year regarding complications ranging from mild to fatal. In the year ending in September 2017, 7,000 patients were transferred from a surgicenter to a hospital following a surgery. No one knows the number of patient deaths because no national organization is responsible for tracing them. But this investigation identified 260 deaths from 2013 to 2017, and some of these occurred in the course of routine procedures such as tonsillectomies (Jewett and Alesia, 2018). Critics charge that some centers perform very risky procedures, overlook high-risk health problems, insufficiently train staff, and sometimes lack lifesaving equipment—all to maximize number of surgeries and profit.

Federally Qualified Health Centers. FQHCs are comprehensive health care programs funded by Section 330 of the Public Health Service Act that provide care for medically underserved populations. The 1,375 clinics operate at more than 11,000 sites, provide more than 110 million patient visits annually, and comprise the following:

- *Community health centers* provide primary care for Americans who are uninsured. They are community based, led by boards of community residents, and include "community health workers" who visit patients in their homes.
- *Migrant health centers* provide health care services for migrant and seasonal agricultural workers.
- *Health care for the homeless programs* provide services for homeless individuals.
- *Public housing primary care programs* are located in and provide services to residents of public housing.

Originally conceived in 1965 as part of the War on Poverty, these centers are located in underserved areas, usually in inner-city neighborhoods and rural areas, and primarily serve uninsured or publicly insured (especially Medicaid) racial and ethnic minorities. Individuals who have purchased a high-deductible health insurance plan (which is the most affordable plan for low-income individuals and families) under the Affordable Care Act have become frequent users of these clinics. Because they have to pay for all of their care until the deductible is reached, they would typically go without care were it not for these clinics.

Care is often provided by nurse practitioners and physician assistants. Services are offered on a sliding-scale fee (i.e., the amount you pay is determined by your income). Studies show that a large majority of the 22 million users each year (at about 9,000 clinics) consider the centers their primary (and sometimes only) source of care. The Affordable Care Act included significant funding to establish new community health centers.

Free Health Clinics. A *free health clinic* movement emerged in the United States in the late 1960s to establish free clinics for people unable to afford private care and/or for those estranged from the conventional medical system. Early clinics targeted people experiencing drug-related illnesses, problem pregnancies, and sexually transmitted infections. They were very much countercultural organizations that highly valued their independence—many even being reluctant to work with each other. They were genuine grassroots clinics started within communities, and they typically worked beside local medical care systems rather than with them.

These clinics evolved from the 1960s and 1970s until today. Their focus has shifted to serving either the very poor or the working poor (i.e., those who are working and are just above the poverty level, but who do not have private health insurance or qualify for Medicaid). Since the inception of the Affordable Care Act, many have modified their eligibility requirements to include those who have high-deductible health insurance. Undocumented immigrants, unable to participate in the health insurance exchanges, often rely on free clinics. Today, in most communities, free clinics are a well-accepted and well-regarded component of the medical system, and they work closely with other medical providers (Weiss, 2006). There are now strong state and regional associations of free clinics, and even a national association (the National Association of Free and Charitable Clinics). The free clinic in Hilton Head, South Carolina, formed in the early 1990s by Dr. Jack McConnell, has created a related organization—Volunteers in Medicine—to assist other communities in establishing free clinics. By 2016, they had helped establish 95 free clinics around the country.

Although there are many variations in the more than 1,200 free clinics nationally, most (1) offer primary health care services; (2) are staffed largely by volunteer physicians, other health care providers, and laypeople (about 90 percent of services are provided by volunteers); (3) serve

people who are unable to afford private medical care; and (4) provide an atmosphere that emphasizes treating each patient with dignity and a supportive, non-judgmental attitude. Many medical schools facilitate their students volunteering at a free clinic, and many now offer their own on-site, student-run free clinic (Fernandez, Kraus, and Olson, 2017). They have become a very important component of the health care system in the communities where they are located, and often receive tremendous support from the professional medical community.

Free clinics provide care to approximately 4 million patients annually. In addition, many have helped set up networks of local physicians who, rather than volunteering at a free clinic, accept free patient referrals from a free clinic in their own office. Financial support comes from several sources, including local and state governments, United Way, corporate donations, church groups, private donations, contributions (often in kind) from the medical community, and patient donations (Weiss, 2006). The accompanying box, "Focus on a Free Health Clinic," describes the evolution of one particular free clinic.

Free clinics emerged in the 1960s, but their numbers have increased rapidly in the last two decades as a community-based means of providing health care for the working poor.

Source: Photo by Gregory Weiss.

IN THE FIELD

FOCUS ON A FREE HEALTH CLINIC

The Bradley Free Clinic in Roanoke, Virginia, was established in 1974 with US$250 in seed money, one volunteer physician, one volunteer nurse, and the free rental of the first floor of an old house (donated by the adjacent church). With the dedication of a small group of concerned citizens and the energy and enthusiasm of a barely paid director, the clinic was able to offer free health services to the local medically indigent 2 nights per week. The commitment of the director and volunteers was noticed in the medical community, by other lay volunteers, and by local governments—important factors in the clinic's subsequent support.

From that beginning, the clinic now provides more than 14,000 patient visits annually at no charge, prescribes more than 25,000 medications (almost all of which are given at no charge out of the clinic's own pharmacy, filled mostly with drugs donated by pharmaceutical companies and local physicians), offers extensive dental services (mostly out of its own fully modern dental operatories supplied by donations from dental equipment companies and local dentists),

provides countless hours of mental health counseling (by local professionals volunteering their time), and performs basic laboratory tests (in its own small laboratory of mostly donated equipment). The clinic is located in its own medical building (purchased with funds from a US$1 million donation by a local philanthropist). The estimated value of annual services provided is more than US$4 million (Weiss, 2006). For every dollar contributed to the clinic, it provides US$4 worth of medical care.

Supplementing a small paid staff are a host of volunteers—more than 250 primary care physicians, dentists, nurses, pharmacists, laboratory technicians, pharmacy and dental assistants, mental health counselors, and medical students who volunteer some time at the clinic, plus 50 specialists who accept free referrals of clinic patients, and scores of lay volunteers. Care is provided at no charge in an atmosphere of respect for the dignity of each patient. By 2015 the Bradley Free Clinic had provided care valued at more than US$60 million.

Reasons for the Emergence of New Ambulatory Care Sites. The emergence of these ambulatory care sites is rooted in several changes within society and the medical profession. Like so many other changes, these new sites represent efforts to offer health care at a lower cost (walk-in clinics, retail clinics, and surgicenters) or to deter the medically indigent from using hospital emergency rooms as a primary care provider (Federally Qualified Health Centers and free health clinics). Lowell-Smith links the development of walk-in clinics and surgicenters (and now retail clinics) to other factors:

Patient-consumers have become more mobile and thus less likely to establish a long term relationship with a physician. Patient-consumers have also become

more knowledgeable in terms of their health needs and thus less likely to rely solely on the advice of a physician. In addition, there is the rise of convenience as a "cultural value." This desire for health care when the patient wants it rather than when the physician is available has aided the growth of walk-in clinics and outpatient surgery centers. . . . [Also] improvements in medical technology have made it possible for many tests and procedures to be performed outside the hospital and in ambulatory settings.

(Lowell-Smith, 1994:277)

NURSING HOMES

A *nursing home* is a long-term residential facility that provides nursing and other therapeutic and rehabilitation care services. Nursing homes serve mainly incapacitated elderly residents, but also some younger adults with significant physical or mental health problems. In 2018, there were about 1.4 million residents of the nation's 15,600 nursing homes. Almost all residents are age 65 or older—about 6 percent of adults 65 and older live in nursing homes. Around 70 percent of residents are women, and 70 percent of them are widowed, divorced, or never married. Dementia is a common problem, with between 50 and 75 percent of residents exhibiting signs of dementia.

Residential care facilities like nursing homes were first developed in the early 1800s. Prior to then, communities offered only almshouses in which incapacitated elderly were placed with the homeless, mentally ill, and chronically inebriated. However, women's and church groups, concerned that some elderly members of their own social class, ethnicity, or religion might end up in the almshouses, began to establish benevolent care centers. These early nursing homes often required a substantial entrance fee and credentials showing good character, and thus were limited to a rather small number (Foundation Aiding the Elderly, 2016).

Throughout the 1800s, communities established a variety of residential facilities such as orphanages, hospitals for the acutely ill, and mental health hospitals, and many residents of the almshouses were moved to more specialized facilities. In this way, the incapacitated elderly became a much larger percentage in almshouses. By the 1930s, society recognized that many elderly people were permanently unable to care for themselves and that an improved system of residential care facilities was necessary. Nursing homes, as we think of them today, grew in number through the middle years of the 1900s and received a significant boost with the passage of Medicare and Medicaid in the 1960s. As the number of homes continued to increase, so did government concern about their quality, and the last 20 years have been marked by increased inspection and required compliance with safety

and quality guidelines (Foundation Aiding the Elderly, 2016).

Types of Nursing Homes

The two main types of nursing homes are "skilled nursing facilities" and "intermediate care facilities." Skilled nursing centers are for residents who require ongoing medical care, such as respiratory therapy, physical therapy, occupational therapy, a feeding tube, or dialysis. These centers are staffed by registered nurses or licensed practical nurses who are available 24 hours a day. Intermediate care facilities basically provide residents with assistance in performing life's daily activities, such as feeding, personal hygiene, toileting, and bathing. These facilities are staffed primarily by certified nursing assistants, many of whom work part-time and for very low wages. The term "nursing home" may also include "assisted living centers," in which seniors live on their own but receive assistance with meals, housekeeping, and medication, and "independent living centers," in which seniors basically live on their own and care for themselves but have someone to check in on them periodically and provide transportation.

Benefits of Nursing Homes

High-quality nursing homes provide a safe, healthy, and stimulating environment for seniors who are not able to live a fully independent life. In addition to basic necessities, they offer programs to help residents avoid loneliness, boredom, and helplessness. The availability of various types of nursing homes means that seniors can receive whatever services are necessary to maximize their independence.

Concerns About Nursing Homes

When nursing homes are of less than high quality, they create living conditions that may be unsafe, unhealthy, and without the desired mental simulation. The Centers for Medicare and Medicaid Services, which conducts periodic evaluations of nursing home quality, rates each home from 1 star (lowest quality) to 5 stars (highest quality). In 2015, 22 percent of nursing homes received 5 stars and 23 percent received 4 stars, but 19 percent received 3 stars, 20 percent received to 2 stars, and 16 percent received 1 star. Thus, more than half were outside the top two levels. In general, non-profits were rated highest, followed by government-owned, followed by the for-profits (Boccuti, Casillas, and Neuman, 2015).

Among the identified concerns in the low-rated nursing homes are:

1. *Neglect.* When the number of staff members is insufficient, staff are not properly trained, or there is an absence of commitment to high-quality care, residents can have problems ranging from medication errors to bedsores, dehydration, and intense boredom.
2. *Abuse.* Periodically, social scientific or clinical research or journalistic exposés uncover cases in which nursing home residents have been abused physically, mentally, or pharmaceutically (e.g., by overuse of antipsychotic medication).
3. *Accidents.* Especially in understaffed homes, residents can be vulnerable to serious accidents (e.g., falls and burns).
4. *The high price of care.* In 2018 it was estimated that the median daily cost of a private room in a nursing home had reached over US$280—that is, about US$8,400 a month or more than US$100,000 per year. Assisted living care averaged about US$48,000 per year. Few individuals or families can afford such extraordinary costs. It has become quite common for individuals to intentionally deplete almost all of their financial resources in order to qualify for Medicaid, because Medicaid pays for long-term care, while Medicare does not. Medicaid is the primary payer for more than 60 percent of nursing home residents. These payments consume nearly a third of Medicaid expenditures, and are a major financial issue for states and federal government.

HOSPICES

The term *hospice* refers to a philosophy of providing care and comfort to people during the dying process. As far back as the eleventh century, the word was used to identify guesthouses and places of shelter for sick and weary travelers. During the 1960s, British physician Dr. Cicely Saunders developed a modern approach to hospice emphasizing professional caregiving and the use of modern pain management techniques to compassionately care for the dying. She worked with others in establishing St. Christopher's Hospice near London, a hospice that significantly influenced the creation of other hospices around the world. The first hospice in the United States was established in New Haven, Connecticut, in 1974.

Hospice has evolved from offering services only on-site in its own locations to offering services within hospitals, nursing homes, and especially in the patient's own home. Surveys indicate that a very large percentage of Americans would prefer to die in their own home. Nationally, only about 25 percent of deaths occur in the home, but about 44 percent of hospice patients die there. There were approximately 4,400 Medicare-certified hospices in the United States in 2016, and they are located in every state. Hospices range in size from small all-volunteer staffs who provide services for fewer than 50 patients per year to large multi-hospice providers that serve several thousand people each day. In 2016, an estimated 1.43 million patients received hospice care, including around 1 million who died that year. Others were still in hospice care at the end of the year or had returned to curative care (National Hospice and Palliative Care Organization, 2018). About 50 percent of all people who died in 2016 were under the care of a hospice at the time of their death.

Benefits of Hospice.   Hospice services are available only to patients who have been attested by two physicians to be in the last 6 months of life. Hospices regard the dying process as a normal part of life. They attempt to make patients as comfortable and pain-free as possible during these months, and they do not do anything to hasten or postpone death. The median time under hospice care in 2016 was 24 days, and the mean time was 71 days. Contrary to popular perception, hospice patients on average live 1 month longer than comparable patients who do not receive hospice care.

Hospice staff may include physicians, nurses, social workers, counselors, home health care aides, clergy, therapists (physical, occupational, massage, recreational, music, art, pet, etc.), dietitians, and volunteers. The services offered to patients and their families include (The Hospice Foundation, 2019):

- Knowledge about medical care and the dying process offered by specially trained professionals, volunteers, and families working in a team approach
- Addressing all symptoms of disease, but with a special emphasis on controlling the patient's pain and discomfort (i.e., palliative care) and treating the patient with concern and dignity
- Dealing with the emotional, social, and spiritual needs of patients and their families
- Offering bereavement and counseling services to families before and after a patient's death.

Hospices provide many services for terminally ill patients and their families, including care and comfort, pain management, physical and emotional support, and grief counseling

Source: Photo by Janet Jonas.

Payment for hospice services is covered by Medicare, Medicaid, and many private health insurers. Hospices work with uninsured patients to determine whether they might qualify for any insurance or financial assistance. Often patients do qualify for this, and if they do not, many hospices will accept them anyway.

Beginning in the 1980s, some hospices converted to an "open-access" model in which terminally ill patients could continue to receive chemotherapy and other curative treatments even while being under hospice care. In part this model was inspired by some AIDS patients who wanted to receive hospice care but also wanted to continue trying other medical options. The Affordable Care Act passed in 2010 directed the Children's Health Insurance Program and Medicaid to immediately cover simultaneous medical care and hospice care for children with terminal illnesses (O'Reilly, 2010).

Several factors have contributed to the growth of hospices in the United States. These include the increasing number of older people who are experiencing and dying from chronic and painful illnesses, the difficulties for patients and their families of contemplating a long dying process, the increasing cultural value of "death with dignity," popular support for the humaneness of the hospice philosophy, the willingness of Medicare to pay for most hospice expenses, and recently, the commitment of veterans' hospitals to offer high-quality hospice care. In addition, quality assessment surveys sent to survivors of hospice patients have shown very high rates of satisfaction with hospice.

Concerns About the Future of Hospice. Although hospice has become an increasingly popular concept and program in the United States, there are pockets of resistance. Some individuals are uncomfortable with any approach that conflicts with doing everything possible to prolong life. The acceptance of death and the dying process that is part of hospice is objectionable to them.

Some hospice enthusiasts strongly prefer the original model of hospice as "an antiestablishment, largely volunteer movement advocating a gentle death as an alternative to the medicalized death many people had come to dread" (Henig, 2005:3). The open-access model, in which patients may be receiving various forms of high-technology care concurrently with hospice care, seems to be a contradiction to the kind of serene environment on which hospice was grounded.

This concern is amplified by the fact that ownership of hospice is shifting rapidly from the non-profit to the for-profit sector. The hospice movement was entirely non-profit in its origin, and as late as 1983 all US hospices were non-profit or government owned. However, by 2016, about 67 percent of all hospice ownership was for profit (29 percent non-profit and 4 percent government). The shift toward for-profit ownership has stimulated higher costs and significantly increased Medicare spending for hospice. In 2011, the nation's fastest-growing for-profit hospice owner agreed to pay US$12.5 million to settle Medicare fraud claims, and in 2013 the nation's largest for-profit hospice owner was sued by the Department of Justice for tens of millions of dollars in Medicare fraud (billing for ineligible patients and inflated services). Discussion of profit margins, productivity adjustments, and market efficiencies seems to many to clash with the original ideals of hospice.

Finally, there is some controversy as to whether or not hospice eliminates any need for euthanasia. Some supporters contend that the pain management and emotional support offered in hospice mean that no one should have to suffer through the dying process and that euthanasia should never be necessary. Other supporters of hospice care argue that, in some cases, relieving significant pain can be very difficult and can only be accomplished through heavy sedation, and some dying patients also experience other unpleasant emotions such as frustration with confinement and psychic pain accompanying the loss of independence and body control. They contend that some of these patients may still prefer euthanasia. This issue, like the others discussed, will be very interesting to watch in the next decade.

HOME HEALTH CARE

Informal Home Health Care

Prior to the widespread development of hospitals and nursing homes, most people with illness and disability were cared for at home by family members. As formal organizations developed for taking care of those needing assistance with basic daily tasks, the family and family setting became somewhat less important. However, people have always relied on *home health care*, and it has once again become more common. About 1 in 5 US households provides informal caregiving for a person aged 18 years or older.

Almost all care for minor illnesses is provided without formal entry into the health care system. Symptoms are monitored, activity may be restricted, medications are taken, and special attention may be given to eating nutritious foods and taking in fluids. These situations may involve temporary inconvenience to family caregivers, but they are typically short term. More intensive home care is provided for people with chronic illnesses, mental, intellectual and other disabilities, and for those who are dying.

Informal home care offers many important benefits. It can be very personal and nurturing, there is continuity of care, and it is usually not as isolating as institutional care. The very high cost of care in hospitals and nursing homes is avoided.

However, there can be disadvantages. Some families are not able to provide the necessary medical or daily living assistance or nurturance. Some family members may be resentful about giving their time, energy, and resources to caring for another. Because this resentment may be difficult or awkward to express, inner tensions may develop that are ultimately vented by verbal or physical abuse.

Even when the caregiving is provided without resentment, the emotional burden can be great. Caregivers often become very stressed, develop health problems of their own, and many are not aware of effective coping and social support techniques. Many communities do have caregiver support groups, but some caregivers are unaware of them or are too physically and emotionally tired to participate. About one-third of caregivers describe their own health as fair to poor.

In addition, family caregiving tends not to be evenly distributed among family members. Studies confirm that in most families the adult woman assumes the caring/nursing role, even if she is employed and despite other commitments outside the home. Employed mothers report three times as many hours missed from work due to family illness as are reported by employed fathers.

The federal and some state governments have taken notice of this situation. Legislation has been passed to give family caregivers paid leave from work. Through the National Family Caregiver Support Program, the federal government now gives state and local governments funding to pass on to families in the form of services and support. Some states have created programs to work with patients as they prepare for discharge from the hospital, to plan for home health care.

Formal Home Health Care

Formal home health care services began 100 years ago with the Visiting Nurse Society of New York. Other home care agencies developed over the years, but by the mid-1960s there were just 1,300 such agencies in all of the United States. The enactment of Medicare in 1965 spurred phenomenal growth in the home care industry—to more than 9,000 Medicare-certified agencies today, which provide about US$60 billion annually of formal home health care. More than 8 million individuals currently receive home care services for acute illness, chronic health conditions, permanent disability, or terminal illness.

About two-thirds of these patients are women, and about two-thirds are aged 65 years or older.

More than 50 percent of the nation's 2 million home care workers are home care aides. Registered nurses constitute the second largest group—about 20 percent of the total—but the field also includes many licensed practical nurses, physical therapists, occupational therapists, social workers, and others. To date, physician involvement in home health care has been minimal. However, physicians are being called upon more frequently to participate in the planning and management of elderly patients at home, and many hospitals have initiated home care departments.

The largest payer for home health care is Medicare (about 37 percent of total payments), but Medicaid and state and local governments (both 19 percent of the total) are also significant payers. About 12 percent of payments are made by private insurers. Over the last 10 years, home health care has become extraordinarily profitable, in part because wages for entry-level home care aides are among the lowest in the health care field.

Several factors are responsible for the growth of this industry, including the increased number of elderly people with chronic conditions, the lower costs associated with home health care compared with institutional care, cost-containment efforts by private insurers and the government that have led to earlier hospital discharges of sicker patients, and significant movement into home health care by large companies, especially health insurers.

Research shows that home health care reduces ER visits, reduces hospital stays, and dramatically reduces costs. The Medicare Payment Advisory Commission reported in 2015, the average Medicare payment was US$18,361 per stay at a skilled nursing facility, US$19,116 per stay at an inpatient rehabilitation center, and US$40,718 at a long-term acute-care hospital, but only US$2,742 per home health care episode (The Medicare Payment Advisory Commission, 2019).

SUMMARY

The sites in which health care services are delivered continue to change with the development of modern medical technology in response to high medical costs and as a result of demands for more convenient services. Although hospitals continue to be a central part of the system, the numbers of hospitals and hospital beds have decreased as cost-containment efforts and managed care have stimulated efforts to deliver care at lower cost. Hospitals today face several critical issues—the relative contributions of for-profit versus not-for-profit hospitals, the survival of public hospitals, the move from inpatient to outpatient services, making more efficient use of the emergency room, new penalties for Medicare readmissions, and the curbing of medical errors.

Ambulatory care is still most often delivered through physicians' offices or clinics. However, the number of freestanding ambulatory care and surgical facilities has increased dramatically in recent years, especially walk-in centers, retail store sites, and surgicenters that appeal to young and middle-aged adults and people without a regular source of care. The number of Federally Qualified Health Centers and free health clinics, which are designed to serve the poor and medically indigent, has also increased in recent years.

The importance of nursing homes within the health care delivery system has increased significantly. When they perform with high quality, they provide a safe, healthy, and mentally stimulating environment for seniors. However, many nursing homes are consistently low-quality performers, and there are serious concerns about neglect, abuse, accidents, and high costs.

Hospice care offers comfort, concern, and palliative care to terminally ill patients. The concept has been very positively received, and many people now enter hospice care during the last days or months of life. Nevertheless, there are concerns about how the large-scale entry of for-profit companies into hospice ownership will affect this model.

Home health care is experiencing a revitalization as the population continues to age and the demands for lower-cost services increase. Home care is much less expensive than hospital and nursing home services. It offers many benefits to patients and their families but also carries with it some important concerns.

HEALTH ON THE INTERNET

1. The American Hospital Association (AHA) is the professional association of hospitals in the United States. One current focus is its "Value Initiative." Log on to this section of the AHA website at:

www.aha.org/value-initiative

Scroll down and click on "Issue Briefs." To get a sense of the AHA's work on this initiative, click on "Framing the Issue of Affordable Health Care." Read this material to answer these two questions: (1) What is meant by affordability? (2) What factors influence affordability?

Return to "Issue Briefs," and click on "What Does Value Mean?" Read this material to answer these two questions: (1) What is the

meaning of "value" in this context? (2) What can be done to improve value?
2. The National Hospice and Palliative Care Organization produced a series of short videos explaining the basics of hospice care. Watch the set of ten short videos, available here:

www.youtube.com/view_play_list?p= BE4D0C4D8E1F663D

Drawing from the videos and text, describe some benefits of hospice care for patients, their families, and the health care system. How is the emergence and growth of hospice similar to the emergence and growth of other ambulatory services? What common issues affect all ambulatory services discussed in this chapter?

DISCUSSION CASE

An important issue within health care systems and one that is discussed both in Chapter 14 and in this chapter relates to the relative benefits of for-profit versus not-for-profit facilities and services. Identify what you consider to be the major advantages and the major disadvantages of for-profit facilities

and the major advantages and disadvantages of not-for-profit facilities. This chapter discusses the fact that hospices are increasingly operated as for-profit companies. Would you expect hospices to change based on the type of ownership? If so, how and why? If not, why not?

GLOSSARY

ambulatory care
charity care

cost shifting
cream skimming

dual line of authority
horizontal integration
hospital consolidation
hospitalist
megamerger
multihospital chains

palliative care
patient dumping
value-based care
vertical integration
walk-in clinics

REFERENCES

Bai, Ge, and Gerard F. Anderson. 2015. "Extreme Markup: The Fifty U.S. Hospitals with the Highest Charge-to-Cost Ratios." *Health Affairs* 34(6):922–928.

———. 2016. "A More Detailed Understanding of Factors Associated with Hospital Profitability." *Health Affairs* 35(5):889–897.

Bannow, Tara. 2019. "Outpatient Revenue Catching Up to Inpatient." *Modern Healthcare* (January 7):6–7.

Berenson, Robert A. 2017. "A Physician's Perspective on Vertical Integration." *Health Affairs* 36(9):1585–1590.

Berenson, Robert A., Paul B. Ginsburg, and Jessica H. May. 2007. "Hospital-Physicians Relations: Cooperation, Competition, or Separation?" *Health Affairs* 26(1):31–43.

Boccuti, Cristina, Giselle Casillas, and Tricia Neuman. 2015. "Reading the Stars: Nursing Home Quality Star Ratings, Nationally by State." *Kaiser Family Foundation*. Retrieved March 8, 2019 (www.kff.org/report-section/reading-the-stars-nursing-home-quality-star-ratings-nationally- and-by-state-issue-brief/.

Centers for Disease Control and Prevention. 2019. "Hospital Statics." *National Center for Health Statistics*. Retrieved March 30, 2019 (www.cdc.gov/nchs/data/hus/2017/082.pdf).

Department of Labor. 1967. *Technology and Manpower in the Health Service Industry*. Washington, DC: Government Printing Office.

Fernandez, Timothy F., Alexandria C. Kraus, and Kristin M. Olson. 2017. "A Call for Residents to Get More Involved with Student-Run Free Clinics." *Academic Medicine* 92(5):577.

Foundation Aiding the Elderly. 2016. "The History of Nursing Homes." Retrieved January 28, 2019 (www.4fate.org/history.pdf).

Giroir, Brett P., and Gail R. Wilensky. 2015. "Reforming the Veterans Administration Hospital—Beyond Palliation of Symptoms." *New England Journal of Medicine* 373(18):1693–1695.

Henig, Robin M. 2005. "Will We Ever Arrive at the Good Death?" *New York Times Magazine*, August 7. Retrieved January 29, 2007 (www.nytimes.com/2005/08/07/magazine/07DYINGL.html).

The Hospice Foundation. 2019. "What Is Hospice?" Retrived March 6, 2019 (www.hospicefoundation.org/whatishospice).

Institute of Medicine. 1999. *To Err is Human: Building a Safer Health Care System*. Washington, DC: National Academy of Sciences.

Jewett, Christina, and Mark Alesia. 2018. "Simple Surgeries: Tragic Results." *USA Today*, March 2, pp. A1,4.

Kenen, Joanne. 2019. "Getting the Facts on Hospital Mergers and Acquisitions." *Association of Health Care Journalists*. Retrieved March 9, 2019 (https://healthjournalism.org/resources-tips-etails.php?id=828#.XOa-fXdFyM8).

Leape, Lucian L., and Donald M. Berwick. 2005. "Five Years After to Err Is Human." *Journal of the American Medical Association* 293(19):2384–2390.

Leape, Lucian L., Miles F. Shore, Jules L. Dienstag, Robert J. Mayer, Susan Edgman-Levitan, Gregg S. Meyer, and Gerald B. Healy. 2012. "Perspective: A Culture of Respect, Part 1: The Nature and Causes of Disrespectful Behavior by Physicians." *Academic Medicine* 87(7):845–852.

Levine, David M., and Jeffrey A. Linder. 2016. "Retail Clinics Shine a Harsh Light on the Failure of Primary Care Access." *Journal of General Internal Medicine* 31(3):260–262.

Light, Donald W. 1986. "Corporate Medicine for Profit." *Scientific American* 255(6):38–45.

Lowell-Smith, Elizabeth G. 1994. "Alternative Forms of Ambulatory Care: Implications for Patients and Physicians." *Social Science and Medicine* 38(2):275–283.

Makary, Martin A., and Michael Daniel. 2016. "Medical Error—The Third Leading Cause of Death in the U.S." *British Medical Journal* 2016;353:i2139.

The Medicare Payment Advisory Payment Commission. 2019. "Medicare Spending and Financing." Retrieved

March 5, 2019 (http://medpac.gov/-research-areas-/medicare-spending-and-financing).

Nanji, Karen C., Amit Patel, Sofia Shaikh, Diane L. Seger, and David W. Bates. 2016. "Evaluation of Perioperative Medication Errors and Adverse Drug Events." *Anesthesiology* 124(1):25–34.

National Center for Health Statistics. 2018. *Health, United States, 2017.* Hyattsville, MD: US Department of Health and Human Services.

National Hospice and Palliative Care Organization. 2018. *NHPCO's Facts and Figures: Hospice Care in America.* Alexandria, VA: NHPCO.

Ofstead, Cori L., Otis L. Heymann, Mariah R. Quick, John E. Eiland, and Harry P. Wetzler. 2018. "Residual Moisture and Waterborne Pathogens Inside Flexible Endoscopes: Evidence from a Multisite Study of Endoscope Drying Effectiveness." *American Journal of Infection Control* 46(6):689–696.

O'Malley, Ann S. 2013. "After-Hours Access to Primary Care Practices Linked with Lower Emergency Department Use and Less Unmet Medical Need." *Health Affairs* 32(1):175–183.

O'Reilly, Kevin B. 2010. "Medicare to Test Allowing More than Palliative Care in Hospice." *American Medical News.* Retrieved March 12, 2019 (www.ama-assn.org/amednews/2010/05/24/prsb0524.htm).

Pitts, Stephen R., Emily R. Carrier, Eugene C. Rich, and Arthur L. Kellermann. 2010. "Where Americans Get Acute Care: Increasingly, It's Not at Their Doctor's Office." *Health Affairs* 29(9):1620–1629.

Pronovost, Peter and Eric Vohr. 2010. *Safe Patients, Smart Hospitals: How One Doctor's Checklist Can Help Us Save Health Care from the Inside Out.* New York: Hudson Street Press.

Rosenberg, Charles E. 1987. *The Care of Strangers: The Rise of America's Hospital System.* New York: Basic Books.

Rudowitz, Robin, Diana Rowland, and Adele Shartzer. 2006. "Health Care in New Orleans Before and After Hurricane Katrina." *Health Affairs* 25(2):393–406.

Slack, Donovan, and Andrea Estes. 2019. "Vets Harmed Under VA Care." *USA Today*, March 29, pp. 1–2.

Todd, Susan. 2015. "10 Years After Katrina, New Orleans Has Transformed Primary Care, Behavioral Health." *Modern Healthcare* 45:27.

Wadhera, Rishi K., Karen E. Maddox, Jason H. Wasfy, Sebastien Haneuse, Changyu Shen, and Robert W. Yeh. 2018. "Association of the Hospital Readmissions Reduction Program with Mortality Among Medicare Beneficiaries Hospitalized for Heart Failure, Acute Myocardial Infarction, and Pneumonia." *Journal of the American Medical Association* 320(24):2542–2552.

Weiss, Gregory L. 2006. *Grass Roots Medicine: The Story of America's Free Health Clinics.* Lanham, MD: Rowman and Littlefield.

Wilensky, Gail R. 2016. "The VA Continues to Struggle—Especially in Terms of Improved Access." *Milbank Quarterly* 94(3):452–455.

Wilson, Jennifer F. 2006. "Health and the Environment after Hurricane Katrina." *Annals of Internal Medicine* 144(2):153–156.

Young, Gary Y, Stephen Flaherty, E. David Zepeda, Simone R. Singh, and Geri R. Cramer. 2018. "Community Benefit Spending by Tax-Exempt Hospitals Changed Little After HCA." *Health Affairs* 37(1):121–124.

CHAPTER 16

The Social Implications of Advanced Health Care Technology

Learning Objectives

- Identify seven key recent advancements in medical technology.

- Identify and discuss five important social implications of rapidly developing medical technology.

- Explain the key arguments for and against patients being able to demand and refuse medical treatment. Identify and explain the

- key arguments for and against the legality of physician-aid-in-dying.

- Discuss the key options for organ donation policy and the strengths and limitations of each.

- Identify and describe four modern assisted procreative techniques. Identify and explain the key arguments for and against the legality of surrogate motherhood.

The development of **technology**—the practical application of scientific or other forms of knowledge—is a major stimulus for social change in most modern societies. Western cultures subscribe to a belief system that prioritizes "technical rationality"—a mindset in which "essentially all problems are seen as manageable with technical solutions, and rationality (reasonableness, plausibility, proof) can be established only through scientific means using scientific criteria" (Barger-Lux and Heaney, 1986:1314). Many social scientists believe that technology is not only influenced by cultural values but in return has a powerful and deterministic effect on culture and social structure—a theory known as **technological determinism**.

Today's health care system reflects the rapid rate of technological innovation in the last few decades. Hospitals and medical clinics contain sophisticated pieces of equipment and specially trained personnel to operate them. The benefits of advanced health care technologies are apparent, including more accurate and quicker diagnoses, effective treatment modalities, and increased life expectancy. However, there are also negative consequences of technological innovations, including increased costs, inequities of access, technological "advancements" that fail (e.g., the artificial heart), and challenging ethical issues (Chang and Lauderdale, 2009).

SOCIETAL CONTROL OF TECHNOLOGY

Advocates view technological development as a means for society to fulfill its needs and create a better life for its citizens. The need for more powerful means of information storage and processing produced the computer revolution. The need for faster food preparation techniques for on-the-go families led to the microwave oven. Automobile air bags are a safety innovation in a society where thousands lose their lives each year in traffic accidents. According to this view (sometimes referred to as a utopian view), society controls the introduction of new technologies, and technological advancements continue because they are beneficial to society.

Others, however, are concerned that technologies also create problems (sometimes referred to as a dystopian view). They critique modern societies (especially the United States) for a failure to systematically assess potential technologies in order to determine whether or not they should be pursued. Instead, American society is said to be controlled by a **technological imperative**—the idea that "if we have the technological capability to do something, then we should do it . . . [it] implies that action in the form of the use of an available technology is always preferable to inaction" (Freund and McGuire, 1999:243).

This technological imperative is clearly demonstrated in medicine—in the desire of individual physicians to perform the newest and most sophisticated procedures (even if more conservative treatment would be just as appropriate), in health insurance companies' greater willingness to pay for high-tech medicine rather than low-tech or non-tech care, and in the march of hospitals to create (and thus be forced to use) high-tech wards (e.g., coronary intensive care units), even when they are shown not to offer any consistent advantage over more conservative, low-tech, and less expensive forms of treatment (Barger-Lux and Heaney, 1986; Freund and McGuire, 1999). Historian David Rothman argues that the middle class's insistence of having unfettered access to medical technologies has been the most important influence on America's health policy for at least the last 60 years (Rothman, 1997).

HEALTH CARE TECHNOLOGY

The pace of technological development in the last few decades has been phenomenal. Key advancements during these years include:

1. *Critical care medicine.* Significant advances have been made in handling intensive care unit (ICU) cardiopulmonary patients (those with insufficient heart and lung capacity). An estimated 20 percent of all hospital patients require some form of respiratory therapy or support, including administration of oxygen to patients who cannot maintain adequate oxygen levels in their blood with their own breathing, performance of physical therapy to break up secretions and mucus in the lungs, and mechanical ventilation for patients unable to breathe on their own.
2. *Cardiac care medicine.* Important innovations include the cardiac pacemaker (which senses the heart's electrical activity and paces it appropriately), the defibrillator (which maintains the rhythmic contractions of the heart to avoid a "heart attack"), increasingly successful heart bypass surgery, and heart transplants.
3. *Cancer care medicine.* Important advances are occurring in the use of blood tests to identify hard-to-find cancers, and new immunotherapy cancer vaccines that trigger the body's immune system to fight cancer cells.
4. *Genomic medicine.* Whereas genetics examines single genes and their function, **genomic medicine** examines the interaction of multiple genes with each other and with the environment. Many diseases, including breast and colorectal cancers, HIV/AIDS, Parkinson's disease, and Alzheimer's disease, can best be understood and addressed using this multifactorial approach.
5. *Personalized medicine.* Based on genetic information (a test that does personal genetic sequencing), medications can be developed for each individual rather than using today's one-size-fits-all approach. These are expected to be extremely expensive but more effective.

6. *Medical imaging.* Non-invasive techniques such as nuclear medicine, ultrasound, computer tomography (CT; also called computerized axial tomography, or CAT), and magnetic resonance imaging (MRI) allow visualization of internal organs. Recent advances provide even more information about bodily tissues.

7. *Health care computers (information technology).* Computers are used throughout the modern health care facility—in the clinical laboratory, in instrumentation, in building patient databases, and in diagnostic support systems. Some analysts believe that in the near future tens of millions of Americans will wear wireless monitoring devices that automatically send vital signs to medical professionals—an extension of devices that now provide automatic fall detection. See the accompanying box, "Telemedicine."

IN THE FIELD

TELEMEDICINE

The information superhighway has created many new opportunities for obtaining, sharing, and discussing information. Research has found that more than 85 percent of physicians and 72 percent of adults in the United States use the Internet for health-related information retrieval (Pew Internet Health Tracking Survey, 2014). Twenty-six states have passed legislation that requires private insurers to cover services that are provided through **telemedicine**. Medicare covers telemedicine, and Medicaid compensates for telemedicine in 48 states. Listed here are some to of the ways in which the Internet is affecting health care.

• Patients can make "virtual" visits to their own physician via a smartphone or online video connection. Many patients find this more convenient than going to a clinic, less expensive, and just as effective for minor health problems. It also enables physicians to see more patients, although quality issues remain a concern. If one's own physician does not provide virtual visits, a patient can contact a "cyberdoc" who has established a website or signed on with a virtual medical company.

• Home health care workers "virtually" visit patients through visual monitors, and they can even check the patient's heart rate (the patient uses a stethoscope, and the nurse uses a headset attached to the computer).

More than 30 states now allow doctors to treat patients and to prescribe drugs online without any personal contact.

• Patients can directly retrieve information health information from Web sources. This reduces the traditional dominance of the physician as gatekeeper to medical knowledge. However, because well-educated middle- and upper-income individuals have the most Internet access, they will continue to obtain the most information. Medical journals can place abstracts or full text of articles on the Internet.

• An estimated 325,000 smartphone health care applications (mHealth) are now available, and they were downloaded an estimated 3.7 billion times worldwide in 2017. mHealth generally refers to any use of mobile telecommunication technologies for the delivery of health care and in support of wellness (Steinhubl, Muse, and Topol, 2013). Especially popular is Epocrates, a drug reference tool that has been consulted by about 1 million health care providers. Some of the apps now come with medical devices, such as an ultrasound wand, in anticipation that eventually a physical examination could be performed virtually.

• The reading of diagnostic tests is sometimes "outsourced" to a physician in another country ("teleradiology"). For example, if a patient in the United States undergoes an emergency

(Continued)

(Continued)

brain scan in the middle of the night, the scan can be electronically sent to a physician—perhaps in India or Australia—for interpretation rather than calling a radiologist into the hospital. Health education online games are being created for children and adolescents to teach them about healthy lifestyles and the importance of taking prescribed medications.

• Public health departments and other health groups make frequent use of social media to provide information, recruit research volunteers, and support healthy lifestyles.

• Electronic support groups ("e-health") and Internet Support Groups (ISGs) are now available for thousands of diseases and conditions and millions of Americans. Research has identified benefits for users, especially for those who create health information through blogging and contributing to social networking on health topics (Oosterveen et al., 2017).

• Electronic mail can be used to enhance communication, especially for those located in rural areas. In 2018, there were about 200 telemedicine networks in the United States connecting to around 3,000 largely rural sites for medical education and consultations.

• Online physician "report cards" are now available, enabling patient evaluations of medical care providers.

• Educational courses can be offered on the Internet to bring more public health information to health professionals and patients in developing countries.

Assessment of these interventions is still in the early stages, but promising results have been obtained. Studies (e.g., Polinski et al., 2016) have discovered very high satisfaction among patients with a telemedicine experience and many even preferring it to an actual visit. Several studies highlight the potential for cost savings. However, it is clear that the accuracy and quality of online health information can vary widely, so some questions remain, and consumers must always be very careful when selecting sites (Chou, Oh, and Klein, 2018).

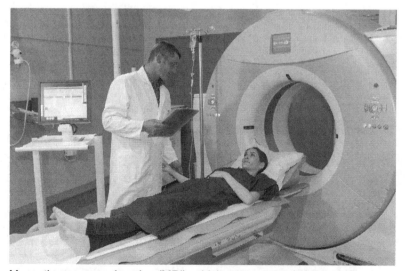

Magnetic resonance imaging (MRI), which uses magnetic fields, radio-wave energy, and sophisticated computer software, creates clearer, more detailed pictures of internal organs. MRI machines can cost up to US$3 million, and an average price per MRI may exceed US$3,000.

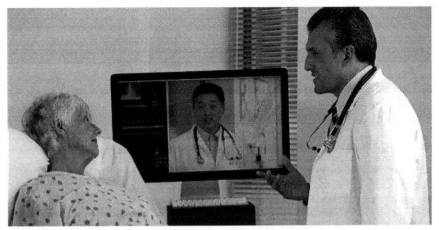

Medical teleconferencing is one of many new forms of telemedicine.

The Social Implications of Advanced Health Care Technology

Advanced health care technologies have many social implications.

First, they create options for people and society that did not previously exist. These range from sustaining a life that once would have expired to creating life through assisted procreation.

Second, they alter human relationships. Technology that is capable of sustaining life after consciousness has been permanently lost have led to family discussions about members' personal wishes, and have created difficult decisions for family members of patients whose wishes are unknown. Physicians and other health care professionals also now engage family members in discussions about "DNR" ("do not resuscitate") or "no code" options.

Many people are concerned that the emergence of advanced health care technologies has led to a dehumanization of patient care. Patients complain that physicians concentrate so much on the disease (in anticipation of selecting the appropriate technology) that they lose sight of the patient as a person. Some patients despair that the warmth and empathy demonstrated by physicians in the pre-high-tech era are being lost (Barger-Lux and Heaney, 1986). Discussion today

of "cyberdocs," "robodocs," and "virtual doctors" reflects the use of modern computer wizardry in medicine, but also suggests to many an increasingly distant physician–patient relationship.

Renée Anspach's ethnographic work *Deciding Who Lives: Fateful Choices in the Intensive-Care Nursery* (Anspach, 1993) illustrates this concern. Anspach discovered that the different ways in which physicians and nurses relate to infants in an intensive care (IC) nursery affect their medical interpretations. Physicians, who have more limited contact with the infants and whose interaction is primarily technologically focused, rely on diagnostic technology to develop prognoses. Nurses, whose contact with the infants is more continuous, long-term, and emotional, develop prognoses more on the basis of their interaction and observations. While Anspach does not suggest that either prognostic technique is superior to the other, her analysis demonstrates that one's position in the social structure of the nursery influences one's perceptions and that, to a certain extent, technology may "distance" the physician from the patient.

Third, they affect the entire health care system. For example, equipment needed to support the new technologies has been the most important stimulus for the rapid increase in health care costs.

The United States is now realizing that it cannot afford every potentially helpful medical procedure for every patient. Increasing the amount of money spent on health care (already considered by many to be unacceptably high) would mean reducing the amount of money spent on education, the environment, and other areas of government funding. When the government or health insurance companies choose to subsidize new technologies, they are explicitly or implicitly choosing not to subsidize other health care programs.

These macro–allocation decisions have led to sophisticated means of **technology assessment** and cost–benefit analysis—efforts to quantify the outcomes of implementing specific technologies and comparing these outcomes with those expected from other options. For example, should the government fund 50 organ transplant procedures or offer prenatal care to 5,000 low-income women? The accompanying box, "Technology Assessment in Medicine," discusses this process.

IN THE FIELD

TECHNOLOGY ASSESSMENT IN MEDICINE

What is health technology assessment (HTA)? According to Lehoux and Blume (2000:1063), it is "a field of applied research that seeks to gather and synthesize the best available evidence on the costs, efficacy, and safety of health technology." Littenberg (1992:425–427) recommends that any proposed medical technology be assessed on the following five levels:

1. *Biological plausibility* assesses whether "the current understanding of the biology and pathology of the disease in question can support the technology."
2. *Technical feasibility* assesses whether "we can safely and reliably deliver the technology to the target patients."
3. *Intermediate outcomes* assess the immediate and specific "biological, physiologic, or clinical effects of the technology."
4. *Patient outcomes* assess "overall and ultimate outcomes for the health of the patient."
5. *Societal outcomes* assess the external effects of the technology on society, including the ethical and fiscal consequences.

A recent example of technology assessment regards the impact of surgical robots. These robots have received much attention in the popular press, and have become very popular in hospital operating rooms and among hospital marketing staffs. Each year, more than 500,000 robotic surgeries are performed in the United States—mostly on prostate glands and uteruses but also on the heart, colon, kidneys, and other organs. However, a recent research study discovered that 144 deaths, 1,391 injuries, and 8,061 device malfunctions were recorded out of a total of more than 1.7 million robotic procedures carried out from 2000 to 2013 (Alemzadeh, 2016). These robots are, of course, very expensive. The typical cost of a surgical robot is US$2.3 million, with an additional annual requirement of US$135,000 for service fees. Using surgical robots adds an estimated US$3,000–6,000 to each surgery (Wilensky, 2016).

However, most assessment research finds no clear benefit of surgical robots over traditional human hands-on surgery (robotic surgery does require smaller incisions). Perhaps additional benefit will occur as the devices evolve, but so far they seem mostly driven by the technological imperative. As health care cost-consciousness further sets in, medical technology firms will need to offer more systematic assessment and price products more affordably (Robinson, 2015).

Fourth, they stimulate value clarification. Medicine continues to raise issues that force individuals to confront provocative value questions. These decisions include value questions such as the amount of money spent on preventive care versus curative care, the amount of money spent on people near the end of life, the amount of money spent on newborns who will require extensive lifetime care, and the amount of money spent on diseases related to "voluntary lifestyles."

A further example relates to the uses of the knowledge gained by mapping the human genome. This knowledge has dramatically increased our understanding of the link between genes and several specific diseases and may eventually lead to the elimination or control of all genetic diseases. However, this process raises value questions. If all genetic diseases can someday be diagnosed and eliminated during fetal development, will such action be required? Would all prospective parents be required to participate in genetic screening programs? Would it be illegal or immoral to produce a child with an unnecessary genetic disease? Could such a child file a "wrongful life" suit against her or his parents? Who should or would have access to genetic information about individuals? Would an employer have a right to check the genetics background of prospective employees? Would health insurance companies be able to require a genetic check-up when deciding whether or not to offer insurance to someone, or when calculating the cost of the insurance policy?

In addition to using prenatal therapy to correct defective genes, will it be permissible to use therapy to provide genetic enhancements? For example, would it be legal to attempt to "boost" the intelligence gene(s), or would it be ethical to abort any (or even all?) fetuses with low intellectual potential? Should the government subsidize prospective parents who want therapy to produce a taller or shorter offspring? What are the long-term implications for altering the gene pool?

These questions exemplify the difficult value questions created by this new knowledge.

Finally, they create social policy questions. Of course, issues that raise difficult value questions for individuals often raise complicated social policy questions for societies. Critics have charged that legislatures and courts have shaped policy regarding ethical issues in medicine prior to adequate public debate. This situation is beginning to change as these issues are now receiving greater public scrutiny.

An example of these social policy considerations occurs with fetal tissue transplants. The vast majority of abortions are performed in the first trimester by the suction curettage method in which the fetus is removed by suction through a vacuum cannula. While the fetus is fragmented in this procedure, cells within tissue fragments can be collected. In about 10 percent of abortions using suction curettage, the fragment containing the fetal midbrain can be identified and retrieved.

Research has found that transplantation of an aborted fetus's midbrain can relieve or even cure certain diseases, including diabetes, Parkinson's disease, and Alzheimer's disease. A high rate of successful transfer is due partially to the fact that this very immature tissue is unlikely to be rejected by the recipient. In the early 2000s the issue focused on stem cell retrieval. The stem cell is a universal cell in embryos and fetuses that can construct hearts, lungs, brains, and other vital organs and tissues. When retrieved, stem cells can be transformed or molded into any type of organ or tissue. The created organ or tissue would potentially be a cure for a wide range of diseases.

However, fetal tissue and stem cell transplants are opposed by most of those who believe that personhood begins at the instant of conception. Because the fetus or embryo is destroyed in the process of obtaining the tissue or stem cells, they believe that the procedure (even for the purpose of a beneficial result) is an act of complicity in the ending of a human life. Presidents Ronald Reagan and George H. W. Bush placed a moratorium on publicly sponsored research on fetal tissue transplants. President Clinton overturned this ban. President George W. Bush enacted a policy that allowed research on a relatively small number of stem cell lines already in existence but prohibited public support for research on additional lines, thus restricting and reducing research in this area. President Obama issued an executive order restoring publicly funded research.

In addition, it is conceivable that this issue will become moot, as recent research is exploring the possibility of converting adult cells (which can easily be obtained by scraping cells off a person's arm) into stem cells, and in turn shaping the stem cells to become a specific kind of cell. For example, a person with a damaged heart could have adult cells converted into healthy heart cells and inserted to replace the damaged heart cells. This work is in the early stages of testing.

Social Issues Raised by Advancing Health Care Technology

The remainder of this chapter examines three issues that raise questions about the rights of individuals and patients versus the force of technology. Each issue has led to serious discussion of the rights of individuals to access or refuse to access modern medical technology, and of the responsibilities of society to control and regulate use of the technology. Questions involving individual choice versus public good and the means by which medical resources are among the important issues created by ever-more sophisticated medical technology.

Do patients have a legal right to refuse medical treatment, including artificial means of nourishment? Can patients demand a particular medical treatment even if physicians judge it to be futile? Can physicians provide aid-in-dying? Should organ donation policies be revised in order to obtain more organs for transplantation? Should there be more investigation of the ways in which human relationships are altered by decisions to

give and receive an organ? Should assisted procreative techniques be made available to anyone who wants them? Is it proper for society to regulate these techniques and/or even to prohibit them?

THE RIGHT TO REFUSE OR DEMAND ADVANCED HEALTH CARE TECHNOLOGY

Health care technology is at a stage of development in which it is often able to keep people alive but without being able to cure their disease, relieve their pain, or at times, even restore consciousness. As critical care technology (especially the artificial ventilator) was incorporated into hospitals, the traditional practice was to use it whenever possible.

Gradually, however, patients and their families have begun to challenge the unquestioned use of technology and have asked (in the words of the book, play, and film) "Whose life is it anyway?" Patients and/or their proxies have become more assertive in requesting, and sometimes demanding, that technology be withheld or withdrawn. In some circumstances, physicians and hospitals have complied, but in other circumstances they have refused. These situations often end in court hearings, and the courts rather than legislators have primarily dealt with the rights of patients and their families versus the rights of hospitals and physicians to determine the use or refusal of advanced health care technologies.

Do Patients Have a Legal Right to Refuse Medical Treatment?

Do competent patients, and incompetent patients through their representatives, have a right to refuse medical treatment? Or are physicians and hospitals required (or, at least, lawfully able) to use all forms of medical treatment, including high-tech medicine, whenever they deem it appropriate? Three landmark court cases have addressed this issue of "fundamental rights."

Karen Ann Quinlan. In April 1975, 21-year-old Karen Ann Quinlan was brought to a hospital emergency room. She had passed out at a party and temporarily stopped breathing (during which time part of her brain died from lack of oxygen). Blood and urine tests showed that she had consumed only a couple of drinks and a small amount of aspirin and Valium, but that significant brain damage had occurred. Karen was connected to an artificial respirator to enable respiration (see the accompanying box, "Defining Death").

After 4 months, the Quinlans acknowledged that Karen was unlikely ever to regain consciousness, and she would be severely brain damaged if she did. Their priest assured them that the Catholic Church did not require continuation of extraordinary measures to support a hopeless life. The family requested the artificial ventilator be disconnected. The hospital refused, arguing that Karen was alive and it was their moral and legal obligation to sustain her life. The Quinlans went to court asking to be designated as Karen's legal guardians in order that the ventilator could be disconnected. Part of the rationale offered by their attorney was that the Constitution contains an implicit right to privacy, which guarantees that individuals (or people acting on their behalf) can terminate extraordinary medical measures even if death results.

The Superior Court ruled against the Quinlan family, but the case was appealed to the New Jersey Supreme Court, which overruled the prior decision and granted guardianship to

---

IN THE FIELD

DEFINING DEATH

The brain consists of three divisions:

1. The *cerebrum* (with the outer shell called the cortex; also called the "higher brain") is the primary center of consciousness, thought, memory, and feeling; many people believe it is the key to what makes us human—that is, it establishes "personhood."
2. The *brainstem* (also called the "lower brain") is the center of respiration and controls spontaneous functions such as swallowing, yawning, and sleep–wake cycles.
3. The *cerebellum* coordinates muscular movement.

Historically, death was defined as the total cessation of respiration and pulsation. Any destruction of the brainstem would stop respiration, preventing the supply of oxygen to the heart, which would stop pulsation, and death would typically occur within 20 minutes.

This definition was rendered inappropriate by the artificial respirator, which in essence replaces the brainstem. It enables breathing and therefore heartbeat.

In 1968, the "brain death" definition of death was developed at Harvard Medical School. It defines death as a permanently non-functioning whole brain (cerebrum and brainstem), including no reflexes, no spontaneous breathing, no cerebral function, and no awareness of externally applied stimuli. Thus if breathing persists, but only through the use of an artificial respirator, the person is officially dead. Many people today would prefer a higher-brain oriented definition of death such as that suggested by Robert Veatch (1993:23), namely "an irreversible cessation of the capacity for consciousness." One effect of this definition would be that patients in a persistent (or "permanent") vegetative state would be declared dead.

Mr. Quinlan. The court ruled that patients have a constitutionally derived right to privacy that includes the right to refuse medical treatment, and this right extends to competent and incompetent persons.

After a protracted series of events, the respirator was disconnected. When this occurred, surprisingly, Karen began to breathe on her own. It was determined that she was in a **persistent vegetative state (PVS)**. In PVS, the patient is not conscious, is irretrievably comatose, must be nourished artificially, *but* is respiring without technical assistance. This happens when the brainstem is functioning but the cerebrum is not. The eyes are open at times, there are sleep–wake cycles, the pupils respond to light, and gag and cough reflexes are normal. However, the person is completely unconscious and totally unaware of surroundings, and will remain in this state until death (which may not occur for many years). At any one time, about 10,000 people in the United States are in PVS. It is not the same as **brain death**, in which neither the cerebrum nor the brainstem is functioning. To be sustained, patients in PVS require artificial nutrition and hydration but no other forms of medical treatment. To be clear, the court ruled about medical treatment in the Quinlan case—not about nutrition and hydration. Karen was moved to a chronic care institution, where she continued breathing for 10 years before expiring.

Nancy Cruzan. Does this right to privacy extend to the refusal to accept artificial means of nourishment? (This is typically administered through a nasogastric tube that delivers fluids through the nose and esophagus, or a gastrostomy in which fluids are delivered by tube through a surgical incision directly into the stomach, or intravenous feeding and hydration in which fluids are delivered through a needle directly into the bloodstream.) Or is the provision of nutrition and hydration so basic that it is not considered "medical treatment"?

In a poignant and lengthy travail through the court system, the case of Nancy Cruzan provided a judicial answer to the question. In January 1983, Nancy was in an automobile accident and suffered irreversible brain damage. She entered a PVS. After 4 years, Nancy's parents asked the Missouri Rehabilitation Center to withdraw the feeding tube. The center refused, and the Cruzans filed suit. They informed the court that Nancy had indicated that she would not want to be kept alive unless she could live "halfway normally." The Circuit Court ruled in favor of the Cruzans, but under appeal, the Missouri Supreme Court overruled, disallowing the feeding tube from being disconnected. The court concluded that there was not "clear and convincing evidence" that Nancy would not have wanted to be maintained as she was. Missouri law required such evidence for the withdrawal of artificial life-support systems.

The Cruzans appealed to the US Supreme Court, and, for the first time, the Court agreed to hear a "right to die" case. On June 25, 1990, the Court handed down a 5–4 decision in favor of the state of Missouri. States were given latitude to require "clear and convincing evidence" that the individual would not wish to be sustained in PVS—meaning that families could not use their own judgment to decide to discontinue feeding.

However, the Court did acknowledge a constitutional basis for **advance directives** (see the accompanying box, "Advance Directives") and the legitimacy of surrogate decision making. Its rationale cited the Fourteenth Amendment's "liberty interest" as enabling individuals to reject unwanted medical treatment. Because the decision did not distinguish between the provision of nutrition and other forms of medical treatment, the feeding tubes could have been removed had the qualifications of the Missouri law been met.

IN THE FIELD

ADVANCE DIRECTIVES

A **living will** is a document signed by a competent person that provides explicit instructions about desired end-of-life treatment if the person is unconscious or unable to express his or her wishes. Legal in all 50 states and the District of Columbia, the living will is commonly used to authorize the withholding or withdrawal of life-sustaining technology and provides immunity for health care professionals who comply with the stated wishes. Approximately 36 percent of adult Americans have completed an advance directive, and most of these are in the form of a living will. Ironically, in most situations, physicians and hospitals ignore the living will if family members request medical treatment.

A *health care power of attorney* can be signed by a competent person to designate someone who will make all health care decisions should the person become legally incompetent. It allows the designee to consider the particulars of the situation before making a decision. Most experts agree that both types of advance directives have some benefit, and encourage people to do both.

The Patient Self-Determination Act (sometimes called the "medical Miranda warning") went into effect in 1991. It requires all health care providers who receive federal funding to inform incoming patients of their rights under state laws to refuse medical treatment and to prepare an advance directive. The law is intended to ensure that people are aware of their rights vis-à-vis life-sustaining medical technology.

Ultimately, another hearing occurred in the circuit court. Friends of Nancy came forward to offer additional evidence that she would not have wanted to be maintained in a PVS, and the judge again ruled for the Cruzans. No appeal was filed, and the feeding tubes were removed on December 14, 1990. Nancy died 12 days later.

Terri Schiavo. In 2004 and 2005, the nation's attention was riveted by a Florida case that once again raised issues regarding persistent vegetative states, the role of proxy decision makers, and the power of the media and politicians to dramatize complex medical issues. On February 25, 1990, 26-year-old Terri Schiavo suffered a cardiac arrest that was, at least in part, brought on by an eating disorder. The disruption to the oxygen supply caused permanent brain damage. Like Nancy Cruzan (and, ultimately, Karen Ann Quinlan), Terri entered a PVS and was kept alive by artificial nutrition and hydration.

For several years her case was like that of thousands of other PVS patients, as both her husband, Michael, and her birth family did all they could to provide support. In 1994, the relationship between Michael and her parents broke down over the manner in which a medical malpractice judgment would be spent. Four years later, in 1998, resigned to the fact that Terri's brain damage was permanent, Michael asked that the feeding tubes be withdrawn. Like Nancy Cruzan, Terri did not have any form of advance directive, and Michael was the legal guardian and proxy.

Her family opposed this decision and filed a series of court cases over the next few years to remove Michael as guardian. All of these found that Michael was acting within his legal rights. In the early 2000s, the media picked up on the case, and details of the situation were reported on a routine basis. Governor Jeb Bush, the Florida state legislature, and eventually President Bush and the Republican leadership in Congress became involved in the case and sought all available means to overturn the several court rulings in the case and to prevent the withdrawal of the feeding tube. Twice the feeding tube was withdrawn and then reinserted. Congressional Republicans passed a bill that pertained just to Terri, but federal judges immediately found it to be unconstitutional. Ultimately, every court involved in the case ruled in favor of Michael's right to decide. The feeding tube was once again removed, and Terri died.

Can Patients Demand a Particular Medical Treatment?

The cases of Karen Ann Quinlan, Nancy Cruzan, and Terri Schiavo illustrate circumstances in which a patient or their proxy refuses medical treatment. In 1991 and in 2013, an unusual twist occurred in the Helga Wanglie and Jahi McMath cases. The hospital wished to stop medical treatment, and the family demanded that it continue. This created the reverse of the usual question: Does a patient or their representative(s) have the right to demand medical treatment?

Helga Wanglie and Jahi McGrath.   In December 1989, Helga Wanglie, an active, well-educated 85-year-old woman, tripped over a rug and broke her hip. During the next few months she experienced several cardiopulmonary arrests. In May 1990, she suffered severe anoxia and slipped into a PVS. Her breathing was reinforced by a respirator, and she was fed through a feeding tube. By year's end, her medical bills were approaching US$500,000.

In December, the medical staff recommended to Oliver Wanglie, her husband of 53 years, that the respirator be disconnected. He refused on the grounds that he and his wife believed in the sanctity of life and that he could never agree to have the respirator disconnected.

The hospital petitioned the court to have Mr. Wanglie replaced as Helga's legal guardian. The

rationale was that Mr. Wanglie had made some statements that indicated that Helga had never voiced an opinion about being sustained in PVS, and that he was not legally competent to serve as her guardian. The hospital justified its request to disconnect by stating that it did not feel it should be obligated to provide "medically futile" medical treatment.

On July 1, 1991, the judge issued a narrow ruling that the hospital had not demonstrated that Mr. Wanglie was incompetent, and therefore he was the most appropriate legal guardian. Without the tubes being removed, Helga died 3 days later.

In December 2013, 13-year-old Jahi McMath underwent surgery for sleep apnea. While recovering in the ICU, Jahi experienced severe bleeding and went into cardiac arrest. She was placed on a respirator. Three days later she was declared brain dead, and the hospital expressed its intention to remove the respirator.

Her mother, Nailah Winkfield, said that she believed her daughter was alive as long as her heart was beating. She went to court twice to secure injunctions that would prohibit the hospital from disconnecting the respirator. However, she refused to order the hospital to fit Jahi with the breathing and feeding tubes that she would need for longer-term care. Eventually, Nailah and the hospital agreed to have Jahi transferred to a facility that would keep her on a respirator. In January that transfer was made. Her condition never changed, and she died in June 2018 at the age of 17.

Medical Futility.   Although the judges in these cases did not directly address the "medical futility" issue, the concept caught the attention of many interested persons. It has proved to be an elusive concept to define. Schneiderman, Jecker, and Jonsen (1990:950) define **medical futility** as "an expectation of success that is either predictably or empirically so unlikely that its exact probability is often incalculable." In a quantitative sense, "when physicians conclude . . . that in the last 100 cases, a medical treatment has been useless, they should regard the treatment as futile" (Schneiderman, Jecker, and Jonsen, 1990:951). In a qualitative sense, "any treatment that merely preserves permanent unconsciousness or that fails to end total dependence on intensive medical care should be regarded as non-beneficial and, therefore, futile" (Schneiderman, Jecker, and Jonsen, 1990:952). If a treatment fails to improve appreciably the person as a whole, they argue, physicians are entitled to withhold the treatment without the consent of family or friends.

While courts have supported patients' "negative rights" to refuse medical treatment, the issue of a "positive right" (the request for a particular intervention) is different in two ways: (1) it is a resource allocation issue—the more dollars spent on non-beneficial treatment, the fewer dollars available to spend on those who would benefit, and (2) the reasonableness of requiring health care practitioners to engage in actions they consider unwarranted (and possibly harmful). A recent article (Dzeng et al., 2016:97) examining studies on attitudes of internal medical residents and fellows about their experiences providing futile care stated:

Our study sheds light on a significant cause of moral distress amongst physician trainees when they felt obligated to provide treatments at the end of life that they believe to be futile or harmful. Their words—"torture," "gruesome," "abuse," "mutilate," and "cruel"—evoke images more befitting penal regimes than hospitals. The moral toll exacted on these physicians is evident in descriptions such as feeling "violated" and "traumatized."

However, successful intervention may be defined differently by different people. Families may be satisfied as long as everything possible is done, even if the patient dies. Their values may rest more on effort than on outcome, and they may never define effort as futile. Some view the issue as showing respect for the autonomy of patients and their families by honoring these value differences but working together to avoid futile treatments.

Physician Aid-in-Dying (PAD)

Physician aid-in-dying (formerly referred to as physician-assisted suicide) occurs when a physician provides both a means of death (e.g., a particular drug) and instructions (e.g., how much of the drug would need to be taken for it to be lethal) to a patient, but does not actually administer the cause of death. This is different than **active euthanasia,** in which the physician directly administers the cause of death.

Dr. Jack Kevorkian. The key figure in this debate in the United States has been Dr. Jack Kevorkian, a retired Michigan pathologist who assisted more than 100 people to end their lives by providing a painless means to do so and by being present at the time of death. Each of these individuals contacted Kevorkian (none of them were patients of his) and convinced him that they had made a rational choice to die. The particular means used varied from case to case. Two juries refused to convict Kevorkian of a crime. Ultimately, however, he sought to push the limits and he engaged in an act of active euthanasia in which he did cause the death to occur. A Michigan jury convicted him in 1999 on this charge and sentenced him to 10 to 25 years in prison. He was released in 2007 after 8 years with a promise that he would no longer assist in dying, although he could continue to advocate for it. He died in 2011.

Actual physician participation in the dying process and physician aid-in-dying are legal in the Netherlands, Canada, Belgium, Luxembourg, India, South Korea, and Colombia. Physician aid-in-dying (but not active euthanasia) is legal in Switzerland, Japan, Germany, and some US states. In 1997, the US Supreme Court ruled unanimously that terminally ill persons do not have a constitutional right to PAD, but that states could enact legislation that allows it. As of 2018, eight states—Oregon, Washington, Vermont, Montana, California, Hawaii, New Jersey, and New Mexico plus the District of Columbia—have legal access to PAD.

Dr. Jack Kevorkian, a retired Michigan pathologist, repeatedly and successfully challenged prohibitions against physician aid-in-dying. Eventually he was convicted of second-degree homicide for directly causing the death of an individual in the late stages of amyotrophic lateral sclerosis (ALS) and had requested Kevorkian's assistance with his death.

To date, the number of people using physician aid-in-dying has been small, and records are not kept the same in all states. Oregon, the first state to legalize, had a total of 1,275 deaths in its first 20 legalized years. People who engaged in PAD were overwhelmingly white and highly educated, and most of them had cancer. By law, all were terminally ill. They mainly feared a loss of their autonomy, a loss of the ability to participate in enjoyable activities, and the loss of dignity (O'Reilly, 2010). The accompanying box, "Advance Directives and Navajo Culture," describes how this concept is considered in a Native American culture.

IN COMPARATIVE FOCUS

ADVANCE DIRECTIVES AND NAVAJO CULTURE

Ethical issues are typically considered within the context of particular cultures so that values specific to each group can be considered. This helps avoid misunderstandings and frustration between health care providers and their patients that might lead to suboptimal care.

This is the case with regard to discussions about advance directives with Navajo patients. An important Navajo cultural norm is avoidance of discussion of negative information. In the Navajo belief system, talking about an event increases the likelihood of that event occurring. This belief obviously comes into conflict with several norms in medical settings—for example, discussing risks as well as benefits of intended procedures, telling patients the truth about a negative diagnosis or prognosis, and preparing an advance directive. Ignoring the cultural values of a Navajo patient almost inevitably means that care and treatment will be interrupted and perhaps discontinued.

On the other hand, acting with cultural sensitivity can enable the values of the patient to be respected while medical responsibilities are discharged. Health care providers who work with the Navajo handle situations of this type in four ways: (1) determining whether the patient is or is not willing to discuss negative information; (2) preparing the patient by building rapport and trust, involving the family, giving an advance warning that bad news is coming, and involving traditional Navajo healers in the encounter; (3) communicating in a kind, caring manner that is respectful of traditional beliefs (e.g., referring to the patient in third-party language rather than directly); and (4) maintaining reasonable hope (Carrese and Rhodes, 2000).

Arguments in Favor of Physician Aid-in-Dying. Proponents of the legalization of physician aid-in-dying offer the following rationale:

1. It is perfectly appropriate to have physicians and other health care professionals create a comfortable and peaceful environment in which death occurs.
2. People have a right to self-determination; if a person has reflected on their life circumstances and made a rational and competent decision to die, the assistance of physicians in the act is appropriate. People should not be required to undergo mental and physical decline, endure emotional and physical pain, and incur sizable medical expenses for treatment that is not desired.
3. In order to prevent abuse, laws could require certain safeguards (e.g., there is intolerable suffering, the patient is mentally competent, provision of a written witnessed request, the patient requests death consistently and repeatedly over time, and two physicians—one of whom has not participated in the patient's care—agree that death is appropriate).
4. An extremely high rate of suicide already exists. In addition to that which occurs without medical contact, it is clear that many deaths in hospitals occur with some "assistance." An estimated 70 percent of the 1.4 million deaths that occur in American hospitals each year involve some agreement not to take aggressive action to sustain the patient.
5. Public opinion polls show that a majority of Americans (73 percent in 2017) favor the legalization of PAD, and in certain circumstances as many as 50 percent would consider it for themselves. Derek Humphry (1991), founder of the Hemlock Society, a national organization in favor of legalized euthanasia and past president of the World Federation of Right to Die Societies, wrote *Final Exit: The Practicalities of Self-Deliverance and Assisted Suicide for the Dying*. It is a how-to-commit-suicide guidebook, and it became an overwhelming bestseller.

Arguments Opposing Physician Aid-in-Dying. Opponents of physician aid-in-dying offer the following rationale:

1. Traditionally, we have considered the physician's responsibility to be to sustain life and relieve suffering. The primary purpose of PAD, however, is to cause death. The American Medical Association, the American Bar Association, and some medical ethicists believe this to be inconsistent with the physician's professional obligations.
2. Patients considering PAD may be sufficiently ill or so worried that they are not capable of genuine contemplative thought or the exercise of true informed consent. The depression that might lead to consideration of this act might itself be treatable.
3. The legal possibility of PAD may interfere with a good physician–patient relationship. A physician's willingness to participate may be interpreted by the patient as confirmation that society (and the physician) would prefer that death occurs. This interpretation may place implicit pressure on the patient to request the act.
4. There could be a slippery-slope argument—that by legalizing PAD for patients with terminal illnesses we increase the likelihood of making it acceptable for other people, such as those with intellectual or physical disabilities and the very old.
5. Significant progress has been made in dealing with the pain that often accompanies late-stage diseases. Many hospitals have developed palliative care programs to manage patients' pain, and many health care providers are receiving training in palliative care. Hospices are increasingly successful in reducing the amount of pain their clients experience.

IN THE FIELD

THE BROKEN END-OF-LIFE CARE SYSTEM

A 2015 report by the well-respected Institute of Medicine (IOM) concluded that end-of-life care in the United States needs significant transformation. The two key problems are (1) a culture that promotes action over inaction and continues to see death as an enemy that should be fought until the last minute and (2) an economic system that rewards procedures over thoughtful decisions. Most people want to die at home, but most die in hospitals. Most want a peaceful setting at death and not to be tethered to countless pieces of high-tech medical equipment, but the final stage of life for many is in an intensive care unit with every effort being made to delay the moment of death. A study in 2011 found that 18 percent of Medicare patients underwent surgery in their last month of life and 8 percent in their last week (Kwok et al., 2011).

Almost one-third of all Medicare dollars are spent on people in their last year of life. Much of it has little benefit and it often makes the patient feel worse. Many have not contemplated their own end-of-life care and have not discussed their wishes with family members or physicians. Increasing numbers of people are using hospice services, but many come to hospice only after all futile efforts have been made to extend their survival (Volandes, 2015).

The IOM panel that published the report included physicians, nurses, insurers, lawyers, religious leaders, and experts on aging. The panel's co-chair, David Walker, stated:

> The bottom line is the health care system is poorly designed to meet the needs of patients near the end of life. The current system is geared towards doing more, more, more, and that system by definition is not necessarily consistent with what patients want, and it is also more costly.
>
> (Cook and Rocker, 2014)

The American College of Physicians (ACP), the specialty section for internal medicine physicians, opposes PAD. While acknowledging the importance of arguments made by PAD proponents, the ACP has concluded that the opposing arguments are more persuasive. Among these are that PAD (1) would undermine the physician–patient relationship, especially the trust that patients have in their physician to do everything in their power to seek cure, (2) is outside the responsibilities of medicine—that physicians cannot control every aspect of disease and illness and death, and providing PAD is inconsistent with physicians' moral responsibilities, and (3) alters fundamentally medicine's role within society (Sulmasy and Mueller, 2017).

ORGAN DONATION AND TRANSPLANTATION

The ability to successfully transplant organs from a cadaver or a living related donor began with a successful transplant in Boston in 1954, when a 23-year-old man received a kidney from his genetically identical twin brother. The recipient recovered completely and lived another 8 years before dying of an unrelated cause. Bone marrow was first successfully transplanted in 1963 (in Paris), the same year as the first liver transplant (in Denver); the first pancreas was transplanted in 1966 (in Minneapolis), the first heart in 1967 (in Cape Town, South Africa), the first heart and lung in 1981 (in Palo Alto, California), the first partial pancreas in 1998 (in Minneapolis), the first hand in 1998 (in Paris), the first partial face in 2005 (in Paris), the first trachea in 2008 (in Barcelona), and the first partial liver from living donor transplant in 2012 (Britain).

Social Policy Issues Related to Organ Transplantation

The success of organ transplantation has prolonged the life of many recipients, but it has also created many complex ethical and social policy issues. Nancy Kutner (1987) and Renée Fox and Judith Swazey (1992) identified the following key issues:

1. Do the medical and quality-of-life outcomes for organ recipients (and donors) justify organ transplantation procedures? Have organ transplants shown sufficient therapeutic value for them to be continued? If the answer to this question is affirmative, then the four following questions need to be addressed.
2. Given that the demand for transplant organs exceeds the supply, how should recipients be selected? Should a complex formula be devised to prioritize potential recipients, or would a first-come-first-served (or random) policy be more consistent with democratic principles?
3. How can the supply of organs be increased? Organ donation policy has evolved during the last 60 years, but demand continues to exceed supply. What policy might increase motivation to donate while maintaining a voluntary nature?
4. How much money should be allocated to organ transplant procedures? How much should be directed to these very expensive procedures (most cost between US$500,000 and US$1,000,000) that benefit a relatively small number of people versus less dramatic, less costly procedures that might benefit a larger number?

5. Who should pay for organ transplant procedures? Should the government pay because these procedures are so expensive? Should health insurance companies guarantee coverage? At the time of writing, the federal government's Medicare program pays for kidney, heart, and some liver transplants, and some health insurance policies cover transplants. People not covered in these ways are on their own, and those unable to pay are turned away.

This section focuses on the evolution of organ donation policy in the United States, assesses the current and alternative policies, and discusses the psychosocial dimension of organ donation.

Organ Donation Policy in the United States

The success of early transplant efforts in the 1950s and 1960s forced the United States to establish a formal organ donation policy. The initial policy was one of *pure voluntarism*—donation was legalized, and it was hoped that volunteers would come forward. Courts ruled that competent adults could voluntarily donate organs to relatives, which at first seemed like the only possibility. Organs could be donated by minors only with parental and judicial consent.

This was an impetus for more donations but as supply increased, so did demand. Increased demand was also prompted by the development of the artificial respirator and the heart–lung machine, and with the discovery of effective immunosuppressive drugs to suppress the body's immune system, thereby making the recipient's body less likely to reject a transplanted organ.

In 1968, the United States adopted "brain death" as the legal standard for death determination. This definition enabled organs to be removed from those who had suffered irreversible loss of brain function (and who therefore were legally dead) but were being sustained on artificial respirators. Death could be pronounced, the organs removed, and then the respirator disconnected.

In 1968, the United States moved to a more assertive policy—*encouraged voluntarism*. This occurred with passage of the Uniform Anatomical Gift Act (UAGA), which was adopted in every state and in Washington, DC, by 1971. The UAGA permitted adults to donate all or part of their body after death through donor cards and living wills, and gave next of kin authority to donate after an individual's death, as long as no contrary instructions had been given. The UAGA was praised for maintaining a voluntary approach and was successful in increasing the number of donors. However, about 90 percent of the 20,000–25,000 people who died in the United States each year in such a way that their organs were transplantable still failed to donate, there was no centralized system for identifying those needing and those willing to make a donation, and hospitals had little involvement in the program.

A dramatic change in organ donation policy occurred in 1987 with the establishment of a *weak required request policy*. In order to receive essential Medicare and Medicaid reimbursements (an essential), each of the nation's hospitals must make patients and their families aware of the organ donation option, and must notify a federally certified organ procurement organization (OPO) when there is consent to donation.

In addition, a national central registry, now called the United Network for Organ Sharing (UNOS), was created in Richmond, Virginia, to maintain a national list of potential donors and recipients. All the country's (now) 300 transplant centers and 58 procurement organizations are required to affiliate with UNOS. When an organ for transplant becomes available, UNOS engages in a matching process, taking into consideration medical need, medical compatibility (size and blood type), and geographic proximity. Much of the physical work is performed by the OPOs, which encourage donation, contact UNOS

when an organ becomes available, send teams to collect and process the organ, and deliver it to its designee.

The weak required request policy maintains the voluntary and altruistic nature of organ donation, but seeks to guarantee that potential donors are aware of the donation option. The request is sometimes handled very sensitively but sometimes with little enthusiasm and little tactfulness. Few physicians and nurses have received any education or training in how to make a request for organ donation, and many feel uncomfortable doing so. These attitudes are extremely important because the comfort level of the requestor has a significant impact on the likelihood of donation. When families are approached with lines such as "I don't suppose you want to donate, do you?" or "The law says I have to ask if you want to donate," a refusal is very likely.

Has the 1987 legislation succeeded? UNOS seems to be well run, and the number of organ donors did increase immediately to a 25 to 30 percent consent level (since then the consent level has increased to just over half). There are now about 35,000 organ transplants annually. Moreover, organ transplants are more likely to be successful than ever before, and recipients are living longer. Yet many families asked to consider donation after a relative has died do not give consent, and many even override the deceased person's desire to donate (hospitals typically accede to family wishes even though all states have laws saying that families cannot override an adult decedent's wishes).

In 2019, there were more than 115,000 people on the UNOS waiting lists who have been medically and financially approved for transplants. Approximately two-thirds of these are likely to receive a transplant (half within 5 years), but one-third will die before an organ for them becomes available. (About 18 people die each day—more than 6,500 per year—while awaiting a transplant.) The American Council on Transplantation estimates that an additional 100,000 people would benefit from an organ transplant but are not on the list because they are unable to demonstrate the means to pay for it. Ironically, research shows that people without health insurance often donate organs but rarely receive them (Herring, Woolhandler, and Himmelstein, 2008).

Alternative Directions for Organ Donation Policy

Many wonder if it is time for the United States to move to a more assertive policy. While many persons believe that altruistic donation is the most morally appropriate policy, they see some alternative policies as also being morally appropriate and able to secure more donated organs. There are five main alternatives.

1. *Strong required request.* Every citizen would be asked to indicate their willingness to participate in organ donation—either on income tax returns or through a mandatory check-off on the driver's license. This policy retains the voluntary and altruistic nature of the system but is more aggressive in forcing people to consider organ donation and take a formal position. Some states already do this and have high donor willingness rates—Montana (93 percent), Alaska (92 percent), and Washington (89 percent). Most states do not, and several of these have a donor rate of less than 40 percent—the lowest rates of donor willingness are in West Virginia, Texas, Mississippi, and New York (Donate Life America, 2019).

2. *Weak presumed consent.* Hospitals would be required by law to remove and use all suitable cadaver organs for donation unless the deceased had expressly objected (through a central registry or a non-donor card) or if family members object. This remains a voluntary and altruistic system but with the significant change that the default position is that donation will occur—that is, a person must take an action to prevent donation. Moving to this type of system typically increases donation by 20 to 30 percent. Most European countries have moved to this policy. Spain has the world's highest countrywide donation rate—between 80 and 85 percent.

3. *Strong presumed consent.* Physicians would be given complete authorization to remove usable organs regardless of the wishes of the deceased or family members. Also referred to as "expropriation," it is the only alternative that eliminates the voluntary dimension of organ donation, but it is also the policy that retrieves the largest number of transplantable organs.

4. *Weak market approach.* In this approach, individuals or next of kin for deceased donors would receive a tax benefit for the donation of organs or a cash payment of sufficient size to offset funeral expenses. This approach adds financial incentive and thus reduces the role of altruism. Proponents argue that offering financial benefit is fair and sensitive, but opponents prefer altruistic motivation. They worry that some likely donors would be so offended by the suggestion of payment that they would choose not to donate. Pennsylvania became the first state to incorporate this technique in 2000, when it began offering US$300 to help families of organ donors to cover funeral expenses.

5. *Strong market approach.* Individuals or next of kin would be able to auction organs to the highest bidder. Like the weak market approach, this system emphasizes increasing the number of organs donated more than retaining altruistic motivation. Critics of the strong market approach worry that the financial incentive may place undue pressure on low-income individuals and those in developing countries to donate. Once organs are on the market, the wealthy clearly would have easier access.

The buying and selling of organs is unlawful in the United States and in all other countries

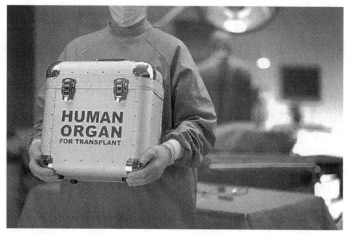

In 2019, there were more than 115,000 people on the UNOS waiting lists who have been medically and financially approved for transplants. Approximately two-thirds of them are likely to receive a transplant, but one-third will die before an organ for them becomes available.

except Iran. The selling of a kidney in Iran is legal and regulated by the government. While many are critical of this approach, Iran does not have a waiting list for kidneys. However, there is an ongoing black market for organs in several countries. A former company in Germany routinely sent a form letter to all people listed in the newspaper as having declared bankruptcy. The individual was offered US$45,000 (plus expenses) for a kidney, which was then sold for US$85,000. This is no longer legal.

The Psychosocial Dimension of Organ Transplantation and Donation

Some very insightful work in medical sociology and medical anthropology pertains to attitudes, motivations, and consequent feelings related to organ donation. Anthropologist Lesley Sharp (2006) wrote not only about medical successes and altruistic motivations but also about the complicated relationships and social injustices related to the gap between supply and demand. Renée Fox and Judith Swazey (1978, 1992), leaders for many years in this field of

study in medical sociology wrote forcefully that the organ donation decision needs to be placed within a social-structural context. Based on years of systematic observation in transplantation settings and countless interviews with physicians, patients, donors, and families, they raise three important concerns about donation and transplantation.

1. There is still some "uncertainty" about the therapeutic value of organ transplantation. Although significant progress has been made, concerns remain: cases of chronic rejection of transplanted organs, organ recipients prone to redeveloping the same life-threatening medical conditions that led to the transplant, and repeated failures with certain transplant modalities (e.g., animal-to-human transplantation).

2. Too little consideration has been given to the psychosocial dimensions of organ donation and receipt, including the human "gift-exchange" dimension of the process. Fox and Swazey contend that the "gift of life" idea needs further study. For example, a study in

Britain (Bailey et al., 2016) found that many organ recipients appreciate not knowing the identity of a live donor in order to avoid feeling a gift reciprocity, but many others wanted to know the donor's identity to be able to express appreciation.

3. The high price of transplant procedures and the fact that more people seek an organ than have been willing to donate one have created real and not yet fully answered questions of distributive justice and public good.

The Donor-Recipient Relationship

The decision to donate and the decision to receive an organ often are governed by unspoken but powerful social norms. Family members may feel an "intense desire" to make a potentially life-saving gift to someone close, and they sometimes feel that donating is a family obligation (even sensing some family pressure). With this "gift of life," an incredible bond can be established between the giver and the receiver. In addition, some cases of "black sheep donors" have surfaced, in which individuals who felt remorse for previous wrongs against the family wished to make amends through donation of an organ (Fox, 1989). Persons who donate to strangers often feel an enhanced self-image—having been helpful and generous.

Just as prevailing norms may motivate organ donation, they also motivate accepting it. Rejection of an offer to donate constitutes a form of rejection of the donor. When the donation and transplant occur, a type of "obligation to repay" may be incurred by the recipient. Having received something so profoundly important, the recipient becomes, in a sense, a debtor—owing something back to the donor (Shaw, 2010). Fox and Swazey (1978) referred to this as the **tyranny of the gift**.

Similar considerations occur in family members' decisions to offer cadaver organs. These decisions are almost always made in traumatic situations, such as automobile accidents, in which the death is sudden and there has been no preparation for it. Family members often consent to donation as a way of bringing meaning or a sense of value to a tragedy. The humanitarian aspects of organ donation become powerful motivating forces (Fox and Swazey, 1978).

ASSISTED PROCREATION

Infertility

The reported incidence of **infertility**, defined as the absence of pregnancy after 1 year of regular sexual intercourse without contraception, is increasing in the United States. An estimated 10 to 15 percent of American couples of childbearing age are considered infertile. However, this percentage may give an exaggerated picture; up to 50 percent of the couples who are not pregnant after 1 year become pregnant on their own in the second year. The increased incidence of infertility is due to several factors, including an actual increase in infertility (probably due to increased exposure to radiation and pollution, ingestion of certain drugs, and higher levels of sexually transmitted infections), the number of older women now trying to get pregnant (peak fertility occurs between 20 and 29 years of age), and more couples seeking assistance with lack of fertility.

The specific reason for a couple's infertility is traceable to the woman in approximately 40 percent of cases. Common causes are inability to produce eggs for fertilization, blocked Fallopian tubes (so the eggs cannot travel to meet the sperm), and a sufficiently high level of acidity in the vagina to kill deposited sperm. Another 40 percent of infertility cases are traceable to the man—typically low sperm count and/or low sperm motility. The specific cause of the remaining 20 percent of cases is either undeterminable or traceable to both partners.

The Development of Assisted Procreative Techniques

Several assisted procreative techniques enable infertile couples to produce children that are biologically related to at least one of the partners. These techniques have in common that at least one of the four traditionally essential steps of procreation—sexual intercourse, tubal fertilization, uterine implantation, and uterine gestation—is eliminated. About 1.5 million assisted procreative techniques are attempted worldwide each year, resulting in the birth of 350,000 babies. As of 2015, more than 5 million births had occurred using assisted procreation; more than 1 million were born in the United States. (It should be noted that few official statistics are recorded for assisted reproduction; therefore, available statistics are estimates.) This section discusses four techniques—intrauterine insemination, in vitro fertilization, ovum donation (surrogate embryo transfer), and surrogate motherhood. The main focus is on surrogate motherhood—the most controversial of the four techniques.

Intrauterine Insemination. Technologically, the least complicated technique is *intrauterine insemination (IUI)*. When the woman is ovulating, sperm is manually inserted via a catheter directly into her uterus (thus bypassing the vagina and cervix). The sperm may be provided by her partner, an anonymous donor, or a mixture of the two. The overall success rate varies widely depending on the cause of the infertility and whether or not fertility drugs are used simultaneously (i.e., oral clomiphene or injectable gonadotropins to stimulate ovulation and the release of several eggs, which also increases the rate of multiples—twins or higher).

Intrauterine insemination is typically used (1) when the man cannot produce a sufficient number of healthy sperm or his sperm lacks motility; (2) when the woman's vaginal environment is biochemically inhospitable to sperm, or the position of the uterus or size of the opening to the uterus is sufficiently small that fertilization is unlikely; (3) if both partners are carriers of a recessive gene for a genetic disorder (e.g., Tay–Sachs disease) or the man is a carrier of a dominant gene (e.g., Huntington's chorea); or (4) increasingly, for single women and lesbian couples.

Precise records are not kept, but approximately 100,000 births per year in the United States occur to women who have been inseminated. The cost of an insemination is in the range of US\$800–\$900, but there are additional costs for initial evaluation and fertility tests, and, when used simultaneously, drug treatments, so the total price is typically higher. As many as three, four, or more cycles may be necessary (if the technique is going to work, it typically does so by the fourth cycle). All states deal with paternity by statute; in most states, insemination by donor sperm for married couples is legal with the husband's consent, and the offspring is considered his legal responsibility.

In Vitro Fertilization. When infertility is due to the woman's blocked Fallopian tubes or to the low motility or low count of the man's sperm, *in vitro fertilization (IVF)* may be used. In this process, the woman is given drugs to stimulate her ovaries to produce multiple eggs. A few hours before ovulation is expected, a small incision is made in the abdomen. A laparoscope (an instrument with a lens and a light source) is inserted to examine the ovaries. Mature eggs are located and removed by a vacuum aspirator and transferred to a petri dish (the so-called test tube) containing sperm and a nutrient solution, where fertilization occurs about 80 to 90 percent of the time. About 2 days later, at an appropriate stage of cell development, the fertilized egg is introduced through the vagina into the uterus. If the cell continues to divide naturally, it will attach itself to the uterine wall.

For women under 35 years of age, about 1 attempt in 2 now results in a pregnancy, although several attempts are necessary before achieving pregnancy. Each attempt may cost US$12,000–15,000. To increase the likelihood of pregnancy, many fertility clinics implant multiple eggs, which has led to a sharp increase in multiple births. In the United States, about 3 percent of births are twins, but about 45 percent of IVF babies are multiples. The concern is that multiple births increase the incidence of life-threatening prematurity (12 percent of US births are preterm, but 37 percent of IVF babies are), low birth weight, and birth defects. More than 65,000 IVF babies are born in the United States each year, about 200,000 through the world.

Among the modifications of IVF is gamete intrafallopian transfer (GIFT), whereby eggs are retrieved from the woman's ovary and implanted with a sample of the man's sperm in her Fallopian tubes where fertilization may occur. This technique may be helpful for couples who have not had success with IVF, but unlike IVF it involves a surgical procedure.

Ovum Donation (Embryo Transfer). Some infertility in women is traceable to the absence of ovaries or to non-functional ovaries. Since eggs are not produced, there can be no genetic offspring. However, if the uterus is functional, there is no biological obstacle to gestating a fetus and giving birth. If the couple wishes to have offspring genetically related to the man, *ovum donation* can be used. This procedure can occur in any one of three ways: (1) transfer of a donor's egg to the woman's Fallopian tube, followed by sexual intercourse, (2) *in vitro* fertilization of a donor's egg with the man's sperm, followed by insertion in the woman, and (3) intrauterine insemination of an egg donor with the man's sperm, resulting in fertilization, and then washing the embryo out of the donor and transferring it to the woman's uterus.

Embryo transfer is the most recently developed technique (early 1980s), the most expensive (approximately US$25,000 per attempt), and the least commonly used, but it has a higher rate of success than IVF. Approximately 16,000 births each year in the United States occur with donated eggs. In most cases, the woman donating the egg(s) receives reimbursement for expenses and some compensation. The average payment ranges from US$6,000 to US$15,000, but some couples who wish to have donor eggs from a woman with a particular background may offer much more.

Surrogate Motherhood. While all assisted procreative techniques carry some controversy, *surrogate motherhood* is the most controversial. In this process, a woman who is not capable or desirous of carrying a pregnancy and her partner contract with another woman—the surrogate— who will supply the egg and carry the pregnancy. The surrogate is artificially inseminated with the man's sperm. If fertilization occurs, the surrogate gestates the fetus, bringing it to term, and then gives it to the couple. The woman receiving the baby must adopt it.

The process usually occurs with the assistance of a lawyer/broker who develops an extensive contract. Early in the history of the technique, a payment of US$10,000 to the surrogate was typical (today the payment is typically in the range of US$48,000–55,000, but the total cost may be two or three times that). Many experts distinguish between surrogate motherhood that is "commercialized" (done for payment) and that which is "altruistic" (most commonly done for a sister or other relative, or a close friend). There are an estimated 1,200 to 1,500 surrogate births annually in the United States.

IN THE FIELD

THE BUSINESS OF EGG FREEZING

Egg freezing ("oocyte cryopreservation") is a reproductive technology that involves extracting and preserving women's reproductive cells (eggs) in anticipation of future infertility. Egg freezing is sometimes used by women who have been diagnosed with cancer or some other condition that might prevent egg production in the future. By freezing eggs before that occurs, the option of having biologically related children is preserved (Inhorn, Birenbaum-Carmeli, and Patrizio, 2017).

A second motivation is to have fertilizable eggs available should a desirable marital/romantic partner not be found until after the peak years of fertility. This prevents pursuing a partnership or settling solely as a means to have children. Brown and Patrick (2018) referred to this motivation as "modifying the relationship between their reproductive and romantic trajectories while still preserving the ideal of eventually having children with a romantic partner."

While the fertility industry has been thriving for many years (it is a US$2 billion dollar industry), a recent development is the creation of egg-freezing boutiques. According to the Society for Assisted Reproductive Technology, just 475 women in the United States froze their eggs in 2009, but the number had grown to nearly 7,300 in 2016. Much of this growth is a result of these boutiques. They often offer packages around US$6,000 per retrieval plus US$3,000 to $5,000 for medical costs—slightly less than at most fertility clinics. Many health insurance plans cover part of the cost. Based on the number of eggs per retrieval and the likelihood of a successful pregnancy, it is likely to take a few to several retrievals for a successful pregnancy (Pflum, 2019). Some groups of women are now travelling to exotic locations with egg-freezing clinics, seeking lower prices and a simultaneous "eggs-cation" (not our term).

Almening (2017) compared and contrasted the manner in which egg banks and sperm banks recruit volunteers. While both recruit young "sellable" donors who will attract recipient clients, and require medical evaluations and a family history, their approach to men and women is very different.

Egg donors must conform to rigorous height/weight ratios; sperm donors do not. Women over 30 are unlikely to be accepted as donors; men can donate until they are 40. Sperm banks require that men be at least 5'8" tall; egg agencies do not set height minimums. Most sperm banks require that men be enrolled in college or have a college degree; egg agencies do not. Most egg agencies require psychological evaluations to assess how women feel about having children out in the world; sperm banks do not.

Considerable public attention was brought to the surrogate motherhood technique in the mid- to late 1980s in the *Baby M* case. A New Jersey couple (the Sterns) contracted through a broker with another New Jersey woman (Mary Beth Whitehead) to be a surrogate. Whitehead had registered to be a surrogate with the Infertility Center of New York, saying that she wanted to help another couple. A contract was signed. The Sterns accepted all responsibilities for the baby even if there were birth defects. Amniocentesis was required, an abortion was agreed to if problems were detected, US$10,000 for Whitehead was put in escrow, and the baby would be given to the Sterns. IUI was performed, and a pregnancy resulted.

After the baby's birth, Whitehead changed her mind about surrendering the baby and refused the payment. When the authorities came to collect the baby, she took her and fled to Florida. This prompted a 3-month search by the FBI, police, and private detectives. When they were caught, the baby was returned to the Sterns, and the legal battle began. Ultimately, the New Jersey Supreme Court ruled that surrogate motherhood contracts are illegal, that both the Sterns and Whitehead had claim to the baby, but that it would be awarded to the Sterns based on the baby's perceived best interests, and that Whitehead would get visitation rights.

Gestational Surrogacy. A modification of surrogate motherhood occurs when a woman is hired only to gestate an embryo created from the sperm and egg of a contracting couple. In other words, the egg is not contributed by the surrogate, who agrees only to have the embryo implanted, to provide gestation, and to give the resulting baby to the contracting couple. An average fee for a gestational surrogate is approximately US$20,000. In the United States about 1,000 births per year occur to gestational surrogates.

Analyzing Surrogate Motherhood

The Case for Surrogate Motherhood. Proponents of surrogate motherhood base their position on two primary points. First, there is a constitutionally protected right to **procreative liberty**. While some recent Supreme Court decisions have limited full access to abortion services, there is a tradition of judicial and legislative action that suggests a fundamental right not to procreate. The right *to* procreate has not received the same explicit judicial endorsement because states have not challenged married couples' efforts to give birth. Nevertheless, the Supreme Court has on several occasions indicated strong support for procreative liberty—especially for married persons.

Proponents of surrogate motherhood and the other assisted procreative techniques contend

that this right to procreate extends to non-coital as well as coital reproduction and extends to the use of donors and surrogates. Non-coital assisted procreation would be supported by the same values and interests that have always supported coital reproduction (e.g., a right to privacy and a belief that families provide emotional and physical support). Infertility ought not to be allowed to prevent a couple from procreating.

Second, the use of surrogate motherhood is an expression of the involved parties' autonomy and may directly benefit everyone involved. Couples who are unable to procreate without such technology are given the option of producing an offspring genetically related to at least one of them. The offspring will be born into a situation where he or she is very much desired, given that the parents have gone to considerable lengths to have the child. The surrogate mother has the opportunity to make a contribution to others' happiness and to earn a not insignificant sum of money (although paltry if considered by the hour). All assisted procreative techniques are freedom-enhancing procedures (Robertson, 1994).

The Case Against Surrogate Motherhood. Opponents of surrogate motherhood level three main criticisms. First, surrogate motherhood is not in the best interests of the surrogate mother, the baby, and even the contracting couple. The deliberate separation of genetic, gestational, and social parentage places everyone involved in an awkward position. Reproductive arrangements are negotiated between non-spouses; the surrogate mother conceives without the intention of raising the baby, who could foreseeably be denied important medical information about lineage and could be psychologically harmed when told about the circumstances surrounding the birth. Both families could experience tension due to the unusual status of the surrogate offspring.

The legal and ethical requirement for an informed consent (see Chapter 13) may inherently be violated in the surrogate motherhood contract. Critics charge that it is impossible for a woman to know at the time when a contract is being signed how she will feel about surrendering the offspring after birth. Moreover, the requirement for voluntariness may be violated by the lure of a payment, especially for low-income women. If so, surrogate motherhood creates the possibility of exploitation of poor women.

Second, surrogate motherhood has a negative effect on the status of women within society. Woliver (1989) is critical of the extent to which discussion of assisted procreation focuses on questions of individual rights and expanding options for women. She contends that they may expand options for individual women, but restrict choices for women as a group.

Women's freedom to make parenting choices must be understood to occur within a culture that remains, in many respects, patriarchal. The zeal with which some women desire children and the vestiges of stigma attached to those who do not are culturally influenced. The growing movement to consider the individual rights of the fetus relative to the mother could restrict women's autonomy over their own bodies. In this environment, technologies have significant potential for abuse and oppression (Rothman, 1989).

Third, surrogate motherhood devalues people and creates a "**commodification of life**—treating people and parts of people as marketable commodities" (Rothman, 1988:95):

> This commodification process is very clearly seen in the notion of "surrogate" motherhood. There we talk openly about buying services and renting body parts—as if body parts were rented without the people who surround the part, as if you could rent a woman's uterus without renting the woman. We ignore our knowledge that women are pregnant with our whole bodies, from the changes in our hair to our swollen feet, with all of our bodies and perhaps with our souls as well.
>
> (1988:96–97)

According to this line of reasoning, the child—the contracted-for baby—is also commodified in that it is the subject of a contract and, in the end, will be surrendered in exchange for a cash payment. The transaction is tantamount to "baby selling" as the potential baby is "ordered precisely as one orders a car or buys pork futures" (Holder, 1988:55).

Surrogate Motherhood and Public Policy. Laws pertaining to surrogate motherhood are the responsibility of each state. Their options are (1) to legalize without restriction, (2) to legalize with restriction, and (3) to prohibit.

Strong proponents of surrogate motherhood believe that it is inappropriate to place any greater restriction on this technique than on coital reproductive methods. If (at the least) married couples have a constitutionally based right to reproduce coitally, and if that right extends to non-coital techniques, then the case is made that these techniques ought to have the same lack of restrictions. However, few states have adopted this approach.

Most advocates of surrogate motherhood acknowledge that one or the other (or both) of two restrictions may be appropriate. The first is that states may restrict the ability of the contracting couple to demand specified behaviors of the surrogate during pregnancy, and that the surrogate has the right until some specified time to change her mind about relinquishing the baby.

The second is that states may prohibit surrogacy for cash payment. The commercial dimension of the technique is the most objectionable part to many people. Macklin (1988) does not believe that surrogacy violates any fundamental moral principle but believes that commercialism in the process does. Rothman (1989) would prohibit the surrogate from selling or trading the offspring, although she would be able to give it to a couple in an arrangement that would be tantamount to an adoption. In this case, all parties would be governed by the traditional rights and responsibilities of an adoption proceeding. Many states have made surrogacy legal but only without financial payment. In the United Kingdom, commercial surrogacy is banned, but the surrogate may receive expenses for time, lost earnings, and costs associated with the pregnancy.

Finally, many states have banned surrogacy altogether and have established a fine or imprisonment for anyone participating in a surrogacy arrangement.

Eric Feldman (2018), a professor of health policy and medical ethics, believes that the United States is at a time when inconsistent laws across states regarding surrogate motherhood need to be addressed. His position is that there has been both sufficient time since the early surrogate cases and a sufficient number of cases that comparable laws across states is in the public interest. He believes that the biggest injustice to low-income women is that many have to travel long distances across state lines in order to find a permissible surrogate motherhood policy.

Feldman proposes that courts and legislatures accept the validity of surrogacy contracts, determine parentage according to intent, and enact appropriate contractual language to minimize potential exploitation of surrogates (e.g., they

cannot be forced to do things they find objectionable) and that surrogacy does not inappropriately commodify reproduction (to emphasize the differences between surrogacy and baby selling and to acknowledge that financial consideration often affects births however conception occurs).

The legal status of gestational surrogacy also varies from state to state. For example, the New Jersey Superior Court in 2009 ruled that the restrictions on surrogacy established in the *Baby M* case also extend to gestational surrogacy. However, passage of the New Jersey Gestational Carrier Agreement Act in 2018 made gestational surrogacy contracts legal and granted significant protections to the parties involved, including automatic parental rights to the contracting couple.

Of further note is the fact that an international surrogacy market has emerged in the last two decades. This multimillion-dollar global industry matches women or couples in wealthy nations with potential surrogates in developing countries. In most cases, the contracting woman or couple and surrogate mother never meet. India, with more than 350 surrogacy clinics across the country, has the largest industry.

SUMMARY

The myriad new health care technologies have several social consequences. They create new options for people, they can alter human relationships, they can affect the entire health care system, they stimulate reflection on important value questions, and they raise social policy questions that must be resolved.

Advances in critical care medicine enable us to keep people alive even though we cannot cure them, relieve all their pain, or sometimes even restore them to consciousness. The cases of Karen Ann Quinlan, Nancy Cruzan, and Terri Schiavo clarified the judicial right for

competent and incompetent persons to refuse medical treatment, and even food and hydration. Despite the reluctance of many health care professionals to provide medically futile treatment—even when demanded by patients' families—the courts refused to allow a hospital to stop treatment for Helga Wanglie and Jahli McMath.

The ability to successfully transplant organs and the demand for transplants have raised complex questions regarding the nation's organ donation policy and the consequences for individuals involved. The United States now has a policy of weak required request, whereby patients or their families must be notified about the option of organ donation, and a request for donation is to be made. Because many people die before an organ becomes available, there is discussion about shifting to a more aggressive policy that presumes people wish to donate, or even shifting to a policy that enables donors to benefit financially.

Many Americans who are infertile seek to use one of the assisted procreative techniques. The most controversial of these is surrogate motherhood. Its proponents argue that there is and should be procreative liberty, and that patient autonomy demands that people have access to this technique. Opponents argue that surrogacy is not in the best interest of the surrogate, the child, or even the contracting individuals, that the process demeans women and reduces them to their reproductive capacity, and that it leads to a commodification of life. Some states have retained the legality of surrogacy, but outlawed payment to the surrogate; other states have banned the practice.

HEALTH ON THE INTERNET

1. The United Network for Organ Sharing (UNOS) makes available to the public updated information about transplant programs and services. Visit their website at

   https://unos.org

   Click on "Data" in the top menu, and then click on "Transplant Trends," and scroll down and click on "National Data" under "Detailed Data." Answer the following questions by clicking on "Donor," "Transplant," and "Waiting List" in "Choose Category." How many transplants have been performed in this calendar year? How many donors were used? Of the donors, how many were deceased and how many were living? How many individuals are currently on the waiting list for a transplant? Go back to "National Data" and click on the link to specific organs. Select an organ and determine the kinds of information that are available about the transplantation of this organ.

2. In 2014, Brittany Maynard, a 29-year-old California woman, was diagnosed with a malignant brain tumor and told that she had between 3 and 10 years to live. Two months later, new tests found an even more aggressive cancer, and she was given less than 6 months. At the time, California did not have legal physician aid-in-dying, so she and her family moved to Oregon, a state where she could legally be prescribed life-ending medications. Before she died, she taped a message to California legislators and put it on YouTube. Access it at "Brittany Maynard Legislative Testimony." It has received more than 185,000 hits. What are her main arguments in favor of aid-in-dying?

DISCUSSION CASES

1. In 1993, the Dutch Supreme Court officially acted to decriminalize active euthanasia, a practice that had been occurring for more than 25 years. The 1993 ruling protects physicians who engage in physician aid-in-dying or in any form of active euthanasia as long as basic guidelines are followed. The guidelines include:

a. The patient's request is the result of sound informed consent (the patient is competent and the request is voluntary and made without undue pressure) and is reviewed, discussed, and repeated.

b. The patient's suffering, both physical and mental, is severe and cannot be relieved by any other means.

c. The attending physician must consult with a colleague regarding the patient's condition and the genuineness and appropriateness of the request for euthanasia.

d. Only physicians may engage in euthanasia.

Requests for active euthanasia performed by physicians come mainly from patients with incurable cancer (70 percent), chronic degenerative neurological disorders (10 percent), and chronic obstructive pulmonary disease. Patients seeking active euthanasia report being in physical and psychological pain. Although Dutch law requires physicians to report the causes of death, some critics charge that active euthanasia is under-reported. In 2017, approximately 7,000 cases of death by active euthanasia or aid-in-dying occurred—more than 4 percent of all deaths. Public opinion polls have found that more than 90 percent of Dutch citizens favor the legalization of physician aid-in-dying and more than 60 percent favor the legalization of active euthanasia performed by physicians.

What arguments favor active euthanasia and what arguments oppose it? How do these compare and contrast with the arguments cited in the text regarding physician aid-in-dying? Should the United States adopt the Dutch policy? What would be the social ramifications of doing so?

2. In the United States, many people who support organ donation (more than 90 percent) do not themselves register to become organ donors (just over 50 percent), and sometimes survivors override the wishes of a deceased family member to donate organs. These factors contribute to the shortage of organs for donation.

An example is with kidney transplants. The kidney is the most frequently transplanted organ and is considered the best treatment option for end-stage kidney disease. In the United States, in 2018, there were 21,167 kidney transplants. About 70 percent of the transplanted kidneys came from deceased donors and 30 percent from donors giving up one of their two kidneys. On average, recipients had been on the transplant list for 3½ years. About 95 percent of kidney transplants are still working well 1 year out, and 92.5 percent are at 3 years out. There are about 103,000 persons on the kidney waiting list (United Network for Organ Sharing, 2019).

Some countries have experimented with incentive-based approaches to increase donation. For example, Singapore gives priority in receiving an organ donation to those who have declared a willingness to donate. When organs become available, priority to receive is given to declared organ donors. Israel has a similar but more elaborate program (that some call "Don't Give, Don't Get"). The system gives priority to those who have already donated from self or family member, then to those who have declared willingness to donate (for at least the prior 3 years), and then to family members of those who have declared donation willingness. Those who have neither donated nor declared a willingness to do so are considered only after the priority individuals.

Surveys indicate that many people believe these policies are effective in increasing organs for transplant, but that they are unsure about their fairness. How would you assess these proposals? Would you support such a proposal in this country?

GLOSSARY

active euthanasia
advance directives
brain death
commodification of life
egg freezing
genomic medicine
infertility
living will
medical futility
persistent vegetative state

personalized medicine
physician aid-in-dying
procreative liberty
technological determinism
technological imperative
technology
technology assessment
telemedicine
tyranny of the gift

REFERENCES

Alemzadeh, Homa, Ravishankar K. Iyer, Zbigniew Kalbarczyk, Nancy Leveson, and Jaishankar Raman. 2016. "Adverse Events in Robotic Surgery: A Retrospective Study of 14 Years of FDA Data." Retrieved March 2, 2019 (https://journals.plos.org/plosone/article?id=10.1371/journal.pone.0151470).

Almening, Rene. 2017. "The Business of Egg and Sperm Donation." *Contexts* 16(4):839–868.

Anspach, Renee. 1993. *Deciding Who Lives: Fateful Choices in the Intensive-Care Nursery*. Berkeley, CA: University of California Press.

Bailey, Phillippa K., Toav Ben-Schlomo, Isabel de Salis, Charles Tomson, and Amanda Owen-Smith. 2016. "Better the Donor You Know? A Qualitative Study of Renal Patients' Views on Altruistic Live-Donor Kidney Transplantation." *Social Science and Medicine* 150(February):104–111.

Barger-Lux, M. Janet, and Robert P. Heaney. 1986. "For Better and Worse: The Technological Imperative in Health Care." *Social Science and Medicine* 22(12):1313–1320.

Brown, Eliza, and Mary Patrick. 2018. "Time, Anticipation, and the Life Course: Egg Freezing as Temporarily Disentangling Romance and Reproduction." *American Sociological Review* 83(5):959–982.

Carrese, Joseph A., and Lorna A. Rhodes. 2000. "Bridging Cultural Differences in Medical Practice." *Journal of General Internal Medicine* 15(2):92–96.

Chang, Virginia W., and Diane S. Lauderdale. 2009. "Fundamental Cause Theory, Technological Innovation, and Health Disparities: The Case of Cholesterol in the Era of Statins." *Journal of Health and Social Behavior* 50(3):245–260.

Chou, Wen-Ying S., April Oh, and William M. Klein. 2018. "Addressing Health-Related Misinformation on Social Media." *Journal of the American Medical Association* 320(23):2417–2418.

Cook, Deborah, and Graeme Rocker. 2014. "Dying with Dignity in the Intensive Care Unit." *New England Journal of Medicine* 370(26):2506–2514.

Donate Life America. 2019. "2018 Annual Update." Retrieved April 25, 2019 (www.donatelife.net/wp-content/uploads/2018/09/DLA_AnnualReport.pdf).

Dzeng, Elizabeth, Alessandra Colaianni, Martin Roland, David Levine, Michael P. Kelly, Stephen Barclay, and Thomas J. Smith. 2016. "Moral Distress Amongst American Physician Trainees Regarding Futile Treatments at the End of Life: A Qualitative Study." *Journal of General Internal Medicine* 31(1):93–99.

Feldman, Eric. 2018. "Baby M Turns 30: The Law and Policy of Surrogate Motherhood." *American Journal of Law and Medicine* 44(1):7–22.

Fox, Renée C. 1989. *The Sociology of Medicine: A Participant Observer's View*. Upper Saddle River, NJ: Prentice Hall.

Fox, Renée C., and Judith P. Swazey. 1978. *The Courage to Fail: A Social View of Organ Transplants and Dialysis* (2nd ed.). Chicago, IL: University of Chicago Press.

———. 1992. *Spare Parts: Organ Replacement in American Society*. New York: Oxford University Press.

Freund, Peter E.S., and Meredith B. McGuire. 1999. *Health, Illness, and the Social Body* (3rd ed.). Upper Saddle River, NJ: Prentice Hall.

Herring, Andrew, Steffie Woolhandler, and David U. Himmelstein. 2008. "Insurance Status of U.S. Organ Donors and Transplant Recipients: The Uninsured Give but Rarely Receive." *International Journal of Health Services* 38(4):641–652.

Holder, Angela R. 1988. "Surrogate Motherhood and the Best Interests of Children." *Law, Medicine, & Health Care* 16(1–2):51–56.

Humphry, Derek. 1991. *Final Exit: The Practicalities of Self-Deliverance and Assisted Suicide for the Dying*. Los Angeles, CA: The Hemlock Society.

Inhorn, Marcia C., Daphna Birenbaum-Carmeli, and Pasquale Patrizio. 2017. "Medical Egg Freezing and Cancer Patients' Hopes: Fertility Preservation at the Intersection of Life and Death." *Social Science and Medicine* 195(December):25–33.

Institute of Medicine. 2015. *Dying in America: Improving Quality and Honoring Individual Preferences Near the End of Life*. Washington, DC: The National Academies Press.

Kutner, Nancy G. 1987. "Issues in the Application of High Cost Medical Technology: The Case of Organ Transplantation." *Journal of Health and Social Behavior* 28(1):23–36.

Kwok, Alvin C., Marcus E. Semel, Stuart R. Lipsitz, Angela M. Bader, Amber E. Barnato, Atul A. Gawande, and Ashish K. Jha. 2011. "The Intensity and Variation of Surgical Care at the End of Life: A Retrospective Cohort Study." *The Lancet* 378(9800):1408–1413.

Lehoux, Pascale, and Stuart Blume. 2000. "Technology Assessment and the Sociopolitics of Health Technologies." *Journal of Health Politics, Policy, and Law* 25(6):1063–1120.

Littenberg, Benjamin. 1992. "Technology Assessment in Medicine." *Academic Medicine* 67(7): 424–428.

Macklin, Ruth. 1988. "Is There Anything Wrong with Surrogate Motherhood? An Ethical Analysis." *Law, Medicine, & Health Care* 16(1–2):57–64.

Oosterveen, Emilie, Flora Tzelepis, Lee Ashton, and Melinda J. Hutchesson. 2017. "A Systematic Review of eHealth Behavioral Interventions Targeting Smoking, Nutrition, Alcohol, Physical Activity and/or Obesity for Young Adults." *Preventive Medicine* 99:197–206.

O'Reilly, Kevin B. 2010. "Assisted Suicide Laws Cited in 95 Deaths in Washington, Oregon." *Amednews.com*. Retrieved April 25, 2019 (www.amednews.com/article/20100325/profession/303259996/8/).

Pew Internet Health Tracking Survey. 2014. "The Social Life of Health Information." Retrieved April 29, 2019 (www. pewresearch.org/fact-tank/2014/01/15/the-social-life-of-health-information/).

Pflum, Mary. 2019. "Investors are Betting Big on the Egg Freezing Market." *NBC News*. Retrieved May 10, 2019 (www.cnbc.com/2019/03/12/investors-are-betting-on-the-continued-growth-of-egg-freezing-startups.html).

Polinski, Jennifer M., Tobias Barker, Nancy Gagliano, Andrew Sussman, Troyen A. Brennan, and William H. Shrank. 2016. "Patients' Satisfaction with and Preference for Telehealth Visits." *Journal of General Internal Medicine* 31(3):269–275.

Robertson, John A. 1994. *Children of Choice: Freedom and the New Reproductive Technologies*. Princeton, NJ: Princeton University Press.

Robinson, James C. 2015. "Biomedical Innovation in the Era of Health Care Spending Constraints." *Health Affairs* 34(2):203–209.

Rothman, Barbara K. 1988. "Reproductive Technology and the Commodification of Life." *Women and Health*, 13(1–2):95–100.

——. 1989. *Recreating Motherhood: Ideology and Technology in a Patriarchal Society*. New York: W.W. Norton.

Rothman, David J. 1997. *Beginnings Count: The Technological Imperative in American Health Care*. New York: Oxford University Press.

Schneiderman, Lawrence J., Nancy S. Jecker, and Albert R. Jonsen. 1990. "Medical Futility: Its Meaning and Ethical Implications." *Annals of Internal Medicine* 112(12):949–954.

Sharp, Lesley A. 2006. *Strange Harvest: Organ Transplants, Denatured Bodies, and the Transformed Self*. Berkeley, CA: University of California Press.

Shaw, Rhonda. 2010. "Perceptions of the Gift Relationship in Organ and Tissue Donation: Views of Intensivists and Donor and Recipient Coordinators." *Social Science and Medicine* 70(4): 609–615.

Steinhubl, Steven R., Evan D. Muse, and Eric J. Topol. 2013. "Can Mobile Health Technologies Transform Health Care?" *Journal of the American Medical Association* 310(22):2395–2396.

Sulmasy, Lois S., and Paul S. Mueller. 2017. "Ethics and the Legalization of Physician-Assisted Suicide: An American College of Physicians Position Paper." *Annals of Internal Medicine* 167(8): 576–578.

United Network for Organ Sharing. 2019. "Transplant Trends." Retrieved March 31, 2019 (https://unos. org/data/transplant-trends/).

Veatch, Robert M. 1993. "The Impending Collapse of the Whole-Brain Definition of Death." *Hastings Center Report* 23(4):18–24.

Volandes, Angelo. 2015. *The Conversation: A Revolutionary Plan for End-of-Life Care*. New York: Bloomsbury USA.

Wilensky, Gail R. 2016. "Robotic Surgery: An Example of When Newer is Not Always Better but Clearly More Expensive." *Milbank Quarterly* 94(1):43–46.

Woliver, Laura R. 1989. "The Deflective Power of Reproductive Technologies: The Impact on Women." *Women & Politics* 9(3):17–47.

CHAPTER 17

Comparative Health Care Systems

Learning Objectives

- Identify and describe the major factors that influence the structure of health care systems.

- Discuss the most important issues for health care systems in developing countries.

- Identify and discuss the concept of "global health."

- Identify and describe the four broad categories of health care systems in the world.

- Compare and contrast the health care systems of China, Canada, England, and Russia.

Studying the health care systems of other countries helps in understanding: (1) the diversity of approaches used to meet health care needs; (2) the variety of factors that shape development of these approaches; and (3) how the health care system in the United States compares and contrasts with those in other countries. Donald Light, who has written extensively on health care systems around the world, maintains that the health care system in the United States "is so unusual that only by comparing it with other systems can those of us who live inside it gain the perspective we need to understand how it works" (Light, 1990:429). See the accompanying box, "Comparing the World's Health Care Systems."

IN THE FIELD

COMPARING THE WORLD'S HEALTH CARE SYSTEMS

Can the United States learn anything about its own health care system by studying other countries?

As discussed in Chapter 14, several well-respected groups that evaluate, rate, and compare the world's health care systems rank the US system very unfavorably compared to health care systems in other modern countries.

In 2000, the World Health Organization evaluated the health care systems of 191 nations on health care delivery. The report took into consideration the overall health of each country, health inequities in the population, how nations respond to problems in their health care systems, how well people of varying economic status within a country are served by their system, and how costs are distributed. Which country earned the highest score? The top scorer was France, followed by Italy, San Marino, Andorra, Malta, Singapore, and Spain. Despite spending much more money

(Continued)

(*Continued*)

on health care than any other nation—in both absolute and relative terms—the United States finished 37th (World Health Organization, 2000).

A joint study by the Organisation for Economic Co-operation and Development and the World Health Organization, conducted around the same time, compared the current performance of the health care systems in 29 modern industrialized nations in 2000 with that in similar studies conducted in 1960 and 1980. The evaluation focused on six performance categories: (1) preventive health care, (2) health care use and services, (3) sophisticated technology, (4) mortality, (5) health system responsiveness, and (6) stability of per capita health spending relative to national income. On most indicators, the United States fared poorly. The overall performance of the United States and its relative performance in most categories declined from 1960 to 1980 to 2000, and the United States

did not improve its relative ranking in a single category (Anderson and Hussey, 2001).

These are the most in-depth studies done, but they were done two decades ago. Have things changed? In 2014, Bloomberg News studied 51 nations with respect to health spending per person, life expectancy, and health care cost as a percentage of the economy. The US health care system ranked 44th (Edney, 2014). In 2015, the Commonwealth Fund compared health care spending, supply, utilization, prices, and health outcomes in 13 high-income countries (Australia, Canada, Denmark, France, Germany, Japan, the Netherlands, New Zealand, Norway, Sweden, Switzerland, the United Kingdom, and the United States). The United States spent far more on health care than any other country but had poorer health outcomes, including lower life expectancy and a higher incidence of chronic conditions (Squires and Anderson, 2015).

MAJOR INFLUENCES ON HEALTH CARE SYSTEMS

Comparative studies of public policy have demonstrated one very clear principle—every public policy in every country is shaped by a wide and complex configuration of forces. Whether the policy is related to education, the environment, or health care, and whether the focus is the United States, China, or Canada, there are many important determinants.

> The range and number of factors that influence or determine what governments do or, for that matter, what they choose not to do, are virtually infinite. Public policy may be influenced by prior policy commitments, international tension, a nation's climate, economic wealth, degree of ethnic conflict, historical traditions, the personality of its leadership, the level of literacy of its people, the nature of its party system, and whether it is governed by civilian or military leaders. . . . Virtually anything can influence or determine what governments do.
> (Leichter, 1979:38)

Social scientists see patterns among these forces and have identified four key influences on the health care and other social systems (Leichter, 1979; Lassey, Lassey, and Jinks, 1997):

1. *The physical environment*, such as climate, availability of natural resources, and level of environmental pollution.
2. *Historical and situational events*, such as the Great Depression in the 1920s and 1930s.
3. *Cultural norms and values*, such as the aggressive "can do" cultural spirit in the United States that encourages American physicians to order more drugs and perform more diagnostic and surgical procedures than their European counterparts (Payer, 1989).
4. *The structure of society*, including political factors (the extent of government centralization), economic factors (the level of national wealth), demographic factors (age structure and degree of urbanization), and social factors (reliance on family versus social organizations).

Not all social scientists assign the same weight to each of these factors. For example, in the United States, many economists hold a *popular choice* position—that is, we have the type of health care system we do because it is the type of system people want. People's preferences are expressed through individual decisions in the marketplace and through voting behavior. Others, including many sociologists and political scientists, favor a *power group* explanation—that health policies have largely been shaped by the power and influence of certain groups (e.g., the AMA, hospitals, and insurance companies). Some analysts emphasize the influence of economic development and demographic makeup (e.g., the influence of available resources and the percentage of elderly within the society). Marxist analysis focuses on the role of class formation, class interests, and the political behavior of social classes, and explains America's lack of universal health care coverage as due to the weakness of labor unions and absence of an influential socialist party.

HEALTH CARE SERVICES IN DEVELOPING COUNTRIES

The world's developing countries experience a doubly difficult situation with regard to providing for public health—more health problems but considerably fewer resources to invest in health care. (See Tables 17.1 and 17.2 for illustrations of this pattern.) They have high rates of many communicable diseases, increasingly high rates of chronic degenerative diseases, and little money to invest in health care.

In the coming years, developing countries are expected to undergo an epidemiological transition as their disease and illness patterns come to more closely resemble that of developed countries. Improved ability to prevent and combat acute infectious diseases should lead to a reduction in infant, child, and overall mortality. But as has occurred in developed countries, this will likely lead to further increases in heart disease, cancer, and other chronic, degenerative

TABLE 17.1   Wealth of Country (2017), Per Capita Gross Domestic Product (2017), and Per Capita Health Expenditures (2016) for Select Countries

	Per Capita GDP (US$)	Per Capita Health Expenditures (US$)
High-Income Countries		
United States	59,930	9,870
Canada	44,871	4,458
United Kingdom	39,954	3,958
Upper-Middle-Income Countries		
Brazil	9,812	1,016
Romania	10,819	476
China	8,827	398
Lower-Middle-Income Countries		
Egypt	2,413	131
Vietnam	2,342	123
Pakistan	1,548	40
Low-Income Countries		
Haiti	766	38
Afghanistan	550	57
Central African Republic	418	16

Source: World Bank. *World Development Indicators*. 2019a and 2019b. https://data.worldbank.org/indicator?tab=all.

TABLE 17.2   Wealth of Country (2017), Life Expectancy (2017), and Infant Mortality Rate (2017) for Select Countries

	Life Expectancy (Years)	Infant Mortality Rate (%)
High-Income Countries		
United States	79	6
Canada	82	5
United Kingdom	81	4
Upper-Middle-Income Countries		
Brazil	76	13
Romania	75	7
China	76	8
Lower-Middle-Income Countries		
Egypt	72	19
Vietnam	76	17
Pakistan	67	61
Low-Income Countries		
Haiti	64	54
Afghanistan	64	52
Central African Republic	53	88

Source: World Bank. *World Development Indicators*. 2019. https://data.worldbank.org/indicator?tab=all.

diseases. Moreover, in some developing countries, these degenerative diseases are striking people at younger ages than has been customary in developed countries, so this is an added problem (Kostova et al., 2017).

It will require a huge financial investment in health care to keep pace with already existing problems and those created by the transition. Most developing countries spend only about 4 or 5 percent of their income on health care—about half of what most developed countries spend. This is creating some of the same issues as in developed countries: access to care, quality of care, and system efficiency. More resources need to be invested in the public health infrastructure, especially in rural areas. Given the government's smaller revenue-raising ability in these countries, pressures mount to turn more of the system over to the private market. This may work to the benefit of the middle and upper classes, but it forces many in the lower classes out of the health care system. The accompanying box, "The Globalization of Health Care," describes the very significant efforts occurring today in the globalization of health care.

IN COMPARATIVE FOCUS

THE GLOBALIZATION OF HEALTH CARE

When many people think about **global health**, they think only of health problems in developing countries. That is only a small part of the concept, as it includes (1) health problems that transcend national borders (e.g., the Zika virus), (2) health problems of such magnitude that they have an impact on economic and political systems around the world (e.g., HIV/

AIDS), and (3) health problems that require cooperative action and solutions by more than one country (e.g., Ebola). Consider the following issues:

1. Health and climate change and other changes in the ecosystem (the countries that will be most negatively affected are those that have contributed the least to the problem).
2. The lack of food security (the world had an estimated 815 million chronically hungry people in 2016—almost 11 percent of the world population).
3. Acute infectious diseases such as malaria and diarrheal diseases that are continuing problems in many areas of the world.
4. Chronic degenerative diseases such as cancer and heart disease that are common causes of death in the developed world and are increasingly common in developing countries.
5. Maternal and child health, as shown in maternal mortality and infant mortality rates.
6. Pharmaceutical company testing of many of their drugs in less developed countries.
7. Inadequate, ineffective, and inequitable health care systems that do not offer the necessary health support to people.
8. Shortages of health care workers—with the accompanying problem that wealthy countries sometimes recruit trained health care workers from developing countries—and shortages of medical equipment and supplies.

Commentators sometimes ask why people in countries like the United States should have any concern about worldwide health problems or problems that occur primarily in developing countries. FamiliesUSA (2010), an organization that promotes global health programs, offers four reasons:

1. Humanitarian reasons—hundreds of millions or more people continue to suffer needlessly.

2. Equity reasons—roughly 90 percent of the world's health care resources are spent on 10 percent of the world's people.
3. Direct impact reasons—in the increasingly connected world, diseases can easily migrate from nation to nation.
4. Indirect impact reasons—countries with significant health problems often experience economic and political instability that has worldwide consequences.

Are global health problems so immense that little can be done? The answer is no. All of the discussions that have occurred in the World Health Organization, FamiliesUSA, Global Health Initiative, and many other groups are a needed step in genuinely addressing these problems. Representatives from disciplines such as public health (which has always had a strong global component), medicine, law, international relations, sociology, anthropology, economics, political science, biology, management, environmental science and policy, and others are combining their expertise to combat global health problems.

Global health partnerships (GHPs) are being developed in other countries by many American and European universities, by private foundations such as the Bill and Melinda Gates Foundation, and by public health/epidemiological groups such as the World Health Organization and the Centers for Disease Control and Prevention. Some schools and programs are affiliating with hospitals, schools, and programs in Africa, Asia, andSouth America. For example, Harvard University has established partnerships in Dubai, Turkey, and India, and the University of Virginia is working with a program in Lesotho. The Global Health Service Partnership sends US physicians and nurses to serve as faculty at medical and nursing schools in low-resource countries such as Malawi, Tanzania, and Uganda. Among other benefits, these programs will improve the medical infrastructure in these countries and hopefully entice more trained health workers to stay in their home country (Kerry and Mullan, 2013).

The Central African Republic, a landlocked nation in the very center of Africa, is a case in point. Once ruled by France, it has been independent since 1960. It has had unstable efforts at autocracy, monarchy, and democracy, but has been locked in civil war since 2012. It is one of the poorest countries in the world despite significant amounts of uranium, crude oil, gold, diamonds, cobalt, lumber, and hydropower. It has the lowest GDP per capita and is considered the unhealthiest country in the world. Population is just under 5 million persons.

Prior to the latest civil war, there were several hospitals and clinics staffed and operated by missionaries that provided relatively good care to those who could reach them. Many of those have been destroyed in the conflict (75 percent of health facilities no longer offer services), and many providers have fled. Now, the only modern health care facilities exist near the largest city, Bangui (which has one sub-standard hospital), and a few other towns.

For the majority of Central Africans, little is offered by the poorly equipped and insufficiently staffed maternity clinics, dispensaries, and first-aid posts available in the countryside. One city of 116,000 people has three physicians. The distribution of medicine is extremely difficult given an inadequate transportation system. Malaria, diarrhea, leprosy, tuberculosis, nutritional diseases, hepatitis A and E, dengue fever, typhoid fever, and HIV/AIDS are major health problems.

There are some significant success stories in the efforts of low- and middle-income countries to create and maintain effective health care systems. As recently as 1970, Mexico's health care system was in disarray, and health indicators were similar to those in many developing countries. However, significant improvements were made in the 1980s and 1990s, and in 2003, Mexico approved landmark health reform legislation that created a government-funded system (*Seguro Popular*) to deliver medical care to all citizens regardless of ability to pay. More than 55 million previously uninsured people have since received health insurance, while health care costs have steadied at 5 to 6 percent of total spending—a very manageable level. Until this time, the only insurance available was through one's employer or through expensive private insurance.

Mexico is now experiencing marked improvement in health indicators for both children and adults. Much remains to be done to close disparity gaps and to make services available in rural areas. But Mexico has used scientific assessments of system effectiveness and health outcomes to improve its health care system (Strouse et al., 2016).

TYPES OF HEALTH CARE SYSTEMS

The world's health care systems can be organized roughly into four categories:

1. *Private and public insurance with private entrepreneurial services.* The United States is the only modern nation in the world to emphasize the private market and profit-making in its health care system. Health insurance companies, pharmaceutical companies, medical equipment companies, and many hospitals are run to make a profit. As we learned in Chapter 14, there has also been a large public (government) sector. Prior to recent health care reform, 47 million people in the United States lacked health insurance. All other modern countries believe that health care is a right, and everyone should receive services at no or minimal cost.

2. *National health insurance with private regulated services.* Some countries rely on a private health care system but with the federal government providing a government-run, health insurance program that covers everyone. There are variations among these plans, but everyone is covered by health insurance and receives care

at no or minimal cost at the point of service. Canada, examined later in this chapter, exemplifies this type of system.

Germany uses a model that is similar in many respects to that in several European countries. The system is based on a belief that people's health care needs should be met regardless of their income. The system is financed by a tax on employers and employees and by general tax revenue surpluses. Everyone is assured of getting health care when they are sick or injured.

The German government requires all individuals to have health insurance (like the individual mandate did under the Affordable Care Act), but it does not directly provide the insurance. Most German people (about 89 percent) buy heavily regulated nonprofit insurance from one of 160 "sickness funds." The government requires these plans to be comprehensive, not to turn anyone away due to a pre-existing condition, and to have premiums based on ability to pay. There are no deductibles, only very small co-payments, and ready access to all health care services. These funds compete with each other for survival rather than for profit. About 11 percent of Germans opt out of these funds and purchase private (for-profit) insurance. Premiums in these plans depend on age and health (older and sicker enrollees pay more).

Most hospitals are government owned (50 percent of all hospital beds) or have non-profit ownership (about 35 percent of beds). Most physicians are salaried and work in private practice or in a hospital. Physician compensation is negotiated by professional medical associations (so that there is a uniform fee schedule), and the government establishes limits on what hospitals can charge.

The German health care system is widely respected around the world, and within the country health indicators are very good, access to services is prompt, and there is much public satisfaction with the system. Health care prices are much lower in Germany than in the United States, but the quality of services is excellent.

3. *National health insurance with public regulated services.* Some countries have public ownership of the health care system and publicly provided health insurance. The government owns health care facilities, employs health care workers, and collects taxes to pay for health care. However, decision making typically is decentralized, with regional and local agencies playing an important role. General practitioners must be seen in order to receive a referral to a specialist. Many of these countries now allow a small private sector for wealthier patients who desire quicker or enhanced service (e.g., a private hospital bed). England is an example of this type of system, and is one of the countries described in detail later in this chapter.

Norway offers a government-owned and government-run health care system with publicly provided health insurance. Health funding is provided to localities, which in turn allocate funds to particular services. After payment of a deductible, all individuals receive comprehensive health care services at no or minimal cost at the point of service. Private insurance is also available, but is rarely used because the public system is so good. Individuals typically purchase private insurance to avoid a hospital waiting list or for services like plastic surgery.

Most physicians are salaried, although some exceptions exist. The government pays for the program from general tax revenues rather than a specially designated tax. Patients are admitted to a hospital through its emergency department or through a physician referral. The quality of hospitals is excellent. While there may be lengthy waiting lists for non-emergency care, receipt of emergency care is prompt. If a physician refers an individual to the hospital, the care is free. The Norwegian health care system is widely respected around the world and within the country, health indicators are very good, and there is much public satisfaction with the system.

4. National health insurance, state-run system (socialized medicine). Some countries have an entirely government-owned and government-funded health care system. All health care workers are employees of the government, and all health care facilities are owned by the government. Theoretically, at least, there is no private health care sector. The government typically conducts extensive health care planning, budgeting, organization, and regulation. In the former Soviet Union, a country covered in detail later in this chapter, patients were assigned to a particular neighborhood physician, and physicians were assigned a particular roster of patients. Patients received health care at no or minimal cost at the point of service. Patient waiting times varied but typically were not long.

Cuba represents an excellent example of **socialized medicine**. The government operates a national health system in which all medical facilities are owned by the government and all medical providers are employed by the government. There are no private facilities or private providers. All medical care is free, and there are no deductibles, coinsurance, or co-payments. The emphasis throughout the system is on prevention.

In part because medical education is free, there are more physicians per capita in Cuba than in the United States. They not only spend more time with each patient, but every patient also receives a home visit once a year. Health providers live in the same community as their patients. Despite being a low-income country, life expectancy is virtually the same as in the United States, the infant mortality rate is lower, and vaccination rates are the highest in the world (Campion and Morrissey, 2013). Moreover, Cuba sends out more than 30,000 medical providers each year to more than 70 developing countries to contribute to health care delivery. Hospitals and other parts of the health care system infrastructure are in serious need of repair, but the system is admired for doing a lot with a little and is appreciated at home.

The US health care system having already been examined, the four countries selected for review in this chapter represent a cross section of other approaches. Many Chinese people are still extremely poor, although there is increasing wealth in the cities. Canada illustrates the national health insurance with a private regulated services approach. England illustrates the national health insurance with a public regulated services model. Russia, when it was part of the Soviet Union, illustrated the national health insurance state-run system (socialized medicine) model.

The health care system of each of these countries is described in terms of (1) its historical, political, and philosophical foundation; (2) the organization of the health care system; (3) the extent to which health services are accessible to the people; (4) indicators of the performance of the health care system; and (5) recent developments in the system. Table 17.3 compares the level of advancement in health care of technology, resources, and access in these countries with that in the United States.

As you are reading about the individual countries, note how each is affected by the same key forces (e.g., rapidly escalating health care costs), and note the similarities and differences in the types of responses that are being made. For each country, consider how its health care system has been influenced by environmental, situational-historical, and cultural norms and values, and the structural factors described earlier.

TABLE 17.3   Comparative Analysis of the Health Care System in Five Countries

Country	Level of Advancement of Health Care System		
	Technology	Resources	Access
China	Low	Low	Moderate
Russia	Low	Low	Moderate
Canada	High	High	High
England	High	Moderate	High
United States	High	High	Moderate

Source: Marie L. Lassey, William R. Lassey, and Martin J. Jinks, *Health Care Systems Around the World* (Upper Saddle River, NJ: Prentice Hall, 1997).

CHINA

The Historical, Political, and Philosophical Foundation

With a population of 1.4 billion people, China has almost 20 percent of all the people in the world and more than any other single country. China's landmass is similar in size to the contiguous United States. Only recently has a majority of China's population been urban-based. China is undergoing rapid modernization, but many Chinese remain very poor.

With regard to health care, three distinct phases are apparent in China's recent history: (1) the focus on improving health care from the time that Mao Zedong came to power in 1949 until 1965; (2) the radical restructuring of the health care system during the Cultural Revolution from 1965 to 1977; and (3) the development of reform efforts and movement toward free-market entrepreneurialism from the 1970s to the present day.

Mao inherited a China in desperate condition. Plagued by years of both civil war and war with Japan, the economy was in shambles, with both agricultural and industrial productivity at low levels. Food shortages were common, as were epidemics of disease. About 1 baby in 5 died in the first year of life, and almost 1 in 3 before the age of 5 years. Hospitals and other health facilities were in desperately short supply in urban areas, with even fewer in rural areas. Most physicians

practiced only traditional Chinese medicine learned through apprenticeships.

At the first National Health Congress, Mao presented four precepts as the ideological basis for health services:

1. Health care must be directed to the working people.
2. Preventive medicine must be given priority over curative medicine. By the mid-1960s, the government had conducted several Patriotic Health Movements in which millions of Chinese worked at getting rid of the "four pests" (flies, mosquitoes, bedbugs, and rats), improving general sanitation, preventing parasitic diseases, and eliminating sexually transmitted infections.
3. Modern health care needed to be added to traditional Chinese approaches. The Chinese adage that "China walks on two legs: one traditional and one modern" is evident in health care.
4. Health workers must be involved with mass movements. An example is the family planning movement in China with the mandatory "one child per family" objective (which has now been discontinued).

Considerable efforts were directed to increasing access to medical care for the massive rural population. Rural areas were divided into *communes* (which averaged between 15,000 and 50,000 people) and further subdivided into *production brigades* (with 1,000–3,000 people), each with its own health center. These health centers were staffed by public health workers, midwives, and barefoot doctors. **Barefoot doctors** (later called *countryside doctors*) were peasants who had received a few months of medical training and then returned to their commune to treat minor illnesses (including colds, gastrointestinal ailments, and minor injuries), provide immunizations and birth control, and improve sanitation. Their existence compensated for the critical shortage of physicians in rural areas.

Within a decade and a half, substantial progress had been made. However, in 1966, frustrated and angered that his ideas were being incorporated too slowly and mistrustful of various societal institutions including medicine, Mao launched the Cultural Revolution—a violent campaign of political and social repression. Those suspected of having ideological differences with Mao were imprisoned, tortured, and sometimes murdered. Schools and medical colleges were closed, medical research was halted, and health expenditures decreased. Mao proclaimed that the health care system was not sufficiently directed toward rural areas, that medical education had become too Westernized and not sufficiently practical, and that many physicians were shunning traditional Chinese medicine in favor of Western approaches.

Following the death of Mao in 1976, China maintained its commitment to a socialist economic system with extensive government control of the economy. This was believed to offer the most effective strategy for ensuring that the basic needs of the people were met. Access to health care was deemed a right of all people, and there was a strong moral commitment to providing health care for free or at very little charge. Emphasis was placed on preventive care, the use of minimally trained health care personnel, and combining traditional and Western-style medicines. The

Chinese health care system became the envy of developing countries around the world.

However, Chinese leaders became frustrated at the slow pace of modernization. Since 1980, leaders have insisted that, while China remains a socialist country politically, efforts to accelerate economic development should occur by shifting from a planned economy with extensive control by the national government to a market-oriented economy with private ownership of enterprises and private investments in all sectors. This created a dramatic transformation for the country—with rapid industrialization and considerable economic growth—but it had dire consequences for health care delivery and health outcomes.

Local governments cut subsidies to rural hospitals and clinics. The decreased funding led to many countryside doctors to enter farming and other occupations where they could make more money, or to enter the private practice of medicine, so they could charge fees. Rural peasants, who had been able to receive services for no or a small payment, became subject to a fee-for-service system in which they paid the village doctor out of pocket. By the year 2000, China's health care system had transitioned from one in which affordable preventive and curative services were accessible to everyone to a system in which most people could not afford basic health care and no government or private health insurance existed (Yip and Hsiao, 2008).

Since that time, China has embarked on a series of modifications to its health care system. Although major changes were introduced in 2003 and 2005, in 2008 Chinese leaders concluded that the private market system had completely failed for health care. Major initiatives were introduced in 2009, 2013, 2014, and 2018 to create more affordable, quality medical care through a government-sponsored insurance system.

Organization of the Health Care System

China comprises five autonomous regions, 22 provinces, four direct-controlled municipalities

(Beijing, Shanghai, Tianjin, and Chongqing), and two largely self-governing regions (Hong Kong and Macau). It is a one-party state (the Communist Party). Since 2013, the National Health and Family Planning Commission has overseen formulation of health care policies, established prices that physicians can charge, and supervised medical research. The health department in each province oversees the actual distribution of health resources, and works with local governments in the financing and delivery of health care services according to local needs.

Primary care is now delivered mostly by village doctors and other health workers in rural (village) clinics and by general practitioners (GPs) in rural (township) hospitals, small urban community hospitals, and multipurpose urban hospitals. Village doctors are not licensed general practitioners and can work only in village clinics. The rural population typically uses the village clinics and township hospitals, and the urban population typically uses the community hospitals. Anyone can see a GP in the multipurpose hospitals. Specialists primarily work out of hospitals. Most township and community hospitals are public, but multipurpose hospitals can be public or private.

Since 1949, China's health care coverage has gone from universal to almost none (in the early 1980s) to now, with the recent health care reforms, about 95 percent. Chinese people have coverage through one of three plans: (1) a compulsory urban employee insurance program, (2) a voluntary but subsidized insurance program for all rural residents, or (3) a voluntary but subsidized program for unemployed urban residents, including students, young children, and the elderly. Combined with other recent changes in the system (e.g., the addition of private insurance plans, greater availability of needed drugs, and the establishment of primary care-based community health centers), significant improvements have occurred.

The government does continue to set the prices that providers can charge for most services,

and this now includes drugs. To recover the money lost when drug costs were restricted, physicians have begun ordering more diagnostic tests and using other additional services with a high-profit margin (Fu, Li, and Yip, 2018).

Accessibility of Health Care

The government continues to affirm its belief that every citizen is entitled to receive basic health care services provided by local governments. Its stated intention is to have 100 percent health insurance coverage by the early 2020s (when it is anticipated that China will spend US$1 trillion annually on health care). Those with insurance are covered for primary, specialist, emergency, hospital, and mental health care, prescription drugs, and traditional Chinese medicine. A few dental and optometry services are provided, but are mostly paid out of pocket, as are home-based and hospice services. Subsidies are available for people with low incomes. Efforts are underway to increase the number of medical facilities and to enhance care coordination and integration among facilities (Fang, 2016).

Performance of the Health Care System

Despite these recent changes, disease patterns in China vary considerably between urban and rural areas and between wealthy and poor people. In urban China, the major health concerns are the same as in the industrialized world—heart disease and cancer. Lung cancer has become a particular problem in China. About 350 million Chinese people smoke cigarettes (70 percent of adult men but just 7 percent of adult women are smokers), 750 million are affected directly by secondhand smoke, and death and illness from smoking-related causes have become a paramount health concern. Smog is a huge problem in cities. In addition, the typical diet contains an increasingly high percentage of fat (there are many fast-food restaurants), lifestyles are becoming much more

The percentage of Chinese citizens with health insurance has climbed back to 95 percent.
Source: Photo by Gregory Weiss.

sedentary, once unheard-of obesity is increasing (30 percent of Chinese people are overweight and 12 percent are obese), and excessive alcohol consumption is becoming more of a problem. HIV/AIDS, long ignored by the government, is now acknowledged as a significant problem. (Although an HIV outbreak in a Hangzhou hospital in 2017—caused by reuse of a needle used on an HIV patient—was not reported by Chinese news stations.) In rural areas, environmental pollution and the absence of safe drinking water (a major source of stomach, liver, and intestinal cancers) continue to be huge problems. Nutrition-related diseases, parasitic diseases, tuberculosis, and hepatitis B are common.

China has rapidly increased its number of physicians in recent years, but a serious shortage remains in both urban and rural areas. With the onset of health insurance coverage there has been a significantly increased demand for services and increased frustration with the shortage of primary care doctors. Health care costs are rapidly increasing. Large pharmaceutical companies, including GlaxoSmithKline, Eli Lilly, and Pfizer have been caught giving kickbacks to physicians using their drugs (in 2014, GlaxoSmithKline paid a fine of US$500 million). Some progress in assimilating advanced medical technology has been made, but expansion has come slowly, and few high-tech services are offered outside large urban areas. Thus many patients go to large cities to receive care, and this has put more pressure on those resources. Overall, China spends about 5.5 percent of its gross domestic product on health care.

Recent Developments in Health Care

The commitment to a private-market health care system created profound problems for health and health care in China. In recent years, however, China's commitment to improving its health care system and providing universal access to effective, safe, and low-cost health care has already had noticeable effects. Since 2009, there has been a financial commitment to building new clinics and hospitals throughout the country. Private facilities account for almost half of medical facilities, although patients prefer public facilities and doctors. State-subsidized health insurance for urban and rural residents enables more than 95 percent of Chinese people to be covered by some form of health insurance. Efforts to increase private market opportunities for international companies to build private hospitals, to engage in research and development, and to sell pharmaceuticals and medical devices in China have been very successful. In 2011, a public-private health care partnership between China and the United States was created to boost health care knowledge and technology and to open lucrative new trade markets (Wang, Zhang, and Hou, 2016).

CANADA

The Historical, Political, and Philosophical Foundation

The nation of Canada is a federal system—its 37 million people are spread across a loose confederation of ten provinces, from Newfoundland off the east coast to British Columbia in the west, and three territories: the Yukon, the Northwest Territories, and Nunavut. Much of the political structure of Canada was created under the British North America (BNA) Act, passed by the British Parliament in 1867. It guarantees considerably greater autonomy to the Canadian provinces than that held by individual American states. The BNA Act allocated to the federal government all matters of national concern and those with highest cost. The provinces were assigned more local and (presumably) less costly activities such as education, roads, and health care.

Throughout the early decades of the twentieth century, limited programs for health insurance were offered by local governments, industries, and voluntary agencies. These programs covered only selected services and left much of the population uninsured. Not until the mid-1940s did Canada begin earnestly to consider universal health insurance. This consideration was stimulated by three factors—high levels of poverty brought on by the Depression, the inability of local governments to offer substantial help due to their own state of near bankruptcy, and the despair of physicians who were frequently not paid. Significant disparities in wealth among the provinces led to additional inequalities in health services.

Although a universal plan was defeated at this time due to fears of federal infringement on provincial authority, the widespread health problems of Canadian people and the inadequacy of available health care facilities were well documented. As a beginning but precedent-setting step, the federal government initiated financial assistance to the provinces to create additional health care resources.

The transition to a universal health insurance plan occurred gradually. In 1946, the Saskatchewan government enacted legislation for a universal compulsory hospital care insurance plan for all its citizens. The success of this program led additional provinces to enact similar programs. These were quite successful and well received but very expensive, prompting the provinces to encourage the federal government to develop a national plan. However, as the concept became more popular with the general citizenry and with political leaders, physicians, fearing loss of professional autonomy, and private insurance companies, fearing their own elimination, expressed increasing reservations.

Finally, in 1968, Canada passed the Medical Care Act, which brought all the provinces together in a universal national health insurance program. The federal government agreed to pay half of the health care costs in each province as long as their health care services complied with four conditions: (1) they provided *comprehensive* services with no benefits limitations; (2) benefits were *universal*—available to all—and provided uniformly; (3) benefits were *portable*, so that citizens were covered wherever they were in Canada; and (4) the plans had to be *publicly financed and administered by an agency accountable to the provincial government.*

Although the system worked well, the federal government soon realized that it not only lacked control over the amount of funds expended by the provinces (and the provinces had little incentive to control costs), but also received little political credit for its substantial contribution. In 1977, a key compromise, Bill C-37, was enacted. This legislation enabled the federal government to reduce its financial contribution (now at about 20 percent) with a corresponding reduction in federal and corporate taxes. The provinces, whose share increased (and is now at 80 percent), were able to increase their taxes to generate sufficient revenue to fund the program. In addition, the provinces were given greater latitude in managing the program, with the desired effect that they would become more cost-conscious.

The law pertaining to health insurance was modified again in 1984 in the Canada Health Act. Concerned that some physicians were "extra billing" (i.e., directly charging patients fees above the reimbursement amount), this law mandated that physicians accept the reimbursement as their total payment. This legislation was not well received in the medical profession. For example, although only about 10 percent of physicians in Ontario were extra billing, a series of general strikes occurred to protest the government's increased regulation of physicians (Lewis, 2015).

Two key values underlie the Canadian national health insurance system. First, Canada has established a "right" to health care for all its citizens and eliminated financial barriers to care. In doing so, the Canadian people have made an important statement about the social unity of the country, the high value placed on social equity, and the worth of people independent of their ability to pay for a service. Many would say that

these values are more reflective of Canadian than American culture.

At the same time, Canada has maintained the private nature of the medical profession. Canadian physicians are not government employees and have considerably greater autonomy than their counterparts in Russia or even England. Canada's intention has been to offer publicly funded insurance for health care in a privately controlled system.

Organization of the Health Care System

Within the national government, the ultimate authority on health care is the health minister who directs national health care policy, works with Parliament on relevant legislation, and serves as an important liaison with the health minister of each of the provinces. Because health is primarily a provincial responsibility, much of the work related to medical education and medical licensure, hospitals, and public health occurs at the provincial level. Although policies, procedures, and standards among provinces tend to be comparable, this is not required and variations do occur.

About 75 to 80 percent of Canadian physicians are in office-based private practice, with most of the remainder based in hospitals. Most office-based physicians (generalists and specialists) have hospital privileges, and admit and tend to patients there. Patients have free choice of physicians, and physicians have the option of accepting or rejecting any new patient.

The national health insurance plan is funded from federal and provincial tax revenues, and insurance premiums are paid by all tax-paying citizens. The government utilizes a variety of "supply-side" cost-containment measures. The most important of these is **prospective budgeting**, whereby hospitals are financed on the basis of annually negotiated prospective budgets within each province. Once a budget is established for the ensuing year, hospitals and other programs and providers are expected to live within it. Capital expenditures are handled separately and do not come out of the assigned allocation but do require government approval.

Other key mechanisms used to regulate costs by controlling the supply of health care services are (1) setting the level of reimbursement for physicians (currently at 75 percent of established fees), (2) controlling the number of physicians by limiting medical school enrollments, and (3) minimizing the presence of private health insurance, which is available only to cover certain supplemental benefits such as a private hospital room, dental and eye care, and prescription drugs.

The degree of physician autonomy remains a key issue. Policy discussions regarding national health insurance have typically been sensitive to preserving the "private" nature of the profession and have avoided language suggesting that physicians are government employees.

In reality, however, the line is not so distinct, and many physicians feel they have been "deprivatized." Physicians are reimbursed directly by the provincial government on a fee-for-service basis. Fees for each medical service are established in annual negotiations between the provincial medical association and the provincial government. The negotiated reimbursement schedules are binding, include little variation by medical specialty or complexity of care delivered, and prohibit extra billing. Even physicians who have entirely "opted out" of national health insurance (an option taken by only a small percentage) are prevented from charging patients more than the specified reimbursement level.

Provincial governments reimburse physicians for only a percentage of the fee schedules set by the medical associations. This has been acceptable to most physicians, however, because they spend considerably less time on billing and other administrative paperwork and pay significantly less for malpractice insurance than physicians in the United States.

Physicians enjoy high esteem in Canada, reflected in salaries in the top 1 percent of all professions. Although some physicians have complained that national health insurance has depressed their incomes, incomes have continued to increase at a reasonable level.

Accessibility of Health Care

All basic hospital services, physician services and surgeries (including dental surgery) are covered for Canadian citizens. Out-of-pocket health care expenses are for prescription medications, eye care, dental care, home care, and private insurance—a somewhat longer list of exclusions than in most countries with universal coverage. Research has documented a greater use of physician and hospital services by Canadians than by Americans, especially among people with lower incomes.

Critics of the Canadian system counter that accessibility to health care is limited by reduced availability of physicians, surgical procedures, and high-tech equipment. The relative lack of equipment and resources means that patients wanting to see a specialist are not seen as promptly as they are in the United States, that queues (i.e., waiting lists) exist for many high-tech procedures, and that fewer of these procedures are provided. Wait times to see a specialist after being referred by a general practitioner can be a few to several months, and wait times for diagnostic imaging services such as MRIs and CTs and non-emergency surgeries (such as hip and knee replacements) are often even longer (Marchildon, Cafaro, and Brown, 2018).

Performance of the Health Care System

Standard health indicators for Canada are very favorable. Canada is among the upper echelon of countries in the world with regard to life expectancy (longer than in the United States) and infant mortality (lower than in the United States). One recent study found that the health of wealthy Americans and wealthy Canadians is about the same, but that the health of low-income persons is much better in Canada (McGrail et al., 2009).

The extent to which Canada maintains control over costs while providing high-quality comprehensive services is a controversial issue. Advocates of the Canadian system emphasize that it guarantees comprehensive services while spending less than in the United States (11 percent of GDP versus 18 percent). Canada's willingness to provide universal coverage for health care has given it bargaining leverage to include mechanisms of cost control. Compared with the United States, Canada invests significantly less money per capita in administrative costs (the uniform billing system alone saves billions of dollars each year), profits, marketing, legal involvement in medicine, and other "medically irrelevant" areas. As noted in Chapter 14, while as much as 30 percent of the American health care dollar goes toward administrative costs, the corresponding figure in Canada is about 16 percent (Woolhandler, Campbell, and Himmelstein, 2004).

Critics of the Canadian system contend that these cost efficiencies come with a price. They argue that even after restricting the availability of services and sacrificing investment in sophisticated high-tech equipment, Canada has not had sufficient money to run the system.

Canadian citizens have long expressed great pride in their health care system, as reflected in public opinion polls. About 75 percent of Canadians consider their health care system to work well or very well. Prior to health care reform, only 25 percent of Americans rated their system as highly. Surveys show that 90 percent of Canadians prefer their health care system to that of the United States. Most people in the United States express a preference for the Canadian system.

Recent Developments in Health Care

The Canadian system needs to address two major pressure points. First, a decision will have to be made about the level of funding. After several years of budget slashing, the government has now committed to increased funding for health care—a development that has been favorably received.

This issue relates to the other pressure point, namely the public–private mix in the health care system. Some medical professionals and ideological conservatives have long sought to reprivatize the system by shifting financial responsibility away from the government and back to patients (through private insurance), establishing less universal and less comprehensive health insurance plans and emphasizing market forces in health care by deregulating the field. This position has not been supported by either a majority of the population or the government.

There is currently increased discussion of allowing a private health care system to develop alongside the public system. Proponents argue that movement in this direction is already occurring. Private health insurance has increased in Canada (about two-thirds of Canadians have private insurance to supplement the public system). Private health insurance and out-of-pocket spending together pay for 30 percent of all health care expenditures. By allowing patients who want to pay for private insurance to do so, some pressure on the public system is relieved (Allin and Rudoler, 2016). Opponents argue that this "two-tier" system will eventually lead to the destruction of the public system by eroding broad-based public support and increasing its costs. This issue will test the commitment of the Canadian people in the coming years to their traditional health care system.

ENGLAND

The Historical, Political, and Philosophical Foundation

England's strong commitment to public responsibility for the health and welfare of its citizens dates back to the mid-1800s. The foundation for today's National Health Service (NHS) was laid in 1867 with passage of the Metropolitan Poor Act—a bill that obligated local governments to provide free hospital care for the poor. The measure appealed both to people's charitable interests and to a desire to protect others from contracting diseases from the untreated sick.

By the turn of the century, however, many were dissatisfied with the limited scope of the Poor Act, as England was confronted with the same pressures that existed throughout Europe to increase social welfare programs. The National Insurance Act of 1911, one of several social reforms sponsored by the Liberal government, provided medical and disability benefits and income protection during sickness. The program was compulsory for all wage earners between the ages of 16 and 65 years earning less than a designated sum per year. However, the plan was less generous than similar programs in Germany and Japan in that it did not cover dependents of wage earners (except for a maternity plan), self-employed people (including farmers), or the unemployed. There was continued interest in a more comprehensive program.

In the early and mid-1940s, England suffered from the devastation of World War II. Major parts of cities were destroyed, the economy was in chaos, a severe housing shortage existed, and the general health of the population was very poor. The prevailing system could not adequately handle these problems.

The Beveridge Report of 1942 analyzed these social problems and recommended major reform through increased government involvement in the economy, education, and health care. Strong Labour Party sponsorship and broad popular support for significant health care reform existed, although not among physicians, who fiercely resisted change. Eventually, the National Health Service Act of 1946 was passed by a wide margin and the National Health Service (NHS) was implemented in 1948. The NHS provided for the entire range of basic health care services to be available at no charge to the entire population

in a system financed by general tax revenues. Despite some major adjustments, the health care system inaugurated in 1948 continues today.

England has a long history of extensive government involvement throughout society's institutions and a commitment to providing for the basic needs of all citizens. Within this "welfare state," the NHS expresses the social value placed on a just distribution of essential resources (such as health care) for its 56 million people. Although the current health care system is not without its critics, the "National" is a source of immense pride.

Organization of the Health Care System

The health care system is largely government-owned and government-run. The government sets health care policy, raises funds and budgets for health care, owns health care facilities, employs physicians and other health care professionals, and purchases medical supplies and equipment. Ultimate authority rests with the Department of Health and the Secretary of State for Health.

The control of costs and cost increases is accomplished through use of a **prospective budget**. The amount of money to be spent on health in a year is determined in advance, and system managers must operate within the budgeted amount. A balanced budget is expected. By limiting expenses (England spends less money per capita on health care than other European countries), the number of health care employees, hospital beds, and high-technology equipment is restricted. Demand for services typically exceeds supply, so immediate access to care can be limited.

The health care system underwent significant change in the 1990s and early 2000s. In the late 1980s, Prime Minister Margaret Thatcher commissioned a report, Working for Patients, which advocated making greater use of private-market forces to increase competition and efficiency while maintaining universal and free access.

At the heart of the reform were two changes. First, as of 2002, decision-making power was decentralized, with localized *primary care trusts (PCTs)* given 75 percent of NHS funds to run the NHS and improve health in their areas. Regional *strategic health authorities* were created to oversee the PCTs and engage in health planning. Second, increased competition among hospitals and other facilities was created, with the aim of reducing costs and increasing quality of services.

Medical settings are like those in the United States. Physicians work out of offices or clinics or in hospitals. As is true in some managed-care networks in the United States, England mandates that an initial contact in the health care system be made with a general practitioner (GP).

The NHS is largely (more than 80 percent) financed by general tax revenues, with only about 4 percent of funds coming from out-of-pocket expenses. Basic health care is provided by physicians and hospitals to all citizens at no charge at the point of service, although there are co-payments for eyeglasses, dentures, and prescription drugs. Certain people (e.g., children and the elderly) are exempt from the fees.

Practicing physicians become either general practitioners or consultants. Patients have a free choice of GPs, but must be on one's roster to be seen. Once on a roster, that is the only GP the patient can use. A patient can switch to another GP by registering with another physician, but this is rare. The GP offers comprehensive primary care and can prescribe medications, but must refer patients to a consultant for hospital care.

GPs contract with the NHS for reimbursement, which occurs in three ways. Each GP receives a base salary to cover the fixed costs of operating a practice, a certain amount of salary based on the number of patients accepted on the roster (called a **capitation system**), and additional income based on services such as vaccinations for which a fee is charged. The capitation system is the most controversial of the three sources. The NHS has established 3,500 patients

as the maximum on a roster, although physicians average only about 1,900. Physicians are obligated to provide care for all patients on the roster, although neither the number of patients actually seen, the duration of the encounter, nor the type of treatment dispensed affects salary. Physicians do receive a supplement for having certain categories of patients (e.g., the elderly, or people on low income) on their roster. Recently, the NHS began experimenting with "pay-for-performance" programs in which physicians receive some compensation when their patients hit designated health targets.

Consultants, all of whom work in hospitals, are physicians trained in a medical or surgical specialty. They are salaried employees of the NHS. Salaries are the same for all specialties in all hospitals, and are determined in an annual negotiation with the NHS. Neither the number of patients seen nor the type of treatments provided affects salary earned.

Traditionally, there has been a small private health care sector, but this has recently become more popular. About 11 percent of the population now supplements their public insurance with private insurance. Physicians are not obligated to register with the NHS (although only a handful have not done so), and registered physicians may accept private patients, although rarely do private patients exceed 5 percent of the total patient load. Private insurance companies sell health insurance for a premium. Hospitals reserve a small number of beds ("pay beds") for private patients. The primary motivations to purchase private insurance are to avoid the long waits ("queues") for services.

Physicians are held in high esteem. Surveys report confidence in physician care, few patients seek a second opinion, and medical malpractice suits are rare. This high prestige is not reflected in salaries to the same extent that it is in the United States. Physicians earn considerably above the national average income, but not several times higher as they do in the United States.

Performance of the Health Care System

Standard health indicators reflect positively on the general health of the people. Overall life expectancy is among the highest in the world (higher than in the United States), and infant mortality is very low (lower than in the United States). Although no person is ever turned away due to an inability to pay, the NHS is considerably less expensive than the US system. In recent years, England has spent a little more than 9 percent of its gross domestic product on health care—about half the US level.

Accessibility of Health Care

Citizens receive comprehensive health care without payment at the point of delivery, although there are some charges for dental care, eye care, and prescription drugs. Moreover, the government offers incentives to physicians who establish practice in medically underserved areas—this has helped to ease the shortage of physicians in rural areas. To help address the problem of long waits for many services, England has developed a new medical group called physician associates. Similar to American physician assistants, they are non-physician advanced practitioners intended to increase the supply of medical providers.

Recent Developments in Health Care

In the last several years, the economic situation in England has led to only very minor increases in the health care budget (less than a 1 percent annual increase)—an unprecedented occurrence. With an increased overall population and an increased elderly population, along with new medical technologies, demand for services has increasingly exceeded supply. Provider shortages, overworked workers, and longer waiting times have resulted. This has created frustration for patients and has put pressure on the government to do better (Montgomery et al., 2017).

In response, several additional changes have recently been introduced. The Health and Social Care Act of 2012 created a new body, NHS England, with overall budgetary control and supervision of both *clinical commissioning groups* (which replaced the primary care trusts) and Monitor (an economic regulator of public and private providers). NHS England also oversees primary care, national immunization and screening programs, health information technology, and some specialized low-volume services (Thorlby and Arora, 2016).

The primary objective of these changes is to increase efficiency, increase the power of physicians in allocating health care dollars, and increase private competition. Efforts have been undertaken to reduce the provision of unnecessary services. Patients have been given increased choice of medical provider, and can choose between public and private facilities. Proponents hope that decentralization and added competition will create a more efficient health care system.

Critics of the changes express concern that the emphasis on competition and profit making will supersede the traditional closeness of the GP–patient relationship. For example, the increased importance of the capitation system gives physicians an incentive to take more patients onto the roster, thereby reducing the time available for each patient.

RUSSIA

The Historical, Political, and Philosophical Foundation

Russia, with a population of about 145 million people (changing little from year to year) falls between the level of modernization of the United States and Western Europe on the one hand and that of developing countries on the other. Since the breakup of the Soviet Union in 1991, Russia has struggled to develop a sound economy and workable health care system.

The roots of Russia's socialized health care system can be traced to the 1917 revolution. Overthrowing the tsar, Lenin and the Bolsheviks moved to establish a working-class society based on Communist principles. Given both the unstable political situation at home and throughout the world and the economic chaos within the country, the Bolsheviks moved quickly to consolidate their power in a totalitarian government.

The health of the people was a primary concern of Lenin and the new government, and one of their priorities was to establish adequate preventive measures to counter the rampant disease epidemics of the time. In 1913, the mortality rate was 29 per 1,000 people, the infant mortality rate was 269 per 1,000, and an average life expectancy was no more than 32 years—all indicators of severe health problems (Leichter, 1979).

Lenin was also determined to reduce sharply the power of the medical profession. Under the tsar, physicians had substantial autonomy and organized themselves into a medical corporation. This body was political as well as medical, and often spoke out against the tsar. Following the 1917 revolution, physicians attempted to alter the structure of medicine to make it more amenable to centralized planning (in accord with Lenin's wishes), but they also attempted to retain extensive professional control over clinical practice. This effort was denounced by the Communists, who were convinced that physicians would always serve the interests of the ruling class. In an effort to deprofessionalize physicians, the government created a medical union in which physicians had no greater say than other health care workers. By the mid-1920s, the medical profession was transformed into a group of medical experts employed and largely controlled by the government.

The philosophical foundation for the health care system was developed in the first years after the revolution. The guiding principles were that (1) the state has responsibility for public health and the provision of health care; (2) administration of the health care system is highly centralized and bureaucratized, but includes public participation; (3) health care is defined as a right of citizenship, and health care services are provided at no cost; (4) preventive medicine is to be emphasized; and (5) medical research must be oriented toward the solution of practical problems—for example, the reduction of industrial absenteeism (Barr and Field, 1996).

These principles guided the health care system in the succeeding decades. Although the government released little information to the outside world about health indicators, the general perception was that the health care system was at least working adequately.

However, when President Gorbachev opened Russian society to the outside world in 1985, it became obvious that the health care system was in a badly deteriorated condition due to underfunding. While Soviet leaders had painted a glowing picture of their health care system, in reality they had concentrated their attention on rapid industrialization and militarization and had failed to adequately support health care. Although the Soviet Union had more physicians and more hospital beds per capita than any other country, their quality was often very low. Unqualified students bribed their way into medical school, severe shortages of pharmaceuticals and other medical supplies existed, and many medical facilities were crumbling (Barr and Field, 1996).

During the summer of 1991, people throughout the Soviet Union demanded an end to centralized government control and insisted on autonomy for the republics. Their focus was largely on political and economic structures, but changes were initiated in every institutional sector. In medicine, highly centralized decision making and planning was ended, and efforts commenced to establish free-market principles in the system. However, the transition to a workable and efficient health care system has been very difficult.

Organization of the Health Care System

Historically, the key organizational characteristic of the health care system was its centralized administration. The ultimate authority in the system resides in the national Health Ministry led by a minister of health (typically a physician) and a Council of Health Ministers. This body has responsibility for (1) all planning, coordination, and control of medical care and medical research; (2) medical education and standards of medical practice; (3) formulating the health care budget and allocating funds to republic, regional, district, and local medical resources. The government owns all health care facilities and employs all health care workers.

In urban areas, a network of large, multiservice polyclinics is the core of the health care system and serves most of the population. Police, railroad employees, university employees, and high-level government officials have their own clinics and hospitals. In rural areas, key providers are the midwife and the feldsher—a midlevel practitioner approximately equivalent to a physician assistant (but with more responsibility), who provides immunizations, primary care, assistance with normal childbirth, and minor surgery.

The hospital sector contains both general and specialized hospitals (e.g., maternity and infectious diseases), most of which are fairly small. Few hospitals contain modern medical technology and adequate pharmaceuticals or have high sanitary standards. Periodic reports of shortages of rubber gloves, surgical instruments, sterile needles, and other necessary supplies still occur. There is also a nursing shortage. The emergency medical system, which was once the pride of the health care system, is in total disarray, with ambulances sometimes arriving half a day after being called.

Physicians enjoy prestige in Russia, but they are not among the highest paid professionals. Salaries are approximately the same as those for starting teachers, but only 70 percent as much as those of industrial workers. In the outlying provinces, salaries are far less. This situation helps to explain under-the-table payments from patients to physicians that are common in order to secure more expedient care or additional services, or even to have an operation performed or medication prescribed. The government does provide physicians with certain fringe benefits, such as preferred apartments, vacation benefits, and access to better schools for their children.

About 70 percent of all physicians in Russia are women, and most of these women work out of the polyclinics. Men physicians are more likely to hold the prestigious specialist positions in hospitals, academic positions, and most positions in the Ministry of Health. These patterns developed during the early 1930s, during a physician shortage. Medicine was determined to be an area where women could adequately replace men. The Soviet government viewed many of these new women physicians (who had been nurses or even hospital orderlies) as being satisfied with a small paycheck and an occupation with little professional status.

Accessibility of Health Care

According to the Russian constitution, free health care is guaranteed to all citizens at the publicly funded polyclinics and hospitals, but only a small part of services is actually free. Services are provided on a first-come-first-served basis (often with long queues), and are limited by the chronic shortage of supplies and equipment. The public system is chronically underfunded; physicians are undertrained; medical equipment, supplies, and drugs are lacking; and some facilities are in extensive disrepair. Russia spends about 6–7 percent of its GDP on health care, and this is not sufficient to elevate standards.

Laws passed in the early 1990s created a two-part government-run health insurance system. Workers are covered under one part (Obligatory Medical Insurance, which is financed by a payroll tax on employers), and non-workers (e.g., the unemployed, retirees, and children) are covered in the second part, which is financed through the national government's budget. All persons are required to have medical insurance.

In recent years, a private system has begun to emerge beside the public system. Physicians are permitted to treat private as well as public patients, and patients with adequate funds may prefer to pay a fee for service in order to get faster, more personalized, or more thorough care. A few pay-polyclinics have been started, and private health insurance is now available to help subsidize these costs. Many patients avoid both the public and private systems by relying on informal access to physician friends or relatives. Not surprisingly, this resource is most readily available to people in upper socioeconomic groups.

Performance of the Health Care System

Despite having significant wealth at its disposal (an estimated 40 percent of the world's natural resources), Russia's health care system is in shambles and health indicators across the board are alarming. Mortality rates are higher than in other industrialized countries. Life expectancy has actually decreased in recent years, and infant mortality rates are two to three times higher than in Western countries. The death rate from heart disease is the highest in the developed world, and the incidence of AIDS has increased rapidly. Epidemics of diseases once thought to be under control in developed countries (e.g., tuberculosis, hepatitis, typhoid, cholera, and diphtheria) are all on the increase and occasionally at epidemic levels. Drug-related health problems have increased while public sanitation, childhood immunizations, and health education programs are down.

These conditions relate to the deterioration of the health care system but are traceable to a variety of other causes. Mark Field (1995) places the problem within the broad context of the collapse of the Soviet empire and the "systemic" breakdown of Russian society (a macro factor). He casts Russia as a country in a "post-war" mindset, having experienced a humiliating national defeat.

The deteriorating economic condition and high rates of inflation, political instability, and feelings of social isolation and alienation have contributed to a tearing of the social fabric.

The high rates of heart disease have been attributed to social stress and to harmful individual behaviors such as alcoholism (among the highest in the world), cigarette smoking (highest rate in the world), drug abuse, high-fat diets, and lack of adequate exercise (Kalinich, 2016). Russia also has high rates of homicide, suicide, traffic accidents, and alcohol poisoning (micro factors). These macro and micro factors have been mutually reinforcing. Poor economic conditions have had a negative impact on population health, and poor health has been one barrier to economic growth (Danton, 2013). King, Hamm, and Stuckler (2009) have shown that rapid implementation of large-scale private market programs reduced available health care resources *and* created considerable psychological stress, which has contributed to poorer health and lifestyles, increased rates of heart disease and suicide, and decreased life expectancy.

Recent Developments in Health Care

Leaders in Russia and many of the countries that once constituted the Soviet Union intend to focus heavily on the application of free-market principles to the health care system. Many health care providers believe the main problems with the system in the past are underfunding and its overly centralized nature. However, the focus to date in Russia has been on the economic system, and little attention has been directed to reforming the health care system and acquiring the basic medical supplies and equipment needed for quality clinical services.

In 2011, Prime Minister Putin announced that the government would contribute $10 billion to the health care system over the next few years, that the medical insurance tax paid by employers would increase in order to add funding to the health care system, and that increased privatization efforts would occur. In 2012, Putin promised to double the (very low) wages of health care workers by 2018. However, deepening economic problems have forced austerity measures throughout the country, and health care funding has been reduced. Privatization efforts thus far seem to be exacerbating the problem, as prices have increased and the quality of services has declined. An "optimization" plan, which commenced in 2014 to try to eliminate waste, has concentrated resources in large hospitals but led to the closing of many smaller facilities. Many hospital staff positions have been cut. A 2014 Bloomberg study rates the Russian health care system as the least efficient among the world's 55 most developed countries (Du and Lu, 2016).

COMMON CHALLENGES TO HEALTH CARE SYSTEMS AROUND THE WORLD

Despite their profound differences, nations around the world are struggling with some of the same issues and questions with respect to their health care systems. The following questions emerge as common and very important issues with which countries are now dealing.

1. What is the optimal level of involvement of the national government in the health care system, and in what ways should the government be involved?
2. Should there be both a public and private health care sector? What is the optimal relationship between the government, employers, insurers, and providers?
3. What is the optimal number of primary care physicians, specialists, and mid-level practitioners within the system?
4. Given considerations of cost and equitable distribution, what is the optimal commitment that should be made to the incorporation of health care technologies?
5. How can continuing large increases in health care costs be controlled?

SUMMARY

Studying health care systems around the world offers insights into policy formation and an ability to understand the forces that shape health care. While every health care system is unique, each is shaped by some configuration of environmental, situational-historical, cultural, and structural factors.

Developing countries are today facing a perfect storm of continued high levels of acute, infectious diseases, increasing rates of chronic, degenerative diseases, and too little money to develop an adequate health care system.

The four systems examined in detail in this chapter represent alternative ways of structuring a health care system. China's urban areas are growing rapidly, but the massive rural population is especially in need of more health care resources. Problems were created when the government abandoned the cooperative system based on

community health workers—a system that was effective in getting medical care to the people—in favor of a more privatized system. This change created a system in disarray, and one in which health care became unobtainable for much of the population. Recently, however, China has committed to a significantly enhanced health care system, and early results are promising.

Canada illustrates the national health insurance with private regulated services model. Canada's health care system has undergone a significant transformation that has shifted more control to the provincial governments, while maintaining a commitment to providing universal access to care. Health personnel in Canada are not government employees, although the federal and provincial governments exercise significant influence on the conditions of medical practice. Health indicators are very positive, but difficult economic times have led to recent system cutbacks.

England illustrates the national health insurance with public regulated services model. It guarantees universal access to health care through a system that is substantially publicly owned and run. Health indicators for the British people are very favorable, and there is considerable pride in the "National." However, rapidly increasing costs have led to organizational changes and focused efforts on using competition and private-market forces to control cost increases.

Russia, when it was part of the Soviet Union, exemplified a state-run system (socialized medicine) model. Russians took much pride in the emphasis on preventive care and on the provision of free care for all citizens. However, the health care system was overcentralized and greatly underfunded. Efforts to address this by transitioning to a private-market economy have been fraught with difficulty. The health care system, like the general economy, is in a desperate condition, and several health indicators remain major concerns.

HEALTH ON THE INTERNET

Throughout this text we have discussed the World Health Organization and used data that it has collected. Learn more about the WHO by checking out its website at

www.who.int

When and by whom was the WHO created? How is the WHO structured and governed? Where is its main office located? What are the WHO's basic principles? What does the WHO have to say about adolescent pregnancy, child maltreatment, and social determinants of health?

DISCUSSION QUESTIONS

1. Determine which of the four major influences on health care systems (physical environment, historical and situational events, cultural norms and values, and the structure of society) had the most impact on each of the four health care systems presented in detail in this chapter.
2. What are the common denominators in these four health care systems? How is each system unique?
3. Identify a major strength and a major concern for each of the four systems. Can you identify at least one feature in the health care system of each country that you would like to see incorporated in health care reform in the United States?

GLOSSARY

barefoot doctors
capitation system
global health

global health partnerships (GHPs)
prospective budgeting
socialized medicine

REFERENCES

Allin, Sara, and David Rudoler. 2016. "The Canadian Health Care System, 2015." In *International Profiles of Health Care Systems*, edited by Elias Mossialos, Martin Wenzl, Robin Osborn, and Dana Sarnak. New York: The Commonwealth Fund.

Anderson, Gerard, and Peter S. Hussey. 2001. "Comparing Health System Performance in OECD Countries." *Health Affairs* 20(2):219–232.

Barr, Donald A., and Mark G. Field. 1996. "The Current State of Health Care in the Former Soviet Union: Implications for Health Care Policy and Reform." *American Journal of Public Health* 86(3):307–312.

Campion, Edward W., and Stephen Morrissey. 2013. "A Different Model—Medical Care in Cuba." *New England Journal of Medicine* 368(4):297–299.

Danton, Christine. 2013. "The Health Crisis in Russia." *Topical Research Digest: Human Rights in Russia and the Former Soviet Republics*. Retrieved May 3, 2019 (www du.edu/korbel/hrhw/researchdigest/russia/health. pdf).

Du, Lisa, and Wei Lu. 2016. "U.S. Health-Care System Ranks as One of the Least-Efficient." *Bloomberg*. Retrieved March 25, 2019 (www.bloomberg. com/news/articles/2016-09-29/u-s-health-care-system-ranks-as-one-of-the-least-efficient).

Edney, Anna. 2014. "U.S. Health Care System Among Least Efficient Before Obamacare." Retrieved May 3, 2019 (www.bloomberg.com/news/articles/ 2014-09-18/u-s-health-system-among-least-efficient-before-obamacare).

FamiliesUSA. 2010. "Why Global Health Matters—Here and Abroad." Retrieved May 2, 2019 (www. familiesusa.org/issues/ global-health).

Fang, Hai. 2016. "The Chinese Health Care System, 2015." In *International Profiles of Health Care Systems*, edited by Elias Mossialos, Martin Wenzl, Robin Osborn, and Dana Sarnak. New York: The Commonwealth Fund.

Field, Mark G. 1995. "The Health Care Crisis in the Former Soviet Union: A Report from the 'Post-War' Zone." *Social Science and Medicine* 41(11):1469–1478.

Fu, Hongqiao, Ling Li, and Winnie Yip. 2018. "Intended and Unintended Impacts of Price Changes for Drugs and Medical Services: Evidence from China." *Social Science and Medicine* 211(August):114–122.

Kalinich, Chaney. 2016. "Russia: The Sickness of a Nation." *The Yale Global Health Review*. Retrieved March 25, 2019 (https://yaleglobalhealthreview. com/2016/12/21/russia-the-sickness-of-a-nation/).

Kerry, Vanessa B., and Fitzhugh Mullan. 2013. "Global Health Service Partnership: Building Health Professional Leadership." *The Lancet* 383(9929):1688–1691.

King, Lawrence L., Patrick Hamm, and David Stuckler. 2009. "Rapid Large-Scale Privatization and Death Rates in Ex-Communist Countries: An Analysis of Stress-Related and Health System Mechanisms." *International Journal of Health Services* 39(3):461–489.

Kostova, Deliana, Frank J. Chaloupka, Thomas R. Frieden, Kelly Henning, Jeremias Paul Jr., Patrick L. Osewe, and Samira Asma. 2017. "Noncommunicable Disease Risk Factors in Developing Countries: Policy Perspectives." *Preventive Medicine* 105(S):1–3.

Lassey, Marie L., William R. Lassey, and Martin J. Jinks. 1997. *Health Care Systems Around the World*. Upper Saddle River, NJ: Prentice Hall.

Leichter, Howard M. 1979. *A Comparative Approach to Policy Analysis: Health Care Policy in Four Nations*. Cambridge, UK: Cambridge University Press.

Lewis, Steven. 2015. "A System in Name Only—Access, Variation, and Reform in Canada's Provinces." *New England Journal of Medicine* 372(5):497–500.

Light, Donald W. 1990. "Comparing Health Care Systems: Lessons from East and West Germany." Pp. 449–463 in *The Sociology of Health and Illness* (3rd ed.), edited by Peter Conrad and Rochelle Kern. New York: St. Martin's Press.

Marchildon, Gregory P., Capri S. Cafaro, and Adalsteinn Brown. 2018. "Myths, Misperceptions, and Policy Learning: Comparing Healthcare in the United States and Canada." *Journal of Law, Medicine, and Ethics* 46(4):833–837.

McGrail, Kimberlyn M., Eddy van Doorslaer, Nancy A. Ross, and Claudia Sanmartin. 2009. "Income-Related Health Inequalities in Canada and the United States: A Decomposition Analysis." *American Journal of Public Health* 99(10):1856–1863.

Montgomery, H.E., A. Haines, N. Marlow, M.G. Mythen, P.W. Grocutt, and C. Swanton. 2017. "The Future of UK Healthcare: Problems and Potential Solutions to a System in Crisis." *Annals of Oncology* 28(8):1751–1755.

Payer, Lynn. 1989. *Medicine and Culture*. New York: Holt, Rinehart and Winston.

Squires, David, and Chloe Anderson. 2015. "U.S. Health Care from a Global Perspective: Spending, Use of Services, Prices, and Health in 13 Countries." Retrieved May 2, 2019 (www.commonwealthfund.

org/publications/issue-briefs/2015/oct/us-health-care-from-a-global-perspective).

Strouse, Carly, Ricardo Petrez-Cuevas, Maureen Lahiff, Julia Walsh, and Sylvia Guendelman. 2016. "Mexico's Seguro Popular Appears to Have Helped Reduce the Risk of Preterm Delivery Among Women with Low Education." *Health Affairs* 35(1):80–87.

Thorlby, Ruth, and Sandeepa Arora. 2016. "The English Health Care System, 2015." In *International Profiles of Health Care Systems*, edited by Elias Mossialos, Martin Wenzl, Robin Osborn, and Dana Sarnak. New York: The Commonwealth Fund.

Wang, Qing, Donglan Zhang, and Zhiyuan Hou. 2016. "Insurance Coverage and Socioeconomic Differences in Patient Choice Between Private and Public Health Care Providers in China." *Social Science and Medicine* 170(December):124–132.

Woolhandler, Steffie, Terry Campbell, and David U. Himmelstein. 2004. "Health Care Administration in the United States and Canada: Micromanagement, Macro Costs." *International Journal of Health Services* 34(1):65–78.

World Bank. 2019a. "World Development Indicators: Per Capital GDP." Retrieved May 2, 2019 (www.data.worldbank.org/indicator/SH.XPD.PCAP/countries).

———. 2019b. "World Development Indicators: Per Capita Health Expenditures." Retrieved May 2, 2019 (www.data.worldbank.org/indicator/NY.GDPRCARCD/countries).

World Health Organization. 2000. *World Health Report 2000—Health Systems: Improving Performance.* Geneva, Switzerland: World Health Organization.

Yip, Winnie C., and William C. Hsiao. 2008. "The Chinese Health System at a Crossroads." *Health Affairs* 27(2):460–468.

Name Index

Subject Index